9518

JX
1391   Hartmann
.H34   World in crisis
1973

DATE DUE

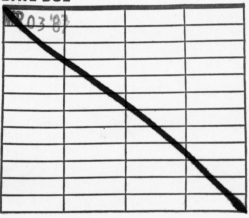

World in Crisis
Readings in International Relations

31

WORLD IN CRISIS

⧓⧓⧓

Readings in International Relations

EDITED BY

Frederick H. Hartmann

Alfred Thayer Mahan Professor, Naval War College

FOURTH EDITION

⧓

The Macmillan Company, New York

The Macmillan Company
866 Third Avenue,
New York, New York 10022

Collier-Macmillan Canada, Ltd.,
Toronto, Ontario

Library of Congress catalog card number: 72–80910

Printing: 1 2 3 4 5 6 7 8   Year: 3 4 5 6 7 8 9

To Lynne Merry, Vicky Carol, and Peter Howard,
who helped sometimes . . .

Preface to the Fourth Edition

TWENTY-ONE YEARS AGO, the first edition of this book was published. Of the articles in that edition, four still survive here, for the truths they tell us are timeless. Of the forty-three selections in the third edition, twelve (including the original four) have been reprinted in this fourth edition. The rest (twenty-nine selections) are here for the first time. Thus almost three quarters of the book is new material, chosen from among hundreds of possibilities considered. (Even the semifinal manuscript was just twice as long—an indication of the quality of readings available today.)

As before, the readings in this book have been chosen because each has something useful, provocative, and basic to say about some major aspect of the relations of nations. Although the organization of the book makes it readily adaptable to standard courses on international relations, rarely was material included merely to inform or to round out the consideration of a particular topic. Thus, in a very real sense, this book represents a choice distillation of really significant and interesting views.

Although the selections incidentally give a fairly complete idea of the methodological controversies in the field, they were chosen with a more basic consideration in mind: to show that the assumptions one makes about the nature of the problem to be analyzed are critical influences on the conclusions reached. This kind of reminder is especially needed for Americans whose approach to problems of foreign policy too often and too quickly stresses problem-solving (what to *do*) rather than conceptual perspectives (what *is* the problem?).

Where significant controversies exist some care has been taken to show both sides. If the book leans to one side of a question it is usually where the opposite point of view is widely shared. Frequent cross references have been included in the chapter introductions to indicate related or opposed viewpoints given elsewhere. In addition, many of the authors themselves cite other authors in the book, either to agree or to disagree with their statements. As a further aid to tying the book together I have included three selections of mine, two published previously elsewhere but one (the first selection) written especially for this edition.

Some editing of selections was needed for clarity or to eliminate repetitions between readings. But very short and heavily edited selections were avoided in favor of readings lengthy enough to do justice to the author's views.

This new edition, as with the previous editions, benefits from the suggestions of numerous colleagues. The burden of the preparation of the manuscript was eased considerably by the able and careful work of my assistants, Don McGowan and Bruce Kelly. Such views and opinions as are expressed in this book are, of course, those of the individuals identified. They do not necessarily represent the views of the Naval War College or any department of government.

F. H. H.

Contents

⚹ Part One

THE FUNDAMENTALS OF THE STATE SYSTEM

⩣ Part Two

THE RELATIONS OF STATES

⊁ Part Three

THE POWER PROBLEM AND THE POWER PATTERNS

≽ Part Four

THE SUPERPOWERS

⊱ Part Five

WORLD IN CRISIS—CONTEMPORARY PROBLEMS

*The Fundamentals
of the State System*

✤1✤

The Nature of
International Relations

BEFORE WE CAN UNDERSTAND a subject we must have some ideas of how to approach it as a field of study. What are the fixed points or principles by which we can judge the meaning of the important developments we are witnessing? To begin at the beginning, what is the proper *unit* of study: the individual nation-state—or the system as a whole? What governs behavior? And are those things identical for every state in the system? How meaningful is the familiar term "power"? If the term is meaningful, is it the goal of states to amass power, to use power, or to escape the possible use of power against them? If all three, in what relation or priority?

Because there are important disagreements on such questions, it will help first to understand these arguments in perspective since they are implied or explicit in almost every selection in this book.

In the first selection, "International Relations Theory: An Overview," written for this book, Frederick H. Hartmann sets the stage by examining the evolution of the main arguments. In the process he sets forth his own theoretical approach in terms of national interest theory. The selection is written both to give the reader a basis of comparison to other approaches in the rest of Chapter 1 and to introduce and clarify what is at issue about the nature of international relations.

In the second selection, "Power and Influence," Charles A. McClelland, of the University of Southern California, an American scholar, gives us a perceptive analysis of the central concept of power,

3

especially as used by "realists." After initial remarks about power which he says will "probably appear to be entirely reasonable," he goes on to show the difficulties which such realist theories contain.

Beginning with a critique of Hans J. Morgenthau's characterization of international politics as "a struggle for power," McClelland next turns to the common textbook device of analyzing elements of national power in terms of capabilities or potential. Such "power calculations at the source" are not as useful in McClelland's view as conceptualizing power as "streams of transactions." Power is not an entity but an effect, a "performance trait of international relations" which should be seen in a "system context." McClelland calls it "poetic—but not informative" to say that "power can be won or lost, distributed and balanced" or to say that "power directs international events, shapes relations among nations." Instead of what he calls the realist theory's focus on national interest defined in terms of power, McClelland argues for behavioral or systems theory which "creates a focus on transactions and relationships occurring in the flow of events." What is needed, he says, are conceptual tools "for identifying 'states' of the system under conditions of fluctuation and change."

In short, McClelland is arguing that a systems approach permits the actual interrelationships of states to be conceptualized without an initial bias being introduced by way of assumptions as to the degree to which relations are conflict-oriented or cooperation-oriented. Much of the emphasis in contemporary national-interest thinking (which is by no means all power-as-goal oriented in the Morgenthau sense) is actually in this same direction, as the first selection indicates. (Compare, for example, the "cardinal principles" at the end of Selection 1 with the "decisional calculus" at the end of Selection 2.)

Behind the arguments discussed by McClelland is an intriguing fundamental question: to what extent are states entities and to what extent are they parts of a "system"? At one extreme there is the simple view aptly characterized by Arnold Wolfers as the "billiard ball" model of international relations in which "every state represents a closed, impermeable and sovereign unit, completely separated from all other states" (*Discord and Collaboration; Essays on International Politics*, p. 19). Analyses from this point of view are likely to overemphasize "free will" (i.e., the degree of discretion a state has over the content of its foreign policy). At the other extreme there are "systems" points of view which concentrate on interactions among sovereign units, and their effects. Analyses from this point of view fall easily into visualizing states as puppets reacting to exterior stimuli. In specific relation to the concept of power, it would appear useful both to examine "capabilities" or potential ("power calculations at the source") *and* to analyze actual nation-state interactions in the international environment. After all, power has one important effect merely by existing as potential—states normally govern the size of their own military forces (if they are able) with reference to perceived potential threats from other states. But, as McClelland would argue, the size of the armies does not tell you who wins a war.

Hedley Bull, Professor of International Relations at Australian National University, Canberra, and a leading Australian scholar, in the third selection, "International Theory: The Case for a Classical Approach," takes issue with the behavioral or "scientific" approach. While not endorsing the "struggle for power" view, Bull believes that the total rejection of what extreme behaviorists have derided as "wisdom literature" is a form of "intellectual puritanism . . . as remote from the substance of international politics as the inmates of a Victorian nunnery were from the study of sex." Bull maintains that the scientific approach, "so far as it [is] intended to encroach upon and ultimately displace the classical approach, . . . is positively harmful." Bull's arguments in support of his view constitute one of the most effective critiques yet made of the "scientific" approach.

These three selections illuminate most of the basic arguments about the nature of international relations. They warn us to be alert as to our assumptions about the nature of man (does he seek power above all else?); as to the perspective from which we observe international behavior (how much discretion does the "system" permit to an "individual" state?); and as to the inevitability of change (but toward what?).

1

INTERNATIONAL RELATIONS THEORY: AN OVERVIEW

Frederick H. Hartmann

1

Progress in the realm of theory is slower than one might think, considering the claims often made. But there *is* progress, more progress than one might judge given the ritual but sad lament of the book reviewers' guild whose best known chorus goes: "But . . . (despite this book's success-failure) . . . we still have far to go before we arrive at an agreed and comprehensive theory of international relations." No matter how hot the controversy, both sides will normally agree on that while the casualties are being carted off the field.

Curiously—or at least, interestingly—there has always been a great deal of disagreement over fundamental questions of theory in the field of international relations. Since World War II controversy has increased even further. Only the main protagonists have changed. No longer is the major battle being fought by idealists vs. realists. Today the prime groupings are said to be traditionalist vs. behaviorist (or the "literary" vs. the "scientific" approach). Like economic man or political man, this simple classification is a rather arbitrary concept, and few who favor the literary approach are prepared to confess to being "unscientific," while not any great number of the "scientists" are prepared to confess incompetence in English usage. The distinction is supposedly based upon the type and rigor of the research designs used and the proof accepted, but here, as in so many things, the variations are often greater *within* the classification than between the two.

Such shifts in the battleground of theory undoubtedly represent change. But change can be of two sorts: shifts in popularity (fad), and progress.

Fad we have always with us. Some years ago, in a very unusual presidential address, the chief officer for that year of the Southern Political Science Association, Jasper Shannon, recounted the scholarly efforts of a mythical professor. This professor, Milquetoast, if memory serves, was writing a book. With each chapter separated from the next by some years—as family and other emergencies intervened—the style and jargon changed fairly radically to keep up with the in-practice. Funny as Shannon's address was, it also contained a shrewd commentary which warned us that innovation in style or method is not necessarily synonymous with progress.

6

If, as asserted above, there *is* progress, the student still has a perfect right to ask, "So what?" The answer is that theory (and the hope for progress) cannot be ignored or downgraded. It is absolutely indispensable to real comprehension as compared to entertainment. Without real comprehension there can be no utility. The rest is pure frivolity, at odds with serious scholarship.

How then does theory serve us? To begin with, theory is the anatomy of a subject matter. It is the bone structure and it indicates the linkages. Fail to grasp the principles and one cannot describe and distinguish the fundamentals from the trivia or illustrations. Worse, as a practical matter, if a foreign policy is attempted on false principles, grief will follow in its wake. Take, for current illustration, former President Johnson's account in his memoirs of why he decided to take the plunge and send U.S. ground forces in large numbers into combat in Vietnam. After one strips away his citations of the earlier actions and views of Presidents Eisenhower and Kennedy, he justifies his decision on the basis of the world as he understood it to be—a view shared with his principal advisers, Secretary Rusk and Secretary McNamara. If Johnson was wrong it was because the problem and the forces at work deviated from his concept of reality. So, when all is said and done, theory is a shorthand statement of what one believes is real, in international relations or in any other field.

Arguments over international relations theory thus come down in the last resort to either being arguments over *methodology* (how to refine out the principles which describe the world and the relations of its component parts) or over *substance* (what role ideology has, for instance, in reshaping or supplanting traditional national interest concerns). All fundamental arguments over theory, reduced to their essence, are ultimately philosophical: they contain conflicting assumptions about the nature of man and the nature of the universe. Controversy over environment vs. heredity and the nature of man is never very far from the surface, whether the nominal focus of the argument is over bringing peace to the world through economic progress for all mankind, or over the possibilities for conflict resolution, peaceful change, and the management of disputes. Questions like this lead to deeper questions. Do men conflict over material things? Or because of the ideas in their heads? Or do they conflict because they are caught up in a tragic system? Are they set at each other's throats and condemned to fear by virtue of the very organization of the world into separate nation-states? Can these conditions be altered (i.e., do men prefer the risks and tensions as they are or do they wish to trade them in on other risks and tensions implicit in some other form of world organization?). Is it believable that risks and tensions can be eliminated or drastically reduced by certain structural changes in the system?

To answer such questions requires some attention to philosophy and psychology. But to assume that meaningful answers to the most serious political questions are possible without an analysis and provisional judgment on these fundamentals is utopian. This is why the earlier arguments in the field, those between the "idealists" and the "realists," focused on opposed interpretations of the roots of human motivation and behavior.

Beginning with the older argument, but spilling over into the present controversy, is a special case of the same problem: whether the rules of politics, whatever they are, are culture-bound and to what extent? For simple illustration, consider whether it is plausible to believe that Russians, Chinese, and Americans have an identical pattern of reaction to threats of nuclear confrontation. To what extent is there a universally valid pattern of thought, decision, and reaction to abstractly identical threats of reciprocal nuclear devastation? Do all men seek peace equally, or some more than others? Is fear a universal commodity producing identical psychological reactions everywhere? If not, then theories of deterrence, concepts drawn from gaming, may be seriously misleading where cultural variations count. In short, can we generalize about mankind as a whole? Or must we distinguish between cultures, confining certain of our observations to the Chinese, others to the Russians, still others to the Americans? Can we say certain things about all, and other things only about some?

2

The first controversies substantially ignored this culture issue, downgrading national differences while emphasizing in large part the environmental-heredity issue. Both the idealists and the realists addressed themselves to supposed innate and universal characteristics of human behavior, as modified or amplified by the effects of the world state system. Generalizations in the idealist-realist argument were very gross indeed. Most men and most nations, even virtually all men in all nations, were conceptualized as wanting essentially the same things. The idealist called it "peace." The realist called it "power." In the sequence of popularity the idealists dominated the field in the 1920s and early 1930s, yielding to the realists only as the shadows of world depression and world rearmament grew too lengthy to be ignored.

Idealism in this form got its popular start with Woodrow Wilson who, unrestrained by his lack of detailed knowledge of world affairs, announced a plan for their reform. He intended to abolish "Germanism"—we would say "going it alone" or unilateralism—and replace it by collective action.[1] Instead of balance of power alliances there would be collective security sanctions. Not that sanctions would be needed often. Few criminals would dare to commit an "aggression" if the whole law-abiding and peace-loving world was ready to punish transgressions both promptly and with overwhelming might. This scheme of Wilson's, embodied in the League of Nations, really rested for its validity on one essential assumption: that widespread conflict

---

[1] Wilson was an academic specialist on congressional affairs whose adult life was lived in a period when American involvement in, or even awareness of, international affairs was minimal.

and general war between equal and powerful groups arose because nations were forced to resort to the balance of power for lack of anything better. Thus they became caught up in a web of intrigue by alliances which existed because no one had previously provided the better alternative of collective security. Wilson did not propose to change the nature of man, only the structural or environmental system. Given a real choice he had no doubt which way man would go. The problem, he thought, was that the choice had not previously existed. So Wilson was an idealist only in one sense. He was not setting out to improve man's nature but only the conditions under which he lived. Wilson wanted to tear down the slum dwellings of balance of power pacts and build model international organization apartments. In the courses in international relations which sprang up in the wake of the League controversy, this lead was faithfully followed.

In a classic book, *The Twenty Years' Crisis, 1919–1939,* published the year World War II began, E. H. Carr, a distinguished British analyst, wrote that the "exposure by realist criticism of the hollowness of the Utopian [Wilsonian] edifice" was "the most urgent task of the moment . . ." But, aware of the danger of replacing one simplistic notion with another, he warned that "when the sham has been demolished . . . we cannot ultimately find a resting place in pure realism." Carr was warning against the notion that desirable change is possible because it is desirable but also against the error of assuming that the future will be a simple projection of the past.

> Indeed, realism itself, if we attack it with its own weapons, often turns out in practice to be just as much conditioned as any other mode of thought. In politics, the belief that certain facts are unalterable or certain trends irresistible commonly reflects a lack of desire or lack of interest to change or resist them. . . . Consistent realism excludes four things which appear to be essential ingredients of all effective political thinking: a finite goal, an emotional appeal, a right of moral judgment and a ground for action.[2]

To paraphrase one aspect of Carr's thought: ideas about the reality of things also form a part of the reality of things. It is as futile to ignore what men are trying to create as to assume that change, if willed to take place, will occur because of sheer determination.

World War II did not eclipse idealist thinking. Much of it focused on the new world organization, the United Nations, founded in 1945. But a new insistence on "realism," especially upon the deep roots of conflict, already present in the literature of the 1930s, began to dominate that of the 1940s and 1950s. When the UN fell into superpower deadlock, with the veto and the Korean "police action" of 1950 ending in an American-Chinese confrontation on the battlefield, the thrust toward a new realism grew greater. "Power politics" and the idea that "international politics" and "the struggle for power" were the same thing said twice, captured front stage center.

---

2 E. H. Carr, *The Twenty Years' Crisis, 1919–1939,* London: Macmillan, 1939, see pp. 113–119.

Such concepts were already gaining popularity when Nicholas John Spykman's book, *America's Strategy in World Politics*, appeared in 1942, but
Spykman's argument was the most influential. Spykman argued that

> States are always engaged in curbing the force of some other state. The truth is
> that states are interested only in a balance which is in their favor. Not an equi-
> librium, but a generous margin is their objective. There is no real security in being
> just as strong as a potential enemy; there is security only in being a little stronger.
> There is no possibility of action if one's strength is fully checked; there is a chance
> for a positive foreign policy only if there is a margin of force which can be
> freely used. Whatever the theory and the rationalization, the practical objective is
> the constant improvement of the state's own relative power position.[3]

Spykman was the last of the prenuclear theorists. By comparison with
Spykman's moderate terms that states are "engaged in curbing the force of
some other state," Hans J. Morgenthau's landmark book, *Politics Among
Nations*, which first appeared in 1949, avoided the emphasis on the use of
force as such, but actually broadened the definitions further by making
power-struggle the central theoretical principle. Morgenthau said: "International politics, like all politics, is a struggle for power. Whatever the
ultimate aims of international politics, power is always the immediate aim."
Because "the aspiration for power [is] the distinguishing element of international politics, as of all politics, international politics is of necessity power
politics."[4] That there is much room for argument about these propositions
was amply attested by the theoretical controversies of the next decade.

What was striking about these "realist" views (i.e., views centering on
power struggle or power accumulation propositions) is what they had in
common with idealist thinking: gross generalization. All or most states were
seen as taking power-oriented actions to improve their relative power position or acquire power. Not being "checked" and having a "margin of force
which can be freely used" become important motivations for states, according to Spykman. Thus, in the realist formulation, all states seek power or
"control" over other states. In the idealists' formulation, all states but the
occasional lawbreaker, seek peace. Both formulations were deficient in that
they inhibited or discouraged resort to further distinctions. Of course, if the
formulations are simply true and accurate descriptions of fundamental and
universal or quasi-universal behavior, then the lack of precision or discrimination in categorizing behavior will not matter. But if it is important to be
precise, and to distinguish degrees, neither idealism nor realism takes us
very far.[5] What would we say?—that Switzerland loves peace 37 per cent

---

[3] Nicholas J. Spykman, *America's Strategy in World Politics*, 1942, see particularly pp.
20–25.

[4] Hans J. Morgenthau, *Politics Among Nations*, 4th ed., New York, Knopf, 1967, pp.
25 and 29.

[5] Morgenthau did provide three distinctive power categories: maintaining power, demonstrating power, and increasing power. Were these precise enough?

more than Communist China but the Soviet Union struggles 216 per cent harder for power? Can such generalizations tell us useful things in the abstract and apart from the situations which specific states confront at specific times and places?

Where realists differed drastically with idealists was in their view of the nature of man, the idealists believing (in Morgenthau's words) in "the essential goodness and infinite malleability of human nature," whereas the realists assumed that this is "inherently a world of opposing interests and of conflict [in which] moral principles can never be fully realized [but can] at best be approximated through the ever temporary balancing of interests and the ever precarious settlement of conflicts."[6] If the idealist vision came to pass man would appear in a full natural goodness previously obscured by the "slum" conditions of his power environment. If the realist vision came to pass man would accept his conflict-prone nature but rationally seek to resolve and accommodate conflict. What "goodness" he would demonstrate would be in efficient thinking or negotiation to avoid "unnecessary" bloodshed, rather than in structured moral terms.

Thus the long contest between idealism and realism raises questions in two directions: one, into the deep philosophical issue of the nature of man as modified by the state system structure in which he presently lives in the world; the other, into the problem of the adequacy of fairly gross categories purporting to describe uniform or universal behavior across the state system and simultaneously including such incongruous pairs as superpower–ministate, and Black unindustrialized–Swiss contemporary. For, if the differences matter, we need at least two sets of categories for our generalizations: those things true of all, and those things true of some but not others. These categories will then need careful alignment with each other.

3

It is exactly for these reasons that another round of controversy became needed. With the idealists' forces decimated by the disappointments of the 1950s (and until their new rally around "peace studies" in the 1960s–1970s), the field was left at first to the realists. Their arguments, although obscured by the later, more eye-catching controversy of the "traditionalists" vs. the "behaviorists," were fairly fundamental because they involved the very point of the grossness of generalizations. Curiously, many of the behaviorists have tended to dismiss or overlook these "neorealist" arguments, perhaps out of some feeling that their own disagreement counts more. Yet there have been important differences in view among contemporary "traditionalists" who have relied on national interest theory as a major source of explanation. Charles McClelland, for example, when he speaks of this group—mentioning Kenneth W. Thompson—indicates that all in this group have

---

[6] Ibid., p. 3.

not agreed with Hans Morgenthau's use of the concept.[7] What McClelland does not dwell on is that the range of use of the concept of national interest is easily as broad as the range in behavioral approaches. Certainly we should all recognize that a mystical or gross invocation of the idea of national interest, without further refinements, is about as useless as the gross generalizations we have already discussed. But that is not the only way national interest theory can be used.

Since the nature of the behaviorist dissatisfaction with power-struggle concepts is amply clarified by McClelland, it will be helpful here to pass over their critique and ask now what a useful theory of international relations, which avoids the grossness and overgeneralization of idealism-realism, must provide.

To understand and discuss international relations we need a theory capable of explaining phenomena and data on three levels. First, such a theory must be able to tell us about the process by which a nation-state decides upon a foreign policy in the first place, and how, when, and why it revises that policy. We need to be able to describe this process to explain why, for example, the United States in 1972 revised its China policy. The first level of analysis must center on what influential interest groups and individuals in the nation as a whole were pushing for policy revision, and what the views in the Congress were, as compared to the arguments in the State Department, Defense Department, and the White House staff. But such views, of course, are not formed in a vacuum, without relevance to events and trends outside the national frontiers. Therefore the argument within the United States cannot be construed, too simply, as a purely "internal" push and shove of opposing American viewpoints occurring in a sealed "national" environment.

Second, such a theory must be able to tell us about the effect of one nation's policies on other nations. When Nixon, for example, visited Peking, the Soviet Union and Japan (to name just two) were as directly affected as was the United States or Communist China. So was Taiwan. On this second level we are dealing with foreign policy reevaluations for specific nations, and the alterations in a complex network of relations among them. The easy error to fall into here is to see any given "bilateral" change as though it were purely bilateral rather than multilateral in its effects.

Third, such a theory must be able to view the entire state system and describe (without overgeneralization) what is true of the whole system. It is with this third level that both idealism and realism tended to be preoccupied, leading to gross generalizations about the system which could not be applied meaningfully to the first and second levels of analysis. These gross generalizations also were open to the criticisms already made: in

---

[7] See Charles McClelland, *Theory and the International System*, New York: Macmillan, 1966. (The second selection in this chapter.)

particular, that they did not accurately describe system-wide behavior. Yet there must be things in principle which are true of the system as a whole since we know, for example, that its tension level rises and falls (i.e., there is more danger or less danger of war at one time compared to another).

Moreover, our theory must be equally applicable to all three levels if it is to serve any useful purpose. The idealist-realist concepts acknowledged this need but assumed that meaningful truths on the first and second levels could be deduced from the systems level generalizations. It is for this reason that the behavioral attack on these propositions was needed. But to the extent that many of these alternative behavioral concepts were limited to one level only, they also fell short of the goal. It was assumed, of course, that bits and pieces of evidence and generalization, built-up "scientifically," would ultimately coalesce into a grand theory. (Also, as Bull brings out in his widely known article in *World Politics*,[8] some of the behavioral model-builders, like the idealists and realists before them, actually concentrated on grand theory—this time more "scientific.")

The difficulties with these assumptions are of two kinds. First, the need for a theory will not wait. As we saw, Johnson and Vietnam did not wait. Rusk acted on the theory he knew. It is supremely ironic that the great period of U.S. involvement in Vietnam is also the period during which the predominant portion of American academic energy was drained into "building" theory "scientifically" while policy questions went by default. Second, there is no guarantee that bits and pieces of theory will ever culminate in a comprehensive whole. Such observations are not meant to deride or discourage the effort, but only to point out that grand theory is needed in the here-and-now which can also be used on the other levels.

What do we do, then, in the meantime? The choice has certain set limits: if we want to affect policy we must at least initially use terms familiar enough to policy-makers (or readily translatable). At this point national interest theory would seem to be an important candidate. With it we can meet practitioners of policy with a common vocabulary which needs only the addition of relatively simple subdivisions and categories to begin to be useful.

It is easy enough to point out that statesmen frequently use national interest terms very loosely. But to dismiss these usages as though they did not exist hardly promises progress. Besides, a content analysis of policy statement around the world shows certain clear uniformities. When something is described as a "vital interest" or "supreme interest" (or sometimes, in Soviet practice, as a "state interest"), it is obvious that the intended message is meant to reflect a judgment about the seriousness of what is at stake: that there is a real threat of, or real possibility of, resort to force.

---

[8] Hedley Bull, "International Theory: The Case for a Classical Approach," *World Politics, 18* (April 1966), pp. 361–377. (The third selection in this chapter.)

Critics of national interest theory are correct, on the other hand, in rejecting the gross generalization that each nation has *a* national interest which it pursues as sort of a guiding star.

Let us apply national interest theory to our three levels and see whether and how well it serves to permit more precise generalizations.

First, on the single nation-state level it will be helpful to consider that policy represents what is chosen at any given time from among divergent and contradictory possibilities. It is not possible simultaneously to attempt to "normalize" U.S. relations with Peking while opposing Peking at every point. Choices are inescapable. What is significant here is to observe at any given time not only the "national interest" chosen for implementation in policy but also the "national interest" rejected for the time being. Each choice is both positive and negative. Thus the calculus of advantage/disadvantage is significant and illuminating from both the positive and negative points of view. Such *counterbalancing national interest* analysis indicates the relative weight of the groups within a nation pushing for a decision. To say that "a policy shift has occurred" can be more precisely rephrased into the statement that a recalculation or reassessment has resulted in substituting a previously rejected interest, incompatible with the first choice, for the one previously implemented. Behind such a recalculation, implied or explicit, is a reshaping of foreign policy strategy (i.e., the conception of what the "game" is about and how it should be played).

Looking at the second level, the interactions of specific nations, we can see that the substitution of one counterbalancing national interest for another in American policy toward China will result in a recalculation not only by China but by all the rest who have made the original calculation of their own interests in the light of America's or China's previous policy. Thus one most important effect of America's new policy toward China is likely to be a change of policy on the part of the Soviet Union. Indeed, this may be the United States' actual objective.

Looking at the third level, the system as a whole, we can conclude that we can make fair sense of the behavior of the total system by realizing that nations, as the major actors, are continually engaged in alternative contingency analysis as the prelude to shifting policies as required. In this process, who the United States is, and how important its policy shifts are to the system as a whole or particular actors within it, will determine the degree of system-wide change which accompanies the American recalculation and shift.

Thus the concept of common and opposed national interests, highly useful in examining the content of a bilateral relationship at any given time, can be seen to be ultimately highly relativistic. Such interests are subject at certain points to significant alteration. One can pass quickly from a highly opposed bilateral relation between Nazi Germany and the Soviet Union in 1938 to the highly common relation of the nonaggression pact (and secret agreement to divide up Poland) of 1939, and to completely hostile relations after the Nazi attack on Russia of 1941.

The existence of counterbalancing national interest calculations (which enable one to analyze the potential shifts in the system) forms one useful guiding principle. A second is to be found in the principle of the "conservation of enemies," by which is meant the usual and common behavior of nations in seeking to avoid the collection of a greater array of enemies or potential enemies than they can readily handle at any one time. Anyone can cite examples of nations who came to grief by disregarding this prudent rule. What rare exceptions exist prove the general truth of the rule as a guide to normal state behavior.

Typically, nations strive to decrease the opposition to their policy or at least hold it to manageable proportions. They accomplish this objective either by recalculating their own counterbalancing interests or by getting other states to recalculate theirs. If, for example, with the U.S. deployed in Vietnam, the Chinese Communists are forced (conservation of enemies) to mute tensions with the Soviet Union because of the possibility of conflict with the United States, the Soviet Union enjoys great freedom of maneuver in the Middle East both because the United States is tied down in a remote theater in Asia and China's passivity in Russia's rear is more or less guaranteed by the American presence. Alter the American deployment in Asia and Soviet behavior is affected on two grounds: the United States is freer and so is China. One could argue that China will not behave prudently in the first circumstance. Some nations do not. In actual fact, China did. If such insights are rejected one has great difficulties in explaining the increased Soviet moderation which has been accompanying the U.S. winddown of its commitment in Southeast Asia and Nixon's visit to Peking. That the Soviet Union is acutely aware of all of this is readily demonstrated from Soviet sources. These two cardinal principles of national interest theory, counterbalancing national interests and conservation of enemies, together form a working model for analysis. Compared to Spykman's model this model has a much higher degree of sophistication and utility.

A survey of theory of this length can hardly do complete justice to a body of arguments compiled over a fifty-year period. The point is to see that the disagreements over the nature of man and the reasons for conflict have not been resolved by the coming of "science" to international relations. Computers are still programmed from initial assumptions just as any other theory model must be. What has been gained is the greater awareness of creating more verifiable hypotheses about the relations of nations and a common commitment in contemporary analysis to more precise and usable generalizations. It does not matter very greatly what labels are attached to these attempts. While it is important not to fall prey to the tempting illusion that dealing with numbers in itself avoids ambiguities, most "scientific" analyses are well aware of these problems. What is highly unscientific about the exceptions is their closed mind to what can be accomplished with other approaches. The truly scientific approach, reflected in the experience of many disciplines before international relations theory came to its present state, has always insisted on imagination in approaching problems, rigor in formulating propositions, and care in explicating both data and its analysis. It can be done in words, it can be done with diagrams, it can be done with numbers.[9] But if the practitioner cannot come to see its relevance it remains highly academic while the world goes on unmoved. Thus, while "pure" research, even if mathematically complicated, serves a purpose, so too does the attempt to formulate a readily understandable body of theory for decision-makers.

---

[9] See, for example, Russell L. Ackoff's imaginative efforts to provide "operational definitions" for conflict and cooperation in "Structural Conflicts within Organizations," in J. R. Lawrence, ed., *Operational Research and the Social Sciences*, London and New York: Tavistock Publications, 1966, pp. 427–438.

2

POWER AND INFLUENCE

CHARLES A. McCLELLAND[*]

Power is an explanatory concept that is applied with equal facility to physical phenomena and human affairs. . . . It is to be expected that interpretations of international relations often will put power in the forefront and that the power concept figures prominently in international theory.

At least three somewhat different images are evoked in the common use of the term power. The first image makes out power to be something akin to a possession or a piece of property. The second causes it to be conceived as a moving force resembling, in social affairs, the functions of an electric current or the flow of a fluid in physical or biological structures. The third image causes power to be viewed as a trait or an attribute appearing in the relations of men. These three images often are interwoven in the interpretations of events with the result that it is usually impossible to separate the references. . . . Let us see if these assertions maintain a general plausibility despite several shifts from one image to another.

Power is something possessed by persons and social groups. Like money, it can be employed for many different purposes. It is something that can be

---

[*] Reprinted with permission of The Macmillan Company from *Theory and the International System*, pp. 61–89, by Charles A. McClelland. © Charles A. McClelland 1966.

used, it is something that can be distributed, it is something that can be won, and it is something that can be lost. Power may be pitted against power; the use of power is intimately associated with conflict. Power is also a force that can be balanced among power-holders or that can be thrown out of balance. Power varies from situation to situation [and] the power of a state decreases as the distance increases between its source and the point of its application.

Power is the motive force in the international system. Each national system possesses an amount of power, and each national system is able to mobilize and use its power by calling on subsystems for assistance. National systems, in interacting with one another, may consume power and generate power. What we previously have called the international system by referring to all the transactions and exchanges among national systems must be, in terms of power, something like an energy system. There is a worldwide distribution of power among the many national systems. Some nations, being more powerful than others, will tend to attract weaker nations. Under the forces of this attraction, groups or camps of nations will be formed. Under the effects of repulsion such camps may break apart. A transformation in the international system will occur as a result of changes in the power situation, either gains or losses or redistribution of power among the members of the system. The uneven gains in power and the consequent redistributions of power are the phenomena behind most international conflicts and behind the instabilities of this age. . . .

In order to control the international system or in order to induce or prevent transformations, one would need to know how to cause changes in power sources, in power relationships, or in both. The theory of the international system is really a theory about power configurations and about the necessary and sufficient conditions for maintaining these configurations or for changing them.

The foregoing remarks about power probably appear to be entirely reasonable, and some readers may feel that an approach to the explanation of the international system in terms of power has the advantage of bringing the subject suddenly into a sharp focus. If power operates in a complicated way in international relations and if several images are required to understand its effects, it might still follow that the power approach explains a great deal about international events within a single frame of reference. Since it has been made abundantly clear in the earlier discussion that it is impossible to know everything about the workings of the international system, should we not exploit the simplification that results from concentrating on the single aspect of the phenomenon of power in international relations? This question has already been answered in the affirmative. A major school of thought has developed around the power concept in the study of international relations, and it has been accepted for several decades by many scholars that power is the organizing idea for the whole discipline of political science.

. . . In order to understand the current status of the power idea, we must give attention to three tasks: (a) to understand the formulation of the power interpretation of the realist school of international relations, (b) to consider the criticisms advanced against realist interpretations, and (c) to assess the place of power phenomena in international relations according to the new perspective.

The Realist Formulation

There is broad agreement that the most comprehensive and successful characterization of international relations in the frame of reference of political power is to be found in the writings of Hans J. Morgenthau. As one might expect, not all realists have espoused each and every statement made by Morgenthau. Kenneth W. Thompson, a leading realist, has observed, in fact, that "much of the literature of international politics is a dialogue, explicit or not, between Morgenthau and his critics. . . ."[1] Many differences in point of view and on details exist within the realist school of thought; we must recognize, however, that the Morgenthau version of the power theory of international politics occupies the center of the stage.

For twenty years, Professor Morgenthau has explained, defended, and reinterpreted his system of ideas on power in a series of books and in scores of essays and articles. He has remained remarkably consistent in his outlook; the result is that his main contentions can be summarized easily, while the detailed lines of his reasoning and the particular elements of his defense can be understood only through an extended study. Thus, only his main contentions are reviewed, in brief, in this treatment.

"International politics, like all politics, is a struggle for power"[2] is the famous statement by which Morgenthau has characterized his subject. . . . In the international environment, . . . restraints are either too weak to exert real controls or are nonexistent. Whenever relations among independent and sovereign political units come into being in history, as in the ancient Greek city-states and in the modern European state system, the power consideration becomes dominant. Morgenthau finds this situation to be inescapable in history and the reflection of an iron law of politics. The unit of the system is always the state, and no other units have any appreciable significance. Further, differences in previous historical experience, the particular structure of a society, and any other national or societal characteristics are not crucial factors in how a state behaves, for the basic reason that the struggle for power is a concern so strong that it will override these factors.

International relations, as a whole, may be conceived to take in a range of interests and activities beyond the power focus, but international *politics*

---

[1] Kenneth W. Thompson, "American Approaches to International Politics," *Yearbook of World Affairs* (1959), p. 222.

[2] Hans J. Morgenthau, *Politics Among Nations; The Struggle for Power and Peace*, 3rd ed. (New York: Alfred A. Knopf, 1960), p. 27.

is that part of the whole that is defined as having *the* central significance. In this age, Morgenthau has contended, the interest in international relations is concentrated on international politics, which is to say, on the struggle for power among nation-states. Every national government is preoccupied with the struggle, and every government must adjust its actions to power requirements. Depending on its relative power position and the overall distribution of power in the system, a nation-state has only a limited number of choices to make among policies. Fundamentally, a state can pursue only three types of policies and can make an appropriate choice among these at any given time according to its power position. The three policies to choose among are (a) the status quo, (b) expansion, or imperialism, and (c) prestige. The latter policy involves the action of demonstrating the power that the state has. The other two are concerned with holding power and increasing it.

There are two reasons, each of which reinforces the other, for such a narrow range of choice for the policy-making of nation-states. One might ask why a state could not invent a fourth fundamental type of policy. Or it could be asked why states could not merely decide to cease the struggle for power. In particular, why could it not happen that the men who run governments would see that conflicts over power are wasteful and destructive for all and would undertake to build international arrangements for cooperation instead of conflict? The first answer is that the will to power is simply a part of human nature; human beings are possessed by that will and reforms are not available to correct an underlying and permanent condition of man-in-society. The second answer is that the logic of the power situation is unassailable. Whenever or wherever a system of relations among separate, sovereign political entities comes into being, the rules of power prevail, without alternative. Moral restraints and the limitations on conduct imposed by legal rules invariably prove to be too weak to change the relations among the political entities to any form other than that of the patterns controlled by power considerations.

Some readers may still wish, at this point, to resist these two fundamental answers to why the world cannot lift itself out of the struggle for power, both domestically and internationally. They may not be content to accept the assertion that it is Utopian to expect anything else. How do Morgenthau and his followers meet resistance of this type? A clue can be found in what was said earlier about the different approaches to the justification of theory— the tests of the literary tradition and the tests of the scientific tradition. Morgenthau is perfectly clear in his mind about these tests; he accepts the literary tradition and rejects the scientific. Essentially, he relies on the force of reasoned arguments based on the lessons of history and the words of earlier authorities to give validity to the power theory of international politics, and he warns others of the dangers and follies that come from rejecting time-honored truths of the long human experience.

Much that has been given attention in this discussion about the need for increased knowledge of international behavior and about the possibilities of matching research findings and intelligent actions to the vast problems of the multiple transformations of the international system is not relevant in the perspective of the realist school of thought. The reason has already been shown: the international system is caught in the meshes of the absolutely basic condition of power competition and power struggle and there is no way to extricate it. The essence of realism is to come to terms with the inevitable and the unchangeable and to find ways to live with the facts. Is Morgenthau, then, a gloomy pessimist who predicts no possible escape from oncoming disasters? The answer seems to be that he is extremely critical of current foreign policies but not at all in despair over the eventual outcome. He is not without hope and solutions.

Intelligent actions by the governments of states have a limited but important capacity to guide the interplay of power. Many different kinds of concrete historical situations confront governments, and, of course, statesmen must deal with these as they occur. Further, a nation will conceive of many desired objectives in international relations. It is natural, especially in democratic countries, to have high hopes that things will turn out well and everybody will live happily ever after. Responsible governments cannot permit themselves the luxury of such sentiments, however. The cardinal rule for the nation-state is to respond to historical situations and to the multitudes of desired national objectives strictly according to its own national interest. Morgenthau refers repeatedly to the national interest defined in terms of power; what this means, simply, is that the concern over the power position of the nation is the primary consideration and that it conditions everything else. Thus, any historical situation or any particular desired national objective is to be evaluated and measured by the yardstick of the nation's power position. The sober calculation of the national interest is the key to a viable system of international relations.

Collaborative relations between nations ensue from a convergence of interests. Coalitions form and endure when several nations are willing to act on their strong common interests. International conflicts are the consequences of clashing national interests. Conflict and collaboration, when firmly based on calculated interests, often can be brought into a desirable condition of equilibrium. A balance of power is a stabilizing arrangement and should be sought in the interplay of the policies of states.

Although the nature of the state system, made up of sovereign states, prevents any final outcomes or permanent arrangements, wise diplomacy often can bring about suitable accommodations among competing states. The extremes of violence in international relations can be avoided. Indeed, the road to peace—and the only real recourse for nations—is to conduct affairs through adept diplomacy. Good diplomats are rare men who can see through the superficialities of daily events, who recognize the limitations on their activities, and who have a deep intuitive grasp on the realities of power.

Great statesmen come on the historical stage only infrequently but when they appear they make a vast difference in the affairs of the world. Great statecraft and efficient diplomacy are practices that belong in the realm of art; the sciences really have nothing to do with these skills. Knowledge that can be produced by the special cultures of science will have little contribution to make to the managing of relations among nations. Along with "moralism" and "legalism," the "scientism" of the social sciences is a misleading influence and is capable of damaging the conduct of international relations to the extent that trust is placed in scientific research to relieve the problems of the international system.

One further point about the realist formulation must be emphasized: at best it is a simplification and an idealization of how relations may be conducted. As a distillation of historical experience, this model is not regarded as an outline of important and unanswered research questions. It contains answers, not questions. Research is important to the realists, however, to discover how current policies and contemporary developments vary from the ideal of the model. That there will be a divergence of actual practice from the ideal is to be expected; but it is the responsibility of the scholar to find the differences and to exhort the practitioners of foreign affairs to reduce the disparities. Thus, a normative tendency in the power approach is persistent.

As long as the basic laws of international politics are known, asserts the realist, there is no reason for the theorist who understands the rules to hesitate to urge other men to bring practices as closely in line with the laws as possible. To the objection sometimes raised that a law of politics could not be violated—that if men are subjected to laws they have no choice but to be bound, as in the case of the law of gravitation—the realist answer is that the model of power politics contains only the ideal rules. Men, being imperfect, can only approach the ideal. When they make errors by moving *away* from the ideal, rather than toward it, however, these shortcomings are to be pointed out and criticized.

The struggle for power among nations is traceable, according to the realist conception, to a trait in human nature. It is human to seek power. If power is so all-encompassing, how do we recognize its presence and its nonpresence and how do we distinguish it from other phenomena? What is power? How is power to be decided and defined?

In writing about power in many places and contexts, Morgenthau has offered numerous descriptions and definitions of what he means by power. The characterization *the struggle for power* suggests, of course, the ideas of power as a possession and of power as a force. Most frequently, Morgenthau defines power as a special value; it is a possession but not in a tangible form like money or real estate. In a definition that has often been singled out for attention, he says that power is an attribute of a relationship between actors, in these terms:

Political power is a psychological relation between those who exercise it and those over whom it is exercised. It gives the former control over certain actions of the latter through the influence which the former exerts over the latter's mind.[3]

It is interesting that Morgenthau often uses the word *control* to indicate the meaning of power.

It is precisely to the point of how to identify power that inquiry has returned, time and again. Neither Morgenthau nor anyone else has been able to satisfy this curiosity. If power is to be used as a central organizing concept of a theory of international relations, then we must discover what it is with sufficient precision that it will not be mixed and confused with other manifestations, whatever the latter may be. If there is nothing but power to be discriminated, understanding will be frustrated. Not everything can be power; we must have at least one other class, perhaps to be called only *not-power*, to provide some contrast or comparison. Thus, in the literature one finds many efforts to say what power is, of what it is composed, and how it is to be recognized.

The Search for Definitions of Power

One familiar method for describing power is to look into its sources. Representative of the approach is the treatment given in the textbook by Norman D. Palmer and Howard C. Perkins. The authors list and discuss seven contributing elements: geography, natural resources, technology, population, ideology, morale, and leadership. That these probably are the sources of national power seems quite obvious. One might think that the actual calculations of the power of nations would be a straightforward process of studying each of these sources in detail. Expert analyses must, by now, have established ratings of power for all nation-states. Indeed, such attempts have been made. The results are not satisfactory, however, for at least two basic reasons.

The elements of power are considered to play back and forth on one another—to affect the set of elements mutually—so that the products of combinations of elements are made difficult to assess. Deficiencies in natural resources may be offset by clever technologies. Leadership may be diminished by a particular ideology. All the elements are so intertwined and the ensuing complexity is so great that some observers have been led to give up all hope of evaluating power with any precision. If there is no way to measure—which is also to say, to assess, estimate, and evaluate—then there is really no way to tell what the power status of a country is. And if there is no way to decide about the power of nations, nothing of importance can be asserted about power distributions. We may *deduce*, however, what the power status of a country once *was*, relative to the power of other countries, by noting the outcomes of historical events. Such findings are also very

---

[3] Hans J. Morgenthau, op. cit., p. 29.

uncertain and are less valuable than one would wish. The more important question is always what the power situation is now or what it will be in the immediate future.

The second reason for finding power calculations at the source unsatisfactory is bound up in the question, power for what? It should be immediately apparent that many of the typical actions of international relations—the negotiating of a treaty is one example—do not require the direct use of much power and do not draw appreciably on the power sources. Further, if psychological efficacy produced by the presence of power is to be taken as a test of power, certain negative consequences are sometimes noticed to occur. The existence of massive power sources in one country sometimes causes adjacent countries to react with fear and anxiety and results in attempts to reduce the possibilities of future control by the powerful neighbor. Here, the power in hand tends to offset the power to control. If a nation's objective is to increase its potential to control through acts of goodwill—by foreign assistance or disaster relief, for instance—morale, the size of the population, geographical location, and other elements of power may not have any connection with the attainment of the goal. Many other observations have been made along this line. Apparently, it is necessary to take into account both the sources of power and the objectives of power; the consideration of only the elements of power does not identify sufficiently the power of nations. . . .

One of the proposed solutions to the troublesome problem of identifying power in terms of the elements at the source has been to employ the concept of *capability* as an additional and essential distinction. National capabilities suggest the potential to be powerful. This notion helps to separate that which *could be* mobilized and brought into play from the actual effort and effect. The effort and the effect can then be characterized as power. An advantage in the idea of separating capability and power lies in the need to identify the *process* of converting potential power at the source into applied and effective power. Some directions for answering the power-to-do-what question take shape in the tracing of the conversion process. An analytic scheme for following the main steps of the conversion can be constructed from the following statements.

1. National capability is a complex of elements, the particular combinations of which lie latent within a national society.

2. The varying situations of international politics require decision-makers to make estimates and judgments on what kinds, combinations, and amounts of the national capability will be needed for future use and, hence, will be mobilized.

3. The capabilities that are allocated for ultimate use as designated by the decision-makers are processed through the channels of relevant political, military, economic, and social organizations. Factors of selection, control, coordination, timing, and phasing are influences that bear on the effective-

ness of the conversion process and, therefore, on the production of power. Power losses may arise from breakdown, overload, miscalculation, interruption, bad timing, and other disorders in the organizational channels. . . .

4. Since the conversion from capability to power involves planning and operations in the channels of organization, there will be, invariably, a passage of time from the moment when a decision to mobilize power is made to the time of its readiness for use. The use of power occurs in the context of some particular international situation. The passage of time and the participation of two or more actors will result, almost always, in changes in the international situation. Thus, a factor influencing the effectiveness of power is the variable of change in the situation. . . .

5. The mobilizing of power, then, is a dynamic process having organizational and situational limits on its uses. Power is limited further at the place and time of its application, by a calculus involving desired objectives and realistic payoffs. Some objectives are always in play provided the activity is not merely aimless. National objectives are, without exception, numerous and complexly ordered with respect to their priorities. Specific international situations, as perceived, will frequently cause a shift in the combinations of active national objectives and will result in temporary rearrangements of their priorities. In rapidly changing international situations, the use of mobilized power in pursuit of certain objectives may, even in a matter of days, become displaced and ineffective simply because a reordering of immediate objectives will accompany changes in the situation. Different kinds of power applied in different ways and amounts may be needed to realize objectives.

Decision-makers do not expect to satisfy a full set of national objectives in every international situation. Instead, they are required to settle for what they can get. They search for the best possible payoffs, given both circumstances and goals. Thus, there is an additional calculus at work that conditions the use of power. How far a nation pushes toward its objectives depends on what the local factors are in the situation, what capabilities are ready in the channels, what level of measures is deemed most appropriate to that situation and to the active values, and what degree of success the decision-makers are willing to accept. Short- and long-term anticipated consequences of the employment of power complicate the choice of objectives further and, hence, these considerations also influence the effectiveness of power in use.

The notion of a conversion process between capability and power leads to a more complicated conceptualization of power in international relations than was suggested at the beginning of the discussion. It has the additional consequence of stimulating questions about the simple idea that power is something possessed and applied. The realization that the presence of power is contingent on the working of a complex process tends to encourage the proposition that the thing called power is a misconception. Theoretical questioning of the power concept has produced the tentative conclusion that power is only an abstract attribute or property connected with interactions and relationships. A brief review of certain aspects of the theory of the international system, as developed earlier, may be helpful in providing the setting for this view of power.

In the definition given in [an earlier part of McClelland's book], it was stressed that the international system is made up of transactions and patterns of transactions. This idea is readily ignored because of a natural tendency to emphasize the sources of the transactions—the national systems—and to consider them as the units of the system. Further, the power approach to international politics makes the nation-state the unit of the state system. To the question, of what the international system is composed, the easy answer is likely to be that the international system is composed of nation-states. This is wrong according to the system outlook. In order to indicate that the nation-state should *not* be thought of either as the constituting part of the international system or as a fixed body, the term *national system* was introduced. It was stressed that the national system, itself being composed of large numbers of interactions of subsystems, should be conceived more in the analogy of the flow of a river, changing its condition according to the environment through which it moves, than in the analogy of some kind of fixed physical structure. Throughout, our concern has been to establish the view that, in considering international relations, we are dealing with activities on the move and impinging on one another to create relationships. The realities that interest us are *acts;* the main facts are reports about acts. References to structures are references to patterned and recurring relationships. If we require units for counting or evaluating purposes, we should look for them in the transactions, and perhaps we should even assign to them a general name such as *transacts*. Units certainly will not be nation-states or national systems. Given these ideas, we can conceive of power only as some characteristic, trait, or property associated with streams of transactions.

Although there is no necessity to fall back on physical analogies, some illustration of the idea of power in the system context is afforded in what most of us know about motors and engines. A certain gasoline engine is said to *have* fifty horsepower. We are not under any illusion, however, that a quantity of fifty horsepower is possessed or owned by that engine. All that we are willing to accept is that it *rates* at fifty horsepower when it is running under certain specified conditions. We understand that horsepower results from interacting processes involving fuel, air, combustion, and mechanical motions, all of which occur in going through the engine. The horsepower of the engine is a performance trait. Similarly, we can say that power is a performance trait of international relations. We repeat the idea by saying that power is to be interpreted as a property of the international system. The old, stubborn question remains, however. What means or methods are to be used to determine when the trait of power is present in an international transaction? What is power?

The Behavioral Inquiry

During recent years a number of students of political behavior have been attracted to the study of power. . . .

. . . The significant advance is . . . in the shift, under the behavioral impact, in the concept of what power is and where to look for it. Harold and Margaret Sprout have remarked in their recent textbook: "The notion of power as a quantifiable mass is giving way to the concept of power as a behavioral relationship."[4] An active theorist of international behavior, J. David Singer, has reached the same conclusion: "The concept does not come to life except as it is observed in action, and that action can be found only when national power is brought into play by nations engaged in the process of influencing one another. Until that occurs, we have no operational indices of power. . . ."[5]

Power in international relations is being reconceptualized as one among other traits that appear in the transactions of nations. The Sprouts call attention to the fact that the transactions of international politics are made up of the demands and responses of governments. Political demands and responses take many forms and occur with different degrees of intensity and urgency. Governments are engaged unceasingly in attempts to influence the actions of other governments and to cope with influence efforts directed at them by others. This shift of focus, apparently slight but actually more radical than it appears at first, leads theory away from the idea of the struggle for power among nations and toward a theory of influence oriented to the transactions—the successions of demands and responses—of governments. This transition is still so new that some serious terminological problems have yet to be resolved.

Some writers have wished to use power and influence as interchangeable terms while others have preferred to preserve a distinction between the two to identify separate behavioral properties. Singer, for example, merely defines power as the capacity to influence, and turns thereafter to an analysis of the influence processes. . . .

Bachrach and Baratz adhere to the notions that "power is relational, as opposed to possessive or substantive"[6] and that a manifestation of power requires the presence of certain conditions in the transactional situation: (1) that there be a conflict of values or interest between the parties of the transaction, (2) that one of the parties of the conflict must actually comply with the other's demands, and (3) that "a power relation can exist only if

---

[4] Harold and Margaret Sprout, *Foundations of International Politics* (Princeton, N.J.: D. Van Nostrand Company, 1962), p. 139.

[5] J. David Singer, "Inter-Nation Influence: A Formal Model," *American Political Science Review*, 57 (June 1963), p. 420.

[6] Peter Bachrach and Morton S. Baratz, "Decisions and Non-Decisions: An Analytical Framework," *American Political Science Review*, 57 (September 1963), p. 633.

one of the parties can threaten to invoke sanctions . . ."[7] They say that the threat to apply sanctions—the holding forth of the prospect of a specified punishment—is the condition that distinguishes power from influence. Further requirements are that the party subjected to the threat of sanctions must understand the nature of the threat, must regard the consequences that would follow from noncompliance as more punishing than other likely outcomes, and must believe in the intent of the threat of sanctions.

The presence of a *power* relationship, according to the Bachrach and Baratz specifications, is marked most impressively and clearly by the occurrence of threats. An *influence* relationship is substantially the same as a power relationship except that it is manifested without the presence of threatened sanctions. They point out, further, that power and influence relationships often co-occur and that one frequently leads to the other. A *force* relationship, on the other hand, involves the carrying out of sanctions and greatly contracts the element of choice that exists in the response in the power relationship. In other words, A no longer waits for a modification in B's behavior but undertakes instead to coerce B into compliance.

Bachrach and Baratz have identified two other classes of behavior in transactional situations. A *manipulative* relationship is defined as one in which one party acts to secure the compliance of another party through measures of which the affected party remains unaware. Thus, manipulation is unlike power and influence, since the recipient does not recognize either the source or the technique affecting his behavior, and therefore is presented with no choices to which he might respond in the relationship. As the theorists suggest, manipulation is related more closely to force than to power and influence. The relationship of *authority* is the last of the categories outlined by Bachrach and Baratz. They argue that authority does not work like power in relational situations. In the authoritative situation, when A makes a demand on B the requirement that B must comply is as strong as in a power situation. The difference is, however, as the authors say, that B complies not because he makes a choice of some lesser evil for the reason that he must but rather "because he recognizes that the command is reasonable in terms of his own values . . ."[8]

Let us make certain at this point that we recognize the significance of the foregoing ideas and classifications of behavior for the study of international relations. First, we need to recognize that as observers we have at our disposal a source of data in the reports of events taking place on the international scene. Our basic facts are, as the Sprouts point out, a succession of demands and responses by the officials of governments. A struggle *is* constantly in progress in which the general objective is to get others to do what we want. Concurrently, the others try to get us to do what they want. The

---

[7] Ibid., p. 633.
[8] Ibid., p. 638.

overall result is an interplay of actions in which demands and responses are the basic data. Now, the observer's purpose is to gain knowledge about what is going on; clearly, if the observer decides to label the whole interplay of demands and responses only a struggle for power among nations, he loses his chance to probe more deeply into the subject. On the other hand, if the observer is able to inspect a body of accumulated demand-response data from the standpoint of several performance traits, his prospects of gleaning additional knowledge are improved. With the help of operational indices, the student may be able to point out with some degree of precision and confidence that, in a given stream of transactions, one type of relationship occurs more often than others or that shifts from one type to another appear. . . .

Power turns out, now, to be one particular kind of relationship in international transactions and not a pervasive quality or force running through all international diplomacy and statecraft. If we use this framework, the analytic questions that we shall apply to a given record of exchanges and transactions between governments will take the form of queries about the manifestations of the

1. Relationship of power.
2. Relationship of authority.
3. Relationship of influence.
4. Relationship of manipulation.
5. Relationship of force.

Let us not assume that the locating of clusters of facts in the appropriate categories will be an easy task; the accomplishment is only that a theoretical addition has been made. One can now see more clearly what would need to be found out in order to understand more exactly what is going on in international relations. In fact, reflection on the problem may cause a person to conclude that we can never find out precisely what is going on because the essential requirement of the Bachrach and Baratz formulation is to know what is going on in men's minds, particularly with reference to their intentions and motives. It is simpler to say that all men are dominated by the will to power [but] the more that we find out about the process through which foreign policy decisions are arrived at, the more closely we shall come to the necessary information about motives and intentions. The more sure we are about motives and intentions, the more accurately can we characterize the nature of international relationships.

Already, the theoretical inquiry into power and influence in international behavior has led beyond the decision-making focus. The tests for the presence of power and influence—as well as for authority, manipulation, and force—all require behavioral evidence of the successful execution of positive acts. Decision-making is, obviously, the taking of the resolve to commit acts and to succeed. In filling out a theoretical framework, we shall wish to account for transactional phenomena that do not fall into the framework as described above. Two additional categories for observable international transactions can be put in place to accommodate those demands and responses that otherwise do not fit in the picture.

A large amount of activity in international politics appears to have no immediate effect. A may undertake to exert influence over B, but A frequently fails. In addition, A often anticipates that the attempt will fail but makes the effort, anyway. Yet, no trace of behavioral effect remains. Further, public announcements are commonly made about the exchange of views between foreign ministers and about conversations being held between heads of states. What fitting characterization will cover the relationships that consist mainly of explorations, efforts to gain up-to-the-minute information on the intentions of other governments, and the influence attempts that fail and are often expected to fail? Such behavior appears to be very common in international politics and deserves, therefore, a category in the scheme of relationship types. It is proposed that evidence of this kind be identified as belonging to the probing relationship. "Probes" are usually preliminary encounters; they seek out immediate opportunities for dealing with an opponent and they provide fresh information.

Both Singer and Bachrach and Baratz have observed a recurring relationship that closely resembles the trait of influence, but yet does not produce any observable change in the behavior of the party being influenced. Bachrach and Baratz have taken note of the efforts that frequently are made in political situations to keep potentially dangerous issues in the background and to avoid confrontations and controversies. The main purpose of such action usually is to avert the development of situations that call for decisions. Hence, the authors refer to a process of *non*decision-making. Singer speaks about the action that may characterize a relationship in the situation where B is already behaving as A wishes but A acts "to insure the continuation of such behavior."[9] There is some resemblance here, of course, between Morgenthau's policy of the status quo and Singer's influence form that he calls perpetuation or reinforcement. It seems appropriate to gather together all the transactions that keep situations in a nondecision state, meant to preserve the status quo and creating the effect of perpetuation and reinforcement, and to group them under the heading of the *maintenance relationship*. As we have already emphasized in the treatment of the theory of systems, the maintenance of a system is an important function.

We arrive, at this point, at the inquiry into ways and means of modifying the global concept of power in its classical form, at seven types of international political behavior—power, authority, influence, manipulation, force, probing, and maintenance. As we view these types in the theoretical perspective of the international system, we should expect a long succession of its transacts to exhibit combinations and mixtures of these behaviors, some

---

[9] Singer, op. cit., p. 421.

of which would be recurrent enough to be regarded as patterns. Theory passes on to research the problem of identifying and interpreting the patterns.

It would be of only limited value to have well-developed theory and research on the mixture of behavioral types in the flows of political transactions among nations without the development of explanations of the process by which national systems introduce behaviors into the stream. On what basis is it ever decided to make an influence attempt, to impose a force situation, or to act to strengthen a maintenance relationship? It will be recalled that the question of similar type in the realist formulation is answered by the concept of the pursuit of the national interest through the arts of diplomacy. Under the theory of the international system, J. David Singer has approached an answer, with special reference to power and influence relationships, through the building of a model that will now be described.

Singer accounts for the persistent efforts of governments to exert influence in international politics by reference to certain basic characteristics of the international system. He points out that nations are interdependent in the international system, yet the system provides virtually no safeguards to protect the welfare of the interdependent parties—"the scarcest commodity in the international system is security . . ." The anxiety over security combines with a very poor ability to predict the future state of the system and impels governments to make repeated influence attempts. Singer concludes that "the international system itself is the key element in explaining why and how nations attempt to influence the behavior of one another."

Given the pressure to undertake influence attempts, what circumstances will cause a government to make a particular attempt? Singer proposes that three fundamental considerations enter into an influence situation. First is the *perception* of the decision-makers of one government of what another government is presently doing. The second consideration of the decision-makers of one government is what they want the future behavior of the other government to be. The third is the *prediction* of the decision-makers of one government of what the future behavior of the other government is likely to be. These three factors—perceived present behavior, preferred future behavior, and predicted future behavior, when brought together in combination with the relevant facts of the situation, give the decision-makers the essential setting within which they exercise choice. In arriving at a choice of whether or not to make an influence attempt, and, when appropriate, in deciding which particular kind of influence attempt to make, the decision-makers face the additional problem of anticipating outcomes. It is not simply a matter of estimating the probability of successful action that faces the decision-makers; they must take into account how much they like and dislike various prospects involved in various approaches and outcomes. They face a *decisional calculus* made up of the variables of *utilities and disutilities,* on the one hand, and of probabilities of outcomes on the other hand.

The nightmarish task of deciding what to do in the setting of such complicated factors is followed by the problem of making choices of actions. It will be remembered that Morgenthau found three fundamental policy choices that can be made—to maintain power, to increase power, and to demonstrate power. Singer shows how policy choices are imbedded in a matrix of possibilities. According to the situation, the influence attempt will be either to persuade or dissuade the party to be influenced. Secondly, it will have to be decided whether to attempt to reinforce or modify the behavior of the other. Then there are four possible modes of action to be employed: to undertake efforts to threaten the other, to hold forth promises to the other, to punish the other, or to reward the other. What line of action will the decision-makers follow and, therefore, what will they contribute to the ongoing stream of transactions of the international system? Singer's answers are theoretical in that they set up problems and questions for research. . . .

Power, Influence, and Other Behavioral Traits in the International System: A Summary

The survey of the ideas of power and influence of this chapter arouses some serious problems. These problems cannot be evaded. It should be entirely apparent from the discussion that a very large investment has been made in the past in the theoretical explanation of international politics in terms of power. A major part of the current understanding of international relations is based squarely on the power concept. . . . It is almost true that if a prohibition were imposed to eliminate the use of the idea of power, the field would be struck dumb. Although there is, fortunately, no sure way either to start or stop the appeal of an idea, the direction of our discussion has been to raise serious doubts about the integrity of the power concept.

To put the matter most radically, we may conclude that, with rare exceptions, the users of power explanations of international politics have only a misty notion of what they are talking about. Power is an arousing and poetic symbol capable of evoking a wide range of feelings, fears, satisfactions, and discontents in people without contributing, however, to any genuine understanding. Under hardheaded and clear-sighted scrutiny, the concept of power is diminished from a commanding theoretical resource to a very modest abstraction for which an occasional legitimate use can be found in theory and research.

It is a reasonable scholarly demand—not only a scientific requirement—to insist that vagueness and ambiguity be reduced to the lowest possible levels in the terms and concepts employed in serious inquiries. Although precision is not, itself, a proper objective of study, neither is the preservation of avoidable confusion. The issue at hand is merely a theory problem: of two intellectual policies, which is the one to be preferred? Will we be further ahead to keep the power concept intact in its classical form and with all its uncertain references, ambiguous definitions, and shadowy explanations or to overthrow it by reducing it to minor proportions so that it will be called upon only when it meets the requirements of specified operational indices?

In order to illustrate the severities lurking in the foregoing question, let us investigate only a few of the consequences that follow from the second choice and from an innocent-appearing proposition that was set forth earlier. As we have seen, several writers subscribe to the statement that power can be defined properly only in relational terms and that is is necessary to *not* consider it as a possession, a substance, or a force. Further, the conception of international relations in the frame of reference of a system of transactions makes the relational definition mandatory and results in the rejection of the other images of power. It does not seem to be too drastic to impose this restriction on the definition of power, in the interests of clarity.

We talk easily about a powerful individual; in personal experience we find, however, that we arrive at the judgment that a certain man is powerful either because others say he is or because we have discovered in our own dealings with him that he is. Of the two ways of identifying the powerful individual, we are far more certain that he is powerful on the evidence of direct dealings than through hearsay. . . . Therefore, let us see what happens to the power explanations of international politics if we set aside notions of possession, force, and substance of power. . . .

Almost everything that was asserted in the first pages of this chapter now must be rejected. Apparently, we are being quite poetic—but not informative—if we say that power can be won and lost, distributed and balanced, and applied and withheld. It is the same if we declare that power directs international events, shapes relations among nations, advances or impedes international transformations, and furnishes the means to control the international system. If we hold firmly to the concept of power as a relational property and continue to reject the possessive and substantive attributions, what happens to the realist conception of international politics? In particular, what are the consequences for the Morgenthau theory?

International politics could not possibly be the struggle of nations *for* power. How could anyone struggle for a relational property—a quality of a relationship? Morgenthau's statement about the importance of the national interest defined in terms of power takes a most peculiar shape when it is poured into the mold of the Bachrach and Baratz definition of power. It seems to have the following meaning: the national interest is the value placed on exerting influence on another nation and securing compliance by exercising threats or sanctions. If this is the great national aspiration and the only fundamental guide to policy, perhaps we should approve only those Administrations that undertake projects to require the compliance of the Soviet Union by the use of potent threats. When the Soviet Union fails to comply, our regret would be great over the loss of national interest, but we would rejoice when the Soviet Union does comply. All this is, of course, a severe distortion. The realist formulations relating to power distributions and to the balance of power seem to be just as irrelevant. Similarly, the will to power would be something like a drive to get into situations characterized by goal conflicts, demands for compliance, and threat attempts. These effects on meaning are simply aberrations resulting from the use of the language of the rejected images of possession, force, and substance of power. Further illustrations are not needed; the status of the realist formulation is not in doubt. Hewing to the definition of power as a relational property has the consequence of undermining the theoretical underpinnings of the Morgenthau theory. Only the foundations are ruined, however, leaving intact a great many of Morgenthau's shrewd observations on the state of foreign policy, wise comments on the condition of international politics, and realistic insights into the follies and errors of men. . . .

It is worthwhile to bear in mind that the recent inquiries that have thrown the integrity of the old concept of power into doubt have not been inspired by any underlying animus against power. The feeling that power is evil or that power corrupts is not a consideration in the latest investigations. Instead, most of the criticisms have come from students whose initial belief was that the power concept is a major tool in the understanding of politics. One result of this positive interest is the likelihood that fresh attempts will be made to restate definitions and to introduce other frames of reference so that the idea will be rehabilitated and the present somewhat pessimistic assessment will be revised. . . .

In the course of the discussion of power and influence in this chapter, a demonstration has been made indirectly of the differences in the approaches of the realist formulation and the international system formulation. Because of some surface similarities, some students of international relations have thought that simple transpositions of ideas could reconcile one with the other. Thus, a statement that was given at the beginning to illustrate the commonsense view that power theory and system theory are about the same must be recalled. It was said at the beginning of the chapter that the "theory of the international system is really a theory about power configurations and about the necessary and sufficient conditions for maintaining these configurations or for changing them." This statement is not true.

While the realist theory makes power and interest the fundamental means of analysis and the basis of explanation, we have seen that system theory creates a focus on transactions and relationships occurring in the flow of events. The problems of system theory are to contrive conceptual tools for the analysis of transactions and relationships and to furnish the means for identifying "states" of the system under conditions of fluctuation and change. Thus, as has been shown, the concept of power, in contrast to its position in the realist theory, is assigned not to a central theoretical role but to a more modest place. The initial assessment that power has only a very minor theoretical value was revised to suggest that it is still too early for severe discounting, in the light of the most recent inquiries. The book has not been closed on the discussion of power. . . .

3

INTERNATIONAL THEORY:
THE CASE FOR A CLASSICAL APPROACH

Hedley Bull*

I

Two approaches to the theory of international relations at present compete for our attention. The first of these I shall call the classical approach. By this I do not mean the study and criticism of the "classics" of international relations, the writings of Hobbes, Grotius, Kant, and other great thinkers of the past who have turned their attention to international affairs. Such study does indeed exemplify the classical approach, and it provides a method that is particularly fruitful and important. What I have in mind, however, is something much wider than this: the approach to theorizing that derives from philosophy, history, and law, and that is characterized above all by explicit reliance upon the exercise of judgment and by the assumptions that if we confine ourselves to strict standards of verification and proof there is very little of significance that can be said about international relations, that general propositions about this subject must therefore derive from a scientifically imperfect process of perception or intuition, and that these general propositions cannot be accorded anything more than the tentative and inconclusive status appropriate to their doubtful origin.

Until very recently virtually all attempts at theorizing about international relations have been founded upon the approach I have just described. We can certainly recognize it in the various twentieth-century systematizations of international theory—in works like those of Alfred Zimmern, E. H. Carr, Hans Morgenthau, Georg Schwarzenberger, Raymond Aron, and Martin Wight. And it is clearly also the method of their various precursors, whose scattered thoughts and partial treatments they have sought to draw together: political philosophers like Machiavelli and Burke, international lawyers like Vattel and Oppenheim, pamphleteers like Gentz and Cobden, historians like Heeren and Ranke. It is because this approach has so long been the standard one that we may call it classical.

The second approach I shall call the scientific one. I have chosen to call it scientific rather than scientistic so as not to prejudge the issue I

* Hedley Bull, "International Theory: The Case for a Classical Approach," *World Politics, 18* (April 1966), pp. 361–377. Reprinted by permission.

wish to discuss by resort to a term of opprobrium. In using this name for the second approach, however, it is the aspirations of those who adopt it that I have in mind rather than their performance. They aspire to a theory of international relations whose propositions are based either upon logical or mathematical proof, or upon strict, empirical procedures of verification. Some of them dismiss the classical theories of international relations as worthless, and clearly conceive themselves to be the founders of a wholly new science. Others concede that the products of the classical approach were better than nothing, and perhaps even regard them with a certain affection, as the owner of a 1965 model might look at a vintage motor car. But in either case they hope and believe that their own sort of theory will come wholly to supersede the older type; like the logical positivists when they sought to appropriate English philosophy in the 1930's, or like Mr. McNamara's Whiz Kids when they moved into the Pentagon, they see themselves as tough-minded and expert new men, taking over an effete and woolly discipline, or pseudo-discipline, which has so far managed by some strange quirk to evade the scientific method but has always been bound to succumb to it in the end.

The scientific approach to the theory of international relations, so defined, is present in the theory of international systems, as developed by Morton A. Kaplan and others, in the various international extrapolations of John Von Neumann and Oskar Morgenstern's theory of games, in Thomas C. Schelling's theory of bargaining, in Karl W. Deutsch's work on social communication, in William H. Riker's study of political coalitions, in the models of foreign policy-making produced by George A. Modelski and others, in Lewis F. Richardson's mathematical studies of arms races and deadly quarrels, and in the theories of conflict developed by Kenneth Boulding and Anatol Rapoport. It also appears to be an important part of the content of what is called "peace research."[1]

The studies I have named vary enormously in the methods they employ and in the questions to which they are addressed. Their authors, indeed, far from facing the outside world with a united front, commonly regard one another with the hostility of leaders of Marxist sects. There are also, it may be argued, great discrepancies among them in the extent to which they have

---

[1] See, for example, Kaplan, *System and Process in International Politics* (New York, 1957); Morgenstern, *The Question of National Defense* (New York, 1959); Schelling, *The Strategy of Conflict* (Cambridge, Mass., 1960); Deutsch and others, *Political Community and the North Atlantic Area: International Organization in the Light of Historical Experience* (Princeton, 1957); Riker, *The Theory of Political Coalitions* (New Haven, 1962); Modelski, *A Theory of Foreign Policy* (New York, 1962); Richardson, *Arms and Insecurity: A Mathematical Study of the Causes and Origin of War*, ed. Nicolas Rashevsky and Ernesto Trucco (Pittsburgh, 1960), and *Statistics of Deadly Quarrels*, ed. Quincy Wright and C. C. Lienau (Pittsburgh, 1960); Boulding, *Conflict and Defense: A General Theory* (New York, 1962); Rapoport, *Fights, Games, and Debates* (Ann Arbor, 1960).

illuminated our subject. What I have called the scientific approach, moreover, is not present in all of them to the same degree. There are dangers in lumping them all together, and it may be inevitable that criticisms directed at the whole of the genre will be unfair to some parts of it. Nevertheless, all of these studies and fashions embody the scientific approach in some measure, and to discuss this it is necessary to confine our attention to what they have in common.

In the United States in the last ten years the scientific approach has progressed from being a fringe activity in the academic study of international relations to such a position that it is at least possible to argue that it has become the orthodox methodology of the subject. The award in 1963 of the American Political Science Association's prize for the best study of the year to a practitioner of the classical approach (to Inis Claude for his *Power and International Relations*) already had the appearance of a perverse action of the rear guard.

In the British academic community, by contrast, the scientific approach to the theory of international relations has had virtually no impact at all. The only Englishmen to have made a major contribution in the new genre— Lewis F. Richardson—worked alone and unrecognized in his lifetime, and when a few years ago his work was exhumed and hailed as that of a great pioneer, it was by American editors addressing themselves to a predominantly American audience. Not only have British students of internation relations not sought to contribute to theory in this vein, but, with one or two exceptions, the work of the American and other writers who have ploughed this field has failed to command their respect or even their attention.

If it were clear that this disdain had been founded upon an understanding of the scientific approach and a considered rejection of it there might be no cause for us to revise our attitude. We might even see in our imperviousness to this fashion the proof of the fundamental soundness and solidity of our own approach. The actual position, however, is that we are largely ignorant of what the new literature contains and that our rejection of it stems much less from any reasoned critique than it does from feelings of aesthetic revulsion against its language and methods, irritation at its sometimes arrogant and preposterous claims, frustration at our inability to grasp its meaning or employ its tools, *a priori* confidence that as an intellectual enterprise it is bound to fail, and professional insecurity induced by the awful gnawing thought that it might perhaps succeed.

There is no doubt that the writing that has emerged from the scientific approach should be taken seriously. Judged by its own standards of logical precision and scientific rigor its quality is sometimes high. Moreover, however adverse a view we take of this literature, it is impossible to examine it with any degree of care and sympathy and yet to conclude that its contribution to the understanding of international relations is nil. Indeed, given the great concentration of energy and talent that has gone into producing it in recent years, it would be extraordinary if this were otherwise.

It is therefore desirable that if we are to reject the scientific approach we should at the same time pay attention to it and formulate such objections to it as we may have. It has now developed so much momentum that silence toward it, or worse, the facile abuse with which it is sometimes greeted by British reviewers, will no longer suffice to keep it at bay. If, as I believe, the scientific approach should be kept firmly in the background, this can only be accomplished by rational criticism.

II

In setting out to provide such a rational criticism one may begin by dismissing a number of complaints commonly directed at the scientific approach which are beside the point.

One such complaint made of these theorists, especially, perhaps, of Morton Kaplan, is that their writing is tortuous and inelegant. But the fact that Morton Kaplan's book is not a pleasure to read is no more a criticism of the theory of international politics it contains than is the difficulty of reading Einstein a deficiency of the theory of relativity. If Kaplan could be charged with deliberately constructing an unnecessarily obscure terminology, or with employing it clumsily and inefficiently, this would be another matter; but such a charge would be quite misplaced. Kaplan's terminology is a vital part of his whole attempt to construct a rigorous system, and his use of it is precise and economical.

Indeed, while one need not go so far as to regard literary mediocrity as a positive merit in a book about politics, Kaplan's work derives much of its originality and force from precisely this disdain of the tradition that regards historical and political writing as a branch of belles lettres. The power of this tradition reflects the fact that historical and political writing, in addition to serving the purpose of communication between specialists seeking understanding of the subject, serves such other purposes as education, persuasion, public entertainment, and the exhibition of gentlemanly accomplishments. Kaplan is surely correct in dismissing the literary embellishment that is a proper element in writing for these latter purposes as an irrelevance and an encumbrance in writing for the former.

Another unsatisfactory line of criticism is that which focuses not upon the doctrine of the scientific theorists but upon the motives that have driven them to propound it. Thus it has been observed that those who follow the scientific approach are new scholastics, who have sought refuge in a world of intellectual constructs essentially in order to escape from political reality; that they are natural scientists, mathematicians, and economists *manqués* who, unable to make careers for themselves in their own fields, have moved into another where the going is easier, bringing their techniques with them; that they are interested in elaborating a mathematical or scientific methodology for its own sake—or for the sake of demonstrating their mastery of it to the uninitiated—rather than in illuminating our subject by the use of it; or even that they represent a new form of the cargo cult.

These observations, or some of them, are true or half true, and they help us to understand the character of the new theorizing as an intellectual movement. It is true of any intellectual style or scholarly fashion that it is pursued for a variety of motives of which the disinterested desire for knowledge is only one, and that some of these motives are much removed from any such desire and are even discreditable. But precisely for this reason a discussion of the motivations of theorists does not provide any basis for the defense of one intellectual style against another. It is too easy for the scientifically-minded theorist to turn the tables. Do not those who adhere to the classical approach do so out of a vested interest in their own techniques, a slothful reluctance to learn new ones? Are they not also wedded to a methodology for its own sake, to the art of judgment over and against measurement, and to literary forms as against symbolic ones, clinging to these instruments of their trade like horse cavalrymen in the age of mechanization? Do they not represent an outgoing generation, trained in one set of techniques, expressing its resentment against an incoming generation trained in another? I should need to be surer than I am that my own motives in preparing this paper are wholly disinterested before inviting criticism of them by attacking those of others. We shall be well advised, therefore, to confine our attention to the doctrines themselves.

Finally, it is a mistake to see in the scientific approach, or in any one of the methods that go to make it up, the instrument of any particular political purpose in foreign or defense policy. In the ranks of the systems theorists, games theorists, communications theorists, and conflict theorists, it is possible to find attitudes ranging from the most conservative to the most radical; nor is there any logical connection between any of the techniques and any particular political attitude. Writers like Herman Kahn, Thomas Schelling, and Morton Kaplan, who may be broadly described as pro-establishment in their attitudes to foreign and defense policy, have been the object of political attacks that hinge upon their use of these techniques. But such attacks take no account of other writers such as Kenneth Boulding, Anatol Rapoport, or J. David Singer, who are dissenters from United States foreign and defense policies but stand intellectually in the same camp. Similarly the current fashion for "peace research" or "conflict resolution" often seems to embody the misconception that the application of these new techniques to the study of international relations is bound to vindicate radical policies or to facilitate their implementation.

However, the scientific approach has contributed and is likely to contribute very little to the theory of international relations, and in so far as it is intended to encroach upon and ultimately displace the classical approach, it is positively harmful. In support of this conclusion I wish to put forward seven propositions.

The first proposition is that by confining themselves to what can be logically or mathematically proved or verified according to strict procedures, the practitioners of the scientific approach are denying themselves the only instruments that are at present available for coming to grips with the substance of the subject. In abstaining from what Morton Kaplan calls "intuitive guesses" or what William Riker calls "wisdom literature" they are committing themselves to a course of intellectual puritanism that keeps them (or would keep them if they really adhered to it) as remote from the substance of international politics as the inmates of a Victorian nunnery were from the study of sex.

To appreciate our reliance upon the capacity for judgment in the theory of international relations we have only to rehearse some of the central questions to which that theory is addressed. Some of these are at least in part moral questions, which cannot by their very nature be given any sort of objective answer, and which can only be probed, clarified, reformulated, and tentatively answered from some arbitrary standpoint, according to the method of philosophy. Others of them are empirical questions, but of so elusive a nature that any answer we provide to them will leave some things unsaid, will be no more than an item in a conversation that has yet to be concluded. It is not merely that in *framing* hypotheses in answer to these empirical questions we are dependent upon intuition or judgment (as has often been pointed out, this is as true in the natural as in the social sciences); it is that in the *testing* of them we are utterly dependent upon judgment also, upon a rough and ready observation, of a sort for which there is no room in logic or strict science, that things are this way and not that.

For example, does the collectivity of sovereign states constitute a political society or system, or does it not? If we can speak of a society of sovereign states, does it presuppose a common culture or civilization? And if it does, does such a common culture underlie the world-wide diplomatic framework in which we are attempting to operate now? What is the place of war in international society? Is all private use of force anathema to society's working, or are there just wars which it may tolerate and even require? Does a member state of international society enjoy a right of intervention in the internal affairs of another, and if so in what circumstances? Are sovereign states the sole members of international society, or does it ultimately consist of individual human beings, whose rights and duties override those of the entities who act in their name? To what extent is the course of diplomatic events at any one time determined or circumscribed by the general shape or structure of the international system; by the number, relative weight, and conservative or radical disposition of its constituent states, and by the instruments for getting their way that military technology or the distribution of wealth has put into their hands; by the particular set of rules of the game underlying diplomatic practice at that time? And so on.

These are typical of the questions of which the theory of international relations essentially consists. But the scientific theorists have forsworn the means of coming directly to grips with them. When confronted with them they do one of two things. Either they shy away and devote themselves to peripheral subjects—methodologies for dealing with the subject, logical extrapolations of conceptual frameworks for thinking about it, marginalia of the subject that are susceptible of measurement or direct observation— or they break free of their own code and resort suddenly and without acknowledging that this is what they are doing to the methods of the classical approach—methods that in some cases they employ very badly, their preoccupations and training having left them still strangers to the substance of the subject.

This congenital inability of the scientific approach to deal with the crux of the subject while yet remaining true to its own terms leads me to an observation about the teaching of the subject in universities. Whatever virtues one might discern in the scientific approach, it is a wholly retrograde development that it should now form the basis of undergraduate courses of instruction in international politics, as in some universities in the United States it now does. The student whose study of international politics consists solely of an introduction to the techniques of systems theory, game theory, simulation, or content analysis is simply shut off from contact with the subject, and is unable to develop any feeling either for the play of international politics or for the moral dilemmas to which it gives rise.

The second proposition I wish to put forward arises out of the first: It is that where practitioners of the scientific approach have succeeded in casting light upon the substance of the subject it has been by stepping beyond the bounds of that approach and employing the classical method. What there is of value in their work consists essentially of judgments that are not established by the mathematical or scientific methods they employ, and which may be arrived at quite independently of them.

Let me take as an example the work of Thomas Schelling, who has contributed as much as and perhaps more than any other thinker of the scientific genre to the theory of international relations. His elaboration of the notion of arms control, the elements of deterrence, the nature of bargaining, the place in international relations of threats of force are of a rare originality and importance and will probably prove to have made a lasting impression on the theory and, indeed, the practice of these matters. At the same time he is an economist by training; he has written studies of a technical nature about game and bargaining theory; and he has sometimes seemed to lend his support to the call for more theory of a scientific sort.

It appears to me that Schelling's illuminating observations about violence and international politics in every case have the status of unprovable and untestable judgments, and that they have not been and could not be demonstrated by his work in formal game and bargaining theory. Schelling happens to combine with his interest in the latter techniques a shrewd political judgment and a philosophical skill in thinking out problems in terms of their basic elements. It is possible that his ideas about international relations have been suggested to him by his technical studies, and he has evidently thought it useful to provide illustrations of his ideas in formal, theoretical exercises. Those of his readers who share his interest in these techniques will find it amusing and perhaps profitable to pursue these illustrations, but they are at best a helpful analogy; they do not represent the foundation of his contribution to international politics or the road that must be travelled in order to arrive at it.

My third proposition is that the practitioners of the scientific approach are unlikely to make progress of the sort to which they aspire. Some of the writers I have been discussing would be ready enough to admit that so far only peripheral topics have been dealt with in a rigidly scientific way. But their claim would be that it is not by its performance so far that their approach should be judged, but by the promise it contains of ultimate advance. They may even say that the modesty of their beginnings shows how faithful they are to the example of natural science: Modern physics too, Morton Kaplan tells us, "has reared its present lofty edifice by setting itself problems that it has the tools or techniques to solve."[2]

The hope is essentially that our knowledge of international relations will reach the point at which it becomes genuinely cumulative: that from the present welter of competing terminologies and conceptual frameworks there will eventually emerge a common language, that the various insignificant subjects that have now been scientifically charted will eventually join together and become significant, and that there will then exist a foundation of firm theory on which newcomers to the enterprise will build.

No one can say with certainty that this will not happen, but the prospects are very bleak indeed. The difficulties that the scientific theory has encountered do not appear to arise from the quality that international relations is supposed to have of a "backward" or neglected science, but from characteristics inherent in the subject matter which have been catalogued often enough: the unmanageable number of variables of which any generalization about state behavior must take account; the resistance of the material to controlled experiment; the quality it has of changing before our eyes and slipping between our fingers even as we try to categorize it; the fact that the theories we produce and the affairs that are theorized about are related not only as subject and object but also as cause and effect, thus ensuring that even our most innocent ideas contribute to their own verification or falsification.

A more likely future for the theory of international politics is that it will remain indefinitely in the philosophical stage of constant debate about fundamentals; that the works of the new scientific theorists will not prove to

---

2 "Problems of Theory Building and Theory Confirmation in International Politics," *World Politics*, XIV (October 1961), 7.

be solid substructure on which the next generation will build, but rather that those of them that survive at all will take their place alongside earlier works as partial and uncertain guides to an essentially intractable subject; and that successive thinkers, while learning what they can from what has gone before, will continue to feel impelled to build their own houses of theory from the foundations up.

A fourth proposition that may be advanced against many who belong to the scientific school is that they have done a great disservice to theory in this field by conceiving of it as the construction and manipulation of so-called "models." Theoretical inquiry into an empirical subject normally proceeds by way of the assertion of general connections and distinctions between events in the real world. But it is the practice of many of these writers to cast their theories in the form of a deliberately simplified abstraction from reality, which they then turn over and examine this way and that before considering what modifications must be effected if it is to be applied to the real world. A model in the strict sense is a deductive system of axioms and theorems; so fashionable has the term become, however, that it is commonly used also to refer to what is simply a metaphor or an analogy. It is only the technique of constructing models in the strict sense that is at issue here. However valuable this technique may have proved in economics and other subjects, its use in international politics is to be deplored.

The virtue that is supposed to lie in models is that by liberating us from the restraint of constant reference to reality, they leave us free to set up simple axioms based on a few variables and thenceforward to confine ourselves to rigorous deductive logic, thereby generating wide theoretical insights that will provide broad signposts to guide us in the real world even if they do not fill in the details.

I know of no model that has assisted our understanding of international relations that could not just as well have been expressed as an empirical generalization. This, however, is not the reason why we should abstain from them. The freedom of the model-builder from the discipline of looking at the world is what makes him dangerous; he slips easily into a dogmatism that empirical generalization does not allow, attributing to the model a connection with reality it does not have, and as often as not distorting the model itself by importing additional assumptions about the world in the guise of logical axioms. The very intellectual completeness and logical tidiness of the model-building operation lend it an air of authority which is often quite misleading as to its standing as a statement about the real world.

I shall take as an example the most ambitious of all the model-builders, Morton Kaplan. He provides us with models of two historical and four possible international systems, each with its "essential rules" or characteristic behavior. He claims that the models enable him to make predictions—only, it is true, of a high level of generality—about characteristic or modal behavior within the present international system, about whether or not transformations of this system into some other are likely and what form they might take.

The six systems that Kaplan identifies, and the "essential rules" or characteristic behavior of each, are in fact quite commonplace ideas, drawn from the everyday discussion of international affairs, about the general political structure that the world has had or might have. They are the international political system of the eighteenth and nineteenth centuries, the present so-called bipolar system, the structure that might exist if the present polarization of power were not moderated by the United Nations and by powerful third parties, the system we might have if the United Nations were to become the predominant political force in a world of still sovereign states, a world state, and a world of many nuclear powers.

In discussing the conditions under which equilibrium is maintained in each of these systems, and in predicting the likelihood and direction of their transformation into different systems, Kaplan appears to resort to a kind of guesswork a good deal more arbitrary than any involved in the style of international theory he wishes to displace. In discussing the two historical systems he uses some pertinent examples from recent history, but there is no reason to assume that behavior in future international systems of this sort is bound to be the same. In discussing the nonhistorical systems, his remarks are either tautological extensions of the definitions he employs, or are quite arbitrarily formulated empirical judgments that do not properly belong to the model at all.

Kaplan's six systems are of course not the only ones possible. He admits, for example, that they do not cover the cases of Greek antiquity or of the Middle Ages, and they do not embrace the infinite variety the future might unveil. What reason, therefore, is there to suppose that transformation of any one of the systems must be into one of the others? The whole enterprise of attempting to predict transformations on the basis of these models requires at every stage that we go outside the models themselves and introduce further considerations.

One objection to Kaplan's models, therefore, is that they are not models; they are lacking in internal rigor and consistency. But even if they possessed such qualities, they would not provide the illumination of reality that Kaplan claims for them. We have no means of knowing that the variables excluded from the models will not prove to be crucial. He has provided an intellectual exercise and no more. I should not wish to contend that someone exploring the question of what changes might take place in the present international system, or the question of what might be the shape and structure of a world of many nuclear powers, is unable to quarry some nuggets of value from Kaplan's work. But how much more fruitfully can these questions be explored, how much better indeed might so gifted a person as Kaplan himself have explored them, by paying attention to the actual variety of events in the real world, by taking note of the many elements that are pushing the present international system this way and that, and the large number of political and technical factors that might contrive to mold a world of many nuclear powers in any one of a dozen shapes different from those that can be confined within the bounds of Kaplan's model.

The fashion for constructing models exemplifies a much wider and more long-standing trend in the study of social affairs: the substitution of methodological tools and the question "Are they useful or not?" for the assertion of propositions about the world and the question "Are they true or not?" Endemic though it has become in recent thinking, I believe this change to have been for the worse. The "usefulness" of a tool has in the end to be translated as the truth of a proposition, or a series of propositions, advanced about the world, and the effect of the substitution is simply to obscure the issue of an empirical test and to pave the way for shoddy thinking and the subordination of inquiry to practical utility. However, this is a theme that requires more amplification than it can be given here, and in introducing it I am perhaps taking on more antagonists than I need do for my present purpose.

A fifth proposition is that the work of the scientific school is in some cases distorted and impoverished by a fetish for measurement. For anyone dedicated to scientific precision, quantification of the subject must appear as the supreme ideal, whether it takes the form of the expression of theories themselves in the form of mathematical equations or simply that of the presentation of evidence amassed in quantitative form. Like the Anglican bishop a year or so ago who began his sermon on morals by saying that he did not think all sexual intercourse is necessarily wrong, I wish to take a liberal view of this matter. There is nothing inherently objectionable, just as there is nothing logically peculiar, in a theoretical statement about international politics cast in mathematical form. Nor is there any objection to the counting of phenomena that do not differ from one another in any relevant respect, and presenting this as evidence in support of a theory. The difficulty arises where the pursuit of the measurable leads us to ignore relevant differences between the phenomena that are being counted, to impute to what has been counted a significance it does not have, or to be so distracted by the possibilities that do abound in our subject for counting as to be diverted from the qualitative inquiries that are in most cases more fruitful.

I should like to take as an example the work of Karl Deutsch and his pupil Bruce Russett. These writers have sought to investigate the bonds of community that link different nations, and in explaining the cohesiveness or mutual responsiveness that exists between different peoples or different groups within a single people they have especially focused their attention upon social communication, that is to say, upon the flow of persons, goods, and ideas, or of the "messages" they carry. Karl Deutsch, together with a number of collaborators, has provided a study of the extent to which the various peoples of the North Atlantic area are linked by such bonds of community, and he is concerned particularly with the question of the measure in which these peoples form what he calls a "security-community" —that is to say, a group of people who agree that their common problems must be resolved by "peaceful change," and who for a long time have had dependable expectations that their problems will in fact be resolved in this way.[3] Bruce Russett has tackled the more manageable subject of community simply in the relationship between Britain and America, and has sought in particular to determine whether these two peoples have become more or less "responsive" to one another as the twentieth century has progressed.[4]

A feature of the work of both these writers is their presentation of quantitative material as an index of the degree of community that exists between one people and another. They produce figures, for example, on resources devoted to trade as a proposition of total resources; mail sent abroad, or to a particular destination, as a proportion of total mail; number of diplomatic agreements arrived at with another country as a proportion of total agreements arrived at; student exchanges; "content analysis" of newspapers and learned journals; and so on.

The work of Karl Deutsch and Bruce Russett in this field is certainly original and suggestive. Moreover, these two writers are not uncritical in their use of quantitative analysis. But the prominence they give to it is a source of weakness rather than strength in their arguments. Their counting often ignores (or, if it does not ignore, skates over) the most relevant differences between the units counted: differences between the content of one item of mail and another, the diplomatic importance of one treaty and another, the significance of one inch of newspaper column and another. Differences in these other relevant respects may cancel themselves out, but they also may not; and in practice we are likely to respect these statistics only in cases where they confirm some intuitive impression we already have, as, e.g., where Russett's figures confirm, as many of them do, the very confident judgment we may make that as this century has progressed America has become relatively more important to Britain than Britain is to America. Even so, such a judgment is quite external to the statistics that are provided, and does not establish that they measure anything relevant.

Deutsch and Russett, furthermore, are inclined to attribute to their statistics a place in the total chain of the argument that they do not have. They often seem to assume that there is something so irrefutable and final about a piece of evidence that can be put into figures that they are absolved

---

[3] Deutsch has, of course, been author or part-author of a number of other works besides *Political Community and the North Atlantic Area*, but apart from his *Political Community at the International Level* (Princeton 1953), this is the one that most comes to grips with the theory of international relations.

[4] *Community and Contention: Britain and America in the Twentieth Century* (Cambridge, Mass., 1963).

of the necessity of showing in detail how it supports the general thesis they are seeking to demonstrate. Foreign trade is foreign trade, and a precise measurement of foreign trade is not a precise measurement of anything else unless an explanation is advanced as to why this is so. A number of the crucial but missing links in Deutsch's chain of argument seem to have been lost to sight because of this tendency of those who have succeeded in producing figures to be blinded by the illumination they cast. Are the figures of "communication flow" an index of political community at the international level, or a cause of it? Does the "communication flow" contribute to producing the vital element, in Deutsch's scheme, of "mutual identification," or does the latter arise in some quite different way?

Finally, even if one may concede that statistics have some place in an inquiry into political community and social communication, it appears to me that Deutsch and Russett have been distracted by them from the more fruitful parts of the subject. By far the most interesting things that these two writers have to say lie in their attempts to think out the distinguishing features of a community, the different sorts of communities that obtain, the elements that make up the cohesion of a community, the determinants of mutual responsiveness between one people and another. And by far the most pertinent evidence they bring forward lies in the qualitative judgments they are able to bring to bear on history and contemporary affairs.

My sixth proposition is that there is a need for rigor and precision in the theory of international politics, but that the sort of rigor and precision of which the subject admits can be accommodated readily enough within the classical approach. Some of the targets at which the scientific theorists aim their barbs are quite legitimate ones. The classical theory of international relations has often been marked by failure to define terms, to observe logical canons of procedure, or to make assumptions explicit. It has sometimes also, especially when associated with the philosophy of history, sought to pursue into international politics implications of a fundamentally unscientific view of the world. The theory of international relations should undoubtedly attempt to be scientific in the sense of being a coherent, precise, and orderly body of knowledge, and in the sense of being consistent with the philosophical foundations of modern science. Insofar as the scientific approach is a protest against slipshod thinking and dogmatism, or against a residual providentialism, there is everything to be said for it. But much theorizing in the classical mold is not open to this sort of objection. The writings of the great international lawyers from Victoria to Oppenheim (which, it may be argued, form the basis of the traditional literature of the subject) are rigorous and critical. There are plenty of contemporary writers who are logical and rigorous in their approach and yet do not belong to the school I have called the scientific one: Raymond Aron, Stanley Hoffmann, and Kenneth Waltz are examples. Moreover, it is not difficult to find cases where writers in the scientific vein have failed to be rigorous and critical in this sense.

My seventh and final proposition is that the practitioners of the scientific approach, by cutting themselves off from history and philosophy, have deprived themselves of the means of self-criticism, and in consequence have a view of their subject and its possibilities that is callow and brash. I hasten to add that this is not true, or not equally true, of them all. But their thinking is certainly characterized by a lack of any sense of inquiry into international politics as a continuing tradition to which they are the latest recruits; by an insensitivity to the conditions of recent history that have produced them, provided them with the preoccupations and perspectives they have, and colored these in ways of which they might not be aware; by an absence of any disposition to wonder why, if the fruits their researches promise are so great and the prospects of translating them into action so favorable, this has not been accomplished by anyone before; by an uncritical attitude toward their own assumptions, and especially toward the moral and political attitudes that have a central but unacknowledged position in much of what they say.

The scientific approach to international relations would provide a very suitable subject for the sort of criticism that Bernard Crick has applied to a wider target in his admirable book *The American Science of Politics*—criticism that would, by describing its history and social conditions, isolate the slender and parochial substructure of moral and political assumption that underlies the enterprise.[5] There is little doubt that the conception of a science of international politics, like that of a science of politics generally, has taken root and flourished in the United States because of attitudes towards the practice of international affairs that are especially American—assumptions, in particular about the moral simplicity of problems of foreign policy, the existence of "solutions" to these problems, the receptivity of policy-makers to the fruits of research, and the degree of control and manipulation that can be exerted over the whole diplomatic field by any one country.

III

Having stated the case against the scientific approach I must return to the qualifications I introduced at the outset. I am conscious of having made a shotgun attack upon a whole flock of assorted approaches, where single rifle shots might have brought down the main targets more efficiently and at the same time spared others that may have been damaged unnecessarily. Certainly, there are many more approaches to the theory of international relations than two, and the dichotomy that has served my present purpose obscures many other distinctions that it is important to bear in mind.

Students of international relations are divided by what are in some cases

---

[5] *The American Science of Politics: Its Origins and Conditions* (Berkeley and London, 1959).

simply barriers of misunderstanding or academic prejudice that cut across the whole field of social studies at the present time. No doubt it is desirable that such barriers be lowered. But in the present controversy, eclecticism, masquerading as tolerance, is the greatest danger of all; if we are to be hospitable to every approach (because "something may come of it some day") and extend equal rights to every cliché (because "there is, after all, a grain of truth in what he says"), there will be no end to the absurdities thrust upon us. There are grains of truth to be had from a speaker at Hyde Park Corner or a man on a Clapham omnibus, but the question is "What place do they have in the hierarchy of academic priorities?"

I hope I have made it clear that I see a good deal of merit in a number of the contributions that have been made by theorists who adopt a scientific approach. The argument is not that these contributions are worthless, but that what is of value in them can be accommodated readily enough within the classical approach. Moreover, the distinctive methods and aspirations these theorists have brought to the subject are leading them down a false path, and to all appeals to follow them down it we should remain resolutely deaf.

≫2≪

National Power and Foreign Policy

IN THE CONTEMPORARY WORLD of nation-states, problems of defense and national security are insistent and endless. While nationalism has erected emotional barriers between peoples, and sovereignty, as a legal concept, has divided the powers of government of one nation from that of another, each state remains affected by the acts of other states. Where other states are near and also great in power, the problem becomes particularly acute, since the ability of other states to affect national security adversely is in proportion to these factors. To meet this danger, states have joined in alliances, formed balances of power, and participated in leagues and in efforts at collective security, but their basic and inescapable reliance for security has been on their own national power. In the ultimate sense, the security of a nation depends on the power (capability) at its disposal multiplied by the degree of effectiveness (positive *or* negative) with which it brings it to bear upon its problems. This is not only the measure of its chances for survival (in the extreme case of world war); it is also the basis on which important aspects of its day-by-day diplomacy rests.

The three selections in this chapter obviously cannot cover all the elements of national power. They are intended as guideposts, as clues to (1) how one begins the task of assessing national power, (2) how national character influences the foreign policy goals to which national power may be devoted, and (3) how modern technology has altered the conditions under which power is used. (The reader should assess

49

the worth of such an approach in the light of McClelland's criticisms in Chapter 1.)

In the first selection, "The Fundamentals of National Power," Salvador de Madariaga, a diplomat of much experience and influence in the League of Nations period, examines the sources of national strength. The great value of his presentation is that he demonstrates very effectively how many *intangible* factors affect national power. The first element he mentions is mass, but this is in turn affected by the technical capacity of a nation. There is then social discipline, which measures the "coordination of effort" of which the community is capable. These elements compromise the "inherent" strength of the nation, the outward symbol of which is armed forces, but the effect of this power on foreign affairs will vary according to what Madariaga calls "political ability for external affairs." He points out that, when a nation has political ability for internal affairs, it will not necessarily have equal ability for foreign affairs. He then examines what this latter ability consists of—including adequate information on international events and a thorough knowledge of world cultures and therefore the background out of which other foreign policies originate.

In the second selection, "National Character and National Policy," Sir Harold Nicolson, a distinguished diplomat and author, explores this last point raised by Madariaga by inquiring into the effect of national character or *style* upon the formulation and implementation of foreign policy. His analysis is both penetrating and amusing. Since he is comparing and contrasting the English and German national characters before an English audience, it is interesting in itself that he feels it possible to dissect the English character so bluntly. His treatment of how Great Britain came to hold Egypt, as seen through foreign eyes and as seen by an Englishman, is particularly revealing. From the foreign point of view it was a diplomatic move "executed with diabolical cunning," while from the English standpoint, "We really did not mean to go in; we did really mean to come out." England occupied Egypt not as the foreseen outcome of logical steps but as the result of English "mental indolence." Turning to the Germans, Nicolson asserts that, if the dominant feature of the English character is "mental lethargy," that of the German is "spiritual uncertainty" arising out of "Germany's perpetual lack of outline." By this he means not only geographical outline (Germany is on an exposed plain) but cultural outline as well. This produces what he terms a "warrior conception" of life. Nicolson's analysis of how these national characteristics affect foreign policy and therefore national power has seldom been equaled (particularly on Germany) in the English language.

If Madariaga's and Nicolson's points are valid, *which* nations are involved in relations with each other makes considerable difference in the nature and outcome of those relations. Is behavioral systems theory taking this factor adequately into account?

In the third selection, "The Frustration of National Power," Walter F. Hahn presents a stimulating analysis of what he calls "the central dilemma of our times," the inability of nations possessing preponderant power to translate it into effective political control. Exploring the restraints imposed by the nuclear age with its stalemates and limitations, Hahn nonetheless argues against the view that traditional elements in national power assessments have lost relevance, such as physical mass or geographic location and configuration. Technological change has altered the meaning of such elements, but not eliminated them. But Hahn's most important point is to warn that "power is not a substitute for purpose or for policy." Is Hahn's perspective, thirty-two years later in time, different basically from Madariaga's?

4

THE FUNDAMENTALS OF NATIONAL POWER

SALVADOR DE MADARIAGA[*]

First as to the inherent power of a nation—apart, let me repeat, from the ability or efficiency with which it is wielded; the inherent power of a nation manifests itself, first, in the guise of such obvious things as the army, the navy, and the air force. A nation from the point of view of its inherent force is generally estimated in the public eye according to whether she possesses one hundred thousand, a million, or five million men. Similarly as to the tonnage of the navy; similarly about the number or power of its airplanes capable of bombing, chasing, or otherwise performing a military activity.

Now this is rather a symptomatic than an essential estimate, for it is evident—it is indeed a truism—that the inherent force of the nation is merely manifesed in these forms of power which are its army, its navy, and its air force. It is not there itself. It is the cause of these things; it is not these things themselves. The cause can be traced back from these external appearances to something already more substantial, though not yet quite essential, namely, the economic and financial strength of the nation concerned; for evidently it is only on economic and financial strength that an army, navy, and air force can be efficiently evolved and possessed.

But even this second stage in our analysis of the inherent force of a nation does not go deep enough, and we have to consider now the elements that constitute the force of a nation as manifested, first, in its financial and economic strength or power, and then in its military, naval, and air power.

The first element is mass. If we compare two nations, such as China and Switzerland, we shall at once realize that mass is not an all-powerful element in the estimate of the force of a nation. There is something else than mass. But if you compare Switzerland and the United States you come back at once to realizing that all the same and in spite of your first observation, mass does count. What is then, exactly, the law that emerges from this double comparison, of China and Switzerland on the one hand and Switzerland and the United States on the other? It is that *all things being equal,* as the mathematicians say, the mass does count. I would even go so far as to say that in certain conditions and when the mass is really overwhelming, it is by

---

[*] Salvador de Madariaga, *Theory and Practice in International Relations*, pp. 21–28. Copyright 1937, by the University of Pennsylvania Press. Reprinted by permission.

its sheer presence already an important element in power. May I draw here on a personal recollection? During the Manchurian question, we were once gathered—the members of the Council, except the parties—by Aristide Briand, in his rooms in the Hotel des Bergnes, in Geneva, for a free and informal discussion. In the course of this gathering, the French Prime Minister and Foreign Secretary, with his inimitable wit and humor, told us he had received the Japanese Ambassador and had said to him, "Mr. Ambassador, I have a friend who is a boxer. He is a very hefty man, a very strong man, and my friend the boxer tells me, 'Well, Mr. Le President, I am afraid of nobody; but I am afraid of a quilt, because I go for the quilt and strike at it with all the might of my fists and the quilt doesn't care at all and I just get tired.' Well, Mr. Ambassador, China is a quilt."

And all that has happened since shows the wisdom of the image struck by the French statesman; the mere fact of mass is already, in itself, an important element of power, of inherent force in the sovereignty of the nation if only because that mass can react in that very efficient way in which its own inertia enables it to react, by passivity. You all remember the enormous effect which the mere mass and distance of Russia produced on the Napoleonic campaigns.

Yet mass of course is not, in spite of all this, the fundamental element in the inherent power of a nation, as shown by the example of very small nations like Belgium and Switzerland, who wield a considerable economic and financial power in spite of their very exiguous mass. What is this, then, due to? It is mostly due to technical capacity, ability, brain-ability, for organizing and leading human beings in the mastering and the controlling of the forces of nature. It is mostly attained through intellectual capacity for the physical, chemical, and mathematical sciences, as well as in the sciences and practical arts of administration and government. This is a force in itself; we need no other definition, and it acts like a powerful factor in the inherent power of a nation.

The next element of power is social discipline; not altogether unconnected with the second, for wherever you find in human beings that technical capacity for controlling the forces of nature, and also for controlling the discoveries of science and even leading them, in which we have seen the second element of power, it generally goes with a predominance of reason over other faculties of the human soul, and therefore an easier coordination of effort in the members of the community, a greater capacity for analyzing events without violence, and consequently the possibility of coordinating all the forces of the community—mass forces and intellectual forces—and enables the government to wield them more firmly in its own hand. With this virtue is very strongly connected the element of patriotism, about which I do not think it is necessary for me to enlarge any further.

So, when closely analyzed, this somewhat dramatic appearance of force as manifested in the armies, the navies, and the air forces of nations, resolves itself into an individual capacity in the members of those nations for reaching a balance, a government of themselves and of their human relations by reason, excluding violence and therefore a well-organized series of virtues, beginning with the right government of personal affairs which enables the accumulation of financial and economic surpluses in banks, those banks gathering up these surpluses, administering them with wisdom and intelligence, and building up a kind of structure of financial and economic stability which in the end has for its apex the government. The governments in their turn are generally intelligent, since they belong to these advanced nations who are advanced because they themselves are intelligent and technically capable; but moreover, they find already a good deal or most of their work done for them by the fact that the nations which they govern are spontaneously well balanced and well organized. So that they have the immense advantage of possessing in their hand an instrument of force consisting of an element of mass, multiplied by an element of ability.

Quite apart from this inherent force, the ability to wield that force is a most important element toward our estimate of sovereignty. It is evident that the political ability to wield the inherent power of the nation enters already as one of the elements of the inherent force of the nation, since we have admitted—we have indeed put forward—the view that a good deal of this inherent force results from the political capacity of the nation in general to organize itself into a well-built construction of financial, economic and political forces. But it enters also as a very important element *outside of it*, as a kind of coefficient of efficiency in the manipulation of this force in external affairs. We would then say that political ability for internal affairs is an element of the inherent force of a nation, while political ability for external affairs is a coefficient, and multiplies this inherent force and gives it its efficiency. The coefficient may, as all who have studied arithmetic know, be greater than the unit or lesser than the unit; that is to say, it may increase the inherent force of the nation, or it may decrease it if the political ability for external affairs is not as high as the political ability for internal affairs.

For, and this is a very important point, it does not follow that when a nation has political ability for internal affairs it has an equal amount of it for external affairs. To be sure, certainly it will not be politically stupid for external affairs, for it is not conceivable that ability should altogether change its sign when crossing the frontier; but there are elements in the management of world affairs outside the frontiers of a nation that do not obtain in the management of affairs inside the national frontiers, and therefore it is quite easy to imagine that a government may be more capable of organizing its own inherent force than of wielding it efficiently in the foreign fields.

Without aiming at an exhaustive analysis of the elements that enter into this ability for external affairs, we may enumerate some of them. To begin with, there is a very important element in the knowledge of what is going on, or in other words, in accurate and up-to-date information. Most of the great powers possess that information as a matter of course. They have the means, the financial means to pay for a sufficient number of foreign representatives, either avowed, such as consuls, or not avowed—they have another name which it is neither necessary nor polite to quote—and these people keep their governments posted with what really is going on.

This factor of accurate information gives to the great powers a tremendous advantage over lesser nations. Take anything that happens in the world nowadays; take, for instance, the Manchurian question; take the Abyssinian question. When the members of the Council gathered in Geneva or Paris or London to discuss these questions, the position of the members of the great powers who had abundant reports as to what had happened or was going to happen, as to who was who and why he was there, as to the exact financial, economic, political, military background, those members had a considerable advantage over the members of the Council who, belonging to smaller nations, did not possess this accurate and complete information. Here is then an element of efficiency in the wielding of sovereignty in which can at once be seen the considerable difference there is between the big nations and the small nations.

The second element is the capacity for acquiring an adequate knowledge of persons, a knowledge of the persons with whom foreign affairs are actually transacted. This in its turn in great part depends on the knowledge of foreign languages and of foreign cultures, that is to say, on the number of foreign-traveled people at the disposal of the nation in question—that is, foreign-traveled *and* capable of profiting by travel, for there is nothing more traveled than a good portmanteau or trunk, and yet it does not gather much knowledge of foreign people. This assumes that foreign-traveled human beings must be able to see with their eyes and to see with their intellect, and to gather their own conclusions. But not even good observation powers, nor even a good intelligence will be of much avail if behind the people used in foreign employ there is not a sound general outlook, and particularly a sound world culture. The people who are sent abroad—not to *lie* for their country, as runs the famous definition of ambassadors—but to work for the country, must be in a position to pick up what is happening and refer it to a general outlook, a general culture, to what the Germans would call a *Weltanschauung*, which is enlightened and really substantial, so that the observations made refer and coordinate in a harmonious whole.

Finally, a very important element in the control of foreign affairs in the ability to wield the internal force of the nation for foreign purposes is a supply of masterful individuals. Now, masterful individuals cannot be made by machinery. They appear, or they do not appear. They are a kind of person about whom every nation is bound to remain in a kind of Mr. Micawber state of mind, expecting that they will turn up. But here again, we find how unfavored small nations are in comparison with big nations. For it is obvious that a nation with a considerable amount of economic and financial power and with a considerable amount of military power—many soldiers and much tonnage and many airplanes—can, more easily than less developed nations, afford to have a stupid foreign secretary.

5

NATIONAL CHARACTER AND NATIONAL POLICY

Sir Harold Nicolson[*]

I now propose to compare the British character and its effect upon British policy with the German character and its effect upon German policy. I take these two instances because they afford me a maximum amount of illustration. . . . I have found that there is a particular quality, or defect if you like, which differentiates the inhabitants of these Islands from the inhabitants of other territories. I have come to the conclusion that the most marked characteristic of the inhabitants of these Islands is mental indolence and mental cowardice. I think that in no country in the world does there exist such cerebral lethargy as there does in England. It always strikes me as strange that the ordinary Englishman who thinks it slightly immoral and decadent not to take physical exercise is apt to regard mental exercises as something Continental and effete. We don't always realise in this country how very lax, how very unformed are our mental biceps. Englishmen are no more cowardly or brave than people in other countries, but mentally they dislike anything that gives them pain, and the whole of English life is largely organised in order to give that very soft shell-fish, the British citizen, spiritual comfort.

If you disagree with me I ask you to consider—though it is rather a digression—the employment not only of the expression "bad taste," but of the expression "affectation." I know very well that if you say anything that might arouse an Englishman's desire to avoid the unpleasant it is said that you have shown bad taste. Anything that makes an Englishman think at all is bad taste; it leaves a nasty taste in his mouth.

Then there is the other expression "affectation." I look back upon my boyhood and I remember that when I was seventeen I realised that I was ex-

[*] Sir Harold Nicolson, *National Character and National Policy,* Montague Burton International Relations Lecture, 1938, University College, Nottingham, pp. 4, 6–13. Reprinted by permission of the University College, Nottingham, England, and Sir Harold Nicolson.

tremely interested in French pictures and deplorably bored by cricket. I felt it ridiculous to waste time hitting one object with another object; had I said that I was bored by this game, but liked French pictures, I should at once have been described as "affected."

If you agree about our intellectual indolence you will agree also that it has produced certain effects, some of them good, some of them bad. I will begin with the good. I think mental indolence does produce a distaste for extreme courses. Extreme courses require thinking out, and one thing that no Englishman would ever do is to think anything out. He always stops before he gets to the extreme. That is called "British commonsense."

The second effect is an excellent effect, and I am not going to sneer at it. It is a hatred of hatred and a hatred of fear. I think that is one of the great virtues of the British race—their good humour. But don't let that be put down as an ethical virtue; it comes mainly from moral and mental indolence. A third good point of mental lethargy is its optimism. I don't see how in this climate, in these islands, in these cities which we built during the Industrial Revolution—I don't see how a country can survive mentally and spiritually without this tremendous injection of optimism.

Then we pass to the bad effects. Obviously the most serious result of our mental indolence is our incapacity to think. We never plan. Our reliance upon instinct implies a refusal to pry into the future or really to grapple with the facts of the future. Always there is this escape from the unpleasant and especially from any form of long-distance planning. This is a grave intellectual, and I would almost say moral, defect in our nature. It is indeed a curious thing to watch a Scotsman or an Englishman faced either by the really unpleasant or by the conjectural.

These are some of the effects of mental indolence. But we have other characteristics. There is our commercial instinct, our shop-keeping instinct, that love of acquisitiveness and materialism. This leads us to the recognition of the realities of a situation; it leads also to extreme elasticity of policy, and it leads to honesty; not honesty because we "are holier than thou," but because we have learnt the great lesson that honesty means credit, and credit means more money. We are infinitely more honest than other countries in our policy, but is this virtue much more than our old-fashioned shop-keeper point of view?

Then there is a third point. There is what I call roughly Puritanism; by which I mean the continuous search, the perfectly sincere search, for the ethical motive, the power of the idea. The Englishman is not happy unless he can find moral reasons for what he is doing; he is only affected by the real moral idea.

Consider, for instance, British policy towards Egypt since 1882. A foreigner would say that it was the most brilliant bit of carefully planned imperialism in the whole history of diplomacy, executed with diabolical cunning. We got the French out of Egypt and then we managed to get the

Turks out; we then bamboozled the Concert of Europe by means of a sham conference in Constantinople; we then sent Wolseley to suppress the Arabi rising at Telel-Kebir; we then occupied Egypt and have been there ever since. That is the foreigner's point of view. They think it an absolute master-piece of carefully thought-out Imperialism. But it was not that. We did not know what was happening. We thought it was a noble mission of civilisa-tion. We really did not mean to go in; we did really mean to come out. We gradually slipped into occupying Egypt and then began to search for moral motives. It was quite obvious that we had occupied the country because of the Suez Canal; because of its strategical value as well as its importance to the bond holders. That was the real reason but it did not sound very nice or very pleasant, so we said we were there for the good of the people, which was true. We did the fellaheen a great deal of good. It can only be explained partly through the shop-keeper instinct, partly through the Puritan instinct of always searching for an ethical motive, and partly from our inability to realise what the proposition really was.

Having indicated what the British character is like, how it influences policy, I must consider the question of whether the British character has changed. I do not think that our character has changed at all, or very little; I think our circumstances are changed. Our character and its manifestations in the nineteenth century was based on the fact that we were absolutely unassailable and that the power of supremacy, the power to crush other people, gave us a great virtue. We have lost that; we have lost our invul-nerability. There are many people who say that our national character of the eighteenth and nineteenth centuries was based on an alliance between the aristocracy and big business and that this has passed. Aristocracy, it is true, has ceased to be aristocracy, and business to be big. The proletariat has come to complete our character. Our unity is no longer an alliance between the Elizabethan and the Victorian spirit; yet our character is fundamentally and essentially the same. We are still shop-keepers.

Now let me pass to Germany and consider the German character and its effect upon policy. And when I have dealt with that, I shall draw certain conclusions as to the difficulties in Anglo-German relations.

If the dominant feature in the English character is mental lethargy, the dominant feature in the German character is spiritual uncertainty. The main cause of this German uncertainty, diffidence and hesitancy is, to my mind, Germany's perpetual lack of outline. By that I mean not geographical out-line only, although being on the edge of other countries does seem to have given the Germans no sharp sense of geographical frontiers. It is also a lack of cultural outline, by which I mean a blurred cultural tradition. It is also a lack of historical outline since Germany suffered much when Augustus with-drew his legions from the Elbe. And it is also a lack of racial outline since the pure German blood has, in the north at least, been diluted by many Slav infiltrations. We who have somewhere at the back of our minds the consciousness that our shores are washed by the silver sea, should try to understand this almost passionate longing of the German to find an outline.

I don't know whether any of you have read a most interesting book on Germany by Frederick Sieburg: it is the most interesting description of the German character I have ever read. The writer says that every German is like a grain of sand blown by the wind, but that in every grain there is a passionate desire to coalesce with others and become one rock. I think that is true. I think if we do not understand this passionate desire for cohesion with other people we shall not for one moment understand the German character. We must always remember that in the German character there are two conflicting tendencies, the one towards international ideas, and the other towards nationalism. The second tendency was developed by Bismarck and led to extreme concentration. I am afraid that ever since 1870 the Bismarck spirit, the spirit of national concentration, the spirit that might is right, has been the dominating spirit of Germany.

Now what is the result of this uncertainty of outline in Germany? I think we must always try to be sympathetic to their spiritual loneliness, their sense of spiritual forsakenness, their desire to do things with other people, especially with their own people, in what we term the spirit of militarism. You will allow me to tell you a little story. I remember very well when I was in Berlin some five years ago in the Embassy, I found myself sitting next to some banker. I said to him, "How do you keep fit?" He said, "I do physical jerks every morning at seven by wireless. But," he added, "it is rather a bore, because the thing is timed for those people who have to be in their offices by eight. I have not to be in my office till nine. I have therefore to get up an hour earlier than necessary." I said, "But you could get what you want on the gramophone and you could turn it on at eight and it would be all right." And he said, "Oh no, I would not do that because I should not have the pleasure of thinking that thousands of people were doing it at the same time." Another German, a German educationalist, remarked to me "How did you organise the week-end movement in England?"

Therefore the first result of this German lack of outline has been to do things with solidarity. Another effect of their uncertainty is their extreme pre-occupation with status. English people never think about status, but the Germans are frightfully pre-occupied with status. That is a point we don't understand.

The final result of their uncertainty and dualism is their militarism; that is a heroic conception of life which is essentially different from our commercial conception. It is important to consider how that affects policy. Let us take first their methods. It is a method of rigid uncertainty, adventurism. It is a method of almost mystical self-sacrifice and the theocracy of the State. It is what Hitler described when he said, "I go forward, inspired by the certainty of a somnambulist."

There is another thing. It is their extreme sensitiveness. I know we think it funny, frightfully funny, that the German should be so sensitive, but we must remember that the Americans are also sensitive; they are very much closer to the Germans than we are.

The German heroic conception of life leads to what I may call a warrior conception of policy and diplomacy. This warrior conception is one of our great difficulties in dealing with Germany. I believe the ordinary German regards diplomacy as a sort of manoeuvre; that he regards it entirely in military terms; that his method is almost entirely a military method. In fact German diplomacy and policy have all the apparatus of manoeuvres.

Let me now bring this argument, this long argument, back to the point where I started, and illustrate it by certain final suggestions. I started by saying that we can never understand policy unless we understand national character; and I went on to indicate how different characteristics existed with certain fundamental similarities in British and German character, and how important it was to understand those defects and differences in the execution of policy.

I would say further, that national policy is coloured and even governed by national character; and I would say that unless we understand that character we cannot understand the policy. I would say that the approach to diplomacy should be above all a psychological approach; and I would go further and say that we must realise that if we adopt the shop-keeper mentality and approach Germans on a mercantile basis—as we have quite recently done—they then accuse us of *kuhhandel;* they would think that we were not treating them as really respectable people. If, on the other hand— and I would say this to the German—if they approach us from the heroic point of view, we do not understand them, we think they are bullying and blustering. I think it is important for us to realise that in dealing with Germans we should bring our most male qualities to bear—and we have got male qualities—and they should try to bring forward their most feminine qualities. In dealing with the French we should reverse this process, and we should be as quiet, gentle and tolerant as we can be.

I am sure if we approach the foreigner with an understanding of their temperament and nature, and they approach us with an understanding of our temperament and nature we shall achieve a far better, a more reasonable, a more sensible and, I hope, a more hopeful interpretation of foreign policy and foreign diplomacy.

6

THE FRUSTRATION OF NATIONAL POWER

Walter F. Hahn*

Not long after the installation of the Nixon administration, the story made the rounds in Washington of the encounter between a highly-placed member of the New Team and a predecessor in the same sensitive job two administrations removed. They compared notes and they argued. The new appointee had the last word. "After all," he asserted, "our situations are different: for the first time, we are *forced* to construct a foreign policy for the United States."

The new policy-maker was not simply trying to score a debating point. The full interpretation of his remark runs something like this: "In past years, the United States did not really have to chart a comprehensive and logically consistent approach to world affairs. Relying, rightly or wrongly, on its massive and largely unchallenged power, it took the luxury of asserting and of reacting to global events. But today the situation is changed. We can no longer rely on sheer power. We must shape meaningful foreign policy."

What the policy-maker was endeavoring to articulate reflects in a significant way upon the central dilemma of our times—a dilemma which bedevils our policies and underlies in good measure the mood of confusion and somber frustration with which the United States is entering the 1970s.

The manifestations of the dilemma are clear. Here is the United States by all yardsticks the most powerful nation in world history, frustrated in Asia in a conflict with a small country, North Vietnam, which in many ways has not even made the turn into the modern industrial age. Here we are in the North Pacific, suffering such mosquito stings as the capture of an intelligence ship and the downing of an American plane without even slapping at the mosquito. Here we are in Europe, unable to maintain cohesion with our closest allies. Here we are in our own hemisphere, frustrated for almost a decade in trying to cope with an adversary on a tiny island nation 90 miles from our shores. Enough said: if a master of old-time power politics, like the 19th Century German Chancellor Otto von Bismarck, were to return to earth today and witness the spectacle, quite probably he would shake his head in total disbelief.

* Walter F. Hahn, "The Frustration of National Power," *World Affairs*, 132 (September 1969), pp. 138–145. Reprinted by permission.

61

Not only has preponderance of power failed to contribute to its wielders political control, but it has not braked the frequency of old-fashioned warfare. In fact, the case can be made that the pace of conflict is accelerating. In a new edition of his book, *Limited War and American Defense Policy*, Seymour Deitschman catalogues 32 limited wars (including civil conflicts) that were waged between 1945 and 1964. By conservative calculation, one can add nine more to that list since 1964, making a total of 41. Moreover, the ferocity of conflict seems to be increasing as well: witness Vietnam and the Arab-Israeli war of 1967. A particularly depressing fact about this list of 41 conflicts is that all but four have flared in the Free World: the notable exceptions are the Hungarian revolt of 1956, the Tibetan rebellion of 1959, the Warsaw Pact invasion of Czechoslovakia in 1968, and the Soviet-Chinese border war of more recent vintage.

Measured by this catalogue, the dilemma has victimized primarily the United States in pursuit of its global interests. This is not to say, however, that the Soviets have escaped unscathed. The mountains of megatons in the Soviet Union did not prevent Communist China from bolting the Soviet embrace, challenging Moscow's preeminence in the world communist movement, and actually engaging Soviet military force in border skirmishes. In August 1968, the Soviets moved brutally in Czechoslovakia when they deemed their vital interests at stake, yet the mountains of megatons in the Soviet Union had not prevented the ideological challenge in Prague from arising in the first place. According to all evidence, massive Soviet power has not exacted loyalty from the communist leadership in Rumania. Nor, for that matter, have Soviet megatons prevented some setbacks in Soviet policy outside the communist world: in Iraq in 1963, in Indonesia, in Guinea, and more recently in the abject defeat of the Soviet Union's Arab clients in the 1967 Arab-Israeli war.

The Measurement of Power

We face, thus, a phenomenon which might be described as the "paradox of power in the nuclear age." But before we grapple with this phenomenon, it is essential first to describe the concept of national power itself.

A common and persuasive definition of national power is "the degree of *influence* which a country is able to bring to bear in the international arena in pursuit of its objectives." If one accepts this definition, one quickly comes face-to-face with an obvious qualification—namely, that national power is not an absolute phenomenon, but a very relative one.

Consider the simple analogy of the man who buys an automobile which boasts a 300-horsepower engine and a top speed of 150 miles per hour. Unless he enters the Indianapolis 500 race, he is not likely ever to experience the thrill of getting his full power's worth. He has to observe speed limits and he has to weave his way through traffic in order to avoid collision.

In international relations, there are no enforced speed limits, nor for that matter are there other clearly defined traffic laws. There is a vague body of rules under the heading of international law, but even the most dedicated international lawyer will confess that international law resembles, at this stage of global evolution, more an Emily Post code of international etiquette than a compelling order of conduct. Yet, even if there are few, if any, enforced traffic rules in international relations, there is a traffic problem. And as has happened on our congested streets and highways, the traffic problem in international relations has become horrendous. More vehicles are on the road in the form of a proliferation of new and unstable countries. The rate of collisions seems to be increasing. More important, the potential cost of collision has soared to the point where safety measures have become urgent.

In any event, if national power is, in essence, the degree of relative influence exerted (or exertable) in the competitive arena of international relations, how is it measurable? In bygone days, the problem was simplified by the implicit measurement of national power in terms of military power. After all, a nation's war-making capacity represented the ultimate expression of influence which a nation could wield on the international stage—it was, and remains, the "punch line" of power. Military power could be conveniently measured in terms of men under arms, seaborne armadas, tanks, guns, and planes. Moreover, military power, supported as it was by a nation's "mobilization base," was a reasonable mirror of the relative strength or weakness of a given society. Thus, the standard sources of national power listed in textbooks on international relations—sources such as the size of a nation, geographical location, possession of national resources, and population—invariably are treated in the context of their contribution to a nation's war-making capability.

The measurement, however, is no longer so convenient or relevant. Two developments have taken their toll. First the stampede of technology has altered some of the traditional criteria of power, downgrading some and elevating others. And more specifically, the advent of nuclear weapons has distorted, at least subjectively, the relationship between real power and its military "punch line."

The Impact of the Technological Revolution

The impact of the revolution in technology upon the traditional yardsticks of national power has been real, but to some extent it has been exaggerated. Consider, for example, the factor of the physical endowments of a nation: its size and its geographical location.

Physical mass has always been a salient element of power. Thus, Russia in modern times owes its survival, let alone its status of superpower, to sheer size: it was often invaded and defeated in battle but never conquered. The armies of Napoleon and Hitler sliced deeply into the Russian land mass. But eventually exhausted, frozen and cut off from supply lines, they had to give up the game and to beat a bloody retreat.

Nuclear warfare has discounted to some extent the value of old-fashioned invading armies—at least in the confrontation between the two superpowers. At the same time, however, intercontinental ballistic missiles *can* conquer the space that was previously denied to marching legions. American missiles can reach any target in the Soviet Union, and Soviet projectiles can span the North American continent.

Yet, even in the age of devastating intercontinental warfare, size and space have not lost their meaning. Its new vulnerability notwithstanding, a spacious country like the United States or the Soviet Union could conceivably disperse its population and resources in order to survive and grope back from a nuclear attack. It could conceivably devise an anti-missile defense for this purpose. Assumptions regarding nuclear survival are admittedly debatable, and neither the United States nor the Soviet Union is likely to focus strategy upon these assumptions. The point is, nevertheless, that the two superpowers, by dint of spaciousness, can speculate about their chances of surviving a nuclear holocaust; the more diminutive, more densely populated countries cannot.

Physical size thus continues to cast its weight upon the scales of national power. More important, size relates even more meaningfully today to economic and technological predominance. It is no accident of history that two of the most sizeable nations in the world, the United States and the Soviet Union, became the world's first two superpowers, and that another massive country, Communist China, is beginning to make its weight felt. Increasingly in modern competition, first-rate technology means technology of scale—the command over vast resources and manpower. The demands of scale technology explain why some of the more technologically proficient countries in the world, such as the nations of Western Europe, have reached the agonizing conclusion that they cannot in the longer run compete by relying on their own national resources, prodigious though these may seem by momentary standards. Acting upon this conclusion, they have taken the first tentative steps to merge their respective capabilities into continental combines. Their conclusion may be rewarded in the long run. In the more foreseeable future, however, the outcome of the race seems, according to qualified prognosticators, to be predetermined. The dizzying pace of the technological revolution is such that it has assumed its own momentum. If anything, the gap between the front-runners in the technological race and their challengers is likely to widen. In terms of overall technological supremacy, the positions of the two superpowers are quite secure.

In addition to sheer size as a criterion of national power, there is the connected factor of geographical "situation," relating to a country's location and to other dimensions of nature's blessings. To what extent have these been revolutionized by events and by technology?

Before the advent of the nuclear age, the factor of geography loomed large among analysts trying to fathom the reasons for national success or failure. Indeed, during the first half of the 20th Century, geography became almost a preoccupation, giving rise to the pseudo-science of geopolitics. The founder of geopolitics, Sir Halford Mackinder, at the turn of the century originated the "heartland" concept of global power politics. Mackinder's "heartland" embraced the territory in which most of history ostensibly had been made: the Eurasian land mass from the Volga to the Yangtze, and from the Himalayas to the Arctic Ocean. Beyond this "heartland" (covering primarily the territory then governed by Russia), Mackinder saw a larger "world island" composed of the continents of Europe, Asia, and Africa. In terms of power, this world island was the pivot around which the rest of the earth's political surface revolved. Mackinder capsuled his concept in his famous formula: "Who rules East Europe commands the heartland; who rules the heartland commands the world island; who rules the world island commands the world." The concept to a large extent shaped history: it is prominently credited with influencing the strategy of Adolf Hitler and his advisers, particularly his fateful decision to invade the Soviet Union.

The theory of geopolitics clearly was illusory—or what Professor Hans Morgenthau terms the "single-factor fallacy," the abortive attempt to attribute national power to a sole source. Exaggerated or not, however, geographical location was a crucial factor in the power politics of the world before 1945. In the days when everything hinged on the thrust of armies, a country's success or failure depended on whether it enjoyed the natural protection of mountain ranges or ocean moats. Spain dominated a good part of the world centuries ago because it operated from a relatively secure base in the southwestern peninsula of Europe, protected by the Pyrenees. Great Britain became a world power largely because the English Channel secured it from attack from the continent. The United States could develop its robust power because no adversary could dream of crossing 3,000 miles of Atlantic Ocean or 5,000 miles of Pacific waters.

Technology obviously has changed this picture drastically. Long-range weaponry, sophisticated means of airlift and sealift, modern logistics and instant communications have shrunken the world. Mountains and oceans no longer assure protection. Nevertheless, geography still asserts its influence.

In some cases, that influence continues to be real. The abiding insecurity of the European members of NATO is a case in point. The planners of the Alliance have been bedevilled by the inescapable fact that the geography of Western Europe renders a defense in depth extremely difficult against potential invading armies from the east. At one point the distance between the Iron Curtain and the Rhine is a mere 90 or so miles. In the event of conflict and assuming an initial breakthrough of communist forces, where between the Rhine and the English Channel would NATO forces regroup in order to muster a second line of defense? It is this palpable prospect which has made Europeans, especially West Germans, abidingly nervous regarding American notions of a conventional or "flexible" defense of Western Europe.

In other cases, while geography has lost its cutting edge, it nevertheless continues to condition national outlook and policy. Consider the example of the Soviet Union. The leaders of the Kremlin, in their wildest nightmares, should not really expect a massive NATO army of invasion, let alone a new German army, sweeping across the European plain into Russia. Nevertheless, the Soviets still seem to be impelled by this fear, which strongly influences their policies in Eastern Europe.

Consider another example: Great Britain. Only 22 miles of Channel or a few minutes' flying time separate the British Isles from the European continent, but psychologically the distance might as well be a thousand miles. Great Britain is just now trying to decide whether politically or economically she will "join Europe." In the meantime, when an Englishman takes off on a holiday to Paris, he still announces to his friends that he is "going to Europe."

Even if national attitudes and policies have not kept pace with the technological revolutions, therefore, the impact of that revolution upon power relationships on the international stage has been profound. The impact, however, does not in itself explain the paradox of power. If anything, as we have seen, the thrust of technology not only has created the phenomenon of superpower, but it is constantly widening the gap between the have and have-not nations. Technology in itself does not explain why, in an age of superpowers, that power appears to be increasingly untranslatable into the ability to control, let alone to dominate. It does not explain why, with all of its massive power, the United States seems incapable of coping with tiny North Vietnam. Nor does it explain why the Soviet Union has difficulty in grappling with the problems of Eastern Europe or with the challenge of Communist China.

One obvious reason for the paradox is the standoff between the two superpowers. In the poker game of international power politics, the principal players have become understandably cautious. The reason is clear: under the shadow of the mushroom cloud, the dimensions of bluff and of "gamesmanship" more generally have narrowed. The destructive power available to the two superpowers, and the diversity of that power have become so enormous that the small, calculated risk has become monstrous in its implications.

Not only has the arena of direct competition between the two superpowers become constrained, but the general terrain has become increasingly dangerous. Mention was made earlier of the fact that nuclear technology has distorted the relationship between overall national power and the military expression of that power. The nuclear genie, having been released from his bottle by the two superpowers, now beckons to others. He promises a shortcut to disproportionate power and prestige. France and Communist China have succumbed to that promise, and other "nuclear threshold nations"— countries like Israel, India, and Japan—eventually may follow suit. The incentives that are pushing toward the nuclear option do not necessarily reside in sinister global ambitions or aspirations for superpower status—although the leadership in Peking may be swayed by such grandiose goals. Rather, the motives of would-be nuclear powers focus essentially on perceived requirements of self-protection and preservation of national identity in an increasingly dangerous world. To that extent, the trend of nuclear proliferation mirrors in itself the paradox of superpower—the inability of the United States and the Soviet Union, respectively or mutually, to provide the kinds of solid pillars of security that would relieve their allies, friends, and clients of the need to find purely national, and often dangerous, solutions to their security problems. Thus, if Israel or India should choose the nuclear route, it will be largely out of despair over superpower protection.

In any event, nuclear proliferation holds out the prospect to the superpowers that, in moving in an already complex and risk-strewn world, they will confront increasingly the tripwires of nuclear conflagration. Yet, the increase in danger, although ominous, would be essentially marginal. The tripwires of conflict already are ubiquitous.

Perhaps one of the salient causes of the growing "impotence of power" in the nuclear age is that, to a large extent, power is no longer taken seriously. This is so partly because military might has become so monstrous as to render incredible any notions of its actual use. Thus, the leaders in Hanoi have been able to steep their strategies against the United States in Vietnam fairly confidently in the assumption that American nuclear power will not be unleashed upon them.

At the same time, also, the impact of power is waning because of the blinders of ideology and emotion. The world today is in the throes of what has been aptly termed a "systemic revolution." The old regulating systems of international order, like the chandelier balance and the colonial empires of the 19th Century, have crumbled and no new embrasive systems have emerged to take their place. In the process, in broad expanses of the world, new and impatient forces have been spawned. They are spurred by the revolution of rising expectations, the convenience of modern communications, by the vulnerabilities of the industrial societies which they challenge, and not least by the examples of success. They are in a real sense irrational forces, unmindful and even contemptuous of existing and predominant power.

Indeed, the revolutionary momentum of these forces is such that it may be questioned whether unchallenged power could control them—whether the United States could cope with them even if the Soviet Union were suddenly to disappear from the globe. Quite probably our moral scruples—especially the American conscience steeped in Hiroshima—and our sensitivity to the judgments of history would render the United States even more constrained in invoking its immense power for political benefit.

The Need for Purposeful Policy

The paradox of power is thus explicable in its major outlines. Yet, understanding the dilemma does not resolve it, nor does it relieve the burgeoning frustration in American society. As has been suggested earlier, the frustration is sponsored not least by the growing recognition that some 24 years of unprecedented American power, combined with righteous ideals, have not produced the "American age"—that, indeed, the rest of the world either is challenging us or turning its back upon us. We sense, on the one hand, that in our confrontation with our principal adversary our massive power may not be enough in the long run. We sense, on the other hand, that in trying to influence global evolution—and, indeed, the evolution of our own society—our power may have become to some extent irrelevant.

Is there no way out of the dilemma? Perhaps in the long (hopefully not too long) run, the vagaries of power in the nuclear age will confirm an old but neglected lesson of history. The lesson, simply expressed, is this: Foreign policy is the harnessing of national power to national purpose. The implements donated by nature and human resourcefulness are necessary to national power. Yet, power is not a substitute for purpose or for policy.

Purpose, moreover, does not spring full-blown from policy-making wisdom. Especially in democratic systems, purpose expresses the values of harmonious society. The stark lesson of history is that great civilizations, empires and nations succumbed not on the battlefield, but because their dynamism was dimmed by internal conflict and confusion.

Perhaps it was this basic thought which the member of the new administration was endeavoring to convey in his remarks regarding the need to construct a foreign policy for the United States. Not only is power not a substitute for policy in the nuclear age, but in many ways power is becoming somewhat irrelevant in the business of winning friends and influencing people on the international stage. Under the nuclear cloud, the emphasis increasingly is not so much on *what* we play the game with, but on *how* we play it. And how we play the game will depend not only on the cogency of American foreign policy, but perhaps more meaningfully on our unity of purpose as a society.

$\mathscr{3}$

Morality, Ideology, and Foreign Policy

THE READINGS in the first two chapters show how skeptical we must be about the simple notion that power equals success in foreign policy. They also warn us that the conceptual approach of nations to foreign policy problems is far from uniform. Ideas and values vary as well as stockpiles of weapons or physical mass.

In the first selection, "Morality and International Politics," Arthur Schlesinger, Jr., Albert Schweitzer Professor of Humanities at The City University of New York, asks whether overt moral principles should decide issues of foreign policy. He answers: "as little as possible." In a compelling essay Schlesinger dissects the role of moral principle in the relations of nations, arguing that "the raw material of foreign affairs is, most of the time, morally neutral or ambiguous." Schlesinger is not saying that moral considerations are irrelevant to political problems, but that their proper role is to give perspective to a nation's view of its national interest, avoiding the error of self-righteousness which so easily (and paradoxically) erodes restraint in the crusade against "evil."

Henry A. Kissinger, former Professor of Government and a member of the Center for International Affairs at Harvard University, and more lately widely known as Special Assistant for National Security Affairs under President Nixon, is the author of the second selection. In "Domestic Structure and Foreign Policy," Kissinger explores the effect of what he calls "the domestic structure" on the conduct of foreign affairs. In a very thoughtful essay he first asserts that what is considered "reasonable" arises out of necessarily shared values. He points out that in a world of change and of conflicting idea systems consensus is eroded. He then examines the impact of domestic structure on the conduct of international affairs from the standpoint of the administrative structure of nations and the formative experience of their leadership groups. Kissinger's treatment of what he calls the political versus the prophetic approach to policy is particularly stimulating. In later chapters we shall see these contrasting approaches in action.

Because Kissinger's article is so wide-ranging, his views can be contrasted or compared with many of the articles in Part One. Consider, for example, to what extent an "idealist" and a "prophetic" approach overlap or are the same.

7

MORALITY AND INTERNATIONAL POLITICS

Arthur Schlesinger, Jr.[*]

For centuries, theologians have distinguished between just and unjust wars, jurists have propounded rules for international conduct, and moralists have worried whether their own nation's course in foreign affairs was right or wrong. Yet the problem of the relationship between morality and international politics remains perennially unsettled. It is particularly difficult and disturbing for Americans today. The Indochina war was first widely justified on moral grounds and is now widely condemned on moral grounds. Both judgments cannot be right. This contradiction and, even more, of course, the shame and horror of the war must surely compel us to look again at the moral question in its relation to foreign policy.

William James used to say that temperaments determined philosophies. People who respond to international politics divide temperamentally into two schools: those who see policies as wise or foolish, and those (evidently in the majority today) who see them as good or evil. One cannot claim an ultimate metaphysical difference here. No one can escape perceptions of good and evil, and no policy can achieve a total separation of political and moral principles. Nor in the impenetrability of one's heart can one easily know when political motives are moral motives in disguise or when moral motives are political motives in disguise. Still the choice of disguise reveals something about temperament and philosophy.

In this time, when both Right and Left yield with relish to the craving for moral judgment, it may be useful to set forth a minority view. Should—as both supporters and critics of the Indochina war have asserted—overt moral principles decide issues of foreign policy? Required to give a succinct answer, I am obliged to say: as little as possible. If, in the management of foreign affairs, decisions can be made and questions disposed of on other grounds, so much the better. Moral values in international politics—or so, at least, my temperament enjoins me to believe—should be decisive only in questions of last resort. One must add that questions of last resort do exist.

[*] Arthur Schlesinger, Jr., *Harper's Magazine*, August 1971, pp. 72–77. Copyright © 1971, by Minneapolis Star and Tribune Co., Inc. Reprinted by permission of the author.

Individual vs. State Morality

How to define right and wrong in dealings among sovereign states? The moralist of foreign affairs relies on the moral code most familiar to him—the code that governs dealings among individuals. He contends that states should be judged by principles of individual morality. As Woodrow Wilson put it in his address to Congress on the declaration of war in 1917: "We are at the beginning of an age in which it will be insisted that the same standards of conduct and of responsibility for wrong done shall be observed among nations and their governments that are observed among the individual citizens of civilized states." John Foster Dulles said it even more bluntly, or naïvely, in the midst of the second world war: "The broad principles that should govern our international conduct are not obscure. They grow out of the practice by the nations of the simple things Christ taught."

The argument for the application of moral principles to questions of foreign policy is thus that there is, or should be, an identity between the morality of individuals and the morality of states. The issues involved here are not easy. Clearly, there are cases in foreign affairs where moral judgment is possible and necessary. But I suggest that these are extreme cases and do not warrant the routine use of moral criteria in making foreign-policy decisions. It was to expose such indiscriminate moralism that Reinhold Niebuhr wrote *Moral Man and Immoral Society* forty years ago. The passage of time has not weakened the force of his analysis.

Niebuhr insisted on the distinction between the moral behavior of individuals and of social groups. The obligation of the individual was to obey the law of love and sacrifice; "from the viewpoint of the author of an action, unselfishness must remain the criterion of the highest morality." But nations cannot be sacrificial. Governments are not individuals. They are trustees for individuals. Niebuhr quotes Hugh Cecil's argument that unselfishness "is inappropriate to the action of a state. No one has a right to be unselfish with other people's interests." Alexander Hamilton made the same point in the early years of the American republic: "The rule of morality . . . is not precisely the same between nations as between individuals. The duty of making its own welfare the guide of its actions is much stronger upon the former than upon the latter. Existing millions, and for the most part future generations, are concerned in the present measures of a government; while the consequences of the private action of an individual ordinarily terminate with himself, or are circumscribed with a narrow compass."

In short, the individual's duty of self-sacrifice and the nation's duty of self-preservation are in conflict; and this makes it impossible to measure the action of nations by a purely individualistic morality. "The Sermon on the Mount," said Churchill, "is the last word in Christian ethics. . . . Still, it is not on those terms that Ministers assume their responsibilities of guiding states." Saints can be pure, but statesmen must be responsible. As trustees for others, they must defend interests and compromise principles. In politics, practical and prudential judgment must have priority over moral verdicts.

The Indifference of God

National societies have joined, to a considerable degree, individual morality and political necessity. The moral sense of a community finds embodiment in positive law. But the shift of the argument from morality to law only strengthens the case against the facile intrusion of moral judgment into foreign affairs.

A nation's law can set down relatively clear standards of right and wrong in individual behavior because it is the product of an imperfect but nonetheless authentic internal moral consensus. International life has no such broad or deep moral consensus. It was once hoped that modern technology would create a common fund of moral ideas transcending the interests of particular nations—common concepts of interest, justice, and comity—either because the revolution in communications would bring people together through hope of mutual understanding or because the revolution in weapons would bring them together through fear of mutual destruction. Such expectations have been disappointed. Until nations come to adopt the same international morality, there can be no world law to regulate the behavior of states. Nor can international institutions—the League of Nations or the United Nations—produce by sleight of hand a moral consensus where none exists. World law must express world community; it cannot create it.

This is not to say we cannot discern the rudiments of an international consensus. Within limits, mankind has begun to develop standards for conduct among nations—defined, for example, in the Hague Conventions of 1899 and 1907; in the Geneva Protocol of 1925 and the Geneva Conventions of 1949; in the Charter and Covenants of the United Nations; in the Charter, Judgment, and Principles of the Nuremberg Tribunal, and so on. Such documents outlaw actions that the world has placed beyond the limits of permissible behavior. Within this restricted area a code emerges that makes moral judgment in international affairs possible up to a point. And within its scope this rudimentary code deserves, and must have, the most unflinching and rigorous enforcement.

But these international rules deal with the limits rather than with the substance of policy. They seek to prevent abnormalities and excesses in the behavior of states, but they do not offer grounds for moral judgment and sanction on normal international transactions (including, it must be sorrowfully said, war itself, so long as war does not constitute aggression and so long as the rules of warfare are faithfully observed). They may eventually promote a world moral consensus. But, for the present, national, ideological, ethical, and religious divisions remain as bitterly intractable as ever.

Moreover, few problems in international politics call for unequivocal ethical approval or disapproval. Most foreign-policy decisions are self-evidently matters of prudence and maneuver, not of good and evil. "I do not think we can conclude," George Kennan noted a decade ago, "that it matters greatly to God whether the free trade area or the Common Market prevails in Europe, whether the British fish or do not fish in Icelandic territorial waters, or even whether Indians or Pakistani run Kashmir. It might matter, but it is hard for us, with our limited vision, to know." The raw material of foreign affairs is, most of the time, morally neutral or ambiguous. In consequence, for the great majority of foreign-policy transactions, moral principles cannot be decisive.

But this is not all. It is not only that moral principles are of limited use in the conduct of foreign affairs. It is also that the compulsion to see foreign policy in moral terms may have, with the noblest of intentions, the most ghastly of consequences. The moralization of foreign affairs encourages, for example, a misunderstanding of the nature of foreign policy. Moralists tend to prefer symbolic to substantive politics. They tend to see foreign policy as a means not of influencing events but of registering virtuous attitudes. One has only to recall the attempt, made variously by Right and by Left, to make recognition policy an instrument of ethical approval or disapproval.

A deeper trouble is inherent in the very process of pronouncing moral judgment on foreign policy. For the man who converts conflicts of interest and circumstance into conflicts of good and evil necessarily invests himself with moral superiority. Those who see foreign affairs as made up of questions of right and wrong begin by supposing they know better than other people what is right for them. The more passionately they believe they are right, the more likely they are to reject expediency and accommodation and seek the final victory of their principles. Little has been more pernicious in international politics than excessive righteousness.

Moral absolutism may strike at any point along the political spectrum. From the standpoint of those who mistrust self-serving ethical stances, the heirs of John Foster Dulles and the disciples of Noam Chomsky are equal victims of the same malady. Both regard foreign policy as a branch of ethics. They end up as mirror images of each other. In the process of moral self-aggrandizement, each loses the humility which is the heart of human restraint. Sir Herbert Butterfield, after observing that "moral indignation corrupts the agent who possesses it and is not calculated to reform the man who is the object of it," makes the essential point: "The passing of what purports to be a moral judgment—particularly a judgment which amounts to the assertion that they are worse men than I am—is not merely irrelevant, but actually immoral and harmful." It is "really a demand for an illegitimate form of power. The attachment to it is based on its efficacy as a tactical weapon, its ability to rouse irrational fervour and extraordinary malevolence against some enemy."

Moralism in foreign policy ends up in fanaticism, and the fanatic, as Mr.

Dooley put it, "does what he thinks th' Lord wud do if He only knew th' facts in th' case." Abroad it leads to crusades and the extermination of the infidel; at home it perceives mistakes in political judgment as evidence of moral obliquity. The issue becomes not self-delusion or stupidity but criminality and treachery; ferreting out the reprobate as traitors or war criminals becomes the goal. Those who are convinced of their own superior righteousness should recall Chekhov's warning: "You will not become a saint through other people's sins."

Losing Crusades

If moral principles have only limited application to foreign policy, then we are forced to the conclusion that decisions in foreign affairs must generally be taken on other than moralistic grounds. What are these other grounds? I believe that where the embryonic international community cannot regulate dealings among nations, the safest basis for foreign policy lies not in attempts to determine what is right or wrong but in attempts to determine the national interest.

Though the idea is an old and honorable one, "national interest," despite the valiant efforts through the years of Walter Lippmann, George Kennan, and Hans Morgenthau, has become an alarming phrase in America in the 1970s. Mention it before students, and the audience shudders. The words should alarm no one. A moment's thought will show that every nation *must* respond to some sense of its national interest, for a nation that rejects national interest as the mainspring of its policy cannot survive. Without the magnetic compass of national interest, there would be no regularity and predictability in international affairs. George Washington called it "a maxim founded on the universal experience of mankind that no nation is to be trusted farther than it is bound by its interest."

This is not to say that national interest is a self-executing formula providing an automatic answer to every perplexity of foreign affairs. Men can argue endlessly about the content of national interest. One man's national interest may be another man's poison. Still the idea is not totally open-ended. Every nation, for example, has a set of fairly definite strategic interests. One has only to reflect on the continuities of Russian foreign policy, whether directed by czars or commissars. When one moves to politics and economics, identification of national interest certainly becomes more debatable. Yet even here one notices that nations often preserve, through changes of government and ideology, an impressive amount of continuity. In any case, the idea of national interest provides the focus and framework within which the debate can take place. It is the debate itself that gives the idea its content, and, in a democracy, its legitimacy.

Obviously a government can take a greedy as well as an enlightened view of its nation's interest. Greed tends to become the dominant motive when there is disparity of power between nations: thus the history of imperialism.

But national interest has a self-limiting factor. It cannot, unless transformed by an injection of moral righteousness, produce ideological crusades for unlimited objectives. Any consistent defender of the idea of national interest must concede that other nations have legitimate interests too, and this sets bounds on international conflict. "You can compromise interests," Hans Morgenthau has reminded us, "but you cannot compromise principles."

This self-limiting factor does not rest only on the perception of other nations' interests. It is reinforced by self-correcting tendencies in the power equilibrium which, at least when the disparity of power is not too great, prevent national interest from billowing up into unbridled national egoism. History has shown how often the overweening behavior of an aggressive state leads to counteraction on the part of other states determined to restore a balance of power. This means that uncontrolled national egoism generally turns out to be contrary to long-term national interest. Can it be persuasively held, for example, that Hitler's foreign policy was in the national interest of Germany? The imperialist states of nineteenth-century Europe have generally been forced to revise their notions as to where national interest truly lies. In time this may even happen to the Soviet Union and the United States.

National interest, realistically construed, will promote enlightened rather than greedy policy. So a realist like Hamilton said (my emphasis) that his aim was not "to recommend a policy absolutely selfish or interested in nations; but to show, that a policy regulated by their own interest, *as far as justice and good faith permit*, is, and ought to be, their prevailing one." And a realist like Theodore Roosevelt could say: "It is neither wise nor right for a nation to disregard its own needs, and it is foolish—and may be wicked— to think that other nations will disregard theirs. But it is wicked for a nation only to regard its own interest, and foolish to believe that such is the sole motive that actuates any other nation. It should be our steady aim to raise the ethical standard of national action just as we strive to raise the ethical standard of individual action."

Double Standard

Both Hamilton and Roosevelt thus tempered their conception of national interest with moral considerations because, as realists, they knew that national self-assertion at the expense of the value and interests of others could lead to national disaster. They did so too, no doubt, because there is something emotionally frustrating about calculations of national interest as the basis for decision. As moral men, we prefer to feel that our actions spring from profound ethical imperatives. The Anglo-American tradition, in particular, has long been addicted to the presentation of egoism in the guise of altruism. And if one has an honest sense of moral concern or moral outrage, it seems idle—indeed, false—to deny this when supporting or censuring a foreign policy. For better or worse, moreover, democratic opinion rebels at the idea of the domination of policy by self-interest. "Let the people get it into their heads that a policy is selfish and they will not follow it," A. J. P. Taylor has wisely written. ". . . A democratic foreign policy has got to be idealistic; or at the very least it has to be justified in terms of great general principles."

Nor is this cynicism. It may well be that the instinct among nearly all nations to justify their actions in terms of abstract moral principle is an involuntary tribute to the existence of a world public opinion, a latent international consensus, that we must all hope will one day be crystallized in law and institutions. This is what Jefferson had in mind when the Declaration of Independence enjoined "a decent respect to the opinions of mankind." It is the point made in a prescient passage in the 63rd Federalist:

An attention to the judgment of other nations is important to every government for two reasons: the one is, that, independently of the merits of any particular plan or measure, it is desirable, on various accounts, that it should appear to other nations as the offspring of a wise and honorable policy; the second is, that in doubtful cases, particularly where the national councils may be warped by some strong passion or momentary interest, the presumed or known opinion of the impartial world may be the best guide that can be followed. What has not America lost by her want of character with foreign nations; and how many errors and follies would she not have avoided, if the justice and propriety of her measures had, in every instance, been previously tried by the light in which they would probably appear to the unbiased part of mankind?

Thus an irrepressible propensity to moral judgment in the field of foreign affairs exists. Nor, despite the perils of moral absolutism, is it without value. It may provide an indispensable reminder that all policies are imperfect and all statesmen capable of self-deception. Indeed, the truly Christian perspective offers the best antidote to the moralistic fallacy of transforming expedients into absolutes. John C. Bennett tells us of the meeting of a delegation from the World Council of Churches with President Kennedy in 1962. The delegation brought a message to heads of states from the New Delhi Assembly of the Council; a paragraph called for the cessation of nuclear tests. When Kennedy read this passage, he responded by discussing his own dilemma: what should the United States do to assure its own security in view of the resumption of tests by the Soviet Union? Impressed, a member of the delegation said, "Mr. President, if you do resume tests, how can we help you?" Kennedy turned to him and said, "Perhaps you shouldn't." Not all statesmen thus recognize the value of separating ultimate from immediate considerations and of preserving ideals in a world of distasteful compromise; if more did, the world would be spared much trouble.

In addition, there are certain problems in foreign policy with so clear-cut a moral character that moral judgment must control political judgment—questions of war crimes and atrocities, of the nuclear arms race, of colonialism, of racial justice, of world poverty. Some have already been defined in international documents. Others define themselves when the consequences of decision transcend the interests of individual nations and threaten the very future of humanity. Modern weapons technology has notably enlarged the number of problems demanding moral priority, for the nuclear bomb, the ICBM and MIRV, by virtue of their unimaginable powers of indiscriminate destruction, have gone far beyond the limits of prudential decision. Still other essentially moral problems arise when civilized values of tolerance and human dignity are menaced by powerful armed fanaticisms whose victory would abolish intellectual and civil freedom. I have in mind such movements as Nazism and Stalinism.

These moral considerations should be brought to bear upon the idea of national interest, but they should not supersede it. Dr. Bennett in his wise and modest book, *Foreign Policy in Christian Perspective*, has made the proper distinction: "We may say that Christian faith and ethics offer ultimate perspectives, broad criteria, motives, inspirations, sensitivities, warning, moral limits rather than directives for policies and decisions." I cannot think of any recent problem in our foreign policy that could not have been adequately and intelligently disposed of on the grounds of national interest, qualified as Hamilton and Roosevelt would have us qualify it. We are asked to consider such questions as when a nation is justified in using force beyond its frontiers or in providing armed support of or opposition to revolutions in other countries. Plainly such questions cannot be answered by *a priori* moral principles but only by careful case-by-case assessment. Burke long ago pointed out the difference between the statesman and the moralist: "the latter has only a general view of society; the former, the statesman, has a number of circumstances to combine with those general ideas, and to take into his consideration. Circumstances are infinite, are infinitely combined, are variable and transient. . . . A statesman, never losing sight of principles, is to be guided by circumstances."

It is through the idea of national interest that moral values enter most effectively into the formation of foreign policy. The moral question arises particularly in a state's observance or nonobservance of its own best standards. Foreign policy is the face a nation wears to the world. If a course in foreign affairs implies moral values incompatible with the ideals of the national community, either the nation will refuse after a time to sustain the policy, or else it must abandon its ideals. A people is in bad trouble when it tries to keep two sets of books—when it holds one scale of values for its internal polity and applies another to its conduct of foreign affairs. The consequent moral schizophrenia is bound to convulse the homeland. This is what happened to France during the Algerian War. It is what is happening to the United States because of the Indochina war.

Moral Slogans, Asian Mud

In order to condemn this horrid conflict it is not necessary to deliver a moral judgment on it. If our policy had been founded on a sober and deliberate calculation of the national interest, we could hardly have sunk so deeply and unthinkingly into a situation where our commitment so far exceeds any rational involvement of that interest or any demonstrable threat to our national security. This is why the analysts who have most consistently invoked the idea of the national interest—Lippmann, Kennan, and Morgenthau—have been skeptical about the Indochinese adventure from the start.

I do not suggest that its advocates did not have a national-interest argument too. This argument in its most sophisticated version was that, with the establishment of nuclear balance between America and Russia, the main source of world instability lay in Third World wars—the kind that Khrushchev called "national liberation" wars in the truculent speech of January 1961 which had so unfortunate an effect on the Kennedy Administration. If the United States proved its ability to deal with such wars, then the world could look forward to an age of peace. Unhappily, this argument assumed that Communist activity everywhere occurred at the behest of and for the benefit of the Soviet Union. It gravely underestimated the strength of national Communism, and it wildly overestimated the capacity of the United States to win guerrilla wars.

Moreover, the argument was thereafter translated into a crude series of political propositions. Our national interest was involved, we were soon given to understand, because the Vietcong and Hanoi were the spearheads of a planned system of Chinese expansion. Therefore, by fighting in Vietnam, we were holding the line against an aggressive Red China. If we did not fight, we would, like Chamberlain at Munich, invite further aggression; and a billion Chinese armed with nuclear weapons (a specter invoked with relish by Secretary Rusk) would overrun Asia and turn the world balance of power permanently in favor of Communism. "The threat to world peace," as Vice President Humphrey summed up this fantasy as late as October 1967, "is militant, aggressive Asian communism, with its headquarters in Peking, China. . . . The aggression of North Vietnam is but the most current and immediate action of militant Asian communism."

The argument that Asian Communism was a monolithic movement run out of Peking was preposterous at the time. It is more preposterous in these days of Ping-Pong diplomacy. As even William Buckley has managed to discern, President Nixon's China policy abolishes the major strategic argument for the Indochina war.

Since it is painful to charge our national leaders with stupidity, one must suppose that this foolish analysis was only a secondary motive for our involvement in Indochina. The primary motive, it seems probable in retrospect, had little to do with national interest at all. It was, rather, a precise consequence of the belief that moral principles should govern decisions of foreign policy. It was the insistence on seeing the civil war in Vietnam as above all a moral issue that led us to construe political questions in ethical terms, local questions in global terms, and relative questions in absolute terms.

The propensity toward thinking big in foreign policy was implicit in the Wilsonian tradition. The habit of ideological escalation grew in the early years of the Cold War. It became rampant in the era of the rigidly Presbyterian Dulles. The Kennedy Administration vacillated between the impassioned rhetoric of the Inaugural Address and Kennedy's own acute sense of the limitations of American power. Then Kennedy was murdered while he was still in the process of giving American foreign policy new precision and restraint. With his successors, moralism triumphed.

Other pressures hastened the Indochina catastrophe—above all, the momentum of the military machine, with its institutional conviction that political problems have military solutions; its institutional desire to try out weapons, tactics, and personnel; and its institutional capacity for self-delusion about the ability of just one more step of escalation to assure military success. Still, the opportunity seized with such avidity by the military was created by those who believed that America was in Vietnam on a moral mission—who applauded when President Johnson cried in 1965:

History and our own achievements have thrust upon us the principal responsibility for protection of freedom on earth. . . . No other people in no other time has had so great an opportunity to work and risk for the freedom of all mankind.

The Indochina war was a morality trip, and moral absolutism was the final stop. As early as 1965, the *New York Times* quoted an American pilot: "I do not like to hit a village. You know you are hitting women and children. But you've got to decide that your cause is noble and that the work has to be done." In this anointed spirit we conceived ourselves the world's judge, jury, and executioner and did our work in Indochina.

Grim Lessons

The moralistic cant of Presidents Johnson and Nixon helped delude a lot of pilots into supposing they were doing God's work. Unfortunately, instead of strengthening the national-interest wing of the opposition to the war, Vietnam seems to have incited an equally moralistic outburst on the part of the war's most clamorous critics. Too many people on both sides of the Indochina debate feel they know exactly what the Lord would do if He only knew the facts in the case.

Yet may not these critics, emotional and extravagant as they often are, have a point? Are not even those quite satisfied to oppose the war as contrary to our national interest still obliged to face the question of whether it may not be an immoral as well as a stupid war? I think they are, if we are ever to extract the full and awful lesson from this catastrophe.

My own answer to the question is yes, it is an immoral war, and it became so, ironically, when our moralistic zeal burst the limitations of national interest. Our original presence in South Vietnam hardly seems immoral, since we were there at the request of the South Vietnam government. Nor does it seem necessarily contrary to our national interest; conceivably it might have been worth it to commit, say, 20,000 military advisers if this could preserve an independent South Vietnam. But at some point the number of troops, and the things they were instructed to do, began to go beyond the requirements of national interest. This point was almost certainly the decision taken in early 1965 to send our bombers to North Vietnam and our combat units to South Vietnam and thus to Americanize the war.

Theologians talk about the principle of proportionality—the principle that means must have a due and rational relationship to ends. The Indochina war became, in my view, what can properly be called an immoral war when the means employed and the destruction wrought grew out of any conceivable proportion to the interests involved and the ends sought.

Enjoined by our leaders as to the sublimity of the mission, we cast ourselves as saviors of human freedom, misconceived the extremely restricted character of our national stake in Indochina, and, step by step, intensified senseless terror till we stand today as a nation disgraced before the world and before our own posterity.

How will our descendants ever understand the mood in which ordinary GIs, inflamed with the belief that anything Americans did was right, virtuously massacred Indochinese women and children—or in which such crimes were condoned, if not concealed, by the theater command? How will they understand the mood in which some American citizens hailed an hysterical killer as a national hero and proposed that, instead of conviction by a military court-martial, he should receive the Congressional Medal of Honor? How will historians explain national decisions, piously taken by God-fearing men in air-conditioned offices in Washington, that resulted in the detonation over this weak and hapless land of six million tons of explosives—three times as much as we dropped on Germany, Italy, and Japan during the second world war?

For years we averted our eyes from what we were doing in Indochina— from the search-and-destroy missions and the free-fire zones; from the defoliation and the B-52s; from the noncombatants slaughtered; the villages laid waste; the crops and forests destroyed; the refugees, one-third of the population of South Vietnam, huddled in unimaginable squalor; from the free and continuous violations of the laws of war. For years we even refrained from pursuing the question of why we were fighting in Indochina— the question that will mystify future historians as they try to figure out what threat to national security, what involvement of national interest, conceivably justified the longest war in American history, the systematic deception of the American people, and the death of thousands of Americans and hundreds of thousands of Vietnamese.

The Calley trial at last compelled the nation to contemplate these questions. The days of pretending were over. No one can doubt that the ordeal of self-interrogation, however damaging it may be to our self-image and self-illusions, will be profoundly beneficial to our nation. If we have the fortitude to carry this process through, history may conclude that the brave men who died in Vietnam did not altogether die in vain.

At the very least, full inquiry into the causes and consequences of the war, as recently suggested by the *New Republic*, would force the nation to contemplate the things we must do to provide reparation for our acts and safeguards against their repetition. But such an inquiry, one must trust, will not result in the vindication of the moral approach to foreign policy. One must hope, rather, that it would increase skepticism about moral judgments promiscuously introduced into international politics. One must hope that the Indochina experience will inoculate the nation against the perversion of policy by moralism in the future. An intelligent regard for one's own national interest joined to unremitting respect for the interests of others seems more likely than the invocation of moral absolutes to bring about greater restraint, justice, and peace among nations.

8

DOMESTIC STRUCTURE AND FOREIGN POLICY

Henry A. Kissinger*

I. The Role of Domestic Structure

In the traditional conception, international relations are conducted by political units treated almost as personalities. The domestic structure is taken as given; foreign policy begins where domestic policy ends.

But this approach is appropriate only to stable periods because then the various components of the international system generally have similar conceptions of the "rules of the game." If the domestic structures are based on commensurable notions of what is just, a consensus about permissible aims and methods of foreign policy develops. If domestic structures are reasonably stable, temptations to use an adventurous foreign policy to achieve domestic cohesion are at a minimum. In these conditions, leaders will generally apply the same criteria and hold similar views about what constitutes a "reasonable" demand. This does not guarantee agreement, but it provides

* Henry A. Kissinger, "Domestic Structure and Foreign Policy." Reprinted by permission of *Daedalus*, Journal of the American Academy of Arts and Sciences, Boston, Mass., Vol. 95, No. 2 (Spring 1966), *Conditions of World Order*, pp. 503–529.

the condition for a meaningful dialogue, that is, it sets the stage for traditional diplomacy.

When the domestic structures are based on fundamentally different conceptions of what is just, the conduct of international affairs grows more complex. Then it becomes difficult even to define the nature of disagreement because what seems most obvious to one side appears most problematic to the other. A policy dilemma arises because the pros and cons of a given course seem evenly balanced. The definition of what constitutes a problem and what criteria are relevant in "solving" it reflects to a considerable extent the domestic notions of what is just, the pressures produced by the decision-making process, and the experience which forms the leaders in their rise to eminence. When domestic structures—and the concept of legitimacy on which they are based—differ widely, statesmen can still meet, but their ability to persuade has been reduced for they no longer speak the same language.

This can occur even when no universal claims are made. Incompatible domestic structures can passively generate a gulf, simply because of the difficulty of achieving a consensus about the nature of "reasonable" aims and methods. But when one or more states claim universal applicability for their particular structure, schisms grow deep indeed. In that event, the domestic structure becomes not only an obstacle to understanding but one of the principal issues in international affairs. Its requirements condition the conception of alternatives; survival seems involved in every dispute. The symbolic aspect of foreign policy begins to overshadow the substantive component. It becomes difficult to consider a dispute "on its merits" because the disagreement seems finally to turn not on a specific issue but on a set of values as expressed in domestic arrangements. The consequences of such a state of affairs were explained by Edmund Burke during the French Revolution:

> I never thought we could make peace with the system; because it was not for the sake of an object we pursued rivalry with each other, but with the system itself that we were at war. As I understood the matter, we were at war not with its conduct but with its existence; convinced that its existence and its hostility were the same.[1]

Of course, the domestic structure is not irrelevant in any historical period. At a minimum, it determines the amount of the total social effort which can be devoted to foreign policy. The wars of the kings who governed by divine right were limited because feudal rulers, bound by customary law, could not levy income taxes or conscript their subjects. The French Revolution, which based its policy on a doctrine of popular will, mobilized resources on a truly national scale for the first time. This was one of the principal reasons for the startling successes of French arms against a hostile Europe

---

[1] Edmund Burke, *Works* (London, 1826), Vol. VIII, pp. 214–215.

which possessed greater over-all power. The ideological regimes of the twentieth century have utilized a still larger share of the national effort. This has enabled them to hold their own against an environment possessing far superior resources.

Aside from the allocation of resources, the domestic structure crucially affects the way the actions of other states are interpreted. To some extent, of course, every society finds itself in an environment not of its own making and has some of the main lines of its foreign policy imposed on it. Indeed, the pressure of the environment can grow so strong that it permits only one interpretation of its significance; Prussia in the eighteenth century and Israel in the contemporary period may have found themselves in this position.

But for the majority of states the margin of decision has been greater. The actual choice has been determined to a considerable degree by their interpretation of the environment and by their leaders' conception of alternatives. Napoleon rejected peace offers beyond the dreams of the kings who had ruled France by "divine right" because he was convinced that *any* settlement which demonstrated the limitations of his power was tantamount to his downfall. That Russia seeks to surround itself with a belt of friendly states in Eastern Europe is a product of geography and history. That it is attempting to do so by imposing a domestic structure based on a particular ideology is a result of conceptions supplied by its domestic structure.

The domestic structure is decisive finally in the elaboration of positive goals. The most difficult, indeed tragic, aspect of foreign policy is how to deal with the problem of conjecture. When the scope for action is greatest, knowledge on which to base such action is small or ambiguous. When knowledge becomes available, the ability to affect events is usually at a minimum. In 1936, no one could know whether Hitler was a misunderstood nationalist or a maniac. By the time certainty was achieved, it had to be paid for with millions of lives.

The conjectural element of foreign policy—the need to gear actions to an assessment that cannot be proved true when it is made—is never more crucial than in a revolutionary period. Then, the old order is obviously disintegrating while the shape of its replacement is highly uncertain. Everything depends, therefore, on some conception of the future. But varying domestic structures can easily produce different assessments of the significance of existing trends and, more importantly, clashing criteria for resolving these differences. This is the dilemma of our time.

Problems are novel; their scale is vast; their nature is often abstract and always psychological. In the past, international relations were confined to a limited geographic area. The various continents pursued their relations essentially in isolation from each other. Until the eighteenth century, other continents impinged on Europe only sporadically and for relatively brief periods. And when Europe extended its sway over much of the world, foreign policy became limited to the Western Powers with the single exception of Japan. The international system of the nineteenth century was to all practical purposes identical with the concert of Europe.

The period after World War II marks the first era of truly global foreign policy. Each major state is capable of producing consequences in every part of the globe by a direct application of its power or because ideas can be transmitted almost instantaneously or because ideological rivalry gives vast symbolic significance even to issues which are minor in geopolitical terms. The mere act of adjusting perspectives to so huge a scale would produce major dislocations. This problem is compounded by the emergence of so many new states. Since 1945, the number of participants in the international system has nearly doubled. In previous periods the addition of even one or two new states tended to lead to decades of instability until a new equilibrium was established and accepted. The emergence of scores of new states has magnified this difficulty many times over.

These upheavals would be challenge enough, but they are overshadowed by the risks posed by modern technology. Peace is maintained through the threat of mutual destruction based on weapons for which there has been no operational experience. Deterrence—the policy of preventing an action by confronting the opponent with risks he is unwilling to run—depends in the first instance on psychological criteria. What the potential aggressor believes is more crucial than what is objectively true. Deterrence occurs above all in the minds of men.

To achieve an international consensus on the significance of these developments would be a major task even if domestic structures were comparable. It becomes especially difficult when domestic structures differ widely and when universal claims are made on behalf of them. A systematic assessment of the impact of domestic structure on the conduct of international affairs would have to treat such factors as historical traditions, social values, and the economic system. But this would far transcend the scope of an article. For the purposes of this discussion we shall confine ourselves to sketching the impact of two factors only: administrative structure and the formative experience of leadership groups.

II. The Impact of the Administrative Structure

In the contemporary period, the very nature of the governmental structure introduces an element of rigidity which operates more or less independently of the convictions of statesmen or the ideology which they represent. Issues are too complex and relevant facts too manifold to be dealt with on the basis of personal intuition. An institutionalization of decision-making is an inevitable by-product of the risks of international affairs in the nuclear age. Moreover, almost every modern state is dedicated to some theory of "planning"—the attempt to structure the future by understanding and, if necessary, manipulating the environment. Planning involves a quest for predictability and, above all, for "objectivity." There is a deliberate effort to reduce the relevant elements of a problem to a standard of average performance. The vast bureaucratic mechanisms that emerge develop a momentum and a vested interest of their own. As they grow more complex, their internal standards of operation are not necessarily commensurable with those of other countries or even with other bureaucratic structures in the same country. There is a trend toward autarky. A paradoxical consequence may be that increased control over the domestic environment is purchased at the price of loss of flexibility in international affairs.

The purpose of bureaucracy is to devise a standard operating procedure which can cope effectively with most problems. A bureaucracy is efficient if the matters which it handles routinely are, in fact, the most frequent and if its procedures are relevant to their solution. If those criteria are met, the energies of the top leadership are freed to deal creatively with the unexpected occurrence or with the need for innovation. Bureaucracy becomes an obstacle when what it defines as routine does not address the most significant range of issues or when its prescribed mode of action proves irrelevant to the problem.

When this occurs, the bureaucracy absorbs the energies of top executives in reconciling what is expected with what happens; the analysis of where one is overwhelms the consideration of where one should be going. Serving the machine becomes a more absorbing occupation than defining its purpose. Success consists in moving the administrative machine to the point of decision, leaving relatively little energy for analyzing the merit of this decision. The quest for "objectivity"—while desirable theoretically—involves the danger that means and ends are confused, that an average standard of performance is exalted as the only valid one. Attention tends to be diverted from the act of choice—which is the ultimate test of statesmanship—to the accumulation of facts. Decisions can be avoided until a crisis brooks no further delay, until the events themselves have removed the element of ambiguity. But at that point the scope for constructive action is at a minimum. Certainty is purchased at the cost of creativity.

Something like this seems to be characteristic of modern bureaucratic states whatever their ideology. In societies with a pragmatic tradition, such as the United States, there develops a greater concern with an analysis of where one is than where one is going. What passes for planning is frequently the projection of the familiar into the future. In societies based on ideology, doctrine is institutionalized and exegesis takes the place of innovation. Creativity must make so many concessions to orthodoxy that it may exhaust itself in doctrinal adaptations. In short, the accumulation of knowledge of the bureaucracy and the impersonality of its method of arriving at decisions can be achieved at a high price. Decision-making can grow so complex that the process of producing a bureaucratic consensus may overshadow the purpose of the effort.

While all thoughtful administrators would grant in the abstract that these dangers exist, they find it difficult to act on their knowledge. Lip service is paid to planning; indeed planning staffs proliferate. However, they suffer from two debilities. The "operating" elements may not take the planning effort seriously. Plans become esoteric exercises which are accepted largely because they imply no practical consequence. They are a sop to administrative theory. At the same time, since planning staffs have a high incentive to try to be "useful," there is a bias against novel conceptions which are difficult to adapt to an administrative mold. It is one thing to assign an individual or a group the task of looking ahead; this is a far cry from providing an environment which encourages an understanding for deeper historical, sociological, and economic trends. The need to provide a memorandum may outweigh the imperatives of creative thought. The quest for objectivity creates a temptation to see in the future an updated version of the present. Yet true innovation is bound to run counter to prevailing standards. The dilemma of modern bureaucracy is that while every creative act is lonely, not every lonely act is creative. Formal criteria are little help in solving this problem because the unique cannot be expressed "objectively."

The rigidity in the policies of the technologically advanced societies is in no small part due to the complexity of decision-making. Crucial problems may —and frequently do—go unrecognized for a long time. But once the decision-making apparatus has disgorged a policy, it becomes very difficult to change it. The alternative to the *status quo* is the prospect of repeating the whole anguishing process of arriving at decisions. This explains to some extent the curious phenomenon that decisions taken with enormous doubt and perhaps with a close division become practically sacrosanct once adopted. The whole administrative machinery swings behind their implementation as if activity could still all doubts.

Moreover, the reputation, indeed the political survival, of most leaders depends on their ability to realize their goals, however these may have been arrived at. Whether these goals are desirable is relatively less crucial. The time span by which administrative success is measured is considerably shorter than that by which historical achievement is determined. In heavily bureaucratized societies all pressures emphasize the first of these accomplishments.

Then, too, the staffs on which modern executives come to depend develop a momentum of their own. What starts out as an aid to decision-makers often turns into a practically autonomous organization whose internal problems structure and sometimes compound the issues which it was originally designed to solve. The decision-maker will always be aware of the morale of his staff. Though he has the authority, he cannot overrule it too frequently without impairing its efficiency; and he may, in any event, lack the knowledge to do so. Placating the staff then becomes a major preoccupation of the executive. A form of administrative democracy results, in which a decision often reflects an attainable consensus rather than substantive conviction (or at least the two imperceptibly merge). The internal requirements of the bureaucracy may come to predominate over the purposes which it was intended to serve. This is probably even more true in highly institutionalized Communist states—such as the U.S.S.R.—than in the United States.

When the administrative machine grows very elaborate, the various levels of the decision-making process are separated by chasms which are obscured from the outside world by the complexity of the apparatus. Research often becomes a means to buy time and to assuage consciences. Studying a problem can turn into an escape from coming to grips with it. In the process, the gap between the technical competence of research staffs and what hard-pressed political leaders are capable of absorbing widens constantly. This heightens the insecurity of the executive and may thus compound either rigidity or arbitrariness or both. In many fields—strategy being a prime example—decision-makers may find it difficult to give as many hours to a problem as the expert has had years to study it. The ultimate decision often depends less on knowledge than on the ability to brief the top administrator—to present the facts in such a way that they can be absorbed rapidly. The effectiveness of briefing, however, puts a premium on theatrical qualities. Not everything that sounds plausible is correct, and many things which are correct may not sound plausible when they are first presented; and a second hearing is rare. The stage aspect of briefing may leave the decision-maker with a gnawing feeling of having been taken—even, and perhaps especially, when he does not know quite how.

Sophistication may thus encourage paralysis or a crude popularization which defeats its own purpose. The excessively theoretical approach of many research staffs overlooks the problem of the strain of decision-making in times of crisis. What is relevant for policy depends not only on academic truth but also on what can be implemented under stress. The technical staffs are frequently operating in a framework of theoretical standards while in fact their usefulness depends on essentially psychological criteria. To be politically meaningful, their proposals must involve answers to the following types of questions: Does the executive understand the proposal? Does he believe in it? Does he accept it as a guide to action or as an excuse for doing nothing? But if these kinds of concerns are given too much weight, the requirements of salesmanship will defeat substance.

The pragmatism of executives thus clashes with the theoretical bent of research or planning staffs. Executives as a rule take cognizance of a problem only when it emerges as an administrative issue. They thus unwittingly encourage bureaucratic contests as the only means of generating decisions. Or the various elements of the bureaucracy make a series of nonaggression pacts with each other and thus reduce the decision-maker to a benevolent constitutional monarch. As the special role of the executive increasingly becomes to choose between proposals generated administratively, decision-makers turn into arbiters rather than leaders. Whether they wait until a problem emerges as an administrative issue or until a crisis has demonstrated the irrelevance of the standard operating procedure, the modern decision-makers often find themselves the prisoners of their advisers.

Faced with an administrative machine which is both elaborate and fragmented, the executive is forced into essentially lateral means of control. Many of his public pronouncements, though ostensibly directed to outsiders, perform a perhaps more important role in laying down guidelines for the bureaucracy. The chief significance of a foreign policy speech by the President may thus be that it settles an internal debate in Washington (a public statement is more useful for this purpose than an administrative memorandum because it is harder to reverse). At the same time, the bureaucracy's awareness of this method of control tempts it to shortcut its debates by using pronouncements by the decision-makers as charters for special purposes. The executive thus finds himself confronted by proposals for public declarations which may be innocuous in themselves—and whose bureaucratic significance may be anything but obvious—but which can be used by some agency or department to launch a study or program which will restrict his freedom of decision later on.

All of this drives the executive in the direction of extra-bureaucratic means of decision. The practice of relying on special emissaries or personal envoys is an example; their status outside the bureaucracy frees them from some of its restraints. International agreements are sometimes possible only by ignoring safeguards against capricious action. It is a paradoxical aspect of modern bureaucracies that their quest for objectivity and calculability often leads to impasses which can be overcome only by essentially arbitrary decisions.

Such a mode of operation would involve a great risk of stagnation even in "normal" times. It becomes especially dangerous in a revolutionary period. For then, the problems which are most obtrusive may be least relevant. The issues which are most significant may not be suitable for administrative formulation and even when formulated may not lend themselves to bureaucratic consensus. When the issue is how to transform the existing framework, routine can become an additional obstacle to both comprehension and action.

This problem, serious enough *within* each society, is magnified in the conduct of international affairs. While the formal machinery of decision-making in developed countries shows many similarities, the criteria which influence decisions vary enormously. With each administrative machine increasingly absorbed in its own internal problems, diplomacy loses its flexibility. Leaders are extremely aware of the problems of placating their own bureaucracy; they cannot depart too far from its prescriptions without raising serious morale problems. Decisions are reached so painfully that the very anguish of decision-making acts as a brake on the give-and-take of traditional diplomacy.

This is true even *within* alliances. Meaningful consultation with other nations becomes very difficult when the internal process of decision-making already has some of the characteristics of compacts between quasi-sovereign entities. There is an increasing reluctance to hazard a hard-won domestic consensus in an international forum.

What is true within alliances—that is, among nations which have at least some common objectives—becomes even more acute in relations between antagonistic states or blocs. The gap created when two large bureaucracies generate goals largely in isolation from each other and on the basis of not necessarily commensurable criteria is magnified considerably by an ideological schism. The degree of ideological fervor is not decisive; the problem would exist even if the original ideological commitment had declined on either or both sides. The criteria for bureaucratic decision-making may continue to be influenced by ideology even after its élan has dissipated. Bureaucratic structures generate their own momentum which may more than counterbalance the loss of earlier fanaticism. In the early stages of a revolutionary movement, ideology is crucial and the accident of personalities can be decisive. The Reign of Terror in France was ended by the elimination of a single man, Robespierre. The Bolshevik revolution could hardly have taken place had Lenin not been on the famous train which crossed Germany into Russia. But once a revolution becomes institutionalized, the administrative structures which it has spawned develop their own vested interests. Ideology may grow less significant in creating commitment; it becomes pervasive in supplying criteria of administrative choice. Ideologies prevail by being taken for granted. Orthodoxy substitutes for conviction and produces its own form of rigidity.

In such circumstances, a meaningful dialogue across ideological dividing lines becomes extraordinarily difficult. The more elaborate the administrative structure, the less relevant an individual's view becomes—indeed one of the purposes of bureaucracy is to liberate decision-making from the accident of personalities. Thus while personal convictions may be modified, it requires a really monumental effort to alter bureaucratic commitments. And if change occurs, the bureaucracy prefers to move at its own pace and not be excessively influenced by statements or pressures of foreigners. For all these reasons, diplomacy tends to become rigid or to turn into an abstract bargaining process based on largely formal criteria such as "splitting the difference." Either course is self-defeating: the former because it negates the very purpose of diplomacy; the latter because it subordinates purpose to technique and because it may encourage intransigence. Indeed, the incentive for intransigence increases if it is known that the difference will generally be split.

Ideological differences are compounded because major parts of the world are only in the first stages of administrative evolution. Where the technologically advanced countries suffer from the inertia of overadministration, the developing areas often lack even the rudiments of effective bureaucracy. Where the advanced countries may drown in "facts," the emerging nations are frequently without the most elementary knowledge needed for forming a meaningful judgment or for implementing it once it has been taken. Where large bureaucracies operate in alternating spurts of rigidity and catastrophic (in relation to the bureaucracy) upheaval, the new states tend to take decisions on the basis of almost random pressures. The excessive institutionalization of one and the inadequate structure of the other inhibit international stability.

III. The Nature of Leadership

Whatever one's view about the degree to which choices in international affairs are "objectively" determined, the decisions are made by individuals who will be above all conscious of the seeming multiplicity of options. Their understanding of the nature of their choice depends on many factors, including their experience during their rise to eminence.

The mediating, conciliatory style of British policy in the nineteenth century reflected, in part, the qualities encouraged during careers in Parliament and the values of a cohesive leadership group connected by ties of family and common education. The hysterical cast of the policy of Imperial Germany was given impetus by a domestic structure in which political parties were deprived of responsibility while ministers were obliged to balance a monarch by divine right against a Parliament composed of representatives without any prospect of ever holding office. Consensus could be achieved most easily through fits of national passion which in turn disquieted all of Germany's neighbors. Germany's foreign policy grew unstable because its domestic structure did little to discourage capricious improvisations; it may even have put a premium on them.

The collapse of the essentially aristocratic conception of foreign policy of the nineteenth century has made the career experiences of leaders even more crucial. An aristocracy—if it lives up to its values—will reject the arbitrariness of absolutist rule; and it will base itself on a notion of quality which discourages the temptations of demagoguery inherent in plebiscitarian democracy. Where position is felt to be a birthright, generosity is possible (though not guaranteed); flexibility is not inhibited by a commitment to perpetual success. Where a leader's estimate of himself is not completely dependent on his standing in an administrative structure, measures can be judged in terms of a conception of the future rather than of an almost compulsive desire to avoid even a temporary setback. When statesmen belonged to a community transcending national boundaries, there tended to be consensus on the criteria of what constituted a reasonable proposal. This did not prevent conflicts, but it did define their nature and encourage dialogue. The bane of aristocratic foreign policy was the risk of frivolousness, of a self-confidence unrelated to knowledge, and of too much emphasis on intuition.

In any event, ours is the age of the expert or the charismatic. leader. The expert has his constituency—those who have a vested interest in commonly held opinions; elaborating and defining its consensus at a high level has, after all, made him an expert. Since the expert is often the product of the administrative dilemmas described earlier, he is usually in a poor position to transcend them. The charismatic leader, on the other hand, needs a perpetual revolution to maintain his position. Neither the expert nor the charismatic leader operates in an environment which puts a premium on long-range conceptions or on generosity or on subordinating the leader's ego to purposes which transcend his own career.

Leadership groups are formed by at least three factors: their experiences during their rise to eminence; the structure in which they must operate; the values of their society. Three contemporary types will be discussed here: (a) the bureaucratic-pragmatic type, (b) the ideological type, and (c) the revolutionary-charismatic type.

BUREAUCRATIC-PRAGMATIC LEADERSHIP

The main example of this type of leadership is the American élite—though the leadership groups of other Western countries increasingly approximate the American pattern. Shaped by a society without fundamental social schisms (at least until the race problem became visible) and the product of an environment in which most recognized problems have proved soluble, its approach to policy is *ad hoc*, pragmatic, and somewhat mechanical.

Because pragmatism is based on the conviction that the context of events produces a solution, there is a tendency to await developments. The belief is prevalent that every problem will yield if attacked with sufficient energy. It is inconceivable, therefore, that delay might result in irretrievable disaster; at worst it is thought to require a redoubled effort later on. Problems are segmented into constituent elements, each of which is dealt with by experts in the special difficulty it involves. There is little emphasis or concern for their interrelationship. Technical issues enjoy more careful attention, and receive more sophisticated treatment, than political ones. Though the importance of intangibles is affirmed in theory, it is difficult to obtain a consensus on which factors are significant and even harder to find a meaningful mode for dealing with them. Things are done because one knows how to do them and not because one ought to do them. The criteria for dealing with trends which are conjectural are less well developed than those for immediate crises. Pragmatism, at least in its generally accepted form, is more concerned with method than with judgment; or rather it seeks to reduce judgment to methodology and value to knowledge.

This is reinforced by the special qualities of the professions—law and business—which furnish the core of the leadership groups in America. Lawyers—at least in the Anglo-Saxon tradition—prefer to deal with actual rather than hypothetical cases; they have little confidence in the possibility of stating a future issue abstractly. But planning by its very nature is hypothetical. Its success depends precisely on the ability to transcend the existing framework. Lawyers may be prepared to undertake this task; but they will do well in it only to the extent that they are able to overcome the special qualities encouraged by their profession. What comes naturally to lawyers in the Anglo-Saxon tradition is the sophisticated analysis of a series of *ad hoc* issues which emerge as problems through adversary proceedings. In so far as lawyers draw on the experience which forms them, they have a bias toward awaiting developments and toward operating within the definition of the problem as formulated by its chief spokesmen.

This has several consequences. It compounds the already powerful tendencies within American society to identify foreign policy with the solution of immediate issues. It produces great refinement of issues as they arise, but it also encourages the administrative dilemmas described earlier. Issues are dealt with only as the pressure of events imposes the need for resolving them. Then, each of the contending factions within the bureaucracy has a maximum incentive to state its case in its most extreme form because the ultimate outcome depends, to a considerable extent, on a bargaining process. The premium placed on advocacy turns decision-making into a series of adjustments among special interests—a process more suited to domestic than to foreign policy. This procedure neglects the long-range because the future has no administrative constituency and is, therefore, without representation in the adversary proceedings. Problems tend to be slighted until some agency or department is made responsible for them. When this occurs—usually when a difficulty has already grown acute—the relevant department becomes an all-out spokesman for its particular area of responsibility. The outcome usually depends more on the pressures or the persuasiveness of the contending advocates than on a concept of over-all purpose. While these tendencies exist to some extent in all bureaucracies they are particularly pronounced in the American system of government.

This explains in part the peculiar alternation of rigidity and spasms of flexibility in American diplomacy. On a given issue—be it the Berlin crisis or disarmament or the war in Vietnam—there generally exists a great reluctance to develop a negotiating position or a statement of objectives except in the most general terms. This stems from a desire not to prejudge the process of negotiations and above all to retain flexibility in the face of unforeseeable events. But when an approaching conference or some other pressures make the development of a position imperative and some office or individual is assigned the specific task, a sudden change occurs. Both personal and bureaucratic success are then identified with bringing the particular assignment to a conclusion. Where so much stock is placed in negotiating skill, a failure of a conference may be viewed as a reflection on the ability of the negotiator rather than on the objective difficulty of the subject. Confidence in the bargaining process causes American negotiators to be extremely sensitive to the tactical requirements of the conference table— sometimes at the expense of longer-term considerations. In internal discussions, American negotiators—generally irrespective of their previous commitments—often become advocates for the maximum range of concessions; their legal background tempts them to act as mediators between Washington and the country with which they are negotiating.

The attitudes of the business élite reinforce the convictions of the legal profession. The American business executive rises through a process of selection which rewards the ability to manipulate the known—in itself a conciliatory procedure. The special skill of the executive is thought to consist in coordinating well-defined functions rather than in challenging them. The procedure is relatively effective in the business world, where the executive can often substitute decisiveness, long experience, and a wide range of personal acquaintance for reflectiveness. In international affairs, however— especially in a revolutionary situation—the strong will which is one of our business executives' notable traits may produce essentially arbitrary choices. Or unfamiliarity with the subject matter may have the opposite effect of turning the executive into a spokesman of his technical staffs. In either case, the business executive is even more dependent than the lawyer on the bureaucracy's formulation of the issue. The business élite is even less able or willing than the lawyer to recognize that the formation of an issue, not the technical remedy, is usually the central problem.

All this gives American policy its particular cast. Problems are dealt with as they arise. Agreement on what constitutes a problem generally depends on an emerging crisis which settles the previously inconclusive disputes about priorities. When a problem is recognized, it is dealt with by a mobilization of all resources to overcome the immediate symptoms. This often involves the risk of slighting longer-term issues which may not yet have assumed crisis proportions and of overwhelming, perhaps even undermining, the structure of the area concerned by a flood of American technical experts proposing remedies on an American scale. Administrative decisions emerge from a compromise of conflicting pressures in which accidents of personality or persuasiveness play a crucial role. The compromise often reflects the maxim that "if two parties disagree the truth is usually somewhere in between." But the pedantic application of such truisms causes the various contenders to exaggerate their positions for bargaining purposes or to construct fictitious extremes to make their position appear moderate. In either case, internal bargaining predominates over substance.

The *ad hoc* tendency of our decision-makers and the reliance on adversary proceeding cause issues to be stated in black and white terms. This suppresses a feeling for nuance and makes it difficult to recognize the relationship between seemingly discrete events. Even with the perspective of a decade there is little consensus about the relationship between the actions culminating in the Suez fiasco and the French decision to enter the nuclear field; or about the inconsistency between the neutralization of Laos and the step-up of the military effort in Vietnam.

The same quality also produces a relatively low valuation of historical factors. Nations are treated as similar phenomena, and those states presenting similar immediate problems are treated similarly. Since many of our policy-makers first address themselves to an issue when it emerges as their area of responsibility, their approach to it is often highly anecdotal. Great weight is given to what people say and relatively little to the significance of these affirmations in terms of domestic structure or historical background. Agreement may be taken at face value and seen as reflecting more consensus than actually exists. Opposition tends to produce moral outrage which often assumes the form of personal animosity—the attitude of some American policy-makers toward President de Gaulle is a good example.

The legal background of our policy-makers produces a bias in favor of constitutional solutions. The issue of supra-nationalism or confederalism in Europe has been discussed largely in terms of the right of countries to make independent decisions. Much less weight has been given to the realities which would limit the application of a majority vote against a major country whatever the legal arrangements. (The fight over the application of Article 19 of the United Nations Charter was based on the same attitude.) Similarly, legal terms such as "integration" and "assignment" sometimes become ends in themselves and thus obscure the operational reality to which they refer. In short, the American leadership groups show high competence in dealing with technical issues, and much less virtuosity in mastering a historical process. And the policies of other Western countries exhibit variations of the American pattern. A lesser pragmatism in continental Europe is counterbalanced by a smaller ability to play a world-role.

THE IDEOLOGICAL TYPE OF LEADERSHIP

As has been discussed above, the impact of ideology can persist long after its initial fervor has been spent. Whatever the ideological commitment of individual leaders, a lifetime spent in the Communist hierarchy must influence their basic categories of thought—especially since Communist ideology continues to perform important functions. It still furnishes the standard of truth and the guarantee of ultimate success. It provides a means for maintaining cohesion among the various Communist parties of the world. It supplies criteria for the settlement of disputes both within the bureaucracy of individual Communist countries and among the various Communist states.

However attenuated, Communist ideology is, in part, responsible for international tensions. This is less because of specific Marxist tactical prescriptions—with respect to which Communists have shown a high degree of flexibility—than because of the basic Marxist-Leninist categories for interpreting reality. Communist leaders never tire of affirming that Marxism-Leninism is the key element of their self-proclaimed superiority over the outside world; as Marxist-Leninists they are convinced that they understand the historical process better than the non-Communist world does.

The essence of Marxism-Leninism—and the reason that normal diplomacy with Communist states is so difficult—is the view that "objective" factors such as the social structure, the economic process, and, above all, the class struggle are more important than the personal convictions of statesmen. Belief in the predominance of objective factors explains the Soviet approach to the problem of security. If personal convictions are "subjective," Soviet security cannot be allowed to rest on the good will of other statesmen, especially those of a different social system. This produces a quest for what may be described as absolute security—the attempt to be so strong as to be independent of the decisions of other countries. But absolute security for one country means absolute insecurity for all others; it can be achieved only by reducing other states to impotence. Thus an essentially defensive foreign policy can grow indistinguishable from traditional aggression.

The belief in the predominance of objective factors explains why, in the past, periods of détente have proved so precarious. When there is a choice between Western good will or a physical gain, the pressures to choose the latter have been overwhelming. The wartime friendship with the West was sacrificed to the possibility of establishing Communist-controlled governments in Eastern Europe. The spirit of Geneva did not survive the temptations offered by the prospect of undermining the Western position in the Middle East. The many overtures of the Kennedy administration were rebuffed until the Cuban missile crisis demonstrated that the balance of forces was not in fact favorable for a test of strength.

The reliance on objective factors has complicated negotiations between the West and the Communist countries. Communist negotiators find it difficult to admit that they could be swayed by the arguments of men who have, by definition, an inferior grasp of the laws of historical development. No matter what is said, they think that they understand their Western counterpart better than he understands himself. Concessions are possible, but they are made to "reality," not to individuals or to a bargaining process. Diplomacy becomes difficult when one of the parties considers the key element to negotiation—the give-and-take of the process of bargaining—as but a superstructure for factors not part of the negotiation itself.

Finally, whatever the decline in ideological fervor, orthodoxy requires the maintenance of a posture of ideological hostility to the non-Communist world even during a period of coexistence. Thus, in a reply to a Chinese challenge, the Communist Party of the U.S.S.R. declared: "We fully support the destruction of capitalism. We not only believe in the inevitable death of capitalism but we are doing everything possible for it to be accomplished through class struggle as quickly as possible."[2]

The wariness toward the outside world is reinforced by the personal experiences which Communist leaders have had on the road to eminence. In a system where there is no legitimate succession, a great deal of energy is absorbed in internal maneuvering. Leaders rise to the top by eliminating— sometimes physically, always bureaucratically—all possible opponents. Stalin had all individuals who helped him into power executed. Khrushchev disgraced Kaganovich, whose protegé he had been, and turned on Marshal Zhukov six months after being saved by him from a conspiracy of his other colleagues. Brezhnev and Kosygin owed their careers to Khrushchev; they nevertheless overthrew him and started a campaign of calumny against him within twenty-four hours of his dismissal.

Anyone succeeding in Communist leadership struggles must be single-minded, unemotional, dedicated, and, above all, motivated by an enormous desire for power. Nothing in the personal experience of Soviet leaders would lead them to accept protestations of good will at face value. Suspiciousness is inherent in their domestic position. It is unlikely that their attitude toward the outside world is more benign than toward their own colleagues or that they would expect more consideration from it.

The combination of personal qualities and ideological structure also affects relations *among* Communist states. Since national rivalries are thought to be the result of class conflict, they are expected to disappear wherever Socialism has triumphed. When disagreements occur they are dealt with by analogy to internal Communist disputes: by attempting to ostracize and then to destroy the opponent. The tendency to treat different opinions as manifestations of heresy causes disagreements to harden into bitter schisms. The debate between Communist China and the U.S.S.R. is in many respects more acrimonious than that between the U.S.S.R. and the non-Communist world.

Even though the basic conceptual categories of Communist leadership groups are similar, the impact of the domestic structure of the individual Communist states on international relations varies greatly. It makes a considerable difference whether an ideology has become institutionalized, as in the Soviet Union, or whether it is still impelled by its early revolutionary fervor, as in Communist China. Where ideology has become institutionalized a special form of pragmatism may develop. It may be just as empirical as that of the United States but it will operate in a different realm of "reality." A different philosophical basis leads to the emergence of another set of categories for the settlement of disputes, and these in turn generate another range of problems.

A Communist bureaucratic structure, however pragmatic, will have dif-

---

[2] "The Soviet Reply to the Chinese Letter," open letter of the Central Committee of the Communist Party of the Soviet Union as it appeared in *Pravda*, July 14, 1963, pp. 1–4; *The Current Digest of the Soviet Press*, Vol. XV, No. 28 (August 7, 1963), p. 23.

ferent priorities from ours; it will give greater weight to doctrinal considerations and conceptual problems. It is more than ritual when speeches of senior
Soviet leaders begin with hour-long recitals of Communist ideology. Even
if it were ritual, it must affect the definition of what is considered reasonable
in internal arguments. Bureaucratization and pragmatism may lead to a loss
of élan; they do not guarantee convergence of Western and Soviet thinking.

The more revolutionary manifestations of Communism, such as Communist China, still possess more ideological fervor, but, paradoxically, their
structure may permit a wider latitude for new departures. Tactical intransigence and ideological vitality should not be confused with structural
rigidity. Because the leadership bases its rule on a prestige which transcends
bureaucratic authority, it has not yet given so many hostages to the administrative structure. If the leadership should change—or if its attitudes are
modified—policy could probably be altered much more dramatically in
Communist China than in the more institutionalized Communist countries.

The Charismatic-Revolutionary Type of Leadership

The contemporary international order is heavily influenced by yet another leadership type: the charismatic-revolutionary leader. For many of the
leaders of the new nations the bureaucratic-pragmatic approach of the
West is irrelevant because they are more interested in the future which
they wish to construct than in the manipulation of the environment which
dominates the thinking of the pragmatists. And ideology is not satisfactory
because doctrine supplies rigid categories which overshadow the personal
experiences which have provided the impetus for so many of the leaders
of the new nations.

The type of individual who leads a struggle for independence has been
sustained in the risks and suffering of such a course primarily by a commitment to a vision which enabled him to override conditions which had
seemed overwhelmingly hostile. Revolutionaries are rarely motivated primarily by material considerations—though the illusion that they are persists
in the West. Material incentives do not cause a man to risk his existence
and to launch himself into the uncertainties of a revolutionary struggle. If
Castro or Sukarno had been principally interested in economics, their
talents would have guaranteed them a brilliant career in the societies they
overthrew. What made their sacrifices worthwhile to them was a vision
of the future—or a quest for political power. To revolutionaries the significant reality is the world which they are striving to bring about, not
the world they are fighting to overcome.

This difference in perspective accounts for the inconclusiveness of much
of the dialogue between the West and many of the leaders of the new
countries. The West has a tendency to believe that the tensions in the
emerging nations are caused by a low level of economic activity. To the
apostles of economic development, raising the gross national product seems

the key to political stability. They believe that it should receive the highest priority from the political leaders of new countries and supply their chief motivation.

But to the charismatic heads of many of the new nations, economic progress, while not unwelcome, offers too limited a scope for their ambitions. It can be achieved only by slow, painful, highly technical measures which contrast with the heroic exertions of the struggle for independence. Results are long-delayed; credit for them cannot be clearly established. If Castro were to act on the advice of theorists of economic development, the best he could hope for would be that after some decades he would lead a small progressive country—perhaps a Switzerland of the Caribbean. Compared to the prospect of leading a revolution throughout Latin America, this goal would appear trivial, boring, perhaps even unreal to him.

Moreover, to the extent that economic progress is achieved, it may magnify domestic political instability, at least in its early phases. Economic advance disrupts the traditional political structure. It thus places constant pressures on the incumbent leaders to re-establish the legitimacy of their rule. For this purpose a dramatic foreign policy is particularly apt. Many leaders of the new countries seem convinced that an adventurous foreign policy will not harm prospects for economic development and may even foster it. The competition of the superpowers makes it likely that economic assistance will be forthcoming regardless of the actions of the recipient. Indeed the more obstrusive their foreign policy the greater is their prospect of being wooed by the chief contenders.

The tendency toward a reckless policy is magnified by the uncertain sense of identity of many of the new nations. National boundaries often correspond to the administrative subdivisions established by the former colonial rulers. States thus have few of the attributes of nineteenth-century European nationalism: common language, common culture, or even common history. In many cases, the only common experience is a century or so of imperial rule. As a result, there is a great pressure toward authoritarian rule, and a high incentive to use foreign policy as a means of bringing about domestic cohesion.

Western-style democracy presupposes that society transcends the political realm; in that case opposition challenges a particular method of achieving common aims but not the existence of the state itself. In many of the new countries, by contrast, the state represents the primary, sometimes the sole, manifestation of social cohesion. Opposition can therefore easily appear as treason—apart from the fact that leaders who have spent several decades running the risks of revolutionary struggle or who have achieved power by a coup d'état are not likely to favor a system of government which makes them dispensable. Indeed the attraction of Communism for many of these leaders is not Marxist-Leninist economic theory but the legitimacy for authoritarian rule which it provides.

No matter what the system of government, many of the leaders of the new nations use foreign policy as a means to escape intractable internal difficulties and as a device to achieve domestic cohesion. The international arena provides an opportunity for the dramatic measures which are impossible at home. These are often cast in an anti-Western mold because this is the easiest way to recreate the struggle against imperial rule which is the principal unifying element for many new nations. The incentive is particularly strong because the rivalry of the nuclear powers eliminates many of the risks which previously were associated with an adventurous foreign policy—especially if that foreign policy is directed against the West which lacks any effective sanctions.

Traditional military pressure is largely precluded by the nuclear stalemate and respect for world opinion. But the West is neither prepared nor able to use the sanction which weighs most heavily on the new countries: the deliberate exploitation of their weak domestic structure. In many areas the ability to foment domestic unrest is a more potent weapon than traditional arms. Many of the leaders of the new countries will be prepared to ignore the classical panoply of power; but they will be very sensitive to the threat of domestic upheaval. States with a high capacity for exploiting domestic instability can use it as a tool of foreign policy. China, though lacking almost all forms of classical long-range military strength, is a growing factor in Africa. Weak states may be more concerned with a country's capacity to organize domestic unrest in their territory than with its capacity for physical destruction.

Conclusion

Contemporary domestic structures thus present an unprecedented challenge to the emergence of a stable international order. The bureaucratic-pragmatic societies concentrate on the manipulation of an empirical reality which they treat as given; the ideological societies are split between an essentially bureaucratic approach (though in a different realm of reality than the bureaucratic-pragmatic structures) and a group using ideology mainly for revolutionary ends. The new nations, in so far as they are active in international affairs, have a high incentive to seek in foreign policy the perpetuation of charismatic leadership.

These differences are a major obstacle to a consensus on what constitutes a "reasonable" proposal. A common diagnosis of the existing situation is hard to achieve, and it is even more difficult to concert measures for a solution. The situation is complicated by the one feature all types of leadership have in common: the premium put on short-term goals and the domestic need to succeed at all times. In the bureaucratic societies policy emerges from a compromise which often produces the least common denominator, and it is implemented by individuals whose reputation is made by administering the *status quo*. The leadership of the institutionalized ideological state may be even more the prisoner of essentially corporate bodies. Neither leadership can afford radical changes of course for they result in profound repercussions in its administrative structure. And the charismatic leaders of the new nations are like tightrope artists—one false step and they will plunge from their perch.

IV. Domestic Structure and Foreign Policy: The Prospects for World Order

Many contemporary divisions are thus traceable to differences in domestic structure. But are there not countervailing factors? What about the spread of technology and its associated rationality, or the adoption on a global scale of many Western political forms? Unfortunately the process of "Westernization" does not inevitably produce a similar concept of reality. For what matters is not the institutions or the technology, but the significance which is attached to them. And this differs according to the evolution of the society concerned.

The term "nation" does not mean the same thing when applied to such various phenomena as India, France, and Nigeria. Similarly, technology is likely to have a different significance for different peoples, depending on how and when it was acquired.

Any society is part of an evolutionary process which proceeds by means of two seemingly contradictory mechanisms. On the one hand, the span of possible adaptations is delimited by the physical environment, the internal structure, and, above all, by previous choices. On the other hand, evolution proceeds not in a straight line but through a series of complicated variations which appear anything but obvious to the chief actors. In retrospect a choice may seem to have been nearly random or else to have represented the only available alternative. In either case, the choice is not an isolated act but an accumulation of previous decisions reflecting history or tradition and values as well as the immediate pressures of the need for survival. And each decision delimits the range of possible future adaptations.

Young societies are in a position to make radical changes of course which are highly impractical at a later stage. As a society becomes more elaborate and as its tradition is firmly established, its choices with respect to its internal organization grow more restricted. If a highly articulated social unit attempts basic shifts, it runs the risk of doing violence to its internal organization, to its history and values as embodied in its structure. When it accepts institutions or values developed elsewhere it must adapt them to what its structure can absorb. The institutions of any political unit must therefore be viewed in historical context for that alone can give an indication of their future. Societies—even when their institutions are similar—may be like ships passing in the night which find themselves but temporarily in the same place.

Is there then no hope for cooperation and stability? Is our international system doomed to incomprehension and its members to mounting frustration?

It must be admitted that if the domestic structures were considered in isolation, the prognosis would not be too hopeful. But domestic structures do not exist in a vacuum. They must respond to the requirements of the environment. And here all states find themselves face to face with the necessity of avoiding a nuclear holocaust. While this condition does not restrain all nations equally, it nevertheless defines a common task which technology will impose on even more countries as a direct responsibility.

Then, too, a certain similarity in the forms of administration may bring about common criteria of rationality. . . . Science and technology will spread. Improved communications may lead to the emergence of a common culture. The fissures between domestic structures and the different stages of evolution are important, but they may be outweighed by the increasing interdependence of humanity.

It would be tempting to end on this note and to base the hope for peace on the self-evidence of the need for it. But this would be too pat. The deepest problem of the contemporary international order may be that most of the debates which form the headlines of the day are peripheral to the basic division described in this article. The cleavage is not over particular political arrangements—except as symptoms—but between two styles of policy and two philosophical perspectives.

The two styles can be defined as the political as against the revolutionary approach to order or, reduced to personalities, as the distinction between the statesman and the prophet.

The statesman manipulates reality; his first goal is survival; he feels responsible not only for the best but also for the worst conceivable outcome. His view of human nature is wary; he is conscious of many great hopes which have failed, of many good intentions that could not be realized, of selfishness and ambition and violence. He is, therefore, inclined to erect hedges against the possibility that even the most brilliant idea might prove abortive and that the most eloquent formulation might hide ulterior motives. He will try to avoid certain experiments, not because he would object to the results if they succeeded, but because he would feel himself responsible for the consequences if they failed. He is suspicious of those who personalize foreign policy, for history teaches him the fragility of structures dependent on individuals. To the statesman, gradualism is the essence of stability; he represents an era of average performance, of gradual change and slow construction.

By contrast, the prophet is less concerned with manipulating than with creating reality. What is possible interests him less than what is "right." He offers his vision as the test and his good faith as a guarantee. He believes in total solutions; he is less absorbed in methodology than in purpose. He believes in the perfectibility of man. His approach is timeless and not dependent on circumstances. He objects to gradualism as an unnecessary concession to circumstance. He will risk everything because his vision is the primary significant reality to him. Paradoxically, his more optimistic view of human nature makes him more intolerant than the statesman. If truth is both knowable and attainable, only immorality or stupidity can keep man from realizing it. The prophet represents an era of exaltation, of great upheavals, of vast accomplishments, but also of enormous disasters.

The encounter between the political and the prophetic approach to policy is always somewhat inconclusive and frustrating. The test of the statesman is the permanence of the international structure under stress. The test of the prophet is inherent in his vision. The statesman will seek to reduce the prophet's intuition to precise measures; he judges ideas on their utility and not on their "truth." To the prophet this approach is almost sacrilegious because it represents the triumph of expediency over universal principles. To the statesman negotiation is the mechanism of stability because it pre-supposes that maintenance of the existing order is more important than any dispute within it. To the prophet negotiations can have only symbolic value—as a means of converting or demoralizing the opponent; truth, by definition, cannot be compromised.

Both approaches have prevailed at different periods in history. The political approach dominated European foreign policy between the end of the religious wars and the French Revolution and then again between the Congress of Vienna and the outbreak of World War I. The prophetic mode was in the ascendant during the great upheavals of the religious struggles and the period of the French Revolution, and in the contemporary uprisings in major parts of the world.

Both modes have produced considerable accomplishments, though the prophetic style is likely to involve the greater dislocations and more suffering. Each has its nemesis. The nemesis of the statesman is that equilibrium, though it may be the condition of stability, does not supply its own motivation; that of the prophet is the impossibility of sustaining a mood of exaltation without the risk of submerging man in the vastness of a vision and reducing him to a mere figure to be manipulated.

As for the difference in philosophical perspective, it may reflect the divergence of the two lines of thought which since the Renaissance have distinguished the West from the part of the world now called underdeveloped (with Russia occupying an intermediary position). The West is deeply committed to the notion that the real world is external to the observer, that knowledge consists of recording and classifying data—the more accurately the better. Cultures which escaped the early impact of Newtonian thinking have retained the essentially pre-Newtonian view that the real world is almost completely *internal* to the observer.

Although this attitude was a liability for centuries—because it prevented the development of the technology and consumer goods which the West enjoyed—it offers great flexibility with respect to the contemporary revolutionary turmoil. It enables the societies which do not share our cultural mode to alter reality by influencing the perspective of the observer—a process which we are largely unprepared to handle or even to perceive. And this can be accomplished under contemporary conditions without sacrificing technological progress. Technology comes as a gift; acquiring it in its advanced form does not presuppose the philosophical commitment that discovering it imposed on the West. Empirical reality has a much different significance for many of the new countries than for the West because in a certain sense they never went through the process of discovering it (with Russia again occupying an intermediary position). At the same time, the difference in philosophical perspective may cause us to seem cold, supercilious, lacking in compassion. The instability of the contemporary world order may thus have at its core a philosophical schism which makes the issues producing most political debates seem largely tangential.

Such differences in style and philosophical perspective are not unprecedented. What is novel is the global scale on which they occur and the risks which the failure to overcome them would entail. Historically, cleavages of lesser magnitude have been worked out dialectically, with one style of policy or one philosophical approach dominant in one era only to give way later to another conception of reality. And the transition was rarely free of violence. The challenge of our time is whether we can deal consciously and creatively with what in previous centuries was adjusted through a series of more or less violent and frequently catastrophic upheavals. We must construct an international order *before* a crisis imposes it as a necessity.

This is a question not of blueprints, but of attitudes. In fact the over-concern with technical blueprints is itself a symptom of our difficulties. Before the problem of order can be "dealt" with—even philosophically— we must be certain that the right questions are being asked.

We can point to some hopeful signs. The most sensitive thinkers of the West have recognized that excessive empiricism may lead to stagnation. In many of the new countries—and in some Communist ones as well—the second or third generation of leaders is in the process of freeing itself from the fervor and dogmatism of the early revolutionary period and of relating their actions to an environment which they helped to create. But these are as yet only the first tentative signs of progress on a course whose significance is not always understood. Indeed it is characteristic of an age of turmoil that it produces so many immediate issues that little time is left to penetrate their deeper meaning. The most serious problem therefore becomes the need to acquire a sufficiently wide perspective so that the present does not overwhelm the future.

❧Part Two❧

The Relations of States

❧4❧

Diplomacy:
Evolution and Uses

B ECAUSE OF THE VITAL ROLE it plays in the affairs of states, diplomacy
is one of the most fascinating and controversial subjects in the study
of international relations. The diplomat has often been painted, in our
democratic age, in the dark role of a villain "secretly" committing his
fellow countrymen to perilous treaties or, alternately, as a social dilet-
tante, occupied with an endless round of parties, dances, and banquets
in the company of very important people. In this stereotyped view the
diplomat is pictured as either scoundrel or wastrel.

Yet the main business of diplomacy is discussion and negotiation; it
is often a tedious business and always a serious one, for the national
interest of a state depends upon its success. The diplomat must not
only thoroughly understand the aims and intentions of his own state;
he must be eternally alert to draw correct conclusions about the
intentions of others, often from insufficient and frequently disconnected evidence. He must know how far to go and when. In over two
thousand years, despite new techniques, new participants, and new
conditions, these fundamentals have not changed.

In the first selection, Dean Rusk, who served in the State Department as Assistant Secretary and Deputy Undersecretary before becoming Secretary of State for eight years in the Kennedy and Johnson
administrations, speaks to the congressional committee charged with
evaluating United States personnel, procedures, and machinery for
foreign affairs. Rusk, in this selection, "The Uses of Diplomacy—A

107

Secretary of State's View," gives a clear and comprehensive picture of the main problems (aside from the substance of policy) in conducting the contemporary diplomacy of the United States. The reader may wish to turn back to the selection by Madariaga in Chapter 2 and compare certain of their observations.

In the second selection, "Codes and Couriers," we are taken behind the gilded façade of the diplomatic great world to see some of the mechanics of diplomacy. Drawing on his long personal experience in the United States Foreign Service, Charles Thayer gives us a fascinating glimpse of some of the security problems involved in modern day diplomacy. Not the least interesting facet of his account is the insight it offers into how the easy-going United States finally evolved security consciousness.

The third selection, "How Nations Negotiate," from the book of the same name by Fred Charles Iklé, is an excellent and provocative analysis of the nature of international negotiation. Compare Iklé's views with Kissinger's remarks in Chapter 3.

9

THE USES OF DIPLOMACY—
A SECRETARY OF STATE'S VIEW

Dean Rusk[*]

In foreign affairs we are dealing with a world which we can influence, but not control, and it is a world of rapid change. . . .

. . . .

. . . Certainly in times of crisis our role is magnified, but in the ordinary flow of events our impact upon other countries is much less than we and others sometimes suppose.

For example, the Alliance for Progress represents about 2 percent of the GNP of Latin America. The 2 percent can influence, but cannot determine what happens with the 98 percent. We cannot buy countries or their policies with 2 percent of their GNP or less than 1 percent of our own, nor would we wish to do so. In any event, minor changes in organization within our own Government will not resolve quarrels between neighbors in distant parts of the world, nor blunt the objectives of international communism, nor make the rest of the world more responsive to our wishes.

The elementary problem of organization, at least to one who has experienced and seen many reorganizations in Government, is to find men of the highest competence to deal with problems which tax human capacity to its limits. The real organization, contrasted with that erected by law and pictured in organization charts, is determined by the flow of confidence from top to bottom and the performance which earns that confidence from bottom to top.

I emphasize the quality of people, and there could be some debate on this, I am sure, because organization seldom stands in the way of good people and seldom converts mediocrity into excellent performance.

Further, I would support the view . . . that the organization of the U.S. Government for the conduct of its foreign relations cannot be effectively studied or significantly improved by an examination of the executive branch alone. The Congress is deeply involved in the conduct of our foreign relations. It plays a decisive role in all actions requiring men or money. It has a great deal to do with the ability of the Government to recruit the best talent

---

[*] From *Hearings*, United States Senate Subcommittee on National Security and International Operations, 88th Cong., 1st sess., Part 6, December 11, 1963, pp. 386–92.

and to move at the speed required by the rapidly changing international environment. . . .

Let me come back now to what seemed to me to be the starting point of our problem. I mentioned doing business with more than 112 countries. I mentioned that in more than 50 of those there would have been elections and changes of government during this calendar year. Now, I suppose there would be 10 or 12 of those changes of government which were unscheduled. I don't say necessarily unpredicted or surprises, but at least unscheduled. That creates a turbulence in our scene which, if anything, is going to increase somewhat, because we will have at least 125 or 130 independent countries before this process ends.

. . . .

But this multiplication of states has greatly changed the conduct of business and foreign policy in the Department of State over the last 30 to 40 years. I am told that the Department of State receives every working day throughout the year about 1,300 incoming cables. I will see 20 to 30 of those on a usual day. We send out 1,000 cables a day, on every working day, and I will see perhaps 6 of those; the White House may see 1 or 2. So when the committee says that delegation is inevitable, this is entirely right. Junior officers in the Department today deal with and have to deal with matters which before World War II would have come to the Secretary of State. The desk officer is the key post in the Department in our bilateral relations with other countries.

I feel myself that we should find ways and means, and I have taken certain steps to do this in some test cases, of upgrading the standing and the experience of the desk officer. He is the man who has the opportunity to brood 24 hours a day about the problems of a particular country. It is he who in Government makes a decision when he puts on his hat at the end of the day and closes the door without having done a particular thing that might have been done that day. It is he who is in the best position to alert the Assistant Secretary or the Secretary that a problem is festering, that it needs attention, that there may be action to be taken to prevent a problem or there may be opportunities where by early attention we can sustain and promote American interests.

. . . .

Then I would emphasize the role of the Assistant Secretaries, the next critical point. The Assistant Secretary at any given time may have 50 or 75 or 100 matters which should be of concern to him which ought to be on his worry list. Again, those higher up are somewhat at the mercy of the judgment of the Assistant Secretary, and his sensing of the art of policy in deciding what matters ought to be dealt with, and when.

I think we could all agree that there is a time for action and a time for letting a situation mature, but which is suitable in a given situation? When is a matter ripe for action? One can look at a worry list, as I have had occasion to do in the past, which is a year old. We used to use these lists when I was Assistant Secretary. If you look at a list that is a year old, it is really quite revealing to see what has happened to that list in the course of a year— which matters improved and which matters got worse, and which matters remained the same—and to find out whether there is any relation between your action or inaction and the course of events, and whether matters improved or worsened. At the end of a year, you can look back and decide that it might have been better to have left a particular item alone and it might have been better to have done something more about some other item. In this respect, the Assistant Secretary is in the crucial post in terms of the art of management of policy in our relations with the rest of the world.

Now, some, or most of our problems, in this tumultuous and, given modern weapons systems, increasingly dangerous world—most of our problems are not so much in the formulation of policy in its broadest sense, in its formulation of objectives. We are a certain kind of nation and we are a certain kind of people. We have some well-established concepts of policy to which we are committed and, indeed, if Government strays too far away from those broadest concepts of policy, the American people have a very effective way of bringing it back into the mainstream of our national policy.

No one, for example, up or down the line thinks that the United States will make an agreement with the intention of breaking it. No one will suppose that we will not try to conduct ourselves to the maximum extent possible in accordance with the norms of international law. No one supposes that we take frivolously the commitments in the preamble and in articles I and II of the United Nations Charter. The general principles of policy are pretty well established and rooted deeply in the nature of our society. But these principles do conflict with each other in a given situation. They compete with each other, and in a tumultuous and highly controversial situation in some part of the world, the problem is how the principles bear upon that particular situation, which principles get priority.

It is the application of policy to particular situations that take almost all of our time. That means that we cannot always be verbally consistent in dealing with one situation as compared with another, because the situations themselves are contradictory. Therefore, if we support American interests in all of these situations, there will be times when our policy appears to be verbally inconsistent.

Now, in this process, it seems to me that there are two or three key points that need attention in addition to those indicated by the committee. The one is the matter of getting accurate and relevant information. The ghost that haunts the policy officer or haunts the man who makes the final decision is the question as to whether, in fact, he has in his mind all of the important elements that ought to bear upon his decision or whether there is a missing piece that he is not aware of that could have been a decisive effect if it became known.

I think we can be proud of the extraordinary improvement in our intelligence- and information-gathering activities in the last 20 years. The need for it has been multiplied many times by the fragmentation of the world political structure, and the breadth, character, and depth of the information we need mounts steadily. When I was assigned to G-2 in 1941, well over a year after the war had started in Europe, I was asked to take charge of a new section that had been organized to cover everything from Afghanistan right through southern Asia, southeast Asia, Australia, and the Pacific. Because we had no intelligence organization that had been giving attention to that area up to that time, the materials available to me when I reported for duty consisted of a tourist handbook on India and Ceylon, a 1924 military attaché's report from London on the Indian Army, and a drawer full of clippings from the *New York Times* that had been gathered since World War I. That was literally the resources of G-2 on that vast part of the world a year after the war in Europe had started.

We have greatly improved our ability to gather relevant information. However, our problem is how to get it to the people at the top. When a crisis occurs, it is then almost too late to educate those who have to make the decision. . . .

· ·

. . . I emphasize the time factor. You can't go back and take a course in the problems of a particular area when you have to move within hours, or make a decision by not moving; so this is of some importance.

Then I think that we have a problem of how to get information to the Congress, since it does play a crucial role in our foreign affairs. I don't think we have fully found the answer to that question. Part of the problem is congressional time, because Senators and Congressmen have not only an interest in or responsibility for having judgments on these very complex matters of foreign relations, they also have a host of domestic problems before them, apart from the political processes by which they remain Senators and Congressmen.

· ·

I would like to underscore what the committee has said about the responsibility of the top leadership for administration. I believe this is important, and I give administration a good deal of my own time because administration should not become a thing in itself, but should know that its purpose is to administer something called foreign policy, and that the end object of administration remains foreign policy. It is not just a machine of its own.

Secondly, administration involves choices in using short resources for potentially unlimited demands—for additional services and additional personnel. The normal trend, not necessarily a happy trend of large organizations, is to grow. Allocation of short resources among different needs and demands itself presents major policy questions in establishing the priorities, and I think only those who are responsible at the top ought to establish those priorities.

Last year, for example, I took a series of Saturdays throughout the fall conducting my own hearings on our budget. I had the responsible officers come in and talk about personnel and personnel assignments and budget, not only to prepare them but to prepare me for the presentations to the Bureau of the Budget and also in preparation for the hearings of the four committees of the Congress. I think the administration itself has a very important responsibility of leadership.

On the role of the Ambassador I might make this comment: I don't believe it is true that the role of an Ambassador has been diminished by the increase in the speed and expansion of communications. If you look back to the period when communications were slow or poor, the role of the Ambassador was not in my judgment nearly so important as his role today. One reason is connected with communications and the other is not.

The speed of communications greatly increases the pace of events. Therefore, the judgment of the man on the spot is just as important today as it was in clipper-ship days, because events are moving that much faster. There is almost never a week that passes when we don't have instances of a judgment that had to be made immediately on the spot by an Ambassador to deal with a situation before he could get this town to comment or give him instructions. I think that we ought to continue to set our sights on Ambassadors who have that capability even though there may be times when he is not called upon to use that capability in the most dramatic sense.

The other factor is that what the United States does in the world is so much more important now than it was 40 or 50 years ago, and this, too, greatly enlarges the responsibility and role of the Ambassador.

The principle reason why Ambassadors have to refer back so many things to Washington is that if he were left alone to decide what should be done to strengthen to the maximum our bilateral relations with the country in which he is posted, we would have accumulated requirements upon the United States for men or money far exceeding the resources available to us. Further, there is a vast complex of relevant legislation on which the Ambassador himself can't be an expert, and he may not know whether we, in fact, are able to do what he would like to see us do.

Then there is a third element—sound foreign policy. This runs directly into important domestic policies and domestic interests. I say this not in a pejorative sense at all, because these domestic interests are real. But an Ambassador has to have judgment from Washington on such a matter as straightening out our problem with Mexico on the salinity of the Colorado River. He can't move on matters involving oil imports or textiles or similar problems without Washington making the decision in the light of all of the factors, domestic and foreign, that might be involved.

On the question of personnel abroad, we are making a very intensive study at the present time on the staffing of our embassies, beginning with some of the larger ones, and particularly regarding the staffing from other agencies of Government. I am concerned that there are at least 44 agencies of Government represented in our Embassy in London. I would hope the committee would give us a little time to sort that one out before it looks too closely at that situation, because I am reminded of a remark that General Marshall made to me when he was Secretary of State. He recalled that in 1923 the Army sent a special task force to Europe to locate a good many officers who were left behind on various missions at the end of World War I, and couldn't be located. They were drawing their pay, but for 5 years they had disappeared from sight, and so the Army sent a mission that was called the "live graves registration team" to locate these individuals.

Well, there is a little of that that has to be looked into at every stage, and we are trying to do something about it.

10

CODES AND COURIERS

CHARLES W. THAYER*

. . . Under the prodding of President Roosevelt several new codes were composed. One of them was the Brown Code. It was popular with code clerks because it contained not only words but whole phrases dear to the hearts of those who drafted cables. "In a note dated today the Foreign Ministry states that" or "it would appear to be" or "It is suggested that" or "I am inclined to believe that," and similar expressions could all be handled by a single code group and at a considerable saving in telegraph bills.

But the Brown Code had a short life. Not long after it had been distributed a cable was flashed from Washington to every embassy and consulate. "The Brown Code," it said ruefully "has been compromised." What had happened was that a gang of Ustachi bandits had invaded the American Consulate in Zagreb and at the points of several machine guns had forced the vice-consul to open the safe, the contents of which they carried off into the forests of Croatia.

Other codes followed the Brown: the A, B, and C codes involved new cryptographic precautions but they greatly added to the time it took to code messages, especially since most telegrams had to be coded and then enciphered. Aside from the technical drawback. . . —the inevitability of repeti-

* Abridged from pp. 144–150, 153–158 in *Diplomat* by Charles W. Thayer. Copyright © 1959 by Charles Wheeler Thayer. Reprinted by permission of Harper & Row, Publishers, Inc.

tions—all codes in book form, like the Brown Code, are susceptible of filching.

During the first months of World War II, I was visiting friends in neutral Stockholm. In the Grand Hotel, then the rendezvous for every eavesdropper, agent and spy in Scandinavia, I ran into a Yugoslav vice-consul with whom I had served at several posts. Enormously fat, a bon vivant and a great raconteur, he joined me at a table in the big central lounge and we ordered drinks.

A woman seated nearby was reading a newspaper which entirely hid her face, but as the Yugoslav started to recount the latest diplomatic gossip, the newspaper slowly descended revealing her listening intently to what he was saying. The vice-consul rose, walked over to her chair, bowed as deeply as his girth-line would permit, and said most politely:

"Madame, you speak English?"

"But of course," she said with a friendly smile, expecting to be invited to join us.

"Et vous parlez français, madame?"

"Mais oui, naturellement, monsieur."

"Und Deutsch auch?"

"Aber natürlich."

"I po-russki?" he went on. But the woman's face went blank. With another deep bow he rejoined me and went on in Russian.

"And have you heard," he asked, "what happened to the Italian codes in Berlin?"

The code room of the Italian Embassy in Berlin, he said, was run by a dried-up spinster who had been in the embassy for thirty years and must have been well into her fifties. With few friends and a face not likely to make many more, she lived a very quiet life in a tiny apartment off the Tiergarten just around the corner from the Italian Chancellery. Occasionally she went to a nearby Italian restaurant for supper or a demi-tasse of espresso. One evening while she was sipping her coffee, a young man dressed in a Tyrolean jacket, whom she had seen once or twice before in the restaurant, joined her and asked to be allowed to finish his coffee in her company.

He was exceedingly good-looking, blond, tall, with an open cheerful smile and could scarcely have been more than twenty-three or four. He explained that he was an Austrian and, he hinted, a member of an old aristocratic family. When they had finished their coffee the Italian clerk excused herself and went back to her rooms. But a few days later she met the Austrian count again and this time he asked her to dine with him. He was lonely in Berlin, he explained, because his only associates were "Prussian swine" whom he detested.

Soon the two were dining regularly together. Then he invited her to a concert and to a theater. A full-blown romance was now in progress between the handsome Austrian count and the deeply infatuated Italian. Eventually they took to spending the weekends at one of the converted Schlösser that before the war Berlin hotelkeepers maintained in the countryside around the capital for just such clients. Then abruptly the count disappeared. The code clerk was sad but bolstered her morale with the happy memories of those blissful months.

Some time later the count showed up in Zurich and let it be known to a few selected foreign governments that the Italian diplomatic codes could be had at a price. My Yugoslav friend had been sent to buy them for a large packet of unmarked dollars on behalf of his government. When the Italian government finally got wind of the affair and investigated, they charged that the code clerk in the Berlin Embassy had "loaned" the codes to her boy friend, who had promptly photographed them. Taken for trial to Rome, she readily confessed, but told the indignant judge she would gladly do it all over again if the count would too.

As totalitarian diplomacy of both Communists and Nazis developed, they became more refined in their operations. Since to blow a safe or leave other traces that a code had been tampered with would warn the user that his code was compromised, Croatian bandits were replaced by expert safe-crackers who could open safes by manipulating the combinations.

How easy this was even with modern safes was demonstrated when, as security officer, I was one day required to alter the combinations of the dozen or more safes in one of our embassies. Having done so and carefully written the new combinations on cards, I put the cards in my safe, slammed the door, twirled the combination and went home. Only the next morning it occurred to me that the new combination of my own safe, which I had forgotten, was safely inside it together with all the other new combinations. For twenty-four hours the embassy was more or less out of business until one of the consuls admitted shyly that he made a hobby of opening safes. Applying a little sandpaper to his finger tips he went to work and simply by feeling the tumblers fall had it open in a few hours.

Since an ultra-powerful telescope in a window across the street might possibly be used to photograph the code books, code clerks are cautioned not to work near windows. The Hotel Crillon in Paris, for example, is directly across a narrow street from the American Embassy. From any of a score of rooms in it an agent could easily see the desks of the embassy's political section.

Microphones are a classic weapon of totalitarian diplomacy, not only to eavesdrop on diplomatic conversations but to record a diplomat's thought as he dictates his telegrams. Easily concealed in curtains or furniture—on one occasion under the connubial bed of an Italian ambassador whose wife was known to wear the ambassadorial pants—their only disadvantage is the wiring they require.

Once while I was inspecting the attic of one of our embassies my flashlight reflected a glint no brighter than a tiny star under the eaves. The wire that had reflected the light could scarcely be seen in normal light. Tracing it with the beam of the flashlight, I found that it led down a ventilation shaft in the wall. I squeezed down the shaft and found a small microphone hanging behind the plaster directly back of the ambassador's desk on the floor below.

To guard against microphones, specialists armed with powerful induction coils to reveal any suspicious live wires in the walls periodically "debug" our diplomatic missions. This method was considered adequate until one day a radio ham on the staff of an American embassy, while twisting the dials of his powerful set, was startled to hear the voice of his ambassador, apparently dictating to his secretary in a building many blocks away. Despite the most thorough debugging of his office no sign of a wire or a mike could be found. Eventually a plaster reproduction of the Great Seal of the United States, presented by a local artist to the ambassador's predecessor to adorn his office, was torn apart and in the plaster backing was found a wireless microphone—a device previously unknown to our security experts. To this day our specialists are not saying what, if any, countermeasure they have devised for this latest contribution to the armory of totalitarian diplomacy.

The totalitarians found other ingenious devices to tap their enemies' communications. When Italy switched sides in 1942, the Italian minister to Kabul, who had up to then been on the enemy side, showed me a photostat of a handwritten message.

"Have you ever seen that?" he asked.

Reluctantly I admitted that it was a penciled draft of a top-secret telegram I had sent some months before, in my own handwriting. He then explained that the German minister in Kabul had given it to him, stating that it had been obtained by a devilish little instrument that could reveal the impression left on a pad through a dozen or more sheets below the original writing.

These products of the totalitarians' ingenuity gradually awakened the State Department to the necessity for greater security. One of the first steps was the Marine guard sent to Moscow in 1934. Slowly similar precautions were extended to other embassies and the Marines soon had replaced all the superannuated night watchmen who had heretofore been almost the only protection against espionage.

As new regulations were issued requiring the locking up first of secret documents, then of stenographers' notebooks, carbon paper and other working papers, and the Marine guards during their night rounds began to enforce them by formal reports of "security violations," the older diplomats complained indignantly that the restrictions were hampering their work. But the appearance of new espionage devices merely strengthened the security measures.

. . . .

Simultaneously, the State Department's codes were tested, with alarming results. In the previous years new coding precautions had tended to add to their cumbersomeness but less to their security and during crises the coding effort in our larger embassies consumed the days and nights of much of the staff. During the Munich Crisis, for example, half the vice-consuls in Berlin were assigned to the code room.

But now, with war practically upon us, the department was finally forced . . . to scrap the sixteenth-century code systems for . . . machines.

. . . .

In the days of the simple colored codes—the Old Gray Code, for example, which preceded the Brown—experienced coding hands eventually memorized most of the more common five-letter symbols in the book. In the late twenties a senior consul who was about to retire was given a testimonial dinner by his staff at the Shanghai Consulate. Rising after the toasts, he made his farewell speech in gray, to the consternation of the uninitiated but to the delight of the old-timers who followed the address with ease. . . .

Despite the coding machine, the basic means of diplomatic communications still remains the classic one of couriers. Since the earliest times one of the basic rights of an embassy has been that of sending couriers whose dispatch cases were immune from search or seizure. The right, however, was not always meticulously observed. Back in 1380 B.C. an Egyptian king, wishing to send a message by courier through an area in which his diplomatic status might not be recognized, had the courier's head shaved, wrote his message on the scalp and waited until the hair had grown over it before sending him. In those days diplomacy apparently operated in a more leisurely fashion than today.

One night over three thousand years later the Nord Express from Paris to Moscow was lumbering slowly across the steppes. The single sleeping car had only a few passengers: an American lady on a visit to her son in the American Embassy in Moscow, a couple of German engineers, and the Japanese diplomatic courier en route to Tokyo from Berlin where a German-Japanese alliance, the text of which was secret, had just been negotiated.

The passengers were all asleep when the train suddenly stopped and the conductor announced that the car had broken an axle. Fortunately, he added, another sleeping car was standing by quite by chance on the adjoining track. Equally fortuitously, a staff of porters were also available—apparently just standing about in the steppe in the middle of the night waiting for a chance to earn an honest kopeck.

Lest the train be late in Moscow, the passengers were told simply to hustle across the track to the new car in their night clothes. Their baggage would be transferred by the waiting porters. After a mad scramble and the confusion that ordinarily accompanies any such operation in Russia, the passengers settled back in their new car. It was hitched to the train and the journey was resumed.

Next morning the Japanese courier joined the American lady at breakfast. Grinning broadly and hissing with mirth, he told her that his dispatch case had disappeared during the midnight transfer.

"But," he added gleefully, "it wasn't my real dispatch case at all. This is where I carry secret messages," he boasted and raised his left arm to which was firmly manacled what looked like a little toilet kit. "And all that 'wreck' for an empty bag!" the little Japanese giggled.

In 1641 the British established the first modern courier service. Known as the king's, or queen's, messengers, these couriers have since traveled around the globe carrying what is known in British diplomatic circles as the "bag." (In American jargon it is the "pouch" and in French the "valise.") Recruited largely from retired police officers, the king's messengers wear a small silver greyhound as a symbol of their proud profession. The symbol predates that of any busline by several centuries.

In his diaries John Quincy Adams, who was American minister to Russia from 1809 to 1814, indicates that most of his correspondence with Washington was carried by the imperial Russian couriers. In fact, on several occasions the Czar's ministers dispatched special couriers to carry the American minister's urgent mail—an undertaking which, in the age of post horses and sailing ships, was not to be compared in simplicity with arranging a transatlantic flight today. It never seems to have occurred to Mr. Adams that his messages might be tampered with but this, of course, was in the days when gentlemen really did not read each other's mail.

During World War I the United States organized a courier system using Marines and soldiers as couriers, but with the end of the war it was disbanded and the pouch was once more sent by mail or entrusted to any American who happened to be going its way. During that chivalrous age even confidential dispatches were often sent through the ordinary mails. Locked and fastened with heavy wax seals, they were not, one presumed, inspected by customs officers or border police. More secret documents were usually turned over to American travelers known to the diplomatic mission, who were given letters appointing them "bearers of dispatches." It was considered quite an honor to be entrusted with diplomatic mail and it also entitled the bearers of dispatches to preferential treatment at frontier stations. They therefore did the work for nothing.

However, the age of totalitarian diplomacy was already forcing itself upon the attention of reluctant State Department officials. Though other governments, too, sent pouches by mail, these generally contained only newspapers, personal mail, and similar nonsecret correspondence. On one occasion in the early thirties the Polish minister in a Balkan country called on the foreign minister to complain about the tampering with his diplomatic mail. He did not, he explained, object to the local authorities opening his mailbags, since they contained only nonconfidential material. However, he considered it an affront that they should have been so thoughtless as to reseal them with the official seal of Finland.

During the London Economic Conference in 1934, President Roosevelt learned for the first time that the State Department had disbanded its courier service years before. Astonished, he ordered that it be reestablished immediately. Small sums were allotted to the embassies in Paris and London to hire one courier apiece. But these single couriers were hardly able to take care of the pouch mail in totalitarian countries, where even personal correspondence could not be entrusted to the public mails because of the censorship.

To supplement them, the personnel of embassies in dictatorships took turns carrying the pouch. It was a somewhat slipshod performance, but somehow no pouches were ever lost—for long. At one Eastern post an elderly consul who was retiring was asked to carry the pouches to a neighboring country on his way home. His departure was celebrated with a large farewell banquet but next day a telegram arrived from his destination reading: "We have the courier. Have you got the pouches?" Fortunately they were still in the pouch room where the consul had forgotten to pick them up after his banquet.

. . . .

During and after the war the U.S. Diplomatic Courier Service was greatly expanded and improved. Today sixty-six couriers cover the globe on courier routes emanating from the three overseas courier centers—Frankfurt, Panama, and Manila. These three centers are connected with Washington by military planes which feed the diplomatic mail to them. In a single year U.S. couriers cover over four million miles—mostly by air. The couriers call only at centrally located missions, from which local couriers distribute the pouches to neighboring posts.

The couriers themselves, unlike their more staid colleagues, the queen's messengers, are young bachelors. They must be college graduates and pass a severe screening, for applications for the positions greatly exceed vacancies. Normally a courier remains with the service for six or seven years, after which he can try for entry into the regular career Foreign Service or return to a less hectic civilian job.

At any large airport a traveler may encounter the tall, thin American with crewcut head and rumpled seersucker suit ambling off a plane behind an airline porter rolling a baggage truck filled with what looks like U.S. mailsacks marked "Dept. of State" and heavily padlocked. Ordering a cup of coffee, he will sit down in a corner surrounded by his pouches, an invoice spread before him, checking and rechecking the little linen bags he has removed from one of the large sacks. Presently another crewcut in a slightly better pressed suit accompanied by a chauffeur in the American Embassy uniform will appear. Together they will check more invoices, exchange little sacks and larger pouches, signing receipts and initialling lists while harassed airline officials cluster about them with warnings that they are delaying the plane. Finally, their paper work completed, they part shouting to each other: "Tell Smitty I'll see him in Lagos Thursday and don't forget to ask Jim about those empty pouches in Tabriz." Preceded by a porter with his pouches, the first courier hurries to his plane. The pouches are not taken to the hold but are stacked beside him on a reserved seat. The plane warms up and he is off on the next leg of his run.

A normal courier run may start from Frankfurt and end there twenty-nine days later. The first stop is Geneva, then Rome, Athens, Cairo, Addis Ababa, and Nairobi. Traveling day and night, pausing only for connections, he reaches Nairobi in two and a half days. There he "stages," that is, another courier, like a relay runner, picks up his pouches and goes on southward while he rests a day or two and flies up to Kampala in Uganda, then to Mogadiscio in the Somali Republic and north to Aden. Thence he flies back to Nairobi, where he in turn picks up the baton from the courier who left Frankfurt a week after he did. He flies south to Salisbury, Rhodesia, and to Pretoria, in South Africa, and then strikes north up the west coast to Leopoldville and finally to Lagos in Nigeria where he stages again, this time for four or five days during which he makes a side trip to Abidjan on the French Ivory Coast and to Duala in the French Cameroons. Then he again relieves the next arrival at Lagos and proceeds to Monrovia, Dakar, Casablanca, Nice and Paris, and finally to Frankfurt. After a day or two of rest there he is off again for Geneva and points south.

Contrary to myth, couriers are seldom overtly attacked and they never carry guns. However, the planes they ride in are occasionally shot at—and down—for violating forbidden territory. One courier, Frank Irwin, was shot down in his plane by Tito's forces in northern Yugoslavia. Though badly wounded, he retrieved his pouches from the burning plane and stayed with them until properly relieved by U.S. officials. Then he was carted off to a hospital, where he remained for over a year recovering from his wounds.

Like the code room, the pouch room, usually next to it, is behind a steel door beyond which innumerable locked gates and iron grills keep out everyone, including embassy officials who are not directly concerned with its operation. In sensitive posts someone is on guard there twenty-four hours a day.

11

HOW NATIONS NEGOTIATE

Fred Charles Iklé*

. . . Negotiation is a subject on which much has been said and written that seems self-evident until examined more closely. To resolve conflict and avoid the use of force, it is said, one must negotiate (Is this always the best

* Abridgement of "What Is Negotiation?" in *How Nations Negotiate* by Fred Charles Iklé. Copyright © 1964 by Fred Charles Iklé. Reprinted by permission of Harper & Row, Publishers, Inc.

way to settle conflict?). Negotiation requires a willingness to compromise (Why?), and both sides must make concessions (According to which law?). Neither side can expect to win all its wants (Not even if its objectives are modest?). If both sides negotiate in good faith (Who judges "good faith"?), they can always find a fair solution (And what is "fair"?). If there is a conflict about many issues, the less controversial ones should be solved first because agreement will lead to further agreement (Or will the postponed issues become harder to solve?). A negotiator should never make a threat he is not prepared to carry out (What is wrong with successful bluffing?). Each side has its minimum beyond which it cannot be moved (But how about moving the opponent's minimum?). . . .

[The present analysis] seeks to relate the *process* of negotiation to the *outcome*. To begin with, two elements must normally be present for negotiation to take place: there must be common interests and issues of conflict. Without common interest there is nothing to negotiate for, without conflict nothing to negotiate about. . . .

One should perhaps distinguish between two kinds of common interests: an *identical common interest* in a single arrangement or object, and a *complementary interest* in an exchange of different objects. In the identical common interest, the parties want to share the *same* object or benefit from the same arrangement, which, however, they can bring about only by joining together. . . . Examples of agreements on such identical common interests are the U.S.-Canadian treaty on the St. Lawrence Seaway, international fishery agreements to protect the supply of fish, and, in a sense, ceasefire agreements.

When parties are interested in an exchange, they want *different* things. These they cannot obtain by themselves but can only grant to each other. The clearest examples are barters and sales. Similarly, commercial aviation agreements, where each country wants to have its planes fly to the other country, have the purpose of settling an exchange. So do agreements for mutual tariff concessions.

In reality, however, most negotiations embrace a combination of identical common interests and complementary interests. When the six European countries set up the European Economic Community, they had complementary interests in the exchange of tariff concessions and common interests in a large, unified European market. The nuclear test-ban treaty between the United States and the Soviet Union can satisfy the complementary interest in slowing down the opponent's development of new weapons and the common interest in preventing an increase in radioactive fallout or in discouraging the proliferation of nuclear weapons. Whether the identical common interests or the complementary interests dominate depends on how the purposes of the agreement are defined.

The process by which two or more parties relate conflicting to common interests is the warp and woof not only of international relations but of human society; individuals, groups, and governments engage in it all the time. We become aware of it only when we call it something special. . . . There seems to be no established term for all the ways in which parties with conflicting and common interests interact—whether explicitly or tacitly— though "bargaining" is sometimes used that broadly.

"Negotiation" in a narrower sense denotes a process that is different from tacit bargaining or other behavior that regulates conflict. As used here, negotiation *is a process in which explicit proposals are put forward ostensibly for the purpose of reaching agreement on an exchange or on the realization of a common interest where conflicting interests are present.* Frequently, these proposals deal not only with the terms of agreement but also with the topics to be discussed (the agenda), with the ground rules that ought to apply, and with underlying technical and legal issues. It is the confrontation of explicit proposals that distinguishes negotiation (as here defined) from tacit bargaining and other types of conflict behavior. . . .

Only part of the frequent changes in relations between countries are the result of negotiation. Governments often revise their expectations and attitudes toward other countries as a result of unilateral actions or tacit bargains. Military and technological developments, growth or decline in economic strength, and internal political changes continually cause the rearrangement of conflicting and common interests between nations, and this happens whether or not diplomats negotiate.

There is no simple rule as to when negotiation is needed, and when tacit bargaining or even less conscious confrontations are more effective to restructure international relations. For certain arrangements negotiation clearly cannot be dispensed with, for others it is optional; and there are some issues which are better settled without it.

Negotiation is necessary for any arrangement that establishes complicated forms of collaboration, such as a joint war effort or Britain's attempted entry into the Common Market. . . . Negotiation is needed for most exchanges, such as exchanges of prisoners or the granting of mutual consular facilities, and for all transactions involving monetary compensation, as in the payment of oil royalties or the leasing of air bases. Negotiation is, of course, necessary for the setting up of formal international institutions and for any arrangement where an *explicit* agreement is essential, such as a peace treaty or an alliance system.

On the other hand, certain undertakings are arrived at in such a delicate way that explicit proposals might interfere with the process. The mutually observed restrictions in the Korean War (for instance, no attacks on the supply lines leading into North and South Korea) is an example of arrangements that would not have been facilitated or might even have been upset by negotiation. The very uncertainties of a tacit understanding may have made these restrictions more stable, because both sides were unwilling to probe and push toward the limits of the "bargain," lest it all be upset. The negotiation of an explicit *quid pro quo* might have given rise to new demands and invited more haggling and tugging than the arrangement which the parties never discussed and never explicitly settled. Furthermore, while soldiers were being killed fighting the enemy, negotiations to establish rules and restraints for the battle or on the interdiction of supplies would have clashed with domestic opinion and perhaps adversely affected the morale of the troops.[1]

Likewise, if there is a deep-seated hostility between the populations of two countries, governments may be unable to negotiate because of public opposition but may work out some arrangements of mutual interest through tacit bargaining. The relationship between Jordan and Israel is an example.

In the field of arms control and disarmament, where we have become so accustomed to large and formal conferences, important understanding can at times be arrived at without negotiation. Formal talks might, in fact, make it more difficult to harmonize some arms policies insofar as they inevitably introduce political issues or questions of prestige and legal precedents.[2]

Negotiation plays an important role in formalizing turning points in international relations, in catalyzing or at least clarifying changes that were caused by tacit bargaining or other processes, and in working out those finer shades in new arrangements between nations that the brute interplay of latent strength cannot define.

Although negotiation is necessary for any new relationship that is based on explicit agreement, an explicit agreement is usually only part of the outcome of negotiation. Negotiation may change the positions of the parties and their mutual relations in many other ways. The outcome may include, for example, tacit understandings between the parties, a clarification of the points of disagreement, a reorientation of national objectives, new commitments to third parties (allies, domestic groups, or world opinion), and propaganda effects. Many of these results may outweigh in importance whatever explicit agreement is arrived at. And even agreements themselves vary widely in their degree of specificity and the amount of disagreement that they leave unsettled.

---

[1] A pioneering analysis of the role of tacit bargaining in limited war is given by Thomas C. Schelling, *The Strategy of Conflict* (Cambridge, Mass.: Harvard University Press, 1960), Chap. 3 and Appendix A. The delicate interaction of tacit limitations on air-attacks in the Korean War is discussed by Morton H. Halperin, *Limited War in the Nuclear Age* (New York: John Wiley, 1963), pp. 53–55.

[2] On the importance of tacit bargaining for arms control, see Thomas C. Schelling and Morton H. Halperin, *Strategy and Arms Control* (New York: Twentieth Century Fund, 1961), pp. 77–82.

❧5❧

The Role of International Law

Fᴏᴍ ᴛʜᴇ ʙᴇɢɪɴɴɪɴɢ of the modern nation-state system international law has played an important although much misunderstood role in the relations of nations. Recurrently dismissed and derided as weak by "hard-headed realists," it has nonetheless continued to play an indispensable part in regulating and regularizing those relations. Without it, given a world of one hundred fifty sovereign states, conflict would escalate beyond tolerance. Consequently, although international law stands on its own merits as an academic discipline with a large and detailed content, its importance for students of international relations is bound up in the first instance with understanding its nature and especially its relation to conflict resolution.

In the first selection, "International Law and the World Community," Louis F. E. Goldie of Syracuse University, a distinguished and prolific contributor to the literature of international law, examines the basic issues. With humor and penetration, Goldie begins by clarifying what international law is *not* by examining "common models" of the legal order. He argues that "international law provides prohibitions which states . . . take into account when calculating the chances of success a given policy may have" and that, even more significantly, "it exists as a system of decision-making, of process, and of communication." He then systematically examines the major arguments advanced as to international law's "weaknesses," and follows with an analysis of the views of the "professional optimists" who conversely "have done international law a major disservice by overstating the case for it." His concluding sections shed light on the probable ulti-

mate consequences of the current unenthusiastic attitude of many of
the newer nations toward traditional international law. He points out
the innovative capability of law in assisting nations to evolve a new
consensus, as in the Alabama Claims Arbitration.

In the second selection, "Law and Legal Institutions May Help,"
Roger Fisher, Professor of Law at Harvard Law School, in a fresh and
stimulating presentation looks at international law as part of "the
process of causing another government to change their mind." He
views legal considerations as elements in influencing the political
decision-making process. Thus his concern is not with what the role of
law ought to be but with its political consequences, given its role as is.
Somewhat like Goldie, Fisher also takes pains to describe the function
of law. His method is to first set forth three essentially false statements
and then, by examining their defects, emerge with a more accurate
conception. Having done this, he then applies his findings to a case
study of the Cuban missile crisis. Fisher's analysis of the role of international law and legal institutions in that crisis is very provocative.

12

INTERNATIONAL LAW AND
THE WORLD COMMUNITY

Louis F. E. Goldie[*]

I. Introduction: Definition and Meaning

Endemic among you there is, I know, . . . skepticism about the claims of international law to reflect a legal order. . . .

Many people ask, when they look at the international order and see that there are none of the regular institutions of a domestic legal order, no legislature, no executive with law-enforcement authority, and no system of courts with compulsory jurisdiction: "How can international law be law at all?" Now this brings me to my first point. Only too often people confuse a significant discussion about the nature of things, or the nature of law, as in this case, with a trivial argument about the meaning of words. Let me illustrate this.

Most people's concept of law, even today, is based on an authoritarian model which can be stated in general terms as a general command issued by a sovereign authority owning no political superior, enforced by the authority of a system of courts, and administered by an executive authority. This is one generally accepted definition of the word "law." But it is a very narrow, restricted view of the law, and it leaves out of account very many kinds of law, even very many kinds of domestic law. On the other hand, its wide acceptance stems from the English Utilitarians of a century and a half ago, especially Jeremy Bentham and John Austin, and their extensive program of domestic legislative reform. One consequence of this positivist, utilitarian definition of law was that international law came to be characterized as "positive morality." This illustrates my point. Stipulate a narrow definition of the word "law," and international law is excluded. On the other hand, if you stipulate a broader definition of law, international law will be included. This reminds me about all the controversy which has been plaguing the world of literature for about a hundred years: "Did William Shakespeare really write those plays he is credited with?" One answer is: "If he did not, then somebody else called William Shakespeare did."

---

[*] Louis F. E. Goldie, "International Law and the World Community: The Meaning of Words, The Nature of Things, and the Face of the International Order," *Naval War College Review*, Vol. 23, No. 6 (February 1971), pp. 8–20. Reprinted by permission.

127

If anyone says to me, "I stipulate a definition of law which will exclude international law. Therefore international law is not law," I will say, "Well, your second sentence, your conclusion, is unnecessary; it was already inherent in your premise. If you stipulate that kind of a definition of law, that is your business. And I do not wish to argue over trivialities. But I would like to point out that you are probably wrong in your concept of what law is." This last is not a trivial point. It is something we should think about—what the nature of law is, what its uses are, how we may best employ it, and how, indeed, it can be utilized to the advantage of . . . the United States, of the world community, rather than treat it as a counter in a parlor game with words.

II. A Legal System at Work—Some "Still" Pictures

I will start my discussion of this topic of finding some common models or pictures of a legal system with the idea that most of us find international law a difficult concept to grasp, or a difficult thing to think about, because our everyday ordinary way of thinking about law is the product of common experiences—these produce the models we have in our heads. For example, a common model of the legal system at work is the picture of a traffic policeman booking us for making a left-hand turn out of a right-hand lane. Now we know there is a rule, we know there is a person in authority, and we know we have done the wrong thing. And this is an easy and simple approach to giving us a model or picture of what law is. Behind the policeman is the State Legislature which authorized the writing of (or indeed may have written itself as is the case in some states) the Rules of the Road, including the strict requirement about not making left-hand turns out of right-hand lanes. The policeman himself is appointed under laws written by the State Legislature, and ultimately his appointment has to be valid, as the legal provision our citizen has offended has to be valid, under the Constitution of the State and that of the United States. There is thus a legal system which bears down on us, possessing the powerful and vast machinery of a sovereign state, complete with legislature, authoritative executive, and, finally, courts with compulsory jurisdiction. (If you make a left-hand turn out of a right-hand lane you will probably find yourself in one of the very minor courts of a great hierarchy of judicial institutions.) In addition to showing our motoring citizen as feeling very sorry for himself while the officer writes out the ticket and says, "You shouldn't have done that, sir," or other words to that effect, there is a vast background which the legal order provides to this trivial legal event. Insofar as this incident has legal significance, it involves the whole domestic legal order and is governed by it. In this way we all see the secure order of great richness in commands or, better, prescriptions, rules, institutions, and validly appointed legal authorities which keep our complex society functioning with the minimum of friction and waste. Then we look to international law and we see none or, at best very little of this institutional richness and depth of legal rules, institutions, experience, authority, and power.

I have gone into some detail with this picture, this common model of the legal order, since many of us and our fellow citizens carry it in their heads as their belief that it constitutes a "hard-core" example of the legal system at work—the citizen in his automobile and the traffic policeman on his motorcycle. This is also in that area of law which most people regard as the paradigm of the legal order—the enforcement of the criminal law. Let us now go a little further. Do you think that in many cases when the U.S. Government, for example, may have to deal with organized crime in the United States, the law enforcement situation is so simple? It seems to me that some research worker could probably uncover an enormous and intricate system of negotiation, concession, surrender, giving ground, claiming ground, and so on, in many of the major cases which the Federal Government or a State government may bring against a major representative of organized crime, successfully prosecute him, and conduct the case ultimately to the conviction and punishment of the accused. It seems that when we observe governments prosecuting major underworld figures we are already a long way from the clear-cut law-enforcement situation of the policeman and the motorcar driver or the policeman and the petty criminal. Let us go another step further.

Outside the realm of criminal law—and you will notice that I have kept my pictures, so far, in the realms of criminal law—we find that there are many more diverse ways in which the law operates than we are apt to expect inside the area of criminal law. We find that the legal system appears, mainly, to provide the citizen with the procedures, with the means, of doing the sort of things he wants to do. The Law of Real Property is not only a law which tells trespassers to keep off your property or be prosecuted; it is also a law, a body of very intricate law, that tells you how you can enjoy what you have and, if you have the right kind of interest, the many ways in which you can transmit that interest or the fruits of it to other people; what it can be worth to you in a money sense—given the state of the market— and how you can enjoy it to its best advantage. This is not telling you not to do something. There is here nothing like an equivalent of disobeying a prohibition—for example, making a left-hand turn out of a right-hand lane or even of belonging to a powerful syndicate of criminals running illegal "business ventures." This area of law tells you what you can do with your own so as to effectuate the maximum of enjoyment to yourself and with maximum advantage to your neighbors.

Again, when a civilian writes a will there are certain rules that he must fulfill; for example, he must have his signature attested to by a certain number of witnesses (the actual number depending on state law); also he must follow certain other basic procedures. It would, therefore, be wrong to say that the law relating to the writing of wills consists of commands given by a legislature and enforced by sanctions—by the threat of prosecution and punishment. After all, what is the sanction if someone writes a will and fails to have it testified to by the right number of witnesses? The will may be invalid, but the citizen will not be punished by any decision to invalidate his will. After all, he is dead! In this kind of a situation, it seems silly to call nullification a sanction—a threat of punishment.

The system, the laws we have on writing wills, are what we may call facultative or facilitating rules. So are all the rules which tell us, and institutions which tell us, how to do what we want to do in 'the best way for ourselves and our fellow citizens.

Thus we see that law—even law within these United States—is something far more pervasive, far less clear-cut, than a prohibition, an offense, a policeman, and a lower court. We need to give it a far wider definition. Now the interesting thing is once we move away from the idea that the legislature, executive, and courts with compulsory jurisdiction are essential to the existence of a legal system, almost any other definition of law includes international law. If, for example, we are prepared to say that a legal system consists of a process of authoritative decision-making, in which basic values become reflected in social action by means of the decisional process and through the agency of the authoritative decision-makers (including courts, but not restricted to them), then we find that international law fits into that definition quite well. Again, if we add thereto the concept of law as a system of facilitative means of social interaction and communication which contains prohibitions only where interaction extends beyond what is permissible in a mutually viable system, then, here too, we find that international law quite clearly fits within our definition. Also, if we state that it is a most important means of directing participants' efforts for the realization of common values, then, again, international law fits in with such a definition of law. Now, I have stressed the problem of definitions because I really want to underline the distinction between the trivial point of arguing about the meaning of words and the important point which calls for an investigation of the nature of things. I must also point out that the definitions of law which I have just indicated seem far closer to the nature of law than the more traditional one which emphasizes power and enforcement at the expense of interaction and direction. I will close this section of my presentation by pointing out to you that international law provides prohibitions which states, like individuals, take into account when calculating the chances of success a given policy may have. In addition, and more significantly perhaps, it exists as a system of decision-making, of process, and of communication. Assuming a knowledge of international law is like assuming a knowledge of language. You can cue your friends and your rivals as to your intentions and then indicate to them those of their options which are acceptable to you—and those which are unacceptable. Your game plans, incidentally, should include the choice of your adversaries' selecting unacceptable options. These, again, should be clearly discernible through the language of international law.

III. The Nature of International Law—Responses to Some Criticisms

A. THE PROBLEM OF STATE SOVEREIGNTY

There is a more sophisticated variant of the skeptics' position which we have just discussed, namely that international law cannot be "law properly so called" since it is not issued by a sovereign commander, is not supported by sanctions, and is not administered by courts with compulsory jurisdiction. That more sophisticated variation takes up the concept of sovereignty from a new point of view. It argues, not on the footing of international law's failure to indicate its own sovereign, but rather, that since it is an order of sovereign nations, it cannot for that reason also be a legal order. More briefly, this argument holds that national sovereignty is inconsistent with international law. The inarticulate premise of such an argument is that if a legal system is itself the child of sovereign authority it cannot, at the same time, incorporate many sovereigns. The restricted definition of law itself, which I outlined earlier, comes up again. It is translated into this new inverted perspective of sovereignty and the international order.

But what do we mean when we talk of national sovereignty? From the point of view of international law, the sovereignty of a state is not an extralegal or metalegal concept. Rather, it is a basic concept of international law and is defined by it. Sovereignty is the term used to describe the competence which the international law ascribes to states. We tend, perhaps, to think of sovereignty in absolute terms. Yet no state is sovereign in the world today in the same sense that the Roman Empire was sovereign in the Mediterranean Basin, in, say, A.D. 100. The difference between then and now is that although every contemporary state is said to be sovereign, each one must recognize and act in terms of the sovereignty of all the others. For all sovereign states act and interact in the common arena of international relations wherein international law facilitates their peaceable interactions and is formulated to limit, where it cannot prevent, states' hostile or violent interactions. International law thus may be seen, at one and the same time, as according and ascribing to states their sovereign authority as the form of competence they enjoy in the international arena and placing the necessary limits on that competence in order to limit, and to humanize, collisions in its mutual and interacting exercise. In contrast with the contemporary world where more than 120 states interact in the same area of action, the sovereign situation of the Roman Empire existed simply because there were no other states interacting with it to limit its sovereignty. By contrast with the example from the Roman world, the contemporary states' interactions calls for the ascription of competences to states. We denominate these competences "sovereignty," which becomes a legally defined and a relative concept. Admittedly, that definition is in extremely wide terms; but there are limits to it. There are limits to it set by treaties and by customary law. Examples of the customary law limitation on state sovereignty are states' universal recognition of the immunity of foreign sovereigns, their diplomats, and their warships in receiving states' ports. At such points as these, and even on the territory of the United States, our legal sovereign power stops short. It meets the opposing and countervailing sovereign competence of a foreign country. Thus, while it is so latitudinarily defined as, possibly, to weaken and undermine the orderliness of the international legal order, the concept of state sovereignty does not contradict that order. It cannot do so, because it is, itself, a derivative of that order.

B. The Problem of Commitment

Tied in with the problems which the looseness of the international order presents is a criticism which looks, at first blush, like a restatement of the argument we have just disposed of when that is freed of its conceptualist impedimenta labeled "sovereignty." This attack on international law, however, in reality comes from a very different group of theorists. Those who argue that national sovereignty is inconsistent with international law, and is a logical denial of it, are concerned about international law's failure to develop into a highly integrated and formalized system of authority. The critics whose position we are now going to review, on the other hand, argue against international law's validity on pragmatic grounds. They argue that because, as it is clear on any view of the way states behave toward each other, no state has an overriding and absolute commitment to the vindication of international law at all costs, international law either does not exist in international reality or, at most, does not reflect a meaningful legal order. I suggest to you that such a thesis is completely beside the point. It is, furthermore, not only based on a cynical, Machiavellian view of the law, it is also based on a misconception of the relation of law and morals and of the morality of obedience to law. Everyone in this room has a sticking point where he would not have an overriding and absolute commitment to the vindication of the domestic law of the United States or of the State of Rhode Island. There may be situations where the law may call upon a citizen to do things that go against his basic moral ideas and which he will withdraw from doing. Thus, once we really start to look at the criticisms involving the issue of commitment which frequently are sagely adduced to deny the existence of international law—including those by such eminent men as Dean Acheson, George Kennan, and Professor Morgenthau—we find that their positions turn on mistaken notions about either the meaning of law or about the expectations people might appropriately entertain of international law itself. Moreover, they do not, perhaps, think sufficiently comparatively in order to evaluate how people, in general, react to certain legal rules which might be imposed before they look at theorists' and states' adverse reactions to specific rules or doctrines of international law.

The cynical position we have just reviewed is, of course, made all the more plausible when we remember that there is an issue many legal philosophers overlook when discussing the way in which legal systems work. The truism is this: there is no legal rule for applying a legal rule. Whenever any legal rule is applied, it is applied by a human being who is applying (a) his knowledge of law; (b) his evaluation and characterization of the facts; (c) his ideas of the relevance of the law he knows to the facts before him; (d) the theory and morality of law he entertains; and (e) the policy goals of the law he holds to be relevant to the case. Now I am coming to one of the points I need to emphasize this morning. You all carry around with you your own moralities of law and your own theories of law. You are all legal philosophers, and you apply your philosophies whenever you face a legal problem or make a legal decision. Your problem may well be that, although you operate from philosophical premises about the nature and morality of law when you apply a rule or discuss the meaning of law, those premises are mainly below the threshold of your articulate thought. But, whether fully articulated and at the forefront of your minds, or operating as inarticulate premises or unconscious prejudices, they exist and they guide your knowledge and your thinking about law in general and your application of law, whether that is to enforce the discipline of a ship, or to identify the relevance of Article 2, paragraph 4, of the Charter of the United Nations to a specific situation or decision you may have to make.

C. THE PROBLEM OF OBLIGATION

This leads me, then, to the third point in our discussion of the meaning and function of international law. At least as significant a question about international law as the question, "Is international law really law?" is the question: "Is international law really binding?" This then leads on to the next question: "And, if so, what is the nature of international law's obligatoriness?" Many critics of international law again show their policeman hangup when we come to this issue. They point to the unsatisfactory means of enforcing international law. Owing to the deadlock of the United Nations Security Council, the only sanction is by the use of force by states. In this context, however, we may tend to underestimate the legal significance of joint action by collective self-defense. This, after all, was the earliest form of law enforcement in domestic legal systems and identified in early Anglo-American law as the "hue and cry." Be that as it may, it is still unfortunately true that the general hue and cry reflected in the United Nations General Assembly's Uniting for Peace Resolution has long been losing whatever effectiveness it may once have had. Again, resort to reprisals by individual states, once a significant sanction, is ceasing to be effective for a myriad of reasons, not the least important of which, perhaps, are such prohibitions as those to be found in Article 2, paragraph 4 of the United Nations Charter which tells us that: "All Members shall refrain in their international relations from the threat or use of force against the territorial integrity or political independence of any state, or in any other manner inconsistent with the purposes of the United Nations."

But to say that because it cannot be enforced, an obligation does not exist, is nonsense. Clearly there are binding obligations today in international law which, if states were to flout them, they would do so with full knowledge of the illegality of their conduct. We should note two well-known facts here. First, while states may act knowingly in breach of international law from time to time, their breaches are generally, indeed standardly, the result of decisions to take calculated risks. That is, states tend to take calculated risks regarding how severe or painful other states' condemnatory reactions will be. Second, no matter how frequently one state may breach its international obligations, it is always indignant at breaches by other states. Hence it is clear that states review both their own and other countries' policies and conduct in the light of a widespread presumption that international law not only exists, but also will be obeyed and followed. Why should this be so? It is clearly because each state anticipates that its own long-term advantage lies more with the compliance of other states with international law than attempting to survive in an international order where international law has no authority and creates no expectations. Such an order would either be one of chaos, where each state is entitled to deny all claims by others not supported by sufficient strength to enforce them, one where there is no law but that of the jungle and where no right can be maintained except that of holding as much as can be physically mastered, or, alternatively, be one governed by the totalitarian authority of a single world empire. (For we may note, parenthetically, that even a world federal system would still need to include much, if not most, of the present order for many years to come, and so should not be viewed as a valid alternative to the present order as much as one possible development of it.)

Neither chaos on the one hand nor subordination in a world empire on the other has much appeal to most states, hence their acceptance of the present order in its broad outline and their indignation at breaches of international law by their fellow subjects of the system. Often, indeed, states' brazenness when charged with breaches of their own obligations appears to reflect their acknowledgment of their duties and their guilt at their evasions. They seem, only too frequently, to remind us of the self-indulgent Roman poet's confession, *videor meliora proboque, deteriora sequor*—I see the better and more honorable course of conduct as I follow the worse.

New states are currently accepting the international legal system as an order, while calling for specific changes to those of the specific rules and doctrines which they consider irksome or anachronistic. This is evidenced by their rejection of the Communists' traditional rejection of international law. It is also reflected at the present time, interestingly enough, in Russia's willingness (together with her satellites, as distinguished from China and hers) to cooperate within the system, to abide by an increasing (if uncertain) number of the existing customary rules of international law in the name of "peaceful coexistence" and to prefer the chicanery of a shabby diplomat over the tactics of an outraged revolutionary.

This review of states' conduct as standardly reflecting a general acceptance of the international legal order as a system should not blind us to the fact that most of the new states are dissatisfied with, and many question the validity of, some of the rules we have inherited from the past as part of customary international law. But the rejection of some traditional rules by some of the new states as irrelevant to the present international order and the questioning of others by many should not be confused with a total rejection of the system. Rather, it is a demand for peaceful legal change to reflect the enormous social change in international society which has gone on over the last two decades. My message in this part of my lecture simply boils down to this: We can, and should clearly distinguish between demands for changing the rules, doctrines, and institutions of international law from demands for the overthrow of the present international legal system. The former note is loudly and sometimes dissonantly struck, the latter is hardly struck at all; except sometimes in the rhetoric of an angry politician speaking, usually, either for home consumption only or in a spirit of malicious gamesmanship.

D. Some Friends of International Law and What They Have Wrought

One of the greatest disservices that has been performed to international law by its supporters is the overstatement of the case for international law by the Great Optimists. In our culture we have a long tradition of being suspicious of politics. . . . We have, since the 17th century, since the English Revolution, the French Revolution, the American Revolution, had a basic philosophical value, namely that science and scientific man should replace politics and that ultimate scoundrel, political man. . . .

Any philosophy which can offer a program for eliminating the unpredictable, temporizing, and covinous qualities of political action and substitute the predictable conduct of "scientific man" in place of it, offers a very attractive dream. Particularly, from the point of view of this lecture, the rise of the science of jurisprudence and of the reasonable man, or *bonus paterfamilias*, gives us a means of replacing politics by codes, constitutions, and treaties. The precision of jurisprudence and of legal logic could then, so the advocates of mechanistic jurisprudence and mechanistic man aver, be called to replace the imprecision of human life and the discretions of myriads of interacting individuals pursuing, in the public arena, their private goals. As I pointed out earlier, this is an old habit in our culture. Let us remember that at the height of the Terror of the French Revolution, France's extremely distinguished "blueprint writer," Abbé Siéyès, believed that all he had to do was to draw up a better Constitution for France, and all that terror, all that bloodshed, all those executions would stop. He quite forgot that people tend to kill other people for reasons which are more compelling than the message of some words on paper, no matter how eloquently, rationally, or elaborately these may be formulated. . . . There is, unfortunately, a spillover of the skepticism these idealists generate toward the drawing of their more wayout blueprints which sometimes seems to threaten to engulf international law in general.

The professional optimists have done international law a major disservice by overstating the case for it. For them, almost every international problem becomes resolvable by a legal formula. Now this, patently, is not true. Lawyers operate on the assumption that all disputes can be formulated clearly and be made the objects of litigation, arbitration, or negotiation on the footing of legal dialectic. Politicians, especially those opposed to this legalistic approach, seek to avoid putting their claims into legal, concrete, and binding form. They prefer to view disputes as tests of nerve and strength and so avoid making their demands rationally explicit. This is sometimes also true of the domestic sphere, especially in business relations. (It may be of interest to suggest that much of the problem the courts face with regard to enforcing the duty of good faith bargaining in labor-management disputes tends to be related to the need to force parties to negotiate on the footing of concrete claims and counterclaims, rather than on the raw basis of nerve and strength.)

The limits of what is appropriately a legal decision are all around us, even in private life. For example, your attorney, whom you wish to instruct to draw up your will, may advise you as to how you should draw up a trust for your children, but he is not going to tell you how to make a detailed distribution of your estate. He may advise you as to what sort of claims should be responded to when you draw your will. He may, in addition, offer advice, in general terms, about whom you should consider appropriate targets of your posthumous bounty. . . . Where he gives you further advice he is not solving your problems, he is helping you make nonlegal decisions on how you could best use the facilities the law offers you. Incidentally, this excursus about the interaction of choices and law when it comes to making a will provides an example of the way society provides us with the means of doing what we want or need to do through law.

We have already seen how international law is facilitative and functional. We now note that it does not prescribe the goals of human action (the goals, for example, of human respect, participation, and dignity and freedom), although it may be formulated in terms of such goals. These goals may be expressed by lawyers and be incorporated in legal documents; but they remain above and beyond the law, and the law provides one of many means of achieving them. For the ultimate demands we make on life and on society are not legal demands. And it is a mistake to try and substitute the needs of life by the criteria of the law.

IV. International Society and Legal Change

We are told that in the "Third World"—the world of the developing countries—the charge is laid against international law that it is simply a form of neoimperialism. Only too often, however, this rhetoric is an attempt to forestall us in indicating to some of the emerging or developing countries what their legal obligations are. This is a piece of gamesmanship we would do well not to heed. On the other hand, these countries are also telling us that they have a demand for legal change. This is something to which we should listen most carefully. But, because we have not been clear-cut in our thinking only too often, our responses to gamesmen's charges have been as conciliatory as those to the people who are making serious claims for legal change. Our own confusion about international law has encouraged others to assert the nonexistence, or the desuetude, of many legal rights which have a lively claim for contemporary respect, recognition, and vindication. It is as if, being careless about its own most valuable legal protection, namely law itself, the United States was encouraging others to be more careless about this country's rights than they would normally be. But this is an aside. We must turn back to our main problem in this part of my lecture, namely, that of legal change in international law.

If, for the sake of an easy and familiar model in its general outline at least, we look at the domestic law of the United States for an example, we see the functioning legislatures as well as the courts and the executives. Now we know the function of a legislature is to keep law in tune with society, or at least we are told this is the function of the legislature. In contrast with this situation, there is no legislature or any similar institution in the international legal order which can be called upon to bring about timely legal change. But this does not necessarily mean that international law is a body of archaic and antiquated rules which can only be found in the doctrines, writings, and practices of 17th century Western Europe which have remained unchanged ever since. Despite its lack of the usual accouterments of legal reform through legislation and despite the fact that the possession of a legislative organ would possibly help international law to be both more elegant and contemporary, international law does change. It can, at times, change with surprising speed. States can change their legal rights and obligations by entering into treaties, and more and more international law is being expressed in multilateral conventions. States may also enter into regional agreements and bilateral treaties. As far as those treaties are concerned, states may also alter and redefine their legal relations amongst themselves very considerably. Again, a trend in bilateral treaties may start a new development in general customary international law. For example, one of the most significant factors of the Alabama Claims Arbitration was not that this was one of the very early arbitrations to which sovereign states resorted, despite the very high and hostile feelings which ran on each side, but also because of its significance in the development of the rules of neutrality. This arbitration was called to decide a dispute between the United States and Great Britain after the defeat of the Southern Confederacy. The United States asserted that Great Britain had allowed the *Alabama* and the *Georgia* and their warlike equipment, to be built and supplied by British yards contrary to the latter's duties as a neutral.

The parties met in head-on dispute over the question of law since, at that time, doubts still existed as to the duties of a neutral state regarding the supply of war vessels to a belligerent. But, by the Treaty of Washington of 1871, the parties agreed to the famous "Three Rules" which have since then come to be regarded as substantially reflecting the customary international law duties of neutrals. . . .

Thus, in addition to their utility as defining, or redefining, the obligations of the parties and to expressing agreement between states on a contractural footing by setting an example for future conduct, bilateral as well as multi-lateral treaties can start new developments in customary international law. Secondly, legal change comes about by what is regarded as a second source of law (as prescribed in Article 38 of the Statute of the International Court of Justice), namely by custom. Old customs can be dispensed with. Long before the challenges of the modern age, for example, the idea that a state could acquire territory simply by discovering it had disappeared well before the end of the 19th century as a result of the technological and population changes of that century. In previous centuries, when explorations had been conducted in leaky wooden hulks, propelled only by sails or oars, an adventurer was able to acquire territory for his sovereign simply by an act of discovery. In the 19th century, with the introduction of iron- and steel-hulled steamships, we find that to recognize this as a basis of title becomes no longer feasible. There would have been too many title-conferring "discoveries"! Something much more came to be required before international law could recognize the acquisition of territory—so occupation came to be developed as a replacement of discovery as a legal concept which could validly provide states with original titles to masterless lands. Occupation called for more activity than discovery did, namely a real "taking" of and exercise of control over the territory in question before it could be said to belong to the claimant. Thus we have here an early example of technological and demographic change effecting a change in customary law. Today, of course, customary law seems almost to be withering before the rapidity of technological and demographic change. But this can be overstated. While some aspects are withering, others, interestingly enough, are acquiring a new vigor and are requiring a new restatement.

V. The Crisis of International Law

My last observation is not intended to palliate the fact that international law is in a state of crisis today. This has many causes and more symptoms. Without any notion of ordering these in a list of importance, I would like briefly to indicate them as follows: the technological revolution; the population explosion; the decolonialization policies of the former European empires—Western European empires, not the Eastern European ones—and the proliferation of new "developing" states; the rise of single-party states as the norm of the developing world instead of the democratic two-party or multiparty politics which had been hoped for and optimistically predicted at the time of the independence of more new countries; and, finally, revolutionary communism. But, as I indicated earlier, these factors have not led to a widespread, root-and-branch denial of international law, but only to disputes as to the meaning, scope, and content of specific rules, to claims for legal change, and to an acceleration of social change. This last, the factor of acceleration, places international law under increasing stress on account of the paucity of its institutions geared towards responding to the needs of accelerated legal change.

On the other side of the coin we find there is a great and very important proliferation of universal and regional agencies. The central organization in international law is the United Nations; but there are many more international agencies than just this one. And these are becoming of increasing importance. There are regional agencies such as the Organization of American States and collective self-defense arrangements like the North Atlantic Treaty Organization. There are important universal agencies such as the Universal Postal Union and the International Telecommunication Union. These, I must emphasize, exist as institutions of international law. Although you may not realize it, they affect your daily lives. The fact that you can have rapid and cheaply mailed letters from anywhere in the world to the United States, the fact that you can send telegrams anywhere in the world from the United States or receive television news items by satellite are due to these and other important international organizations.

Lastly, there is the peace-enforcing function of regional organizations. I will just give you, as my time is running out, one example. The Cuban Missile Crisis in 1962, and the defensive quarantine which was imposed in response thereto were achieved through the procedures and processes of the Organization of American States. The reason why the U.S. Navy could act as it did was through the intelligent utilization of the United Nations Charter and the Rio de Janeiro Pact. Our trump card was the agreement of the Organization of American States that the Soviet missiles in Cuba were a threat to this hemisphere. We may hope that it is through the regional and universal organs of peace and progress that desirable legal change can be brought about in a timely way and that they will increasingly carry the burden which has come to be too heavy for customary international law and traditionally drafted treaties to bear alone.

It is for this reason that it is now possible to discern an emerging quasi-competence on the part of international organizations, and especially the United Nations, to indicate, by their practice and by their formulations of generally held basic values and programs of legal change, emerging doctrines and precepts. These enjoy, in international law, at least the equivalent of the "directive principles" of the Indian and Irish constitutions. In some cases, furthermore, they may have a more direct "self-executing" effect. They may offer a new source of law responsive both to the interests calling for change and those promoting the values of stability and continuity. To do so they must, however, reflect a general, if not a universal, consensus.

13

LAW AND LEGAL INSTITUTIONS MAY HELP

ROGER FISHER*

It is worth while considering explicitly how international law and institutions fit into the process of causing another government to change their mind. Here the going gets rough, because there is such widespread misunderstanding of how law works—misunderstanding both among advocates of international law and among its detractors. Although I cannot expect in a few words to convert anyone from a deeply held belief, I can at least articulate my own views. I will do so by setting up and dealing with three straw men—men who may, in fact, not be made exclusively of straw. I will then illustrate in terms of the Cuban missile case the kind of diverse roles which law and legal institutions can be expected to play in exerting influence upon another government.

The following three statements reflect the views of a substantial number of people:

1. "Law works because it is a command backed up by force."
2. "It takes force to influence another government."
3. "Law operates as a restraint, and it cannot restrain a government from doing what they want."

Each of these statements is essentially false. In each case there is an element of truth underlying the statement, but the generalization is wrong. It would be a serious mistake to rely on any one of these propositions in deciding what to do. Let us look at them one at a time.

FALLACY NO. 1: "LAW WORKS BECAUSE IT IS A COMMAND
BACKED UP BY FORCE."

There is a tendency to make a distinction between international law and "real" law, which is backed up by force. The argument then goes that since international law is not backed up by force, the kind of law which works

---

* "Law and Legal Institutions May Help" in *International Conflict for Beginners* by Roger Fisher. Copyright © 1969 by Roger Fisher. Reprinted by permission of Harper & Row, Publishers, Inc.

domestically cannot be expected to work internationally. But the premise is wrong. For those in whose conduct we are interested—national governments—domestic law is backed up by less force than is international law. The process by which national governments are controlled by domestic law is more than an analogy; it demonstrates the susceptibilities of the very governments we are interested in.

The command theory of law, which was used to distinguish the law that *is* from the law that *ought to be,* was developed out of an examination of the typical private action for a tort or on a contract. If a court declared that a defendant must pay a plaintiff a stated amount, the sheriff and the marshal stood ready to enforce the judgment with the full power of the state.

That was the situation envisioned by the legal philosopher John Austin when he spoke of laws as commands. But his definition of law did not apply to rules restraining the behavior of a state. The "power of the government," he said, "is incapable of *legal* limitation." It followed that, in his view, a government had neither legal rights nor legal duties.

Such a definition of law has no relevance to our problem. We are concerned exclusively with the conduct of governments. In a typical year, more than half the cases before the United States Supreme Court involve the rights or duties of the federal government, all of which are considered legal and are dealt with by legal institutions. The command theory of law—the notion that domestic law works because it is backed up by superior force— is plainly wrong when dealing with public law. Governments regularly comply with adverse court decisions. This is true not only for constitutional law, administrative law, and tax law, but even for criminal law. When a man charged with crime is acquitted, and the court orders the government to release him, the government does so, and they do so not because they are compelled to do so by a threat of force superior to that of the government. When a judgment is entered against the United States in the Court of Claims, no superior sovereign compels Congress to vote the appropriation. Legal limitations upon a government, whether they be those of constitutional law or international law, succeed or fail for reasons other than the existence of superior military force. By and large law with respect to governments works because it affects political consequences, not military ones.

During the course of the Korean War, the steel industry of the United States was threatened with a strike. Considering the pros and cons as they then looked, President Truman decided to seize the steel industry in order to keep it operating and did so. The steel companies disputed the government's right to seize the industry and took the matter to court. After a few weeks of litigation the Supreme Court ordered the Secretary of Commerce, who had taken charge of the steel mills at the President's request, to return them to their private owners.

The Supreme Court had no regiments at its command. It had no greater force vis-à-vis the government than does the International Court of Justice sitting at The Hague. Yet the steel mills were returned. There can be little doubt that in a showdown between "the government" and the Supreme Court, the government would have won. If the President had wanted to continue to hold the steel mills, the army would have obeyed him.

The government had a choice when taking over the steel mills. They decided that the national interest made the action desirable. The legal process worked because it changed the question with which the government were confronted—in a number of respects.

Before the Court spoke, the demand upon the government was both vague and general. If articulated by the management of the steel companies, it would have been that the government must never seize private property without specific legal authority. So far as the demand came from the Constitution, it was a general rule, coming from no one in particular and going to no one in particular. So far as the demand came from the steel companies, it came from biased persons with a personal interest in the outcome. The consequences to the government of yielding to the demand may have looked serious. To allow steel production to stop because of a strike while American soldiers were dying in Korea would have produced a hostile political reaction within the United States. It also might have affected the conduct of the war. To accept the proposition that in time of emergency the government could do nothing to keep the most important industry operating would establish a disastrous precedent. The consequences of seizing the steel industry were more attractive. At the worst, somebody might take the case to court, and the government could face that problem when and if it arose.

The decision of the Court changed the demand. It now came from a respected and disinterested body and was directed to a named individual, the Secretary of Commerce. The decision was not in the form of a general restriction against interfering with private property, but a narrow and explicit demand that he refrain from asserting further authority over the steel companies' property. The fact and form of the demand also changed the consequences of the government's decision. So far as internal politics was concerned, it now made more sense to go along with the Supreme Court than to defy it. Further, the precedent which would be established by going along with the Court's decision became a favorable one from the point of view of the government rather than an unfavorable one. On the other hand, to defy the Court's decision would establish a disastrous precedent which others might follow. Finally, the decision of the Court was narrowly directed at the particular way in which the government had acted. To accept the decision was merely to take one step back. The same end could be pursued by the government by other means.

Law enforcement against a government involves not a command backed up by force. Rather it involves so changing the choice with which the government is confronted that their long-range interest in orderly settlement of disputes outweighs their short-run interest in winning this particular dispute.

This is also, I believe, a more useful way of understanding the process than to talk of shared values and a sense of community. Shared values and a sense of community will help the legal process operate and will set limits on what it can do, but they fail to shed light on the process itself. Shared values and a sense of community, by themselves, are not enough to cause a government to respect the law. The routine violation of law by federal officers in the cases of wire tapping and unlawful searches and seizures amply demonstrates that the United States government cannot be counted on to comply with the law whenever they know what it is. I am convinced that the same officers who would violate a general restriction would comply with a narrow and explicit court injunction ordering them by name not to tap a particular telephone. Such a demand would shift the political situation. A court decision can be looked at as influencing a government to change their mind not so much by adding new weight to one side of a question as by shifting the fulcrum so that political forces which were previously on one side of the balance now find themselves on the other.

Domestic courts may thus be taken as a model not only for how international courts may be expected to exert influence on governments but for other international institutions as well. Although we may not expect the statement of an international body to carry the same political impact upon a government as does the legally binding decision of their own court, its impact will be greater the more its statement resembles that of a domestic court. The steel companies influenced the United States government not by threatening to hurt the government by retaliatory action but by going through third-party procedures which changed the question. The steel companies took the risk that the decision would not be to their liking. In exchange, they gained the effective political support which followed a decision in their favor.

FALLACY NO. 2: "IT TAKES FORCE TO INFLUENCE ANOTHER GOVERNMENT."

Although we can accept the idea that our own government is influenced by considerations other than force in "domestic" questions, we tend to believe that on international questions it takes force to exert influence on other governments. But every decision of a government is a domestic one in the sense that it is made by a domestic government. Whatever the nominal subject, governmental officers are affected by the anticipated consequences of a decision both within and without the territorial limits of the country. In terms of the character of the considerations which affect a decision there is no sharp line between domestic decisions and international decisions. And underlying this entire book is the idea that no one ingredient of the influence process is either all-important or unimportant. Force is relevant but not all-important. In some cases it will be necessary, in others insufficient. A government will take into account the whole picture as they see it. In one situation the greatest hope of exerting influence may lie in changing one element; in another situation it will lie in changing another element, or in changing several at the same time.

To confirm the limited role which force plays—and to suggest opportunities for law and legal institutions—let me pull together from previous chapters some conclusions about other things that do exert influence upon another government:

Make the desired decision explicit. The more unambiguous the request the easier it is for a government to deal with.

Make the request one for inaction rather than action. If the decision desired is not only reformulated but is reformulated in such a way that, rather than requiring a new decision, the request will be met if the other government fails to make a decision to act contrary to the request, the chance of success is further increased.

Have the request come from a neutral party. If the revised request comes from an impartial source, there is a greater likelihood that the government will make the desired decision. The political cost of going along with a neutral request is far less than that of "giving in" to an adversary. In fact, under these circumstances, to decide as desired tends to establish a helpful procedural precedent, rather than a harmful one.

Have the request formed in terms of principles accepted by the other government. If the proposed decision is formulated as one which is required by standards, policies, or rules accepted by the government we are trying to influence, it will be more readily acceptable to that government's officers. They may even regard it as their duty to go along with it.

Have the request narrowly limited to the next step. The immediate cost of yielding to a request will be less if less is asked.

Change the decision desired. To present a government with a different decision than the one they had previously declined to make both provides an occasion for decision and permits a decision we would like without requiring a reversal of position.

Such actions tend to increase the chance of success. They do so by altering the three basic elements of demand, offer, and threat. They reform the decision we want into one that is institutionally easier for a government to make; they tend to reduce the political cost of acting in accordance with our wishes and to increase the political cost of not doing so.

The above summary of important ways to exert influence on governments turns out to be also a summary of important ways in which international institutions can deal with an international dispute. These elements of the process of exerting influence are those which international institutions are in general equipped to perform. Other elements of the process of exerting influence upon a government, in particular increasing a risk of military action, tend to be those at which international institutions are not very good. Much of the current lack of regard for the capabilities of international organizations stems from misperceiving the task to be done. Only if the crucial task in exerting influence upon a government were to increase the military threat would it be correct to minimize the role which international organizations might be expected to play.

When a dispute is referred to an international institution, whether it be the General Assembly, the Security Council, the International Court of Justice, or an *ad hoc* tribunal, commission, or committee of any kind, the foundation has been laid for changing the question facing each government. Each government will be more influenced by what the international institution asks than by what an adversary asks. This does not, of course, mean that governments will always do what they are asked to do by an international institution or that they will never do what they are asked by another government.

A decision or recommendation of an international institution typically asks of a government something less than what was asked of them by their adversary. A neutral institution is freed from the temptation to include something extra in its demand to give it negotiating room. On the contrary, no further bargaining is usually anticipated, and the institution will recognize that the less it asks, the greater the chance of compliance with its request.

Even where it asks no less, the institution can be extremely explicit about what it is asking for. The demand also comes from a neutral. Each of these facts tends to make it politically easier for a government to yield to the demands.

It has long been pointed out that if governments have agreed to international arbitration, they usually abide by the result. This fact is sometimes cited in support of the proposition that all governments ought to agree to compulsory arbitration or adjudication. Others cite it to support the proposition that arbitration only works where governments are prepared to abide by the result. From our point of view the interesting fact is that governments find it much easier to go along with a request if it is made by an impartial body of recognized authority than if a comparable request is made by an adversary. If prior to an arbitrator's decision a government's weighing of the pros and cons results in a political decision not to do what it is being asked to do, and after the arbitrator's decision the government's weighing of the pros and cons comes out differently, this may be because they are being asked to do something different. Whether or not that is true, the consequences of the choice have been changed.

From the point of view of a lawyer there is a black-and-white difference between international decisions which are legally binding upon a government and those that are not. From the point of view of the student of government behavior the matter is one of degree. One of the features of a decision which gives it political power is the quality of being regarded by some as legally binding. Other features are also important, and in terms of political consequences even the legal question tends to be one of degree.

FALLACY NO. 3: "LAW OPERATES AS A RESTRAINT, AND IT CANNOT RESTRAIN A GOVERNMENT FROM DOING WHAT THEY WANT."

There are two parts to this statement. That law and legal institutions do exert influence suggests what is wrong with the second part of the statement. In one sense law cannot restrain a government from doing what they want, but law affects what they want. In the absence of a legal rule to the contrary, the United States government might well conclude that they wanted to take over the oil fields of Kuwait. The existence of a rule of international law which makes it improper for the United States to seize the oil fields of Kuwait results in the United States government's not wanting to seize the fields. Law, by affecting what governments want, does restrain them from doing things which they would otherwise want to do.

The first part of the statement is also misleading. Law, to be sure, does operate as a restraint, but it does far more than that. To think of law only as a restraint on behavior is to underestimate its potential. Law and legal institutions play many roles. Unfortunately, from the point of view of exposition by an international lawyer, law and legal institutions become relevant in a number of quite disconnected ways at different points in the international political process. And at each one of these points nonlegal considerations may be more important than legal ones. There may be good reason to rely not on the law or on the courts but on other norms and other institutions. We may choose to rely not on a legal contract but on a gentleman's agreement. A man's reputation may provide us with more security than could any remedy at law. A recommendation from the governing board of a stock exchange may have more impact than a court decision.

Lawyers are rightly skeptical about a book such as "Law of the Theater" which tries to pull together the diverse roles which law and legal institutions play in a particular business. Such a book will cover bits and pieces of law dealing with copyright, options, the leasing of theaters, the making and breaking of contracts, local regulation and censorship, liability for negligence, the right of privacy, and perhaps something on slander and libel. If a man wishes to put on a theatrical performance which is artistically and financially successful, the law and its institutions may help him to do so, but they are unlikely to be the most important consideration. What theater he rents is likely to be more important than the terms of the lease, what actors he hires more important than the terms of their contracts, and what the critics say about the play more important than what the lawyers say about it. Yet to ignore the law would be risky. It provides both opportunities for making success easier and defenses against problems which might otherwise lead to failure.

The role of law and institutions in the pursuit by a government of an international objective is not unlike their role in the pursuit by a businessman or theatrical producer of some objective of his. Law is not just a restraint. To ask only the question "will our conduct be legal" is to omit consideration of most of the ways in which law can serve the enterprise. In influencing another government as in putting on a play, law is not the most important consideration, but a knowledgeable use of the opportunities which law and legal institutions offer can make success more likely.

The variety of ways in which international law and legal institutions do and do not affect government decisions can be illustrated by looking at the predominantly nonlegal decisions of the United States government in October, 1962, on what to do about the Soviet introduction of intermediate- and long-range missiles into Cuba. The following brief analysis is based on the accounts of the missile crisis by Elie Abel and Theodore Sorensen.

The motive for United States action was not primarily to maintain or improve the international system, but rather to pursue political and military objectives within the system. We should expect law to play modest roles in decisions which were primarily concerned with things other than the law.

International law implicitly affected what the United States wanted. The action which caused the United States government to have a problem on its hands was the secret placing in Cuba of intermediate- and long-range missiles and bomber aircraft by the Soviet Union after they had previously assured the United States that they were not doing so and were not going to do so. Officials of the United States knew that they did not like what had happened and what was going on. In the discussions, they apparently did not consider separately alternative objectives that the United States might pursue, but only alternative courses of action the United States might follow. In a general way the objective was clear. The United States wanted the missiles not to become operable with nuclear warheads and wanted to be confident that this was the case. Alternative formulations of the objective might have been to have the missiles come into United States possession or to be destroyed or damaged or removed from Cuba.

International law had little to do with this objective. The United States wanted the missiles to become inoperable independent of its legal rights. But international law did play a crucial role in creating the problem. What made the United States response so difficult was the fact that the Soviet Union had apparently acted within its legal rights under international law. If the Soviet Union had installed the missiles on an island in the Caribbean belonging to the United States, or on an unoccupied corner of Alaska—in clear violation of international law—the United States would have been presented with a problem that looked totally different. The fact that the provocative act of the Soviet Union was not illegal and the fact that the objective desired by the United States was not one to which it was automatically entitled as a matter of international law were both central to the crisis.

International law affected what the United States decided to try for. It affected, implicitly if not explicitly, the selection of the three narrow objectives: having the weapons now in Cuba removed, having no further offensive weapons sent to Cuba, and having some form of international verification. No doubt the United States military authorities would have liked to acquire the Soviet missiles, both those in Cuba and those heading toward Cuba, and studied them. But the Soviet Union still had legal ownership of the missiles. If the Soviet Union were willing to withdraw the missiles from Cuba, the United States had no legal right to seize those missiles, or even to destroy them. There was no legal case for saying that missiles on board a ship bound for Cuba had thereby become contraband and forfeited to the United States government.

International law provided a set of tools. Influence requires communication. One of the functions of law is to serve as a language. International law helps one government communicate to another about the choice with which they are confronted and about the consequences of making or not making the desired decision. If a government has embarked upon a course of action, as the Soviet government had in Cuba, the issue must be reopened. Law and legal institutions can help present a government with a new occasion for decision. They can also clarify and alter both the decision that is required and the consequences of making and of not making that decision.

Legal documents tend to be far more precise than most political statements. A simple reference to an established rule of law can convey a great deal of meaning because of what is incorporated.

The resolution adopted by the Organization of American States, the draft resolution submitted to the United Nations, and the proclamation of a naval quarantine issued by the President identified clearly that action by the Soviet government was called for. Although international institutions and a formal proclamation were used, the finger could have been and was pointed with equal explicitness by nonlegal documents, such as the President's letter to Chairman Khrushchev.

There were essentially three substantive demands: the stopping of shipment of offensive weapons to Cuba, the removal of such weapons already there, and verification. The law as such played little role in the formulation of these demands, except that the demands were limited to those on which the United States had the strongest ground. Like a judicial decree, the requests were for no more relief than that to which the action complained of would entitle the United States. The requested relief was not to eliminate Communism from the Western Hemisphere, to oust Castro, to stop all shipments to Cuba, or even to stop all shipments of arms to Cuba. It was narrowly limited to stopping shipments of offensive weapons at a designated point on the high seas and to remove forty-two missiles and other offensive weapons from Cuba.

The political demands with respect to "offensive" weapons might well have profited if language closer to legal precision had been used. The ambiguity in the concept of "offensive" weapons caused the United States some difficulty by permitting the Soviet Union to argue that their missiles were in Cuba for defensive purposes only and that there had been no deception. The Kennedy-Khrushchev letter of October 27 clarified the demand by stating that the first thing that needed to be done was "for all weapons systems in Cuba *capable of offensive use* to be rendered inoperable."[1] (Italics mine.)

Governments will typically postpone a decision unless there is some good reason not to. The United States forced a decision with respect to the ships going toward Cuba by establishing the quarantine as of a precise moment, with sufficient advance notice to allow the ship captains time to receive orders from Moscow. The legal concept of signing a proclamation at one time to come into effect at another served well to give the Soviet Union both time for a decision and the necessity of a decision. The deadline for the decision to withdraw the missiles already in Cuba was less clear and was set wholly by nonlegal methods. Apparently Robert Kennedy explained orally to the Soviet ambassador on Saturday, October 27, that time was running out and that the United States was ready to begin military action by the first of the next week.[2] There was no deadline for the desired decision to accept appropriate UN inspection, and such a decision was never made.

A major way in which law operates as a tool to help one government influence another is in making more legitimate what is being asked. Legality is not simply window dressing; it can be crucial to success.

The essential demand of the United States—that the Soviet Union not have nuclear missiles in Cuba—was converted by the OAS vote from the purely political demand of a nuclear adversary to the unanimous request of twenty countries of the Western Hemisphere, acting through formal procedures and pursuant to a pre-existing treaty. Countries such as Mexico and Brazil, which had demonstrated their independence of the United States, supported the resolution. The existence of the Rio Treaty and the Organization of American States made it possible to strengthen and make more reasonable the United States demand in this way.

Robert Kennedy regarded this vote as crucial:

It was the vote of the Organization of American States that gave a legal basis for the quarantine. Their willingness to follow the leadership of the United States was a heavy and unexpected blow to Khrushchev. It had a major psychological and practical effect on the Russians and changed our position from that of an outlaw acting in violation of international law into a country acting in accordance with twenty allies legally protecting their position.[3]

Taking the case to the Security Council of the United Nations also operated to strengthen the legitimacy of the United States position. Going

---

[1] T. Sorensen, *Kennedy* (New York: Harper & Row, 1965), p. 714.
[2] E. Abel, *The Missile Crisis* (Philadelphia: J. B. Lippincott, 1966), p. 199.
[3] *McCall's*, November, 1968, p. 172.

as a plaintiff to the United Nations rather than as a defendant tended to make the United States position appear more defensible.

The particular demand with respect to the quarantine and the stopping of ships was undoubtedly strengthened by having it done with proper care to legalities. A formal proclamation was used, and it was issued only after the vote of the Organization of American States.

Abel reports that Ambassador Llewellyn Thompson "made the point that the Russians were impressed by legalities" and that "If, for example, the Organization of American States should pass a resolution endorsing the blockade, Moscow might be inclined to take it seriously" (p. 87).

Making the quarantine as legal and legitimate as possible was important not only for its direct effect on the Russians. The more legitimate the quarantine appeared to third states, the greater would be the indirect effect of their views on the Soviet Union.

The demand for international inspection of Cuba was never supported by a good—or even plausible—legal case. American insistence on inspection was supported by a Soviet promise, but the Soviet Union clearly had no legal right to invite international inspectors to Cuba. The OAS case against the Soviet Union, demanding the removal of the missiles, was not an equally good case for Cuba's permitting international inspection.

One fear of the United States was that the Soviet Union could, if its planes had a stop en route, fly nuclear warheads to Cuba. The United States relied on international law (and the consequent high cost to the Soviet Union of violating it) to block this contingency. The Soviet Union had a month before requested landing rights in Guinea for a once-a-week flight from Moscow to Havana. The United States asked the President of Guinea to refuse the Russian request, and he agreed to do so (Abel, p. 137). It was assumed that if it were illegal for the Russians to land at Conakry, they would not do so; if it were legal, they might. Similar action was taken by the United States with respect to the legality of Soviet aircraft landing at Dakar in Senegal (Abel, pp. 136, 137). The implicit American demand that the Soviet Union not fly warheads into Cuba was thus made extremely legitimate. The Soviet Union could not fly warheads without violating the law.

By making offers and threats more legitimate, the law not only made them more acceptable; it also made them more credible. The United States supported each of its three demands with a separate threat. The demand that Soviet ships stop was supported by the threat of shooting them (and the consequent risk of escalation) if they did not. The demand that the missiles be removed was supported by the threat of an air strike or an invasion (and the risk of escalation) if the missiles were not removed. The demand for international inspection was supported by the threat of continued unilateral aerial reconnaissance (and perhaps more) if such inspection was not established. The stronger the United States legal case, the more credible each of these threats, and the less costly it would have been to the United States to carry them out. The international procedures followed and the legal rhetoric advanced in support of the United States position thus operated to make the threats more influential.

Law provided an international mechanism. The fact that the Organization of American States and the United Nations existed made it possible for them to be used to make more legitimate the demands of the United States. But neither organization was in a position to take on the job itself. There was no inter-American naval force which could take on the quarantine function. If there had been one, it certainly would have been used.

There was also no international observation team in existence which could have taken on the verification function. Kennedy interpreted Khrushchev's letter as a proposal to remove weapons systems from Cuba "under appropriate United Nations observation and supervision." Kennedy also wanted "the establishment of adequate arrangements through the United Nations to ensure the carrying out and continuation of these commitments" before the United States removed the quarantine and gave the desired no-invasion pledge (Abel, p. 198). There was no established international machinery for carrying on these functions, and it proved impossible to create such machinery at the time. The world was lucky that this fact did not upset the resolution of the crisis.

Despite Khrushchev's assertion that for the United States Navy to stop Soviet ships on the high seas would be "piracy," it did not look like piracy to the Soviet Union or to anybody else. The formal proclamation, the designated zones, the limited list of what would be stopped—in short, the "legalistic" aspects of what was being done—were tools used by the United States better to accomplish its task.

An exchange of promises was used as the means for settling the crisis. Although both sides were ultimately interested in what was done rather than what was said, the Soviet Union decided that it would adopt as an intermediate goal a formal pledge from the United States not to invade Cuba. The United States was interested in the physical removal of weapons but found that in the first instance it should settle for the exchange of promises—an informal legal arrangement.

The effectiveness of an action often depends upon its legality. In discussing the quarantine, Sorensen reports:

We could not even be certain that the blockade route was open to us. Without obtaining a two-thirds vote in the OAS—which appeared dubious at best—allies and neutrals as well as adversaries might well regard it as an illegal blockade, in violation of the UN Charter and international law. If so, they might feel free to defy it [p. 687].

It was on October 22 that President Kennedy announced that "All ships of any kind bound for Cuba from whatever nation or port will, if found to contain cargoes of offensive weapons, be turned back." Nevertheless, recognizing that the effectiveness of the quarantine might depend upon its legality, Kennedy held up the signing of the formal proclamation until after the Organization of American States had authorized it. Abel writes:

The President was fully prepared to act alone if necessary. But he understood the importance of holding back the proclamation until the OAS had voted. It was, therefore, not until seven o'clock [October 23rd] that the President signed the proclamation, basing the blockade squarely on the unanimous OAS vote invoking Articles 6 and 8 of the Rio Treaty of Reciprocal Assistance [p. 135].

Sorensen has reported the fear that illegality might make the quarantine ineffective:

. . . Llewellyn Thompson . . . had emphasized the fundamental importance of obtaining OAS endorsement of the quarantine. . . . Thompson's interest was the added legal justification such endorsement would give to the quarantine under international and maritime law as well as the UN Charter. That was important, he said, not only to our maritime allies but to legalistic-minded decision-makers in the Kremlin [p. 706].

Law thus operates as a restraint by making certain courses of action, if illegal, either ineffective or counterproductive. That illegality operates as a restraint is the obverse of the fact that legality may serve as a tool.

International law may also operate as a restraint by raising the political cost which a country pays for engaging in certain conduct. There can be little doubt that one of the considerations which restrained the United States from an immediate air strike against the missile sites in Cuba was the gross illegality of such action. The Attorney General is reported to have compared such a surprise attack with Pearl Harbor and stated, "My brother is not going to be the Tojo of the 1960's" (Abel, p. 64). The legal consideration, of course, was not operating independently of general considerations of what is right and what is wrong, or of the facts that an air strike could not be sure to be 100 per cent effective and would result in killing a number of people, including Russians. Abel reports that ". . . it began to appear that the blockade advocates might prevail. Legalities had less to do with this than the practical argument that a naval blockade would avoid killing Russians and give the Kremlin time to reflect" (p. 73).

There was a good argument that even the blockade was a violation of international law. The Soviet Union tried to raise the cost to the United States of its quarantine (as well as to accomplish other objectives) by charging it with piracy and "unheard of violation of international law" (Abel, pp. 127–128). The reputation of the United States as a lawabiding country was no doubt somewhat damaged by the conclusions of Indian newspapers in New Delhi, Bombay, and Calcutta that in blockading Cuba the United States was "violating international law" (Abel, p. 145).

The illegality of engaging in U-2 overflights also, apparently, had operated to reduce the number of flights made and to restrict discussion of them. The United States was undoubtedly concerned, at least in part, with the political cost it would suffer for being found to be acting contrary to international law.

Law also operates as a restraint by raising for each country the fear of setting a harmful precedent. This kind of cost is one that governments often minimize. At least they fail to take it into account to the extent that many international lawyers would like. Abel quotes Dean Acheson as taking "the position that legal niceties were so much pompous foolishness in a situation where the essential security of the United States, its prestige, its pledged word to defend the Americas, was threatened" (p. 72).

For the United States to act unilaterally to the extent that it did could not help but set precedents for unilateral action in the future. One modest way in which fears of damage to the international system did restrain the United States is described by Abel:

Abram Chayes, the State Department legal adviser, suggested a language change. Instead of basing the blockade on Article 51 of the United Nations Charter, which assures each nation's inherent right of self-defense in case of armed attack, Chayes argued that its legal basis should be the right of the OAS to take collective measures in guarding the security of the Americas. To an international lawyer, the distinction had its importance in avoiding the establishing of a self-defense precedent the Russians might use in the future (Abel, p. 115).

Probably the decision not to engage in an immediate air strike on Cuba reflected concern not only for the reputation of the United States but also for the impact which such lawlessness might have on the future of international relations.

The decisions consciously taken during the Cuban missile crisis were ones in immediate pursuit of the substantive objective of removing missiles from Cuba. The various roles which international law played in the decision process of the United States government is not fully appreciated without considering some of the decisions which had previously been made by default—decisions which had not been made because questions were not raised. There are a limitless number of "might-have-beens" which are suggested by the missile crisis. One way to appreciate them is to ask these questions: What rules of substantive international law and what changes in international machinery would the United States have liked to have had on hand when the missile crisis started? Why was it that the United States had decided not to press for these substantive rules and this international machinery?

The United States would have been in a stronger position if some international conduct to which it was going to object as violently as it did to the Soviet introduction of missiles into Cuba had been not merely objectionable but also illegal. Prior action by the United States designed to improve the international system might have been able to bring the rules into closer conformity with the rules which the United States intended to "enforce." This might have been done through the establishment of a Latin American nuclear-free zone, through OAS action outlawing non-Western Hemisphere military bases in the Western Hemisphere, or perhaps through agreement between the Soviet Union and the United States regarding the deployment of missiles. Such an agreement might have been possible in August, 1962, when President Kennedy first decided to withdraw United States nuclear missiles from Turkey (Abel, p. 191).

The United States might have been better off if the United Nations had had in existence a small stand-by inspection staff, with standard operating practices that the Cuban government could have been asked to accept. Rather than being confronted with the task of working out new arrangements acceptable to the Soviet Union, United States, Cuba, and the United Nations, there would have been a greater change of international inspection if some such facility had been in existence. The United States had previously "decided" (perhaps by ignoring the possibility) not to press for the establishment of such an international inspection staff.

The Cuban missile crisis suggests that in appraising the role of international law in government decision making we should look not only at its role in the decisions which consciously were made but also at its role in decisions which were made by default.

❧6❧

Strategy, War, and
Arms Control

WARFARE HAS BEEN ACCEPTED in the relations of states for hundreds of years. In times past man has occasionally asked himself whether he could afford it, as during the slaughter of the Thirty Years' War. The distinctive change today is that man in the twentieth century asks that question all the time—and he knows he can hardly afford it.

Since the end of World War II and the beginning of the nuclear age strategic thinking has concentrated on a novel and difficult problem: the transformation wrought by the advent and spread of nuclear weapons. Speculation and analysis has had to center on first questions: Will these weapons be used where retaliation in kind is almost inevitable? Would civilization survive such an exchange? Are arms control agreements possible and under what conditions? Is limited war possible between nuclear powers?

In the first selection, "Lessons of the Nuclear Age," Louis J. Halle of the Graduate Institute of International Studies at Geneva, attempts an assessment of the main lessons "that may be drawn from the experience of living with nuclear weapons." He sees six, of which the most important is the need to keep war in a nuclear environment limited. While Halle sees no assurance that war will in fact be limited, he points out means by which that hope can be made more realizable—especially the need for "good communication between antagonists."

Foremost among groups sponsoring the study of strategic questions is the International Institute for Strategic Studies, with headquarters in London but with worldwide membership. To its annual meetings come scholars, statesmen, generals, and admirals to grapple with these issues. The papers presented to this distinguished audience are of a very high order of merit. The second selection, "The Classical Strategists," by the distinguished British scholar, Michael Howard, Fellow in Higher Defense Studies, All Souls College, Oxford, was presented at the 1968 meeting.

By "classical strategists," Howard means those "thinkers who assume that the element of force exists in international relations, that it can and must be intelligently controlled, but that it cannot be totally eliminated." With that definition laid down, Howard surveys the evolution of classical strategic thought from the end of World War II. The quality of his synthesis would be difficult to match; it is made more worthwhile by the sweep of its scope, which surveys much of the significant thinking around the world over more than two decades of time.

14

LESSONS OF THE NUCLEAR AGE

Louis J. Halle[*]

For centuries, up to 17 July 1945, the power of weapons had been increasing at an exponential rate. That morning at 5:30, however, it took a quantum jump. The device that was exploded at Alamogordo, New Mexico, had two thousand times the blast-power of the largest bomb ever before used in the history of warfare. One despairs of recapturing for a new generation the awe and the terror we felt at the time before an event that seemed to spell the doom of mankind.

Barring a few insiders, all any of us knew at first about this monstrous device was that it could destroy a city in a flash. As far as we knew, any garage-mechanic would now be able to manufacture it in his own cellar, any maniac could carry it in his vest-pocket. What defence could civilization have against such a weapon?

Even when the nightmare of the home-made vest-pocket device had been dissipated, the potentialities of the real bomb, as reported by the scientists who had invented it, were such as to lead to the conclusion that this was not a weapon mankind could live with. If it were not abolished or somehow proscribed as a weapon in national armaments, while there was still time, mankind had little chance of an acceptable future.

The eminent physicist, Dr. Edward U. Condon (then Director of the National Bureau of Standards in Washington), told us:

> In the insecurity of a world of national atomic armaments, every bit of metal carried by every incoming foreign traveller will have to be inspected in a laborious and sophisticated way. . . . The beginning of a new war will surely involve not only the launching of the missiles, but the explosion of the mines that have been secretly set near key targets . . .[1]

This warning represented the authoritative opinion of the day. Nevertheless, twenty-two years later we see that it was wrong. Today we do live in a world of "national atomic armaments," and the bomb has become thousands of times more powerful, and we have had quite a few new wars. Happily, however, the consequences Dr. Condon foresaw have not been realised.

---

[*] Louis J Halle, "Lessons of the Nuclear Age," *Encounter,* Vol. 30, No. 3 (March 1968), pp. 17–25. Reprinted by permission.

[1] Dexter Masters (ed.), *One World or None,* New York (1946), pp. 40–41.

The implication of predictions like this, which were altogether plausible in 1946, was that abolition or control of the bomb required the nations of the world to give up some part of their sovereignty forthwith, and to submit themselves to a world government that would police mankind, prevent any further wars, and hold a monopoly of atomic energy to be used for peaceful purposes only. An approach to this objective, at least, was what lay behind the Baruch Report to the United Nations Atomic Energy Commission in 1946—this, rather than a Machiavellian plot (as some alleged) to steal a march on Stalin and get the Cold War started.

Today we can be sure of one thing. The problem, from the beginning, was not that of abolishing or uninventing nuclear weapons. It was, rather, that of learning to live with them—as it still is. Our initial impulse to get rid of them possessed our minds, and it follows a consistent pattern of precedents in the history of weapons-technology. When the rules and limits of chivalric warfare were threatened by the advent of the cross-bow, which dealt death at a distance and anonymously, the Second Lateran Council in 1159 prohibited its use against Christians "under penalty of anathema."[2] When fire-arms arrived, that same reaction was symbolically dealt with by Ariosto's Orlando, who, having wrested the devilish device from his adversary's grasp, took it out and cast it into the depths of the ocean, exclaiming:

O! curs'd device! base implement of death!
Fram'd in the black Tartarean realms beneath!
By Beelzebub's malicious art design'd
To ruin all the race of human kind. . . .
That ne'er again a knight by thee may dare,
Or dastard cowards, by thy help in war,
With vantage base, assault a nobler foe,
Here lie for ever in th' abyss below!

Some of us are old enough to remember the attempt in our own century to abolish or outlaw the submarine.

One reason why we thought that the survival of civilisation depended on the abolition of the bomb was our assumption that any new war would bring it into play. We believed that any new war would bring it into play because we assumed that any new war would be a total war in which the belligerents would use every weapon in their armouries that might prevent defeat and contribute to victory. In 1945, as World War II drew to its end, the American Chief of Staff, General George C. Marshall, said: "We can be certain that the next war, if there is one, will be even more total than this one."[3]

Happily this prediction, too, was wrong. For there have been quite a few new wars since it was made, and they have not been "even more total" than

---

[2] C. and J. Hefele, *Histoire des conciles* (1912), vol. V, p. 733.
[3] Trumbull Higgins, *Korea and the Fall of MacArthur* (1960), p. 4.

World War II, and they have not brought the terrible new armaments into play at all.

Our belief, in the beginning, was that nuclear weapons were more usable than in fact they have proved to be. In the absence of experience, an abstract reasoning made it easy to believe that a sovereign state with nuclear weapons, having a quarrel with another sovereign state (let us say over a canal connecting the Mediterranean with the Red Sea), would blow the other state off the map with nuclear bombs rather than accept defeat. It was equally plausible that Nuclear State A, having a quarrel with State B, would smuggle some bombs into B's cities—perhaps in the holds of ships, if the cities were coastal—and then tell it that unless it surrendered forthwith its cities would vanish in so many mushroom clouds.

Today we can see, as we could not then, that there is a complex of reasons why the uses of nuclear weapons are severely limited, why they cannot be made to serve as all-purpose weapons for all occasions. A weapon may simply be too powerful for use on the actual occasions of conflict that arise in reality. I can use my open right hand on a child who refuses to eat his spinach, but I cannot use a revolver.

The first lesson of the nuclear age, then, is that the uses of a nuclear armament for actual combat are severely limited—so limited as to be almost non-existent.

One citation will show how far we were from appreciating this in the mid-1940s. In August 1943, at the first Quebec Conference, the head of the scientific Research Committee of the British War Cabinet, Sir John Anderson, told Prime Minister Mackenzie King of Canada that the country which first succeeded in producing atomic bombs would have control of the world. Two years later the United States did become the first country to succeed in producing atomic bombs, but this did not give it control of the world. Even in the years in which it still had them to control the large part of the world ruled by Stalin, it could not use them to prevent . . . Mao Tse-tung from taking China away from Chiang Kai-shek; it could not use them to prevent Moscow from blockading Berlin; it could not use them to stop the invasion of South Korea. It could not use its nuclear monopoly even to prevent Stalin's Russia from going through the process of breaking that monopoly.

The discovery that nuclear weapons are too powerful for actual use in almost any situation that arises is closely associated with another lesson of the nuclear age. In the mid-1940s we had all assumed that any new war would be a total war. What this represented was a long-established and virtually unquestioned attitude toward war and peace. We assumed that there were two alternative and mutually exclusive states of being. The normal state was one of peace. In this state, international relations were conducted through foreign offices and corps of diplomats, while the military men, like firemen between fires, spent their time exercising or playing cards. However, when the state of peace gave way, as it occasionally did, to the alternative state of war, then the diplomats retired while the generals and admirals took over and addressed themselves, in each belligerent nation, to the irreducible objective of victory. That objective achieved or lost, and the war over, the diplomats emerged from retirement to take command again.

In this established conception, war was properly total. Once a state resorted to it, or was thrown into it by an attack, it would have been shameful for it not to go all-out for military victory. It would have been shameful for it to allow the political schemes of the scheming politicians to interfere with the achievement of the irreducible objective. It would have been shameful for it to "pull its punches" in the hope of some negotiated political compromise. We know how outraged the Prussian generals were at Bismarck's disposition to fight limited wars and to end them with a political compromise. During World War II, General Marshall was firmly opposed to the British inclination to formulate miliary strategy with political ends in view: as when Churchill wanted to campaign up through the Balkans for the ulterior political purpose of blocking the expansion of his Russian ally.

Finally, the central issue of the debate that raged in the United States over the Korean War was the Truman Administration's determination to keep it limited—not to risk expanding it into a world war, not to bomb beyond the Yalu, not to use nuclear weapons. The older generation of military men were morally outraged by this political interference with the achievement of the only proper objective. "In war," said General MacArthur, "there is no substitute for victory."

This either-or conception, of absolute peace or absolute war, explains why the American military authorities made their war plans, after 1945, only for the contingency of a third world war. And this in turn explains why, in the eighteen months before the Korean War, first General MacArthur and then Secretary Acheson publicly revealed that the American "defensive perimeter" in the Pacific ran through the off-shore islands of East Asia, from the Aleutians to the Philippines, excluding all mainland territory like Korea.[4] The anticipated contingency was that of a world-wide total war in which it would have been folly for the United States, which had reduced its ground forces in 1948 to little more than half-a-million men, to attempt to hold any position on the mainland of Asia.

Until the 1950s, the term "limited war" was hardly in the military lexicon of the West at all. It was certainly not in common use, although the historians may have applied it, often nostalgically, to the quaint wars of the eighteenth century. Consequently, the United States was not conceptually prepared to fight the kind of war that it did find itself fighting in Korea.

---

[4] MacArthur's interview in *The New York Times* for 2 March 1949; and Acheson's address before the National Press Club in Washington on 12 January 1950.

The either-or concept was one of the factors that led us Americans to reduce our ground forces so drastically. If any new war would inevitably be a total war, fought with the big nuclear armaments, then it was plausible that the role of these old-fashioned conventional forces would be secondary. Victory or defeat would be decided in the air. Britain, too, sacrificed ground forces for nuclear power, only to find that nuclear power was useless to meet her obligations east of Suez and in Germany.

We were all quite wrong in our expectations, and *the second lesson of the nuclear age, which stems from the first, is that the only kind of war that can be contemplated in the nuclear age is limited war.* If nations cannot use their most powerful armaments for actual combat it follows quite simply that they cannot fight a total war.

This second lesson conforms to a principle that, in addition to being supported by a simple logic, is exemplified in the fighting behaviour of vertebrates generally. While all-out conflict may be consonant with limited weapons, unlimited weapons require that conflict be limited. This principle, in its application to vertebrates, has been exemplified in the writings of Dr. Konrad Lorenz and discussed in a scholarly fashion by Dr. Irenaus Eibl-Eibesfeldt, who points out that fighting among vertebrates of the same species almost never ends in death and rarely results in serious injury to either combatant.[5] The reason is that, while species without deadly weapons, such as pigeons with their soft bills and weak feet, may fight each other all-out, those that have the means to do each other mortal injury never fight all-out. Male rattlesnakes, which can kill each other with a single bite, never bite each other in their combats.

The two snakes [Dr. Eibl-Eibesfeldt writes] glide along, side by side, each with the forward third of its length raised in the air. In this posture they push head against head, each trying to force the other sideways and to the ground. . . . The successful snake pins the loser for a moment with the weight of his body and then lets the loser escape.

The loser accepts the verdict, and so the dominance of the winner is established.

This behaviour has had striking parallels in the behaviour of nations since the nuclear age began. While the United States and the Soviet Union, in the great conflict between them, have had the ability to kill each other with one bite, they have shown an instinctive inhibition against biting—an inhibition greater than ever before in history. In Berlin during the winter of 1948–49, and again in the winter of 1958–59, and again in 1961, the confrontation of Russia and the West was like that of the two snakes who push against each other head to head but refrain from biting. Both sides used tear-gas bombs freely, but never the nuclear bombs that each also had available.

---

[5] Konrad Lorenz, *King Solomon's Ring: New Light on Animal Ways* (1952), Chapter 12; "The Fighting Behaviour of Animals," *Scientific American,* December 1961.

This parallel between the behaviour of vertebrates and the behaviour of nations is not merely metaphoric. Precisely the same logic as applies to the one applies to the other. It has, by genetic evolution, endowed rattlesnakes with certain behavioural inhibitions conducive to their survival as a species; for they would quickly become extinct if they did not have these inhibitions. In the case of nations, the governing logic, directly appreciated, inspires behavioural inhibitions conducive to the survival of the human species. But it is the same logic that has imposed itself on the instincts of rattlesnakes and on the reasoning powers of men, to the same end, and so far with the same result in each case.

We have found that nuclear weapons are virtually unusable in combat, and that the wars of the nuclear age must therefore be limited. The only time that nuclear weapons actually have been used in combat was in the context of an essentially unlimited war that had begun in the pre-nuclear age, when unlimited wars were still practicable. But this is a situation that could never rise again—unless, of course, it were possible to abolish nuclear weapons, in which case an unlimited war might start and lead, again, to the production of the nuclear weapons that would be used to end it.

To say that nuclear weapons are virtually unusable in combat, however, is not to say that they are unusable as a contingent threat in diplomacy. When we refer to national nuclear armaments as "deterrents" we indicate that they are, in fact, usable in diplomacy. A wise Frenchman recently remarked that his country's so-called *force de frappe* (a term translated from the English "striking force") was misnamed, that it should have been called *force de dissuasion* (after the English "deterrent force"), since it could be used to deter but it could not possibly be used to strike. There is, here, a paradox to which we shall have to return. For the moment we may simply note that nuclear armaments have proved less useful than expected even in diplomacy. The practice of what we too crudely call "nuclear blackmail" has not had a history of success.

During the first half of the 1950s, when Moscow was in the process of developing a great nuclear armament of its own, the best minds in the West laboured under dire forebodings because of an altogether plausible logic that they applied to the approaching future. Up to then there had seemed to be a sort of balance of power in the Cold War. On the one hand, it was thought that the American nuclear monopoly deterred the Red Army from marching to the Channel. On the other hand, the overwhelming superiority of the Red Army to the ground forces opposing it in Europe deterred the United States from using its nuclear armament against Russia, for that (as the Russians warned) might be expected to provoke the occupation of West Europe by the Red Army. The situation, then, was one of mutual deterrence.

However, once Russia had acquired a nuclear armament of its own to deter, by itself, the American nuclear armament, what would then prevent the Red Army from marching on to the Channel with impunity? Surely the balance of power would then have been decisively upset in favour of the Russians, and as a matter of simple realism the change would have to be registered in a series of diplomatic concessions to Moscow. The West would no longer be able to defend Berlin because its nuclear armament would be rendered unusable by the Russian nuclear armament, which could retaliate in kind for any nuclear attack, while the Western ground forces would not be able to stand up against the now undeterred Communist ground forces. Under these rapidly approaching circumstances, diplomatic pressure by Moscow should alone suffice to compel the abandonment by the West of Berlin—and perhaps of Turkey, and then Greece, and an indefinite succession of other positions besides.

It is clear that the men in Moscow saw the same prospect. After the mid-1950s, as their nuclear capacity grew, they began with increasing assurance to practice a diplomacy of nuclear threat. Russia's first *sputnik* (launched on 4 October 1957) demonstrated that the Russians had stolen a march on the Americans, getting ahead of them in the development of long-range missiles for the delivery of nuclear warheads. Within a week Moscow began to raise an outcry about an alleged plot whereby Turkey, as cat's paw for the United States, was to attack Syria, a Russian protégé at the time. On 9 October Khrushchev told James Reston of *The New York Times* that if war broke out over Syria

we are near Turkey and you [the U.S.A.] are not. When the guns begin to fire the missiles can begin flying, and then it will be too late to think about it.

On 12 October he wrote a letter to the British Labour Party (and *mutatis mutandis* to the respective socialist parties of the other European members of NATO) in which he said:

One cannot ignore the fact that Britain is a member of the North Atlantic bloc, and a military gamble by Turkey and the United States against Syria would in effect predetermine Britain's participation in it. Any extension of the conflict around Syria may plunge Britain into a new devastating war, with all its terrible consequences for the population of the British Isles.

This was the beginning of an ominous campaign to break up the North Atlantic alliance by detaching countries like Britain that supposedly lay, now, at the mercy of the new Russian nuclear armament.

It did not succeed, and perhaps Moscow concluded that the attempt had been premature. A year later (in November 1958) it renewed its campaign of nuclear diplomacy, this time with an air of absolute assurance. On 27 November Khrushchev issued his famous ultimatum, which in effect gave the Western allies just six months to get out of Berlin. In abstract terms it seemed reasonable that the allies, taking the new calculus of power into account, should retreat from Berlin; for they no longer had the military means to defend it, and any attempt to do so seemed likely to lead to their own destruction and, perhaps, the destruction of Berlin as well.

Now, however, a curious thing happened. The Western allies did not obey the dictates of reason. They stood firm, announcing their intention not to retreat. Faced with this stubbornness, Khrushchev at last decided to give himself more time, and in March 1959 he withdrew his ultimatum. In 1961 Khrushchev renewed his ultimatum and set off the series of demonstrative nuclear explosions that culminated in one estimated at 57 megatons—only to withdraw it again when again the West proved intransigent.

What this experience shows is that not only are nuclear weapons virtually unusable in combat, they are of more limited usefulness in diplomacy than we had expected them to be. This has a certain obvious logic of which, however, we must be wary: for, if a weapon is virtually unusable in combat, then the threat to use it will lack credibility, and to the degree that it lacks credibility it will be limited in its effectiveness. So *the third lesson of the nuclear age is that a nuclear armament is of highly limited use in diplomacy.*

Since the diplomatic effectiveness of the nuclear armament is limited by its credibility, we are brought to ask what are the limits of its credibility. By now we all know the answer. When a nuclear power threatens to use its nuclear armament in response to an aggression that would imminently endanger its very survival, its threat will be more credible than if it should threaten to use that armament in response to some remote provocation by which its vital interests are not directly endangered.

By 1954 U.S. Secretary of State John Foster Dulles resorted, however obliquely, to the threat of massive nuclear retaliation if the Communists should take Dien Bien Phu in Indo-China, which they were besieging. Presumably it was incredible to the Communists that the United States would start a nuclear war over anything as remote as Dien Bien Phu. So they were not deterred; they went ahead and took it anyway.

Why should it not have been the same at Berlin? Certainly Berlin, although it was far more important to the United States than Dien Bien Phu, was not worth a great nuclear war. Berlin, however, unlike Dien Bien Phu, was at the centre of the Cold War, not only geographically but politically and symbolically as well. The area of Berlin was, consequently, so sensitive that any shock there might have led to loss of control by the contesting governments.

There is a basic principle that applies here: the greater the stakes, the less the risk that can be accepted. Where one stands to lose one's life one cannot take as big a gamble as where one stands to lose only a dollar bill. If there was only one chance to fifty that, in going through with their attempt to capture Berlin, the men in Moscow would set off a nuclear war in which their own society would be destroyed, then they could not reasonably take that chance.

Although we agree that there are virtually no situations in which a nuclear power would be rationally justified in firing off its nuclear armament, situations might easily arise in which one could not be quite sure that such a power would not do so nevertheless. In such a situation, the power that was contemplating the act of provocation might feel almost certain, but not quite certain, that it would not thereby set off a nuclear war. And, where the survival of one's own society was at stake, even a slight uncertainty would have a powerful inhibiting effect. Uncertainty is the great deterrent. By virtue of it, governments are, in the final test, deterred from extreme acts of provocation. So nuclear armaments, as the Cold War has proved, are powerful influences for keeping the peace. This is their diplomatic use. They serve this purpose simply by their passive presence on the scene.

If nuclear armaments are effective for the maintenance of the *status quo*, they are ineffective for upsetting it. The basic situation at Berlin was that Moscow was using its nuclear threat in an attempt to upset the *status quo*, while the West, also with a nuclear armament, was defending it. In a nuclear confrontation the challenger is at a disadvantage simply because he is the one taking the initiative: because it is his move. He, rather than the defender, is the one who, if he carries out his threat, takes the action that might set off the nuclear fireworks. Consequently, when the moment for that action comes, he is likely to have second thoughts.

A fourth lesson of the nuclear age, then, is that the presence of nuclear armaments in the world's landscape has tended to strengthen the status quo. This is illustrated by the fact that the fantastic territorial anomalies left at the end of World War II, which no one expected to last more than a few weeks or months, are still with us almost a generation later. Korea is still divided. Germany is still divided. West Berlin is still an enclave a hundred miles inside hostile territory. Since the great confrontation began, every attempt to upset the essential *status quo* between the two camps by an abrupt use of force or the threat of force has failed. The attempts from each side to overcome the division of Korea by force failed. The three Russian attempts to get the West out of Berlin failed. The attempt to mount Russian power in Cuba failed. The attempt to seize the Suez Canal failed.

We should recognise at this point that the advent of nuclear armaments is only one among several factors that have been tending increasingly throughout this century to limit the possibilities of using force, or the threat of force, to bring about abrupt changes in the *status quo*. It is, however, a factor of the first importance.

The solidifying of the *status quo* by nuclear armaments is a consequence of the fact that their only function is deterrence. And deterrence does not create change, it prevents change.

In the old days it was assumed that a nation's military security depended largely on defence, on the military ability to stop an invading force. This is part of the reason why we got into such a panic when nuclear weapons first appeared on the scene. For it was in everyone's mind that no defence against these weapons was possible. If an enemy launched a substantial number of nuclear weapons against one's cities there was no way of stopping enough of them to prevent the cities from being destroyed. This was part of the reason why it was thought that the only possible salvation lay in abolishing such weapons forthwith. But deterrence has always been a better alternative to defence, since it prevents any attack at all rather than stopping an attack already begun. The experience of twenty-two years shows that this better alternative has been immensely strengthened by the advent of nuclear armaments.

Deterrence has always been primary in the domain of military security, although never before practised so consciously and explicitly. The balance of power, to which the world has looked in times past for peace and stability, has in fact been nothing but a system of mutual deterrence. In a constellation of rival states with claims against each other, or with ambitions that could be fulfilled only at each other's expense, each has been deterred from aggression against the others by the spectacle of the power that would oppose it.

In the pre-nuclear age, however, we all knew that only a multilateral balance of power could be stable, that a bipolar balance was like a chair with only two legs. The logic of this was that, in a balance-of-power situation involving many independent centres of power, there were possibilities of adjustment that tended to prevent any one power from upsetting the balance. An increase of weight by one power could be compensated for by shifting the weights of others against it. But such adjustment is not possible in a confrontation of two powers only. There are no supplementary weights to rectify the balance. Therefore, as soon as one of the two powers gains a distinct advantage over the other the balance is definitively upset. In the classic case (which it was no comfort to recall in the 1950s), Carthage was utterly destroyed by Rome.

With this logic and this precedent in mind, we were naturally alarmed after 1945 by the development of a bipolar balance between the two superpowers and their respective associates. It was under the circumstances of this bipolar confrontation that the arms race got under way, and one could plausibly ask how it could end in anything but the destruction of half the world. During the last years of the 1950s we lived in the terror that an acute enough crisis, say over Berlin, would eventuate in a surprise disarming attack by one side against the other.

Then, however, the situation began to improve. Each side began to feel itself more secure. The bipolar balance began to seem less unstable. What had happened was that both sides had been able to achieve protection for their respective nuclear panoplies by putting them under the ground or under the sea. After that it was evident that a surprise disarming attack would not disarm its victim, who would retain, still, the means of cataclysmic retaliation. Neither side could expect to destroy the other, then, without being destroyed itself. In direct contradiction of the traditional principles upon which our minds had been formed, a bipolar stability ensued.

What had changed the classical situation was the advent of "absolute" weapons. Nuclear armaments are "absolute" in the sense that they have the capacity for extinguishing any organized society, no matter how big, at one blow. Between such absolute armaments—as between a big and a little rattlesnake, each of which can kill the other with one bite—the balance of power is bound to remain perfect regardless of limited increments on one side or the other. If two men stand with pistols at each other's temples, their fingers on the triggers, the balance between them is perfect even though one pistol is a .45 while the other is only a .22.

The fifth lesson of the nuclear age, then, is that, where the power on either side is absolute, a bipolar balance is relatively stable.

One cannot say that it is absolutely stable. There is the theoretical possibility, at least, of some sensational scientific or technological "breakthrough," such as the development by one side of an effective defence against massive nuclear attack. However, although this would destabilise it in theory—let us say, in games-theory—it seems likely that the element of uncertainty, together with other inhibitions on the use of nuclear weapons, might ensure that it would not be seriously destabilised in practice.

It is not implausible that, in a nuclear environment, the classical situation has been completely reversed: that a bipolar balance of power is stable while a multilateral balance would be unstable or less stable. Is it not precisely the apprehension of this that makes us worry, today, about the possibility of nuclear proliferation?

In summary, the five main lessons that may be drawn from the experience of living with nuclear weapons are:

1. That nuclear weapons are virtually unusable in combat.
2. That in a nuclear environment wars must be limited.
3. That the usefulness of nuclear armaments in diplomacy is limited to deterrence and defence of the *status quo*.
4. That nuclear weapons have, consequently, strengthened the *status quo*.
5. That in a nuclear environment a bipolar balance of power may have a greater stability than the classical balances of the pre-nuclear age.

Of these five interrelated lessons, the one we should concentrate on and develop in all its implications is the second, that wars must be limited. We can feel no assurance that they will in fact be limited, because the existence of nuclear armaments does not, in itself, automatically limit them. There is always the possibility that a nation or a ruler might go too far beyond the bounds of prudence, that diplomatic "brinkmanship" might end in loss of control. Therefore, in order to keep our wars limited hereafter, we shall have to develop the concepts, the modalities, and the institutions required to keep them from going out of control.

These concepts, modalities, and institutions are all those that contribute to the maintenance of reciprocal understanding between the opposed parties in a limited war. The parties must have a tacit if not an explicit understand-

168

THE RELATIONS OF STATES

ing about going too close to the brink of an all-out war. And they must have means of communicating with each other intelligibly and meaningfully when it becomes necessary to draw back from the brink—as in the Cuban missile crisis of October 1962.

I have already noted that the old concept of total war was of a situation in which the military men replaced the diplomatic policy-makers at the levers of command. In limited war, however, the diplomatic policy-makers have to remain in full and active command. For the parties to a limited war use military force essentially as an instrument of diplomacy for the realisation of diplomatically attainable objectives. This means that diplomatic negotiation between the antagonists should if possible be going on concurrently with the fighting, or at the least that diplomatic contact between them should not be lost.

One implication of this is that the ideological element in conflict has to be minimized. It is almost a contradiction in terms to fight a limited ideological war, for the ultimate objectives of the belligerents in an ideological war are total. Moreover, to the extent that the issue in a conflict is ideological rather than strategic, there is no possibility of meaningful communication, of understanding, or of compromise, between the opposed parties. If the issue is the nominal issue of whether the ideas attributed to Karl Marx or those attributed to John Locke shall rule the world, then the contest will tend to be all-out, directed to the unlimited objective that requires total victory. But if the issue is one of the balance of power, perhaps involving spheres of influence, then the two sides may be able to understand each other very well, and to negotiate a reasonable compromise—as was the case on the night of 9 October 1944, when Churchill and Stalin agreed that Russia was to be predominant in Rumania and Bulgaria while Britain was to be predominant in Greece.

Closely associated with the dangerous ideological view of the world is the myth, which takes many forms, that mankind is divided into two opposed and mutually irreconcilable species, the Good and the Wicked. The two species may be the Servants of God identified with Christendom and the Servants of Satan identified with Islam; or they may be the virtuous Proletarians and the wicked Capitalists; or they may be, as in World War II, the Peace-loving Nations and the Aggressor Nations. Since the virtuous species cannot make deals with the wicked species, and communication to achieve mutual understanding between them is impossible, the confinement of war to limited objectives is implicitly impossible.

Today ideological passion has abated to a considerable extent in the West and in Russia. We must look forward to its abatement in China with the passage of time and, perhaps, the sobering possession of a nuclear arsenal. We must look forward to the time when Washington is effectively represented in Peking, and Peking in Washington. The avoidance or limitation of war depends more on good communication than on any other operational factor.

The whole history of the Korean War, until it was at last brought under control, is a history of the failure of communication. For it was not intended or desired by any of the parties to it; it came about and was continued and enlarged purely because of successive failures of communication between the two sides; and at the cost of something approaching two million casualties it settled nothing.

Item. What General MacArthur and Secretary Acheson meant by their public statements defining the "defensive perimeter" of the United States as running through the islands off the east coast of Asia, and thus excluding Korea, was simply that this was the line it would try to hold in the contingency of a third world war. But Moscow, reading them in the light of the concurrent withdrawal of American forces from Korea, must have interpreted the statements as an assurance that the United States would not defend South Korea even against a local aggression and in the absence of general war. So, because of a failure in communication, it gave its North Korean puppet the signal to move into South Korea.

Item. When the Inchon landing of 15 September resulted in the rout and destruction of the North Korean Army, of which only a remnant was able to make its way back to North Korea, the issue arose whether the victorious forces under MacArthur should counter-invade North Korea and liberate it up to the Chinese and Russian frontiers. The issue hung on whether the Chinese armies massed in Manchuria would intervene if they did so. MacArthur's orders were that, if Peking communicated such an intention in time, he was to desist. But Peking did not communicate such an intention, or did not communicate it clearly, until it was too late.

On 22 September the Foreign Ministry in Peking issued a statement in which it said: "We clearly reaffirm that we will always stand on the side of the Korean people . . . and resolutely oppose the criminal acts of American imperialist aggressors against Korea." As a warning, this piece of bombast was much too vague to provide a basis for restraining MacArthur's forces.

Again, on 30 September, Prime Minister Chou En-lai said in a public address that the Chinese people will not "supinely tolerate seeing their neighbours being savagely invaded by the imperialists." What this seemed to represent was the deliberate avoidance of any explicit commitment to intervene militarily if MacArthur marched north across the 38th parallel.

Only then, when it was too late, when the invasion of North Korea was already under way, did Chou En-lai ask the Indian ambassador in Peking to inform Washington that, if American troops (as distinct from the South Koreans who had already done so) should cross the parallel, China would enter the war. But by now the whole movement of invasion was going full tilt. It was too late to check and reverse it. So, because of another failure in communication, MacArthur's forces, including Americans, went up to the Yalu, three hundred thousand Chinese troops came in against them, and the war that no one wanted was catastrophically enlarged.

One may speculate on how different the situation might have been if Chou En-lai had issued his explicit warning a week earlier than he did, or if Washington had had in Peking an ambassador to find out and to warn it in time that, if MacArthur proceeded north, the Chinese would come in.

The sixth and last lesson to be set down here, then, is that in the nuclear age it is even more important to have good communication between antagonists than between allies.

This was recognised after the Cuban missile crisis of October 1962. During that crisis President Kennedy and Prime Minister Khrushchev had communicated with each other through diplomatic channels that required several hours for the transmission of each message. By contrast, missiles carrying thermonuclear warheads could span the distance in a few minutes. It was conceivable that, in another crisis, both nations would be destroyed unless the words travelled faster than the missiles. Consequently, the so-called "hot line" was set up as a rapid-communications link between Moscow and Washington. It has since demonstrated its utility by the use that President Johnson and Premier Kosygin made of it during the Arab-Israeli war of June 1967.

Similar communications links have now been set up between Paris and Moscow and between London and Moscow. We may reasonably look forward to the day when there are hot lines running from the Western capitals to Peking as well.

When the nuclear age first burst upon us it seemed as if nothing short of a miracle could save human civilisation from a terrible doom. Now, however, we have lived with nuclear weapons for over twenty-two years. We have seen how they have tended to keep wars limited. We have seen how they have produced a certain stability in the balance of power, and how they have tended to stabilise international relations as a whole.

This is not to deny the danger that still persists, the danger against which we must take all possible measures, the danger by which we must constantly govern our thinking. It is hard to believe that mankind has been rising in consciousness, understanding, and vision for a million years only to go smash in the end. But accidents happen that cut off the most promising lives of individuals, and cataclysmic disaster brought on by itself has often been the lot of mankind. It is precisely because we have so much reason to look forward to a larger future that we should cultivate an understanding of the factors that make for the limitation of conflict.

15

THE CLASSICAL STRATEGISTS

Michael Howard[*]

I

It may help to begin with a definition of "classical" strategy. Liddell Hart has provided us with one which is as good as any, and better than most: "The art of distributing and applying military means to fulfil the ends of policy."[1] Whether this remains adequate in the nuclear age is a matter of some controversy. André Beaufre, for example, has adumbrated the concept of an "indirect strategy," to be considered later, which embraces more than purely military means;[2] but even he still gives as his basic definition of the term "the art of the dialectic of two opposing wills using force to resolve their dispute."[3] It is this element of *force* which distinguishes "strategy" from the purposeful planning in other branches of human activity to which the term is often loosely applied. When other elements such as economic pressure, propaganda, subversion and diplomacy are combined with force, these elements may also be considered as "strategic"; but to apply this adjective to activities unconnected with the use, or threatened use, of force would be to broaden it to such an extent that it would be necessary to find another word to cover the original meaning of the term as defined by Liddell Hart, and as considered in this paper.

It need hardly be said that students of strategy have generally assumed that military force is a necessary element in international affairs. Before World War I, there were few who questioned even whether it was desirable. After 1918, many regretted its necessity and saw their function as being to ensure that it should be used as economically, and as rarely, as possible. After 1945, an even greater proportion devoted themselves to examine, not how wars should be fought, but how they could be prevented, and the study of strategy merged into that of arms control, disarmament and peace-keeping. There the "classical strategists" found themselves working with scholars of a different kind; men who believed that the element of force was *not* a

---

[*] Michael Howard, "The Classical Strategists," *Adelphi Papers*, No. 54 (February 1969), pp. 18–32. Reprinted by permission.
[1] B. H. Liddell Hart, *Strategy: The Indirect Approach* (London: Faber, 1967), p. 335.
[2] André Beaufre, *An Introduction to Strategy* (London: Faber, 1965), *passim*, esp. pp. 107–130.
[3] Ibid., p. 22.

necessary part of international intercourse, but could be eliminated by an application of the methodology of the social sciences. . . . This paper will . . . concern itself solely with the thinkers who assume that the element of force exists in international relations, that it can and must be intelligently controlled, but that it cannot be totally eliminated. Further, it is confined to the men who have primarily used the methodology of history or traditional political science; though it includes such figures as Schelling and Morgenstern, who have made considerable contributions in the newer disciplines as well.

The art* of strategy remains one of such complexity that even the greatest contributors to its study have been able to do little more than outline broad principles; principles which nevertheless must often be discarded in practice if the circumstances are inappropriate, and which must never be allowed to harden into dogma. Even when these principles appear self-evident, it may be extraordinarily hard to apply them. In World War II "command of the sea" as advocated by Mahan and "command of the air" as advocated by Douhet were certainly necessary preliminaries to the military victory of the Western powers. The problem was how to obtain them with resources on which equally urgent calls were being made for other purposes. The academic strategist could not help the Chiefs of Staff much, for example, in deciding how to allot a limited number of long-range aircraft between the conflicting needs of the strategic offensive against Germany, the war against German submarines, interdiction bombing of German railways, the requirements of the Pacific theatre and support for guerrilla activities in occupied Europe. Operational research and systems-analysis could simplify the problem without ever eliminating it. In the last resort the quality termed by Blackett "the conventional military wisdom"[4] remained the basic factor in making the decision; and that decision was determined by what could be done rather than by what ideally should. The military commander is always primarily conscious of the constraints under which he operates, in terms both of information and of resources. He is, therefore, likely to be impatient with the advice of the academic strategist which may appear to him either platitudinous or impracticable. His decisions must be based at best on educated guesses.

But the academic strategist does have one vital role to play. He can see that the guesses *are* educated. He may not accompany the commander to battle, as Clausewitz expressed it, but he forms his mind in the schoolroom, whether the commander realizes it or not. In World War II the Allied High Command did operate in accordance with certain very definite strategic principles. It is tempting to link these principles with the names of

---

* The term seems appropriate. Strategy deals with too many imponderables to merit the description "science." It remains, as Voltaire described it two hundred years ago, "murderous and conjectural."

[4] P. M. S. Blackett, *Studies of War* (London: Oliver & Boyd, 1962), p. 128.

specific theorists: General Marshall's desire for concentration against the
enemy army with Clausewitz, General Brooke's desire to enforce dispersal
on the enemy with Liddell Hart, the doctrine of the Allied air forces with
Douhet: tempting, but difficult to prove. The name of Douhet was virtually
unknown in the Royal Air Force.[5] The most eminent thinkers sometimes do
no more than codify and clarify conclusions which arise so naturally from
the circumstances of the time that they occur simultaneously to those
obscurer, but more influential figures who write training manuals and teach
in service colleges. And sometimes strategic doctrines may be widely held
which cannot be attributed to any specific thinkers, but represent simply
the consensus of opinion among a large number of professionals who had
undergone a formative common experience.

Of this kind were the doctrines which were generally held in the armed
forces of the Western world in the mid-1940s as a result of the experiences
of World War II. It was considered, first, that the mobilization of superior
resources, together with the maintenance of civilian *morale* at home, was a
necessary condition for victory; a condition requiring a substantial domestic
"mobilization base" in terms of industrial potential and trained manpower.
It was agreed that, in order to deploy these resources effectively, it was
necessary to secure command of the sea and command of the air. It was
agreed that surface and air operations were totally interdependent. And it
was agreed that strategic air power could do much—though *how* much remained a matter of controversy—to weaken the capacity of the adversary to
resist. The general concept of war remained as it had been since the days of
Napoleon: the contest of armed forces to obtain a position of such superiority that the victorious power would be in a position to impose its political
will. And it was generally assumed that in the future, as in the immediate
past, this would still be a very long-drawn-out process indeed.

II

The advent of nuclear weapons, to the eyes of the layman, transformed
the entire nature of war. But certain eminent professionals suggested that
they made remarkably little difference, at least in a conflict between two
powers of the size of the United States and the Soviet Union. These weapons
obviously would make it possible to inflict with far greater rapidity the
kind of damage by which the strategic bombing offensive had crippled
Germany and Japan. But the stockpiles of bombs were small—how small
is still not known. The bombs were vulnerable to interception; and they
had to operate from bases which had to be protected by land armies which
would have in their turn to be supplied by sea. All this was pointed out to
the general public by, among others, two scientists with long experience in

---

[5] Sir John Slessor, "Air Power and the Future of War," *Journal of the Royal United
Service Institution*, August 1954.

military planning—the British Professor P. M. S. Blackett and the American Dr. Vannevar Bush. Blackett, on the basis of careful calculations from un-classified material, concluded in 1948 that "a long-range atomic bombing offensive against a large continental Power is not likely to be by itself decisive within the next five years."[6] Bush, a figure closely associated with the American military establishment, described in 1949 a conflict barely dis-tinguishable from the last.

The opening phases would be in the air soon followed by sea and land action. Great fleets of bombers would be in action at once, but this would be the opening phase only . . . They could undoubtedly devastate the cities and the war po-tential of the enemy and its satellites, but it is highly doubtful if they could at once stop the march of great land armies. To overcome them would require a great national effort, and the marshalling of all our strength. The effort to keep the seas open would be particularly hazardous, because of modern submarines, and severe efforts would be needed to stop them at the source. Such a war would be a contest of the old form, with variations and new techniques of one sort or another. But, except for greater use of the atomic bomb, it would not differ much from the last struggle.[7]

It was along these lines that planning went forward when the framework of the North Atlantic Treaty Organization was established at the end of the 1940s. Such ideas were legitimate deductions from the then "state of the art." NATO planners had to think what could be done with the weapons they had available, not with those which might or might not be developed in ten years' time. But many scientists and academic strategists, particularly in the United States, were already thinking ahead. Because their views ap-peared to have no immediate relevance, or because of the pressures of inter-service politics, they had little immediate influence on Western policy; and they were usually set out in papers or articles which enjoyed only a limited circulation within the academic world.[8] An adequate account of these seminal discussions would require a separate paper. We can, however, salvage and admire the shrewd insights shown by two thinkers who had al-ready established their reputation in the pre-nuclear era: Bernard Brodie and Sir Basil Liddell Hart. Both of them, in works published in 1946, made prophecies which twenty years later were to be commonplaces of strategic thinking.

---

[6] P. M. S. Blackett, *The Military and Political Consequences of Atomic Energy* (Lon-don: The Turnstile Press, 1948), p. 56.

[7] Vannevar Bush, *Modern Arms and Free Men* (New York: Simon and Schuster, 1949), pp. 115–16.

[8] As for example Jacob Viner's paper on "The Implications of the Atomic Bomb for East–West Relations," the influence of which is acknowledged by Brodie and many others. Albert Wohlstetter gave an impromptu account, at the ISS Conference, of the main lines along which these discussions ran. Some account will also be found in Richard G. Hewlett and Oscar E. Anderson, *The New World* (Vol. I of the History of the United States Atomic Energy Commission, Pennsylvania, 1962), and in the early issues of the *Bulletin of the Atomic Scientists*.

In the final chapter of *The Revolution in Warfare*,[9] Liddell Hart suggested that, failing disarmament, attempts should be made "to revive a code of limiting rules for warfare—based on a realistic view that wars are likely to occur again, and that the limitation of their destructiveness is to everybody's interest." "Fear of atomic war," he wrote, "might lead to indirect methods of aggression, infiltration taking civil forms as well as military, to which nuclear retaliation would be irrelevant. Armed forces would still be required to fight 'sub-atomic war,' but the emphasis should be on their mobility, both tactical and strategic."

The great armies of the past would be irrelevant to the needs of the nuclear age. Liddell Hart did not, at this stage, consider the problems and contradictions of limited war, including the possibility which emerged fifteen years later, that it might be necessary to have large conventional forces precisely in order to keep war limited.

Neither did he explore the implications and requirements of deterrence. Brodie, however, with his collaborators in the Yale Institute of International Studies' publication *The Absolute Weapon*, did exactly this, and with remarkable prescience. Much that he wrote was to become unquestionably valid only with the development of thermonuclear weapons, but his insights were none the less remarkable for that. He rejected, for example, the whole concept of a "mobilization base." "The idea," he wrote, "which must be driven home above all else is that a military establishment which is expected to fight on after the nation has undergone atomic bomb attack must be prepared to fight with the men already mobilized and with the equipment already in the arsenals."[10] More important, he outlined the concept of a stable balance of nuclear forces.

If the atomic bomb can be used without fear of substantial retaliation in kind, it will clearly encourage aggression. So much the more reason, therefore, to take all possible steps to assure that multilateral possession of the bomb, should that prove inevitable, be attended by arrangements to make as nearly certain as possible that the aggressor who uses the bomb will have it used against him . . .

. . . Thus, the first and most vital step in any American programme for the age of atomic bombs is to take measures to guarantee to ourselves in case of attack the possibility of retaliation in kind. The writer in making that statement is not for the moment concerned about who will *win* the next war in which atomic bombs are used. Thus far the chief purpose of our military establishment has been to win wars. From now on its chief purpose must be to avert them. It can have almost no other useful purpose.[11]

Not until thermonuclear weapons had been developed and the Soviet Union had shown itself to possess an inter-continental delivery system did

---

[9] B. H. Liddell Hart, *The Revolution in Warfare* (London: Faber, 1946), p. 87.

[10] Bernard Brodie (ed.), *The Absolute Weapon* (New York: Harcourt, Brace, 1946), p. 89.

[11] Brodie, op. cit., pp. 75–76. He did not, however, deal with the problem of vulnerability of retaliatory forces, and the consequent dependence of stability on an effective second-strike capability.

the U.S. Joint Chiefs of Staff accept Brodie's logic; though it is significant that shortly after the publication of this work Brodie joined the newly formed RAND Corporation, where with the support of the U.S. Air Force the full implications and requirements of his ideas, and others current in the United States academic community, were to be exhaustively studied. The first Western government to adopt the concept of "deterrence" as the basis of its military policy was that of the United Kingdom in 1952; very largely thanks to the thinking of Marshal of the Royal Air Force, Sir John Slessor, the then Chairman of the Chiefs of Staff.[12]

Giving a late account of his stewardship at Chatham House in 1953, Slessor was to say:

> The aim of Western policy is not primarily to be ready to win a war with the world in ruins—though we must be as ready as possible to do that if it is forced upon us by accident or miscalculation. It is the prevention of war. The bomber holds out to us the greatest, perhaps the only hope of that. It is the great deterrent.[13]

This doctrine of "the great deterrent" was to unleash within the United Kingdom a debate which foreshadowed that set off in the United States by the comparable "New Look" strategy which Mr. Dulles was formally to unveil there in January 1954. Among its earliest and ablest critics were the men who, four years later, were to be primarily responsible for the foundation of the Institute for Strategic Studies: Rear-Admiral Sir Anthony Buzzard, Mr. Richard Goold-Adams, Mr. Denis Healey, and Professor P. M. S. Blackett. In its public presentation by Ministers and senior officers, the doctrine of "massive retaliation" provided its critics in England with an even easier target than it did in the United States. No official distinction was made between the use of Bomber Command as a first-strike force in response to a Soviet "conventional" invasion of Western Europe and as a second-strike force to retaliate after a Soviet nuclear attack. In face of the growing strength of Soviet nuclear-strike forces, the first role appeared to lack political, the second technical, credibility. Liddell Hart had already pointed out in 1950 that defence against nuclear weapons would be credible only if accompanied by massive civil-defence measures of a kind which no government showed any sign of being prepared to carry out.[14] Britain's military leaders indeed at first assumed that the civilian population might be induced to grin and bear the nuclear holocaust as cheerfully as they had endured the German blitz. The inhabitants of areas which contained no protected installations, suggested Slessor, "must steel themselves to risks and

---

[12] Richard N. Rosecrance, *The Defense of the Realm* (New York and London: Columbia University Press, 1967), p. 159.

[13] "The Place of the Bomber in British Policy." Reprinted in *The Great Deterrent* (London: Cassell, 1957), p. 123.

[14] B. H. Liddell Hart, *The Defence of the West* (London: Cassell, 1950), pp. 97, 134, 139, 140.

take what may come to them, knowing that thereby they are playing as essential a part in the country's defence as the pilot in the fighter or the man behind the gun."[15] This attitude presumably remained the basis of British official thinking until the acquisition of the *Polaris* missile system gave the United Kingdom a second-strike weapon which was technically if not politically credible. The validity of this thesis however gave rise to widespread doubts, and not only among the members of the Campaign for Nuclear Disarmament. In a famous lecture to the Royal United Service Institution in November 1959, after Mr. Duncan Sandys had, in two Defence White Papers, laid yet greater stress on the importance of "the deterrent," Lieutenant-General Sir John Cowley was to ask a question unusual for a senior serving officer:

> The choice of death or dishonour is one which has always faced the professional fighting man, and there must be no doubt in his mind what his answer must be. He chooses death for himself so that his country may survive, or on a grander scale so that the principles for which he is fighting may survive. Now we are facing a somewhat different situation, when the reply is not to be given by individuals but by countries as a whole. Is it right for the Government of a country to choose complete destruction of the population rather than some other alternative, however unpleasant that alternative may be?[16]

As a coherent theory of strategy in the traditional sense, the doctrine of deterrence by the threat of massive retaliation, in the simple form in which it was set out by the British and American governments in the early 1950s, is not easy to defend, and its exponents tended at times to use the vocabulary of exhortation rather than that of rational argument in their attempts to justify it. But three points should be noted if we are to appreciate their standpoint. First, the British Chiefs of Staff from the beginning saw Bomber Command as a supplement to rather than a substitute for the United States Strategic Air Command, with the task of striking at targets of particular significance for the United Kingdom. Its strategic utility and its credibility as a deterrent were thus to be judged within the context of the Western deterrent force as a whole.[17]

Second, it was an attempt, like the American "New Look" two years later, to solve the problem—and one far more difficult for the United Kingdom than for the United States—of maintaining an effective military force in a peace-time economy. The burden of rearmament assumed in 1950 had proved not only economically crippling but politically unacceptable; and since the political objective of the United Kingdom was the maintenance, *virgo intacta*, of the *status quo* in Europe, a policy which imposed the maximum penalty for *any* violation of that *status quo* was not so irrational as it

---

[15] Sir John Slessor, *Strategy for the West* (London: Cassell, 1954), p. 108.

[16] Lt-Gen. Sir John Cowley, "Future Trends in Warfare," *Journal of the Royal United Service Institution*, February 1960, p. 13.

[17] Rosecrance, op. cit., pp. 160–61.

appeared. For the United Kingdom not one inch of Western Europe could be considered negotiable.

Third, as British officials repeatedly said later in the decade, "The Great Deterrent" existed not to fight but to deter war: "If it is used, it will have failed." This argument was open to the rejoinder that a strategy which was not militarily viable was not politically credible, but this rejoinder is by no means conclusive. The concept of "deterrence" takes us out of the familiar field of military strategy into the unmapped if not unfamiliar territory of political bargaining, where total rationality does not invariably reign supreme. Schelling and others were only then beginning their studies of "the strategy of conflict"; but even without the help of game-theory techniques, it could be reasonably argued that, even if there was only one chance in a hundred that a political move would really be met by the threatened nuclear response, that chance would be an effective deterrent to any responsible statesman.* "The most that the advocates of the deterrent policy have ever claimed for it," said Slessor in 1955, "is that it will deter a potential aggressor from undertaking total war as an instrument of policy, as Hitler did in 1939, or from embarking upon a course of international action which obviously involves a serious risk of total war, as the Austrian Government did in 1914."[18]

Certainly the British advocates of the "deterrent policy" in the 1950s did not underrate the continuing importance of conflicts which would *not* be deterred by nuclear weapons. Liddell Hart repeatedly pointed out that nuclear stalemate would encourage local and indirect aggression which could be countered only by conventional forces; a lesson which British armed forces tied down in operations from Cyprus to Malaya had no need to learn. Faced with the double burden of deterring total war and fighting small ones, it was natural enough for British strategists to adopt the doctrine later termed "minimal deterrence." This was stated with uncompromising clarity by Blackett in 1956:

I think we should act as if atomic and hydrogen bombs have abolished total war and concentrate our efforts on working out how few atomic bombs and their carriers are required to keep it abolished. In the next few years I see the problem not as how many atomic bombs we can afford but how few we need. For every hundred million pounds spent on offensive and defensive preparations for global war, which almost certainly will not happen, is so much less for limited and colonial wars, which well may.[19]

British strategic thinkers in fact—even Slessor after his retirement—tended to take the existence of stable deterrence very much for granted. In

---

* This of course begs the whole question so carefully examined by Stephen Maxwell in Adelphi Paper No. 50: *Rationality in Deterrence* (London: ISS).

[18] Slessor, Lecture at Oxford University, April 1955, reprinted in *The Great Deterrent*, p. 181.

[19] P. M. S. Blackett, *Atomic Energy and East–West Relations* (Cambridge: Cambridge University Press, 1956), p. 100.

view of the highly classified nature of all information relating to Bomber Command and the absence of any serious intercourse at that time between Ministry of Defence officials and free-lance strategic thinkers, this was not altogether surprising. It enabled them to concentrate, not only on problems of limited wars (Liddell Hart) but on graduated deterrence and restraints on war (Buzzard) and, in the atmosphere of *détente* which followed the Geneva Summit Meeting of 1955, on "disengagement," disarmament and arms control (Blackett and Healey). When a few years later American thinkers questioned the validity of the doctrine of "minimal deterrence" they evoked from Blackett a forceful rejoinder,[20] in which he expressed the fear that to depart from such a policy would only lead to an endless and increasing arms race. But by the end of the 1950s it was becoming clear that any doctrine of deterrence depended for its validity on technical calculations which stretched far beyond the orthodox boundaries of strategic thinking; and on which it was difficult for thinkers who did not enjoy access to the facilities available in the United States to pronounce with any degree of authority.

III

Within the United States the controversy was now well under way. It had been got off to an excellent start by Mr. John Foster Dulles, whose definition of the doctrine of "massive retaliation" in January 1954 had been far more precise and dogmatic than the statements emanating from Whitehall to the same effect during the past two years. This, it will be remembered, announced the intention of the United States Administration to place its military dependence "primarily upon a great capacity to retaliate, instantly, by means and at places of our own choosing," thereby gaining "more basic security at less cost."[21] The rationale behind this policy was of course political and economic: American weariness with the Korean War, and the desire of the Republican Party to return to financial "normalcy" after what they regarded as the ruinous spending spree of the last four years.[22] It should perhaps be judged, not as a coherent strategic doctrine, but as a political expedient—or even as a diplomatic communication, itself a manoeuvre in a politico-military strategy of "deterrence." By these criteria the policy must be pronounced not ineffective. But its logical fallacies were too glaring to be overlooked. The assumption of American invulnerability to a pre-emptive or a retaliatory strike was unconvincing in the year in which the Soviet Union first unveiled her inter-continental bombers. Even when that assumption

---

[20] P. M. S. Blackett, "Critique of Some Contemporary Defence Thinking." First published in *Encounter* in 1961, this article is reprinted in *Studies of War*, op. cit., pp. 128–46. See also Blackett's dissenting note in Alastair Buchan: *NATO in the 1960's* (London: Chatto & Windus, 1960).

[21] Text in *The New York Times*, 13 January 1954.

[22] See the analysis " 'The New Look' of 1953" by Glenn H. Snyder, in Warner R. Schilling, Paul Y. Hammond and Glenn H. Snyder, *Strategy, Policy and Defense Budgets* (New York: Columbia University Press, 1962), pp. 379–524.

had been justifiable four years earlier, American nuclear monopoly had not deterred the Korean conflict; and in that very year American nuclear power was to prove irrelevant to the conflict in Indo-China. These, and other points, were rapidly made with force and relish by Democrat politicians and sympathizers out of office, by academic specialists, and by members of the armed services which were being cut back to provide greater resources for the Strategic Air Command.

There has perhaps never been a strategic controversy which has not been fuelled by political passions and service interests. It is entirely understandable, and for our purposes quite unimportant, that the U.S. Air Force should have sought every argument to justify the doctrine of massive retaliation while the U.S. Army powerfully supported its opponents. What is significant, however, is that the latter included every strategic thinker of any consequence in the United States; and the failure of the present writer to find any serious academic defence of the doctrine may not be entirely due to unfamiliarity with the literature. Among the first critics was that pioneer of deterrence-theory, Bernard Brodie, who published in November 1954 one of the earliest analyses of the place of "limited war" in national policy;[23] but the first really formidable public broadside was fired by a group of scholars at the Princeton Center of International Studies under the leadership of William W. Kaufmann, in a collection of essays published in 1956 under the innocuous-sounding title *Military Policy and National Security*. In this work Kaufmann himself stressed the need for the United States to have the capacity to meet, and therefore deter, Communist aggression at every level;[24] that "spectrum of deterrence," in fact, which Mr. Robert McNamara was to develop, not without some assistance from Dr. Kaufmann himself, when he became Secretary for Defense four years later. In the same work Dr. Roger Hilsman discussed the actual conduct of nuclear war; both making the distinction between counter-force and counter-value targets in total war, and considering the tactics of war with nuclear weapons fought on the ground;[25] and Professor Klaus Knorr gave one of the earliest published estimates of the kind of civil defence policy which might be feasible and necessary if the United States were really to employ the kind of nuclear strategy implied in Mr. Dulles's statement.[26] Finally Mr. Kaufmann emphasized the necessity for ensuring that military force should be tailored to the actual requirements of foreign policy: a point which was to be expanded more fully in two important books published the following year.

---

[23] Bernard Brodie, "Unlimited Weapons and Limited War," *The Reporter,* 18 November 1954. For an indispensable annotated bibliography of the whole controversy, see Morton H. Halperin: *Limited War in the Nuclear Age* (New York and London: John Wiley, 1963).

[24] William W. Kaufmann, ed., *Military Policy and National Security* (Princeton, N.J.: Princeton University Press, 1956), pp. 28, 38, 257.

[25] Ibid., pp. 53–7, 60–72.

[26] Ibid., pp. 75–101.

These were Dr. Robert Osgood's study of *Limited War* and Dr. Henry Kissinger's *Nuclear Weapons and Foreign Policy*.[27] Neither author had any significant experience of military operations or operational research. Their intellectual training was in the disciplines of history and political science; but with the shift of strategic thinking from the problem of waging war to that of its prevention, this background was at least as relevant as any more directly concerned with military affairs. Both analysed the traditional rigidity of the American attitude towards war and peace, contrasting it with the flexibility of Communist theory and, as they saw it, practice. Both emphasized the irrelevance of strategic nuclear weapons to the conduct of foreign policy in peripheral areas. Both stressed, as had Kaufmann, the need to provide the appropriate forces for the fighting of limited wars; and both considered that tactical nuclear weapons should be regarded as appropriate for this purpose—a view shared by Mr. Dulles himself,[28] and by the Joint Chiefs of Staff under the Chairmanship of Admiral Radford.

Osgood based his belief in the need to use nuclear weapons in limited wars largely on the difficulty of preparing troops to fight with both nuclear and conventional weapons.[29] Kissinger, whose study developed out of panel discussions at the Council on Foreign Relations in which a number of professional soldiers took part, went into the question more deeply, discussing both the possible *modus operandi* of tactical nuclear forces and the kind of limitations which might be agreed between two belligerents anxious not to allow their military confrontation to get out of hand.[30] In doing so he aligned himself with the views of Rear-Admiral Sir Anthony Buzzard, who was energetically canvassing before British audiences both the value of tactical nuclear weapons in making possible graduated deterrence at acceptable cost, and the feasibility of negotiating agreed limitations on the conduct of war.[31] But Buzzard's views were hotly contested in England. Slessor gave them general support, but Liddell Hart was highly sceptical (believing the capabilities of conventional forces to be unnecessarily underrated) and Blackett, after some hesitation, came out flatly against them.[32] In the United States the same controversy blew up. Brodie, writing in 1959, was prepared

[27] Robert E. Osgood: *Limited War: the Challenge to American Strategy* (Chicago: University of Chicago Press, 1957). Henry A. Kissinger, *Nuclear Weapons and Foreign Policy* (New York: Houghton Mifflin, 1957).

[28] J. F. Dulles, "Challenge and Response in United States' Policy," *Foreign Affairs*, October 1957.

[29] Osgood, op. cit., p. 258.

[30] Kissinger, op. cit., pp. 174–202.

[31] Anthony Buzzard et al., *On Limiting Atomic War* (London: Royal Institute of International Affairs, 1956); and "The H-Bomb: Massive Retaliation or Graduated Deterrence," *International Affairs*, 1956.

[32] Slessor: "Total or Limited War?" in *The Great Deterrent*, pp. 262–84. Liddell Hart, *Deterrent or Defence: a Fresh Look at the West's Military Position* (London: Stevens, 1960), pp. 74–81. Blackett, "Nuclear Weapons and Defence," *International Affairs*, October 1958.

to admit only that there might be *some* circumstances in which tactical nuclear weapons might be appropriate, but considered that "The conclusion that nuclear weapons *must* be used in limited wars has been reached by too many people, too quickly, on the basis of too little analysis of the problem." Schelling the following year suggested that the break between conventional and nuclear weapons was one of the rare "natural" distinctions which made tacit bargaining possible in limiting war.[33] By this time Kissinger himself had had second thoughts, and agreed that, though tactical nuclear weapons were a necessary element in the spectrum of deterrence, they could not take the place of conventional forces.[34] Within a year Mr. McNamara was to take the debate into the council chambers of NATO, where the advocates of tactical nuclear weapons had already found staunch allies among officials grimly conscious of the unpopularity and expense of large conventional forces. Throughout the 1960s the debate was to continue, in three major languages, about the place of tactical nuclear weapons in the defence of Europe.[35] Only the sheer exhaustion of the participants keeps it from continuing still.

It will be seen that the major American contributions to strategic thinking published in 1956–67 were distinguished by two main characteristics. They attempted to reintegrate military power with foreign policy, stressing, in contradiction to the doctrine of massive retaliation, the need for "a strategy of options." And they tended to be the work of academic institutions; Kaufmann's group at Princeton, Osgood from Chicago, Kissinger working with the Council on Foreign Relations. Their authors were thus concerned less with the technicalities of defence (Hilsman at Princeton, a former West Pointer, was an interesting exception) than with its political objectives. Over what those objectives should be, they had no quarrel with John Foster Dulles. Although British thinkers, like British statesmen, had been exploring possibilities of *détente* ever since 1954, in the United States the cold war was still blowing at full blast. The Soviet Union was still, in the works of these scholars, considered to be implacably aggressive, pursuing its objective of conquest in every quarter of the globe, its machinations visible behind every disturbance which threatened world stability. As Gordon Dean put it in his introduction to Kissinger's book, "Abhorrent of war but unwill-

---

[33] Brodie, *Strategy in the Missile Age* (Princeton, N.J.: Princeton University Press, 1959), p. 330. Thomas C. Schelling, *The Strategy of Conflict* (Cam., Mass.: Harvard University Press, 1960), pp. 262–66. But the debate continued. Brodie in *Escalation and the Nuclear Option* (Princeton, N.J.: Princeton University Press, 1966) was to argue strongly against what had by then become known as the "firebreak" theory, and emphasize the deterrent value of tactical nuclear weapons.

[34] Kissinger, *The Necessity for Choice* (London: Chatto & Windus, 1960), pp. 81–98.

[35] The literature is enormous, but three outstanding contributions are Helmuth Schmidt, *Verteidigung oder Vergeltung* (Stuttgart, 1961); Alastair Buchan and Philip Windsor, *Arms and Stability in Europe* (London: Chatto & Windus, 1963); and Raymond Aron, *Le Grand Débat* (Paris: Calmann-Lévy, 1963).

ing to accept gradual Russian enslavement of other peoples around the world, which we know will eventually lead to our own enslavement, we are forced to adopt a posture that, despite Russian military capabilities and despite their long-range intentions, freedom shall be preserved to us."[36] The strategy of options which they urged had as its object, not the reduction of tensions, but the provision of additional and appropriate weapons to deal with a subtle adversary who might otherwise get under the American guard.

IV

Two years later, in 1959–60, the major works on strategy in the United States showed a slight but perceptible change of emphasis. As it happened, the most significant of these were the work, not of full-time academics in universities, but of men drawn from a wide variety of disciplines—physicists, engineers, mathematicians, economists and systems analysts—who had been working in defence research institutes on classified information, particularly at RAND Corporation. As a result they analysed the technical problems of deterrence with an expertise which earlier works had naturally lacked. These problems appeared all the more urgent to the general public after the launching of the Sputnik satellite in 1957; which revealed the full extent of the challenge which the United States had to meet from Soviet technology. For the first time in its history the United States felt itself in danger of physical attack, and the question of civil defence, which had for some time agitated academic specialists, became one of public concern. Yet at the same time there was beginning to emerge in some quarters a new attitude to the Soviet Union. This saw in that power not simply a threat to be countered, but a partner whose collaboration was essential if nuclear war through accident or miscalculation was to be avoided. It recognized that Soviet policy and intentions might have certain elements in common with those of the United States, and that its leaders faced comparable problems. This attitude was by no means general. For scholars such as Robert Strausz-Hupé and William Kintner the conflict still resembled that between the Archangel Michael and Lucifer rather than that between Tweedledum and Tweedledee. But the concept, not only of a common interest between antagonists but of a joint responsibility for the avoidance of nuclear holocaust became increasingly evident after the new Administration came into power in 1961.[37]

The view which commanded growing support among American strategic thinkers was, therefore, that the "balance of terror" was a great deal less stable than had hitherto been assumed, but that if it could be stabilized (which involved a certain reciprocity from the Soviet Union) there would

---

[36] Kissinger, *Nuclear Weapons*, p. vii.

[37] For an analysis of the various attitudes of American strategic thinkers to the question of *détente* see Robert A. Levine, *The Arms Debate* (Cam., Mass.: Harvard University Press, 1963), *passim*.

be reasonable prospects of lasting peace. The technical instability of the balance was described by Albert Wohlstetter in the famous article which appeared in *Foreign Affairs* at the begining of 1958, describing on the basis of his classified studies at RAND Corporation, the full requirements of an invulnerable retaliatory force: a stable "steady-state" peace-time operation within feasible budgets, the capacity to survive enemy attacks, to make and communicate the decision to retaliate, to reach enemy territory, penetrate all defences and destroy the target; each phase demanding technical preparations of very considerable complexity and expense.[38]

The following year the mathematician Oskar Morgenstern was to suggest, in *The Question of National Defense*, that the best answer to the problem as defined by Wohlstetter, and the best safeguard against accidental war, was to be found in the development of seaborne missiles; and that it would be in the best interests of the United States if such a system could be developed by both sides. "In view of modern technology of speedy weapons-delivery from any point on earth to any other," he wrote, "it is in the interest of the United States for Russia to have an invulnerable retaliatory force and vice versa."[39] Whether Morgenstern reached this conclusion entirely through applying the game-theory in which he had made so outstanding a reputation is not entirely clear. Professor Thomas Schelling, who also brought the discipline of game-theory to bear on strategy, reached the same conclusion at approximately the same time;[40] but even by cruder calculations its validity seemed evident, and the concept of a "stable balance" was central to Bernard Brodie's *Strategy in the Missile Age*, which also appeared in 1959.[41] This study pulled together all the threads of strategic thinking of the past five years and set them in their historical context. Brodie reduced the requirements of strategy in the missile age to three: an invulnerable retaliatory force; "a real and substantial capability for coping with local and

---

[38] Albert Wohlstetter, "The Delicate Balance of Terror," *Foreign Affairs*, January 1958. The article is reprinted in Henry A. Kissinger (ed.), *Problems of National Strategy* (New York and London: Praeger and Pall Mall, 1965). The principal relevant studies were *Selection and Use of Air Bases* (R-266, April 1954) and *Protecting U.S. Power to Strike Back in the 1950s and 1960s* (R-290, April 1956) by Albert Wohlstetter, F. S. Hoffman, and H. S. Rowen. Wohlstetter in a private communication to the present writer has stressed the significant part played in these studies by experts in systems-analysis such as J. F. Pigby, E. J. Barlow, and R. J. Lutz.

[39] Oskar Morgenstern, *The Question of National Defence* (New York: Random House, 1959), p. 75.

[40] See particularly his "Surprise Attack and Disarmament" in Klaus Knorr, (ed.), *NATO and American Security* (Princeton, N.J.: Princeton University Press, 1959). Schelling's whole work on the problem of dialogue in conflict situations is of major importance. His principal articles are collected in *The Strategy of Conflict* (Cam., Mass.: Harvard University Press, 1960).

[41] Brodie, *Strategy in the Missile Age*, op. cit., Chapter 8. Brodie and Schelling, like Wohlstetter, were at the time working at RAND Corporation, as also was Herman Kahn. All have acknowledged their mutual indebtedness during this formative period in their thinking.

limited aggression by local application of force"; and provision for saving life "on a vast scale" if the worst came to the worst.[42] About how, if the worst did come to the worst, nuclear war should be conducted, he did not attempt to offer any guidance beyond suggesting that the most important problem to study was not so much how to conduct the war, but how to stop it.

Not all of Brodie's colleagues at the RAND Corporation were so modest. The following year, 1960, saw the publication of Herman Kahn's huge and baroque study *On Thermonuclear War;*[43] the first published attempt by any thinker with access to classified material to discuss the action which should be taken if deterrence *did* fail. The horrible nature of the subject, the broad brush-strokes with which the author treated it, his somewhat selective approach to scientific data and the grim jocularity of the style, all combined to ensure for this study a reception which ranged from the cool to the hysterically vitriolic. Many of the criticisms, however, appear to arise rather from a sense of moral outrage that the subject should be examined at all than from serious disagreement with Kahn's actual views. In fact Kahn basically made only two new contributions to the strategic debate. The first, based on the classified RAND *Study of Non-Military Defense* for which he had been largely responsible, was that a substantial proportion of the American population could survive a nuclear strike, and that this proportion might be considerably increased if the necessary preparations were made. The second was that the United States should equip itself with the capacity to choose among a range of options in nuclear as well as in non-nuclear war; that rather than relying on a single spasm reaction (von Schlieffen's *Schlacht ohne Morgen* brought up to date) the United States should be able to conduct a controlled nuclear strategy, suiting its targets to its political intentions—which would normally be, not to destroy the enemy, but to "coerce" him.[44] Kahn in fact reintroduced the concept of an operational strategy which had been almost entirely missing, at least from public discussion, since the thermonuclear age had dawned ten years earlier. For smaller nuclear powers any such notion, as applied to a conflict with the Soviet Union, was self-evidently absurd. Between the super-powers it was—and remains—a perfectly legitimate matter for analysis. Kahn may have exaggerated the capacity of the social and political structure of the United States to survive a nuclear holocaust; certainly many of his comments and calculations were oversimplified to the point of naïveté. But it is hard to quarrel with his assumption that that capacity, whatever its true dimensions, could be increased by appropriate preliminary measures; while the position adopted by some of his critics, that even to contemplate the possibility of

---

42 Ibid., pp. 294–97.
43 Herman Kahn, *On Thermonuclear War* (Princeton, N.J.: Princeton University Press, 1960).
44 Ibid., pp. 301–2.

deterrence failing might increase the possibility of such failure, is hardly one that stands up to dispassionate analysis.

At the beginning of 1961 President Kennedy's new Administration took office and Mr. Robert McNamara became Secretary of Defense. Not entirely coincidentally, the great period of American intellectual strategic speculation came to an end, after five astonishingly fruitful years. The military intellectuals were either drawn, like Kaufmann and Hilsman, into government, or returned to more orthodox studies on university campuses. Most of them continued to write. Kahn has produced two further works refining some of the views expounded in *On Thermonuclear War*.[45] Kissinger has remained a sage observer of and a prolific commentator on the political scene, and is at the moment of writing President Nixon's adviser on international security affairs. Osgood, Wohlstetter and Brodie have all produced notable work of synthesis or criticism. Perhaps the most interesting work has been that of Knorr and Schelling, who have broadened their studies to embrace the whole question of the role of military power in international relations;[46] a remarkably little-explored field in which a great deal of work remains to be done. It would be absurdly premature to suggest that any of these scholars—many of them still comparatively young men—have no more substantial contributions to make to strategic studies; but they are unlikely to surpass the intellectual achievement for which they were individually and jointly responsible in the 1950s. Between them they have done what Clausewitz and Mahan did in the last century, during times of no less bewildering political and technological change: laid down clear principles to guide the men who have to make decisions. Like Clausewitz and Mahan they are children of their time, and their views are formed by historical and technological conditions whose transformation may well render them out of date. Like those of Clausewitz and Mahan, their principles are likely to be misunderstood, abused, or applied incorrectly, and must be subjected by each generation to searching examination and criticism. Debate will certainly continue; but at least we now have certain solid issues to debate about.

The principles established by the thinkers of the 1950s were to guide Mr. McNamara in his work of remoulding American defence policy during the eight years of his period of office in the Department of Defense. "The McNamara Strategy" had a logical coherence—almost an elegance—which may have commanded rather more admiration among academics than it did in the world of affairs.[47] An invulnerable second-strike force was built up on a

---

[45] *Thinking the Unthinkable. On Escalation: Metaphors and Scenarios* (London: Pall Mall, 1965).

[46] Knorr, *On the Uses of Military Power in the Nuclear Age* (Princeton, N.J.: Princeton University Press, 1966). Schelling, *Arms and Influence* (New Haven: Yale University Press, 1966).

[47] William W. Kaufmann, *The McNamara Strategy* (New York: Harper & Row, 1964) provides a useful if uncritical account. It should be read in association with Bernard Brodie's dry commentary "The McNamara Phenomenon," *World Politics,* July 1965.

considerably larger scale than that considered adequate by the believers in "minimal deterrence." These forces were endowed with the capability, even after a surprise attack, of retaliating selectively against enemy forces rather than against his civilian population, so that "a possible opponent" would have "the strongest imaginable incentive to refrain from striking our own cities."[48] Forces for "limited wars" at all levels were created, armed both with nuclear and with conventional weapons. This involved an increase in expenditure, but it was an increase which was not grudged by Congressmen alarmed by an alleged "missile gap" and happy to see fat defence contracts being placed within their home states; and the techniques of systems analysis which had also been developed at RAND Corporation were employed to keep this increase within bounds.[49] Overtures were made, official and unofficial, to the Soviet Union to establish arms-control agreements based on the principle of a stable balance resting on invulnerable second-strike forces on either side. And plans were put in hand for civil defence projects on a massive scale.

McNamara was able to carry out much of his programme, but not all. The Russians were remarkably slow to absorb the reasoning which appeared so self-evident to American academics. The American public was even slower to co-operate in the sweeping measures necessary to provide effective insurance against holocaust. The ideal of a second-strike counter-force strategy seemed to many critics to be one almost intrinsically impossible of realization. And America's European allies flatly refused McNamara's requests that they should increase their conventional forces to provide the necessary "spectrum of deterrence." The Germans saw this as a diminution of the deterrent to any invasion of their own narrow land, and besides had their own not particularly enjoyable memories of "conventional war." The British, struggling to maintain a world presence on their obstinately stagnant economy, could not afford it; while the French had ideas of their own. None of them, perhaps, could produce a coherent theoretical framework to sustain them in their arguments, but they remained unconvinced. Several of Mr McNamara's emissaries received, in consequence, a somewhat gruelling introduction to the refractory world of international affairs.

For the American strategic programme was based on two assumptions which were not accepted by all the major allies of the United States; first, that America was the leader of "The Free World" and had both the right and the power to shape its strategy; and second, it was in the interests of the

---

[48] McNamara speech at the University of Michigan at Ann Arbor, 16 June 1962. Kaufmann, op. cit., p. 116.

[49] See Charles Hitch and Roland McKean, *The Economics of Defense in the Nuclear Age* (Cam., Mass.: Harvard University Press, 1960) for the promise. The performance was examined in *Planning—Programming—Budgeting: Hearings before the Subcommittee on National Security and International Operations of the Committee on Government Operations*, United States Senate, 90th Congress, 1st Session (U.S. Government Printing Office, 1967).

world as a whole that the United States and the Soviet Union should enter into an ever closer dialogue. Neither of these assumptions was challenged by the British; though not all their countrymen admired the assiduity with which successive British Prime Ministers set themselves up as "honest brokers" between the super-powers the moment they set foot inside Downing Street. Indeed the most substantial British contribution to the strategic debate in the early 1960s, John Strachey's *On the Prevention of War*, quite explicitly advocated a Russo-American diarchy as the best guarantee of world peace.[50] But on the Continent reactions were different. The Chancellor of the Federal German Republic took a glum view of a Russo-American *détente* which could only, in his view, confirm the division of his country and might even threaten the position of Berlin; and long before Mr. McNamara had appeared on the scene the President of the French Fifth Republic had made clear his own attitude to the American claim to act as leader and the spokesman of "The Free World."

V

Too much should not be made of the personality of General de Gaulle in shaping the French contribution to the strategic debate which began to gain in importance towards the end of the 1950s. French military experience during the past twenty years had been distinctive and disagreeable. They had their own views on the reliability of overseas allies as protectors against powerful continental neighbours—neighbours who might in future comprise not only Russia but a revived Germany or, in moments of sheer nightmare, both. The decision to develop their own nuclear weapons had been taken before De Gaulle came into power, though perhaps it took De Gaulle to ensure that they would not be integrated, like the British, in a common Western targeting system. General Pierre Gallois, the first French writer to develop a distinctive theory of nuclear strategy,[51] advanced the thesis that nuclear weapons rendered traditional alliance systems totally out of date since no state, however powerful, would risk nuclear retaliation on behalf of an ally when it really came to the point. In a world thus atomized (in the traditional sense of the word) the security of every State lay in its capacity to provide its own minimal deterrence. The more States that did, indeed, the greater the stability of the international system was likely to be.

Extreme as Gallois's logic was, it probably reflected the sentiments of a large number of his countrymen and a substantial section of the French Armed Forces. In spite of innumerable official expressions to the contrary, there is every reason to suppose that many influential members of the British governing establishment felt very much the same about their own nuclear force. A more subtle variant of this doctrine was presented by General

---

[50] John Strachey, *On the Prevention of War* (London: Macmillan, 1962).
[51] Pierre Gallois, *Stratégie de l'Age nucléaire* (Paris: Calmann-Lévy, 1960).

André Beaufre, who argued powerfully in his work, *Deterrence and Strategy*, that a multipolar nuclear balance in fact provided greater stability than a bipolar, since it reduced the area of uncertainty which an aggressor might exploit. So far from atomizing alliances, argued Beaufre, independent nuclear forces cemented them, "necessarily covering the whole range of their vital interests."[52] He was careful to distinguish between multipolarity and proliferation. "The stability provided by the nuclear weapon" he argued, "is attainable only between *reasonable* powers. Boxes of matches should not be given to children";[53] a sentiment which one can endorse while wondering what Beaufre would define, in international relations, as the age of consent. As for the Russo-American diarchy welcomed by Strachey, Beaufre specifically identified this as a danger to be avoided. "The prospect of a world controlled by a *de facto* Russo-American 'condominium' is one of the possible—and menacing—results of nuclear evolution" he wrote. "Looked at from this point of view, the existence of independent nuclear forces should constitute a guarantee that the interests of the other nuclear powers will not be sacrificed through some agreement between the two superpowers."[54]

The doctrine of "multipolarity" was thus one distinctive contribution by French theorists to the study of strategy in the nuclear age. The second was their analysis of revolutionary war: a subject virtually ignored by American strategic thinkers until the Vietnam involvement brutally forced it on their attention. For the French it had been inescapable. For nearly ten years after World War II the flower of their armies had been involved, in Indo-China, in operations of far larger scope than the various "imperial policing" activities which absorbed so much of the attention of the British Armed Forces, and one which imposed on the French nation a longer and perhaps even more severe a strain than the Korean War imposed on the United States. The war in Indo-China was lost. It was followed by six years of struggle in Algeria which ended, for the French Armed Forces, no less tragically. The outcome of these wars significantly altered the balance of power in the world, but the strategic concepts being developed in the United States appeared as irrelevant to their conduct as those which guided —or misguided—the French armies during the two world wars. The concepts which *were* relevant of course were those of Mao Tse-tung; those precepts evolved during the Sino-Japanese struggles of the 1930s and developed into a full theory of revolutionary warfare whereby a strongly-motivated cadre operating from a position of total weakness could defeat a government controlling the entire apparatus of the state.

The theories of Mao lie outside the scope of this study, though there is little doubt that he is among the outstanding strategic thinkers of our day.

---

52 André Beaufre, *Deterrence and Strategy* (London: Faber, 1965), p. 93.
53 Ibid., p. 97.
54 Ibid., p. 140. Beaufre's experience as commander of the French land forces in the Suez operation of 1956 may have had some relevance to his views on this point.

Certainly the French paid him the compliment of trying to imitate him. The literature on the subject is so considerable that it may be only by hazard that the earliest French study to receive widespread recognition was Colonel Bonnet's historical analysis, *Les guerres insurrectionnelles et révolutionnaires*.[55] Bonnet in this work gave a definition which has since been generally accepted: "Guerre de partisans + guerre psychologique = guerre révolutionnaire." "Poser cette équation," he went on to claim, "c'est formuler une loi valable pour tous les mouvements révolutionnaires qui, aujourd'hui, agitent le monde."[56] On the basis of this definition and their own experiences, French military thinkers, true to their national intellectual traditions, attempted to formulate *une doctrine*. (It is interesting to note that the pragmatic British, whose cumulative experience in counter-insurgency campaigning was certainly no less than that of the French, thought more modestly in terms of "techniques.")[57] As worked out by such writers as Bonnet himself, Hogard, Lacheroy, Nemo, and Trinquier,[58] this *doctrine* set out the object, both of revolutionary and counter-revolutionary war, as the gaining of the confidence and support of the people, by a mixture of violent and non-violent means directed both at "military" and at "non-military" targets. It was not enough to suppress guerrillas: it was necessary to destroy the basis of their support among the population by eliminating the grievances which they exploited, by giving protection against their terroristic activities and, insisted the French writers, by a process of intensive indoctrination to combat that of the revolutionary cadres themselves.

It would be painful to record in detail where and why these excellent recommendations went wrong. The use of undifferentiated violence by legitimate authority undermines the basis of consent which is its strongest weapon against revolutionary opponents. Indoctrination of a population can be done only by men who are themselves indoctrinated; and since the whole essence of the "open societies" of the West is virtually incompatible with the concept of ideological indoctrination, the men thus indoctrinated rapidly found themselves almost as much at odds with their own society as the revolutionaries they were trying to combat. In Algeria the French Army applied its doctrines with a fair measure of at least short-term success, but in so doing it alienated the sympathies of its own countrymen. The main fault of its theorists—and of their imitators in the United States—was to

---

[55] Gabriel Bonnet, *Les guerres insurrectionnelles et révolutionnaires de l'antiquité à nos jours* (Paris: Pavot, 1955). Important unpublished studies by Colonel Lacheroy were in circulation at the same time.

[56] Ibid., p. 60.

[57] See, for example, Julian Paget, *Counter-Insurgency Campaigning* (London: Faber, 1967) and Sir Robert Thompson, *Defeating Communist Insurgency* (London: Chatto & Windus, 1966).

[58] For a good select bibliography see the excellent and highly critical study by Peter Paret, *French Revolutionary Warfare from Indo-China to Algeria* (London: Pall Mall, 1964).

overlook the element of simple *nationalism* which provided such strength for the insurgent forces: a curious failing in the country which was the original home of that immensely powerful force. They accepted the propaganda of their adversaries, and saw the conflict simply in terms of a global struggle against the forces of world Communist revolution. Marxist categories of thought make it impossible for their theorists even to consider that the most potent revolutionary force in the world may be not the class struggle but old-fashioned "bourgeois" nationalism. The French theorists were no doubt equally unwilling to take into account a consideration which boded so ill for their own side. But there is good reason to suppose that the FLN won in Algeria, not because they were Marxist but because they were *Algerian,* and the French were not. *Mutatis mutandis* the same applied—and applies still—in Indo-China. Marx and Lenin may provide the rationale of insurgency warfare; Mao Tse-tung may provide the techniques; but the driving power is furnished by the ideas of Mazzini. It is therefore difficult for foreign troops, however well-intentioned, to apply counter-insurgency techniques among a people which has awoken to a consciousness of its national identity with any chance of success.

In addition to the doctrines of multipolarity and revolutionary war, France has produced yet a third contribution to strategic thinking: the doctrine of indirect strategy. This was not totally novel. A group of American thinkers based on the Center of Foreign Policy Research at the University of Pennsylvania had long been working on the assumption that "The Free World" and the Communists were locked in a protracted conflict which could end only in the victory of one side or the other and in which force was only one element out of many which might be used.[59] It was an assumption that could certainly be justified by reference to the works of Marx–Leninist theoreticians. But the publications of these writers tended to be as emotional and tendentious as those of the Marxists themselves. Certainly they had never formulated their theories with the clarity, reasonableness and dispassionate precision of General André Beaufre and his colleagues at the Institut d'Études Stratégiques in Paris.[60] For Beaufre the whole field of international relations constituted a battlefield in which the Communist powers, thwarted in the use of force by the nuclear stalemate, were attacking the West by indirect means. Strategy had progressed from the "operational" (Clausewitz and Jomini) through the "logistic" (the great build-ups of World War II) to the "indirect." Political manoeuvres should therefore be seen as strategic manoeuvres. The adversary attacked, withdrew, feinted, outflanked, or dug in, using direct force where he could and infiltration

---

[59] Robert Strausz-Hupé, et al., *Protracted Conflict; A Challenging Study of Communist Strategy* (New York, 1959) and *A Forward Strategy for America* (New York, 1961).

[60] André Beaufre, *An Introduction to Strategy* (London: Faber, 1965); *Deterrence and Strategy* (London: Faber, 1965); *Strategy of Action* (London: Faber, 1967).

where he could not. The West should respond accordingly, devise a single overall political strategy and use economic, political, and military means to implement it.

The trouble with this is that it is not simply a theory of strategy but also a theory of international relations. If it is correct, Beaufre's recommendations follow naturally enough; but Beaufre states his assumptions rather than argues them, and to most students of international relations they are not self-evident. Such a view leaves too many factors out of account. The world is not really polarized so simply. Communist leaders do not control events so firmly. Whatever the ideologues may say, in practice interests are not so implacably opposed. Strategy must certainly be shaped by the needs of policy; but policy cannot be made to fit quite so easily into the Procrustean concepts of the professional strategist.

Perhaps the most significant conclusion to be drawn from this survey is the extent to which the quality of strategic thinking in the nuclear age is related to an understanding of international relations, on the one hand, and of weapons technology on the other. There is of course nothing new in this dependence. Clausewitz emphasized the first, though he never fully adjusted his purely strategic thinking to take account of the political environment whose overriding importance he quite rightly stressed. The second has been evident, particularly in naval and air operations, at least since the beginning of the twentieth century. But strategic thinkers, from the pioneers of the eighteenth century to Liddell Hart in his earlier writings, were able to assume a fairly simple model of international relations within which armed conflict might occur, as well as a basically stable technological environment. Neither assumption can now be made. No thinking about deterrence is likely to be of value unless it is based on a thorough understanding of "the state of the art" in weapons technology. Any thinking about limited war, revolutionary war, or indirect strategy must take as its starting point an understanding of the political—including the social and economic—context out of which these conflicts arise or are likely to arise. Inevitably the interaction works both ways. Strategic factors themselves constitute an important element in international relations: the statesman can never be a purely despotic law-giver to the strategist. Similarly, strategic requirements have inspired scientists and technologists to achievements they would normally consider impossible. Increasingly the three fields overlap. That is why strategic studies owe at least as much to the work of political scientists at one end of the spectrum, and of physical scientists, systems analysts and mathematical economists at the other, as they do to the classical strategist. One may indeed wonder whether "classical strategy," as a self-sufficient study, has any longer a valid claim to exist.

International Organization:
The United Nations

THE UNITED NATIONS (like its predecessor, the League of Nations) was deliberately designed to be the focal point around which contemporary international relations would center. It was to have primary responsibility for preserving both international peace and international security. If it became necessary, as a consequence of flagrant aggression, the organization was to use sanctions, up to and including force, against the offending nation or nations. Such security actions (*collective security*, to be examined in Chapter 8) were conceived as rare. The greater part by far of UN activity was expected to fall within the category of "peaceful settlement" procedures (Chapter VI of the Charter) where the role of the UN was to encourage solutions through investigation, compromise formulas, etc., and where the object of UN activity was to resolve the dispute rather than punish disputants. Peaceful settlement techniques, designed to bring shooting to an end in ambiguous circumstances where clearcut aggression was not involved, were utilized by the UN from the beginning. Truce observation teams for the Palestine War illustrate. But beginning in 1956 the UN went well beyond these more traditional peace-keeping devices to the establishment of substantial *ad hoc* "peace-keeping forces." These forces, composite armies in form, were of course capable of limited but coercive action even though they were not designed for fighting as such. The first major experiment in this connection, the United Nations Emergency Force (UNEF), was a clear success in terminating the

hostilities of the Suez War of 1956. With the consent of the belligerents the UN force was interposed between the rival armies who had
agreed to cease fire. Thus encouraged, the UN had recourse to the
device a second time in 1960 with the creation of the United Nations
Congo Force (ONUC). But because of the unusual and complex problems involved in the insertion of an international force to keep order
in a nation torn by civil strife, and the ultimate employment of ONUC
for purposes not accepted as valid by the Soviet Union, the Congo
Force experiment led to a severe crisis in the UN.

In a UN in which a two-thirds vote by 1964 could be marshalled
from members representing only ten percent of the population of UN
members and only five percent of contributions to the regular budget,
long, expensive, and precedent-shattering operations such as the Congo
can and do raise widespread fears that the organization may be committed to activities without real power backing from the membership.
Thus an argument over financing these UN operations is much more
than technical, for budgets in a real sense represent policy decisions.

In the first selection, "The United Nations Financial Crisis and the
Superpowers," John G. Stoessinger, professor at CUNY as well as
Director of the UN Political Affairs Division since 1957, gives us a
perceptive and informed analysis of the development of the United
Nations financial crisis. The beginning of financial difficulties of the
UN coincide with the establishment of the UNEF. But what really
compounded the difficulties were the much larger expenses of the
ONUC. The important nations, such as the Soviet Union and France,
who refused to pay special assessments levied for these operations, did
not oppose for lack of funds. What they questioned was the legitimacy
of the UN involving itself in such operations. (The Soviet objections
were tied specifically to those parts of the operations not determined
by the Security Council.) Stoessinger traces the argument through
the bond issue to meet the emergency, and the curious "no vote" procedures of the Nineteenth General Assembly. He concludes with the
observation that no state will willingly, if at all, pay for policies it considers contrary to its national interest—UN majority or no.

In the second selection, "The Symbolic Significance of the United
Nations," Inis L. Claude, Jr., Stettinius Professor of Government and
Foreign Affairs at the University of Virginia and one of the best known
scholars in the field, analyzes American attitudes toward the UN. As
he points out, the question "has frequently been put in terms of believing *in* rather than believing *that* . . ." He observes a more recent

growth in a matter-of-fact attitude, coincident with a recession in the belief in a withering away of state sovereignty into an ever-stronger UN. Discussing the UN's contribution, he sums up by calling it "not a competitor of states but a stimulator," not designed "to put them out of business, but to help them to help themselves" and handle their business more effectively. (Compare this analysis with Goldie's view of international law and change in Chapter 5.)

Note that both Stoessinger and Claude belong to what we saw called the "wisdom literature" school of approach to international relations outlined in Chapter 1.

16

THE UNITED NATIONS FINANCIAL CRISIS
AND THE SUPERPOWERS

John G. Stoessinger*

While the United Nations was engaged in major peace-keeping responsibilities, there was never a shortage of Cassandras predicting that the Organization would end with a bang. However, during the height of the UN
Operation in the Congo there existed a real possibility that it might have
ended with a whimper. A fiscal crisis developed in the early 1960's that became a threat to the life of the Organization. The cause of this crisis was the
refusal of the Soviets and others to pay for the two operations that the
United Nations had mounted to keep the peace: the United Nations Emergency Force in the Middle East (UNEF) and the United Nations Congo
Force (ONUC).

Never had so many people argued so much about so little money. The
financial crisis was in reality a political crisis over the proper role for
the UN to play in the national policies of its member states, particularly the
superpowers. Only secondarily was it a crisis over the costs of UN membership.

The United Nations Emergency Force

As we have seen, the General Assembly authorized UNEF by a vote of
64–0–12 in November, 1956 and, after much delicate negotiation, over 6,000
men—contingents from ten countries (Brazil, Canada, Colombia, Denmark,
Finland, India, Indonesia, Norway, Sweden, and Yugoslavia)—were ready
for action. But it was clear that unless the question of financing was solved,
the Force would not get beyond the paper stage. Hence the Secretary-General, in his proposals to the General Assembly, gave the matter of financing
the Force his most careful attention.

On November 21, 1956, the Secretary-General recommended that a Special Account outside the regular budget be set up for UNEF and that the
costs of the Force be shared by the member states on the basis of the scale
of assessments to be adopted for the 1957 budget. In addition, he suggested
an initial appropriation of $10 million to meet the immediate cash needs of
the Force.

---

* From *The United Nations and the Superpowers*, Second edition, by John G. Stoessinger. Copyright © 1970 by Random House, Inc. Reprinted by permission of the publisher.

On December 3, the Secretary-General faced the problem of allocating the balance of the expenses of the Force and indicated to the Assembly that the only equitable way of meeting the costs henceforth was to share them according to the 1957 scale of assessments. Although UNEF costs were financed under a Special Account, the Secretary-General nevertheless considered them as "United Nations expenditures within the general scope and intent of Article 17 of the Charter." Other states disagreed sharply with this proposal, however, and it profoundly divided the Fifth Committee of the Assembly. The superpowers took opposing positions immediately.

The United States delegates agreed with the Secretary-General and pointed out that the Committee's decision would be of crucial importance for the future of the Organization. He was supported by most of the Western nations. This view was sharply challenged by the delegates from the Soviet bloc, who insisted that the entire cost of the Operation should be borne by those countries which had precipitated the crisis—Britain, France, and Israel.

Between these two opposing views, yet a third emerged: most of the smaller nations claimed that everyone should pay something, but that the Great Powers, which had special privileges under the Charter, should also shoulder special responsibilities and pick up the major portion of the bill.

This formula won the day in the General Assembly and was adopted by a vote of 62 in favor, 8 against, and 7 abstentions. Only the Soviet bloc voted against. Under the terms of the Resolution, everyone was expected to contribute, but nations with limited capacities to pay received rebates of up to 50 percent of their assessments. The United States pledged itself to make voluntary contributions in order to cover the deficits created by these rebates.

The decision to assess the member states by this "rebate formula" did not solve the problem of financing UNEF. The heart of the problem was how to collect the assessments. Each year, arrears and defaults amounted to roughly one-third of the total assessment. The largest single debtor was the Soviet Union, which justified its nonpayment with two arguments: first, that "the aggressors must pay" and, second, that UNEF was illegal in a fundamental sense, since only the Security Council had the right to authorize peace-keeping operations.

The Secretary-General's position was clear: all member states had a legal obligation to pay. This view was supported by a majority of the membership, and most adamantly by the United States.

Although the numerous arrears and defaults had put the United Nations into serious financial straits by 1960, UNEF never threatened the financial structure of the Organization itself. It was the Congo crisis which was to shake that structure to its very foundations.

The United Nations Congo Force

After the two superpowers had both voted for the authorization of a peace force in the Congo in the Security Council on the night of July 13–14, 1960, and a tenuous consensus had thus been attained, the Secretary-General set about to put together and finance the new Force. On October 24, 1960, the Secretary-General estimated the cost of the Congo Force for 1960 at $66,-625,000. Once again, he defended the principle of collective responsibility as the most equitable method of sharing the financial burden. The United States supported him, but the Soviet Union stated its intention not to contribute to any part of ONUC's expenses since, in its opinion, "the main burden . . . should be borne by the chief culprits—the Belgian colonizers." The rest of the money should be raised through voluntary contributions.

At this point, the Secretary-General presented his view to the Fifth Committee. After strongly endorsing the principle of collective responsibility, Mr. Hammarskjöld deplored the tendency of some delegations to approve courses of action for the United Nations without following through financially:

Will this organization face the economic consequences of its own actions and how will it be done? Further, if it is not willing to face the financial consequences of its own decisions, is it then prepared to change its substantive policies? There is no third alternative.

He then pointed up the resulting dilemma:

The Secretariat finds itself in a difficult position. On the one hand, it has to pursue "vigorously" the policy decided upon by the General Assembly and the Security Council. On the other hand, it is continuously fighting against the financial difficulties with which these decisions under present circumstances face the Organization. Of course, the Organization cannot have it both ways.

Finally, the Fifth Committee, by a vote of 45 to 15, with 25 abstentions, approved a draft resolution proposed by Pakistan, Tunisia, and Senegal and supported by the United States. The resolution recommended an *ad hoc* account of $48.5 million for the expenses of ONUC, to be assessed on the basis of the 1960 scale; stressed that these assessments would be "binding legal obligations" on member states within the meaning of Article 17 of the Charter; called on the government of Belgium to make a substantial contribution; and recommended that voluntary contributions be applied to reduce by up to 50 percent the assessment of states with the least capacity to pay. On December 20, this recommendation was adopted by the General Assembly by a vote of 46 to 17, with 24 abstentions.

The second round was fought over the 1961 assessment of $100 million. Again, the Fifth Committee was deeply divided. Since the sum under consideration was the largest ever to be assessed by the United Nations for a single operation and since the decision would obviously have far-reaching consequences, more fundamental and elaborate arguments were raised by the superpowers than over the 1960 assessment. Moreover, the very solvency of the Organization depended on the outcome of the discussion. The United States once again favored the principle of collective responsibility on the basis of the 1960 assessment, although it offered to waive its reimbursement rights of over $10 million and to make a voluntary cash contribution of up to $4 million to be used to reduce the assessments of governments with limited capacity to pay.

The Soviet Union insisted that since ONUC was a Security Council "action" in the sense of Article 48 of the Charter, the General Assembly had no right to reach a decision on the matter. Article 11 of the Charter provided that any question involving peace and security on which action was necessary must be referred to the Security Council by the Assembly. Hence, in the Soviet view, ONUC financing should be governed not by Article 17 but by the unanimity principle in the Security Council. The Secretary-General stated in rebuttal that once the Security Council had taken a decision, the implementation costs fell clearly within the meaning of Article 17 and therefore within the bailiwick of the Assembly. The Soviet position, he argued, would have the effect of extending the unanimity principle of the Big Five to matters of finance, which would clearly lead to the paralysis of the entire operation in the Congo.

Finally, the Fifth Committee adopted a draft resolution originally sponsored by Ghana, Liberia, Pakistan, and Tunisia, and supported by the United States, which apportioned $100 million for the period January 1 to October 31, 1961 according to the 1960 assessment scale, "pending the establishment of a different scale of assessment" to defray ONUC's expenses. This time reductions of up to 50 percent were granted the poorer nations in order to obtain the necessary two-thirds majority in the plenary Assembly. Voluntary contributions were to be applied to offset the resulting deficits. The Big Five and Belgium were called upon to make substantial voluntary contributions. The final vote, taken at dawn on the last day of the session, was 54 in favor, 15 against, with 23 abstentions. The Soviet bloc, Mexico, and Belgium cast negative votes, while France and South Africa abstained and subsequently refused to contribute.

The third round was fought in December, 1961 over the 1962 ONUC budget. The Fifth Committee delegates went over much the same ground as in the previous debates and recommended an appropriation of $80 million to cover ONUC costs from November 1, 1961 to June 30, 1962. On' December 20, 1961, the General Assembly, by a vote of 67 in favor, 13 against, with 16 abstentions, appropriated this amount, with the same provisions for reductions as were approved in April.

The only nation which made voluntary contributions in cash to the Congo Operation was the United States. The sums contributed between 1960 and

1962 totalled more than $30.6 million and were used to cover the deficits created through rebates given to the poorer nations.

At the time of the opening of the Sixteenth General Assembly in 1961, UNEF and ONUC arrears had brought the United Nations to the brink of bankruptcy. In the case of UNEF, forty-one members owed all or part of their assessments for the 1960 budget, bringing arrears to almost 25 percent, and sixty-five members owed all or part of their 1961 assessments, bringing the combined shortage to almost 30 percent of the total. In the case of ONUC, sixty-six members had accumulated a combined shortage of nearly 40 percent of the 1960 budget, and only twenty-four had paid their 1961 assessments. The accumulated arrears for UNEF and ONUC by the end of 1961 exceeded $80 million, which was a sum larger than the annual regular budget. Two of the five permanent powers of the Security Council—the Soviet Union and France—had declared their intention not to make payment, and a third—Nationalist China—had defaulted.

As a result, the two peace-keeping operations had become heavily dependent on one of the two superpowers—the United States. Although the United States was assessed less than one-third of the 1961 UNEF budget, in effect, since its voluntary contribution was used to offset the reductions granted to fifty-one countries with limited capacity to pay, it was paying 43 percent of the total. In 1962, these reductions were increased and the United States assumed responsibility for a portion of the assessment of seventy-nine member states, which brought its share of the total cost to 48 percent. In the case of ONUC, the United States had assumed this larger share from the very beginning.

Such dependence on one superpower was not desirable and, more important, the failure of other states to pay their assessments was reaching alarming proportions. The UN debt now exceeded $100 million. In April, 1961, a Working Group of Fifteen was established which attempted to construct a special scale of assessment for peace-keeping operations. On November 15, 1961, this Working Group reported its findings to the Fifth Committee. In essence, the report was a catalogue of individual opinions largely retracing the ground that had been covered in earlier debates on UNEF and ONUC financing. Only one positive recommendation emerged from the discussions —a suggestion to ask the International Court for an advisory opinion on the applicability of Article 17 of the Charter to peace-keeping operations. In order to settle at least one argument in the financing controversy, the Assembly decided on December 20, 1961, by a vote of 52 to 11, with 32 abstentions, to ask the International Court for an advisory opinion on the question: Did the expenditures authorized by the General Assembly for UNEF and ONUC constitute expenses of the Organization within the meaning of Article 17 of the Charter? Acting Secretary-General U Thant also warned the Assembly at that time that the United Nations was faced with imminent insolvency if arrears and current assessments were not paid promptly. He estimated that, by June 30, 1962, the gap between the debts of the Organization and its available net cash resources would exceed $100 million. Quite obviously, drastic emergency action was necessary to finance the peace-keeping operations beyond June, 1962.

The Bond Issue: The United Nations As Borrower

On December 20, 1961, the General Assembly also adopted Resolution 1739 authorizing the Secretary-General to issue bonds in the amount of $200 million. The Resolution provided that the bonds were to bear interest at 2 percent per annum and that the principal was to be repaid in twenty-five annual installments by including in the regular budget each year beginning in 1963 an amount sufficient to pay installments of principal and interest charges. The bonds were to be offered to member states of the United Nations, members of the specialized agencies and of the International Atomic Energy Agency, and, if the Secretary-General with the concurrence of the Advisory Committee on Administrative and Budgetary Questions should so determine, to non-profit institutions or associations. The sale of bonds was to continue until December 31, 1963.

The debate in the Fifth Committee which preceded the passage of Resolution 1739 was animated, and frequently heated. The superpowers took opposing positions. Strong support for the bond issue came from the delegates of the United States, Canada, Australia, Ireland, Ethiopia, Ghana, Ceylon, Burma, and the Netherlands. Philip M. Klutznick of the United States said that if all members paid their arrears on the peace-keeping operations, the Organization could forget about the proposal; but since the exact opposite seemed to be true, the Committee could not leave the Acting Secretary-General with a political mandate but without the means to carry it out. Any amount less than $200 million would be insufficient to put the United Nations house in order. The proposal was to be seen as a one-time emergency arrangement to keep the Organization alive. The opposition was led by A. A. Roschin of the Soviet Union, who declared that the deficit in the United Nations existed not because certain states failed to pay their contributions but because UNEF and ONUC were illegal under the Charter. A bond issue would make the United Nations a tool of the bondholders. It was a maneuver to enable the United Nations to engage in similar illegal "peace-keeping" activities in the future.

The passage of the bond Resolution by the General Assembly was only the first step in securing the $200 million loan for the United Nations. In many member nations only legislative approval could authorize subscription to the bond issue. Most crucial, of course, was to be the decision of the Congress of the United States. When the United States delegate to the United Nations voted in favor of the bond Resolution, he stated at the time that only the Congress could authorize the purchase of such bonds and that his vote was to be considered as subject to this condition. Indeed, the fiercest legislative battle over the bond issue took place in the Congress of the United States.

On January 30, 1962, President Kennedy sent a special message to Congress to appropriate $100 million for the purchase of the bonds. Exhaustive hearings on the bill were held in the Senate Committee on Foreign Relations during February and March. The bond issue was defended by top-level members of the Administration, including Secretary of State Dean Rusk; Assistant Secretary of State for International Organization Affairs Harlan Cleveland; the United States Representative to the United Nations, Adlai Stevenson; and the United States Representative to the Economic and Social Council, Philip Klutznick. The merits of the bond plan were seriously questioned, however, by several members of the Committee on Foreign Relations, particularly Senators George D. Aiken (Republican, Vermont), and Bourke B. Hickenlooper (Republican, Iowa). These debates in the Committee were perhaps the most crucial phase in the history of the bond issue.

There were several strong arguments adduced in favor of the bond proposal. First, it was claimed that the bond issue would ensure the principle of collective responsibility since the principal and interest payments on the bonds would come out of the regular budget, thus compelling nations to pay or risk the loss of voting privileges in the General Assembly. Second, it was asserted that the United States would save money in the long run because, since the bonds would be paid back out of the regular budget over a twenty-five year period, the United States would contribute to UNEF and ONUC operations on the basis of 32 percent instead of 48 percent as heretofore. Third, since the Secretary-General would be permitted to sell bonds not only to member states of the United Nations but also to members of specialized agencies and possibly to nonprofit institutions, the bond issue offered the prospect of new financial resources. Germany and Switzerland, for example, two nonmembers, would, it was hoped, purchase some of the bonds. Fourth, it was argued that the twenty-five years permitted for repayment would make each annual installment small enough for the burden on some of the smaller countries not to be unreasonable. Finally, the Administration defended the view that the bond proposal appeared to be the best temporary device for financing the two peace-keeping operations until a pay-as-you-go plan could be agreed upon. Moreover, the bond issue was not to be deemed a precedent for United Nations financing, nor was it intended to relieve nations in arrears of their responsibilities toward the two peace-keeping operations. The proceeds were expected to be large enough to carry UNEF and ONUC until the end of 1963.

While no member of the Committee proposed that the United States withhold emergency financial assistance from the United Nations, there was considerable concern about whether the bond technique was the wisest course of action. Senators Aiken and Hickenlooper suggested as an alternative that the United States should make a three-year loan of $100 million, with an annual interest rate of 3 per cent, to help the United Nations over its financial emergency. The two Senators, who received considerable support in the Committee, questioned the bond device on a number of grounds. First, it was felt that, even though the bond issue was not to become a precedent, it would nevertheless encourage further fiscal irresponsibility by member states who were in arrears. Many might decide that if the United States bought one-half of the bonds, this amount would suffice and thereby relieve them of their own responsibilities. Hence, a short-term loan coupled with a vigorous attempt to collect arrears on past assessments would be preferable. The bond issue would simply postpone the moment of truth and encourage irresponsible nations to shift their burdens to others. Second, support for the bond issue in the General Assembly itself had not been overwhelming. While it was true that 58 nations had voted in favor of the bond resolution, 13 had voted against it, and 33 had abstained or had been absent, indicating that perhaps as many as 46 states did not support the bond proposal. Finally, it was feared that a bond issue would merely be a disguised form of assessment under which subscribing states would first pay up the arrears of delinquent states; then, when the bonds came due, the redemption money would come not from the states in arrears but from those which had both paid their assessments faithfully and subscribed to the bonds as well.

After weighing these conflicting considerations, the Committee on Foreign Relations, by an 8 to 7 vote, reported favorably on the bond bill. The alternative of a straight $100 million loan was narrowly rejected. The majority, however, decided to protect the United States by including the proviso that the President would be authorized to purchase $25 million worth of bonds without limitation, but that the purchase of additional bonds up to a total of $100 million would have to be matched by the aggregate amount purchased by other nations. Furthermore, in order to ensure repayment of the bonds, it was decided to deduct from the annual contributions of the United States to the regular budget amounts corresponding to principal and interest payments owed to the United States. Finally, it was made clear that the bond issue was not to set a pattern for the future financing of peace-keeping operations, but was to be regarded as an extraordinary one-time remedy for the financial ills of the United Nations.

The narrowness of the vote was a source of considerable anxiety to the Administration. It was feared that a hostile majority might develop on the floor of the Senate. Even if the bill did pass the Senate, passage in the House of Representatives was highly uncertain. Consequently, the White House supplanted the State Department as the intermediary with the Senate, in the hope of achieving an overwhelming Senate majority for the President's proposal. The result was agreement on a revised form of the bill; the money was to be designated as a loan but still made available for the purchase of United Nations bonds by the President at his discretion. This compromise, in which the President maintained the substance of his proposal and the Senators won their semantic point of designating the fund as a loan, produced a favorable vote on the Senate floor of 70 to 22. The bill as finally passed retained the original matching proviso as well as the condition that bond repayments be deducted annually from the United States contribution to the regular budget. It also included a clause to the effect that the United States should use its best efforts to promote a pattern of United Nations financing that would make unnecessary any future large-scale borrowing.

The telling argument against a straight $100-million loan that finally won over the opposition was the fact that such a loan would certainly have precipitated a financial crisis after three years. It would have been a pistol pointed at the head of the United Nations since, in all likelihood, the world organization would have had no resources to repay the loan at the end of the three years. Moreover, the Senate shared the hope of the Administration that the bond plan would compel all members to pay their share of the costs of peace-keeping operations. The Aiken-Hickenlooper loan project would not have furthered the principle of collective responsibility. The battle in the United States Senate over the bond proposal was not solely, not perhaps even primarily, the result of a difference of opinion over the respective merits of a bond issue or a straight loan. The bond controversy became a catalyst and brought into the open a good deal of doubt, suspicion, and ambivalence about the United Nations as a whole. The role of the United Nations in Katanga, the rising power of the African and Asian nations in the General Assembly, and the increasing intransigence of the Soviet position—all these stimulated a broad reassessment of the world organization. The difficulties which the bond proposal experienced in the United States Senate were largely to be explained in terms of a genuine and serious questioning of the role of the United Nations—especially its peace-keeping function—in the foreign policy of the United States.

The battle in the House of Representatives was no less intense. In September, 1962, that body, by a vote of 256 to 134, settled on a bill which permitted the United States merely to match bond purchases of other UN members up to $100 million. The Senate version would have permitted outright United States purchase of $25 million. In the last analysis, the more restrictive version was adopted by the Congress. Hence, the full $200 million worth of bonds authorized by U Thant could be raised only if members other than the United States should buy $100 million.

By late 1965, 65 states had subscribed to the bond issue, many of them subject to legislative approval. The total amount purchased had reached almost $150 million, of which the United States had bought almost $75 million. Only in the United States had the condition of legislative approval posed a serious threat. Everywhere else, parliaments approved the pledges of their delegations with relative ease.

Superpower Showdown

It had always been clear to even the strongest supporters of the bond issue that the measure would have to be regarded as a stopgap emergency device pending a permanent solution of the problem of financing peace-keeping operations. One ray of hope appeared when, on July 20, 1962, the World Court declared in a 9 to 5 Advisory Opinion that the costs of UNEF and ONUC were to be considered as legally binding obligations upon the entire membership. The Seventeenth General Assembly, on December 19, 1962, after a debate which covered familiar ground, decided to "accept" the Advisory Opinion by a vote of 76 in favor, 17 against, and 8 abstentions. As a result, a considerable number of smaller nations cleared their accounts, but the Soviet Union and France refused to abide by the opinion. Since France was paying for UNEF, it became increasingly obvious to all concerned that the first major nation to fall under the penalty provisions of Article 19 would be the Soviet Union. Under the terms of this Article, member states delinquent in their assessed contributions for two years or more could lose their votes in the General Assembly unless that body specifically waived that penalty.

In the meantime, the General Assembly re-established the Working Group and increased its membership from 15 to 21. The enlarged Working Group continued to search for a solution to the impasse. The Soviet bloc countries stuck to their contention that only the Security Council had the right to impose assessments for peace-keeping operations. The United States stiffened its position and declared its opposition to any special scale of assessments for UNEF and ONUC for the last six months of 1963 which would involve an assessment percentage for the United States in excess of 32.02 percent. The new United States position was based on the assumption that the regular scale made ample adjustments for low per-capita-income countries and the belief that the financing of UNEF and ONUC for the last six months of 1963 should be handled on an *ad hoc* basis by methods which would not necessarily constitute a pattern for the future.

The bond money was virtually exhausted by early 1963. Hence, the Assembly had to meet in emergency session in May, 1963. It assessed $42.5 million for the two peace forces for the last six months of 1963 according to the regular scale, with a 55 percent reduction to the developing countries. In December, it appropriated $17.75 million for UNEF for 1964, but decided to allot only $15 million to carry ONUC through June, 1964.

While conditions in the Congo had improved somewhat, the Assembly's action was taken with at least one eye on its own problems. The accumulated Soviet debts for UNEF and ONUC were rapidly reaching the point at which the USSR would run the risk of losing its vote in the General Assembly under Article 19 of the Charter. The Assembly had no desire to precipitate a major political and constitutional crisis at a time when its military and financial problems in the Congo were still considerable. It was hoped that, after the Congo operation was concluded, some compromise might be arranged concerning the Soviet payments and that the Article 19 crisis could be avoided. Thus, the Assembly was in an increasingly conservative mood and the combined cash appropriations for UNEF and ONUC for 1964 amounted to less than one-fourth of those appropriated for 1963.

The threat of a constitutional and political crisis over Article 19 had another and, perhaps in the long run, more important impact upon the Assembly than reducing the appropriations for ONUC in late 1963 and 1964. New threats to the peace arose in 1962 in West New Guinea, in 1963 in Yemen, and in 1964 in Cyprus, and the UN had to make some provisions to meet its responsibilities. In West New Guinea, the UN established the UN Temporary Executive Authority (UNTEA) and arranged to have the costs shared jointly by the Netherlands and Indonesia. Similarly, in 1963, the expenses of a UN Observer Group in Yemen were split between Saudi Arabia and Egypt without cost to the UN. The expenses of the UN peace-keeping force in Cyprus were met by voluntary contributions every three months. In September, 1964, Secretary-General U Thant had a hard time raising the modest sum of $7 million needed to keep the 6,400 man force in Cyprus for another three-month period. The original motive behind the move to split the costs between the involved nations in UNTEA and in Yemen was probably to spare the UN additional financial strain at this critical juncture and to try to wrap up the Congo operation *before* Article 19 fell on the Soviets, in the hope that the latter would make some sort of voluntary payment once the operation was over. In these three cases, however, the UN took an important step away from the collective responsibility principle upon which it had insisted previously. In two cases it was only the "involved" countries that paid. In Cyprus the voluntary contributions further underscored the disintegration of the collective responsibility principle. In sum, in an effort to postpone a showdown on this principle, the UN, with United States support, created three precedents that undermined it.

By 1964, even the Secretary-General admitted that "if the UN does not settle its past, it may not have much of a future." In June, 1964 the last UN troops left the Congo, and the operation to which the USSR had been so much opposed was thus brought to an end. It was now hoped that some compromise could be reached on the Soviet debt. The usual September opening of the General Assembly was postponed until December 1 in order to give diplomats an opportunity to work behind the scenes. The United States, unsure of the support of the Afro-Asian countries and fearful of a showdown, decided not to fight the issue on its merits and would have agreed to a voluntary, unspecified Soviet payment sufficiently large to escape the sanction of Article 19. The United States and other members proposed numerous face-saving compromises to the USSR which would permit that country to make a payment without yielding its basic position that the peace-keeping operations were illegal violations of the Charter. However, no compromise was reached and as December 1 approached, positions hardened. The United States took the stand that the penalty should go into effect automatically and was determined to enforce it against the Soviet Union if the latter withheld payment. The USSR, on the other hand, insisted that a decision to suspend a member from voting could be obtained only by a two-thirds vote of the members present and voting. It based its case on Article 18 of the Charter which requires a two-thirds majority for Assembly decisions on "important" issues, including "the suspension of the rights and privileges of membership." A week before opening day, the United States declared that it would withhold pledges to the Special Fund until the Soviet Union paid enough of its arrears to avoid the application of Article 19 and the latter stated that, if it were stripped of its voting rights, it would leave the United Nations.

In order to avoid a head-on collision between the superpowers, the Secretary-General proposed on opening day that the Assembly conduct its business on a "no objection" basis, that is, without taking formal votes until some compromise on the debt issue could be hammered out. This proposal was accepted and established an uneasy truce between the superpowers during which further possibilities for compromise could be explored. The Afro-Asian nations proposed a "rescue fund" to which all members, including those in arrears on their peace-keeping assessments, would make voluntary contributions. After protracted and laborious negotiations, the Soviet Union committed itself to the Secretary-General to pledge an unspecified voluntary contribution, but refused to name the amount and date of payment, demanding in return that the Assembly resume normal business and voting procedure. The United States refused to accept this proposal, describing it as a "pig in the poke." In effect, the Soviet Union demanded the right to vote now and pay later, while the United States insisted that the Soviet Union pay first and vote later.

In the meantime, the tenuous "no vote" procedure threatened to break down when a sharp disagreement arose over one of four nonpermanent Security Council seats to be filled by December 31, 1964. While three candidates were unopposed, the fourth seat was hotly contested by Jordan and Mali. Since neither candidate was prepared to yield, the President of the Assembly, Mr. Alex Quaison-Sackey, proposed a special "consultation" procedure which, in effect, was tantamount to voting, with the single difference that the location of the ballot box was outside the Assembly hall. When three of these "straw polls" failed to break the deadlock, the two candidates reluctantly agreed to split the term.

New Year's Day of 1965 added France and ten other states to the list of members that were in danger of losing their voting rights under Article 19. Thus the crisis assumed more serious proportions since, by now, over 10 percent of the membership, including two great powers, fell under Article 19.

The "no vote" procedure continued, but under it none of the important agenda items could be touched. Shortly before the Assembly was to adjourn, the delegate of Albania threatened the precarious superpower truce by demanding an immediate resumption of normal voting procedure. The Assembly, however, in an overwhelming vote of 97 to 2, with 13 abstentions, overruled the Albanian demand, both superpowers voting with the majority. The United States, in a tactical retreat, permitted this one vote, declaring that it was merely procedural and thus did not compromise the American position on Article 19. On February 18, the General Assembly adjourned until September 1, 1965, with the main problem—the issue of Article 19— as far from solution as ever.

The Nineteenth General Assembly had thus managed to avoid an open confrontation between the superpowers over the application of Article 19. The Afro-Asian group had tried desperately to find some middle ground and had succeeded in making modest headway. The Soviet Union did offer to pledge a voluntary contribution, though it refused to name the amount and date of payment under "American blackmail." And the United States had to look on while the Soviet delegate cast his "vote" in the "consultation" over the seating of Jordan and Mali on the Security Council and had to permit a General Assembly vote to continue the "no vote" procedure.

As the Nineteenth General Assembly adjourned, a curious situation prevailed. The superpowers continued to be at odds with one another over the issue of Article 19. But the Afro-Asians were becoming increasingly frustrated with the superpowers since no important UN business could be transacted on a "no vote" basis. Hence, by early 1965, the confrontation between the two superpowers on the one hand and almost everyone else on the other had become almost as important as the U.S.-Soviet confrontation itself. The financial crisis had become a mirror of a significant political fact: the United States and the Soviet Union, if they chose to, could still virtually paralyze the more than one hundred other member states of the General Assembly. But finally, and perhaps most important, almost the entire membership *including* the superpowers made a common front against one member, Albania, which—probably prompted by Communist China—tried to precipitate a showdown that neither superpower wanted. Hence, there emerged a partial community of interest between the superpowers which made both of them rally to the defense of the United Nations itself.

What was basically at stake in the tug of war during the Nineteenth General Assembly was the principle of collective responsibility. The USSR opposed it and the United States chose not to fight for it on its merits. While the USSR's opposition was understandable, the problem of the United States was far more complex. On the one hand, the United States had a clear commitment to the principle; its support of the UNEF and ONUC financing patterns and its approval of the World Court Advisory Opinion left little doubt on that score. On the other hand, from a tactical point of view, the

United States feared that it would lose a showdown vote or, if it won, that the victory might be indecisive or even Pyrrhic. The Afro-Asians were most eager to avoid a confrontation and were deeply divided on the merits of the American position. Second, there was the nagging fear that the collective responsibility principle might not always be congruent with the United States national interest in the future. Indeed, the right to pick and choose the peace-keeping operations one supported might one day be to the Americans' advantage. These conflicting considerations led to the ambivalence that characterized the United States position.

Finally, shortly before the opening of the Twentieth General Assembly, the United States gave up the fight over Article 19. On August 16, 1965, Ambassador Arthur J. Goldberg announced that "the United States regretfully accepted the simple and inescapable fact of life that a majority of the 114 member states was unready to apply Article 19." Thus it now became unlikely that the UN would soon again venture into massive peace-keeping operations against the will of a superpower. It seemed, instead, that future operations would have to be based on a broader political consensus and be more modest in scale. It also seemed that the financial counterpart of collective responsibility, the assessment principle, would be superseded, at least temporarily, by that of voluntarism. The UN would require a period during which past gains would have to be consolidated before new advances could be made.

Conclusions

The financial crisis of the United Nations has aroused acute anxiety among many observers, who see it as the unmistakable symptom of an early death of the Organization. They point to the history of the League of Nations, maintaining that, in its case, financial atrophy was the first harbinger of doom, and claim that the same omens are now gathering over the United Nations: the penury of states and the Organization's mounting deficits.

On closer scrutiny, this analogy does not hold up. Many of the symptoms are similar, to be sure, but the root causes are quite different. The fiscal plight of the League had been the symptom of a struggle over its very existence. Many states had questioned the *raison d'être* of the League; others had tolerated it; certainly very few states wanted it to move beyond the concept of a "static conference machinery." In that sense, the League's chronic financial anemia had been the result of a struggle between nihilists and conservatives: those who would deny its existence altogether and those who would relegate it to the peripheries of their national policies. The former attitude had led to active hostility, the latter to political neglect and indifference.

The UN's financial plight is not the expression of a struggle over the Organization's existence. All states, including the Soviet Union, have accepted its presence. The struggle has moved onto a higher plane. It is now being waged between the conservatives and the liberals: those who wish to maintain the UN as a "static conference machinery," and those who wish to endow it with increasing strength and executive authority. Viewed in this light, the financial crisis of the United States does not indicate that the Organization has fallen into political collapse, but rather that the membership has not yet been willing to ratify and sustain its rise to a higher plane of development.

If one examines the superpowers' attitude in detail, it is clear that the "liberal" and "conservative" labels must be used with caution in the areas of peace-keeping and financing. It is true that the United States has generally favored the creation of peace-keeping machinery as a collective responsibility of the membership, whereas the USSR has tended to reject the assessment principle for UN peace forces. But as we look at specific cases, it is clear that the Soviet Union has not always said "no" with equal vigor. In fact, until 1963 the Soviet Union paid for a considerable number of minor peace-keeping operations that were financed through the regular budget. It acquiesced in the establishment of UNEF and actually voted for the creation of the Congo Force and only later tried to destroy it. Finally, and under great pressure, it came close to offering a payment toward UNEF and ONUC costs, although ostensibly as an unspecified and general contribution to the United Nations. Hence, the Soviet attitude has varied and can be portrayed in terms of a spectrum ranging from acquiescence through passive resistance to active obstruction. Moreover, these attitudes often changed during one operation. The changing Soviet position toward the Congo Force is a case in point.

Similarly, the states favoring UN peace-keeping operations do not always say "yes" with the same degree of enthusiasm. Some states, like the United States, support the political resolutions authorizing the establishment of the peace forces, then vote for the financing resolutions, and make payment as well. Others have second thoughts at the second stage and abstain or even vote against the financing resolutions. And some that vote "yes" in the first two stages finally refuse to make payment after all. The liberal position on peace-keeping forces also extends along a fluid continuum: enthusiastic support, moral support, and tacit consent. The more cautious form of liberalism and the permissive form of conservatism often meet in voting terms, if not in principle, on the common ground of abstention.

Thus, both "liberals" and "conservatives" have varied their position over a broad spectrum. In fact, most states have responded to specific peace-keeping cases in terms of national interest rather than abstract principle. This is particularly true of the superpowers. From the United States point of view UNEF and ONUC sealed off a "no man's land" in the cold war from a possible East-West military confrontation and reduced the likelihood of unilateral intervention by the Soviet Union. The Soviet Union could reason that UNEF and ONUC prevented Soviet bridgeheads in the Middle East and Africa. Since, in the latter case, a bridgehead had already been established and had to be liquidated under UN pressure, Soviet opposition to ONUC may have taken a more active form. Thus, the financial crisis over UNEF and ONUC is really a political crisis over the proper role and control over these forces. The Soviet Union did not oppose UNEF and ONUC because it did not want to pay for them; it did not want to pay for them because it opposed them.

No one knows how the United States would react to a UN peace-keeping operation that conflicted with its national interests, because to date the United States has never been on the wrong end of a UN police action. In part, this fact is due to good luck. If Kasavubu had been killed in the Congo instead of Lumumba, the ONUC operation might have provided an interesting test of the American commitment to the principle of collective responsibility in the financing of peace-keeping operations. American voting supremacy in the UN . . . has also been important in preventing issues like the 1954 coup in Guatemala from being considered at any length by the UN. What the United States would do in a minority position against a UN operation is difficult to estimate, but . . . the U.S. has not hesitated to attack UN operations contrary to its national interest in the far less sensitive economic and social areas of the organization's work. The point here is not to indict the policies of the superpowers, but to suggest that in peace-keeping matters it is misleading to associate the United States or Soviet Union too closely with any philosophical position toward the UN in the abstract. Each case is decided in accordance with the national interest as it arises.

While the positions of the superpowers have had little to do with finances per se, in the case of many of the middle and smaller powers, a weak financial position and the relatively large sums involved have played a far larger, and in some instances, even a decisive role. It is a fact, for example, that in terms of percentages of their gross national products twenty-one nations are called upon to make larger contributions to total UN costs than the United States. Hence, while the financial crisis of the UNEF and ONUC is caused primarily by the political conservatism of the few, it has been deepened by the financial limitations of the many.

The toughest problem, therefore, is that of coming to grips with the politically motivated deficits. One way to face up to the challenge completely would be to construct a scale which permitted a member to refuse payment for a peace-keeping operation it opposed. Such a solution would ignore the message of the Advisory Opinion that *all* member states should pay and would instead squarely confront the political reality that no power, certainly no great power, can be coerced into payment. It is also important to make a distinction between passive and active opposition. If opposition to nonpayment remains limited, as was the Soviet Union's opposition to UNEF, supporters may wish to override it provided they are ready to pay the share of the recalcitrant power. But if they override active opposition, they may drive

the obstructionist power out of the UN altogether unless they are reasonably sure that the opposition will revert to a milder form, as the USSR's did
in the Congo. The central truth that emerges is that the launching of an
operation in the face of either passive or active opposition by a major power
is in fact to ask for a financial crisis and any state which asks for such a crisis
may have to be prepared to bail the Organization out. At the heart of this
problem is the stark fact of international life that no power, least of all a
superpower, will adopt or easily acquiesce in paying for a policy which it
considers inimical to its national interest.

17

THE SYMBOLIC SIGNIFICANCE OF
THE UNITED NATIONS

Inis L. Claude, Jr.*

For twenty-five years, the United Nations has been a part of the American scene. . . . As the host country and the most prominent and powerful
member, the United States has displayed an unusual degree of interest in
and concern about the world organization. While such sentiments as pride
of authorship and presumption of ownership may have entered into the
American attitude toward the United Nations, the dominant factor making
for strong interest and active concern has probably been the novelty of the
engagement of the United States in a massive effort to organize the operation
of the international system. . . .

The attitudes and expectations directed toward the world organization by
interested Americans have, naturally enough, been mixed and variable. Considerable currency has been gained by the notion that the United Nations
was oversold to the American people in the beginning. . . . As I read the
record, the potentialities of the United Nations were described by most
officials and commentators with restrained optimism and were regarded by
most Americans with moderate pessimism. The United Nations appears to
have been presented and accepted as an experiment worth trying, not as a
panacea worthy of uncritical confidence. The mood of 1945 was one of resolution to make a determined effort to save the world from chaos, not one of
naïve conviction that an easy and infallible method had been found. Never-

* Inis L. Claude, Jr., "The Symbolic Significance of the United Nations," *The Virginia
Quarterly Review*, Vol. 47, No. 4 (Autumn 1971), pp. 481–504. Reprinted by permission.

theless, it is true that many Americans, both in official positions and in private life, initially approached the United Nations in a spirit of idealism. . . .

From the inception of the United Nations, Americans have been strongly inclined to treat the question of the attitude one should adopt toward the organization as an ideological matter, an issue of political faith and morals. This suggests that the appropriate imagery of the United Nations is that of a church rather than a political institution. The organization has its creed of orthodoxy, its conventional liturgy, its component of hypocrisy, and its gap between the performance willed by the spirit and that dictated by the weakness of the flesh. The question of conviction about the United Nations has frequently been put in terms of believing *in* rather than believing *that,* thus indicating that the issue is thought to fall within the realm of political theology. The ecclesiastical image is further reflected in the assumption of true believers that political righteousness consists in faithful attendance at and generous support of the United Nations; a properly fervent supporter can be counted on to take both his troubles and his offerings to the United Nations and leave them there. The United Nations has attracted an ample quota of Americans dedicated to the idea that it is not merely a Good Thing but a Holy Cause, and prepared to wage evangelical campaigns on its behalf. Whether imbued with faith that it will save mankind from disaster or motivated by hope that it might be enabled to do so, they have invested a great deal of idealism in support of the United Nations.

Negative attitudes toward the United Nations within the United States have been no less ideological in character. If the United Nations is a church, it is for some Americans the wrong church, leading its adherents to whore after false gods and to abandon the true faith. Friends of the organization approve it as a symbol of progress toward One World; enemies deplore it as a symbol of the destruction of National Sovereignty, or the insidious advance of International Communism, or the undermining of European Civilization. The view of the United Nations as the embodiment of lofty idealism is countered if not matched in American public opinion by the conception of it as a manifestation of nefarious conspiracy or utopian foolishness. Against the vision of the organization as the hope of mankind is set the notion that it is a snare, a delusion, and a confounded nuisance.

If enthusiastic dedication to the United Nations has declined in the United States, as I think it has, the trend has run not toward militant ideological opposition but toward the dominance of indifference; the organization has tended to be neglected, not rejected. Ideological passions regarding the United Nations have cooled, not so much because agreement has been reached as to the values that the organization should or does epitomize as because it has come to be considered less relevant to the important issues of world affairs. The United Nations has been relegated to a less prominent place on the agenda of public interest and concern.

Is this an unfortunate development? It is if it reflects an actual decline in the usefulness and usability of the United Nations for worthwhile international purposes. To some degree, this is the case; some of the loss of popular interest in the United Nations, favorable and unfavorable, must be considered symptomatic of the diminishing effectiveness of the organization in producing results that excite either strong approval or strong disapproval. On the other hand, this development may tell us more about the ideologically-based attitudes of friends and enemies of the United Nations than about the evolution of the organization itself. If the organization has not achieved what its supporters hoped or its critics feared, and has thus contributed to the lessening of their pro and con passions, this may well reflect not upon its performance but upon their expectations, and it may mean not that the United Nations is in decline but that its viewers are in process of receiving salutary re-education as to how they should look at and what they can reasonably and realistically expect from international institutions.

On the whole, I am inclined to regard public indifference to the United Nations, involving the diminution of both dedicated support and passionate distrust, as a healthy development. This judgment is based on the premise that the world organization is inappropriately cast as an object of ideological fervor. . . .

Nobody asks whether I am "for" or "against" Congress, or the state board of education, or the local fire department. I am presumed, correctly, to take the view that such agencies as these are parts of the necessary mechanism for carrying on the public business, to regard it as normal that their policies and acts should sometimes win my approval and sometimes arouse my wrath, and to consider that it is more sensible for me to ponder the question of how I can influence their performance than to raise the question of whether they should continue to exist. We take such agencies of domestic government for granted. We have no illusions that they will achieve the definitive solution of the problems with which they deal, and we are frequently dissatisfied with their efforts, but few of us are tempted to imagine that a complex society could dispense with the imperfect apparatus that they constitute. Despite the important truth that it asserted, Ernest Renan's famous maxim that the existence of a nation is "un plébiscite de tous les jours" was profoundly wrong in one respect: no nation, certainly not one that has become a state, can afford the persistent reopening of the question of the propriety of its existence; if it is necessary constantly to ask the question, the answer is assuredly negative.

The analogy is applicable, I think, to the United Nations. That organization will have achieved a firm footing when it has come to be taken for granted, when it is routinely regarded as a part of the apparatus for the conduct of international relations, when nobody feels compelled to consider or announce whether he is "for" or "against" it—when, in short, it comes to be treated and evaluated as a political institution, in pragmatic terms, rather than as a Cause, in ideological terms. This is the proposition that underlies my belief that popular indifference toward the United Nations is essentially a good thing. . . .

To a considerable degree, the recent decline of popular interest in the United Nations does, I think, represent the development of a more matter-of-fact attitude toward the organization. At the very least, it tends to free responsible American public officials to treat the United Nations less as the symbol of an ideological crusade and more as an instrument to be appraised according to estimates of its utility. The shift is a partial one; from the beginning, American popular opinion and public policy have been influenced in some measure by calculations of the practical merits of the United Nations. Despite verbal emphasis upon what the organization has been thought to stand for, the actual behavior of the United States in and toward the United Nations has never been altogether divorced from consideration of what practical objectives can and cannot be achieved within the network of facilities that it provides for the managers of international affairs. The weakening of pressures against the dominance of such an instrumentalist view is, from my standpoint, to be welcomed.

Nevertheless, it would be unrealistic to deny that the United Nations has had, still has, and will continue to have symbolic significance that is only imperfectly related to the shifting boundaries of its potentialities and accomplishments as a working institution. What it is believed, or hoped, or feared that the organization symbolizes is no less important an object of study than its operating experience. The symbolic meaning attributed to the United Nations by Americans has some impact upon the character of American participation in the processes and programs of the organization. More than this, it provides a valuable clue to American perceptions of the nature of the international system and of the necessary and proper rôle of the United States in that system. Recognizing the persistence of the ideological, as distinguished from the pragmatic, approach to the United Nations, I propose to exploit its analytical value. This requires brushing aside such questions as what the United Nations is, what it does, and how it can be used, in favor of questions pertaining to its symbolic significance. What is it taken to *mean?* What image of the world does it convey? What changes in the world does it stand for? . . .

II

During the period of the designing, building, and launching of the United Nations, the organization symbolized above all the commitment of the United States to permanent involvement and reliably continuous and vigorous leadership in global affairs. In sponsoring its creation, in joining it, and in accepting the rôle of host state, Americans were deliberately affirming such an intention; they regarded the United Nations as a vehicle for the solemnization and the institutionalization of the resolve that the United States should henceforth play a major rôle in international relations.

The self-consciousness of this symbolic act can be understood only in the light of American history and of the reaction of Americans to the results of their twentieth-century performance in world affairs. The United States had a tradition of isolationism, dating back to its origin as an independent state, that argued against any avoidable involvement in the central arena of international politics. It had undertaken, in the early twentieth century, to play an auxiliary rôle in that arena, exercising the discretion to intervene on an emergency basis, but without the expectation of sustained involvement. Although President Wilson had led the United States into World War I on that basis, he had changed his mind before the fighting was finished; pondering the future requirements of world order, he had concluded that the avoidance of major war would depend heavily upon the willingness of the United States to serve continuously as a leading member of an organized community of states, conspicuously dedicated to upholding world order against all who might attempt to disrupt it. This was, in my view, the central meaning of Wilson's scheme for the League of Nations. For him, the League was to be a symbol of the transformation of American foreign policy, of America's adoption of the position and rôle that he had come to consider requisite for the maintenance of global peace and order. Wilson's campaign for American adhesion to the League conveyed this message; he warned that the investment of blood and treasure in World War I would prove to have been wasted, that the horrors of major war would recur, if the United States did not, by joining the League, commit itself to the policy that he advocated. . . .

. . . .

[But Wilson's advice was rejected. The League failed; World War II broke out.] What conclusions did Americans draw from [this experience]? Isolationism was discredited. It had neither prevented wars nor prevented American involvement in those wars. The isolation of the United States from the disasters of international politics no longer appeared feasible. The auxiliary rôle seemed hardly more attractive. The United States had eventually intervened in both global conflicts, but it had risked doing so too late to save the situation, and the uncertainty as to whether it would intervene at all or in time to be effective had encouraged aggressors to drive ahead. The United States had helped to cause these terrible wars by not helping to prevent them; if it had not tempted potential disrupters of the peace to disregard the weight of American opposition, the United States might well have forestalled the execution of their plans. By its refusal to commit itself to join in action against aggression, the United States had not avoided the necessity to fight, but had contributed to the emergence of that necessity. A contrary policy of promising and threatening to fight in resistance to aggression, to do what in fact it ultimately did, might well have averted the occasions for fighting. In the acid of this logic, the virtues of the auxiliary rôle were converted to vices. The retention of national freedom of action took on the appearance of international irresponsibility; desirable flexibility of policy came to appear as disastrous indecisiveness; commendable maneuvering to avoid being drawn into other peoples' wars was translated as giving the green light to those ambitious for global conquest. The United States should deter aggressors, not defeat them by belated and unpredictable entry into the ranks of their opponents. Through all of this ran the confident assumption that American power was formidable enough to make the decisive difference; in two World Wars, the military strength of the United States had turned the tide. The tragedy lay in the fact that this power had been used only to affect the ending of the struggles, not to inhibit their beginning.

This analysis boiled down to the conclusion that Wilson had been right as to what the United States could and should do in the world. He had urged the country to symbolize its adoption of a new rôle of leadership in keeping the world at peace by joining the League of Nations; the League now became the symbol of the folly and irresponsibility of the United States, of America's relinquishment of the task that only it could have performed. Small wonder then that the United Nations became the symbol of America's repentance, its enlightenment as to what was required for maintaining world order, and its determination to undertake the responsibility that it had previously spurned! Among Americans, the dominant meaning attached to ratification of the United Nations Charter was that it proclaimed the acceptance by the United States of the global rôle that it now believed it should have accepted in Wilson's time and at his urging.

This was not a matter of arrogant self-assertion, of claiming a right to run the world. Rather, it was a matter of acceding to international demand, of acknowledging a duty to take the lead in saving the world. . . . The twin themes of the San Francisco Conference in 1945 were that the defection of the United States had doomed the League to failure and that only the loyal adherence of the United States to the new organizational plan could give the world a chance to achieve peace and order under the United Nations. Getting the United States firmly and irrevocably committed to playing an active rôle in world politics was generally regarded as the central task of that Conference. If ever an international leader was "elected," it was the United States at San Francisco. Fears directed toward the United States related to what it might refrain from doing; hopes directed toward it related to what it might be prepared to do. . . . Many Americans, impressed by Woodrow Wilson but influenced by Henry Cabot Lodge, had been willing to say "Yes, but" to the League. A generation later, the prevailing assumption was that nothing short of a rousing American "Yes, indeed!" would suffice to breathe life into the United Nations.

A second—and, as I shall argue, secondary—element in the early symbolism of the United Nations was the view that the new organization stood for, and promised, a new and better kind of international system. The United Nations was identified with One World. Some men thought in terms of structure and process; World Federation was on the way, a universal Rule of Law was in prospect, or a system of institutionalized International Cooperation was being established. Others concentrated more on policy and program; aggression was to be frustrated, national self-determination was to be promoted, human rights were to be safeguarded, and economic and social welfare was to be fostered. The Charter was widely regarded as a definitive affirmation of the ideals of a nascent international community. One could retain his doubts and fears, even his sophisticated awareness of complexities and difficulties, and yet treat the United Nations as a powerful symbol of human hopes and aspirations for peace, justice, and welfare. . . .

. . . .

After World War I, British and French leaders had been convinced that a drastic change in American foreign policy was the key to future stability. Given such a change, the system might be improved and even transformed; without such a change, the system was doomed to operate in the bad old way. This was the gist of the argument that they addressed to Wilson: only a steadfastly committed United States could prevent the recurrence of international disaster. Wilson countered by turning the argument around. His position was, in effect, that only a transformation of the system would induce the United States—or induce or enable him to induce the United States—to take a leading part in the regular operation of the system. He insisted that America would not and probably should not join the old system, but held out the hope that he might persuade his country to join a new, more reputable, and more promising system. The Allies sought the transformation of American foreign policy in order to effect the transformation of the global system; Wilson sought the transformation of the system as the prerequisite for the transformation of America's rôle in the world. The fundamental revision of the system that was symbolized by the League was probably necessary, as Wilson believed, to induce American participation, but events proved that it was not sufficient, as Wilson hoped, to produce that result. Moreover, the experience of the interwar period tended to confirm the conviction of the Allies that the system could not be successfully transformed unless the United States were willing to undertake a new rôle.

This background provided the basis for the strategy of peace-building that was adopted during and after World War II. The objective remained that of securing the commitment of the United States to active international leadership. The method employed was to assure the United States that its leadership was sought not in the bad old system but in a bright new system. In short, Wilson's prescription was again applied—and this time it worked. The United Nations symbolized the purification of international relations, the creation of a global system fit for American participation and worthy of American dedication. The United States responded, as Wilson had vainly hoped that it would do a generation earlier, by taking the position that membership involved not the abandonment but the fulfillment of its principles, that the engagement represented not the world's dragging the United States down to the level of old-style power politics but America's lifting the world up to the level of co-operative endeavor to achieve justice and peace. The two transformations, of American foreign policy and of the international system, were envisaged as having been successfully linked in this second attempt. The United Nations was the symbol of this dual success.

In this original conception of the symbolic significance of the United Nations, the emphasis lay upon the positive, constructive tasks that were to be performed in order to promote the realization of a just and stable world order. One thought in terms of building a peaceful world. States were to join as partners, with the United States taking the leading rôle, in assuming the responsibilities and carrying the burdens entailed by this ambitious project. The evils of international relations—anarchy, oligarchy, and wide-spread misery—were to be reduced by a vigorous and concerted multilateral effort. The anarchic element, war, was to be tackled directly by the mobilization of persuasion, pressure, and—where required—coercion, an enterprise in which the power of the United States ranked as a critical resource. International oligarchy, identified as colonialism and other forms of imperialism, was to be ameliorated by programs looking toward the preparation of suppressed and underprivileged peoples for the exercise of national self-determination. The inadequacies of the resources and capabilities of these and other peoples for liberating themselves from the bonds of poverty and associated ills were to be remedied by co-operative assistance, in which the contribution of the United States would be a vital element. In all of these undertakings, heavy reliance would have to be placed upon the power, the wealth, the political initiative, and the political support of the United States. The United Nations was viewed as the symbol and vehicle of a campaign to create the conditions of peace by the positive action of states. . . .

III

This version of the meaning to be attached to the United Nations and to American membership in that organization has not been abandoned, but it has lost its standing as the unquestionably orthodox view. The chief contender for predominance is one that has a distinctly negative flavor, as contrasted with the positive emphasis of the originally dominant viewpoint. Positive and negative elements have always been, and continue to be, mixed in the symbolism of the United Nations. The point I wish to make is that the former have tended to become less, and the latter to become more, prominent.

The negative syndrome may be analyzed, first, with reference to its implications concerning the position and policy of the United States, both in the United Nations and in the world at large. American membership in the organization is interpreted less as a proclamation of commitment to act than as a registration of restraint. What the United States is willing to refrain from doing replaces what it is prepared to do as the key question. The United Nations Charter is conceived mainly as a list of restrictions laid upon states, and the contribution of the United States to the success of the organization is measured by its acceptance of limitations and prohibitions stated in the Charter or in the resolutions adopted by organs of the United Nations. The ultimate responsibility of the United States is to refrain from intervening, particularly with military force, in external situations unless such intervention is authorized or demanded by the United Nations. The proper rôle of the United States in the world organization is no longer conceived as that of doing what no other state can do, but, in this version, as that of refraining from doing what every other state should also refrain from doing. What is wanted from the United States is not dynamic leadership but faithful followership.

It is hardly surprising that this shift of emphasis concerning the symbolic significance of American membership in the United Nations should have occurred among leaders of other states. International political memories are notoriously short, and a quarter of a century has gone by since the world was preoccupied with the urgent importance of securing a guarantee that the United States would assume primary responsibility for action to maintain world order. For most states, the world has come to seem more settled and the need for a vigilant and powerful protector of the global system less pressing; the possibility of worrying about irresponsible American action instead of irresponsible American inaction is a luxury of this situation. Acknowledgment of the special status of a great power never comes easily, and there is gratification in being able to put such a power in its proper place, which is of course the place shared by ordinary states. The natural discomfort of dependence is to be endured only so long as abnormal circumstances require it; when the sense of need for protection diminishes, the great power's contribution is likely to be recorded as the imposition of imperialist rule.

America's performance of the rôle that it was elected to play at the end of World War II has not been flawless. . . . On balance, however, the record of the United States as the leader of postwar efforts to achieve a modicum of international order has been, in my view, a creditable one. The fact that this leadership was essential is now obscured by the fact that it has been successful. Widespread doubts that it is now being exercised wisely, whether justified or not, are permitted by the fact that it has been exercised faithfully. American leadership is regarded as eligible for harsh criticism less because it is considered unnecessary than because its availability is taken for granted. While it may be unrealistic to expect the world to express appreciation for what the United States has done in the past twenty-five years, it is by no means unthinkable that the world's true evaluation of American leadership may be revealed by insistent demands for more of the same. It is not difficult to conceive of developments that might elicit evidence that most statesmen's concern about the misuse of American power is subordinate to their fear of its disuse. For the present, however, the international emphasis lies upon the dangers posed by American activity on the global stage, and the United Nations is widely conceived as the symbol of the multilateral constraint that ought to be brought to bear upon, and accepted by, the United States.

The shift to negative symbolism has been quite as pronounced among Americans as among foreigners, and its importance is probably greater on the domestic than on the foreign scene. For a variety of reasons, the general American disposition to engage in strenuous international activity has diminished. The fear that the United States might fail to do what it should do has largely given way to the conviction that it has been doing what it should have abstained from doing. Preventing unwise or improper American action looms as more important than facilitating necessary and proper action.

The reasons for this alteration of attitude are numerous and complex, and only a sketchy analysis will be offered here. One generation of Americans is tired and discouraged—weary of the carrying of burdens and the running of risks, nostalgic for the blissful days of freedom from responsibility for the state of the world, wistful for a "normalcy" that shows no signs of arriving, apprehensive about the domestic costs of continuing the effort to hold the world together, and resentful of America's being too little assisted, too little understood and appreciated, and too much suspected and condemned. Here we encounter the self-image of the overworked, underpaid, and much-maligned policeman. Another generation has never known an America that threatened world peace by weakness, neglect, and indifference, and it tends to interpret postwar American policy as that of a bumptious imperialist, ambitious to dominate and enamored of military action. From this perspective, the American image is that of the overweening tyrant, not the over-burdened policeman; what happened at the end of World War II was that the United States arrogated to itself the right to run the world, not that it accepted the duty to save the world. The problem is defined in terms of police brutality rather than of police fatigue. The United States is not so much overextended as underdisciplined, and its situation calls less for sympathy and relief than for repentance and restraint. These two points of view are imperfectly aligned with age groups, though they are related to the different experiences of Americans divided by the rough category of generation. Contradictory as they are, they point in the same direction: whether impelled by weariness in well doing or by a sense of guilt for wrong doing, whether it be undertaken as a prudent reduction of obligations or as a penitent renunciation of pretensions, the United States should restrict its engagement in international affairs.

This conclusion, however reached, finds expression in a drastically revised version of the meaning that should be attached to American membership in the United Nations. The world organization becomes, for Americans, a symbol of the inhibitions that their country should respect, of the limitations that it should observe, in the conduct of foreign policy. Membership should be taken to imply America's surrender of the right of unilateral intervention in situations external to itself, and acknowledgment of multilateral authority to restrict and regulate American activism. It is not clear whether the United States should do what the United Nations authorizes or orders it to do—would the approval or sponsorship of the organization have been recognized as having purified and justified the American entanglement in Vietnam, or would it have been cited as evidence that the United States had corrupted the United Nations? It is certain, however, that, according to this view, the United States should not intrude into external situations without the blessing of the organization. The United Nations is the symbol of what the United States must not do.

It is also, for those of this persuasion, a symbol of what the United States *need* not do. Advocates of American retrenchment, thinking more wishfully than realistically, have displayed an inclination to regard the United Nations as a substitute for the United States, eligible to take up the burdens that this country might cast off. "Let the United Nations do it" is a slogan of those who are more weary of bearing responsibility than concerned about the responsibility's being successfully borne, whose eagerness for abdication surpasses their interest in the problem of succession. There is a certain irony in the fact that the United Nations, originally conceived as a device for insuring steadfast American involvement in world affairs, is now increasingly regarded by Americans as a means for encouraging and facilitating their retreat from such involvement.

More broadly, this newly prominent syndrome represents a shift toward an essentially negative conception of the task of achieving international peace. It substitutes pacifism for peace-building. The American contribution to peace is put in terms of withdrawing from foreign entanglements, minimizing international commitments, minding one's own national business, reducing military expenditures, and limiting executive authority to respond to international exigencies. Peace is seen as a function of what states are incapacitated for doing and resolved not to do. The United Nations is conceived no longer as a state-building, state-activating, state-mobilizing enterprise, but as an agency for restraining, limiting, and—in some vague sense —replacing states. The state is regarded as an evil to be suppressed and supplanted. A sort of zero-sum game is thought to be in progress between the United Nations and its member states, a game in which a gain in the strength and effectiveness of one side involves a corresponding loss on the other side; the attainment of world peace is considered dependent upon the flourishing of the United Nations—which means the withering away of the state. In these terms, the United Nations is the symbol of a movement to achieve peace and order by controlling and subordinating states, and ultimately by putting them out of business. In such a scheme, submissiveness is the criterion of the loyalty of the performance of any state, including the United States.

IV

In my judgment, the first of the two versions of the symbolic significance of the United Nations that I have discussed is both more realistic as a description of the enterprise in which the world is engaged and more convincing as an approach to peace. The United Nations is in fact not a competitor of states but a stimulator of states; its business is not to put them out of business, but to help them to help themselves and each other to develop their capacities for handling their business. The antithesis between positive and negative approaches to peace is ultimately false, since they are related as the two sides of a coin, but placing emphasis upon the responsibilities that states should assume, rather than upon the restraints that they should accept, seems to me a sound approach to the ordering of international relations. World peace is not so much a status quo to be protected by the dictates of a multilateral nay-sayer as a situation to be promoted by the action of states cognizant of their stake in the state of the world. Such success as the United Nations may have in the building of a peaceful world will depend upon its ability to inspire the positive action of states.

In particular, the success of the United Nations will be determined by what the United States is able and willing to do. American restraint is obviously essential; both in the national interest and in the interest of world peace, it is important that the United States refrain from acting foolishly or wickedly. To say that not just any American action will conduce to international order is not to say, however, that the prime requirement for peace is to establish safeguards, domestic and international, against improper or imprudent action by the United States. An America preoccupied with the problem of avoiding mistakes and abuses will not break the peace, but is very likely to permit it to be broken. American innocence is not enough; American responsibility is the critical ingredient in any workable formula for world peace in our time. The world is more likely to survive unwise American activity than unwise American passivity.

No formula is available for the easy and certain calculation of what the United States should and should not do to enhance the prospects for a stable international order. The standard conception of "good citizenship" in the United Nations demands that a member state be respectful of and deferential toward the organization, obey its rules, accept its decisions, and support its programs. These things are important, but perhaps less so than another contribution that falls peculiarly within the province of a major power such as the United States: to work at establishing and maintaining the kind of world situation that permits the United Nations to survive and to have the chance to accomplish something. Performance of this task may not be consistently compatible with observance of the rules of "good citizenship" described above. It may sometimes require taking actions that are unpopular among members of the United Nations and that constitute bypassing rather than utilization of the organization. The truest form of great-power support for the United Nations may involve not heeding its resolutions or funding its programs but providing a favorable international context for its operation.

This is clearly not a task for the United States alone, but for all major powers, including particularly the Soviet Union. Despite all the global troubles that can be attributed to antagonism between the United States and the Soviet Union, it must be said that these two superpowers have performed the task rather well, in rivalry more than in partnership. In pursuing the arms race, for instance, they have ignored or violated many resolutions of the General Assembly, but they have stabilized the international situation to the degree necessary for the survival and development of the United Nations. Rivalry between the giants, originally dreaded as the nemesis of the world organization, has in fact proved to be its principal dynamic force. Thus far, the survival of the United Nations has depended far more upon the kind of world we have than the survival of the latter has depended upon the United Nations. The maintenance of the kind of world in which it has been possible for the United Nations to take root has been, under all the circumstances, a remarkable achievement—which should be credited primarily to the United States and the Soviet Union.

To divide this credit between the superpowers is not to insist or to concede that it should be distributed equally. Both have contributed something, positively and negatively, but the record seems to me to confirm the general international judgment expressed at the end of both World Wars: the conviction that the basic requirement for global order is the firm and resolute commitment of the United States to active leadership in world affairs. No alternative leader, equally dedicated to generally acceptable international ideals and equally capable of promoting them, has appeared; the United Nations has neither found nor demonstrated the potentiality to become a substitute for the United States.

Americans today are tired, disillusioned, confused, and divided. They are a captive audience for a "peace movement" that conceives peace in narrow and negative terms—that interprets peace as the immediate or nearly immediate cessation of fighting by one of the two sides involved in the Indochinese struggle, that concentrates on peace *now* and peace *there,* and that defines the essential American contribution to peace in terms of what the United States should stop doing, refrain from undertaking again, and diminish its capability for attempting in the future. They are confronted with a "peace movement" that seeks to intimidate those whom it may not be able to persuade, that asks while arrogantly refusing to take "No" for an answer, that proclaims the right of dissent while rejecting the possibility that decent and responsible men might dissent from its dissent, and that threatens to destroy the capacity of the United States to follow any approach to peace other than its own. Understandably, Americans are tempted to adopt a short-range and narrow view of peace, and one that requires only that the United States exhibit a virtuous passivity.

Peace, however, is too important a matter to be left to those who think that they are pacifists. It is not a "whether" issue but a "how" problem. It is not a matter of local cease-fire but of global stability. It is not an immediate withdrawal but a long-term building project. Nobody knows with certainty how to achieve world peace; there is no necessary correlation between passionate commitment to the idea of peace and intelligent understanding of the problem of peace. . . . Only one thing seems to me reasonably certain: the future peace of the world depends more heavily upon the vigilance, far-sightedness, wisdom, courage, persistence, and power of the United States than upon any other factor. The founders of the League of Nations and the United Nations were on the right track, I think, when they undertook to make those organizations serve as symbols of an American commitment to active leadership in the quest for a just and lasting peace.

≥Part Three≤

The Power Problem and
The Power Patterns

❧8❧

Collective Security
and Sanctions

So long as a multiple state system continues to exist, and with it the danger for any state that it may be attacked or involved in hostilities with others, the problem of security is always of prime concern. States have three basic security options in a multiple system: unilateralism ("to go it alone"), alliances with states threatened by the same enemies (balance of power), or collective security via a League or United Nations. While neither the League Covenant nor the UN Charter envisaged frequent need to resort to collective security, both contained clear pledges of collective support against any unprovoked aggression, if the need arose. One vital difference between such pledges and the support due allies under alliance pledges was that the aggressor, since unknown before the event, could turn out to be a nation not otherwise hostile. One might even be expected to fight a friend.

President Woodrow Wilson had the most to do with creating the League and therefore the most to do with launching this new, experimental pattern for assuring national security on a collective, world basis. In the first selection, "Collective Security vs. Balance of Power," Wilson, in one of his best remembered speeches in favor of the new approach, argues that Germany would "never have begun the war" (World War I) could she have foreseen the great coalition she would be opposed by. Wilson was certain that neither unilateralism as isolationism (with each nation for itself), nor balance of power alliances (which he considered tended to produce evenly divided blocs) could

229

prevent new wars. While he did not believe that the use of force by nations could be abolished, he did think that force could be collectivized in order to bring maximum pressure against an aggressor from the outset of hostilities. If an aggressor was almost certain of the armed opposition of a worldwide coalition *from the beginning,* in most cases aggression would not even occur. Where it did occur, it could be suppressed more readily and effectively.

The second selection, "A Critique of Collective Security," is by Roland N. Stromberg, who has written extensively on this subject. Stromberg's selection, taken from the concluding chapter of his book, has the advantage of including a perspective based on some four decades of experience with collective security, including the Korean War which was the first full venture in armed sanctions. Stromberg's comment that collective security becomes "feasible only where a very old and stable political delimitation of peoples, with boundaries long unchallenged, exists," should be compared against Wilson's assumptions on "land titles." Both Wilson and Stromberg, in order to assess collective security's possibilities, are led to analyze the basic nature of international relations and the dilemmas confronting states in following reasonable security-oriented foreign policies. Compare their thinking against the writers in Chapter 1 and against the argument over the Vietnam War in later chapters.

Note that the newer tendencies of the UN, as brought out in Chapter 7, reveal a stress on UN nonfighting forces which can help end hostilities in the many cases where fighting occurs but the right and wrong of the situation are obscure. It is for these kinds of hostilities that collective security is most obviously inappropriate for reasons which Stromberg gives. (Compare his remarks with Claude's views given in Chapter 7.) With these analyses in mind we can appreciate better why collective security has been so little attempted in practice.

Collective sanctions may not be taken all the way to armed force, either because economic sanctions are considered sufficient to curb the behavior of the wrong-doer, or because there is no willingness to take the final step. The League's sanctions against Italy over Ethiopia were restricted to economic measures. And in the UN's efforts to force Rhodesian compliance with its resolutions, the same restrictions have been in effect.

In the third selection, the "Third Report of the UN Committee on Rhodesian Sanctions," the nature of the argument is revealed in the debate over that report in the Security Council's committee. Whether Rhodesia's actions, entirely confined within her own frontiers—and however reprehensible on a moral basis—should properly have been considered a "threat to the peace" is another question altogether.

18

COLLECTIVE SECURITY VS. BALANCE OF POWER

WOODROW WILSON[*]

If Germany had dreamed that anything like the greater part of the world would combine against her, she never would have begun the war, and she did not dare to let the opinion of mankind crystallize against her by the discussion of the purposes which she had in mind. What I want to point out to you to-night is that we are making a fundamental choice. You have either got to have the old system, of which Germany was the perfect flower, or you have got to have a new system. You cannot have a new system unless you provide a substitute, an adequate substitute, for the old, and when certain of our fellow citizens take the position that we do not want to go into any combination at all but want to take care of ourselves, all I have to say to them is that this is exactly the German position. . . .

The old system was, Be ready, and we can be ready. I have heard gentlemen say, "America can take care of herself." Yes, she can take care of herself. Every man would have to train to arms. We would have to have a great standing army. We would have to have accumulations of military material such as Germany used to have. We would enjoy the luxuries of taxes even higher than we pay now. We could accumulate our force, and then our force would have to be directed by some kind of sufficiently vigorous central power. You would have a military government in spirit if not in form. No use having a fighting Nation if there is not somebody to swing it. If you do not want your President to be a representative of the civil purposes of this country, you can turn him into merely a commander in chief, ready to fight the world. But if you did nobody would recognize America in those strange and altered circumstances. All the world would stand at amaze and say, "Has America forgotten everything that she ever professed?" The picture is one that every American repudiates; and I challenge any man who has that purpose at the back of his thought to avow it. If he comes and tells you that America must stand alone and take care of herself, ask him how it is going to be done, and he will not dare tell you, because you would show him the door and say, "We do not know any such America."

[*] Woodrow Wilson, Address at Coliseum, Sioux Falls, South Dakota, Sept. 8, 1919, from *Addresses of President Wilson,* Senate Document No. 120, 66th Congress, 1st Session, Government Printing Office, Washington, 1919, pp. 83, 85–86, 88.

Yet we cannot do without force. You cannot establish land titles, as I have expressed it, and not maintain them. Suppose that the land titles of South Dakota were disturbed. Suppose the farm lines were moved, say, ten feet. You know what would happen. Along every fence line you would see farmers perching with guns on their knees. The only reason they are not perching now is that there are land deeds deposited in a particular place, and the whole majesty and force and judicial system of the State of South Dakota are behind the titles. Very well, we have got to do something like that internationally. You cannot set up Poland, whom all the world through centuries has pitied and sympathized with, as the owner of her property and not have somebody take care that her title deeds are respected. You cannot establish freedom, my fellow citizens, without force, and the only force you can substitute for an armed mankind is the concerted force of the combined action of mankind through the instrumentality of all the enlightened Governments of the world. This is the only conceivable system that you can substitute for the old order of things which brought the calamity of another war upon us. Your choice is between the League of Nations and Germanism. I have told you what I mean by Germanism—taking care of yourselves, being armed and ready, having a chip on your shoulder, thinking of nothing but your own rights and never thinking of the rights of anybody else, thinking that you were put into this world to see that American might was asserted and forgetting that American might ought never to be used against the weak, ought never to be used in an unjust cause, ought never to be used for aggression; ought to be used with the heart of humanity beating behind it.

Sometimes people call me an idealist. Well, that is the way I know I am an American. America, my fellow citizens—I do not say it in disparagement of any other great people—America is the only idealistic Nation in the world. When I speak practical judgments about business affairs, I can only guess whether I am speaking the voice of America or not, but when I speak the ideal purposes of history I know that I am speaking the voice of America, because I have saturated myself since I was a boy in the records of that spirit, and everywhere in them there is this authentic tone of the love of justice and the service of humanity. If by any mysterious influence of error America should not take the leading part in this new enterprise of concerted power, the world would experience one of those reversals of sentiment, one of those penetrating chills of reaction, which would lead to a universal cynicism, for if America goes back upon mankind, mankind has no other place to turn. It is the hope of Nations all over the world that America will do this great thing. . . .

I can not understand the psychology of men who are resisting it. I can not understand what they are afraid of, unless it is that they know physical force and do not understand moral force. Moral force is a great deal more powerful than physical. Govern the sentiments of mankind and you govern mankind. Govern their fears, govern their hopes, determine their fortunes, get them together in concerted masses, and the whole thing sways like a team. Once get them suspecting one another, once get them antagonizing one another, and society itself goes to pieces. We are trying to make a society instead of a set of barbarians out of the governments of the world.

19

A CRITIQUE OF COLLECTIVE SECURITY

ROLAND N. STROMBERG*

"Collective security" has never been precisely defined,[1] and it has meant several different things, some of them nearly opposites. We have certainly noted at least three meanings: (a) the original, pristine, and idealistic "universal alliance" aiming to abolish war, a messianic hope launched amid the apocalypse of World War I; (b) the big-power dictatorship foreshadowed in the structure of the League of Nations and definitely intended by the Big Three architects of the United Nations; and (c) the intimate alliance systems of a divided world after 1945. We are not including the last meaning in this analysis.

It may be worth-while to review and sum up the flaws exposed in collective security. First of all, the major states had not been willing to make binding commitments for future action, as the theory demanded. What an American delegate to the United Nations referred to as "making commitments in disregard of future military, strategic, and political realities" was too much of a risk. It was this fact that underlay the somewhat confused debate of 1919 in the United States and that continued to plague the League and the United Nations. Based as it was on recognition of the sovereignty of the member states, the collective-security organization could not bind its members, and they would not bind themselves. In fact, there was no point in insisting upon a promise that clearly would not be honored in all circum-

---

* Roland N. Stromberg, *Collective Security and American Foreign Policy.* (New York: Frederick A. Praeger, 1963), pp. 230–247. Reprinted by permission of Frederick A. Praeger, Inc.

[1] "Collective security is not a conception, much less a technical term of international law; it has never been defined by treaty, or by the supreme international tribunal which has been functioning at The Hague since 1922. The conception is political, the words vague and ambiguous." Andrew Martin, *Collective Security: A Progress Report* (Paris: UNESCO, 1952), p. 14.

stances. Democratic and constitutional governments, the natural bulwark of antiwar idealism in most respects, were peculiarly unfitted to undertake agreements that might involve future war, for they were bound to consult their peoples and their parliaments at the time of any such grave decision. One could hope that a sense of duty and higher interest would develop and persuade peoples to back such decisions, but the deterrent power of certain action—"swift, automatic, and overwhelming"—could never be there. This in turn made nations reluctant to rely upon such a system for their security. Practice showed rather persistently that states were "shortsighted" and "realistic"; it seemed to show that they had to be where the possibility of war was involved and where their very security was at stake. This reflex has been called "almost biological." Collective security was occasionally applied, as in Korea in 1950 and (incompletely) against Italy in 1935, but the pattern of application has been shifting and irrational, and unpredictable. Thus, it does not differ in this respect from national reactions leading to war in the older manner. Effective collective security presumably demands consistency and certainty in its application.

Reasons for the reluctance to make the necessary full commitment to action under a collective-security system reveal other classic objections. Chief of these was the problem of the *status quo,* or the problem of peaceful change—or of justice. Nations hesitated to sign up in advance because of doubts about the permanence and justice of the existing political order to the defence of which, as against violent change, collective security is committed. Thus, between the wars, many felt that the Paris peace settlement was unjust and unnatural and that the League existed to perpetuate a not altogether holy alliance of the victors. Collective security seems based on the proposition that peace is the highest end. But this is a false proposition because virtually everyone will prefer to fight for "rights" or justice under severe enough provocation. It is impossible to insist that change cease with the latest war; and so, collective security always recognized the legitimacy of change "by peaceful means." As a leading journal once put it, "It is as if a successful gambler were to rise with his winnings from the table and say to his fellows: I intend to stop playing, and gambling from now on is immoral. But I will keep my winnings." It is worth noting that both the Japanese in 1932 and the Italians in 1935 forcefully repeated exactly this idea, in much the same imagery. But no international organization based on sovereignty could have the power to compel or induce necessary change. Unless there were a satisfactory world government based on law and having its authority acknowledged by almost all, one had to recognize the possibility and even the legitimacy of change by violence. The point was once made by James T. Shotwell, a distinguished American internationalist: "Unless there is provision for peaceful change, we have to accept the possibility of warlike change, because the worst of all injustices would be to hold nations down within the iron framework of past conditions." And according to another famous authority on international organization: "As long as the States of the world have not agreed upon a legal method of peacefully settling all disputes which may arise between them, war will remain an inevitable expedient which in certain extreme cases may be considered legitimate." It might be added that the development of such a legal method of settling disputes—the World Court way—has declined rather than increased in recent years.

A fallacy that seems to accompany collective security is that there is some sort of final, permanent, basic "agreement" possible in world affairs. Thus, we find Secretary Stimson holding, back in 1945, that the great powers should *first* "thresh out" the "underlying issues," agreeing on their major lines of policy for the postwar world, and *then* create the United Nations—otherwise they would quarrel within the United Nations. . . . It was thought that, after a happy agreement had been reached, the United Nations could preside over it. It appears that, with one part of their minds, at least, the believers in the United Nations knew that the harder task had to be accomplished by diplomacy, outside that organization. This view seems to diminish very considerably the importance of the United Nations—at least, it is not very consistent with the collective-security approach as it is generally understood. . . .

The impossibility of guaranteeing existing borders as largely final or closed against any future revision is even more evident in the "new" countries of the world so prominent in recent years—in Africa, especially. Here is a situation so fluid that guarantees would be simply out of the question. Collective security becomes feasible only where a very old and stable political delimitation of peoples, with boundaries long unchallenged, exists. But the permanence of any such situations must always be problematical in a dynamic world.

It is this difficulty, no doubt, that has driven advocates of collective security to assume that all or most wars are the products of deliberate acts of aggression by states that may be considered hardened criminals ("bandit nations"). Much of the trouble thus far indicated is removed if this is true. The assumption is that except perhaps in "extreme cases," good, "peaceloving" nations do not go to war; they exercise enormous restraint and even give in to the claims of justice against themselves, while aggression is easily recognized and is the proper target of collective action. Men of good will—the majority—will readily recognize such immoral behavior and will readily perceive that it has forfeited all claim to receiving ordinary justice. Thus, the problems of commitment and justice disappear if the aggressor is wicked enough and if this is the usual cause of war. There is no question that collective security was revived from a languishing state by Hitler and revived again by the fairly clear case of North Korean aggression.

But there remains a serious problem of aggression that has proved annoying for collective security. That there are certain perennial criminals among

nations is an outrageous assumption, and the West is now paying for adopting it.[2] Men labored in vain both at Geneva and at New York to define aggression. It is believed by the cruder popular proponents of collective security that nothing is easier than to define aggression: "A national boundary is
crossed with armed force." But it is not always easy to decide which state
did in fact first do this, and the definition leaves out of account raids, and
other hostile acts not even related to the frontier (boycotts, for example), as
well as earlier provocations. The Arab-Israel violence over the last ten years
offers a classic example of the difficulties. No informed person believes that
the above definition will do. "What two nations were ever at war, and did
not obstinately charge the aggression, each on the other?" Coleridge mused.
The worst is that the honest historian, with all the time in the world, can too
seldom tell which it was. The difficulty is not solely in establishing the facts,
but in interpreting them.

People take for granted, also, that the U.N. Charter "defined aggression."
No one has yet been able to do that: Exhaustive efforts, lately by the U.N.
Special Committee, have always led to a blind alley. The Special Committee
finished its work in 1956 without reaching a definition, having labored on
the problem since 1953. Before that, the International Law Commission had
the job. In the 1920's, Geneva went through a similar process. After all this,
it seems safe to say that a general definition of aggression will never be
adopted by the United Nations. The reason was long ago indicated in the
well-known dictum that any definition would be "a trap for the innocent and
a signpost for the guilty"—to which it is necessary to add the fear that it
might also be a trap for the policemen. (The refusal to define aggression
relates closely to the unwillingness of states to commit themselves to future
action that might prove embarrassing.)

There is a belief that, while for technical reasons it may be impossible to
write a comprehensive definition (and Anglo-Saxon law, at least, typically
leaves some discretion to the courts), aggression will be recognized when it
occurs. But the great majority of wars are not that clear. It may well be
doubted whether most wars have a determinable "aggressor." Determination in the United Nations becomes lost in fatal subjectivity, with political
motives all too obviously entering in. Who is to decide? Again, an impartial,
universally trusted World Court, administering an international law that all
had helped to make, could make this sort of determination: in brief, if we
had world government. But if we had *that*, there would have been no problem in the first place. Collective security is designed to function in the absence of world government. It requires that nations recognize and act against

---

[2] An appropriate comment on this "heresy, smelling to high heaven" is made by G. A.
Borgese in his book *Common Cause* (1954), p. 383. Apart from its morality, such a
diagnosis assumes away the whole problem of war. If it has no rational causes, being
confined to the insane and the criminal, war can hardly be a pressing problem.

aggression and assumes that aggression is obvious and recognizable.[3] Unfortunately, it is usually not. It should be realized that judicial determination of crime is not *less* difficult in the case of states than of individuals, but far more so. (We are not speaking here of the enormous difficulties encountered in the Nürnberg effort to assign individuals criminal blame for state actions, but simply of the effort to establish aggression against a state as the basis for some legal action under a collective-security system.) Quarrels between nations involve the actions, frequently, of thousands of individuals, who may or may not be said to act on behalf of their states (consider again the typical border incident), whereas, in an individual case, this is obviously not so. Quarrels between nations usually involve also the interpretation of rights whose legal basis is far less clear than would ordinarily be the case between individuals under municipal law (disputed territory, for example, that is inhabited by numerous individuals and may have been transferred by treaty extorted under the duress of the last war). The collective life of a nation ranges in time through centuries and embraces millions of people; the collisions of these entities raise problems that are on an entirely different level from those of private individuals. It may well be doubted whether even the aggressions of Nazi Germany, backed as they were by the complex emotions of a historic people, could be judged in the same category as crimes of persons. In any event, these cases of national aggression were rarely as apparent as they should have been if they were merely criminal actions. The case of Japan in Manchuria in 1931, it will be recalled, which *later* seemed so obvious, was not, at the time; even Hitler committed no readily identifiable act of aggression during 1935–38, when he was securing the domination of Europe.

It might be added that if the world offered as clear a picture of the good and the bad as is assumed, we would have no real need of a system of collective security per se. By a natural moral law, the decent would turn on the monstrous, just as Hitler and then Stalin provoked spontaneous alliances against themselves, without need of the League of Nations or any special machinery or philosophy of international relations.

For many other conflicts, however, there is no satisfactory answer. The United Nations recognizes the obvious fact that some disputes require conciliation and not suppression. The international organization is both "a security system and a peace system," it must seek to harmonize honest disputes as well as crush malevolent aggressions. It can, in practice, distinguish between the two only with difficulty. In 1931, as well as on other occasions, the

---

[3] The view, held by some, that only the technical fact of aggression is relevant and all other factors—past history, present circumstances, moral and cultural elements—may be dismissed is inadequate, as experience reveals continually and as logic indicates. Even in a court case under municipal law, circumstances are relevant, more so in international affairs.

first and natural instinct was to settle the question by compromise, an approach that clashed with the application of sanctions against one side. In sum, the problem of the aggressor, after a vast amount of discussion (raising issues that we have here but touched upon), remains a formidable one for collective security, solvable only when a veritable monster of wickedness obligingly appears. It is a stumbling block because conflict in the world is not, unfortunately, due only to sheer malevolence on one side.

Despite all these difficulties, one can cut the Gordian knot if there is enough power. Impatience with the slowness of growth of a legal order and a world community (while war ravaged the world) was what impelled men to the idea of collective security, which at its birth was compared to the vigilantes committee, or self-appointed lynch gang. The idea was that there was no time to wait for the courts and that one must revert to the cruder methods of the posse. If so, legal niceties may be irrelevant. Let all the great powers get together, and aggression is what they say it is. They will impose the canons of justice and law like a Solon, and we shall have peace, though some causes may be handled roughly. No omelet without broken eggs, and peace in this age is worth a great price. From the League to the United Nations, as we have observed, the trend was toward giving a small number of the great powers more authority and discretion to preserve peace.

The only trouble with this is that it is a complete *reductio ad absurdum* of the whole idea. For, if power is so monopolized and those who possess it are so united in their aims, what need do we have for security organizations? A preliminary miracle has been assumed. "When solidarity existed, the organizations were needless. When it did not, they were impotent." Formal association, the invoking of Charter or Covenant as talisman, could not appreciably alter the relationships of states in this respect.

The effort to force the superpowers into a common mold looked like a very desperate last resort. The gamble was great: If they did not harmonize, but quarreled (as superpowers have had a persistent habit of doing), then the United Nations was useless. It soon became obvious that the cleavage between the two great ones had done just this. The paradox always latent in using force to preserve peace (witness its emergence earlier, in the case of Manchuria) became a gigantic absurdity when one thought of one of the two huge power blocs into which the world was virtually divided launching a "police action" against the other. Conceivably, "a major coalition of overwhelming might" could frighten or easily subdue an "aggressive minority," but this condition did not prevail. Events since 1945 have shown that although it is not impossible for the United States and the U.S.S.R. to agree in their policies toward a warlike action (witness the Middle East crisis of 1956), it is very unusual, to say the least. Korea, which apparently changed the pattern of U.N. impotence, was, in fact, a trial of strength, or a maneuver of some sort between the two blocs. That the United Nations would be used by whichever of the blocs could exploit it was obvious, but the hope of a peaceful world presided over by the superpowers acting in unison was hardly in the realm of the possible. The danger then became that the two mighty power blocs would clash in major war and tear the world to shreds, and collective security became something to be avoided. For in the era of nuclear rocket warfare, anything that threatened "peaceful coexistence" was to be dreaded.

It is perhaps logical to ask next why the dream of the united great powers failed so completely. It certainly seemed plausible once, however fatuous we must now regard those hopes. (This hope was not a new one in history. One is struck by its frequent recurrences, for instance, in the dreams of a permanent Anglo-French union that flourished in the 1850's. There were other examples, including Theodore Roosevelt's vision of Anglo-American dominion. The hope seems, indeed, to have gathered strength whenever large powers for some reason felt a temporary glow of good will toward each other.) As the most satisfied of the satisfied states, the giants could not seriously prefer war to peace, for they had much more to lose than to gain. This was the one realistic argument. With it went much loose talk about naturally "peace-loving" nations. Such talk was assisted by illusions about the causes of war including a tendency to think in terms of natural criminals and natural policemen, villains and heroes—the world, one might say, as a cowboy movie.

There was also a flagrant neglect of the realities of power. It is a notable fact that the leading proponents of collective security assailed the balance of power as an iniquitous principle. They were not merely blind to it, they did not like it, and they thought it could somehow be abolished. "The system of the balance of power is bound to fail," wrote Anthony Eden. The balance of power is not a system but an ultimate fact that no system can escape. The task of keeping peace is not automatically solved by having a favorable balance of power, but it is made easier, while an unfavorable balance can make it very difficult. This contempt for the balance became the source of most of the postwar difficulties. "I would know of no basic issues of genuine gravity between Russia and the West other than those arising directly from the manner in which the recent war was allowed to come to an end," George F. Kennan has remarked. One might venture the emendation that the way the war was fought—to the total defeat and utter destruction of the "bandit" states—had more to do with it. Beginning, middle, and end, the war was handled without thought of the future power situation. This must be charged principally against the particular view of affairs that collective security encouraged.

This disregard of realities in favor of an abstract formula has done more than anything else to discredit the doctrine in official circles. Innocent at one time, the United States has taken some intensive course work in international politics in recent years, and it would no longer occur to most thinking Americans to adopt some attitudes that were formerly pervasive. The disparagement of power, the mistrust of diplomacy, and the "fetishism of ideology" (James Burnham), which made foreign policy consist of "the periodic enunciation of elevated sentiments" (Hans Kohn)—these have not quite vanished but have very much diminished. Discovery of the world in all its dimensions has destroyed faith in simple rules and general formulas that cover every subject. Hull and Hornbeck used to teach that foreign policy consisted in the steady application of a few basic moral principles to every part of the globe. Kennan and Lippmann now counsel us to avoid "doctrines" and rethink our policies every morning. The difference is the measure of the distance America has traveled (for better or worse) along the road to being a mature world power. Nothing so general, so vague in its concrete implications, and so uncertain in its grasp of immediate power realities could serve any longer as the chief guide to American policy.

As a practical guide to policy, the injunctions of collective security turn out to be not very helpful. The general assertion that great wars can and should be prevented by a strong show of force the first time an incident occurs might be true sometimes but it might not be true. One must judge each question on its merits, and thus the general injunction is virtually worthless as a guide. It can indeed induce a habit of looking for an aggressor's conspiracy in every show of violence. But a trained diplomatic staff must look to the facts and not the theory. . . .

A further factor in the discrediting of collective security may be mentioned: the explosion of myths about the road to World War II. Collective security revived from a fairly low status to become the most fashionable of ideologies almost exclusively because of a belief that its application could have prevented that war. Careful scholarship has since cast doubt on this popular theory. Such studies as Reginald Bassett's made it clear that only after the event was it revealed, by an almost entirely legendary version of the Manchurian affair, that collective security could have easily set all to rights. Few competent historians of the period would now pass such sweeping judgments on Neville Chamberlain's European policies or hold that the opposite course would have solved our problems. From a recent article by G. Barraclough, the following may be cited: "Who save politicians who have learnt nothing and forgotten nothing would dare to assert that an opposite policy [than Chamberlain's] would necessarily and beyond peradventure have checked Hitler or averted war?" The literature here is too large to be cited readily; it may be enough to record the judgment that almost every scholarly book that appears has prompted the reflections that things were not so simple as they seemed, a view that would apply to such matters (at a random selection) as the 1936 German reoccupation of the Rhineland, the Ethiopian affair, the nature of the relations between Germany and Japan, the Sino-Japanese conflict of 1937, and so on. The simplified popular reconstruction of the road to war as one long bout of cravenness in the face of a conspiracy of evil always involved myths. Some were almost self-evident;

others have been exposed by the patient march of scholarship (and publication of at least some of the records and sources, which unhappily comes only long afterwards).

The espousal of collective security was often connected with that type of thinking that not only made the mistake of trusting in Stalin's benevolence but also expected an abandonment of force altogether in international relations. It could be held responsible for the grim outlook that confronted the United States and the world in 1947. "All nations," the Atlantic Charter had announced, "must come to the abandonment of the use of force." Although as late as 1957 President Eisenhower still held that the use of force by individual states in solving international disputes was inadmissible, American policy since then has surely been based on another and more realistic view. The remarkable effort to identify the ideal of 1945 with the reality of 1949, and to describe the system of alliances as collective security, could result only in proving that the phrase is too slippery to have any clear meaning. Collective security has become the system of partial alliances based on national power that it was originally designed to replace and, as such, is no different in principle from traditional methods of keeping the peace or defending national security. The curious migration of the idea to mean just having allies against Russia has enabled it to keep a favorable connotation—for everyone wants allies against Russia—at the cost of either destroying its classic principles or rendering it hopelessly unclear. For many good people, no doubt, the phrase carries connotations of supporting the United Nations and being for cooperation as much as possible. As such, it has lost all precision of meaning and can expect to vanish from the vocabulary of intelligent men within a few years.

A formidable list of charges against collective security might be drawn up, alleging grave damage to the world as a result of its counsels and exhortations. Professor E. M. Borchard, a tireless foe of the heresy of collective security, presented such an indictment some years ago: The "disastrous" effects included diminishing, by the stress on compulsion, the attention paid to peaceful processes, extending war by the abolition of neutrality, making conciliation and compromise more difficult, and exacerbating international tensions by self-righteous moralism, which passes condemnatory judgment on national ambitions and interests with explosive results. By a philosophy of unlimited intervention, collective security threatened to universalize every conflict and by a philosophy of unlimited denunciation, it tended to maximize the bitterness. These particulars have frequently recurred in criticism of collective security. Mussolini's reported rejoinder to Litvinov's "peace is indivisible"—that indivisible peace means indivisible war—is a familiar hit against the doctrine. The view that the United States should pay a great deal more attention to constructive peace-building processes and less to punishment and condemnation is widely accepted today. Many have deplored the "smudging of the borderline between war and peace," which seems a retrogression, not an advance. And the most searching criticism has persistently found the largest chink in collective security's armor to be its sin of pride: a dangerous assumption of moral superiority that not only heats the passions that lead to war but turns the war into one of annihilation. And wars of annihilation destroy the equilibrium of power and lead to fresh wars in "chain reaction."

If both sides adopt the collective-security outlook, a peaceful compromise is likely to be difficult. In connection with the Berlin crisis, Khrushchev announced that the aggressor must be rebuffed, otherwise he becomes "brazen," but if "rebuffed he calms down." Many in the West also believe that peremptory rebuff is the medicine for Soviet aggression. Two antagonists each of whom believes he is bound to deal severely with the other, as an aggressor who must be taught a lesson, represent unpromising material for negotiations.

On the other hand, some hold that the United Nations ought to function more as the conscience of world opinion, not hesitating to inflict the sternest judgments on international immoralists, provided that it eschew penalties. If this is done by a large majority of the General Assembly, representing as it does, now, almost all the peoples of the world, it has a force that it could not have coming from a Security Council dominated by a few great powers. The chief trouble, after all, with condemnation by the Council under League and U.N. theories of collective security was that it seemed like self-serving on the part of the judges and thus intolerably pharisaical. One great power cannot sit in judgment on another. The entire world perhaps can.[4]

It does not seem that many have much faith, however, in such efforts to salvage a useful role for U.N. collective action. In functioning as a court of world opinion and in supplying its good offices to disputants it can surely do much to oil the frictions of an abrasive world. But impatient idealism has moved on toward world government once more and is increasingly aware that the United Nations is not a halfway house to that goal but is rather "in almost every respect the very antithesis of world government"; "a voluntary association of States which cling desperately to their sovereignty," an association that today is most notably a forum where the new nationalisms of the world like to announce themselves. The goal of world government may be unreal. Even if Communism's unfriendly fanatics were abolished from the earth, it is hard to believe that all the new, aspiring peoples would resign control over their destinies to any outside agency. Obviously, the rising force in Africa and Asia is nationalism, not supranationalism.

However that may be, there were always many supporters of collective

---

[4] It ought not to be overlooked that the "new" and "neutralist" nations have generally opposed the idea of the United Nations as a coercive, peace-enforcement agency, preferring to stress its functions of conciliation and building good will. For an example, see the volume on *India and the United Nations* in the Carnegie series on the United Nations (New York: Manhattan Publ. Co., 1957).

security who overlooked the contradictions and anomalies in the system because they thought it would grow up to be a real world government. Thus a
communication of October 8, 1945, signed by Owen J. Roberts and a long
list of distinguished internationalists, had declared: "Everyone knows that
the Charter is only a beginning. It does not guarantee peace." This view was
widespread. Most of them finally became aware that it would not, and began
to call for a wholly new approach. There has lately been a significant revival
of such schemes, and a somewhat related concern for the World Court approach (building a basic structure of international law), with pointed reminders that under the U.N. system of political police, this portion of the
task has been sadly neglected. It can hardly be doubted that the conception
of the United Nations as a big-power policing agency directly clashed with
the world-government or growth-of-international-law approach. It has already been noted that the United States and Britain as well as the U.S.S.R.
displayed a positively retrograde attitude on the World Court in 1945 when
they ratified the U.N. Charter: They withheld from it, more jealously even
than the "isolationists" of the 1920's, any power to bind them. Collective
security, in its 1945 model, looked toward the giving of all power to each of
the policemen. It is a fact that none of them, the United States included, has
shown much inclination to hand over to the United Nations any important
practical duties: The record in such areas as economic development funds
and international economic cooperation affords evidence of this. Those who
think in terms of evolving a world "sense of community" through the practice
of real international law as well as the evolution of vital international political institutions are usually gloomy these days not merely about the Communist refusal to play any such game but about the trend in the rest of the
world, too.

Yet, those accustomed to dismiss schemes of world government as the
airiest of cloud-cuckooland utopias might not have been quite so sure in
1960. The 1958 Defense White Paper of the British Government, *not* composed by cranks, said flatly that the only answer to the nuclear stalemate
(which might keep the peace for a generation, with luck, but could not be
endured permanently) was a world state, controlling all arms. . . .

This was one possibility. Another, much discussed, was to explore seriously
the possibilities of recovering the institutions of limited war, on the eigh-
teenth-century model. . . . The historian of collective security could record
only that this former idol had become irrelevant in the debate. In neither
scheme was there any apparent place for the sort of U.N. system established
in 1945.

Images and ideas drawn from that system, however, undeniably continued
to influence foreign policy thinking in various ways. One commonly criticized
feature of American policy was its tendency to stress military power and to
refuse to consider an accommodation with the Soviet-Chinese bloc, along
with its inclination to see the entire world as affected by nothing else but
the struggle with a Communist conspiracy. (Some of this criticism was ir-

responsible, but by no means all of it.) The vision of standing firm at every point against the "aggressor," meeting him with overwhelming power and not a willingness to truck and bargain, and seeing in every crisis his hand probing for a weakness, which, if found, would lead him on to greater aggressions—this picture seemed to have had its influence in policy-making circles. "Appeasement" was still a nasty word. Whenever a problem arose, the instinct of American politicians was still to compare it to Munich. . . .

The Communists have their own version of "collective security." It is a story we have not been concerned to tell, but it is well known that collective security had no more faithful backers than the Soviets in the era of Maxim Litvinov when, in the 1930's, it suited the interest of the U.S.S.R. to build ideological bridges toward an alliance with the Western powers. And Communism has its own peculiar theory of aggression and war. Aggression is, by definition, what a Socialist state cannot do: It is, in Mr. Khrushchev's words, "alien to the very nature of the socialist system," and he has explained that what happened in Hungary in November, 1956, was that the working people of Hungary smashed a counterrevolutionary conspiracy with some degree of "fraternal" help from Soviet troops who were performing a "sacred international duty." On the other hand, the "imperialist powers," as we learn from the Chinese Reds, are "aggressive by nature," capitalist society being predestined to war. Since opposition to capitalistic imperialism constitutes a "just war," it is easy to rationalize any use of force against it as essentially "defensive." This sort of double talk dwarfs any similar tendency in the Western world though it is essentially only an exaggeration of the same thing: the use of such terms as "collective security," "aggression," "resistance to aggression," "police action in behalf of peace," etc., to mean what one's prejudices and interests want them to mean at any given time.

Schemes for eternal peace form a mournful chapter in the history of human thought. They are approximately as old as war and have been just as futile. Lord Acton once observed that such political writings "remained without influence, and never passed from literary into political history, because something more than discontent and speculative ingenuity is needed to invest a political idea with power over the masses of mankind." Lacking such power, such general ideas cannot be of much use to practical men of affairs, who must struggle with a world far too rough and contingent to yield to their prescriptions. But Acton's remark suggests that such ideas would become influential and "pass from literary into political history" if they could acquire "power over the masses of mankind," i.e., if they could become an effective myth. Collective security came close to becoming a potent myth at moments during both world wars. Around it clustered strong emotions; it was a rallying cry and a symbol. With it, one could overlook the cruel dilemmas of policy and point to a simple solution, one requiring only faith and courage. One could paint a rosy picture of the future with which to make the ghastliness of total war tolerable.

But a myth, to survive, must yield some results; in other words, it must be applicable to reality in some degree. Collective security would seem to have failed because of its contradictions and errors. The strength of its appeal lay, obviously, in the horror and hatred of war in the modern age and the impelling need to end it. With the potency and the worth of this impulse, no one can quarrel. Because of it, there is urgent need for some formula, other than that of drift and hope, around which to rally modern man's quest for peace and security. It is too large a topic to be pursued here. Rethinking the basic concepts of foreign policy is one of the more important intellectual adventures of our times. Perhaps, out of this activity, currently going on, new and more valid mental constructs will arise.

The modern psyche seems to demand slogans and general ideas. Long ago, Edmund Burke taught those who were willing to be taught, that "nothing universal can rationally be affirmed of any moral or political subject," that statecraft will submit to no set of logically satisfactory principles, and that the politician should content himself with working from civilized standards on the material that lies at hand. The democratic era is little suited to such sanity and restraint. Foreign policy, like everything else, must be dramatized and made glamorous for the masses. This accounts for the appeal of collective security—a myth or ideology, simplifying and moralizing the complex materials of life.

A kind of apocalyptic faith in the "second coming" of Woodrow Wilson recurs from time to time. Thus, we have Richard W. Leopold, in his study of Elihu Root (1954), urging that, though Wilson was wrong in 1919, he was or will be vindicated by the "whirligig of time"; and Dexter Perkins writing (1952) that "the idea of collective security furnishes the context in which American diplomacy is likely to operate as time goes on." These are authorities worthy of respect; similar quotations are abundant. The bald facts seem more nearly to approximate Hans J. Morgenthau's conception of foreign policy as "a struggle for power," which "by its very nature is never ended, for the lust for power, and the fear of it, is never stilled." But the American democratic ideology is inclined to insist that *realpolitik* is fatal to democratic ideals. This strain of thought, deriving ultimately from Puritanism, demands the moralization of politics as the price of continuing the American political tradition. To drop collective security and embrace the balance of power, to follow Hans Morgenthau and George Kennan, would be, in the rather representative view of Frank Tannenbaum, to "destroy a hundred and fifty years of democratic life" and "abandon the faith we have lived by." Whereas Senators Borah and Taft were isolationists because they believed that all foreign policy poisons republican government, Professor Tannenbaum and others are international collectivists because they feel that foreign policy can be made safe for democracy in no other way. Despite the weakness of that system, they will not abandon it, and can even contemplate further ideological wars to force their morality upon the unenlightened, because of their strong feeling that we are lost without the faith of our fathers—lost with Morgenthau and Kennan, those worldly wise men who dwell in the realm of "carnal policy."

There is doubtless a grave problem here. The present study cannot undertake to resolve the great issues of democracy and foreign policy, of morals and politics. But one might comment that to cling to fallacies because they conflict with your faith is folly. It is like the Church's condemnation of Galileo. The real issue is not whether collective security squares better with items of a political faith, important as that may be; it is whether collective security is sound, true, and workable. If it is not, then, with whatever reluctance, we must surely abandon it and set about to square our faith with reality rather than try to make over reality in the image of our faith. It is futile to say democracy will not associate with the balance of power, if the balance of power is a fact. Like Carlyle's friend, we had better accept the universe.

Considerable movement of thought in America and elsewhere away from "utopianism" and toward a conservative realism that abandons the absolute quest for peace and security and is ready to settle for something much less is in evidence. One writer has referred to the solutions of those who do not look at the real world, but are concerned with "the arbitrary dismantling or reconstruction of the world, in such a way that these problems will not arise. They represent a corruption of thinking about international relations, and a distraction from its proper concerns." Whether such a revolt against utopia presages a return to concepts long since seen to be inadequate (among such people, the balance of power has suffered a rediscovery) or whether it is the beginning of progress, of true science rising on the ruins of ideology, cannot yet be determined. What seems fairly certain is that the hour is not a propitious one for such ideological theories as collective security.

20

THIRD REPORT OF THE UN COMMITTEE ON RHODESIAN SANCTIONS OF 15 JUNE 1970*

Mr. Tarassov (Union of Soviet Socialist Republics) said that the report should note that, as a result of the adoption of Security Council resolution 277 (1970), the Committee had been entrusted with the additional respon-

---

* UN Security Council Document S/9844 of 15 June 1970, from Appendix III, Summary Records of the Thirty-Fourth Meeting of the Committee, pp. 41–48.

sibility of studying ways and means of which Member States could carry out more effectively the decisions of the Security Council regarding sanctions against the illegal régime of Southern Rhodesia and make recommendations to the Council. In addition, it should be noted in the report that . . . the Republic of South Africa and Portugal were continuing to give active assistance to Southern Rhodesia and were thus reducing the effectiveness of the sanctions called for by the Security Council. The Rhodesian economy was being developed only because a number of States, primarily the United States, the United Kingdom, the Federal Republic of Germany, Japan and certain other countries, maintained extensive trade and economic relations with the Republic of South Africa, which nullified the effect of the sanctions against Southern Rhodesia. There were many facts to demonstrate that most of the goods imported and exported by Southern Rhodesia were being shipped through the Republic of South Africa. It was very revealing that, for eight months of 1969 alone, United States exports to the Republic of South Africa had been $18.8 million higher than for the corresponding period of 1968, that exports from Western Germany had increased by $38.4 million, from Japan by $48 million and from the United Kingdom by $17.5 million. Obviously, the Committee should state that the measures taken by the Security Council, including the sanctions imposed on Southern Rhodesia, had not led to the liberation of the people of Zimbabwe [the UN name for Rhodesia] from the murderous tyranny of the Southern Rhodesian racist régime, which was their main objective. The development of the Rhodesian economy could also be explained by the continuing use of foreign capital. For example, United States investments in Southern Rhodesia amounted to $55 million and those of the United Kingdom to $200 million.

In its recommendations, the report should refer to the desirability of enlarging the membership of the Committee. An unjustifiable situation had arisen in which the Committee, which now consisted of seven members—most of whom were from the Western countries—had only one representative from Africa. The report should also mention the need to give wider publicity to the work of the Committee and to abandon the practice of holding closed meetings. The overwhelming majority of Member States supported the sanctions against Southern Rhodesia and there was no reason for the Committee to conceal its work from other Members of the United Nations.

Another reason why the sanctions had failed to achieve their objective was that they were essentially selective and piecemeal measures which could hardly produce effective results even if they were fully implemented. Accordingly, the report should recommend the Security Council to apply all the sanctions provided for in Article 41 of the Charter, including the complete interruption of economic relations and of rail, sea, air, postal, telegraphic, radio and other means of communication. It was also clear that Portugal and the Republic of South Africa had given and would continue to give Southern Rhodesia all possible assistance in order to offset the effects of the sanctions. It was therefore imperative to request the Security Council to extend sanctions to Portugal and the Republic of South Africa, particularly sanctions which would prohibit all States from supplying South Africa and Portugal with goods which were then forwarded to Southern Rhodesia. He realized that appropriate steps had not been taken in the Security Council because of the veto exercised by the United Kingdom and the United States. Nevertheless, the Committee had been instructed to ascertain how sanctions were being implemented and it should state its belief that sanctions should be extended to those countries which were assisting the illegal régime in Southern Rhodesia.

The Security Council should also draw the attention of States to the fact that failure to comply with its resolutions 253 (1968) and 277 (1970) was a violation of the obligations assumed under Articles 25, 48 and 49 of the Charter. Although the States at fault were aware of that fact, such a reminder might be of some additional moral and political value. Similarly, the report could express the wish that the Security Council should recommend to States that monopolies and companies registered in their territories should terminate activities of all kinds in Southern Rhodesia, should stop investing capital in the Rhodesian economy and withdraw their existing investments. It also seemed desirable, as suggested in the note submitted by Nepal, to prepare a report on action taken by Governments or their legal authorities against monopolies and companies which continued to trade illegally with Southern Rhodesia, a report which should be given the widest publicity. Lastly, the measures provided for in Article 41 of the Charter were inadequate and the Committee should recommend that the Council propose that the United Kingdom, as administering Power, should take action by armed force to put an end to the domination of the racist group in Southern Rhodesia.

His delegation recognized that the Committee could not have carried on its work without the information on suspected violations provided by the United Kingdom. Nevertheless, he was not convinced that the United Kingdom itself had not violated the sanctions. With an enlarged membership, the Committee would be more objective in its consideration of cases. At present, it acted as a kind of screen for the United Kingdom, which was endeavouring to conceal its own policy of condoning the régime in Southern Rhodesia.

Mr. Hildyard (United Kingdom) agreed that the report should point to the fact that some Member States had failed to co-operate in the implementation of sanctions and that the measures taken thus far had not led to positive results, although he would prefer to say, as had the USSR representative, that the sanctions had not achieved their main objective—which was of course political.

Many members had pointed out that the Security Council had decided to revert to the question of enlarging the membership of the Committee after the latter had submitted its third report. In his view, that decision was a reasonable one. It had been stressed that, in the United Nations, the alternatives were a small and a practical working body or a large but unwieldy committee which was merely a forum for endless discussion. His delegation had always felt that the Committee had been efficient precisely because it was small. Moreover, it had been objective in its deliberations and he questioned the assertion that a larger membership would lead to greater objectivity.

If the United Kingdom had considered that it was in a position to take effective steps against the Southern Rhodesian régime, it would not have appealed to the United Nations for assistance and the whole question of sanctions would not have arisen in the Security Council. Moreover, it had sought United Nations help because it could not contemplate using armed force against the rebellious Smith régime. At the time, it had explained that it was almost fifty years since the United Kingdom had exercised control over the internal affairs of Southern Rhodesia.

If the Committee were to abandon the practice of holding closed meetings as recommended by the Soviet Union, its sources of information might dry up, with the result that its work would be less effective. Like the question of the size of the Committee, the matter of open or closed meetings could only be decided by the Security Council, and not the Committee. He did not agree with the Soviet representative that the sanctions provided for in resolutions 253 (1968) and 277 (1970) were "limited and piecemeal," particularly since resolution 277 (1970) called for a total economic embargo of Southern Rhodesia. To extend the sanctions to South Africa and Portugal, as recommended by the USSR, would be a major step and only the Security Council itself could take a decision on such an important question.

The investments by a number of Western countries, including the United Kingdom, in Southern Rhodesia had been made by independent companies which could not and did not now receive funds from the United Kingdom or remit funds to it. It was meaningless to talk of removing fixed capital assets from Southern Rhodesia. Moreover, it had long been accepted that associate companies should not be subordinate to their parent companies and should act independently in accordance with the laws of the country in which they conducted their business. Since trade with South Africa was most important to it, the United Kingdom, like many other States, could not contemplate action against that country. The figures quoted by the USSR representative concerning the increasing trade of certain Western countries with South Africa did not take inflation into account; in order to be truly meaningful, the figures should indicate the percentage increase and thus show which countries had increased their trade with South Africa most significantly. Such an approach would show that the countries mentioned by the USSR were not the ones with the biggest percentage increases. Besides, no causal connexion had been established between increased trade with South Africa and violations of the sanctions against Southern Rhodesia. Replying to the USSR allegation that the United Kingdom was violating the sanctions, he said that this was totally unwarranted; there had been a very few violations by individual British firms, but the United Kingdom Government had taken action against those firms.

With regard to the suggestions submitted by the United Kingdom for the final section of the report, he said that the wording was less important than the substance. The Committee's observations should draw attention to the increased number of cases of suspected violations of sanctions notified since the last report and the need for more United Nations members to report suspected violations where they had reliable evidence. The observations should also stress the need for the Committee to receive full details, the incomplete nature of many Government replies to requests for information and the lack of co-operation on the part of certain countries. It should also be stated that it was desirable for some Members of the United Nations urgently to take legislative measures to control their shipping in accordance with paragraph 3 (e) of Security Council resolution 253 (1968) so that those countries would be in a better position to take action when they were informed of possible violations of the sanctions. Lastly, the observations should stress the desirability of the national authorities at transshipment ports and free ports investigating carefully the origin of any goods which might be suspect in origin.

The table drawn up by the Secretariat showed that many points in the three lists of suggestions for the final section of the report had a good deal in common and it was to be hoped that the Committee would be able to reach agreement on a single text.

Mr. Finger (United States of America) said that no proof had been offered for the statement made in the USSR paper that the extensive trade and economic relations of certain Western Powers with the Republic of South Africa were "nullifying the effect of the sanctions against Southern Rhodesia." The trade figures quoted in the Soviet paper were meaningless since they did not indicate percentage increases or support the allegation that that trade was being diverted to Southern Rhodesia in violation of the sanctions. His country had faithfully applied the sanctions and its trade with Southern Rhodesia was now almost non-existent. Only one case of sanctions violations had been established and the company concerned had been prosecuted.

The USSR representative's choice of the countries for which he had given trade statistics was completely arbitrary and based solely on political considerations. The countries named were not the only ones which still traded with South Africa. For example, an article which had recently appeared in *Pravda* on 10 June revealed that mainland China bought a considerable amount of chrome from Rhodesia and that, in 1969, its trade with Rhodesia had been three times that of the previous year. Rhodesian chrome was sent to Beira in Mozambique, and from there Portuguese ships take it to the Portuguese enclave of Macao on Chinese territory. The United States, on the other hand, bought chrome at a more expensive rate elsewhere in order to apply the sanctions. If the Soviet representative were really interested in sanctions enforcement, rather than making political propaganda, the countries selected for citation in this paragraph certainly would have been quite different, and he would have reported the Peiping violations to the Committee. Furthermore, in the interest of preserving the stability of the world economy, the United States had opposed South Africa's efforts to raise the price of gold; if the price had been raised, it would have been profitable for both South Africa and for the USSR.

He agreed with the USSR representative that the report should state that the sanctions had so far not accomplished their main objective. However, he was opposed to the use of the word "murderous" in speaking of the Southern Rhodesian régime; other tyrannies had behaved more scandalously in that respect. As to foreign investments in Southern Rhodesia, he pointed out that there had been no new United States investments in that country and that even before the sanctions had been applied, United States investments in Southern Rhodesia were insignificant and amounted to less than .0001 of total United States investments throughout the world. His Government had no control over those funds.

Since there was no consensus on the question of enlarging the membership of the Committee, he felt that that question should be considered after the report had been submitted. The question whether the Committee should have open or closed meeings should be decided later after a decision had been taken on enlargement of the membership.

With regard to the USSR proposal that the Security Council should apply all the sanctions provided for under Article 41 of the Charter, he had serious objection to the application of sanctions to posts and telecommunications, which were not yet mandatory. Approximately 1,000 United States citizens were living in Southern Rhodesia, almost all of them missionaries working with the African population. The United States had been reluctant to close its consulate because it wanted to protect its own nationals, but it had eventually done so when Southern Rhodesia proclaimed itself a Republic. It would not be fair to those United States citizens in Southern Rhodesia to cut off all means of communication with the rest of the world and all means of leaving the country. Application of such aspects of Article 41 of the Charter was therefore neither realistic nor practical in the present situation.

With regard to extending the sanctions to South Africa and Portugal, Ambassador Yost had already stated in the Security Council that the United States believed that such a procedure would lead to additional grave complications and would be very unwise. He agreed with the USSR representative that all States should comply with Council resolutions 253

(1968) and 277 (1970). With regard to the use of force against Southern Rhodesia, he emphasized that there was no way to force a permanent member of the Security Council to go to war against its wishes. The United Kingdom had already stated that it was not prepared to use force against the Smith régime and it would be particularly dangerous to embark on such a course in southern Africa. He agreed with the USSR recommendation that a report should be prepared on action taken by national Governments or courts against companies continuing to trade illegally with Southern Rhodesia.

He agreed with the United Kingdom recommendations and found them very helpful. The same was true of most of the recommendations made by Nepal. However, he did not agree with the suggestion made in the working paper submitted by Nepal that Article 2 (5) of the Charter could be invoked, since Southern Rhodesia was not legally a State. As to the Nepalese proposal that the Committee should recommend that all Governments refuse to recognize the new Rhodesian postage stamps, he said it would be unthinkable for the United States to refuse to deliver a missionary's letter to his family in the United States merely because the only postage stamp he could buy happened to be a "Rhodesian" stamp.

In sum, Mr. Chairman, if the Committee were to leave out those proposals which had essentially partisan political motivations, and certain proposals which obviously could not command a consensus, there were significant common elements in all three drafts which could be adopted, could make very helpful recommendations to the Security Council and which his delegation would be prepared to support.

Mr. Hildyard (United Kingdom) said, with regard to the Nepalese proposal that all Governments should refuse to recognize the new Rhodesian postage stamps, that his Government had informed the Universal Postal Union that the stamps were invalid.

Mr. Bhatt (Nepal) said that the proposals which his delegation had circulated to the members should be considered as having been formally submitted.

Mr. Ortega-Urbina (Nicaragua) felt that the Committee's membership should not be enlarged since that would mean altering an established system. It was for the Security Council to decide whether the Committee's meetings should be open or closed. He felt that it would not be a humanitarian act to cut off all communications with Southern Rhodesia and that nothing was to be gained from isolating the indigenous population from the rest of the world. On the contrary, if those people were aware of the rights and freedoms that existed elsewhere they would be in a better position to remedy their own situation. The question of extending the sanctions to Portugal and South Africa was a very important one and it would be better for the Security Council itself, and not the Committee, to take a decision on the matter. The Committee should ensure that no new investments were made in Southern Rhodesia, but it should not recommend the use of force or any other measures which could lead to loss of human life.

The Chairman suggested that the representatives of Nepal, the United Kingdom and the USSR might meet informally with a view to arrive at an agreed text . . . of the report for consideration by the Committee at its next meeting.

It was so decided.

❧9❧

Balance of Power

THE FACT that decisions which may drastically affect the national well-being and vital interests of a nation can be taken in other independent states means that one important objective of its foreign policy must be to neutralize the power threat implicit in such a state system. We have already examined one "solution" to this power problem in Chapter 8. A second solution—indeed, the most frequently adopted solution—is for each nation to seek allies who will counterbalance the power of its principal rival and its allies. This creates an alliance system which may preserve national security by the balancing of rival nations and rival power blocs. Under conditions of a true balance neither group could afford to make the decision to attack the other, since it is a first principle of military strategy never to attack without superior force and some assurance of "victory."

Within the whole field of international relations no concept is superficially so capable of definition and yet so elusive and subtle in its implications and workings as the balance of power. To compound the problem, since the idea is very old (and even the term dates back three centuries), many authors have had an opportunity to use it with successively contrasting meanings. No wonder that the concept is frequently dismissed or derided. Goldie's complaint in Chapter 5 about a failure to understand the nature of international law, or Claude's similar observations (in Chapter 7) about what the UN is or is not, could be doubled and underscored for the balance of power.

Sometimes it has been used to imply or reject a supposed automatic tendency of competing nations to arrive at a condition of equilibrium. Sometimes it has meant a given distribution of power in the state system. Sometimes it has been defined to exist only when there are three or more fairly equal powers, or only when a "balancer" is present to keep the scales from tipping. If the balance of power theory was not absolutely essential to describe fundamental phenomena in international relations, it would have long ago disappeared from view, weighted down by these conflicting meanings.

Many special and limited definitions of the balance of power have been consciously posed as straw men, set up to be demolished. What the student should remember is that so long as nations enter into alliances or attempt to manipulate relations between alliance blocs, the balance of power is very much in existence. Obviously, the results of such efforts can either encourage or restrain would-be upsetters of a *status quo,* depending on the particular form the balance may take. Thus the results can be looked at either from the standpoint of an individual actor (nation-state) or from the viewpoint of the effects on the state system as a whole.

In the first selection, "The Balance of Power in Action," Sir Eyre Crowe, for many years a senior permanent Foreign Office official, describes the diplomatic revolution of 1904 from both points of view. In that year an era came to an end when Great Britain, in the face of the growing German threat, came to an understanding with her historic enemy, France. The 1904 entente with France represented a complete reversal of policy toward that nation and was done for balance of power reasons which involved the British abandoning their "splendid isolation" or "balancer" position for an integral part in the balance proper.

The selection, from Crowe's official pre-World War I memorandum, is a classic statement of the balance of power. His analysis sheds much light on how Britain has historically regarded the operation of the balance of power. Especially interesting is the way in which Crowe links the balance of power to the necessity for Britain's safeguarding the independence of small states—a refutation, certainly, of the common American assumption that the balance of power represents a "selfish" or narrow policy.

In the second selection, "International Structure, National Force, and the Balance of World Power," Kenneth N. Waltz of California (Berkeley), examines whether in the nuclear age "the affairs of the world can any longer be conducted or understood according to the balance-of-power concept." He particularly raises the question, given two superpowers, whether the balance concept is at all applicable. Waltz concludes that the specific form of the contemporary balance of power is different from its typical, classic form, but that it is still very much at the center of the relations of nations. (How do Waltz's views on power and its uses compare to McClelland's in Chapter 1? Waltz says that "force is most useful . . . when it need not be used in . . . warfare.")

When the reader has finished both selections he should be well aware that the theory of the balance of power is not at all as simple as it appears to begin with. Balance of power theory is essentially a generalized description of how the national power of a number of states, interacting out of frequently divergent strategies, produces particular kinds of systems results. Whatever the national strategy, the intent of any one "player" or participant is always to influence the conditions under which a potential opponent may be tempted to resort to force. While the chips in the game are ultimately military, the emphasis in the play is psychological and political.

21

THE BALANCE OF POWER IN ACTION

Sir Eyre Crowe[*]

The Anglo-French Agreement of the 8th April, 1904, was the outcome of the honest and ardent desire, freely expressed among all classes and parties of the two countries, that an earnest effort should be made to compose, as far as possible, the many differences which had been a source of perpetual friction between them. . . .

The conviction that the removal of causes of friction, apart from having an independent value of its own, as making directly for peace, would also confer on the Governments of both countries greater freedom in regulating their general foreign relations, can hardly be supposed to have been absent from the mind of the British and French negotiators. Whenever the Government of a country is confronted with external difficulties by the opposition of another State on a question of national rights or claims, the probable attitude of third Powers in regard to the point in dispute must always be a matter of anxious concern. The likelihood of other Powers actively taking sides in a quarrel which does not touch them directly may reasonably be expected, and, indeed, is shown by experience, very much to depend, quite apart from the merits of the dispute, on the general trend of relations existing between the several parties. It is impossible to overestimate the importance in such a connection of the existence of a firmly established and broadly based system of friendly intercourse with those Powers whose position would enable them to throw a heavy weight into the balance of strength on the other side. If a country could be imagined whose foreign relations were so favourably disposed that, in the defence of its legitimate interests, it could always count upon the sympathy of its most powerful neighbors, such a country would never—or at least not so long as the national armaments were maintained at the proper standard of efficiency—need to entertain those fears and misgivings which, under the actual conditions of dominant international jealousies and rivalries, only too often compel the abandonment of a just cause as the only alternative to the more serious evil and risk of giving suspicious and unfriendly neighbors a welcome opportunity for aggression or hostile and humiliating interference. If both France and England were

---

[*] Sir Eyre Crowe, "Memorandum," *British Documents on the Outbreak of the War,* edited by Gooch and Temperley. Vol. III, 1928, pp. 397–400, 402–403, 417.

acutely conscious that, in the contingency of either of them being involved in a quarrel with this or that Power, an Anglo-French understanding would at least remove one serious danger inherent in such a situation, patriotic self-interest would, on this ground alone, justify and encourage any attempt to settle outstanding differences, if and so far as they were found capable of settlement without jeopardizing vital interests. . . .

The maintenance of a state of tension and antagonism between third Powers had avowedly been one of the principal elements in Bismarck's political combinations by which he first secured and then endeavoured to preserve the predominant position of Germany on the continent. . . . The conclusion of the Franco-Russian alliance some time after Bismarck's fall filled Germany with concern and anxiety, and she never ceased in her efforts at least to neutralize it by establishing the closest possible relations with Russia for herself. . . .

It was, in fact, soon made apparent that, far from welcoming . . . an Anglo-French rapprochement, the Emperor's Government [Germany] had been thoroughly alarmed at the mere disappearance of all causes of friction between the two Western Powers. . . . Nor is it possible to be blind to the fact that Germany is bound to be as strongly opposed to a possible Anglo-Russian understanding. . . .

The general character of England's foreign policy is determined by the immutable conditions of her geographical situation on the ocean flank of Europe as an island State with vast overseas colonies and dependencies, whose existence and survival as an independent community are inseparably bound up with the possession of preponderant sea power. . . . Sea power is more potent than land power, because it is as pervading as the element in which it moves and has its being. Its formidable character makes itself felt the more directly that a maritime State is, in the literal sense of the word, the neighbor of every country accessible by sea. It would, therefore, be but natural that the power of a State supreme at sea should inspire universal jealousy and fear, and be ever exposed to the danger of being overthrown by a general combination of the world. Against such a combination no single nation could in the long run stand, least of all a small island kingdom not possessed of the military strength of a people trained to arms, and dependent for its food supply on oversea commerce. The danger can in practice only be averted—and history shows that it has been so averted—on condition that the national policy of the insular and naval State is so directed as to harmonize with the general desires and ideals common to all mankind, and more particularly that it is closely identified with the primary and vital interests of a majority, or as many as possible, of the other nations. Now, the first interest of all countries is the preservation of national independence. It follows that England, more than any other non-insular Power, has a direct and positive interest in the maintenance of the independence of nations, and therefore must be the natural enemy of any country threatening the independence of others, and the natural protector of the weaker communities. . . .

History shows that the danger threatening the independence of this or that nation has generally arisen, at least in part, out of the momentary predominance of a neighboring State at once militarily powerful, economically efficient, and ambitious to extend its frontiers or spread its influence, the danger being directly proportionate to the degree of its power and efficiency, and to the spontaneity or "inevitableness" of its ambitions. The only check on the abuse of political predominance derived from such a position has always consisted in the opposition of an equally formidable rival, or of a combination of several countries forming leagues of defence. The equilibrium established by such a grouping of forces is technically known as the balance of power, and it has become almost an historical truism to identify England's secular policy with the maintenance of this balance by throwing her weight now in this scale and now in that, but ever on the side opposed to the political dictatorship of the strongest single State or group at a given time.

If this view of British policy is correct, the opposition into which England must inevitably be driven to any country aspiring to such a dictatorship assumes almost the form of a law of nature. . . .

By applying this general law to a particular case, the attempt might be made to ascertain whether, at a given time, some powerful and ambitious State is or is not in a position of natural and necessary enmity towards England; and the present position of Germany might, perhaps, be so tested. . . .

So long as England remains faithful to the general principle of the preservation of the balance of power, her interests would not be served by Germany being reduced to the rank of a weak Power, as this might easily lead to a Franco-Russian predominance equally, if not more, formidable to the British Empire. There are no existing German rights, territorial or other, which this country could wish to see diminished. Therefore, so long as Germany's action does not overstep the line of legitimate protection of existing rights she can always count upon the sympathy and good-will, and even the moral support, of England.

22

INTERNATIONAL STRUCTURE, NATIONAL FORCE, AND THE BALANCE OF WORLD POWER

Balance of power is the hoariest concept in the field of international relations. Elaborated in a variety of analyses and loaded with different meanings, it has often been praised or condemned, but has seldom been wholly rejected. In a fascinating historical account of balance-of-power concepts, Martin Wight has distinguished nine meanings of the term.[1] For purposes of theoretical analysis a tenth meaning, cast in causal terms, should be added.

Balance-of-power theory assumes that the desire for survival supplies the basic motivation of states, indicates the responses that the constraints of the system encourage, and describes the expected outcome. Beyond the survival motive, the aims of states may be wondrously varied; they may range from the ambition to conquer the world to the desire merely to be left alone. But the minimum responses of states, which are necessary to the dynamics of balance, derive from the condition of national coexistence where no external guarantee of survival exists. Perception of the peril that lies in unbalanced power encourages the behavior required for the maintenance of a balance-of-power system.

Because of the present narrow concentration of awesome power, the question arises whether the affairs of the world can any longer be conducted or understood according to the balance-of-power concept, the main theoretical prop of those traditionally called realists. Even many who share the realist concern with power question its present relevance. They do so for two reasons.

It is, in the first place, widely accepted that balance-of-power politics requires the presence of three or more states. Political thought is so histori-

* Kenneth N. Waltz, "International Structure, National Force, and the Balance of World Power." Copyright by the Trustees of Columbia University. Permission to reprint from the *Journal of Internationl Affairs*, Vol. 21, No. 2, pp. 215–231, 1967, is gratefully acknowledged to the Editors of the *Journal*.
1 Martin Wight, "The Balance of Power," in *Diplomatic Investigations: Essays in the Theory of International Politics*, ed. by Herbert Butterfield and Martin Wight (Cambridge: Harvard University Press, 1966), p. 151.

cally conditioned that the balance of power as it is usually defined merely reflects the experience of the modern era. In Europe for a period of three centuries, from the Treaty of Westphalia to the Second World War, five or more great powers sometimes sought to coexist peacefully and at other times competed for mastery. The idea thus became fixed that a balance of power can exist only where the participants approximate the customary number. But something more than habit is involved. Also mixed into ideas about necessary numbers is the notion that flexibility in the alignment of states is a requirement of balance-of-power politics. The existence of only two states at the summit of power precludes the possibility of international maneuver and national realignment as ways of compensating for changes in the strength of either of them. Excessive concentration of power negates the possibility of playing the politics of balance.

Second, war or the threat of war, another essential means of adjustment, is said to be of only limited utility in the nuclear age. In balances of power, of course, more is placed on the scales than mere military force. Military force has, however, served not only as the *ultima ratio* of international politics but indeed as the first and the constant one. To reduce force to being the *ultima ratio* of politics implies, as Ortega y Gasset once noted, "the previous submission of force to methods of reason."[2] Insufficient social cohesion exists among states and the instruments of international control are too weak to relegate power to the status of simply the *ultima ratio*. Power cannot be separated from the purposes of those who possess it; in international politics power has appeared primarily as the power to do harm.[3] To interdict the use of force by the threat of force, to oppose force with force, to annex territory by force, to influence the policies of other states by the threat or application of force—such uses of force have always been present at least as possibilities in the relations of states. The threat to use military forces and their occasional commitment to battle have helped to regulate the relations of states, and the preponderance of power in the hands of the major states has set them apart from the others. But, it is now often said, nuclear weapons, the "best" weapons of the most powerful states, are the least usable. At the extreme, some commentators assert that military force has become obsolete. Others, more cautious in their claims, believe that the inflated cost of using military force has seriously distorted both the balance between the military strong states and the imbalance between the strong and the weak ones. National military power, though not rendered wholly obsolete by nuclear weapons, nevertheless must be heavily dis-

---

[2] Quoted in Chalmers Johnson, *Revolutionary Change* (Boston: Little, Brown, 1966), p. 13.

[3] I do not mean to imply that this exhausts the purposes of power. In this essay, however, I cannot analyze other aspects of power either in themselves or in relation to the power to do harm.

counted. The power of the two nuclear giants, it would seem, is then seriously impaired.[4]

A weird picture of the political world is thus drawn. The constraints of balance-of-power politics still operate: each state by its own efforts fends for its rights and seeks to maintain its existence. At the same time, the operation of balance-of-power politics is strangely truncated; for one essential means of adjustment is absent, and the operation of the other is severely restricted. In the nineteenth-century liberals' vision of a world without power, force was to be banished internationally by the growing perfection of states and their consequent acceptance of each other as equals in dignity. The liberal utopia has reappeared in odd form. The limitation of power— or in extreme formulations, its abolition—is said to derive from the nuclear armament of some states; for nuclear armament makes at once for gross inequality in the power of states and for substantial equality among all states through the inability of the most powerful to use force effectively. Those who love paradox are understandably enchanted. To examine the ground upon which the supposed paradox rests is one of the main aims of this essay.

I

The first reason for believing that balance-of-power politics has ended is easy to deal with, for only its relevance, not its truth, is in question.

If the balance-of-power game is really played hard it eventuates in two participants, whether states or groupings of them. If two groupings of states have hardened or if the relation of major antagonism in the world is simply between two nations, the balance-of-power model no longer applies, according to the conventional definition. This conclusion is reached by placing heavy emphasis on the process of balancing (by realignments of states) rather than on altering power (which may depend on the efforts of each state).[5] In a two-power world, emphasis must shift from the international process of balancing to the prospect of altering power by the internal efforts of each participant.

---

[4] The point has been made most extensively by Klaus Knorr and most insistently by Stanley Hoffmann. See Knorr, *On the Uses of Military Power in the Nuclear Age* (Princeton: Princeton University Press, 1966). See also Hoffmann, "Obstinate or Obsolete? The Fate of the Nation-State and the Case of Western Europe," *Daedalus*, Vol. XCV (Summer 1965), especially pp. 897, 907; "Europe's Identity Crisis: Between the Past and America," *Daedalus*, Vol. XCIII (Fall 1964), especially pp. 1287–88; "Nuclear Proliferation and World Politics," in *A World of Nuclear Powers?*, ed. by Alastair Buchan (Englewood Cliffs, N.J.: Prentice-Hall, 1966); and two essays in *The State of War* (New York: Praeger, 1965), "Roulette in the Cellar: Notes on Risk in International Relations," especially pp. 140–47, and "Terror in Theory and Practice," especially pp. 233–51.

[5] See, for example, Inis L. Claude, Jr., *Power and International Relations* (New York: Random House, 1962), p. 90; and Morton A. Kaplan, *System and Process in International Politics* (New York: John Wiley & Sons, 1957), p. 22.

Admittedly, the old balance-of-power model cannot be applied without modification to a world in which two states far exceed all others in the force at their disposal. Balance-of-power analysis, however, remains highly useful if the observer shifts his perspective from a concentration upon international maneuver as a mode of adjustment to an examination of national power as a means of control and national effort as a way of compensating for incipient disequilibria of power. With this shift in perspective, balance-of-power politics does not disappear; but the meaning of politics changes in a manner that can only be briefly suggested here.

In a world of three or more powers the possibility of making and breaking alliances exists. The substance of balance-of-power politics is found in the diplomacy by which alliances are made, maintained, or disrupted. Flexibility of alignment then makes for rigidity in national strategies: a state's strategy must satisfy its partner lest that partner defect from the alliance. A comparable situation is found where political parties compete for votes by forming and reforming electoral coalitions of different economic, ethnic, religious, and regional groups. The strategies (or policies) of the parties are made so as to attract and hold voters. If it is to be an electoral success, a party's policy cannot simply be the policy that its leaders may think would be best for the country. Policy must at least partly be made for the sake of party management. Similarly in an alliance of approximately equal states, strategy is at least partly made for the sake of the alliance's cohesion. The alliance diplomacy of Europe in the years before World War I is rich in examples of this. Because the defection or defeat of a major state would have shaken the balance of power, each state was constrained to adjust its strategy and the deployment of its forces to the aims and fears of its partners. This is in sharp contrast to the current situation in NATO, where de Gaulle's disenchantment, for example, can only have mild repercussions. Though concessions to allies will sometimes be made, neither the Soviet Union nor the United States alters its strategy or changes its military dispositions simply to accommodate associated states. Both superpowers can make long-range plans and carry out their policies as best they see fit, for they need not accede to the demands of third parties. That America's strategy is not made for the sake of de Gaulle helps to explain his partial defection.

Disregarding the views of an ally makes sense only if military cooperation is relatively unimportant. This is the case in NATO, which in fact if not in form consists of unilateral guarantees by the United States to its European allies. The United States, with a preponderance of nuclear weapons and as many men in uniform as all of the Western European states combined,[6] may be able to protect her allies; they cannot possibly protect her. Because of the vast differences in the capacities of member states, the approximately

---

[6] See "The Text of Address by McNamara to American Society of Newspaper Editors," *The New York Times*, May 19, 1966, p. 11.

equal sharing of burdens found in earlier alliance systems is no longer conceivable. The gross inequality between the two superpowers and the members of their respective alliances makes any realignment of the latter fairly insignificant. The leader's strategy can therefore be flexible. In balance-of-power politics, old style, flexibility of alignment made for rigidity of strategy or the limitation of freedom of decision. In balance-of-power politics, new style, the obverse is true: rigidity of alignment in a two-power world makes for flexibility of strategy or the enlargement of freedom of decision.

Those who discern the demise of balance-of-power politics mistakenly identify the existence of balances of power with a particular mode of adjustment and the political means of effecting it. Balances of power tend to form so long as states desire to maintain their political identities and so long as they must rely on their own devices in striving to do so. With shrinking numbers, political practices and methods will differ; but the number of states required for the existence and perpetuation of balance-of-power politics is simply two or more, not, as is usually averred, some number larger than two.

II

The reduction in the number of major states calls for a shift in conceptual perspective. Internal effort has replaced external realignment as a means of maintaining an approximate balance of power. But the operation of a balance of power, as previously noted, has entailed the occasional use of national force as a means of international control and adjustment. Great-power status was traditionally conferred on states that could use force most handily. Is the use of force in a nuclear world so severely inhibited that balance-of-power analysis has lost most if not all of its meaning?

Four reasons are usually given in support of an affirmative answer. First, because the nuclear might of one superpower balances that of the other, their effective power is reduced to zero. Their best and most distinctive forces, the nuclear ones, are least usable. In the widely echoed words of John Herz, absolute power equals absolute impotence.[7] Second, the fear of escalation strongly inhibits even the use of conventional forces, especially by the United States or the Soviet Union. Nuclear powers must fear escalation more than other states do, for in any war that rose to the nuclear level they would be primary targets. They may, of course, still choose to commit their armies to battle, but the risks of doing so, as they themselves must realize, are higher than in the past. Third, in the nuclear age enormous military power no longer ensures effective control. The Soviet Union has not been able to control her Asian and European satellites. The United

---

[7] John Herz, *International Politics in the Atomic Age* (New York: Columbia University Press, 1959), pp. 22, 169.

States has found it difficult to use military force for constructive purposes even against weak opponents in Southeast Asia. Political rewards have not been proportionate to the strength of the states that are militarily most powerful. Finally, the weak states of the world, having become politically aware and active, have turned world opinion into a serious restraint upon the use of force, whether in nuclear or conventional form. These four factors, it is argued, work singly and in combination to make the use of force more costly and in general to depreciate its value.

Never have great powers disposed of larger national products, and seldom in peacetime have they spent higher percentages of them on their military forces. The money so lavishly expended purchases more explosive power and more varied ways of delivering it than ever before in history. In terms of world distribution, seldom has military force been more narrowly concentrated. If military force is less useful today, the irony of history will have yet another vivid illustration. Has force indeed so depreciated as to warp and seriously weaken the effects of power in international relations? The above arguments make it seem so; they need to be re-examined. The following analysis of the use of force deals with all four arguments, though not by examining them one by one and in the order in which they are stated.

E. H. Carr long ago identified the error of believing "in the efficacy of an international public opinion," and he illustrated and explained the fallacy at length.[8] To think of world opinion as a restraint upon the military actions of states, one must believe that the strong states of the world—or for that matter the weak ones—would have used more military force and used it more often had they not anticipated their condemnation. Unless in a given instance world opinion can be defined, its source identified, and the mode of its operation discerned, such a view is not plausible. To believe in the efficacy of world opinion is to endow a non-existent agent and an indefinable force with effective restraining power. Not world opinion but national views, shaped into policies and implemented by governments, have accounted for past events in international relations. Changes that would now permit world opinion, whatever that might be, to restrict national policies would have to lie not in the operation of opinion itself but in other changes that have occurred in the world. With "world opinion," as with Adam Smith's "invisible hand," one must ask: What is the reality that the metaphor stands for? It may be that statesmen pay their respects to world opinion because they are already restrained by other considerations.

Are such considerations found, perhaps, in changes that have taken place in the nature and distribution of force itself? If the costs of using military force have lessened its value, then obeisance paid to world opinion is merely a cloak for frustration and a hypocritical show of politeness. That the use of

---

[8] Edward Hallett Carr, *The Twenty Years' Crisis, 1919–1939*, 2nd ed. (New York: Harper & Row, 1964), p. 140.

force is unusually costly, however, is a conclusion that rests on a number of errors. One that is commonly committed is to extend to all military force the conclusion that nuclear force is unusable. After listing the changes effected by nuclear weapons, one author, for example, concludes that these changes tend to restrict "the usability and hence the political utility of national military power in various ways."[9] This may represent merely a slip of the pen; if so, it is a telling one. A clearer and more interesting form of the error is found in the argument that the two superpowers, each stalemated by the other's nuclear force, are for important political purposes effectively reduced to the power of middle-range states. The effective equality of states apparently emerges from the very condition of their gross inequality. We read, for example, that "the very change in the nature of the mobilizable potential has made its actual use in emergencies by its unhappy owners quite difficult and self-defeating. As a result, nations endowed with infinitely less can behave in a whole range of issues as if the difference in power did not matter." The conclusion is driven home—or, rather, error is compounded —by the argument that the United States thinks in "cataclysmic terms," lives in dread of all-out war, and bases its military calculations on the forces needed for the ultimate but unlikely crisis rather than on what might be needed in the less spectacular cases that are in fact more likely to occur.[10]

Absolute power equals absolute impotence, at least at the highest levels of force represented by the American and Soviet nuclear armories. At lesser levels of violence many states can compete as though they were substantially equal. The best weapons of the United States and the Soviet Union are useless, and the distinctive advantage of those two states is thus negated. But what about American or Soviet nuclear weapons used against minor nuclear states or against those who are entirely without nuclear weapons? Here again, it is claimed, the "best" weapon of the most powerful states turns out to be the least usable. The nation that is equipped to "retaliate massively" is not likely to find the occasion to use its capability. If amputation of an arm were the only remedy available for an infected finger, one would be tempted to hope for the best and leave the ailment untreated. The state that can move effectively only by committing the full power of its military arsenal is likely to forget the threats it has made and acquiesce in a situation formerly described as intolerable. Instruments that cannot be used to deal with small cases—those that are moderately dangerous and damaging—remain idle until the big case arises. But then the use of major force to defend a vital interest would run the grave risk of retaliation. Under such circumstances, the powerful are frustrated by their very strength; and although the weak do not thereby become strong, they are, it is said, nevertheless able to behave as though they were.

Such arguments are often made and have to be taken seriously. In an ob-

---

[9] Knorr, *On the Uses of Military Power*, p. 87.
[10] Hoffmann, "Europe's Identity Crisis," pp. 1279, 1287–88.

vious sense, part of the contention is valid. When great powers are in a stalemate, lesser states acquire an increased freedom of movement. That this phenomenon is now noticeable tells us nothing new about the strength of the weak or the weakness of the strong. Weak states have often found opportunities for maneuver in the interstices of a balance of power. This is, however, only part of the story. To maintain both the balance and its by-product requires the continuing efforts of America and Russia. Their instincts for self-preservation call forth such efforts: the objective of both states must be to perpetuate an international stalemate as a minimum basis for the security of each of them—even if this should mean that the two big states do the work while the small ones have the fun. The margins within which the relative strengths of America and Russia may vary without destroying the stalemate are made wide by the existence of second-strike retaliatory forces, but permissible variation is not without limit. In the years of the supposed missile gap in America's disfavor, Khrushchev became unpleasantly frisky, especially over Berlin and Cuba. The usefulness of maintaining American nuclear strength was demonstrated by the unfortunate consequences of its apparent diminution.

Strategic nuclear weapons deter strategic nuclear weapons (though they may also do more than that). Where each state must tend to its own security as best it can, the means adopted by one state must be geared to the efforts of others. The cost of the American nuclear establishment, maintained in peaceful readiness, is functionally comparable to the costs incurred by a government in order to maintain domestic order and provide internal security. Such expenditure is not productive in the sense that spending to build roads is, but it is not unproductive either. Its utility is obvious, and should anyone successfully argue otherwise, the consequences of accepting his argument would quickly demonstrate its falsity. Force is least visible where power is most fully and most adequately present.[11] The better ordered a society and the more competent and respected its government, the less force its policemen are required to employ. Less shooting occurs in present-day Sandusky than did on the western frontier. Similarly in international relations, states supreme in their power have to use force less often. "Non-recourse to force"—as both Eisenhower and Khrushchev seem to have realized—is the doctrine of powerful states. Powerful states need to use force less often than their weaker neighbors because the strong can more often protect their interests or work their wills in other ways—by persuasion and cajolery, by economic bargaining and bribery, by the extension of aid, or finally by posing deterrent threats. Since states with large nuclear armories do not actually "use" them, force is said to be discounted. Such reasoning is fallacious. Possession of power should not be identified with the use of force, and the usefulness of force should not be confused with its usa-

---

[11] Cf. Carr, The Twenty Years' Crisis, pp. 103, 129–32.

bility. To introduce such confusions into the analysis of power is comparable to saying that the police force that seldom if ever employs violence is weak or that a police force is strong only when policemen are swinging their clubs. To vary the image, it is comparable to saying that a man with large assets is not rich if he spends little money or that a man is rich only if he spends a lot of it.

But the argument, which we should not lose sight of, is that just as the miser's money may grossly depreciate in value over the years, so the great powers' military strength has lost much of its usability. If military force is like currency that cannot be spent or money that has lost much of its worth, then is not forbearance in its use merely a way of disguising its depreciated value? Conrad von Hötzendorf, Austrian Chief of Staff prior to the First World War, looked upon military power as though it were a capital sum, useless unless invested. In his view, the investment of military force was ultimately its commitment to battle.[12] It may be permissible to reason in this way, but it makes the result of the reasoning a foregone conclusion. As Robert W. Tucker has noted, those who argue that force has lost its utility do so "in terms of its virtually uncontrolled use." But, he adds, "alter the assumption on which the argument proceeds—consider the functions served by military power so long as it is not overtly employed or employed only with restraint—and precisely the opposite conclusion may be drawn."[13]

In the reasoning of Conrad, military force is most useful at the moment of its employment in war. Depending on a country's situation, it may make much better sense to say that military force is most useful when it deters an attack, that is, when it need not be used in battle at all. When the strongest state militarily is also a status-quo power, non-use of force is a sign of its strength. Force is most useful, or best serves the interests of such a state, when it need not be used in the actual conduct of warfare. Again, the reasoning is old-fashioned. Throughout a century that ended in 1914, the British navy was powerful enough to scare off all comers, while Britain carried out occasional imperial ventures in odd parts of the world. Only as Britain's power weakened did her military forces have to be used to fight a full-scale war. By being used, her military power had surely become less useful.

Force is cheap, especially for a status-quo power, if its very existence works against its use. What does it mean then to say that the cost of using

---

[12] "The sums spent for the war power is money wasted," he maintained, "if the war power remains unused for obtaining political advantages. In some cases the mere threat will suffice and the war power thus becomes useful, but others can be obtained only through the warlike use of the war power itself, that is, by war undertaken in time; if this moment is missed, the capital is lost. In this sense, war becomes a great financial enterprise of the State." Quoted in Alfred Vagts, *Defense and Diplomacy: The Soldier and the Conduct of Foreign Relations* (New York: King's Crown Press, 1956), p. 361.

[13] Robert W. Tucker, "Peace and War," *World Politics*, Vol. XVII (Jan. 1965), p. 324 fn. For a comprehensive and profound examination of the use of force internationally, see Robert Osgood and Robert Tucker, *Force, Order, and Justice* (forthcoming).

force has increased while its utility has lessened? It is highly important, indeed useful, to think in "cataclysmic terms," to live in dread of all-out war, and to base military calculations on the force needed for the ultimate but unlikely crisis. That the United States does so, and that the Soviet Union apparently does too, makes the cataclysm less likely to occur. But not only that. Nuclear weapons deter nuclear weapons; they also serve as a means of limiting escalation. The temptation of one country to employ larger and larger amounts of force is lessened if its opponent has the ability to raise the ante. Conventional force may be used more hesitantly than it would be in the absence of nuclear weapons because it cannot be assumed that escalation will be perfectly regulated. But force can be used with less hesitation by those states able to parry, to thrust, and to threaten at varied levels of military endeavor.

Where power is seen to be balanced, whether or not the balance is nuclear, it may seem that the resultant of opposing forces is zero. But this is misleading. The vectors of national force do not meet at a point, if only because the power of a state does not resolve into a single vector. Military force is divisible, especially for the state that can afford a lot of it. In a nuclear world, contrary to some assertions, the dialectic of inequality does not produce the effective equality of strong and weak states. Lesser states that decide to establish a nuclear arsenal by slighting their conventional forces render themselves unable to meet any threat to themselves other than the ultimate one (and that doubtfully). By way of contrast, the military doctrine of the United States, to which the organization of her forces corresponds, is one of flexible response. Great powers are strong not simply because they have nuclear weapons but also because their immense resources enable them to generate and maintain power of all types, military and other, at different technological levels.

Just as the state that refrains from applying force is said to betray its weakness, so the state that has trouble in exercising control is said to display the defectiveness of its power. In such a conclusion, the elementary error of identifying power with control is evident. Absence of control or failure to press hard to achieve it may indicate either that the would-be controller noticed that, try as he might, he would have insufficient force or inappropriate types of force at his command; or it may indicate that he chose to make less than a maximum effort because imposition of control was not regarded as very important. One student of international relations has remarked that "though the weapons of mass destruction grow more and more ferociously efficient, the revolutionary guerrilla armed with nothing more advanced than an old rifle and a nineteenth-century political doctrine has proved the most effective means yet devised for altering the world power-balance."[14] But the revolutionary guerrilla wins civil wars, not inter-

---

[14] Coral Bell, "Non-Alignment and the Power Balance," *Survival*, Vol. V (Nov.-Dec. 1963), p. 255.

national ones, and no civil war can change the balance of power in the world unless it takes place in the United States or the Soviet Union. Enough of them have occurred since the Second World War to make the truth of this statement clear without need for further analysis. Even in China, the most populous of states, a civil war that led to a change of allegiance in the cold war did not seriously tilt the world balance.

Two states that enjoy wide margins of power over other states need worry little about changes that occur among the latter. Failure to act may then not betray the frustrations of impotence; instead it may demonstrate the serenity of power. The United States, having chosen to intervene in Vietnam, has limited the use of its military force. Because no realignment of national power in Vietnam could in itself affect the balance of power between the United States and the Soviet Union—or even noticeably alter the imbalance of power between the United States and China—the United States need not have intervened at all. Whether or not it could have safely "passed" in Southeast Asia, the American government chose not to do so; nor have its costly, long-sustained efforts brought success. If military power can be equated with control, then the United States has indeed demonstrated its weakness. The case is instructive. The People's Republic of China has not moved militarily against any country of Southeast Asia. The United States could successfully counter such a move, one would expect, by opposing military force with military force. What has worried some people and led others to sharpen their statements about the weakness of the powerful is that the United States, hard though it has tried, has been unable to put down insurrection and halt the possible spread of Communist ideology.

Here again old truths need to be brought into focus. As David Hume long ago noted, "force is always on the side of the governed."[15] The governors, being few in number, depend for the exercise of their rule upon the more or less willing assent of their subjects. If sullen disregard is the response to every command, no government can rule. And if a country, because of internal disorder and lack of coherence, is unable to rule itself, no body of foreigners, whatever the military force at its command, can reasonably hope to do so. If Communism is the threat to Southeast Asia, then military forces are not the right means for countering it. If insurrection is the problem, then it can hardly be hoped that an alien army will be able to pacify a country that is unable to govern itself. Foreign troops, though not irrelevant to such problems, can only be of indirect help. Military force, used internationally, is a means of establishing control over a territory, not of exercising control within it. The threat of a nation to use military force, whether nuclear or conventional, is pre-eminently a means of affecting an-

---

15 "The soldan of Egypt or the emperor of Rome," he went on to say, "might drive his harmless subjects like brute beasts against their sentiments and inclination. But he must, at least, have led his *mamalukes* or *praetorian bands,* like men, by their opinion." "Of the First Principles of Government," in *Hume's Moral and Political Philosophy,* ed. by Henry D. Aiken (New York: Hafner, 1948), p. 307.

other state's external behavior, of dissuading a state from launching a career of aggression and of meeting the aggression if dissuasion should fail.

Dissuasion or deterrence is easier to accomplish than "compellence," to use an apt term invented by Thomas C. Schelling.[16] Compellence is more difficult to achieve than deterrence, and its contrivance is a more intricate affair. In Vietnam, the United States faces not merely the task of compelling a particular action but of promoting an effective political order. Those who argue from such a case that force has depreciated in value fail in their analyses to apply their own historical and political knowledge. The master builders of imperial rule, such men as Bugeaud, Galliéni, and Lyautey, played both political and military roles. In like fashion, successful counter-revolutionary efforts have been directed by such men as Templer and Magsaysay, who combined military resources with political instruments.[17] Military forces, whether domestic or foreign, are insufficient for the task of pacification, the more so if a country is rent by faction and if its people are politically engaged and active. To say that militarily strong states are feeble because they cannot easily bring order to minor states is like saying that a pneumatic hammer is weak because it is not suitable for drilling decayed teeth. It is to confuse the purpose of instruments and to confound the means of external power with the agencies of internal governance. Inability to exercise *political* control over others does not indicate *military* weakness. Strong states cannot do everything with their military forces, as Napoleon acutely realized; but they are able to do things that militarily weak states cannot do. The People's Republic of China can no more solve the problems of governance in some Latin American country than the United States can in Southeast Asia. But the United States can intervene with great military force in far quarters of the world while wielding an effective deterrent against escalation. Such action exceeds the capabilities of all but the strongest of states.

Differences in strength do matter, though not for every conceivable purpose. To deduce the weakness of the powerful from this qualifying clause is a misleading use of words. One sees in such a case as Vietnam not the *weakness* of great military power in a nuclear world but instead a clear illustration of the *limits* of military force in the world of the present as always.

III

Only a sketch, intended to be suggestive, can here be offered of the connections between the present structure of the global balance of power, the relations of states, and the use of force internationally.

---

[16] Thomas C. Schelling, *Arms and Influence* (New Haven: Yale University Press, 1966), pp. 70–71.

[17] The point is well made by Samuel P. Huntington, "Patterns of Violence in World Politics," in *Changing Patterns of Military Politics,* ed. by Samuel P. Huntington (New York: The Free Press of Glencoe, 1962), p. 28.

Unbalanced power is a danger to weak states. It may also be a danger to strong ones. An imbalance of power, by feeding the ambition of some states to extend their control, may tempt them to dangerously adventurous activity. Safety for all states, one may then conclude, depends upon the maintenance of a balance among them. Ideally, in this view, the rough equality of states gives each of them the ability to fend for itself. Equality may then also be viewed as a morally desirable condition. Each of the states within the arena of balance will have at least a modest ability to maintain its integrity. At the same time, inequality violates one's sense of justice and leads to national resentments that are in many ways troublesome. Because inequality is inherent in the state system, however, it cannot be removed. At the pinnacle of power, only a few states coexist as approximate equals; in relation to them, other states are of lesser moment. The bothersome qualities of this inevitable inequality of states should not cause one to overlook its virtues. In an economy, in a polity, or in the world at large, extreme equality is associated with instability. To draw another domestic analogy: where individualism is extreme, where society is atomistic, and where secondary organizations are lacking, government tends either to break down into anarchy or to become highly centralized and despotic. Under conditions of extreme equality, the prospect of oscillation between those two poles was well described by de Tocqueville; it was illustrated by Hobbes; and its avoidance was earnestly sought by the authors of the *Federalist Papers*. In a collection of equals, any impulse ripples through the whole society. Lack of secondary groups with some cohesion and continuity of commitment, for example, turns elections into auctions with each party in its promises tempted to bid up the others. The presence of social and economic groups, which inevitably will not all be equal, makes for less volatility in society.

Such durable propositions of political theory are lost sight of in the argument, frequently made, that the larger the number of consequential states the more stable the structure of world politics will be.[18] Carried to its logical conclusion, the argument must mean that perfect stability would prevail in a world in which many states exist, all of them approximate equals in power.

The analysis of the present essay leads to a different conclusion. The inequality of states, though not a guarantee of international stability, at least makes stability possible. Within the structure of world politics, the relations of states will be as variable and complex as the movements and patterns of bits of glass within a kaleidoscope. It is not very interesting to ask whether destabilizing events will occur and disruptive relations will form, because the answer must always be yes. More interesting are such questions as these: What is the likely durability of a given political structure, whether

---

[18] By "structure" I mean the pattern according to which power is distributed; by "stability," the perpetuation of that structure without the occurrence of grossly destructive violence.

international or domestic? How does it affect the relations of states, or of groups and individuals? How do the relations of constituent units and changes within them in turn affect the political structure? Within a state, people use more violence than do governments. In the United States in 1965, 9,814 people were murdered, but only seven were executed.[19] Thus one says (with some exaggeration, since fathers still spank their children) that the state enjoys a monopoly of *legitimate* violence. Too much violence among individuals will jeopardize the political structure. In international relations it is difficult to say that any particular use of violence is illegitimate, but some states have the ability to wield more of it. Because they do, they are able both to moderate others' use of violence and to absorb possibly destabilizing changes that emanate from uses of violence that they do not or cannot control. In the spring of 1966, Secretary McNamara remarked that in the preceding eight years there had been "no less than 164 internationally significant outbreaks of violence. . . ."[20] Of course, not only violence is at issue. To put the point in more general terms, strong structures are able to moderate and absorb destabilizing changes; weak structures succumb to them.

No political structure, whether domestic or international, can guarantee stability. The question that one must ask is not whether a given distribution of power is stable but how stable different distributions of power are likely to be. For a number of reasons, the bipolar world of the past two decades has been highly stable.[21] The two leading states have a common interest in stability: they would at least like to maintain their positions. In one respect, bipolarity is expressed as the reciprocal control of the two strongest states by each other out of their mutual antagonism. What is unpredictable in such a two-party competition is whether one party will try to eliminate the other. Nuclear forces of second-strike capacity induce an added caution. Here again force is useful, and its usefulness is reinforced in proportion as its use is forestalled. Fear of major war induces caution all around; the Soviet Union and the United States wield the means of inducing that caution.

The constraints of duopolistic competition press in one direction: duopolists eye each other warily, and each is very sensitive to the gains of the other. Working in the opposite direction, however, is the existence of the immense difference in power between the two superpowers and the states of middle or lesser rank. This condition of inequality makes it unlikely that any shifts in the alignment of states would very much help or hurt either of the two leading powers. If few changes can damage the vital interests of either of them, then both can be moderate in their responses. Not being de-

---

[19] U.S. Bureau of the Census, *Statistical Abstract of the United States: 1966* (Washington, D.C.: Government Printing Office, 1966), p. 165.

[20] *The New York Times*, May 19, 1966, p. 11.

[21] For further examination of the proposition, see Kenneth N. Waltz, "The Stability of a Bipolar World," *Daedalus*, Vol. XCIII (Summer 1964), pp. 881–909. On the possibility of exercising control, see Waltz, "Contention and Management in International Relations," *World Politics*, Vol. XVII (July 1965), pp. 720–44.

pendent upon allies, the United States and the Soviet Union are free to design strategies in accord with their interests. Since the power actually and potentially at the disposal of each of them far exceeds that of their closest competitors, they are able to control in some measure the possibly destabilizing acts of third parties or to absorb their effects. The Americans and Russians, for example, can acquire the means of defending themselves against the nuclear assaults that the Chinese and French may be able to launch by the mid-1970's. Anti-ballistic-missile systems, useful against missiles launched in small number, are themselves anti-proliferation devices. With considerable expectation of success, states with vast economic, scientific, and technological resources can hope to counter the armaments and actions of others and to reduce their destabilizing effects.[22] The extent of the difference in national capabilities makes the bipolar structure resilient. Defection of allies and national shifts of allegiance do not decisively alter the structure. Because they do not, recalcitrant allies may be treated with indifference; they may even be effectively disciplined. Pressure can be applied to moderate the behavior of third states or to check and contain their activities. The Suez venture of Britain and France was stopped by American financial pressure. Chiang Kai-shek has been kept on a leash by denying him the means of invasion. The prospective loss of foreign aid helped to halt warfare between Pakistan and India, as did the Soviet Union's persuasion. In such ways, the wielding of great power can be useful.

The above examples illustrate hierarchical control operating in a way that often goes unnoticed because the means by which control is exercised are not institutionalized. What management there now is in international relations must be provided, singly and occasionally together, by the duopolists at the top. In certain ways, some of them suggested above, the inequality of states in a bipolar world enables the two most powerful states to develop a rich variety of controls and to follow flexible strategies in using them.

A good many statements about the obsolescence of force, the instability of international politics, and the disappearance of the bipolar order are made because no distinction has been clearly and consistently drawn between international structure, on the one hand, and the relations of states on the other. For more than two decades, power has been narrowly concentrated; and force has been used, not orgiastically as in the world wars of this century, but in a controlled way and for conscious political purposes. Power may be present when force is not used, but force is also used openly. A catalogue of examples would be both complex and lengthy. It would contain such items, on the American side of the ledger, as the garrisoning of Berlin, its supply by airlift during the blockade, the stationing of troops in Europe, the establishment of bases in Japan and elsewhere, the waging of

---

[22] On the limitations of a small nuclear force, see Waltz, *Foreign Policy and Democratic Politics* (Boston: Little, Brown, 1967), pp. 145–48.

war in Korea and Vietnam, and the "quarantine" of Cuba. Seldom if ever has force been more variously, more persistently, and more widely applied; and seldom has it been more consciously used as an instrument of national policy. Since the war we have seen, not the cancellation of force by nuclear stalemate, but instead the political organization and pervasion of power; not the end of balance of power owing to a reduction in the number of major states, but instead the formation and perpetuation of a balance *à deux*.

❧Part Four❦

The Superpowers

≫10≪

Approaches to United States Foreign Policy

ANY NATION's foreign policy will reflect some blend or mix of two factors: its attitudes growing out of its own past experience, plus its conception of the nature of the world outside its frontiers. Each nation will play the role it thinks it ought to play as seen through those two perspectives. If either changes, the foreign policy, too, will change. Thus substantial changes in either attitude or direction are relatively infrequent and are normally the result of traumatic and dramatic experiences.

World War II was such a turning point. After 1945 United States foreign policy became just about the reverse of what it was before. The American people had been told, and told recurrently, that they had undermined the League by nonmembership and nonparticipation in sanctions; that they had held aloof from alliances and thereby prevented a truly effective antiaggressive coalition; that they had tried to ignore the world and that it could not be done. Thereupon, during and after 1945, America helped found the UN, entered into not one alliance but many, gave arms and aid to scores of nations, issued doctrines laying claims to interests all over the world—and, in short, got involved.

While the majority of the American people was convinced of the correctness of this policy it was hardly equally happy with its results. It brought war and death in Korea, further advances of communism despite heroic measures taken, higher taxes, perennial military service, and an unpopular war in Vietnam. The results were disappointing

279

because the predominant American attitude, arising from the easy optimism of much of America's experience, was that enough dedication, dollars, good will, and faith, spell success whatever the odds or task.

It was the Vietnam experience which, above all, led to the search for new and less costly alternatives. The debate over Vietnam raised two closely connected issues even more dramatically than the debate over the Korean War two decades earlier: (1) whether the U.S. should "go it alone" rather than try to act in unison and collectively with allies, and (2) what degree of involvement and forward deployment of U.S. military forces was needed to protect legitimate American interests abroad.

Leaving the debate over Vietnam as such for Chapter 11, we are concerned in this chapter with the evolving attitudes (and their causes) with which Americans approached post-World War II problems.

In the first selection, "War, Crisis and Intellectuals," Robert Nisbet, Professor of Sociology at the University of California, Riverside, writes provocatively of what he sees as the different political style of Democrats and Republicans. In Nisbet's view, "political intellectuals" have a great "proneness toward crisis-mentality." Since the Democratic party in recent decades has surrounded itself with a host of intellectuals at the policy-making level, he sees the Democratic tendency to involve the U.S. in foreign crises as reflecting their preconceptions and attitudes. By contrast, says Nisbet, Eisenhower, "much to the distress of many political intellectuals, had refused to see 'crisis' even in the Hungarian uprising and the Suez disturbance." Nisbet's preliminary verdict on President Nixon: elected with a mandate to disengage from Vietnam, he nonetheless "identifies with the intellectual class in a way that neither Hoover nor Eisenhower ever did." Nisbet might have added that Nixon has some intellectuals around him, too. Perhaps the intellectuals are no longer so certain that the sword is an adequate cure for a "crisis"?

In the second selection, continuing this theme of probing our attitudes, Senator J. William Fulbright, Chairman of the Senate Foreign Relations Committee, looks back over the evolution of American viewpoints after 1945. In his article, "Reflections in Thrall to Fear," he makes an extraordinarily frank appraisal of the development of his own views, showing what he thought at the time, counterpointed with what he thinks now. With an intellectual honesty and a capability for reflection somewhat unusual in a public figure, he has contributed a document well worth study. In many ways it represents, for better or for worse, a picture of a whole generation of American leadership and how they conceptualized the world outside our frontiers. Compare Fulbright's conclusion that "romantic, aggressive 'realism'" has failed to provide useful answers, and his thought that idealism has never been tried, with the selections in Chapters 1, 7, and 8.

In the third selection, "Alternative Strategies for U.S. Policy," Frederick H. Hartmann provides an analytical framework for comparing two alternate foreign policy strategies: bloc containment versus opponent-isolation. Through this analysis Hartmann seeks to answer the question: if the U.S. cannot in a practical sense withdraw or "go it alone," how much of the burden need it carry on its own shoulders? In this selection Hartmann applies the national interest theory explained in Chapter 1. Is Hartmann's "neo-realistic" approach more useful or is Fulbright's wish to implement idealism more suitable for American problems?

Although the book from which the third selection is drawn appeared in 1970, not very long ago, the foreign policy of the United States has been shifting sufficiently rapidly in the direction advocated in the selection that much of the "bloc containment" strategy the selection rejects is rapidly being phased out.

23

WAR, CRISIS AND INTELLECTUALS

Robert Nisbet[*]

In his "Who Needs the Democrats?" John Kenneth Galbraith muses that "wars, just or unjust, have come with devastating reliability every time the Democrats have been in power." Four times America has gone to war this century, and in each of them a Democratic Administration has been in power.

It is possible that we are dealing only with coincidence. No one suggests that the Democrats actually start the wars. It would be absurd to believe that there is any more war-mindedness among Democrats than among Republicans. Assuming that there may be more than coincidence in what Professor Galbraith notes, though, there is one striking difference between the two parties that may shed light on the matter. This lies in a propensity toward crisis-mindedness among Democrats, and in particular among the academic-political intellectuals that have been among that party's brightest ornaments.

The "Tender" and the "Tough"   .

William James once divided minds into the "tender" and "tough." The tender-minded, James wrote, seek refuge in systems, which may be religious or non-religious, in which rational articulation and intellectual symmetry is the essence. The tough-minded on the other hand are empiricists, usually willing to accept experience in its own terms, rarely requiring the anodyne of either system or someone's charisma. I am inclined to think that proneness to see problems as crisis rather than as problems is a further mark of James' tender-minded category.

Not strangely it is among intellectuals, especially political intellectuals, that we find greatest proneness toward crisis-mentality. As brilliance, rather than profundity or knowledge, is the style of the intellectual, so a high sensitivity to the existence of "crisis" is the hallmark of this thought.

Among modern intellectuals, further, there is a frequently observed fondness for the uses of power, especially centralized, bureaucratized power in service to large-scale moral objectives. In a modern nation state, war is the

* Robert Nisbet, "War, Crisis and Intellectuals," *The Wall Street Journal,* January 25, 1971, p. 10. Reprinted by permission.

supreme crisis, the highest expression of a complex of elements including love of large-scale undertakings involving masses of people, power, centralization, bureaucracy and chronic political moralism.

The Democratic Party, on the record, has been rich in these elements since the time of Woodrow Wilson. This was when the liaison between the party and academic intellectuals began in this country. Wilson was himself the perfect academic-political intellectual, the true believer, with the State his temple. He had a strongly developed sense of crisis, moral crisis, political crisis, crisis in the human condition. When he ordered American troops across the Mexican border in chase of bandits he did it, he informed the world, in the interest of mankind. Earlier, while president of Princeton, he had seen crisis involving all of higher education in America in his altercation with Dean West over the precise location of the graduate school.

Who but Wilson—not, certainly, Clemenceau and Lloyd George—would have converted the war in Europe between the Allies and the Central Powers into a total crusade for democracy everywhere? Who but Wilson could have whipped patriotism up to the frenzy it reached by 1918, continuing on through the notorious Palmer raids? To the very end of his Administration Wilson refused pardon for Eugene Debs, in prison on long sentence for pacifism. (Harding pardoned Debs almost immediately, without fanfare.)

Not much of Wilson's political Calvinism stayed with the Democratic Party. His nearly god-like image did, though. So did a few other legacies, among them liaison with academic intellectuals, fondness for large moral objectives, fascination with centralized power and bureaucracy, and, not least a tradition of crisis-mindedness.

Under Franklin D. Roosevelt, members of the academy flocked to Washington, with all the predictable results. Where Hoover was prone, rightly or wrongly, to see only problems, FDR saw or soon came to see the world as a constantly escalating series of crises. From the New Deal with its NRA and Supreme Court-packing bill it was an easy ascent to early involvement in Europe, with the moralistic crescendo reached in FDR's doctrine of unconditional surrender.

After the war, under the Democratic Truman Administration, came not normalcy but the Cold War and a large scale, politically centralized humanitarianism that ranged all the way from the Point 4 Program to the Korean "police action." It was Eisenhower, who very probably never perceived anything as a "crisis" in his entire life, who got America out of Korea.

Vietnam: Its Origins

We come to Vietnam and the Kennedy Administration. Although it is a byword in the New Left that our military engagement there springs from a corrupt middle class and an imperialistic business order, the facts are the very reverse. Not business-oriented, profits-minded leaders of the middle class in Congress, but rather academy-sprung, political intellectuals of the familiar Wilsonian pattern are the ones we are obliged to look to for understanding of how the war in Vietnam came about.

Under Eisenhower, who will do well enough in the history books as a prime representative of the middle class in America, with its business and commercial orientation, involvement in Saigon was rigorously limited to a few hundred, loosely attached, advisers in civilian dress. Eisenhower, much to the distress of many political intellectuals, had refused to see "crisis" even in the Hungarian uprising and the Suez disturbance. Understandably, he had earlier rejected proposals to intervene in support of the French at Dienbienphu, and kept a short leash on the Calvinism of John Foster Dulles. Anything resembling a commitment, military or political, would have been hard to extract from America's position in Vietnam prior to 1960.

Things changed decisively after Kennedy's election. The campaign atmosphere had been filled with the political intellectuals' references to "crises" in missiles, economic growth, higher education, scientific research (though not poverty and civil rights—not then). One might have, knowing the ways of academic-political intellectuals, who well before the election had switched from Stevenson to Kennedy, where the power was, predicted fairly easily that crisis of some kind would quickly emerge once Kennedy was in the White House. And it did.

The flow of intellectuals to Washington—to State, to Pentagon, to all key Executive offices—became a torrent. Overnight America had become, once again, government by academic-political intellectuals: Bundy, Rostow, McNamara, Rusk, Goodwin, Schlesinger, Hilsman, to name the more powerful and illustrious of them. Anything remotely resembling a "crisis" of missiles, of economic growth, or higher education, or scientific research could not be found. Cuba was shortlived. That left the situation in Vietnam.

What happened, under the aegis of Kennedy's political intellectuals, was a simultaneous *militarization* and *politicization* of Washington's relation to Saigon. From a few hundred civilian-clad advisers, loosely attached to Saigon, we moved in a rather short time to several thousand armed, uniformed troops under a four star general. It is hard for the military in such circumstances to be loosely attached, wherever they are, regardless of their number.

The politicization of our relationship was the more fundamental phase, however. Nothing could have seemed more odious to academic-political intellectuals than such a government as Diem's. It had to be managed, directed, run—from Washington, and in accord with Western moral ideals. And that proving difficult, it had to be overthrown. The Diem coup was, beyond any doubt, the decisive action. The Washington intellectuals, having, in effect, destroyed a government many thousand miles away, were honorbound, not to say politically delighted, to govern South Vietnam themselves. Once again political intellectuals were in the delicious position of being able, through centralization of command, through computer-rationalism, through large scale undertaking, with crisis-mentality regnant, to take charge. This was the real, and very nearly irreversible beginning of the American war in Vietnam.

After that came substantial enlargement, growing intensity of White House commitment, and President Johnson's Tonkin Gulf Resolution superbly executed to seal off Congressional opposition. Political intellectuals, predictably, flipped and flopped, with some of them, such as Hilsman and McNamara revealing comical ability to walk down both sides of the street without breaking stride. But despite carefully nurtured myth, Kennedy and his intellectuals, not Johnson and his Texas intimates, are the real architects of Vietnam.

None of this, to anyone familiar with the history of the Democratic Party and its liaison with academic *politiques*, presents any mystery. What is baffling in many ways is the failure of a conservative, middle class, business-oriented, above all Republican opposition to the Intellectuals' War. Where were the Congressional leaders, representatives of war-hating middle America, few of whom ordinarily relish White House intellectuals and their works? Where were the leaders of American business, or the middle classes, which detest war as they do internal revolution? Why was opposition left to noisy, arrogant and militant college students?

One can only speculate. No doubt, after the Diem coup, many a war-disliking conservative in Congress felt that, through whatever wretched misjudgments, we were nonetheless committed by national honor. There was also the residue of the seek-and-destroy mentality toward communism everywhere in the world that Truman's Cold War had done so much to create.

Beyond these two points is the fact that Kennedy and his intellectuals confronted Congress with an accomplished fact. In November of 1964, after the coup but before President Johnson's massive 1965 escalation, Senator Richard Russell emerged from a briefing session to remark: "We either have to get out or take some action to help the Vietnamese. . . . We made a mistake in going there, but I can't figure out any way to get out without scaring the rest of the world."

Finally, once the more violent and obscene of student-faculty demonstrations against Vietnam had disgusted the vast majority of Americans, few relished the thought of seeming to think along the same lines.

So much is true. It doesn't, however, offset the considerable damage that has been done by failure of opposition to the Vietnam war to emerge from those business and middle class elements of America where everything we know about them would lead us ordinarily to expect such opposition. Unyielding opposition to communism is sound and vital. But military forays into each and every part of the world where some form of Communist aggression is to be found is, plainly, suicidal to the American nation. Patriotism is indispensable to the American nation. Nothing, however, corrupts and damages patriotism like war that is without relation to clear and compelling national interest. Not for some time will American patriotism recover from Vietnam.

Mr. Nixon's Presidency

Nixon's election in 1968 was in response to popular feeling much like that behind Harding's victory in 1920 and Eisenhower's in 1952. If any mandate can be found in Nixon's victory over Humphrey it must surely be quick and full disengagement from Vietnam. President Nixon has incontestably made moves in this direction. Why, then, does doubt of Nixon persist?

Such doubt springs from the curious existence in Nixon of a strongly Wilsonian thrust of mind. One does not expect this in the Republican tradition. But we know that Nixon has an almost reverential regard for Wilson, and we know too that while Vice President he had rather different views from Eisenhower on sending troops into Indochina. His extraordinary manner of announcing entry into Cambodia last spring was unmistakably Wilsonian-Democratic, not Eisenhower-Republican. If Nixon did not actually say "mankind" and "crisis," the words could certainly be heard between the lines of his spoken text. It was, in every respect, a Wilson-Roosevelt-Kennedy type of announcement; emphatically not the kind we might expect from Coolidge or Hoover or Eisenhower.

Nor should one underestimate the power of the political intellectuals on Mr. Nixon's mind and temper. Despite the vilification he has had to endure for a quarter of a century from academy and press, the latter sector as rich in crisis-mentalities as the former, Nixon identifies with the intellectual class in a way that neither Hoover nor Eisenhower ever did. In a McLuhanesque age one dares not dismiss the importance to any Wilsonian mind of image, as this *image* is picked up or created by political intellectuals of the press or the universities.

It would be supremely ironic, but by no means beyond rational belief, were Richard Nixon to reveal himself as the least Republican of Presidents this century. The Wilsonian *mystique* is a powerful one, and we live, for good or bad, in the Intellectuals' Age.

24

REFLECTIONS
IN THRALL TO FEAR

J. WILLIAM FULBRIGHT[*]

For reasons still not wholly known and understood, the grand alliance of the Second World War broke up almost as soon as victory was won, and the powers that had called themselves "the United Nations" fell into the pattern of hostility, periodic crisis, and "limited" war that has characterized world politics for the last twenty-five years. At Yalta in February, 1945, the United States, Great Britain, and the Soviet Union pledged to maintain and strengthen in peace the "unity of purpose and of action" that was bringing victory in war. Just over two years later, on March 12, 1947, President Truman proclaimed the doctrine that came to be recognized as the basic rationale, from the American standpoint, for the Cold War. President Truman based the appeal he made to Congress for support of Greece and Turkey not primarily on the specific circumstances of those two countries at that time but on a general formulation of the American national interest which held that "totalitarian regimes imposed on free peoples, by direct or indirect aggression, undermine the foundations of international peace and hence the security of the United States." President Truman went on to say that at that moment in world history "nearly every nation must choose between alternative ways of life"—the one based on democratic institutions, like our own, and the other based on "terror and oppression," for which the model, of course, was the Soviet Union.

Most of us thought we knew how and why this great transition—from "unity of purpose and of action" to Truman's declaration of ideological warfare—had come about in so short a time. The cause was Soviet Communist aggression, limited at the outset to Stalin's subjugation of Eastern Europe but shown by Marxist-Leninist doctrine to be universal in design, aimed at nothing less than the Communization of the world. American policy and opinion were profoundly influenced in the early postwar period by the thesis that George Kennan, signing himself "X," set forth in *Foreign Affairs* for July, 1947, which depicted Soviet policy as relentlessly expansionist, committed by a fanatical ideology to filling "every nook and cranny avail-

* J. William Fulbright, "Reflections in Thrall to Fear," *The New Yorker,* January 8, 1972. Reprinted by permission; © 1972 The New Yorker Magazine, Inc.

287

able . . . in the basin of world power," and "stopping only when it meets with some unanswerable force." Warning against bluster and excessive reliance on military force, Kennan nonetheless called for an American policy of "unalterable counter force," of "firm and vigilant containment," which he anticipated would "increase enormously the strains under which Soviet policy must operate," and encourage changes within Russia leading to "either the break-up or the gradual mellowing of Soviet power."

From Korea to Berlin to Cuba to Vietnam, the Truman Doctrine governed America's response to the Communist world. Tactics changed—from "massive retaliation" to "limited war" and "counterinsurgency"—but these were variations on a classic formulation based on assumptions that few really questioned. Sustained by an inert Congress, the policymakers of the forties, fifties, and early sixties were never compelled to reëxamine the premises of the Truman Doctrine, or even to defend them in constructive adversary proceedings.

Change has come not from wisdom but from disaster. The calamitous failure of American policy in Vietnam has induced on the part of scholars, journalists, and politicians a belated willingness to reëxamine the basic assumptions of American postwar policy. Induced by the agitations of the present moment, this new look at old events may well result in an excess of revision, or of emotion, but the corrective is much needed if we are to profit from experience and recast our policies. It cannot be said that the assumptions underlying the Truman Doctrine were wholly false, especially for their time and place. But there is a powerful presumptive case against their subsequent universal application—the case deriving from the disaster of our policy in Asia—and it seems appropriate to look back and try to discover how and why the promise of the United Nations Charter gave way so quickly to ideological warfare between East and West.

Until fairly recently, I accepted the conventional view that the United States had acted in good faith to make the United Nations work but that the Charter was undermined by the Soviet veto. In retrospect, this seems less certain, and one suspects now that, like the League of Nations before it, the United Nations was orphaned at birth. Whereas Woodrow Wilson's great creation was abandoned to skeptical Europeans, Franklin Roosevelt's project was consigned to the care of unsympathetic men of his own country. President Roosevelt died only two weeks before the opening of the meeting in San Francisco at which the United Nations was organized. Truman, as a new and inexperienced President, was naturally more dependent on his advisers than President Roosevelt had been; among these, so far as I know, none was a strong supporter of the plan for a world organization, as Cordell Hull had been. The Under-Secretary of State, Dean Acheson, was assigned to lobby for Senate approval of the United Nations Charter, and he recalled later that "I did my duty faithfully and successfully, but always believed that the Charter was impractical." And, with even greater asperity and candor, he told an interviewer in 1970, "I never thought the United Nations was worth a damn. To a lot of people it was a Holy Grail, and those who set store by it had the misfortune to believe their own bunk."

Disdaining the United Nations, the framers of the Truman Doctrine also nurtured an intense hostility toward Communism and the Soviet Union. Stalin, of course, did much to earn this hostility, with his paranoiac suspiciousness, the imposition of Soviet domination in Eastern Europe, and the use of Western Communist parties as instruments of Soviet policy. All this is well known. Less well known, far more puzzling, and also more pertinent to our position in the world today is the eagerness with which we seized upon postwar Soviet provocations and plunged into the Cold War. If it be granted that Stalin started the Cold War, it must also be recognized that the Truman Administration seemed to welcome it.

By early 1947—a year and a half after the founding of the United Nations —the assumptions of the Cold War were all but unchallenged within the United States government. It was *assumed* that the object of Soviet policy was the Communization of the world; if Soviet behavior in Europe and northern China were not proof enough, the design was spelled out in the writings of Lenin and Marx, which our policy-makers chose to read not as a body of political philosophy but as the field manual of Soviet strategy. It is true, of course, that by 1947, with the United States virtually disarmed and Western Europe in a condition of economic paralysis, the Soviet Union might plausibly have tried to take over Western Europe through the manipulation of Communist parties, through military intimidation, through economic strangulation, and possibly even through direct military action. The fact that Stalin could have done this, and might well have tried but for timely American counteraction through the Marshall Plan and the formation of NATO, was quickly and uncritically taken as proof of a design for unlimited conquest comparable to that of Nazi Germany. Neither in the executive branch of our government nor in Congress were more than a few, isolated voices raised to suggest the possibility that Soviet policy in Europe might be motivated by morbid fears for the security of the Soviet Union rather than by a design for world conquest. Virtually no one in a position of power was receptive to the hypothesis that Soviet truculence reflected weakness rather than strength, intensified by memories of 1919, when the Western powers had intervened in an effort—however halfhearted—to strangle the Bolshevik "monster" in its cradle. Our own policy was formed without the benefit of constructive adversary proceedings. A few brave individuals, like former Vice-President Henry Wallace, offered dissenting counsel—and paid dear for it.

When Great Britain informed the United States in February, 1947, that it was no longer able to provide military support for Greece, the American government was ready with a policy and a world view. The latter was an early version of the domino theory. Knowing, as we thought we did, that

Russian support for Communist insurgents in Greece was part of a grand design for the takeover first of Greece, then of Turkey, the Middle East, and so forth, we were not content simply to assume the British role of providing arms to a beleaguered government; instead, we chose to issue a declaration of ideological warfare in the form of the Truman Doctrine. It may well be true that the grand phrases were motivated in part by a desire to arouse this nation's combative spirit, and so to build congressional support for the funds involved, but it is also true—at least, according to Joseph Jones, the State Department official who drafted President Truman's appeal to Congress, under Acheson's direction—that the new policy was conceived not just as a practical measure to bolster the Greeks and Turks but as a historic summons of the United States to world leadership. "*All* barriers to bold action were indeed down," as Jones has written. Among the State Department policymakers, Jones reports, it was felt that "a new chapter in world history had opened, and they were the most privileged of men, participants in a drama such as rarely occurs even in the long life of a great nation."

The Truman Doctrine, which may have made sense for its time and place, was followed by the Marshall Plan and NATO, which surely did make sense for their time and place. But as a charter for twenty-five years of global ideological warfare and unilateral military intervention against Communist insurgencies the Truman Doctrine has a different set of implications altogether. It represents a view of Communism, of the world, and of our role in the world that has had much to do with the disaster of our policy in Asia. Even in the country to which it was first applied, President Truman's basic formulation—that "we shall not realize our objectives . . . unless we are willing to help free peoples to maintain their free institutions"—has been reduced to a mockery. But who remembers now (surely not Mr. Agnew) that the Truman Doctrine was initially designed to preserve democracy in Greece?

Acheson, who prided himself on being a realist, may not have taken all that ideological claptrap seriously, but his successors Dulles and Rusk certainly did, and they framed their policies accordingly. Whatever merit the Truman Doctrine may have had in the circumstances of early-postwar Europe, the bond with reality became more and more strained as the Doctrine came to be applied at times and in places increasingly remote from the Greek civil war. Operating on a set of assumptions that defined reality for them—that as a social system Communism was deeply immoral, that as a political movement it was a conspiracy for world conquest—our leaders became liberated from the normal rules of evidence and inference when it came to dealing with Communism. After all, who ever heard of giving the Devil a fair shake? Since we know what he has in mind, it is pedantry to split hairs over what he is actually doing.

Political pressures at home intensified the virulence of the anti-Communist ideology. In retrospect, the surprise Democratic victory in the election of 1948 was probably a misfortune for the country. The Republicans, frustrated and enraged by their fifth successive defeat, became desperate in their search for a winning issue. They found their issue in the threat of Communism, at home and abroad, and they seized upon it with uncommon ferocity. They blamed the Truman Administration for Chiang Kai-shek's defeat in the Chinese civil war; they attacked President Truman for the bloody stalemate in Korea, although they had strongly supported his initial commitment; and they tolerated and in many cases encouraged Senator Joseph R. McCarthy's attacks on reputable, and even eminent, Americans. Every American President since that time has been under intense pressure to demonstrate his anti-Communist orthodoxy.

More by far than any other factor, the anti-Communism of the Truman Doctrine has been the guiding spirit of American foreign policy since the Second World War. Stalin and Mao Tse-tung and even Ho Chi Minh replaced Hitler in our minds as the sources of all evil in the world. We came to see the hand of "Moscow Communism" in every disruption that occurred anywhere. First, there was the conception of Communism as an international conspiracy—as an octopus with its body in Moscow and its tentacles reaching out to the farthest corners of the world. Later, after the Sino-Soviet break, sophisticated foreign-policy analysts disavowed the conspiracy thesis, but at the same time they disavowed it they said things that showed that the faith lingered on. Secretary Rusk and his associates professed to be scornful of the conspiracy thesis, but still they defended the Vietnam war with references to a world "cut in two by Asian Communism," the only difference between the earlier view and the later one being that where once we had seen one octopus we now saw two.

If you accepted the premise, the rest followed. If Moscow and Peking represented centers of great power implacably hostile to the United States, and if every local crisis, from Cuba to the Congo to Vietnam, had the Communist mark upon it, then it followed logically that every crisis posed a threat to the security of the United States. The effect of the anti-Communist ideology was to spare us the task of taking cognizance of the specific facts of specific situations. Our "faith" liberated us, like the believers of old, from the requirements of empirical thinking, from the necessity of observing and evaluating the actual behavior of the nations and leaders with whom we were dealing. Like medieval theologians, we had a philosophy that explained everything to us in advance, and everything that did not fit could be readily identified as a fraud or a lie or an illusion. The fact that in some respects the behavior of the Soviet Union and of China and North Vietnam lived up to our ideological expectations made it all the easier to ignore the instances in which it did not. What we are now, belatedly, discovering is not that the Communist states have never really been hostile to us but that they have been neither consistent nor united in hostility to us; that their hostility has by no means been wholly unprovoked; and that they have been willing from time to time to do business or come to terms with us. Our ideological blinders concealed these instances from us, robbing us of useful information and of promising opportunities. The perniciousness of the anti-Communist ideology of the Truman Doctrine arises not from any patent falsehood but from its distortion and simplification of reality, from its universalization and its elevation to the status of a revealed truth.

Psychologists tell us that there is often a great difference between what one person says and what another hears, or, in variation of the old adage, that the evil may be in the ear of the hearer. When Khrushchev said, "We will bury you," Americans heard the statement as a threat of nuclear war and were outraged accordingly. The matter was raised when Chairman Khrushchev visited the United States in 1959, and he replied with some anger that he had been talking about economic competition. "I am deeply concerned over these conscious distortions of my thoughts," he said. "I've never mentioned any rockets."

We will never know, of course, but it is possible that an opportunity for a stable peace was lost during the years of Khrushchev's power. As we look back now on the many things he said regarding peaceful coexistence, the words have a different ring. At the time, we did not believe them: at best, they were Communist propaganda; at worst, outright lies. I recalled recently, for example, the visit of Chairman Khrushchev to the Senate Foreign Relations Committee on September 16, 1959. Suggesting that we lay aside the polemics of the past, Mr. Khrushchev said:

> We must face the future more and have wisdom enough to secure peace for our countries and for the whole world. We have always had great respect for the American people. We have also been somewhat envious of your achievements in the economic field, and for that reason we are doing our best to try to catch up with you in that field, to compete with you, and when we do catch up to move further ahead. I should say that future generations would be grateful to us if we managed to switch our efforts from stockpiling and perfecting weapons and concentrated those efforts fully on competition in the economic field.

Now, in retrospect, one wonders: why were we so sure that Khrushchev didn't mean what he said about peace? The answer lies in part, I believe, in our anti-Communist obsession—in the distortions it created in our perception of Soviet behavior, and in the extraordinary sense of threat we experienced when the Russians proclaimed their desire to catch up and overtake us economically. In our own national value system, competition has always been prized; why, then, should we have been so alarmed by a challenge to compete? Perhaps our national tendency to extoll competition rather than coöperation as a social virtue and our preoccupation with our own primacy—with being the "biggest," the "greatest" nation—suggest an underlying lack of confidence in ourselves, a supposition that unless we are "No. 1" we will be nothing: worthless and despised, and deservedly so. I am convinced that the real reason we squandered twenty billion dollars or more getting men to the moon in the decade of the sixties was our fear of something like horrible humiliation if the Russians got men there first. All this suggests that slogans about competition and our own primacy in that competition are largely hot air—sincerely believed, no doubt, but nonetheless masking an exaggerated fear of failure, which, in turn, lends a quality of desperation to our competitive endeavors. One detects this cast of mind in President Johnson's determination that he would not be "the first American President to lose a war," and also in President Nixon's spectre of America as "a pitiful, helpless giant."

This kind of thinking robs a nation's policymakers of objectivity and drives them to irresponsible behavior. The distortion of priorities involved in going to the moon is a relatively benign example. The perpetuation of the Vietnam war is the most terrible and fateful manifestation of the determination to prove that we are "No. 1." Assistant Secretary of Defense for International Security Affairs John T. McNaughton, as quoted in the Pentagon Papers, measured the American interest in Vietnam and found that "to permit the people of South Vietnam to enjoy a better, freer way of life" accounted for a mere ten per cent and "to avoid a humiliating U.S. defeat" for up to seventy per cent. McNaughton's statistical metaphor suggests a nation in thrall to fear; it suggests a policy-making élite unable to distinguish between the national interest and their own personal pride.

Perhaps if we had been less proud and less fearful, we would have responded in a more positive way to the earthy, unorthodox Khrushchev. Whatever his faults and excesses, Khrushchev is recognized in retrospect as the Communist leader who repudiated the Marxist dogma of the "inevitability" of war between Socialist and capitalist states. Understanding the insanity of war with nuclear weapons, Khrushchev became the advocate of "goulash" Communism, of peaceful economic competition with the West. During his period in office, some amenities were restored in East-West relations; the Berlin issue was stirred up but finally defused; and, most important, the limited-nuclear-test-ban treaty was concluded. These were solid achievements, though meagre in proportion to mankind's need for peace, and meagre, too, it now appears, in proportion to the opportunity that may then have existed. One wonders how much more might have been accomplished—particularly in the field of disarmament—if Americans had not still been caught up in the prideful, fearful spirit of the Truman Doctrine.

Even the crises look different in retrospect, especially when one takes into account the internal workings of the Communist world. A leading British authority on Soviet affairs, Victor Zorza, has traced the beginning of the Vietnam war to a "fatal misreading" by President Kennedy of Khrushchev's endorsement of "wars of national liberation." The Kennedy Administration interpreted Khrushchev's statement as a declaration that the Soviet Union intended to sponsor subversion, guerrilla warfare, and rebellion all over the world. Accordingly, the Administration attached enormous significance to

Soviet material support for the Laotian Communists, as if the issue in that remote and backward land were directly pertinent to the world balance of power. It was judged that Khrushchev must be shown that he could not get away with it. We had taught Stalin that "direct" aggression did not pay; now we must teach Khrushchev—and the Chinese—that "indirect" aggression did not pay. In Zorza's view, Khrushchev's talk of "wars of national liberation" was not a serious plan for worldwide subversion but a response to Communist China, whose leaders were then accusing Khrushchev of selling out the cause of revolution and making a deal with the United States.

In the spirit of the Truman Doctrine, the Kennedy Administration read the Soviet endorsement of "wars of national liberation" as a direct challenge to the United States. Speaking of Russia and China, President Kennedy said in his first State of the Union Message, "We must never be lulled into believing that either power has yielded its ambitions for world domination —ambitions which they forcefully restated only a short time ago." I do not recall these words for purposes of reproach; they represented an assessment of Communist intentions that most of us shared at that time, an assessment that had been held by every Administration and most members of Congress since the Second World War, an assessment that had scarcely—if at all— been brought up for critical examination in the executive branch, in congressional committees, in the proliferating "think tanks," or in the universities. Perhaps no better assessment could have been made on the basis of the information available at that time, but I doubt it. I think it more likely that we simply chose to ignore evidence that did not fit our preconceptions, or— as is more often the case—when the facts lent themselves to several possible interpretations we chose to seize upon the one with which we were most familiar: the Communist drive for world domination.

In the amplified form it acquired during the Johnson years, the conception of "wars of national liberation" as part of the Communist design for world domination became the basic rationale for the Vietnam war. All the other excuses—defending freedom, honoring our "commitments," demonstrating America's resolution—are secondary in importance and are easily shown to be fallacious and contradictory. But no one can *prove* that Mao Tse-tung and Brezhnev and Kosygin—or Khrushchev, for that matter—have not harbored secret ambitions to conquer the world. Who can prove that the desire or the intention was never in their minds? The truly remarkable thing about this Cold War psychology is the totally illogical transfer of the burden of proof from those who make charges to those who question them. In this frame of reference, Communists are guilty until proved innocent— or simply by definition. The Cold Warriors, instead of having to say how they knew that Vietnam was part of a plan for the Communization of the world, so manipulated the terms of public discussion as to be able to demand that the skeptics prove that it was not. If the skeptics could not, then the war must go on—to end it would be recklessly risking the national security. We come to the ultimate illogic: war is the course of prudence and sobriety until the case for peace is proved under impossible rules of evidence —or until the enemy surrenders.

Rational men cannot deal with each other on this basis. Recognizing their inability to know with anything like certainty what is going on in other men's minds, they do not try to deal with others on the basis of their presumed intentions. Instead, rational men respond to others on the basis of their actual, observable behavior, and they place the burden of proof where it belongs—on those who assert and accuse rather than on those who question or deny. The departure from these elementary rules for the ascertainment of truth is the essence of the Cold War way of thinking; its weakened but still formidable hold on our minds is indicative of the surviving tyranny of the Truman Doctrine.

In a decade's perspective—and without the blinders of the Truman Doctrine—it even seems possible that the Cuban missile crisis of 1962 was not so enormous a crisis as it then seemed. Khrushchev in the early sixties was engaged in an internal struggle with the Soviet military, who, not unlike our own generals, were constantly lobbying for more funds for ever more colossal weapons systems. Khrushchev had been cutting back on conventional forces and, largely for purposes of appeasing his unhappy generals, was talking a great deal about the power of Soviet missiles. President Kennedy, however, was applying pressure from another direction: unnerved by Khrushchev's endorsement of "wars of national liberation," he was undertaking to build up American conventional forces at the same time that he was greatly expanding the American nuclear-missile force, even though by this time the United States had an enormous strategic superiority. Khrushchev's effort to resist the pressures from his generals was, of course, undermined by the American buildup. It exposed him to pressures within the Kremlin from a hostile coalition of thwarted generals and politicians who opposed his de-Stalinization policies. In the view of a number of specialists in the Soviet field, the placement of missiles in Cuba was motivated largely, if not primarily, by Khrushchev's need to deal with these domestic pressures; it was meant to close or narrow the Soviet "missile gap" in relation to the United States without forcing Khrushchev to concentrate all available resources on a ruinous arms race.

Lacking an expert knowledge of my own on these matters, I commend this interpretation of Khrushchev's purpose not as necessarily true but as highly plausible. As far as I know, however, none of the American officials who participated in the decisions relating to the Cuban missile crisis seriously considered the possibility that Khrushchev might be acting defensively or in response to domestic pressures. It was universally assumed that the installation of Soviet missiles in Cuba was an aggressive strategic move against the United States—that, and nothing more. Assuming Khrushchev's aggressive intent, we imposed on the Soviet Union a resounding defeat, for which Khrushchev was naturally held responsible. In this way, we helped to strengthen the military and political conservatives within the Soviet Union, who were to overthrow Khrushchev two years later. If we had been willing to consider the possibility that Khrushchev was acting on internal considerations, we would still have wished to secure the removal of the missiles from Cuba, but it might have been accomplished by means less embarrassing to Khrushchev, such as a *quid pro quo* under which we would have removed our Jupiter missiles from Turkey.

Khrushchev had paid dear for his "softness on capitalism" in an earlier encounter with President Eisenhower. After his visit to the United States in 1959, Khrushchev apparently tried to persuade his skeptical, hard-line colleagues that Americans were not such monsters as they supposed and that President Eisenhower was a reasonable man. This heretical theory—heretical from the Soviet point of view—was shot out of the sky along with the American U-2 spy plane in May, 1960. When President Eisenhower subsequently declined the opportunity Khrushchev offered him to disclaim personal responsibility, Khrushchev felt compelled to break up the Paris summit meeting. The U-2 incident was later cited by Khrushchev himself as a critical moment in his loss of power at home. It shattered his plans for President Eisenhower to pay a visit to the Soviet Union—for which, it is said, he had already had a golf course secretly constructed in the Crimea.

There were, of course, other factors in Khrushchev's fall, and perhaps more important ones; nor is it suggested that his intentions toward the West were necessarily benevolent. The point that must emerge, however—more for the sake of the future than for history's sake—is that if we had not been wearing ideological blinders, if our judgment had not been clouded by fear and hostility, we might have perceived in Khrushchev a world statesman with whom constructive business could be done. When he fell, his successors put an end to de-Stalinization, began the military buildup that has brought the Soviet Union to a rough strategic parity with the United States, and greatly stepped up their aid to Communist forces in Vietnam.

While our response to Soviet Communism has been marked by hostility, tensions, and fear, our response to Communism in Asia has been marked by all these and, in addition, by a profound sense of injury and betrayal. Russia never was a country for which we had much affection anyway; it was the bleak and terrible land of the czars, which, when it went to the Communist devils, was merely trading one tyranny for another. But China had a special place in our hearts. We had favored her with our merchants and missionaries and our "open door" policy; we had even given back the Boxer indemnity so that Chinese students could study in America. In the Second World War, we fought shoulder to shoulder with "free" China; we were filled with admiration for its fighting Generalissimo Chiang Kai-shek, and utterly charmed by his Wellesley-educated wife.

When the Chinese darlings of our patronizing hearts went to Communist perdition, we could only assume that they had been sold or betrayed into bondage. It was inconceivable that our star pupils in the East could actually have willed this calamity; it had to be the work of Chinese traitors, abetted by disloyal Americans, joined in an unholy alliance to sell out China to those quintessential bad people the Russians. A white paper on China was issued in 1949, and Secretary of State Acheson's letter of transmittal recounted accurately the intense but futile American effort to salvage a Kuomintang regime whose officials and soldiers had "sunk into corruption, into a scramble for place and power, and into reliance on the United States to win the war for them and to preserve their own domestic supremacy." Then, having exonerated the United States from responsibility for the loss of China, Secretary Acheson wrote:

The heart of China is in Communist hands. The Communist leaders have forsworn their Chinese heritage and have publicly announced their subservience to a foreign power, Russia, which during the last 50 years, under czars and Communists alike, has been most assiduous in its efforts to extend its control in the Far East. . . . The foreign domination has been masked behind the façade of a vast crusading movement which apparently has seemed to many Chinese to be wholly indigenous and national. . . .

However tragic may be the immediate future of China and however ruthlessly a major portion of this great people may be exploited by a party in the interest of a foreign imperialism, ultimately the profound civilization and the democratic individualism of China will reassert themselves and she will throw off the foreign yoke. I consider that we should encourage all developments in China which now and in the future work toward this end.

In these words, the United States government enunciated what became its Truman Doctrine for Asia. By the end of 1950, we were at war with China in Korea, but even then our belief in Moscow's control of the "Communist conspiracy" or our sentimental unwillingness to believe that China of its own free will would make war on the United States, or some combination of the two, made it difficult for us to believe that the Chinese Communists had intervened in Korea for reasons directly related to their own national interest. The fact that General MacArthur's sweep to the Yalu was bringing American ground forces within striking distance of China's industrial heartland in Manchuria was not at that time widely thought to be a factor in China's intervention in the war. The view of Dean Rusk, then the Assistant Secretary of State for Far Eastern Affairs, was that "the peace and security of China are being sacrificed to the ambitions of the Communist conspiracy," and that "China has been driven by foreign masters into an adventure of foreign aggression which cuts across the most fundamental national interests of the Chinese people." Mr. Rusk went on to say, "We do not recognize the authorities in Peiping for what they pretend to be. The Peiping regime may be a colonial Russian government—a Slavic Manchukuo on a larger scale. It is not the government of China."

Nonetheless, for the first time in our history we were coming to regard

China as our enemy, departing from a half century's policy of supporting a strong, independent China. One of our leading young China scholars, Warren I. Cohen, has provided this summary in his recent book, "America's Response to China":

The great aberration in American policy began in 1950, as the people and their leaders were blinded by fear of Communism and forgot the sound geopolitical, economic, and ethical basis of their historic desire for China's well-being. Having always assumed that China would be friendly, Americans were further bewildered by the hostility of Mao's China, leading them to forsake their traditional support of Asian nationalism, not only in China, but wherever Marxist leadership threatened to enlarge the apparent Communist monolith. With the full support of the American people, Truman and his advisors committed the United States to a policy of containing Communism in Asia as well as in Europe—and in practice this policy became increasingly anti-Chinese, an unprecedented campaign of opposition to the development of a strong, modern China. There was no longer any question of whether the United States would interpose itself between China and her enemies, for the United States had become China's principal enemy.

Over the years, the notion of a "Slavic Manchukuo" gave way to a recognition of the Chinese Communists as the authors of their own deviltry. This was not a fundamental change of outlook toward "international Communism" but an accommodation to a fact that had become obvious to all save the most fanatical and self-deluded Cold Warriors: that, far from being an instrument in Moscow's hands, the Chinese Communist leaders had become defiant and hostile toward Soviet leadership of the Communist world. Now, from the American viewpoint, there were two "Communist conspiracies," and of the two great Communist states China was judged to be the more virulent and aggressive. The Chinese had withdrawn their troops from Korea in 1958, limited themselves to a border adjustment with India in 1962 (when they could have detached a large area after defeating the Indian Army), and assumed no direct combat role in the developing conflict in Vietnam. But these facts were judged to be less important than the fact that they were Communists, who openly advocated subversion and "wars of national liberation." Communist China was not judged to be aggressive on the basis of its actions; it was presumed to be aggressive because it was Communist.

In much the same way that Khrushchev terrified us with his talk of "burying" us, the Chinese sent us into a panic with their doctrine of "wars of national liberation." While the Russians had become relatively benign, contained by America's nuclear deterrent, China claimed to be impervious to the horrors of nuclear war and was still intensely revolutionary itself, committed to the promotion and support of "wars of national liberation" throughout the world. The Kennedy and Johnson Administrations concluded that still another gauntlet had been flung down before the United States. To meet this presumed threat, our military planners invented the strategy of "counterinsurgency," which they undertook to put into effect in Vietnam.

None of this is meant to suggest that China would have been friendly to us if we ourselves had not been hostile. I do not know whether the Chinese Communists would have been friendly or not; nor, I think, does anyone else know, since we never tried to find out. Most probably, in the turmoil of revolutionary change, the Chinese Communists would have been deeply suspicious and verbally abusive of the citadel of capitalism and the leader of the Western "imperialist camp" even if the United States had been willing to come to terms with them. Be that as it may, an objective observer must admit that on the basis of their actual behavior the Chinese Communists have never proved the Hitlerian menace we have taken them to be. They have not tried to conquer and subjugate their neighbors. Nor, upon examination, does the doctrine of "wars of national liberation," as set forth by Lin Piao, constitute a charter of Chinese aggression. It stresses self-reliance and the limitations of external support. Lin Piao wrote:

> In order to make a revolution and to fight a people's war and be victorious, it is imperative to adhere to the policy of self-reliance, rely on the strength of the masses in one's own country and prepare to carry on the fight independently even when all material aid from outside is cut off. If one does not operate by one's own efforts, does not independently ponder and solve the problems of the revolution in one's own country, and does not rely on the strength of the masses, but leans wholly on foreign aid—even though this be aid from Socialist countries which persist in revolution—no victory can be won, or be consolidated even if it is won.

The sudden reversal of American policy toward China in 1971 necessarily invites our attention back to the basic causes of these two decades of conflict between the United States and the Communist countries of Asia. In the course of these two decades, we have engaged in armed conflict with all three of these countries—with Communist China, North Korea, and North Vietnam—but we have never fought a war with the Soviet Union, which is the only Communist power capable of posing a direct strategic threat to the United States. Although it was assumed from the outset of the Cold War that our real strategic interests lay in Europe rather than in Asia, it has been in Asia that we have thought it necessary to fight two wars to enforce the Truman Doctrine. Looking back, one is bound to ask whether these conflicts were inescapable. Having avoided war in the region we judged more important, and with the power we judged the greater threat, why have we found it necessary to fight in Asia, at such enormous cost in lives and money and in the internal cohesion of our own society? Is it possible that if Mao Tse-tung and Ho Chi Minh had not borne the title of "Communist" but otherwise had done exactly what they have done in their two countries, we would have accepted their victories over their domestic rivals and lived with them in peace? I think it quite possible that we would have come to terms with both. Apart from the North Korean invasion of South Korea, which was a direct violation of the United Nations Charter, the Communist countries of Asia have done nothing that has threatened the security of the United States and little, if anything, that has impaired our legitimate interests. We intervened in the Chinese and Vietnamese civil wars only because the stronger side in each case was the Communist side and we assumed that, as Communists, they were parties to a conspiracy for world domination, and were therefore our enemies. We intervened against them not for what they *did* but for what they *were* and for what we assumed to be their purpose.

There were Americans in official positions who provided a more objective, less ideologically colored view of the Chinese Communists back in the days before they won their civil war. These wartime observers in China, who included John S. Service, John Paton Davies, and Colonel David D. Barrett, were themselves sympathetic to the Nationalist government of Chiang Kai-shek, at least to the extent of urging it to make the reforms that might have allowed it to survive. Nonetheless, they reported objectively on the weakness and corruption of the Kuomintang and on the organization and discipline of the Communists in their headquarters in Yenan. They also provided information suggesting that at that time Mao Tse-tung and his associates had no intention whatever of becoming subservient to the Soviet Union and hoped to coöperate with the United States. Not only did the observations of these men go unheeded; they themselves were subsequently denounced and persecuted. Colonel Barrett did not attain the promotion to brigadier general that his service in the Army merited, and Service and Davies were hounded out of the Foreign Service, charged with advocacy of, and even responsibility for, the Chinese Communist victory that they had foreseen. The nation was deprived thereafter of their accurate observations and valuable insights, and, what is more, their surviving colleagues in the bureaucracy got the unmistakable message that it was unhealthy to deviate from the anti-Communist line. To survive and get ahead, it was necessary to see the world as the world was defined by the Truman Doctrine.

Having been thoroughly educated in the catechism of the Cold War, we look back now with astonishment on the reports of Service, Barrett, and others from China in 1944. Barrett and Service came to know the Chinese Communist leaders well through the Dixie Mission, which was the name given to the mission of the United States Army Observer Group, headed by Colonel Barrett, at Chinese Communist headquarters in Yenan in late 1944 and early 1945. Their assignment was to assess the potential contribution of the Chinese Communists to a final assault against Japanese forces in China. They came to know and respect the Communists, not for their ideology but for their discipline, organization, fighting skills, and morale.

In his recent book "Dixie Mission," Colonel Barrett comments, "The Chinese Communists are our bitter enemies now, but they were certainly 'good guys' then, particularly to the airmen who received their help." Colonel Barrett found that as sources of information about the Japanese the Communists were "all we had hoped they would be and even more"—

among other reasons, because they "could almost always count on the co-operation and support of a local population." American observers sent out into the countryside from Yenan "all expressed the belief that the Communists were being supported by the entire civil population." In retrospect, Colonel Barrett felt that he had been "oversold" on the Communists in Yenan, but nonetheless he comments, "The overall look of things there was one which most Americans were inclined to regard with favor." American observers were impressed by the absence of sentries around the leaders, in contrast with the Nationalist capital in Chungking, where there were "police and sentries everywhere;" by the tough, well-nourished, and well-dressed troops, in contrast with the poorly nourished, shabbily uniformed Kuomintang soldiers; and by the general atmosphere of roughhewn equality and shared sacrifice. "As a whole," Colonel Barrett comments, "the Communist outlook on life was old-fashioned and conservative."

Even the flamboyant and volatile General Patrick J. Hurley—Roosevelt's special emissary and, later, Ambassador to Chungking—was at first favorably impressed by the Chinese Communists' terms for a settlement with Chiang Kai-shek. In November, 1944, Hurley flew to Yenan, where he signed an agreement with Mao Tse-tung calling for a coalition government; Hurley pronounced the agreement eminently fair, and even told Mao—in Barrett's hearing—that the terms did not go far enough in the Communists' favor. Chiang Kai-shek rejected Hurley's plan out of hand; nonetheless, Hurley thereafter supported Chiang as the sole leader of China and publicly blamed the failure of his mediation on his Embassy staff, whom he accused, in effect, of being pro-Communist. Although he contended in November, 1944, that "if there is a breakdown in the parleys it will be the fault of the Government and not the Communists," and although he told President Truman in May, 1945, that the Communists were holding back "in my opinion with some degree of reasonableness," Hurley still backed the Nationalist regime to the hilt, and in the spring of 1945 even reimposed the ban on nonmilitary travel by Americans to the Communist headquarters in Yenan. Thus began the process, culminating in the failure of the mission undertaken in 1946 by General George C. Marshall through which, without having ascertained their attitudes and intentions toward us, the United States government came to identify the Chinese Communists as enemies of the United States—presaging the policy of isolation and containment that was to endure at least until 1971.

This was not at the outset the result of decisions made at the highest level. President Roosevelt wrote a friend on November 15, 1944, "I am hoping and praying for a real working out of the situation with the so-called Communists." And in March, 1945, in reply to a question from Edgar Snow about whether we could work with two governments in China for purposes of prosecuting the war with Japan, Roosevelt said, "Well, I've been working with two governments there. I intend to go on doing so until we can get them together." Within a few weeks after that interview, Roosevelt was dead and the conduct of American foreign policy had passed into the hands of the inexperienced President Truman. Neither Roosevelt nor Truman, however, seems in the last days of the Second World War to have given serious and sustained thought to the internal problems of China. Both Presidents were preoccupied with the defeat of Japan, and it had been clear for some time that China was unlikely to play a decisive role in bringing that about.

There was no lack of information available to the United States government in 1944 and 1945 about either the weakness and corruption of the Kuomintang or the strength and aspirations of the Chinese Communists. The views of the professional diplomats were rejected, however, and their reports ignored—that is, until the witchhunters in the State Department and Congress got hold of them. In June, 1944, for example, a warning was conveyed to Washington in a memorandum written principally by John Service:

> The situation in China is rapidly becoming critical. . . . There is a progressive internal breakdown. . . . The fundamental cause of this suicidal trend is that the Kuomintang, steadily losing popular support . . . is concentrating more and more on putting the preservation of its shrinking power above all other considerations.
>
> These policies, unless checked by the internal opposition they evoke and by friendly foreign influence, seem certain to bring about a collapse which will be harmful to the war and our long-term interests in the Far East.

At the same time that American observers in China were reporting the enfeeblement of the Kuomintang, they were providing detailed accounts of the growing military and political strength of the Communists. Service summed up the importance of these circumstances for the United States:

> From the basic fact that the Communists have built up popular support of a magnitude and depth which makes their elimination impossible, we must draw the conclusion that the Communists will have a certain and important share in China's future.

His colleague John Paton Davies put it even more succinctly:

> The Communists are in China to stay. And China's destiny is not Chiang's but theirs.

The Communists were not only strong but—at least, so they said—willing and eager to coöperate with the United States. In his recent book "The Amerasia Papers: Some Problems in the History of U.S.-China Relations," Service reports on a long conversation he had with Mao Tse-tung in Yenan on August 23, 1944, in which Mao emphasized that the Chinese Communists were "first of all Chinese," and appealed for American help for China after the war. "The Russians," Mao said, "have suffered greatly in the war and will have their hands full with their own job of rebuilding. We do not expect Russian help." America, he thought, could help China, and he told Service:

> China must industrialize. This can be done—in China—only by free enterprise and with the aid of foreign capital. Chinese and American interests are corre-

lated and similar. They fit together, economically and politically. We can and must work together.

The United States would find us more coöperative than the Kuomintang. We will not be afraid of democratic American influence—we will welcome it. We have no silly ideas of taking only Western mechanical techniques. . . .

America does not need to fear that we will not be coöperative. We must coöperate and we must have American help. This is why it is so important to us Communists to know what you Americans are thinking and planning. We cannot risk crossing you—cannot risk any conflict with you.

We do not know, of course, whether Mao was sincere in his repeated appeals for American friendship. The reason we do not know is that we never tried to find out. In our postwar anti-Communist hysteria, we assumed that the Chinese Communists were hostile simply because they were Communists, and we also assumed, despite impressive evidence to the contrary, that they were subservient to the Soviet Union. We thereupon made our fateful commitment to the losing side in the Chinese civil war—the side of whose weakness and probable defeat full warning had been provided by our own highly competent observers. From these events followed two wars and a quarter century of bitter hostility, which might have been avoided if we had remained neutral in the Chinese civil war.

This is not to say that Mao might have been expected to put Sino-American relations back on their prewar basis. He most assuredly would not have done that. Certainly our pretensions to a benevolent paternalism toward China would have been given short shrift; the age of missionaries and the "open door" was at an end. But whatever our relations might have been if we had not intervened in the civil war, they would at least have been initiated on a more realistic and more promising basis. We might have long ago established a working relationship at least as tolerable, and as peaceful, as the one we have had with the Soviet Union: the sort of relationship toward which—belatedly but most commendably—the Nixon Administration now seems to be working.

The anti-Communist spirit that governed our relations with China after the Second World War also shaped—and distorted—our involvement in Vietnam. Our interest in China's civil war, though tragic in consequence, was attenuated and limited in time. Vietnam was less fortunate. In a test application of the new science of "counterinsurgency," it has been subjected to prolonged, though inconclusive, devastation. But for the American intervention, the Vietnamese civil war would have ended long ago—at infinitely less cost in lives, money, and property—in a nationalist Communist victory under the leadership of Ho Chi Minh.

In retrospect, it is difficult to understand how we could have accepted the "loss" of China but not the "loss" of the small, undeveloped countries on China's southern border. Only in the context of the assumptions of the Truman Doctrine could the Vietnamese war ever have been rationalized as having something to do with American security or American interests. Looking through our anti-Communist prism, we saw Ho Chi Minh not as a Vietnamese nationalist who was also a Communist but as a spear-carrier for the international Communist conspiracy, the driving force for a "world cut in two by Asian Communism." The Johnson Administration, as Mr. Johnson's memoirs show clearly, believed itself to be acting on President Truman's doctrine that "totalitarian regimes imposed on free peoples, by direct or indirect aggression, undermine the foundations of international peace and hence the security of the United States." President Johnson and his advisers believed this despite a set of facts that did not fit the formula: the fact that the issue was not between a "free people" and a "totalitarian regime" but between rival totalitarian regimes; the fact that the war was not one of international aggression, "direct" or otherwise, but an anti-colonial war and then a civil war; and the fact that, in any case, the country was too small and the issue too indigenous to Vietnam to pose anything resembling a threat to "the foundations of international peace," much less to "the security of the United States." In practice, the issue had resolved itself into a corruption of the Truman Doctrine—into the fear of a "humiliating" defeat at the hands of Communists. It was not so much that we needed to win, or that there was anything for us to win, as that our leaders felt—for reasons of prestige abroad and political standing at home—that they could not afford to "lose." President Johnson said soon after he took office, "I am not going to be the President who saw Southeast Asia go the way China went."

The notion that a country is "lost" or "gone" when it becomes Communist is a peculiarly revealing one. How can we have "lost" a country unless it was ours to begin with—unless it was some part of an unacknowledged American imperium? To my eye, China under Mao is in the same place on the map that it was in the days of Chiang. Where, then, has it "gone"? To the moon? Or to the devil? The "lost" and "gone" concept is indicative of a virulent sanctimoniousness that is only now beginning to abate. In October, 1971, members of the Senate gave President Tito of Yugoslavia a cordial reception at an afternoon tea. In September, 1959, a similar reception was held for Chairman Khrushchev, but one senator refused to sit in the room with him —for fear, apparently, of ideological contamination. As the President now moves toward lifting the "quarantine" of China, as we recognize at long last that there really still is a China, Communist though it may be, the tragic irrationality of the Vietnam war is thrown once again into high relief. All that bloodletting—not just for ourselves but for the Vietnamese—could have been avoided by an awareness that Communism is not a contagious disease but a political movement and a way of organizing a society.

In the case of Ho Chi Minh, as in the case of Mao Tse-tung, we might have come to this awareness twenty-five years—and two wars—ago. Ho, in fact, was a lifelong admirer of the American Revolution, of Lincoln, and of Wilson and his Fourteen Points. As a young man, in 1919, he went to the Versailles Peace Conference to appeal for self-determination for his country in accordance with President Wilson's principles, but no attention was paid to him, and Vietnam remained within the French empire. In 1945, Ho Chi Minh started his declaration of independence for Vietnam with words taken from our own: "All men are created equal." In 1945 and 1946, Ho addressed a series of letters to the United States government asking for its mediation toward a compromise with France, but none of these letters were ever answered, because Ho was, in Dean Acheson's words, "an outright Commie."

President Roosevelt, during the Second World War, had favored independence for Indo-China, or a trusteeship, but in any event he was opposed to letting the French recover Indo-China for their colonial empire. Roosevelt's attitude was spelled out in a memorandum to Secretary of State Hull dated January 24, 1944, which appears in the Pentagon Papers:

> I saw Halifax last week and told him quite frankly that it was perfectly true that I had, for over a year, expressed the opinion that Indo-China should not go back to France but that it should be administered by an international trusteeship. France has had the country—thirty million inhabitants—for nearly one hundred years, and the people are worse off than they were at the beginning.
>
> As a matter of interest, I am whole-heartedly supported in this view by Generalissimo Chiang Kai-shek and by Marshal Stalin. I see no reason to play in with the British Foreign Office in this matter. The only reason they seem to oppose it is that they fear the effect it would have on their own possessions and those of the Dutch. They have never liked the idea of trusteeship because it is, in some instances, aimed at future independence. This is true in the case of Indo-China.
>
> Each case must, of course, stand on its own feet, but the case of Indo-China is perfectly clear. France has milked it for one hundred years. The people of Indo-China are entitled to something better than that.

British intransigence and the requirements of military strategy prevented Roosevelt from acting on his anticolonialist preference, which was so wholly in keeping with the traditional American outlook. When the Truman Administration took office, American policy was changed, and the French were officially assured by our State Department that the United States had never questioned, "even by implication, French sovereignty over Indo-China." The United States would advocate reforms but would leave it to the French to decide when, or even whether, the people of Indo-China were to be given independence: "Such decisions would preclude the establishment of a trusteeship in Indo-China except with the consent of the French Government."

Whether this initial commitment to France—and therefore against Ho— was the result of growing anti-Communist sentiment within the Truman Administration or of friendly feelings toward the colonial powers on the part of President Truman's old-line advisers, or both, American policy was constant and firm from that time on. Later, when Acheson and his colleagues were attempting to build up France as the centerpiece of the anti-Communist coalition in Europe, the commitment to France's position in Indo-China became stronger than ever. By 1951, the United States was paying forty per cent of the cost of France's war against the Vietminh, and by 1954 eighty per cent. After the Geneva settlement, American military aid to South Vietnam averaged about two hundred million dollars a year between 1955 and 1961. By 1963, South Vietnam ranked first among the recipients of our military assistance, and only India and Pakistan received more in economic assistance. In this way, foreign aid served as a vehicle of commitment, from our initial support of French colonial rule in Indo-China to sending an American force of over half a million men to fight in a war that is still going on.

As with China, it might have been different. The Pentagon Papers show that between October, 1945, and February, 1946, Ho Chi Minh addressed at least eight communications to the President of the United States or to the Secretary of State asking America to intervene for Vietnamese independence. Earlier, in the summer of 1945, Ho had asked that Vietnam be accorded "the same status as the Philippines"—a period of tutelage to be followed by independence. Following the outbreak of hostilities in Vietnam in the early fall of 1945, Ho made his appeals to President Truman on the basis of the Atlantic Charter, the United Nations Charter, and Mr. Truman's Navy Day speech of October 27, 1945, in which the President expressed the American belief that "all peoples who are prepared for self-government should be permitted to choose their own form of government by their own freely expressed choice, without interference from any foreign source." In November, 1945, Ho wrote to the Secretary of State requesting the initiation of cultural relations through the sending of fifty Vietnamese students to the United States. On February 16, 1946, in a letter to President Truman, Ho referred to American "complicity" with the French, but he still appealed to the Americans "as guardians and champions of world justice" to "take a decisive step" in support of Vietnamese independence, and pointed out that he was asking only what had been "graciously granted to the Philippines." On September 11, 1946, Ho communicated directly with the United States government for the last time, expressing to an American Embassy official in Paris his own admiration for the United States and the Vietnamese people's respect and affection for President Roosevelt; again he referred to America's granting of independence to the Philippines.

As far as the record shows, neither President Truman nor any of his subordinates replied to any of Ho Chi Minh's appeals. He got his answer nonetheless, clearly and unmistakably. By late 1946, with the first Vietnam war under way, American military equipment was being used by the French against the Vietnamese. As far as the United States government was concerned, Vietnam was a sideshow to the real struggle against Communism, in Europe. If the price of French support in that struggle was American support of French colonialism in Southeast Asia—and we seem never to have questioned that it was—the Truman Administration was ready to pay that price. Ho, after all, was just another "Commie." In a cable to the United States representative in Hanoi in May, 1949, Acheson said:

QUESTION WHETHER HO AS MUCH NATIONALIST AS COMMIE IS IRRELEVANT. ALL STALINISTS IN COLONIAL AREAS ARE NATIONALISTS. WITH ACHIEVEMENT NAT'L AIMS (I.E., INDEPENDENCE) THEIR OBJECTIVE NECESSARILY BECOMES SUBORDINATION STATE TO COMMIE PURPOSES.

In February, 1950, the recognition of Ho Chi Minh's government by the Communist powers moved Secretary Acheson to declare that this recognition "should remove any illusion as to the nationalist character of Ho Chi Minh's aims and reveals Ho in his true colors as the mortal enemy of native independence in Indochina."

As with China under Mao Tse-tung, we might have got along tolerably well—maybe even quite well—with a unified, independent Vietnam under Ho Chi Minh if our leaders' minds had not been hopelessly locked in by the imprisoning theory of the international Communist conspiracy. Ho was an authentic Vietnamese patriot, revered by his countrymen. He had led the resistance to the Japanese within Vietnam and had welcomed the Allies as liberators. His unwillingness to submit to foreign domination was clear—or should have been clear—from the outset. But if the evidence of Ho Chi Minh's Vietnamese nationalism ever reached the American policymakers, it certainly did not persuade them. Acting Secretary of State Acheson instructed an American diplomat in Hanoi in December, 1946, "KEEP IN MIND HO'S CLEAR RECORD AS AGENT INTERNATIONAL COMMUNISM." In February, 1947, by which time the war between France and the Vietminh was well under way, Secretary of State Marshall conceded, in another cable, that colonial empires were rapidly becoming a thing of the past but, as to Vietnam,

WE DO NOT LOSE SIGHT FACT THAT HO CHI MINH HAS DIRECT COMMUNIST CONNECTIONS, AND IT SHOULD BE OBVIOUS THAT WE ARE NOT INTERESTED IN SEEING COLONIAL EMPIRE ADMINISTRATIONS SUPPLANTED BY PHILOSOPHY AND POLITICAL ORGANIZATIONS EMANATING FROM AND CONTROLLED BY KREMLIN.

General Marshall's words were prophetic of what became a guiding principle—or, more accurately, a guiding aberration—of American foreign policy for at least two decades: where Communists were involved, the United States would depart from its traditional anti-colonialism and support the imperial powers. Assuming as we did that Communists by definition were agents of an international conspiracy, we further assumed that a Communist leader could not be an authentic patriot no matter what he said or did. If the choice was to be—as we then rationalized it—between the old imperialism of the West and the new imperialism of the Kremlin, we would side with the former. Where possible, we told ourselves, we would support or nurture "third forces"—genuine independence movements that were neither colonialist nor Communist—and where such movements existed, as in India, we did support and welcome independence. Where they did not exist, as in Vietnam and Cuba and the Dominican Republic, we intervened, making these countries the great crisis areas of postwar American foreign policy and, in the process, earning for the United States the reputation of foremost imperialist power.

The role is one to which we are unsuited by temperament and tradition. Until a generation ago, America was regarded throughout the world—and deservedly so—as the one great nation that was authentically anti-imperialist. It was Woodrow Wilson who introduced into international relations the revolutionary principle of "justice to all peoples and nationalities, and their right to live on equal terms of liberty and safety with one another, whether they be strong or weak." Perhaps it was a utopian dream, but Americans meant it at the time, and the world believed we meant it, and we had plans for realizing it: first the Covenant of the League of Nations and then the United Nations Charter, both purporting to introduce the rule of law into international relations, both purporting to supplant the old imperialist anarchy with the principle of trusteeship for the weak and the poor, both purporting to supplant the old balance of power with a new community of power.

The dismay and disillusion that have overtaken so many of us in America are the result, I believe, of our departure from these traditional American values. The corrosive, consuming fear of Communism has driven us into a role in the world which suits us badly and which we deeply dislike. I think that the American people have sensed this all along and are moving now to an active, conscious awareness of their own real preferences. It is no easy matter for us to knock over the household gods we have been taught for a generation to worship, but I think the American people have all along had an uneasy awareness that the dictators and warlords with whom we have been in league for so long are not really our kind of people. I suspect, too, that if Khrushchev and Mao and Ho had not had the name of "Communist" we might have recognized them as men we could respect: tough and sometimes ruthless, but patriots nonetheless; committed to an ideology we would not want for ourselves, but also committed to the well-being of their own people. With China's entry into the United Nations and the President's imminent trip to Peking, we may find that we can do business with the Chinese, just as we have done with the Russians. We may even find it possible to be cordial, as we have been with the Yugoslavs. Eventually (who knows?), we may even kick over the household gods once and for all and become friends. Huck Finn, when he helped Jim escape, knew it was a sin and knew he was going to go to Hell for it, but he liked Jim, so he did it anyway.

History is filled with turning points that are not easily identified until long after the event. It seems almost inevitable that Vietnam will prove to have been a watershed in American foreign policy, but it is by no means clear what kind. Before it can represent anything of a lasting historical nature, the war, of course, will have to be ended—not just scaled down but ended, and not just for Americans but for the tortured Vietnamese as well. One assumes that it will be ended—if not by our present leaders, then by their successors—and that when at last it is, the American people will once again in their history have the opportunity and the responsibility of deciding where they want to go in the world, of deciding what kind of role they want their country to play, of deciding what kind of country they want America to be.

The Truman Doctrine, which made limited sense for a limited time in a particular place, has led us in its universalized form to disaster in Southeast Asia and demoralization at home. In view of all that has happened, it seems unlikely that we will wish to resume the anti-Communist crusade of the early postwar years. Yet it is not impossible: memories will fade, controversies may recur, pride may once again be challenged and competitive instincts aroused. The Truman Doctrine is frayed and tattered, but it is still an influence upon our policy and outlook.

I do not think we are going to return to isolationism. I will go further: I do not think there is or ever has been the slightest chance of the United States' returning to the isolationism of the prewar years. It will not happen because it cannot happen: we are inextricably involved with the world politically, economically, militarily, and—in case anyone cares—legally. We could not get loose if we wanted to. And no one wants to. The people who are called "neo-isolationists" are no such thing; the word is an invention of people who confuse internationalism with an intrusive American unilateralism, with a quasi-imperialism. Those of us who are accused of "neo-isolationism" are, I believe, the opposite: internationalists in the classic sense of that term—in the sense in which it was brought into American usage by Woodrow Wilson and Franklin Roosevelt. We believe in international coöperation through international institutions. We would like to try to keep the peace through the United Nations, and we would like to try to assist the poor countries through institutions like the World Bank. We do not think the United Nations is a failure; we think it has never been tried.

In the aftermath of Vietnam, it is America's option—not its "destiny," because there is no such thing—to return to the practical idealism of the United Nations Charter. It is, I believe, consistent with our national tradition and congenial to our national character, and is therefore the most natural course for us to follow. It is also the most logical, in terms of our interests and the interests of all other nations living in a diverse and crowded but interdependent world in the age of nuclear weapons.

The essence of any community—local, national, or international—is some degree of acceptance of the principle that the good of the whole must take precedence over the good of the parts. I do not believe that the United States (or any of the other big countries) has ever accepted that principle with respect to the United Nations. Like the Soviet Union and other great powers, we have treated the United Nations as an instrument of our policy, to be used when it is helpful but otherwise ignored. Orphaned at birth by the passing from the political scene of those who understood its potential real usefulness, the United Nations has never been treated as a potential world-security community—as an institution to be developed and strengthened for the long-term purpose of protecting humanity from the destructiveness of unrestrained nationalism. The immediate, short-term advantage of the leading members has invariably been given precedence over the needs of the collectivity. That is why the United Nations has not worked. There is no mystery about it, no fatal shortcoming in the Charter. Our own federal government would soon collapse if the states and the people had no loyalty to it. The reason that the United Nations has not functioned as a peace-keeping organization is that its members, including the United States, have not wished it to; if they had wanted it to work, it could have—and it still can. Acheson and his colleagues were wholly justified in their expectation of the United Nations' failure; their own cynicism, along with Stalin's cynicism, assured that failure.

Our shortsighted, self-serving, and sanctimonious view of the United Nations was put on vivid display in the reaction to the General Assembly's vote to take in mainland China and expel Nationalist China. Mr. Nixon expressed unctuous indignation, not at the loss of the vote but at the "shocking demonstration" of "undisguised glee" shown by the winners, especially those among the winners to whom the United States had been "quite generous"—as the President's press secretary was at pains to add. Mr. Agnew at least spared us the pomposities, denouncing the United Nations as a "paper tiger" and a "sounding board for the left," whose only value for the United States was that "it's good to be in the other guy's huddle." The Senate Minority Leader was equally candid: "I think we are going to wipe off some of the smiles from the faces we saw on television during the United Nations voting." The revelations are striking. Having controlled the United Nations for many years as tightly and as easily as a big-city boss controls his party machine, we had got used to the idea that the United Nations was a place where we could work our will; Communists could delay and disrupt the proceedings and could exercise the Soviet veto in the Security Council, but they certainly were not supposed to be able to win votes. When they did, we were naturally shocked—all the more because, as one European diplomat commented, our unrestrained arm-twisting had turned the issue into a "worldwide plebiscite for or against the United States," and had thereby made it difficult for many nations to judge the question of Chinese representation on its merits. When the vote went against us nonetheless, the right-wingers among us saw that as proof of what they had always contended—that the United Nations was a nest of Red vipers.

The test of devotion to the law is not how people behave when it goes their way but how they behave when it goes against them. During these years of internal dissension over the war in Vietnam, our leaders have pointed out frequently—and correctly—that citizens, however little they may like it, have a duty to obey the law. The same principle applies on the international level. *"Pacta sunt servanda,"* the international lawyers say: "The law must be obeyed." The China vote in the General Assembly may well have been unwise, and it may have shown a certain vindictiveness toward the United States, but it was a legal vote, wholly consistent with the procedures spelled out in the Charter.

The old balance-of-power system is a discredited failure, having broken down in two world wars in the twentieth century. The human race managed to survive those conflicts; it is by no means certain that it would survive another. This being the case, it is myopic to dismiss the idea of an effective world peace-keeping organization as a visionary ideal—or as anything, indeed, but an immediate, practical necessity.

With the coöperation of the major powers—and there is no reason in terms of their own national interests for them not to coöperate—the conflict in the Middle East could be resolved on the basis of the Security Council resolution of 1967, to which all the principal parties have agreed, calling for a settlement based upon, among other things, the principle of "the inadmissibility of the acquisition of territory by war." Similarly, I believe that the Security Council should have interceded to prevent war between India and Pakistan. This proved impossible largely because of the self-seeking of the great powers, each of which perceived and acted upon the situation not on its merits, and certainly not in terms of human cost, but in terms of its own shortsighted geopolitical interests. Moreover, the Security Council waited until war had actually broken out and an Indian victory seemed certain before attempting to intervene. The time for the United Nations to act on the crisis in East Pakistan was many months earlier, when the Bengalis were being brutally suppressed by the armed forces of the Pakistani government. The United Nations, it is true, is proscribed by Article 2 of the Charter from intervention in "matters which are essentially within the domestic jurisdiction of any state," but Article 2 also states that "the principle shall not prejudice the application of enforcement measures" under the peace-enforcement provisions of the Charter. By any reasonable standard of judgment, the mass killing of East Bengalis and the flight of ten million refugees across the Indian border constituted a "threat to the peace" as that term is used in the Charter, warranting United Nations intervention. I do not think it likely under present circumstances that the United Nations could play a mediating role in the war in Indo-China, the disabling circumstance being that the belligerents, including the United States, almost certainly would not permit it. But, looking ahead to the time when the Vietnam war is finally ended, I think it would be feasible for the United Nations to oversee and police a general peace settlement, through a revived International Control Commission, and perhaps through the assignment of peace-keeping forces.

When a conflict presents what Article 39 of the Charter calls a "threat to the peace, breach of the peace, or act of aggression," it makes no sense to leave the issue to the caprices of the belligerents. I have never understood why it is so widely regarded as outrageous or immoral for external parties to impose a solution to a dangerous conflict. Under the United Nations Charter, the Security Council has full authority—possibly even an obligation—to impose a settlement upon warring parties that fail to make peace on their own. The very premise of the Charter is that warring nations can no longer be permitted immunity from a world police power. As far as the United States is concerned, it is worth recalling that the United Nations Charter is a valid and binding obligation upon us, ratified as a treaty with the advice and consent of the Senate. And as far as the parties to various conflicts are concerned—Arabs and Israelis, Indians and Pakistanis—it needs to be recognized that they, too, are signatories to the Charter and are therefore obligated, under Article 25, "to accept and carry out the decisions of the Security Council in accordance with the present Charter."

In this century of conflict, the United States led in the conception and formulation of plans for an international peace-keeping organization. We did not invent the idea, nor have we been its only proponents, but without our leadership the ideal embodied in the Covenant of the League of Nations and the United Nations Charter would not have attained even the meagre degree of realization it has attained. It is this idea of world organization—rather than our democratic ideology, or our capitalist economy, or our power and the responsibilities it is supposed to have thrust upon us—that entitles the United States to claim to have made a valuable and unique contribution to the progress of international relations. Coming as we did on the international scene as a new and inexperienced participant, with a special historical experience that had sheltered us from the normal pressures of world politics, we Americans pursued our conception of a rational world order with uncritical optimism and excessive fervor. As a consequence, the first encounter with disappointment, in the form of Stalin and his ambitions in Eastern Europe, sent us reeling back from Wilsonian idealism. And from the practical idealism of the United Nations Charter we reverted to the unrealistic "realism" of the Truman Doctrine in its universalized application. We made the conversion from Wilson to Machiavelli with zeal.

At no point, of course, did the leading architects of Vietnam or the Bay of Pigs or the participants in the Cuban missile crisis conceive of themselves as power brokers pure and simple. Having themselves been reared in the tenets of Wilson-Roosevelt internationalism, and having lived through the disaster of appeasement in the inter-war years, they came to regard themselves as "tough-minded idealists," as "realists with vision," and, above all, as practitioners of collective security against aggression. What the United Nations could not do the United States could and would do, with allies if possible, alone if necessary. We, after all, were the ones who bore the burden of the "responsibilities of power." It was up to us, if all else failed, to curb aggression at its outset, to accept whatever sacrifices had to be made in order to defend the "free world" against the new Communist predator. We, in effect, were the successors to an enfeebled United Nations, and were forced by fate and circumstance to endure the glory and agony of power.

In this heady frame of reference, Vietnam and its consequences might be conceived as the ripe harvest of the American era of romantic "realism." Primarily, no doubt, because of its military failures, the war in Vietnam has brought many Americans to an awareness of the sham idealism of the "responsibilities of power," and of the inadequacies of the new "realism" once it is stripped of its romantic façade. Many young Americans, and some older ones, are appalled not only by the horrors of the Vietnam war but by the deterministic philosophy, espoused by the intellectuals who came into government in the sixties, of a permanent, purposeless struggle for power and advantage. We seem to be discovering once again that without a moral purpose and frame of reference there can be no such thing as "advantage."

America may be coming near to the closing of a circle. Having begun the postwar period with the idealism of the United Nations Charter, we retreated in disillusion to the "realism" of the Cold War, to the Truman Doctrine and its consummation in Vietnam, easing the transition by telling ourselves that we were not really abandoning the old values at all but simply applying them in more practical ways. Now, having failed most dismally and shockingly, we are beginning to cast about for a new set of values. The American people, if not their leaders, have come near to recognizing the failure of romantic, aggressive "realism," although a new idealism has yet to take its place. Perhaps we will settle for an old idealism —the one we conceived and commended to the world but have never tried.

25

ALTERNATIVE STRATEGIES FOR U.S. POLICY

Frederick H. Hartmann[*]

A balance sheet for U.S. foreign policy in the new age of increasing involvements after World War II must give full marks to much that was constructive in conception and capable in execution. Conversely, the important mistakes could be traced predominantly to our limited and unusual experi-

---

* Reprinted with permission of The Macmillan Company from *The New Age of American Foreign Policy*, by Frederick H. Hartmann, 1970, pp. 259–281.

ence as a nation. Views as to what the world is like, what kinds of solutions will cure its ills, what our constructive contribution can be (and its limitations), and through what methods, strategies, and tactics that contribution can best be made, naturally are profoundly influenced by experience—an experience that U.S. policy-makers of both major parties share. Where the limitations of our experience had greatest negative consequences was in our failing to ask the right strategic questions in the right order. That, plus our impatience, inclined us almost automatically to ask first what we should do, rather than what we want done and who might do it. If U.S. errors after 1945 were in the direction of assuming unilaterally too much of the burden, these errors stem from a failure to understand the conditions under which other nations would and could be forced to act in our essential interests. Before attempting . . . to analyze our major military, socioeconomic, and political policy dilemmas, it will be useful here to look systematically at the assumptions behind our approach to world problems.

The Strategic Questions Debated

[Earlier] we made the point that the three most important strategic decisions involve where to deploy politico-military power to hold the line, whom the line should be held against, and how the line should be held. Deciding these three aspects of strategy wisely is indeed the proof that one has a well-conceived set of objectives implemented through a strategic policy that takes account of and advantage of the basic forces at work in international relations.

When, as in *The New York Times* (February 26, 1967), a round-up of largely critical views by prominent individuals before the Senate Foreign Relations Committee and elsewhere is presented, it is these questions they are asking. The article title is "Are We Overextended?—Six Views," but its content thrust is less on whether we have the power to pursue "globalist" commitments (although no nation *is* unlimited in its power) and more on whether these many commitments are desirable or necessary. They are asking what we *should* be attempting in Europe, Asia, and elsewhere. (Compare with Rusk's comments which follow, noting how central the adequacy of his guiding formulas—defend freedom, stop communism, deter aggression—is to this debate.)

In the *Times* article Senate Majority Leader Mike Mansfield's views on Europe are reported. Speaking before Soviet occupation of Czechoslovakia dashed hopes for détente, Senator Mansfield called for "a selective but substantial reduction of our troop commitments to NATO" which "could become central to furthering" bridge-building efforts. Former ambassador George F. Kennan noted, "We stand today at something of a parting of the ways with respect to our approach to the Communist world. If we . . . carry our differences against individual Communist powers as though we

were still dealing . . . with the grim monolith of Communist power that confronted us in the days of Stalin, we may be neglecting and discarding the
only chance that I can see to spare ourselves . . . the immeasurable ca-
tastrophes of a world war among nuclear powers." Professor Henry Steele
Commager recorded his "feeling that we do not have the resources, material,
intellectual or moral, to be at once an American power, a European power,
and an Asian power. . . . It is not our duty to keep peace throughout the
globe, to put down aggression wherever it starts up, to stop the advance of
communism or other isms which we may not approve of. It is primarily the
responsibility of the United Nations to keep the peace . . . if that organization is not strong enough to do the job we should perhaps bend our major
energies to giving her the necessary authority and the tools."

Retired General James E. Gavin saw the "United States' troop commitment to Europe [as] far in excess of today's needs." Although NATO was
necessary, Gavin stressed the need to encourage a stronger, more independent Western Europe. Senator J. W. Fulbright, Chairman of the Senate
Foreign Relations Committee, noted the "quite fundamental changes . . .
in the world during the past twenty years [but] we continue to apply the
vocabulary created two decades ago to the shape of current events. . . .
We know only that aggression is usually an action that Communist countries
take and that the United States abjures. Equally, we therefore appear to
know instinctively that fighting in Lebanon or the Dominican Republic,
for instance, somehow does not involve aggression."

Former Ambassador to Japan Edwin O. Reischauer said: "The threat of
unitary world communism sweeping Asia has largely faded, and the menace
of Chinese domination—if ever it was a real menace in the military sense—
is growing weaker. . . . We should seek to minimize our military involvement and military commitments in Asia, because our vital interests are not
likely to be threatened in most of Asia, because our type of military strength
is not very effective in meeting subversion and guerrilla warfare . . . and
because our military presence is likely to stir up anti-American reactions."

A debate is not complete without the opposing views. No one has more
ably enunciated the basis for the [pre-Nixon] policy than former Secretary of
State Dean Rusk. One of the clearest defenses he made deserves quotation
at length. Dated January 4, 1967, in form it is a response to a letter from
student leaders on the U.S. policy in Vietnam, but in fact it contains a complete intellectual justification for how U.S. strategic problems have been
conceptualized in the 1950's and 1960's by successive administrations.

There is no shadow of doubt in my mind that our vital interests are deeply
involved in Vietnam and in Southeast Asia.

We are involved because the nation's word has been given that we would be
involved. On February 1, 1955, by a vote of 82 to 1 the United States Senate
passed the Southeast Asia Collective Defense Treaty. That Treaty stated that
aggression by means of armed attack in the treaty area would endanger our own

peace and safety and, in that event, "we would act to meet the common danger." There is no question that an expanding armed attack by North Vietnam on South Vietnam has been under way in recent years; and six nations, with vital interests in the peace and security of the region, have joined South Vietnam in defense against that armed attack.

Behind the words and the commitment of the Treaty lies the lesson learned in the tragic half century since the First World War.

After that war our country withdrew from effective world responsibility. When aggressors challenged the peace in Manchuria, Ethiopia, and then Central Europe during the 1930's, the world community did not act to prevent their success. The result was a Second World War—which could have been prevented. . . .

This was also the experience President Truman had in mind when—at a period when the United Nations was incapable of protecting Greece and Turkey from aggression—he said: "We shall not realize our objectives unless we are willing to help free peoples to maintain their free institutions and their national integrity against aggressive movements that seek to impose upon them totalitarian regimes."

These are the memories which have inspired the four postwar American Presidents as they dealt with aggressive pressures and thrusts from Berlin to Korea, from the Caribbean to Vietnam.

In short, we are involved in Vietnam because we know from painful experience that the minimum condition for order on our planet is that aggression must not be permitted to succeed. For when it does succeed, the consequence is not peace, it is the further expansion of aggression. . . .

Look back and imagine the kind of world we now would have if we had adopted a different course. What kind of Europe would now exist if there had been no commitment to Greece and Turkey? No Marshall Plan? No NATO? No defense of Berlin? Would Europe and the world be better off or worse? Would the possibilities of détente be on the present horizon?

Then turn the globe and look at Asia. If we had made no commitments and offered no assistance, what kind of Asia would there now be? Would there be a confident and vital South Korea? A prosperous and peaceful Japan? Would there be the new spirit of regional cooperation and forward movement now developing throughout Asia? . . .

. . . We regret all the loss of life and property that this conflict entails. We regret that a single person, North or South, civilian or soldier, American or Vietnamese, must die.

And the sooner this conflict can be settled, the happier we and the Vietnamese people will be.

The differences in opinion are obvious; the question is who is right? Do the formulas which worked well in Europe work equally well in Asia? Has the European situation changed so that even there adjustments in U.S. policy have become necessary? What fundamental considerations must be taken into account to answer such questions?

Looking at the record of commitment and involvement which marks the new age of U.S. foreign policy and such debates over its wisdom, one is struck by the centrality of four functional problem areas. Today, in each of these four problem areas there are substantial differences of opinion over the most useful and realistic way to conceptualize what is involved. *First* is communism. We have been torn between seeing it as a unified, militant, subversive, revolutionary bloc bent on undermining and destroying "free world" democracy, and thinking of it alternatively as a competing ideology taking different forms in different states loosely united by their common outlook. *Second* is foreign aid and the uncommitted. We have been torn between seeing foreign aid as an instrument to retard the spread of communism and seeing it as a moral obligation of the wealthy nations to the poorer peoples of the world. We have similarly hovered between the view that "he who is not with me, is against me," and the view that "he who is not against me, is with me"—meaning that we have not been sure whether we could or should convert the uncommitted, enroll them in one of our many alliance blocs. *Third* is the United Nations, conflict resolution, and the whole area of "peace-keeping." We have moved back and forth from considering the UN as the main focus of U.S. policy efforts to the other extreme. We have not always been certain whether UN peace-keeping activities could and should be strengthened, and our attitude has varied especially as the organization itself has changed. *Fourth* is military security. We have altered our doctrines from "massive retaliation" to "graduated response"; we have tried to outrun the Soviet armaments program on the one hand and urged them to settle for an equal destructive capability on the other (and to refrain from antimissile systems). We have sought to unravel the complex interrelations among armaments, arms control, weapons systems (both defensive and offensive), and strategy.

All four functional problem areas have been approached in quite different ways at various times in this postwar quarter century. Partly this was inevitable simply because we live in a world of constant change. Partly we have been uncertain of the correct approach because there have been substantial differences among the American people as to which approach corresponded most closely to American needs and which approach was most useful and realistic in the world as we saw it. In other words, an important part of the argument has turned on the *perception* of the problem and its world environmental setting. It is here where Rusk's views most importantly clashed with those of his critics.

Arguments over U.S. objectives necessarily include disagreements over perceptions (i.e., an objective appears more or less realistic depending on what one thinks reality is). Arguments over alternate strategies to attain these objectives will again inevitably reflect differences over perceptions. Even arguments over tactical implementation of strategy in some part reflect differences in perception.

It is of limited utility to examine U.S. objectives apart from perceptions, or strategies apart from objectives, or tactics apart from strategy. If we could agree on what the world is like and on what makes it "tick," we could presumably agree on what objectives the U.S. could hope to obtain, which strategy would be most appropriate, and which tactics were necessary. The problem of analysis of U.S. foreign policy therefore includes all four parts, and the sequence of consideration is important: perceptions, objectives, strategy, and tactics.

Perceptions

What is the world like with which foreign policy must cope? What makes it "tick"?[1] It is a world presently divided into more than 130 sovereign units, varying from the city-state modesty of the Vatican to the geographic and demographic hugeness of China. Although varying tremendously in national power, each sovereign unit is the same in two respects: (1) its government makes decisions for itself (taking into account whatever factors it wishes in reaching its decisions), and (2) each unit must face the possibility of becoming involved in war. The international "system," then, has a very large number of actors who have greatly varying characteristics (location, size, and so forth) but who will also have certain similar behavioral traits (the need to make security-conserving or security-enhancing decisions). The historical experience of a nation will affect very importantly how that nation perceives its security problem and what kinds of actions (or lack of actions) that nation may decide on. Two factors limit the strategic choices to a fairly narrow range of alternatives.

First, the amount and kind of national power which gives backing to foreign policy decisions already is a significant practical limitation on freedom of selection. Being sovereign, any nation, however small, could choose to attack alone a much more powerful neighbor. Such behavior in fact does not occur. Location tends to focus security decision-making: those who are near enough as neighbors, or those whose great power mobility allows them to deploy forces in the area, are of most concern. No nation is worried over conflict with more than a relatively few other nations.

Second, a nation's choices among structural or organizational patterns as "solutions" to its security problem are very limited in number, although each has more than one form. Only three basic options are available: to go it alone," making no alliances (the pattern of *unilateralism*); to make alliances by joining other nations who have similar security concerns, either on a "regional" basis or otherwise (the pattern of the *balance of power*); or to rely for protection on the collective security features of a world organization such as the United Nations (the pattern of *collective security*).

An important fact is that the range of organizational alternatives is narrow; equally important is the fact that the range of consequences that flow from the choice of such alternatives is broad. Looking at the balance of power pattern, for example, since alliance networks can and do take various forms, they can and do produce varying results. The choice of a

---

[1] It is not necessary for the reader to agree with the analysis here; it is necessary for him to decide whether he does agree or not. For the assumptions made here lead in the next sections to conclusions whose validity rests on these assumptions.

unilateralist pattern may have effects on other nations (or on the system as a whole), which may vary tremendously (as when Switzerland remains neutral compared with U.S. "isolationism"). Therefore, although the range of basic *options* is very limited, the results are far less so. Various kinds of total power systems will emerge, depending on the options chosen and the form in which they are implemented. Alliance systems, for example, may and do vary widely in their form—and effects.

Any option chosen by any nation will reflect its own conception of its security problem in view of the total power system and especially that part that affects it most directly. The system is anything but static, since individual choices of options will be continually reviewed in the light of the total system at any one time. Thus it is misleading to think of any "actor" as a "set piece" except in a transitory sense. This means that, at a given time, the policy being pursued by Indonesia and the security choices she has made cannot be regarded as absolute and unchanging but, rather, relative and flexible. Cambodian policy likewise can be expected to reflect changing Cambodian conclusions as to how well its interests are served by a given course of action. If each nation makes its choices out of a calculus of interests which frequently needs review, and alternative choices are available, what behavior, if any, is typical of nations confronted by severe threats?

We come at this point to a critical question, reaching to the very heart of the American foreign-policy problem. Do nations that have realistic reasons to be concerned about their security capitulate and make their peace with the nearer power or powers, who are the apparent source of their concern, unless they are guaranteed by great powers located quite far away? Or, in the absence of such guarantees, do they pool their strength and strive to maintain national integrity as best they can? Will the answer to this question be the same for Cambodia as for Japan and India, or for France and West Germany? How valid is the "domino theory"; and, if valid at all, under what circumstances?

This is not an easy set of questions to answer concerning any individual nation. Cambodia, for instance, has fears clustering on Thailand, Vietnam, China, and the United States and might therefore act in a number of ways. How much specific concern she feels about the actions of any one of these other states and what policy courses they are following will influence her decision. All we can be sure of is that Cambodia will know she has no hope of matching Chinese or American power, although she might hope to compete on more equal terms with either Thailand or the Vietnams (but again, probably not with both areas acting in concert—if this were to occur). Larger powers are less dependent on guile and agility. India is hardly likely to allow herself to become a Chinese puppet, whatever the Asian policy of the U.S. One can say that India is too weak to resist, but one would have to reserve judgment on this point. How easy would it be to occupy and hold India even if India could not prevent the occupation? And what are still other powers such as the Soviet Union doing while China is taking over India? In Europe, de Gaulle's independent policy toward NATO was not an indication of French conviction that security is unobtainable.

Looking at 1938 we see Czechoslovakia giving up without a fight; but in 1939, Poland fought against hopeless odds.

Answering the question on response to security threats (capitulation vs. opposition) for any individual nation necessitates careful and complex analysis, of its friends and foes as well as of its location and political stability and power. We can more confidently and simply answer the question for the international system as a whole. Unless one wants to argue that the advent of nuclear weapons now makes possible what never proved possible before, one must conclude from the historical evidence that the system as a whole rejects one-power control. No one nation has ever come near taking over the whole world. Those who have by their actions shown a desire for gross territorial expansion have invariably been repulsed by a union of those threatened. Nuclear weapons may make possible world destruction; they do not necessarily make possible world conquest. At this point we reach the realm of balance-of-power theory.

As with any ancient concept, the mere passing of many years allows simplistic notions, heresies, and false generalizations to cluster around it like the barnacles on a ship's bottom. The resulting travesty of good sense exposes the concept to easy ridicule. Yet if the concept endures, it is likely to have some real meaning. Without going into an extensive discussion of the many questionable things said in the name of balance-of-power theory, we can rest the case on its essence—which is that nations tend ultimately to combine against the most radical disturber of the territorial *status quo*. It is easy to point to cases where they did not when they should have. (Consider the failure in the 1930's of Great Britain, France, and Russia—let alone the United States—to combine against Nazi Germany.) Yet in the end they tend to do so, even be forced into it by the recklessness of their opponent. (Hitler attacked Russia of his own will and took the initiative in declaring war on the U.S.)

What causes the ultimate tendency to combine against the most radical disturber of the peace is that those who combine do so because they are confronted by a common and inescapable threat. The nearer and more immediate the threat, the greater the tendency. In neither world war did the U.S. feel threatened before Britain, France, and Russia did, because we were geographically more remote from its source. Hitler's real threat to U.S. interests depended on his ability to defeat first the powers who stood as a barrier to German expansion. Today, although the existence of ICBM's theoretically allows the destructive power of the Soviet Union to be launched against the U.S. even without a Soviet attack on her European great power neighbors, the basic workings of the balance of power tell us this action is highly unlikely. The Soviets would have no reason for such action unless they wished to conquer Europe. An attack on the U.S. alone, even if it were considered feasible by the Soviets, would be tantamount to a declaration of intent to take over Europe.

One can argue that Western Europe might seek peace at any price to avoid nuclear devastation. But if Europe's will to defend itself was that weak, the Soviets would surely choose to take advantage of that weakness and impose their hegemony directly on Europe, foregoing the presumably mutual nuclear devastation a war with the U.S. would entail. If convinced that Europe would not fight in her own defense, the U.S. would have to decide whether to fight at that point on its own.

Assuming this nightmare problem arose, would not the enormous growth in Soviet power automatically force other large, non-European power centers to weigh making common cause with the U.S.?

Speculations of this kind—assuming a supine attitude by proud European states toward their own national integrity—are far from reality. The fact of the matter is that the U.S., geographically remote from both Europe and Asia (except in ICBM terms), has a fortunate security position conferred by nature. Nations can (as the Soviets can) directly attack the U.S., but they have no reason to do so apart from interdicting U.S. interference in actions nearer their own frontiers. They cannot otherwise erode the security flanks of the U.S. without expanding nearer at home into the territories of near neighbors. If the Soviet Union or China were to do this, they would threaten all the rest of the nations in their immediate area, and threaten them far more immediately than they threatened the United States. In short, geography guarantees the U.S. allies; and nuclear weapons do not alter that fact.

If it is not logical to assume that a Soviet threat to Europe would be resisted by Europe or that a Chinese threat to Asia would be resisted by Asia, why is it logical to assume that if the U.S. were confronted by one or both of these dire possibilities she would nonetheless fight and die? What would make all the rest cowards while we remained heroes?

These observations about balance of power behavior tell us a great deal about the pros and cons of alternative strategies available to us. Let us consider U.S. objectives in this perspective. Here we must discuss what alert readers will have already noted by its heretofore conspicuous absence: the role of ideology.

Foreign Policy Objectives

What should be the U.S. goals? Is it enough for the U.S. to survive in an insecure world, or must we make each part of it share our own beliefs? How far-reaching should be our objectives? How many sets of beliefs do we think there are in the world: two, three, as many as there are nations, or even more? What is the relation of our tendency to give a small-number answer to this question with our tendency to conceptualize our prime strategy in the simple and restricted terms of containing a Communist bloc?

Early in this book we sketched the particular and unusual nature of American historical experience and its results in American national characteristics as well as in the specific qualities of American nationalism. Pains were taken to stress the sources of American optimism, pragmatism, and idealism. We pointed out that American idealism in the form of a view of the proper functioning of government among men (consent of the májority, American freedoms, and so forth) had an obverse side in the Yankee practicality of these formulas for settling many novel questions in a very novel setting, among men from many national backgrounds. Because of this, ideas as systems have bulked large in American history. One finds one root here of the tendency toward slogans and formulas that adorn (or distort) our foreign policy. We take ideas seriously because our very system of government is abstract in orientation. A "government of laws, not of men" is a tribute to ideas about government, and by holding to this abstract *procedure or method* we have been able to arrive at specific successive *contents* or policies acceptable to the majority. Thus our habit is to proceed from the general to the particular.

Similarly, when we approach world problems, we like to reason from the general to the particular. When Eisenhower reportedly said at the time of the 1956 Suez Crisis that the U.S. would do whatever the UN majority thought just, he was acting on that belief, and in accordance with well-worn American patterns of thought. When we try, recurrently, to reduce foreign policy problems to formulas, we are illustrating the same tendency: "Communist aggression in Asia must be stopped."

A people prone above the norm to value ideas, abstractions, systems of ideas, are likely to take what they understand of the idea systems of other nations with the utter seriousness with which they take their own. Such a people are likely to undervalue the "sea change" that occurs in ideas transplanted in alien environments. And because their own idea system of "democracy" shares with communism pretensions of universality, they are prone to generalize on the largest and most abstract scale, seeing the world as engaged in a struggle "between two ways of life." (Even if they up the number to four or five, would it be adequate?) A weak historical sense will encourage this tendency further.

Coming back to the opening questions in this section, do we think that other peoples do share or can come to share American beliefs? And does it really matter? Asked another way the question becomes: do we think that peoples stand together against enemies because they share similar ideas and values, or because they fear similar foes? Or do we think that only those who think alike could have similar enemies? (If so, how do we explain Nazi-Soviet collaboration in 1939–1941 and Soviet-American collaboration in 1941–1945?) Should Portugal be expelled from NATO because of her authoritarian regime, and Spain excluded, even if they think their enemies are the same as those of the U.S., and on that ground alone?

If security problems are strictly classifiable along lines of categories of idea systems and values, a simple line could be drawn: Communists on this side, non-Communists on that. Is this workable? Apart from Castro's insults to the U.S. and the strategic location of Cuba off the Florida coast, does it threaten U.S. security that the Cuban people today are made to say they are Communists? Or even if they were all sincere and happy in their Communist faith? Do we worry much about the fact that Albania is Communist?

The problem with mixing categories based on idea systems with categories based on national interests and security threats is that they do not match. Should a prime U.S. objective then be opposing communism, or should it be focused on achieving U.S. national interests and preserving American security? Which is the correct objective?

That the international Communist movement has run into the same dilemma does not mean that the question need not be faced. What can be concluded instead is that both communism and anticommunism are too simple as conceptions that will automatically advance the national interest and achieve national security. At the Communist Consultative Conference (March 1968) in Budapest (where 66 Communist parties were represented) the Czech delegate reaffirmed opposition to West Germany's claim on areas of Western Poland, while insisting that "there is still an honest role for maneuver in our policy." Vladimir Koucky, the Czech delegate and a Secretary of the Central Committee, urged "closer collaboration with socialist parties in Western Europe," arguing that such opportunities had "not been fully exploited." He particularly hoped to see overcome "the tendency toward an overly sectarian approach." At the same conference—at which the Romanian delegation walked out—the Romanians were criticized by the Hungarians for their refusal to put ideological conformity above national interest: for "sprouting phenomena of nationalism, the trend for isolation, the artificial confrontation of party independence with internationalism and the weakening of international solidarity." While the Hungarian speech had anti-Soviet barbs, too, it also contained this passage: "Unacceptable in principle and ineffective in practice is the striving of a Communist party, whether in power or fighting for power, to present [its] anti-Soviet attitude as a piece of evidence for [its] own independence."[2] (With appropriate substitutions, this is exactly how many Americans felt about de Gaulle's policies in 1968!)

One can respond to these observations by saying: "Yes, of course, now that there are divisions in the Communist movement, and wherever such divisions do exist, American foreign policy must be adjusted to take them into account." Such a reformed and elastic point of view will be a definite improvement over simple anticommunism as a foreign-policy objective, but it tends too much to assume that although the Communist movement

---

[2] Quoted from *The New York Times* (March 3, 1968).

is now polycentric, it used to be the reverse and the U.S. was perfectly justified earlier in treating it as a monolith. A careful study of communism shows that it has always been riddled with schisms. It is only that in the post-Stalin era, with the relaxation of terror, one can see more clearly that this is so. Granted the differences in the Communist world are now more evident than before. One may ask whether the doctrinaire policy of anticommunism really served U.S. interests in the period *before* the differences became public. Did not the U.S., exactly because it tended to treat the Communist movement as a solid bloc, help to keep it one? By espousing this view, did not the U.S. generally voluntarily restrict itself from efforts to exploit the diversive tendencies in the Communist world? (U.S. policy toward Tito is the one real exception.)

A major question in relation to the Vietnam War is appropriately raised here. While there is significant evidence that the war in 1967–1969 caused certain Sino-Soviet disagreements to be raised to a caustic pitch, did it not in its larger effects softpedal those differences? The Soviet need to show support for the Viet Cong—if only to preserve the Soviet revolutionary image—certainly led to parallel support actions for Ho Chi Minh by the Soviet Union and Communist China. When Chinese distrust of the Russians erupted, it was usually over whether the Soviets were engaged in an effort to help the U.S. find a way to disengage in Vietnam. By contrast the Chinese had no quarrel with the Soviets' sending aid, as long as it was massive. Did the U.S. weigh this loss in Sino-Soviet frictions against its gains in repulsing communism in Vietnam? Even more serious: did the U.S. properly weigh whether its interests were ultimately best served by a continuation of war in Vietnam? The vast destruction must weaken Vietnam's ability to resist Chinese domination. Do we care most whether Vietnam is Communist or whether it falls under Chinese control? Or do we assume that the one thing is exactly equal to the other?

Should the major U.S. policy objective be to contain communism anywhere and everywhere, relying heavily on direct and massive U.S. counterforce? Is it possible to do that in view of the example just given? And do we seriously believe that the only appropriate foreign policy strategy is one of organizing a "democratic bloc" to oppose a "Communist bloc"? Should not our major objective be a peaceful and secure world in which each nation, as long as it does not overtly threaten others, is allowed to develop as it sees fit? If this is our objective, the foreign policy strategy we have been following [in the 1960s] is not likely to achieve it—at least at reasonable costs.

Alternative Strategies for U.S. Policy

The conventional American view of the world—that ideological belief indicates and delineates basic national interests—almost automatically results in a strategic conception of containment with special features. We will contain the enemy or potentially enemy states, *seen as a bloc*. We shall do so by creating a direct counter-bloc, or counter-blocs; we shall do so even if we have to act and use force largely alone (because of the timidity or weakness or preoccupation of those who should aid us). In the older phrase, we would build "positions of strength" at least equal to and hopefully surpassing that of the "Communist bloc." The alliance pattern the U.S. has evolved from this strategic conception is extensive but varied. Its stronger features include a viable Inter-American system, a still important NATO, and direct alliances with states such as South Korea, New Zealand, and Australia. Its weaker features include SEATO, which is so restricted in its Asian membership, and the security guarantee to Formosa. Thus its weaker features are in Asia, which is precisely where U.S. blood has been shed fairly frequently since 1941.

The U.S. has embraced these many alliances, and alliances are at the heart of the balance of power; therefore, the U.S., although in the habit of verbally condemning the balance of power as a security option, has nonetheless apparently become a foremost practitioner of the balance of power. Since bedrock "realists" normally espouse the balance of power alliance as far more effective for security than such loosely-organized alternatives as the United Nations, how could U.S. policy be considered unrealistic? After all, the UN has shown no great ability to solve the problems of Asia.

Here we arrive at a critical point. It is quite true that, of the three organizational forms or responses among which a great power can choose in seeking security in a multipower system (unilateralism, balance of power alliances, universal collective security), only alliances generally represent a realistic choice. It does not follow that, simply by choosing the correct power-organizational *option,* the proper consequences will automatically follow—any more than electing a candidate as President of the United States ensures that campaign pledges will be realized. Alliances take many forms and yield diverse results. The simple generalizations often made about the balance of power, imputing a "standard behavior" for nations in alliance and positing the inevitable formation of rival and opposed blocs, are too pat. Actually the formation of mutual opposition blocs represents only one form the balance can take—and not the most effective form at that. We said earlier that combination of those threatened is the essence of normal balance of power behavior. We did not say that it is inevitable for the disturber of the balance to have a bloc. It can happen that way, of course, but neither Napoleon nor Hitler was able to enlist great powers in support.

Woodrow Wilson's vigorous condemnation of bloc versus bloc alliances at the time of World War I had a certain justification. They *had* become entangling in the worst sense. Moreover, in the years just prior to World War I, the ineptitude of Germany (who had the crucial role to play) directly produced this worst (i.e., tension-enhancing) form of the balance. Kaiser Wilhelm brought a simple, two-bloc system into existence, with the one bloc arrayed against the other in direct opposition. Under these circumstances members of each bloc felt forced to support each other in crises, if only to preserve the alliance. The premium was on bloc cohesion rather than on the adjustment of problems or the lessening of tensions. Wilhelm, had he lived to see it, would have felt quite at home in the era of the Cold War.

It is ironic that this Wilhelminian balance is so often thought to be the archetype or sole model. Bismarck, as we saw earlier, created a very different, complex set of alliances and alignments, tied to Germany, and designed for one prime purpose: to *isolate* his major enemy (France). To accomplish this purpose Bismarck devised many ingenious arrangements, but the thrust of what he did in principle was to "take care" of certain essential interests of those nations who might have alternatively allied with France. He thus controlled the one alliance bloc existing among the great powers and kept the potential "French bloc" from coming into existence in the first place. When Wilhelm later refused to give Russia the same protection Bismarck gave her (assurance of German neutrality if Austria attacked Russia), she entered an alliance with France. That action created an anti-German bloc where none had existed before—a harbinger of Germany's defeat on the battlefield in World War I. This alliance of Russia with France, postponed so long as Germany would meet minimum Russian needs, was Russia's *second* choice.

Our excursion into nineteenth century European politics is to reaffirm a principle: there are always alternatives open to nations, and they may be induced to take second choices if their first choices are foreclosed. Various alliance systems are possible, producing quite discernibly different balances of power with drastically different results.

A nation never has only one set of interests, but many. Considerations supporting one choice are *counterbalanced* by factors arguing for its alternative. "Trade-offs" are inevitable. When any one choice is made because it seems best under the circumstances, something else is always temporarily suppressed. When France joined NATO, she suppressed her wish to have greater independence in handling her own problems. When she left the organized features of NATO (but not the alliance itself), she gained independence and lost certain support. When Romania publicly walked out on a Communist conference (1968), she risked retaliatory Soviet pressures, but she advertised she was her own master. How much Communist China keeps her quarrel with the Soviets in bounds, depends in part on how much U.S. power remains adjacent to her territory. When America takes on involvement in Vietnam, she diminishes the chance to exploit the common interest of the U.S. and the Soviets by lowering super power tensions. These new effects stem from alternative choices and may or may not be accurately gauged by those making the choices or observing the choices made. What is always true, however, is that the new choice, like the old choice, always has certain drawbacks: regardless of the course chosen certain counterbalancing interests must, as before, be suppressed.

From these observations follow two conclusions. Actual or potential alliances or blocs are always vulnerable to political attack, especially attacks focused on the suppressed counterbalancing national interests. A strategy which accepts an enemy bloc as inevitable or indissoluble, or assumes that ideology (or any other single factor) by itself assures bloc unity, has thrown away an important tactical card. While a nation may desire to erect an opposition bloc centered on itself, it is hardly warranted in denying itself opportunities to dismantle the enemy coalition, especially since the enemy coalition may well reject such tactical self-denial in its own maneuvers.

The second conclusion is that no nation should be considered a set-piece. It is open to blandishment, to inducement, to pressure. Whether it yields to these depends on how much these reach to the core of its suppressed counterbalancing interests. So the whole international system is *far more fluid* and the balance of power can take many more shapes than most Americans tend to believe. Not just any change is possible of course. There must be something to appeal to, to react to.

The balance of power in the 1930's illustrates these observations. It lacked organized coherence through much of the decade which led up to World War II; it was allowed to be far more fluid than was good for peace. For example, in 1934 Italy played a prime role in frustrating Hitler's first attempt to seize Austria. To Britain and France's satisfaction, Mussolini mobilized; and Hitler—whose rearmament program was still in its early stages—backed down. Yet by mid-1935 the anti-Hitler *de facto* coalition had come apart. Somewhat overcoming her distrust of communism, France entered (May 2, 1935) into a five-year alliance with the Soviet Union. For her part Great Britain (June 18, 1935) agreed to a naval rearmament program with Germany, which permitted Germany to set aside the provisions of the Versailles Treaty. Where France was attempting to contain Germany with Soviet help, Britain was simultaneously attempting to reconcile Germany through changes in the *status quo*. Not only did these efforts cancel each other out, but when Mussolini defied the League shortly thereafter and attacked Ethiopia, the League (and Britain and France) was forced to do *something* by way of sanctions against Italy; Italy for revenge joined the Hitler camp. Then in 1938, Britain and France appeased Hitler at Munich by sacrificing part of Czechoslovakia. Stalin had not been invited to Munich. Alarmed, he made a 1939 pact with Hitler to divide Poland. And, once World War II began, Britain and France attempted to aid the Finns against the Russians—an effort frustrated by Hitler's invasion of Scandinavia. But for that it would have resulted in Britain and France simultaneously fighting both Germany and the Soviet Union! The whole story is an object lesson in confusion. Critical to the problem was a joint agreement by Britain and France either to appease Germany in the West (and thus at least implicitly encourage a Nazi-Soviet war) or to arrange with also-threatened Russia for a common containment of Hitler. A choice was necessary but was not made.

An inconsistent policy among those concerned with restraining expansion (where there is more than one nation suspected of desiring expansion) can be very dangerous. It can induce those who would expand to set aside their own differences for a time. If differing assessments of the likelihood of Soviet or Chinese expansion moves are currently being made by non-Communist great powers, this can be highly dangerous and calls for a re-examination by all concerned. But there is a deeper point, and that is that the wish for expansion of any two powers is not only an inducement for them to use each other for a time, but also itself a potentially serious cause for friction between the two expanding powers—especially if they are neighbors or near-neighbors.

Today, for example, any great expansion of Soviet influence would also have serious negative connotations for the Chinese, and vice versa. Confronted with disarray by the other powers, China and Russia might cooperate for a time. Yet they also worry about each other. Thus, to refine more closely the Soviet attitude during the Vietnam War, they did not want a decisive upgrading of Chinese influence to result; they did want a struggle without dangerous escalation, which continued to confine both American and Chinese attention to this area remote from the Russian frontier.

In the meantime, since U.S. efforts in Vietnam appeared in Asian eyes generally to be morally ambivalent in involving great destruction in what must be considered at least in part a civil war, Japan, India, and Indonesia refrained from any effective part, citing their own weakness or whatever else would do. If China *was* engaged in a dangerous expansion via Vietnam, U.S. involvement protected these larger Asian nations and permitted their own noninvolvement. If, instead, American involvement in Vietnam was a tragic mistake that had little to do with any Chinese expansion (real or assumed), then the major Asian nations could not help by also becoming involved in the war. Either way the result is that the very large Asian nations which the U.S. presumably was protecting by the Vietnam War played no role. Neither were Sino-Soviet frictions basically intensified. (Serious Sino-Soviet border clashes only began *after* it was obvious that the U.S. was liquidating the Vietnam War.) One must conclude that this strategy leaves much to be desired.

If the U.S. bloc containment policy, in Asia especially, contains a serious strategic flaw, of what does that flaw consist? What alternative strategy might provide a more efficient use of the balance of power in U.S. interests, and thus better results?

A Better Alternative

The U.S. strategy of bloc containment in Asia fails not so much on the grounds that the largely American counterforce cannot be made sufficiently available (although this is serious, too) as that the counterforce is largely furnished by the U.S. If the U.S. premise was correct, that our intervention in Vietnam was "saving" Asia, then why did Asia make so little effort to save itself? And if the U.S. were to get into war with China, would its power be sufficient considering that China has huge masses, is acquiring modern nuclear capabilities, and might under certain circumstances have Soviet tactical nuclear weapons made available to her? A consideration of these points might still yield the conclusion that the U.S. cannot afford to stand passively by no matter what happened in Asia. Yet a conclusion favoring action is by no means a conclusion that the bloc containment, force–direct counterforce strategy of the U.S., is appropriate to the problem.

A sober strategic judgment must turn on the response to two related questions. First, could U.S. strategy be altered so that the U.S. played a supporting rather than primary role? Second, if a supporting role was chosen, would it not necessitate a quite different assessment of the worth to the U.S. of maintaining land-force beachheads on the Asian mainland?

The idea of playing a supporting rather than primary role can be objected to on two grounds. First, it can be argued that no one else has the capacity or strength to play the primary role, so it becomes ours by default. But this is manifestly untrue. The Pacific phase of World War II was fought by the U.S. against a Japan who had overrun most of the area. Japan then held much of China and positions as far east as the Aleutians and as far south as New Guinea. Today, Japan has greater potential strength than then. Even India and Indonesia have far more potential than they have used so far. There is also the Soviet Union against whom Communist China has important territorial claims. Almost any one of these nations by itself could preoccupy China if it chose.

Second, it can be argued that, regardless of the capacity of Asian nations to play the primary role in Asian affairs, they lack the will now to step forward and play it, so it comes to the U.S. by default. This is a curious argument, for its essence is that Asian nations will not take actions that are in their own best interests and therefore the U.S. must save them from their own shortsightedness by taking up the burdens that they decline. Given this breathing space for reflection or for improvements in their military capacity, these Asian nations are then supposed to react by ultimately thanking us for our demonstration of how it should be done and relieving us in the front lines. The argument might be given some serious consideration if there were any evidence that U.S. actions in Asia are producing such results. But there is no evidence that this is so. Should we wait longer? How long? Should we continue to fight Vietnam wars until the Asian "awakening" comes?

Among reasons *not* usually advanced by the U.S. as justifying this primary role in Asia is that Americans—seeing a task to be done—are temperamentally impatient to step in and do it. But clearly there is some feeling that the large Asian nations may too slowly or never come really around to doing what they ought to do, and that the U.S. cannot allow "Asia to be lost." Yet national impatience will need to be balanced off against the blood-tax that it brings. Common sense suggests that if the large Asian nations cannot be brought to act to stabilize Asia, then the U.S. as an outsider will never accomplish it.

An entirely different perspective on the problem is given if one assumes that the major non-Communist Asian nations do have a prudent regard for their own security and are already acting in ways which, under the circumstances, they believe to be in their interests. Suppose that they consider the U.S. (for whatever reasons) to have plunged into an unwise military involvement in a remote corner of Southeast Asia, an involvement that could escalate into major war. Would they on the whole be grateful for the U.S. actions? Would they want themselves to escalate it by sending troops? Suppose that they considered the Vietnam War as a testing ground for whether Communist China or "communism generally" could expand by force. Would they be likely to choose to meet the test at that particular geographical point (Vietnam)? India would not feel directly threatened until or unless more of Southeast Asia fell under Chinese control, nor would Indonesia, and certainly not Japan. Because China in any case is already geographically adjacent to both India and Japan and is building a missile capability, the question of how much more threatened either would be if Vietnam were under Chinese control is a moot point. If it is only "communism generally" that is seen as expanding and not China in particular, no major non-Communist Asian nation is likely to feel that much is at issue.

On the whole the very point that gave strength to NATO (U.S. backing of the major West European nations' security) is what is conspicuously lacking in Asia. If China is believed to be to Asia what Russia is to Western Europe (i.e., the main serious threat), then the remedy ought to be U.S. backing of attempts by major Asian nations to build a common defense. For the U.S. to believe that the Vietnam effort was really worthwhile she must think of it as something like aid to Greece (1947), which was followed by the Western Union Alliance of Western Europe (1948) and by NATO (1949). Yet, to continue the analogy, it was not U.S. aid to Greece that brought Western Europe to unite and then also join NATO; rather, it was the fall of Czechoslovakia and the Soviet squeeze on Berlin. Really meaningful threats to Western Europe brought really meaningful responses by Western Europe.

To continue the analogy, if Greece had proved so vulnerable to revolt that it took more than a half-million U.S. troops merely to hold parts of it, one wonders whether—especially if Russia had not made the Czech and Berlin moves—Western Europe would have been encouraged by that example to unite.

Of course again, the ultimate argument for U.S. involvement is that (whether the U.S. is supported in Asia by the large non-Communist Asian nations or not) the U.S. must act as she has been acting—and even alone—

in her own interests. This argument is simply not convincing, if only because China cannot destroy the Asian balance of power without first taking on one or more of the major non-Communist Asian powers. China can *alter* the balance short of such a drastic move, but she cannot *overturn* it. Should the U.S. try to prevent alteration which does not overturn? The answer would appear to be clearly *no*—or at least that the U.S. should not attempt this overly ambitious task by playing the primary role. Strategically the U.S. should *support* the large non-Communist Asian nations; it should not *supplant* them.

If the U.S. seeks to support rather than supplant, the whole question of U.S. beachheads on the Asian mainland changes focus. In the first place, any beachheads would not be "U.S." beachheads. Any military action taken on the Asian mainland with U.S. land forces would be supplementary to other significant land forces contributed by other large Asian powers. Even here it would be well to remember that the most flexibly effective U.S. power is in the sea and air forces. A U.S. contribution in an Asian war in which we supplemented other large nations would be or should be far more in air and sea power and logistical support. If the U.S. is the back-up power rather than the prime contestant she will concentrate on controlling the approaches to Asia rather than on holding Asian territory. An offshore strategy (except where direct support of U.S. supplemental land forces is needed) will be the normal requirement.

What of the example, then, of the Korean War? There the U.S. took quite contrary action to what has just been described. Indeed, many who have thought the Vietnam War in the real interests of the U.S. have argued that it is "like" Korea. Yet the U.N. never authorized a U.S. war in Vietnam, as it did in Korea. One can say that made no real difference since only 16 UN members exerted force in Korea, but it made a real difference. Consider that U.S. action in Vietnam was roundly condemned in the UN rather than largely supported. And 16 allies are far better than three or four (as in Vietnam). Other differences, however, between the two conflicts are significant. Korea is a true peninsula and susceptible to U.S. air, sea, and land power in a way which Vietnam never can be. Korea is of vital concern to Japan (who was happy to provide the "privileged sanctuary" near at hand from which the U.S. forces were staged). The South Koreans also wanted their independence. In short, U.S. actions there had support and were feasible.

To sum up, the U.S. strategy of bloc containment (with its emphasis on force–counterforce) worked relatively well in Europe to prevent Soviet advances (although not to solve pressing problems like German reunification or exploit the fissures in the Soviet "bloc"). It worked well in stabilizing the balance, because the U.S. worked together with major European nations, sharing a similar conception of their vital interests. Even at its best this strategy was deficient, however, in exploiting the counterbalancing national interests *within* the opponent group because of American overvaluing of ideological considerations. The same bloc-containment strategy applied in Asia has suffered not only from the same deficiencies as in Europe (a failure to solve pressing problems such as the "China question" or to exploit the Sino-Soviet dispute) but has also had the added defects that it has been applied in a geographical area of limited concern to the major non-Communist Asian nations and has failed to associate those nations with it.

An alternative strategy, capable of gaining more widespread support and burden-sharing in Asia, is badly needed. Using this principle is impossible without taking an open-minded approach to who in the nature of things has a need to help restrain Chinese ambitions. Since this group obviously includes the Soviet Union, whose bond of communism with China (for whatever it is worth) is counterbalanced by Soviet concern over growing Chinese power, care should be taken not to place the Soviets in positions where, as in Vietnam, they feel compelled to soft-pedal differences with China. Vietnam on these grounds alone would have to be questioned as counterproductive to basic U.S. interests. The *objective* of U.S. strategy in Asia is properly the creation of conditions constraining any forceful Chinese expansion; and each of the major Asian nations (except naturally China) has a definite interest in seeing this condition accomplished. The alternative strategy argued for here is designed to isolate a major opponent by utilizing the counterbalancing interests of its potential major allies. It is an *opponent-isolating* or *limiting strategy*. It answers the question of what the U.S. should do only after first asking what we want accomplished and who could be made to do it.

An opponent-isolating strategy obviously is quite complex. China, for example, may not be successfully isolated from Soviet or other support under every circumstance. But that is not what is sought. What is sought (i.e., the objective) is to isolate the opponent from support for expansive purposes— and this could be obtained, since China cannot expand far in any direction without encroaching on the territory of one of her major neighbors. Here we see again why Vietnam was an inopportune occasion for the U.S. to make a test case. Since China had not injured her major neighbors by this move, neither were these neighbors disposed toward serious retaliation. (That South Vietnam would be worthwhile for the U.S. to defend simply because the *status quo* was being altered by other Vietnamese, or because communism was involved, might be argued by some—but consider the price in terms of what strategically have to be considered more major objectives.)

It is very difficult in principle for the U.S. in effect to isolate both the Soviet Union in Europe and Communist China in Asia from great power allies, because on the face of it this suggests that they will ally together. But if the isolation of the Soviets is accomplished as it has been (with U.S. and NATO forebearance from attempts to shrink the Soviet sphere by force), and if the expansion of China if it occurs would threaten Soviet interests too, it is possible to achieve this aim unless both Communist great powers can agree on supporting each other's expansion—a very dangerous but highly unlikely possibility. (What the Soviets eventually got from their agreement with Hitler to expand together into Poland was an assault by Germany without any assured Soviet allies.)

The opponent-isolating strategy assumes that seven features of the nation-state system are of fundamental importance. First, although Communist nations may allow their views of their own national interests to be shaped to some extent by ideology, if a clearcut choice must be made between tangible, immediate, and important national assets and the unity of the Communist movement, the former will outweigh the latter. Second, nations should not be considered as set-pieces but rather as responding to conflicting needs in a variety of ways in different periods of time. Third, the security goals of states are sought through alliances and alignments whose consummation necessitates the suppression of certain counterbalancing interests. Fourth, because situations change (no set-pieces) and because certain counterbalancing interests have always by a given course been suppressed, alliance blocs are always vulnerable to political attack. Fifth, great nations attempting to overthrow an existing *status quo* will ordinarily find difficulty in gaining support from other nations who might thereby be threatened. Sixth, expansive nations can therefore be isolated by adroit appeal to the interests of the others. Seventh, such appeal to be effective must take into proper account the counterbalancing interests of all the major nations whose roles can make a real difference in the outcome.

Since these seven features, if they are true descriptions of the nation-state system we live in, [were] not considered by American policy-makers generally as all true, it is apparent why we would follow a bloc-containment strategy in preference to an opponent-isolating strategy. Yet if these seven features are true, they make possible a more rewarding alternative strategy.

One important reason why Americans have tended toward the bloc-containment strategy is because of their conviction that there is indeed a "democratic bloc" and a "Communist bloc" (plus whatever else is left over). But in view of all the evidence, is this belief warranted? The second important reason is that Americans have . . . been asking the wrong questions in the wrong order, in the process becoming confused as to what we want, who opposes, and how to succeed.

If the world and how it operates is different in important features from what are apparently generally-held American views, it is not only necessary to change strategies. It is also necessary to deal with major problems of American foreign policy on an altered tactical basis which would implement the new strategy. [This] is the main moral to be drawn from the U.S. experience [since World War II].

↘11↙

Vietnam Issues,
the Senate, and the President

No issue in American postwar foreign policy, with the possible exception of the Korean War, has aroused such intense public interest and debate as the Vietnam War, and especially the United States combat role in that war. As we have seen, crises involving the United States have come about since 1945 with fair frequency. But in many of these crises, issues were much more clear-cut even if the dangers were just as real, and there was extensive popular consensus. Most of these crises revolved around commitments of fairly long standing, as over Berlin. Or, as in the Cuban missile crisis, the issue was immediately perceived by the American people to be whether the United States would accept a Soviet step clearly calculated to change the military balance drastically. American involvement in Vietnam, by contrast, sparked a widespread and continuing debate over the facts about Vietnam itself, and about the wisdom of the American commitment.

That debate was slow in developing. Initially the majority of the American public and the majority of the Senate were at one with the President. It was taken more or less for granted that the war was just and necessary and would be won. Most intellectuals agreed. Only after a time did a reaction set in, leading to a reappraisal. That reevaluation began with "teach-ins" on college campuses. It gradually spread to a Congress which, in the name of a "bipartisan" foreign policy, had failed after World War II in its constitutional duty to debate foreign policy. Once the Senate realized the extent of its abdication of responsibility, a continuing dialogue began. In this chapter, with all our selections drawn from official sources, we shall see how this debate changed between 1966 and 1972.

It was certainly true that Congress, in the after-shock of the "McCarthy era," did not effectively debate Far Eastern policy except perhaps for the foreign aid and informational programs. So that by 1965–1966 some more systematic Congressional efforts in depth were overdue. Consequently, when the Senate Committee on Foreign Relations began a series of hearings, they aroused great and intense interest. Especially when certain hearings were put on national television. These hearings, conducted by the Committee under the chairmanship of Senator Fulbright, brought much of the hitherto scattered and fragmentary debate into initial focus. From this rich treasury of materials it is possible to include only a small sampling in the selections which follow. Both of these presentations came in February 1966 when the hearings reached a climax.

The first selection, "The United States Commitment in Vietnam," by Secretary of State Dean Rusk, is interesting not only for the Secretary's comments on Vietnam itself but even more for the way in which he approaches the problem. For the real heart of the controversy, as we saw in Chapter 10, is over conceptualization and strategy. How should the U.S. conceive the relationship of Communist China to the Vietnam War? What is the effect of that war on the Sino-Soviet dispute? And what should be the strategic objective of the U.S. toward China and the Communist "bloc?" Rusk, for example, speaks of a "Communist world" which "has returned to its demand for . . . a 'world revolution,' a world of coercion . . ." Thus he sees Vietnam essentially as the present particular geographical theatre in which the larger struggle is joined, where the "freedom" of a particular people is threatened. But at times Rusk seems to equate the threat with Peking as such. "Peking—and the Communist states living under its shadow— must learn that they cannot redraw the boundaries of the world by force." Important questions are involved here. Is the "Communist world" really a "bloc," is the Vietnam War essentially Peking-controlled, and is it fairly irrelevant *where* (and perhaps *how*) the struggle is joined?

In the second selection, "A Critical Appraisal of Vietnam Policy," George F. Kennan, former diplomat (Ambassador to the Soviet Union, and later to Yugoslavia), historian, and author, raises serious questions on the particular points of conceptualization and strategy. When

Kennan says that "if we were not already involved as we are today in Vietnam, I would know of no reason why we should wish to become so involved" and "several reasons why we should wish not to," he is asking that kind of question. Kennan says "Vietnam is not a region of major military industrial importance" and that "there is every likelihood that a Communist regime in South Vietnam would follow a fairly independent course." These views are directly contrary to Rusk's on important points since Rusk believes that Vietnam's importance is that it is the point being attacked by communism (and any such point therefore becomes important by that reason) and that Peking would control any Communist regime in South Vietnam.

Many more of these direct (and stimulating) disagreements exist; space precludes further illustration. Consider in reading these selections how you would "type" Rusk and Kennan. Is Rusk an "idealist?" Is Kennan's general reluctance to think in terms of a Communist "bloc" a consequence of the "national interest" frame of reference with which he is usually identified? Note Kennan's concern with effects on relations with the Soviet Union, and his comments on Japanese viewpoints. Note also how the trend of his thinking emerges clearly from his answers to questions.

President Johnson's comment the next day was that "there is not a great deal of difference" between what Kennan said and "what the government is doing." Both agreed, for example, that the U.S. could not, as a matter of tactics, simply pull out. But are the Kennan and Johnson views the same on conceptualization and strategy?

In the third selection, "The Secret Talks on Vietnam," President Richard Nixon gives his own views after three years in office struggling to disengage. That his views can be demonstrated to have changed in those three years is not at all necessarily an adverse comment, for certainly that could also be said of the nation over which he presided. What is most interesting to note is the relatively small amount of disagreement left by early 1972 between Nixon's critics and himself. This speech of Nixon caused quite a sensation because the press was astounded to find that Kissinger had held so many secret meetings without their knowledge! (In May, simultaneously with mining North Vietnamese ports, Nixon further lowered U.S. terms to a requirement that prisoners be returned, and an internationally supervised cease-fire throughout Indochina be established. Then all U.S. forces would leave Vietnam within four months.)

That the Vietnam War is rapidly being phased out of the active

American consciousness will not be a good thing if the nature of the argument (and the assumptions on which it was based) are also forgotten. Those who forget the errors of the past repeat them in the future.

26

THE UNITED STATES COMMITMENT
IN VIETNAM

Dean Rusk*

South Vietnam is a long way from the United States, and the issues posed may seem remote from our daily experience and our immediate interests. It is essential, therefore, that we clearly understand—and so far as possible agree on—our mission and purpose in that faraway land.

Why are we in Vietnam? Certainly we are not there merely because we have power and like to use it. We do not regard ourselves as the policeman of the universe. We do not go around the world looking for quarrels in which we can intervene. Quite the contrary. We have recognized that, just as we are not gendarmes of the universe, neither are we the magistrate of the universe. If other governments, other institutions, or other regional organizations can find solutions to the quarrels which disturb the present scene, we are anxious to have this occur. But we are in Vietnam because the issues posed there are deeply intertwined with our own security and because the outcome of the struggle can profoundly affect the nature of the world in which we and our children will live.

The situation we face in Southeast Asia is obviously complex but, in my view, the underlying issues are relatively simple and utterly fundamental.

What are our world security interests involved in the struggle in Vietnam?

They cannot be seen clearly in terms of Southeast Asia only or merely in terms of the events of the past few months. We must view the problem in perspective. We must recognize that what we are seeking to achieve in South Vietnam is part of a process that has continued for a long time—a process of preventing the expansion and extension of Communist domination by the use of force against the weaker nations on the perimeter of Communist power.

This is the problem as it looks to us. Nor do the Communists themselves see the problem in isolation. They see the struggle in South Vietnam as part of a larger design for the steady extension of Communist power through force and threat.

---

* Dean Rusk, "The United States Commitment in Vietnam: Fundamental Issues." Testimony Before the United States Senate Committee on Foreign Relations, February 18, 1966. *Department of State Bulletin*, March 7, 1966. Department of State Publication 8054.

I have observed in the course of your hearings that some objection has been raised to the use of the term "Communist aggression." It seems to me that we should not confuse ourselves or our people by turning our eyes away from what that phrase means. The underlying crisis of this postwar period turns about a major struggle over the very nature of the political structure of the world. . . . The Communist world has returned to its demand for what it calls a "world revolution," a world of coercion in direct contradiction to the Charter of the United Nations. There may be differences within the Communist world about methods, and techniques, and leadership within the Communist world itself, but they share a common attachment to their "world revolution" and to its support through what they call "wars of liberation."

So what we face in Vietnam is what we have faced on many occasions before—the need to check the extension of Communist power in order to maintain a reasonable stability in a precarious world. That stability was achieved in the years after the war by the valor of free nations in defending the integrity of postwar territorial arrangements. And we have achieved a certain stability for the last decade and a half. It must not be overthrown now. . . .

Checking Communist Ambitions

The United States first faced the menace of Communist ambition in Europe, when one after another of the nations on the boundaries of the Soviet Union fell under the dominion of Moscow through the presence of the Red Army.

To check this tidal wave the United States provided the Marshall Plan to strengthen the nations of Western Europe and then moved to organize with those nations a collective security system through NATO. As a result, the advance of Soviet Communist power was stopped and the Soviet Union gradually adjusted its policies to this situation.

But within a year after the establishment of NATO, the Communists took over China. This posed a new and serious threat, particularly to those weak new nations of the Far East that had been formed out of colonial empires.

The problems in Asia were, of course, different from those in Europe. But the result was much the same—instability, uncertainty, and vulnerability to both the bully and the aggressor. Western Europe, with its established governmental and traditional social institutions, recovered quickly. But certain of the new nations of Asia—particularly those that had not known self-government for a century or more—continued to face a far more formidable problem, which they still face.

The first test in Asia came in Korea. . . .

We fought the Korean War, which like the struggle in Vietnam occurred in a remote area thousands of miles away, to sustain a principle vital to the freedom and security of America—the principle that the Communist world should not be permitted to expand by overrunning one after another of the arrangements built during and since the war to mark the outer limits of Communist expansion by force.

Before the Korean War had ended, the United States, under President Truman, moved to settle and consolidate the situation in the Pacific through a peace treaty with Japan, and through bilateral security treaties with Japan and the Philippines, and through the ANZUS treaty with Australia and New Zealand.

Hardly had the Korean War been finished when France, which had been fighting a protracted struggle in Indochina, decided to relinquish its political presence in Southeast Asia. After a brief negotiation it came to terms with the Communist forces that had captured the nationalist movement. The result was the division of Indochina into four parts: a Kingdom of Cambodia, a Kingdom of Laos, and Vietnam divided at the 17th parallel between the Communist forces in the North and a non-Communist Vietnamese government in the South.

Recognizing that the Communists had not abandoned their ambitions, the United States Government, under President Eisenhower, took steps to secure the situation by further alliances. Bilateral treaties were concluded with the Republic of Korea and the Republic of China on Formosa....

In order to give support to the nations of Southeast Asia, the United States took the lead in the creation of an alliance embodied in a treaty and reinforced by a collective security system known as SEATO—the Southeast Asia Treaty Organization. In this alliance the United States joined with Great Britain, France, Australia, New Zealand, Thailand, Pakistan, and the Philippines to guarantee the security not only of the member nations but also to come to the aid of certain protocol states and territories if they so requested.

South Vietnam was included in this protocol. The United States had not been a party to the agreements made in Geneva in 1954, which France had concluded with the Communist Vietnamese forces known as the Viet Minh. But the Under Secretary of State, Walter Bedell Smith, stated under instructions that the United States would not disturb the agreements and "would view any renewal of the aggression in violation of the . . . agreements with grave concern and as seriously threatening international peace and security."

Under Secretary Smith's statement was only a unilateral declaration, but in joining SEATO the United States took a solemn treaty engagement of far-reaching effect. Article IV, paragraph 1, provides that "each Party recognizes that aggression by means of armed attack . . . would endanger its own peace and safety, and agrees that it will in that event act to meet the common danger in accordance with its constitutional processes."

It is this fundamental SEATO obligation that has from the outset guided our actions in South Vietnam.

The language of this treaty is worth careful attention. The obligation it imposes is not only joint but several. The finding that an armed attack has occurred does not have to be made by a collective determination before the obligation of each member becomes operative. Nor does the treaty require a collective decision on actions to be taken to meet the common danger. If the United States determines that an armed attack has occurred against any nation to whom the protection of the treaty applies, then it is obligated to "act to meet the common danger" without regard to the views or actions of any other treaty member.

The far-reaching implications of this commitment were well understood by this committee when it recommended, with only the late Senator [William] Langer dissenting, that the Senate consent to the ratification of the treaty. The committee's report states:

> The committee is not impervious to the risks which this treaty entails. It fully appreciates that acceptance of these additional obligations commits the United States to a course of action over a vast expanse of the Pacific. Yet these risks are consistent with our own highest interests. There are greater hazards in not advising a potential enemy of what he can expect of us, and in failing to disabuse him of assumptions which might lead to a miscalculation of our intentions.

Following this committee's recommendation, the Senate gave its advice and consent to the treaty by a vote of 82 to 1, the late Senator Langer dissenting. All members of this distinguished committee who were then Senators voted for that treaty.

Our multilateral engagement under the SEATO treaty has been reinforced and amplified by a series of bilateral commitments and assurances directly to the Government of South Vietnam. On October 1, 1954, President Eisenhower wrote to President Diem offering "to assist the Government of Vietnam in developing and maintaining a strong, viable state, capable of resisting attempted subversion or aggression through military means." In 1957 President Eisenhower and President Diem issued a joint statement which called attention to "the large build-up of Vietnamese Communist military forces in North Vietnam" and stated:

> Noting that the Republic of Vietnam is covered by Article IV of the Southeast Asia Collective Defense Treaty, President Eisenhower and President Ngo Dinh Diem agreed that aggression or subversion threatening the political independence of the Republic of Vietnam would be considered as endangering peace and stability.

On August 2, 1961, President Kennedy declared that "the United States is determined that the Republic of Vietnam shall not be lost to the Communists for lack of any support which the United States can render."

On December 14, 1961, President Kennedy wrote to President Diem, recalling the United States declaration made at the end of the Geneva conference in 1954. The President once again stated that the United States was "prepared to help the Republic of Vietnam to protect its people and to preserve its independence." This commitment has been reaffirmed many times since.

These, then, are the commitments we have taken to protect South Vietnam as a part of protecting our own "peace and security." We have sent American forces to fight in the jungles of that beleaguered country because South Vietnam has, under the language of the SEATO treaty, been the victim of "aggression by means of armed attack."

There can be no serious question as to the existence and nature of this aggression. The war is clearly an "armed attack," cynically and systematically mounted by the Hanoi regime against the people of South Vietnam.

The North Vietnamese regime has sought deliberately to confuse the issue by seeking to make its aggression appear as an indigenous revolt. But we should not be deceived by this subterfuge. It is a familiar Communist practice. Impeded in their efforts to extend their power by the use of classical forms of force such as the invasion of Korea, the Communists have, over many years, developed an elaborate doctrine for so-called "wars of national liberation" to cloak their aggressions in ambiguity.

A "war of national liberation," in the Communist lexicon, depends on the tactics of terror and sabotage, of stealth and subversion. It has a particular utility for them since it gives an advantage to a disciplined and ruthless minority, particularly in countries where the physical terrain makes clandestine infiltration relatively easy.

At the same time the Communists have a more subtle reason for favoring this type of aggression. It creates in any situation a sense of ambiguity that they can exploit to their own advantage.

Nature of the Conflict in South Vietnam

Yet, in spite of Communist efforts to confuse the issue, the nature of the conflict in South Vietnam is very clear.

Let me review the facts.

With the benefit of hindsight no one can doubt that, in agreeing to the 1954 accords, the regime in Hanoi fully expected that within a relatively short period the South Vietnamese would fall under their control. The South seemed overburdened with troubles. Its formidable economic problems were complicated by the need to absorb almost 1 million North Vietnamese, who—having seen the true face of communism—fled South after the 1954 accords. The North, moreover, had concealed resources in the South. At the time of the accords in 1954, many Communists fighting with the Viet Minh had been directed by the Lao Dong Party in Hanoi to stay in the South, to hide their arms, and to devote their efforts to undermining the South Vietnamese Government. These efforts of subversion were in the initial years quite unsuccessful.

Much to the dismay of the Hanoi regime, South Vietnam made substantial progress in spite of the extraordinary problems it faced, while North Vietnam lagged far behind. As a consequence the Communist leaders in North Vietnam were forced to conclude that more active measures were necessary if the subversion of South Vietnam were to succeed.

During the 5 years following the Geneva conference the Hanoi regime developed a secret political-military organization in South Vietnam based on the cadres who had been ordered to stay in the South. Many of the activities of this organization were directed toward the assassination of selected South Vietnamese civilians. More than 1,000 civilians were murdered or kidnapped from 1957 to 1959. In 1960 alone, terrorists assassinated 1,400 local government officials and kidnaped 700 others, while armed guerrillas killed 2,200 military and security personnel.

. . . .

In the 3-year period from 1959 to 1961, the North Vietnam regime infiltrated 10,000 men into the South. In 1962, 13,000 additional personnel were infiltrated. And by the end of 1964, North Vietnam may well have moved over 40,000 armed and unarmed guerrillas into South Vietnam.

Beginning over a year ago, the Communists apparently exhausted their reservoir of Southerners who had gone North. Since then, the greater number of men infiltrated into the South have been nativeborn North Vietnamese. Most recently, Hanoi has begun to infiltrate elements of the North Vietnamese army in increasingly larger numbers. . . .

I have reviewed these facts—which are familiar enough to most of you—because, it seems to me, they demonstrate beyond question that the war in Vietnam is as much an act of outside aggression as though the Hanoi regime had sent an army across the 17th parallel rather than infiltrating armed forces by stealth. This point is important since it goes to the heart of our own involvement. Much of the confusion about the struggle in South Vietnam has arisen over a failure to understand the nature of the conflict.

For if the war in South Vietnam were—as the Communists try to make it appear—merely an indigenous revolt, then the United States would not have its own combat troops in South Vietnam. But the evidence is overwhelming that it is, in fact, something quite different—a systematic aggression by Hanoi against the people of South Vietnam. It is one further effort by a Communist regime in one-half of a divided country to take over the people of the other half at the point of a gun and against their will.

Up to this point I have tried to describe the nature of our commitments in South Vietnam and why we have made them. I have sought to put those commitments within the framework of our larger effort to prevent the Communists from upsetting the arrangements which have been the basis for our security. These policies have sometimes been attacked as static and sterile. It has been argued that they do not take account of the vast changes which have occurred in the world and are still in train.

These contentions seem to me to miss the point. The line of policy we are following involves far more than a defense of the *status quo*. It seeks rather to insure that degree of security which is necessary if change and progress are to take place through consent and not through coercion. Certainly, as has been frequently pointed out, the world of the mid-20th century is not standing still. Movement is occurring on both sides of the Iron Curtain. Communism today is no longer monolithic; it no longer wears one face but many, and the deep schism between the two great power centers of the Communist world—Moscow and Peking—is clearly one of the major political facts of our time.

There has been substantial change and movement within the Soviet Union as well—and perhaps even more among the countries of Eastern Europe. These changes have not been inhibited because of our efforts to maintain our postwar arrangements by organizing the Western alliance. They have taken place because of internal developments as well as because the Communist regime in Moscow has recognized that the Western alliance cannot permit it to extend its dominion by force.

Over time the same processes hopefully will work in the Far East. Peking —and the Communist states living under its shadow—must learn that they cannot redraw the boundaries of the world by force.

What we are pursuing, therefore, is not a static concept. For, unlike the Communists, we really believe in social revolution and not merely in power cloaked as revolution. We believe in constructive change and encourage it. That was the meaning of President Johnson's initiatives at the Honolulu conference—to encourage the efforts of the South Vietnamese Government to transform the country in a way that will correct ancient injustices and bring about a better life for all the people.

A Limited and Well-Defined Objective

In meeting our commitments in South Vietnam we are using substantial military forces. At the same time, we are making it quite clear to North Vietnam and to the world that our forces are being employed for a limited and well-defined objective.

What we seek in South Vietnam is to bring about a restoration of the conditions contemplated by the accords of 1954. We seek, in other words to restore the integrity of the settlement made between the French Government and the Communist forces under Ho Chi Minh—a settlement which was joined in by the United Kingdom, Communist China, the Soviet Union, Laos, and Cambodia. This settlement forms a part of the structure of arrangements that are the key to stability in the present-day world.

Unfortunately, the limited nature of our purpose is foreign to the philosophy of the Communist world. It may be hard, therefore, for them to realize that the United States seeks no territorial aggrandizement in South Vietnam or anywhere in Southeast Asia. We do not wish to maintain our troops in that area any longer than is necessary to secure the freedom of the South Vietnamese people. We want no permanent military bases, no trade advantages. We are not asking that the Government of South Vietnam ally itself with us or be in any way beholden to us. We wish only that the people of South Vietnam should have the right and the opportunity to determine their future in freedom without coercion or threat.

. . . .

This is the simple message that we have tried to convey to Hanoi through many channels. We have sought in every way to impress upon the Communist world the ease with which peace could be attained if only Hanoi were willing.

We have used every resource of diplomacy. I know of no occasion in history where so much effort has been devoted—not only on the part of the United States but of many other nations—in an effort to bring about a political solution to a costly and dangerous war. I know you are generally familiar with the record.

But to this point the sounds from the other side have been harsh and negative. The regime in Hanoi has been unwilling to accept any of the possibilities open to it for discussion. All we have heard is the constant insistence that they will not negotiate unless we accept in advance their four points. Yet the effect of those four points, as propounded by Hanoi, would be to give away the very purposes for which we are fighting and to deliver the people of South Vietnam against their will to the domination of a Communist regime.

To understand the situation realistically, we should not underestimate the harshness of the Communist side or overestimate the ease of a political solution.

From time to time we have heard it suggested that we should seek a Geneva conference, or enlist the good offices of the conference cochairmen, or take the problem to the United Nations, or invite the mediation efforts of neutral nations. Well, we have done all of these things, and in most cases we have done them repeatedly—with no result.

We heard it suggested also, by governments and individuals on both sides of the Iron Curtain, that no peace was possible so long as American planes were flying bombing missions over North Vietnam but that negotiations might be possible if the bombing were discontinued. We did that also—not once but twice. The last pause, as this committee will recall, lasted more than 37 days. And again with no response.

The "14 Points"

Certainly we shall do everything consistent with our national objectives to seek a solution through diplomacy. There is no doubt as to the elements for an honorable peace as we see it. We have made them clear again and again. Most recently we have summarized them in the form of "14 points."

1. The Geneva Agreements of 1954 and 1962 are an adequate basis for peace in Southeast Asia;

2. We would welcome a conference on Southeast Asia or on any part thereof;

3. We would welcome "negotiations without pre-conditions" as the 17 nations put it;

4. We would welcome unconditional discussions as President Johnson put it;

5. A cessation of hostilities could be the first order of business at a conference or could be the subject of preliminary discussions;

6. Hanoi's four points could be discussed along with other points which others might wish to propose;

7. We want no U.S. bases in Southeast Asia;

8. We do not desire to retain U.S. troops in South Vietnam after peace is assured;

9. We support free elections in South Vietnam to give the South Vietnamese a government of their own choice;

10. The question of reunification of Vietnam should be determined by the Vietnamese through their own free decision;

11. The countries of Southeast Asia can be non-aligned or neutral if that be their option;

12. We would much prefer to use our resources for the economic reconstruction of Southeast Asia than in war. If there is peace, North Vietnam could participate in a regional effort to which we would be prepared to contribute at least one billion dollars;

13. The President has said "The Viet Cong would not have difficulty being represented and having their views represented if for a moment Hanoi decided she wanted to cease aggression. I don't think that would be an insurmountable problem."

14. We have said publicly and privately that we could stop the bombing of North Vietnam as a step toward peace although there has not been the slightest hint or suggestion from the other side as to what they would do if the bombing stopped.

These 14 points are on the public record. Our Government has made quite clear what kind of peace we are prepared to accept—a peace that will guarantee the security of South Vietnam, a peace that will stop armed aggression in violation of international agreements and international law.

This is the position that we have made known to the other side both directly and through intermediaries. How does this compare with the position of the Hanoi regime?

Hanoi's Four Points

Both Hanoi and Peking have repeatedly rejected our proposal for unconditional discussions. They have insisted instead that before any discussions can take place our side must agree in advance to the four points of Hanoi's program. The words that they have used have differed from formulation to formulation. Sometimes they have said their points are the "sole basis" for negotiations, sometimes the "most correct basis." But the effect is the same. What they are insisting upon is that we accept in advance their substantive position and then discuss only the ways in which it shall be given effect. The technique of demanding such substantive agreement in advance is a familiar Communist negotiating tactic. It does not mean that the basic points are open for discussion or that they can be loosely interpreted. It means just what it says.

We have subjected these four points to the most careful scrutiny. What do they reveal?

The first point calls for "recognition of the fundamental national rights of the Vietnamese people: sovereignty, independence, unity, and territorial integrity." This point also calls for the withdrawal of U.S. forces, dismantling of our military bases, and abolition of our military alliance with the Government of South Vietnam, "in strict conformity with the Geneva Agreements."

The United States has made clear that we, too, are prepared to support a restoration of the provisions of the Geneva agreements and that we are prepared to withdraw our troops and dismantle military bases once there is compliance with the accords by all parties. We have said also that we would not expect or require a military alliance with a free South Vietnam.

The second point relates to the military clauses of the Geneva agreements, and these, too, we could agree to under the conditions I have indicated.

The fourth point provides that the issue of peaceful reunification should be settled by the Vietnamese people without foreign intervention. This also we could accept if it be clearly understood that conditions must first be created both in the North and South that will make it possible for truly free elections to be held.

It is in the third point that the core of the Communist position is disclosed. That point provides that "The internal affairs of South Vietnam must be settled by the South Vietnamese people themselves in accordance with the program of the National Liberation Front."

Character of the National Liberation Front

. . . .

What are the implications of this proposal, and why are the Communists urging it so insistently?

The evidence is overwhelming that the National Liberation Front is exactly what its name implies—a Communist front organization intended to give support to the deliberate fiction that the war in Vietnam is an indigenous revolt. The Front is, as the facts make clear, an invention of the Communist Party of North Vietnam, to serve as a political cloak for its activities in the South.

. . . .

And so the Communists . . . insist on our recognition of the Front as the sole spokesman for the people of South Vietnam since our acceptance of the Front in that capacity would in effect mean our acceptance of the Communist position as to the indigenous nature of the conflict and thus our acceptance of a settlement on Hanoi's terms—which would mean delivering South Vietnam into the control of the Communist North.

In spite of these clear realities, we have not asserted nor do we assert an unreasoning attitude with regard to the Front. The President said in his State of the Union message, "We will meet at any conference table, we will discuss any proposals—4 points or 14 or 40—and we will consider the views of any group"—and that, of course, includes the Front along with other groups.

To the extent then that the Front has any validity as a representative of a group, the views of that group can be heard and the issue of the Liberation Front should, as the President has said, not prove "an insurmountable problem."

It remains a problem only because Hanoi insists on using it to establish its own substantive position—that the Front represents the hopes and aspirations of the South Vietnamese people—and hence should control them.

The significance of this issue is clearly seen when one examines the so-called "Program of the National Liberation Front" as it was announced from Hanoi on January 29, 1961, and revised and amplified in a second publication on February 11 that same year. The first point of this program discloses the full Communist intention. It calls for the overthrow of the South Vietnamese Government in Saigon and the establishment of a coalition government from which the government in Saigon would be totally excluded.

In other words, the Hanoi regime is demanding the following preconditions to which the United States must agree before the Communists will even condescend to negotiate:

First, that the South Vietnamese Government be overthrown;

Second, that the Liberation Front, the creature and agent of Hanoi, be accepted as the sole bargaining representative for the South Vietnamese people;

Third, that South Vietnam be put under the control of a coalition government formed by the Communists and from which the South Vietnamese Government would be excluded.

May I conclude, therefore, Mr. Chairman, with certain simple points which are at the heart of the problem and at the heart of United States policy in South Vietnam.

1. The elementary fact is that there is an aggression in the form of an armed attack by North Vietnam against South Vietnam.

2. The United States has commitments to assist South Vietnam to repel this aggression.

3. Our commitments to South Vietnam were not taken in isolation but are a part of a systematic effort in the postwar period to assure a stable peace.

4. The issue in Southeast Asia becomes worldwide because we must make clear that the United States keeps its word wherever it is pledged.

5. No nation is more interested in peace in Southeast Asia or elsewhere than is the United States. If the armed attack against South Vietnam is brought to an end, peace can come very quickly. Every channel or forum for contact, discussion, or negotiation will remain active in order that no possibility for peace will be overlooked.

27

A CRITICAL APPRAISAL OF VIETNAM POLICY

George F. Kennan[*]

The Chairman [Mr. Fulbright]: We are very fortunate, indeed, this morning to have the Honorable George F. Kennan as our witness. Mr. Kennan today is with the Institute for Advanced Study at Princeton. He has had an outstanding record with 30 years observance of our foreign affairs. . . . He has no present connection with the government and is, therefore, quite independent to express himself in any way he sees fit.

Ambassador Kennan: Mr. Chairman, and distinguished members of the Foreign Relations Committee, the subject on which I am invited to give my views this morning is, as I understand it, the complex of problems connected with our present involvement in Vietnam. I would like to explain in undertaking to speak to this subject, that Southeast Asia is a part of the world for which I can claim no specialized knowledge. I am not familiar with the official rationale of our policy there except as it has been revealed in the press. I cannot recall that I have ever, either during my official service in government or subsequently, been drawn by the Executive Branch of our government into consultation on the problem of our policy in Southeast Asia, or even been made privy to the official discussions by which that policy was decided.

I am sure that there are many data that are relevant to any thoroughly founded judgment on these matters which are not available to me, and this being the case, I have tried in recent weeks and months not to jump to final conclusions even in my own thoughts, to remain sympathetically receptive, both to our government's explanations of the very real difficulties it has faced and to the doubts and questions of its serious critics.

I have not been anxious to press my views on the public but I gladly give them to you for whatever they are worth, claiming no particular merit for

[*] George F. Kennan, Testimony Before the United States Senate Committee on Foreign Relations, February 10, 1966.

them except perhaps that they flow from experience with Communist affairs that runs back now for some 38 years, and also from the deepest and most troubled sort of concern that we should find the proper course, the right course, at this truly crucial moment.

The first point I would like to make is that if we were not already involved as we are today in Vietnam, I would know of no reason why we should wish to become so involved, and I could think of several reasons why we should wish not to.

Vietnam is not a region of major military, industrial importance. It is difficult to believe that any decisive developments of the world situation would be determined in normal circumstances by what happens on that territory. If it were not for the considerations of prestige that arise precisely out of our present involvement, even a situation in which South Vietnam was controlled exclusively by the Viet Cong, while regrettable, and no doubt morally unwarranted, would not, in my opinion, present dangers great enough to justify our direct military intervention.

Given the situation that exists today in the relations among the leading Communist powers, and by that I have, of course, in mind primarily the Soviet-Chinese conflict, there is every likelihood that a Communist regime in South Vietnam would follow a fairly independent course.

There is no reason to suspect that such a regime would find it either necessary or desirable in present circumstances to function simply as a passive puppet and instrument of Chinese power. And as for the danger that its establishment there would unleash similar tendencies in neighboring countries, this, I think, would depend largely on the manner in which it came into power.

In the light of what has recently happened in Indonesia, and on the Indian subcontinent, the danger of the so-called domino effect, that is the effect that would be produced by a limited Communist success in South Vietnam, seems to me to be considerably less than it was when the main decisions were taken that have led to our present involvement.

Let me stress, I do not say that that danger does not exist, I say that it is less than it was a year or two ago when we got into this involvement.

From the long-term standpoint, therefore, and on principle, I think our military involvement in Vietnam has to be recognized as unfortunate, as something we would not choose deliberately, if the choice were ours to make all over again today, and by the same token, I think it should be our government's aim to liquidate this involvement just as soon as this can be done without inordinate damage to our own prestige or to the stability of conditions in that area.

It is obvious on the other hand that this involvement is today a fact. It creates a new situation. It raises new questions ulterior to the long-term problem which have to be taken into account; a precipitate and disorderly withdrawal could represent in present circumstances a disservice to our own interests, and even to world peace greater than any that might have been involved by our failure to engage ourselves there in the first place.

This is a reality which, if there is to be any peaceful resolution of this conflict, is going to have to be recognized both by the more critical of our friends and by our adversaries.

But at the same time, I have great misgivings about any deliberate expansion of hostilities on our part directed to the achievement of something called "victory"—if by the use of that term we envisage the complete disappearance of the recalcitrance with which we are now faced, the formal submission by the adversary to our will, and the complete realization of our present stated political aims.

I doubt that these things can be achieved even by the most formidable military successes.

There seems to be an impression about that if we bring sufficient military pressure to bear there will occur at some point something in the nature of a political capitulation on the other side. I think this is a most dangerous assumption. I don't say that it is absolutely impossible, but it is a dangerous assumption in the light of the experience we have had with Communist elements in the past.

The North Vietnamese and the Viet Cong have between them a great deal of space and manpower to give up if they have to, and the Chinese can give them more if they need it. Fidelity to the Communist tradition would dictate that if really pressed to extremity on the military level, these people should disappear entirely from the open scene and fall back exclusively on an underground political and military existence rather than to accept terms that would be openly humiliating and would represent in their eyes the betrayal of the future political prospects of the cause to which they are dedicated.

Any total rooting out of the Viet Cong from the territory of South Vietnam could be achieved, if it could be achieved at all, only at the cost of a degree of damage to civilian life and of civilian suffering generally, for which I would not like to see this country responsible.

And to attempt to crush North Vietnamese strength to a point where Hanoi could no longer give any support for Viet Cong political activity in the South, would almost certainly, it seems to me, have the effect of bringing in Chinese forces at some point, whether formally or in the guise of volunteers, thus involving us in a military conflict with Communist China in one of the most unfavorable theaters of hostility that we could possibly choose.

This is not the only reason why I think we should do everything possible to avoid the escalation of this conflict. There is another one which is no less weighty, and this is the effect the conflict is already having on our policies and interests further afield. This involvement seems to me to represent a grievous misplacement of emphasis on our foreign policies as a whole.

Not only are great and potentially more important questions of world affairs not receiving, as a consequence of our involvement in Vietnam, the attention they should be receiving, but in some instances assets we already enjoy and, hopefully, possibilities we should be developing, are being sacrificed to this unpromising involvement in a remote and secondary theater. Our relations with the Soviet Union have suffered grievously as was to be expected, and this at a time when far more important things were involved in those relations than what is ultimately involved in Vietnam and when we had special reason, I think, to cultivate those relations. And more unfortunate still, in my opinion, is the damage being done to the feelings entertained for us by the Japanese people. The confidence and the good disposition of the Japanese is the greatest asset we have had and the greatest asset we could have in East Asia. As the greatest industrial complex in the entire Far East, and the only place where the sinews of modern war can be produced on a formidable scale there, Japan is of vital importance to us and indeed to the prospects generally of peace and stability in East Asia.

There is no success we could have in Vietnam that would conceivably warrant, in my opinion, the sacrifice by us of the confidence and goodwill of the Japanese people.

Yet, I fear that we abuse that confidence and goodwill in the most serious way when we press the military struggle in Vietnam, and particularly when we press it by means of strategic bombing, a process to which the Japanese for historical reasons are peculiarly sensitive and averse.

I mention Japan particularly because it is an outstanding example, both in importance and in the intensity of the feelings aroused, of the psychological damage that is being done in many parts of the world by the prosecution of this conflict, and that will be done in even greater measure if the hostilities become still more bloody and tragic as a result of our deliberate effort.

It is clear that however justified our action may be in our own eyes, it has failed to win either enthusiasm or confidence even among peoples normally friendly to us.

Our motives are widely misinterpreted, and the spectacle, the spectacle emphasized and reproduced in thousands of press photographs and stories that appear in the press of the world, the spectacle of Americans inflicting grievous injury on the lives of a poor and helpless people, and particularly a people of different race and color, no matter how warranted by military necessity or by the excesses of the adversary our operations may seem to us to be or may genuinely be, this spectacle produces reactions among millions of people throughout the world profoundly detrimental to the image we would like them to hold of this country. I am not saying that this is just or right. I am saying that this is so, and that it is bound in the circumstances to be so, and a victory purchased at the price of further such damage would be a hollow one in terms of our world interests, no matter what advantages it might hold from the standpoint of developments on the local scene.

Now, these are the reasons, gentlemen, why I hope that our government will restrict our military operations in Vietnam to the minimum necessary to assure the security of our forces, and to maintain our military presence there until we can achieve a satisfactory peaceful resolution of the conflict, and these are the reasons why I hope that we will continue to pursue vigorously, and I may say consistently, the question—the questions for such a peaceful resolution of the conflict—even if this involves some moderation of our stated objectives, and even if the resulting settlement appears to us as something less than ideal.

I cannot, of course, judge the military necessities of our situation. But everything that I can learn about its political aspects suggests to me that General Gavin is on the right track in his suggestions that we should, if I understood him correctly, decide what limited areas we can safely police and defend, and restrict ourselves largely to the maintenance of our position there. I have listened with interest to the arguments that have been brought forward in opposition to his views, and I must say that I have not been much impressed with some of them. When I am told that it would be difficult to defend such enclaves it is hard for me to understand why it would be easier to defend the far greater areas to which presumably a successful escalation of our military activity would bring us.

I also find it difficult, for reasons that I won't take time to go into here, to believe that our allies, and particularly our Western European allies, most of whom themselves have given up great territories within recent years, and sometimes in a very statesmanlike way, I find it hard to believe that we would be subject to great reproach or loss of confidence at their hands simply because we followed a defensive rather than an offensive strategy in Vietnam at this time.

In matters such as this, it is not, in my experience, what you do that is mainly decisive. It is how you do it, and I would submit that there is more respect to be won in the opinion of this world by a resolute and courageous liquidation of unsound positions than by the most stubborn pursuit of extravagant or unpromising objectives.

And finally, when I hear it said that to adopt a defensive strategy in South Vietnam would be to rat on our commitment to the government of that territory I am a little bewildered. I would like to know what that commitment really consists of, and how and when it was incurred. What seems to be involved here is an obligation on our part not only to defend the frontiers of a certain political entity against outside attack, but to assure the internal security of its government in circumstances where that government is unable to assure that security by its own means.

Now, any such obligation is one that goes obviously considerably further in its implications than the normal obligations of a military alliance.

If we did not incur such an obligation in any formal way, then I think we should not be inventing it for ourselves and assuring ourselves that we are bound by it today.

But if we did incur it, then I do fail to understand how it was possible to enter into any such commitment otherwise than through the constitutional processes which were meant to come into play when even commitments of lesser import than this were undertaken.

Now, just two concluding observations: I would like it understood that what I have said here implies nothing but the highest respect and admiration for the fighting qualities of our forces in the field. I have the greatest confidence in them, men and commanders alike. I have no doubt, in fact, that they can and will, if duty requires, produce before this thing is over military results that will surprise both our skeptical friends and our arrogant adversaries. It is not their fighting qualities, it is the purpose to which they are being employed that evokes my skepticism.

Secondly, I would like to say I am trying to look at this whole problem not from the moral standpoint but from the practical one. I see in the Viet Cong a band of ruthless fanatics, partly misled, perhaps by the propaganda that has been drummed into them, but cruel in their purposes, dictatorial, and oppressive in their aims. I am not conscious of having any sympathy for them. I think their claim to represent the people of South Vietnam is unfounded and arrogant and outrageous. A country which fell under this exclusive power would have my deepest sympathy, and I would hope that this eventuality, at any rate, would be avoided by a restrained and moderate policy on our part in South Vietnam.

But, our country should not be asked, and should not ask of itself, to shoulder the main burden of determining the political realities in any other country, and particularly not in one remote from our shores, from our culture, and from the experience of our people. This is not only not our business, but I don't think we can do it successfully.

In saying this, I am only paraphrasing, and very poorly, the words once uttered by one who had at one time been a member of the United States Senate, and who, had a Foreign Relations Committee existed in his day, would unquestionably have been a member of it. This was John Quincy Adams, and I would like your permission to recall, before I close, the words of his that I have in mind. They were spoken in [Washington] 145 years ago on the 4th of July, 1821. Some of you may be familiar with them but they stand repeating at this moment:

"Wherever the standard of freedom and independence has been or shall be unfurled, there," Adams said, "will be America's heart, her benedictions, and her prayers. But she goes not abroad," he went on, "in search of monsters to destroy. She is the well-wisher to the freedom and independence of all. She is the champion and vindicator only of her own. She will recommend the general cause by the countenance of her voice, and by the benignant sympathy of her example. She well knows that by once enlisting under other banners than her own, were they even the banners of foreign independence, she would involve herself beyond the power of extrication, in all the wars of interest and intrigue, of individual avarice, envy and ambition, which assume the colors and usurp the standards of freedom. The fundamental maxims of her policy would insensibly change from liberty to force. . . . She might become the dictatress of the world. She would no longer be the ruler of her own spirit."

Now, gentlemen, I don't know exactly what John Quincy Adams had in mind when he spoke those words, but I think that without knowing it, he spoke very directly and very pertinently to us here today.

Questions and Answers

Senator Hickenlooper: What do you think the result of a sudden precipitate withdrawal of our activities in South Vietnam would be?

Mr. Kennan: I think it would be exploited mercilessly by the Chinese and the North Vietnamese. . . .

Senator Hickenlooper: Do you think it would have an effect on Cambodia and Laos?

Mr. Kennan: I should not think that it would have a great effect on Cambodia because it seems to me that the government of that country is already so concerned to stay close to the Chinese that I don't think they could get much closer without submitting to inclusion into the Chinese state. I think that probably the most dangerous effect of this might be on Thailand, but I don't know. I agree that the effect would be unfortunate.

Senator Hickenlooper: Do you think there would be an ascertainable effect on the Philippines? . . .

Mr. Kennan: Senator, I ought to emphasize as I answer these questions that in my opinion a great deal depends on how these things are done. If we get out in a gradual way, if there is some sort of political compromise which can help to explain our departure, that is one thing. But if we simply turned tail and fled the scene, obviously we would do great damage around, and I am not advocating anything of that sort.

I personally think that even if we were to withdraw at an early date from South Vietnam, there is no reason for the Filipinos to get jittery. The Viet Cong have no amphibious capacity and are not going to pursue us across the Philippine Islands or anything like that. It depends largely on the Filipinos themselves. They have the wherewithal to assure their own security if they want to do it; it is a question of their morale and their determination. They have done it before and they can do it again if they had to. . . .

Senator Gore: Mr. Ambassador, for reasons which you have stated more eloquently and with more erudition than I have been able to summon, I have long thought this was an unadvisable adventure for the United States. Behind the closed doors of the Senate Foreign Relations Committee, a long while ago, I asked this question of Secretary Rusk. I cannot give his reply now, but I would like to ask you the same question today: "Now to view this problem in the context of a decade hence, what is your assessment of its bearing upon the possibility that the Soviet Union may or may not continue on the course of rapprochement with the Western powers which has been underway now since the confrontation of 1961, thus possibly reentering the European society or conversely becoming more closely aligned with Red China, not only in a push into the Pacific but aligned more closely in a more aggressive international Communist thrust?"

Mr. Kennan: Senator Gore, a year ago this month . . . I tried to make the point that if we pressed our intervention in Vietnam, the Soviet government would see no choice but to come down strongly against us, and to enter into a sort of a competition with the Chinese to see who could look most critical of our policies, and most dedicated and violent in their defense of the Viet Cong. I said that they would do this even if it had to proceed at the expense of Soviet-American relations. This is exactly what has happened. The effect of the Vietnamese crisis, conflict, is not to restore the unity between the Soviet Union and Communist China. I think things have gone too far for that. But it is to give to their rivalry a form very undesirable from the standpoint of our interests and the interests of world peace, namely, the form of a contest to see who can look the most anti-American, the most critical of our policies, who can appear to be the most violent defender of what they call the national liberation movements.

The reasons why the Soviet leaders have seen themselves compelled to move in this direction are ones for which I can take no responsibility; they don't commend themselves to my sympathies but I can see why they exist if you try to look at it from their point of view, and this seems to me a most unfortunate development of world affairs generally.

I think that we must have more important problems than Vietnam to thrash out eventually with the Soviet Union, problems of disarmament, and problems of the halting of the proliferation of nuclear weaponry, and the still great and vital problem of Germany, which is, to my mind, the most important specific political-geographic problem in the world. All of this, as I see it, is in suspense while this Vietnam conflict proceeds, and the effect of the Vietnam conflict on the Soviet Union has been, I fear, to make it more difficult for us to discuss these things in a useful way with the Soviet leaders.

I am not saying that if Vietnam, if the Vietnam conflict, did not exist, I am sure that we could have agreements with the Soviet leaders on these points. I think this would take a long time, and a great deal of patience, but I think we should have kept the pressure on, and I think we might make progress slowly. At any rate, that was the way things looked a year or so ago. Unfortunately, they do not look that way today, and I attribute this to the operation of the logic of the situation which we have in South Vietnam. . . .

Senator Carlson: Why have the Soviets appeared to be reluctant to play any sort of peacekeeping role similar to the one that they played at Tashkent recently?

Mr. Kennan: I believe it is because they are being pushed so hard by the

Chinese. It is my observation that any Marxist detests being outflanked to the left by any other Marxist. And they are very sensitive to criticisms that they are aiding the imperialists, doing the work of the imperialists. . . .

Senator Carlson: What are your thoughts on Chinese intervention?

Mr. Kennan: I think the Chinese, too, obviously would like to stay out of it, and will unless they feel that our military operations are taking forms that become really dangerous to them, either in the straight military sense or in the sense of prestige. I think that if we bomb too freely or if we get operating too close to their borders, it will bring them in. Now, whether it will bring them in in a formal sense, as I have already said, or whether they will do what they did in Korea and send troops in under the flimsy and shabby excuse that these are volunteers, I couldn't say. I would suspect it might be the latter.

But it doesn't matter much from the standpoint of the problem this presents for us, whether they come as volunteers or as regular Chinese troops.

Senator Lausche: Would you advocate allowing the people of South Vietnam by open, free elections, supervised by the United Nations or by an international body so authorized to hold elections and determine whether they want a Communist government or a government leaning to the free world?

Mr. Kennan: I think it would be very fine if one could have such a test of opinion, but I doubt that it would be possible in the conditions that prevail to date. . . .

Senator Lausche: If we do pull out, let's assume that we determined that, would that be the end of our troubles or would we be confronted with new troubles in Thailand and Burma and Malaysia and Indonesia and other places?

Mr. Kennan: I think it is likely that we would certainly be confronted with new troubles because this is a very troubled part of the world and conditions there generally are not favorable from our standpoint.

Senator Williams: Had you been in a position of authority at the time, what decisions do you think you would have made that were any different from those that were made?

Mr. Kennan: . . . I think probably if there was any point where we went wrong it was in putting fighting men ashore for purposes of combat. Possibly even the instructors for the South Vietnamese forces were warranted by the situation. It is difficult for me as an outsider far away to tell. But . . . perhaps we should have thought much more carefully before we put combat units ashore. It has been my belief for many years, and it is a belief based on the fact that I had at one time to make a very careful study of our difficulties in connection with the intervention in Russia in 1918, it has been my belief that one should be very, very careful about ever putting American forces ashore into a situation of this sort, unless one can see clearly how and at what point one can get them out again. . . .

Senator Williams: Well . . . recognizing that we are at this point, we do have a couple of hundred thousand men in there, what would you recommend that we do now?

Mr. Kennan: I would recommend that we not expand either our own commitment of men [or] resources to this conflict, that we try to limit the conflict rather than to expand it, that we adopt in general a defensive strategy and put ourselves in a position where we cannot be hurried, where we cannot be panicked, where we can afford to wait, and let the logic of this situation then gradually sink in on our opponents, and I think then there is a possibility that with a little greater patience than we have shown thus far, possibilities for an acceptable resolution of the conflict may open up. By an acceptable resolution of it, I do not say that this will be one which will hold any triumphs or indeed any great satisfaction from our standpoint. . . .

Senator Clark: In my opinion, the major thrust of our American foreign policy today should be the most difficult task of arriving at an overall *détente* with the Soviet Union in the interests of world peace. I wonder if you would agree with that and whether you would care to elaborate?

Mr. Kennan: I agree very strongly with that because I think that the greatest dangers to world peace still lie in the area of our relations with the Soviet Union. Not that I think that either of us wants a great war, but when you still have such unresolved problems as the continuing proliferation of nuclear weaponry, and the great outstanding differences over Germany, differences which are becoming, after all, potentially more explosive and dangerous from year to year as the military strength of the Western German government increases, so long as you have those problems, I think that the most important questions we have to face lie in the field of our relations with the Soviet Union.

Senator Clark: I take it, sir, that you would also be of the view that Russia's present problems and needs, economic and social, are not so different from our own but that such a *détente* would be in the realm of a very skillful diplomacy exercised over a considerable period of time.

Mr. Kennan: Yes, in the realm of a skillful but a very patient diplomacy. I don't think these successes are to be had at any early date. I think some sort of a resolution of the Vietnam conflict is a prerequisite for them, but I am not unhopeful about the long-term future of our relations with Russia. May I just say here that I have never looked for any Utopia in our relations with Russia. We are two great different nations in different situations in different parts of the globe. The relations between two such peoples are always complicated and there always will be elements in which we do not see eye to eye. . . . But, when I look back on those days when the so-called containment policy was formed, it seems to me we have made a good deal of progress in our relations with Russia since that time, and that things are better than they were then, and this is a very important recognition, and if we could make that sort of progress over the past 20 years, I think there are possibilities that we could make it over the next 20 and we ought to cherish them.

Senator Clark: You would agree, I take it, that the Soviet leaders and, indeed, the Soviet people, need both peace and reasonably good relations with Western countries almost as much as we need the same thing from them.

Mr. Kennan: They do, and I think they are conscious of that need.

Senator Clark: Now, my understanding is that you feel the present situation in Communist China is somewhat different on the ground that they are in the early stages of a revolution, a belligerent stage. . . .

Mr. Kennan: I think that at the moment the Chinese Communist leaders are in an extremely difficult and almost hysterical state of mind. They have had frustrations of one sort and another both internally and externally over the course of recent years. I believe they are really weaker than they like to admit. They are very troubled by what does seem to them to be a sort of encirclement, and an exclusion for which admittedly they are themselves mainly to blame, from the councils of the world. But this puts them into a highly excitable and irritated state of mind, and I think there is very little opportunity of talking with them or dealing effectively with them today. On the other hand, I do not feel that they have the capability to create much mischief beyond the Asian land mass. I am not really too terribly worried about the island territories of the Pacific. I think [Peking has] suffered an enormous reverse in Indonesia, and one of great significance, and one that does rather confine any realistic hopes they may have for the expansion of their authority, confine it pretty much to the Asian land mass, most of which in East Asia they already occupy.

I think it will take a long time before we could deal with them effectively. But meanwhile, I think that we should leave them alone. I don't think that it is necessary . . . or desirable for us to try to solve this vast problem by military means. I don't think it is susceptible to solution by military means any more than the problem of Vietnam is. I am quite prepared to recognize that we face a great and serious problem in the cultivation by the Chinese Communists of a nuclear striking capacity. I don't wish to minimize that for a moment. But I would prefer to see us tackle that problem and approach it by finding as soon as we can an acceptable ending to the conflict in Vietnam, and then pursuing with the Soviet government and even with the French, agreements which would permit us to bring the pressure of world opinion to bear a little more effectively on the Chinese. . . . Things will change in China, as they changed in Russia. They always do. A new generation of Chinese leaders will come. They could scarcely be worse in their attitude toward us than the present one, and as I look over the history of international affairs, it seems to me that the counsels of patience and restraint have been more effective as a general rule, than the counsels of violence and unleashing unlimited violence.

Senator Symington: I have heard in other briefings that it is estimated the number of American casualties in this war is about the same as the number of North Vietnamese casualties . . . our bombing has resulted in, in North Vietnam. Would not that figure tend to show that we have tried to be very careful not to kill or wound people in North Vietnam?

Mr. Kennan: It would, and I have no doubt that this is the case. But unfortunately in this world, what things seem is often more important than what things are, and we stand under certain handicaps. Anything that a great big powerful white nation such as ours does, is going to be interpreted to our disadvantage, if there is any way to do it. . . .

Senator Case: I take it that one of our problems here is that we are facing a kind of aggression which is not so easy to recognize and not so clear perhaps, what the Communist Chinese particularly call wars of national liberation, as opposed to the kind of aggression where armies mobilize along a frontier and then cross and we have this very direct physical occupation of foreign territory. Now, I take it you do not disagree that the former, that is the kind we face now, is just as much aggression as the latter, is that correct?

Mr. Kennan: Senator Case, I think the use of the word "aggression" with what we are facing today in Vietnam is confusing. I think that this present conflict has so complicated a background, so long a background, so much of it does result from things that have happened within South Vietnam and not outside of it. Not only that, but the border between North and South Vietnam is of a curious quality. It was not meant originally to be the border between states. All these things seem to me to indicate that when one uses the term "aggression" as our—some of the people in our own government have been using it—one confuses the issue. This is, of course, in part, if you will, the invasion of one country, if one wants to describe it that way, by forces of another country, although all of these things involve stretching of terms. But in any case, it is not just that. It is also a civil conflict within South Vietnam, and one of greater seriousness, I think. I do not think that we can afford to delude ourselves that the Viet Cong are simply an external force or a force that would not exist if there were not external encouragement. They might not be so strong, but all accounts indicate that they were fairly strong years ago before they had this help from the North Vietnamese. . . .

Senator Sparkman: In your statement you refer to a satisfactory peaceful resolution of the conflict, and you have referred to it here. Could you state to us what the elements of such a settlement would be?

Mr. Kennan: . . . Eventually there must be some sort of a political compromise between the various factions involved in South Vietnam. And I am afraid that others, as I say, are going to have to work this out—and the South Vietnamese themselves. But there are a number of factions there. It is not [just] Viet Cong and their opponents. There are Catholics, there are Buddhists, there are Montagnards, and there are a lot of people who have fingers in that pie and at some point, perhaps they, who I must say are rarely lacking in political resourcefulness when they want to do something, they may cook up compromises which today look impossible to us. I do not think that anything of this sort can occur in the present atmosphere of sharp conflict and great nervousness on both sides, and this is why I would like to see things quiet down. . . .

Senator Aiken: . . . Assuming that we do have a commitment there [in Vietnam] would you say there is any point beyond which we should not go in meeting that commitment?

Mr. Kennan: Senator, I cannot imagine that anyone with any degree of responsible concern for the fortunes of the people of this country, could ever have given to any foreign political authority an unlimited commitment on our resources and our manpower. I just do not see how this is conceivable. There are a great many countries in the world besides Vietnam, and we have many other obligations and responsibilities, and it seems to me out of the question that we should assume any such obligation toward anyone else or feel that we had it even in a moral sense.

After all, our first duty is to ourselves and to the life of our own people here, and to their prosperity, and I would be strongly averse, I would fight with every fiber of my own being against the suggestion that we should ever give to any foreign political authority anything in the nature of an indefinite commitment on the resources of this country. . . . I always find myself caught up short when I see the way that this struggle is often referred to today in our public debates, and people talk about our living up to our commitments, and we must fulfill our commitments to these people.

Well, these commitments as we now interpret them, go very far indeed. They go, as I pointed out here, farther than the normal military alliance. To commit yourself in any way to assure the internal security of another government, means to commit yourself to interference in the most vital process of its own internal political life, and this seems to me a commitment of such seriousness that it should not be lightly or casually slipped into . . . .

Senator Case: What I had in mind, just to pursue the balance of my time at least in this round, was your thoughts about the extent to which we have a responsibility in the world for world peace, the extent to which in the absence of world order run by law with courts and a system of enforcing court orders, this country has to act as Britain did at [a] time gone by. . . . Now, the other side of the coin, I suppose, would be to say we have no function, no responsibility in this matter at all. So long as our fairly immediate security is not involved we can wash our hands of the world. Do you move in this direction in your thinking? . . .

Mr. Kennan: Senator, that question goes very deep, and it puts me in a sense on the defensive because I find that . . . now that I am behind the barrier of 60 years I find myself with more and more sympathy for the concepts of foreign policy that prevailed in this country in an earlier time, and I find myself, if you will, in many respects sort of a neo-isolationist. . . .

We have an enormous responsibility with regard to world peace. We are in many respects the most powerful nation in the world, and in most important respects, and there certainly is no nation which, if its affairs are handled prudently and well and thoughtfully, can contribute more than we can to preserving the peace of the world. I do think, though, what we have to bear in mind here mainly is preserving the peace between the great powers. . . .

I do not have any illusions that we can stop all violence everywhere in the world. I think that the slogan which Litvinoff, the Soviet foreign affairs commissar, used to mouth so frequently in the '30s, that peace is indivisible, that this is not correct; it is in fact a horrendous doctrine. Men have always fought, they are always going to. We must hope now that the great powers such as ourselves and Russia are aware of the fact that the weapons in our hands are of such terribleness that we cannot afford to do this any more. And I think we are coming to this realization, that . . . what we have in our hands is so terrible that we cannot afford the luxury of settling affairs with each other the way people have traditionally all through human history. But there are a great many new nations, small nations, nations with inexperienced governments, nations with shallow traditions of national life, dotted all around this world.

Believe me, they are going to fight with each other, and it seems to me that our role here as a great power must be to try to isolate, to moderate these conflicts, to settle them as quickly and as easily as we can, not to worry too much about the issues, because there will be right and wrong on both sides, but to try to keep these local conflicts from doing great damage to world peace.

Now, the problem we face with relation to Vietnam today is how do we best serve world peace at this moment? Do we serve it best by increasing the measure of our involvement in Vietnam? By trying to root out the Viet Cong by fire and sword? By increasing the intensity of this conflict in a single area to the neglect, I must say, of our world responsibilities, our responsibilities in other areas? Or do we serve it better by trying, as best we can, to bring about some sort of a resolution of the fighting in Vietnam and applying ourselves then again imaginatively and courageously and enthusiastically to the solution of the great, really great, and fateful problems that we still have outstanding with the Soviet Union. . . .

Senator Morse: We hear a lot of comparison [of] the situation in Vietnam with Munich. Those of us who . . . are against this escalation and this unilateral American war in Vietnam, we are told we are a bunch of Chamberlains. Would you give us your view as to what the analogous relationship, if anything, between this war and situation at the time of Munich or between Mao and Hitler might be?

Mr. Kennan: I think they are entirely different things, and I think that no episode, perhaps, in modern history has led to, has been more misleading than that of the Munich conference. It has given to many people the idea that never must one attempt to make any sort of a political accommodation in any circumstances. This is, of course, a fatally unfortunate conclusion. Hitler was, thank heaven, a unique phenomenon, I think, and circumstances existed there that did indeed make it fatuous to think that you could arrive at that point at an agreement with him, that would preserve the peace of Europe.

But these were specific circumstances and I think the wrong conclusions can be drawn and have been drawn time and time again from this. Hitler was a man who had made up his mind that he was going to conquer Europe by force of arms according to a certain timetable. I have never seen the evidence of anything comparable to that state of mind on the part of our Communist opponents, and for this reason, I have had to struggle for years against the attempt of people to apply the Munich precedent to the problem of containing Soviet power.

Senator Hickenlooper: Do you consider that the Chinese abandoned the idea of international Communism—that force and force of arms is the ultimate weapon which may be necessary to advance their international aims and ambitions?

Mr. Kennan: Not at all. On the contrary, I think they are quite committed to such means, and I don't doubt that Chinese Communist leaders would love to unleash the bloodiest sort of revolutions in every country that they can think of that is not Communist.

Senator Hickenlooper: I will get down to the wars of liberation in just a moment. But I am trying to see what you think about the Chinese at the present time. . . . Isn't it reasonable to assume that the Chinese are, in effect, urging the North Vietnamese on as a part or as a cat's paw in this idea of advancing Communism clear down the end of the peninsula?

Mr. Kennan: Oh, yes, it is. . . . I think it is unquestionable they are urging the North Vietnamese on, but, of course, this situation suits the Chinese book very well. They have someone, they have us, locked into a conflict there with somebody else, and they want these people to bleed us as long and as profusely as possible.

Senator Hickenlooper: You mean they follow the philosophy of let's you and him fight?

Mr. Kennan: Senator, I think the Chinese are the passionate partisans of a war between anybody else and the United States, anybody else except China.

Senator Hickenlooper: . . . We are in, we are like the fellow who is out in the water drowning, we don't necessarily stand on the bank and quarrel as to how he got in there, the job is to get him out, and it is in that context that I want to discuss this with you for just a moment. . . . What choices do we have?

Mr. Kennan: I see three basic choices: One is to multiply our military effort in the hope that somehow or another we can overcome all the resistance with which we are faced in that area, and settle things according to our own ideas. This means an escalation of the war. It means from what I pick up from the press, that is all I have to go on, it means at least the doubling of our forces there and possibly more so, and it means a great deal more physical damage done within the country. It means—

Senator Hickenlooper: Would you say that that particular line would, if successful, mean the military defeat of North Vietnam?

Mr. Kennan: That would be its purpose, I should think eventually, because we would have to stamp that source of resistance out. That is one alternative.

Senator Hickenlooper: Go on with the others.

Mr. Kennan: A second alternative is—probably it was better stated here by General Gavin in the military sense than I could state it—but that is to adopt basically a defensive strategy, to try to give an opportunity there for a simmering down of hostilities, to let the whole situation quiet down, to hang onto certain areas as a bargaining counter for the future, and see what gives. And to strive in every way possible for a peaceful resolution of the conflict. . . .

Senator Hickenlooper: That would involve the enclaves?

Mr. Kennan: That would involve the enclaves idea. The third alternative would be to just get right out. I would like to say one thing that I have not had occasion to say today, that I favor the second of these alternatives, of course. . . . But if these alternatives were to be narrowed down to two, only to an unlimited commitment to something called victory which I don't quite understand in this area, or to a withdrawal, then I am not sure that I would not prefer the second. Fortunately, they are not that today.

Senator Hickenlooper: All the evidence I have seen is that the Viet Cong, unless it has changed within the last few days or weeks, holds more than 50 percent while we may control some of the other area, some of the other cities, but this is what puzzles me about the enclave theory. It seems to me that in the enclave theory we would be holding certain strong points at certain places, and [in] the rest of the country around there the Viet Cong could run wild and organize the country and what would we be doing in there. We would be merely sitting and holding and subject to periodic and frequent attacks at their convenience.

Mr. Kennan: Of course the South Vietnamese themselves, according to the figures again that are published in the paper have forces considerably larger numerically than do the Viet Cong. I was surprised to see a day or so ago in a column in the papers written by a friend of mine, and opposing the idea of the enclaves, the statement that if we settle down to a defensive strategy there such as General Gavin proposed, we could just wipe out the entire South Vietnamese forces as a factor in the situation; that they would become demoralized and nonexistent as a factor in the situation overnight. I can only say if this is true, if this is so weak a reed as this, then I would very, very seriously question how much we wanted to have our fate linked to these people. . . .

Senator Symington: Of course, there are 700,000 South Vietnamese fighting with us over there today, and their casualties are a great deal heavier than ours. If you go to the enclave theory then you automatically give up the assistance of 700,000 people, of whom only 5 percent are draftees, the rest are volunteers. Do you think that that would be a wise move from the standpoint of the additional casualties we would have in American forces that would be carried on without the assistance of the 700,000?

Mr. Kennan: Senator, I would be very interested to know why one of those things follows from the other. Why should we give up the support of the 700,000 and some Vietnamese because we concentrated on defending enclave areas?

Senator Symington: Well, of course, they hope ultimately that their villages will be free, and if we retire to these coastal enclaves and give up all the land that their families live on, and give their families up to the Viet Cong, what reason would there be for them wanting to continue to fight the war strictly in order to protect the Americans in the enclaves?

Mr. Kennan: Well, after all, it is their country, and these places that they hold are, if I am correct, over three times numerically what the Viet Cong have. If they have any extent of determination and resolve, can they not fight on their own behalf? Must they have us at their side?

Senator Symington: In the first place, I do not think they are over three times, but that is a detail.

Mr. Kennan: Yes.

Senator Symington: But in any case, they would be continually supported heavily by the Communists from the north and, therefore, they would find it extremely difficult to protect their villages against terrorism. . . . Morally, do you think we have the right to desert them and go to the coastal enclaves?

Mr. Kennan: Senator, if their morale is so shaky that without an offensive strategy on their part they are simply going to give up the fight, I do not think they are worth helping anyway. And, as for the question of our having a moral obligation to them, they have had enormous help from us to date. I mean, goodness, they have had help in billions and billions of dollars. How many countries are you going to give such a claim on our resources and our help? If they cannot really do the trick with this, I feel strongly that the trouble lies somewhere with them and not with us, and I am not inclined to take the exclusive blame for this whole situation on to the United States and say that everything that goes wrong there or anything that cannot be done, it is our fault because we have not given it enough. . . .

Senator Symington: May I ask one more question on my time?

The Chairman: I will yield to you my time if you like.

Senator Symington: That is very kind of you, but I would like to pursue this because I am not quite clear.

Then you do not feel that Red China—and I ask it with great respect—is a serious menace to the United States today; is that a fair question?

Mr. Kennan: This is correct, except insofar as we have involved ourselves in the situation in Southeast Asia where we meet [China] on its own land mass. But in any place outside of that land mass today, I do not think it is a serious threat to us as things stand now. . . . I think there might be better ways of approaching on our part the problem created by the Chinese approach to the acquisition of a nuclear striking capacity than by trying to fight Vietnamese in Southeast Asia.

Senator Symington: Well, surely you do not mean that you would attack the nuclear developments.

Mr. Kennan: No.

Senator Symington: Then would you state what you mean?

Mr. Kennan: I think I would like to see us get back to the cultivation of our world relationships and to the pursuit of this whole question of the proliferation of nuclear weapons in talks with the Russians and with others, because I think that if we could develop the general agreement elsewhere in the world on this subject we might begin to bring some pressure to bear on the Chinese.

Senator Symington: I agree with you on that. But aren't we doing that? Isn't Mr. Foster in Geneva now trying very hard to reach some agreement with respect to proliferation?

Mr. Kennan: I think we could do a lot better if we did not have the complication in Vietnam, with the burden that that places on our relationships with other people.

Senator Symington: In other words, if we would get out of South Vietnam you think that would improve our possibilities of making a proliferation treaty with the Soviet?

Mr. Kennan: If the conflict there could be terminated, I think we could address ourselves to other problems of world affairs in a much more hopeful way. This is indeed my view.

28

THE SECRET TALKS ON VIETNAM

President Richard M. Nixon[*]

I have asked for this television time tonight to make public a plan for peace that can end the war in Vietnam.

The offer that I shall now present on behalf of the Government of the United States and the Government of South Vietnam, with the full knowledge and approval of President [Nguyen Van] Thieu, is both generous

---

[*] Text of statement by President Nixon on nationwide TV and radio, January 25, 1972.

and far-reaching. It is a plan to end the war now. It includes an offer to withdraw all American forces within six months of an agreement. Its acceptance would mean the speedy return of all the prisoners of war to their homes.

Three years ago when I took office, there were 550,000 Americans in Vietnam; the number killed in action was running as high as 300 a week; there were no plans to bring any Americans home, and the only thing that had been settled in Paris was the shape of the conference table. I immediately moved to fulfill a pledge I had made to the American people to bring about a peace that could last, not only for the United States but for the long-suffering people of Southeast Asia.

There were two honorable paths open to us:

The path of negotiation was—and is—the path we prefer. But it takes two to negotiate; there had to be another way in case the other side refused to negotiate. That path was called "Vietnamization." What it meant was training and equipping the South Vietnamese to defend themselves, and steadily withdrawing Americans as they developed the capability to do so.

The path of Vietnamization has been successful. Two weeks ago you will recall that I announced that by May 1 American forces in Vietnam would be down to 69,000. That means almost one-half million Americans will have been brought home from Vietnam over the past three years. In terms of American lives, the losses of 300 a week have been reduced by over 95 per cent—to less than 10 a week. But the path of Vietnamization has been the long voyage home. It has strained the patience and tested the perseverance of the American people.

What of the short cut—the short cut we prefer—the path of negotiation? Progress here has been disappointing. The American people deserve an accounting of why it has been disappointing, and tonight I intend to give you that accounting—and in so doing, I am going to try to break the deadlock in the negotiations.

We have made a series of public proposals designed to bring an end to the conflict. But early in this Administration, after 10 months of no progress in the public Paris talks, I became convinced that it was necessary to explore the possibility of negotiating in private channels to see whether it would be possible to end the public deadlock.

After consultation with Secretary of State [William P.] Rogers, our Ambassador in Saigon [Ellsworth Bunker], our chief negotiator in Paris [Henry Cabot Lodge], with the full knowledge and approval of President Thieu, I sent Dr. [Henry A.] Kissinger to Paris as my personal representative on Aug. 4, 1969—30 months ago—to begin these secret peace negotiations.

Since that time, Dr. Kissinger has traveled to Paris 12 times on these secret missions. He has met seven times with Le Duc Tho, one of Hanoi's top political leaders, and Minister Xuan Thuy, head of the North Vietnamese delegation to the Paris talks. And he has met with Minister Xuan Thuy five times alone.

I would like, incidentally, to take this opportunity to thank President [Georges] Pompidou of France for his personal assistance in helping to make the arrangements for these secret talks.

Now, this is why I initiated these private negotiations: Privately, both sides can be more flexible in offering new approaches. And also, private discussions allow both sides to talk frankly, to take positions free from the pressure of public debate.

In seeking peace in Vietnam, with so many lives at stake, I felt we could not afford to let any opportunity go by—private or public—to negotiate a settlement. As I have stated on a number of occasions, I was prepared and I remain prepared to explore any avenue—public or private—to speed negotiations to end the war.

For 30 months, whenever Secretary Rogers, Dr. Kissinger or I were asked about secret negotiations, we would only say we were pursuing every possible channel in our search for peace. There was never a leak, because we were determined not to jeopardize the secret negotiations. Until recently, this course showed signs of yielding some progress.

Now, however, it is my judgment that purposes of peace will best be served by bringing out publicly the proposals we have been making in private.

Nothing is served by silence when the other side exploits our good faith to divide America and to avoid the conference table. And nothing is served by silence when it misleads some Americans into accusing their own Government of failing to do what it has already done. And nothing is served by silence when it enables the other side to imply possible solutions publicly that it has already flatly rejected privately.

The time has come to lay the record of our secret negotiations on the table. Just as secret negotiations can sometimes break a public deadlock, public disclosure may help to break a secret deadlock.

Some Americans who believed what the North Vietnamese led them to believe have charged that the United States has not pursued negotiations intensively. As the record that I now will disclose will show, just the opposite is true.

Questions have been raised as to why we have not proposed a deadline for the withdrawal of all American forces in exchange for a cease-fire and the return of prisoners of war; why we have not discussed the seven-point proposal made by the Viet Cong last July in Paris; why we have not submitted a new plan of our own to move the negotiations off dead center.

As the private record will show, we have taken all these steps and more—and have been flatly rejected or ignored by the other side.

On May 31, 1971—eight months ago—at one of the secret meetings in Paris, we offered specifically to agree to a deadline for the withdrawal of all American forces in exchange for the release of all prisoners of war and a cease-fire.

At the next private meeting, on June 26, the North Vietnamese rejected our offer. They privately proposed instead their own nine-point plan, which insisted that we overthrow the Government of South Vietnam.

Five days later, on July 1, the enemy publicly presented a different package of proposals—the seven-point Viet Cong plan.

That posed a dilemma: Which package should we respond to—the public plan or the secret plan?

On July 12, at another private meeting in Paris, Dr. Kissinger put that question to the North Vietnamese directly. They said we should deal with their nine-point secret plan because it covered all of Indo-China including Laos and Cambodia, while the Viet Cong seven-point public proposal was limited to Vietnam.

And so that's what we did. But we even went beyond that—dealing with some of the points in the public plan that were not covered in the secret plan.

On August 16, at another private meeting, we went further. We offered the complete withdrawal of U.S. and Allied forces within nine months after an agreement on an over-all settlement. On September 13, the North Vietnamese rejected that proposal. They continued to insist that we overthrow the South Vietnamese Government.

Now, what has been the result of these private efforts? For months, the North Vietnamese have been berating us at the public sessions for not responding to their side's publicly presented seven-point plan.

The truth is that we did respond to the enemy's plan, in the manner they wanted us to respond—secretly. In full possession of our complete response, the North Vietnamese publicly denounced us for not having responded at all. They induced many Americans in the press and the Congress into echoing their propaganda—Americans who could not know they were being falsely used by the enemy to stir up divisiveness in this country.

I decided in October that we should make another attempt to break the deadlock. I consulted with President Thieu, who concurred fully in a new plan. On October 11, I sent a private communication to the North Vietnamese that contained new elements that could move negotiations forward. I urged a meeting on November 1 between Dr. Kissinger and Special Adviser Le Duc Tho, or some other appropriate official from Hanoi.

On October 25, the North Vietnamese agreed to meet, suggested November 20 as the time for meeting. On November 17—just three days before the scheduled meeting—they said Le Duc Tho was ill. We offered to meet as soon as he recovered—either with him, or immediately with any other authorized leader who could come from Hanoi.

Two months have passed since they called off that meeting. The only reply to our plan has been an increase in troop infiltration from North Vietnam, and Communist military offensives in Laos and Cambodia. Our proposal for peace was answered by a step-up in the war on their part.

That is where matters stand today.

We are being asked publicly to respond to proposals that we answered—and in some respects accepted—months ago in private. We are being asked publicly to set a terminal date for our withdrawals when we have already offered one in private. And the most comprehensive peace plan of this conflict lies ignored in a secret channel while the enemy tries again for military victory.

That is why I have instructed Ambassador [William J.] Porter to present our plan publicly at this Thursday's [January 27] session of the Paris peace talks, along with alternatives to make it even more flexible.

We are publishing the full details of our plan tonight. It will prove beyond doubt which side has made every effort to make these negotiations succeed. It will show unmistakably that Hanoi—not Washington or Saigon—has made the war go on.

Here is the essence of our peace plan; public disclosure may gain it the attention it deserves in Hanoi:

Within six months of an agreement—

1. We shall withdraw all U.S. and Allied forces from South Vietnam;

2. We shall exchange all prisoners of war;

3. There shall be a cease-fire throughout Indo-China;

4. There shall be a new presidential election in South Vietnam.

President Thieu will announce the elements of this election. These include international supervision and an independent body to organize and run the election, representing all political forces in South Vietnam including the National Liberation Front.

Furthermore, President Thieu has informed me that within the framework of the agreement outlined above he makes the following offer: He and Vice President [Tran Van] Huong would be ready to resign one month before the new election. The Chairman of the Senate, as caretaker head of the Government, would assume adminstrative responsibilities in South Vietnam, but the election would be the sole responsibility of the independent election body I have just described.

There are several other proposals in our new peace plan.

For example, as we offered privately on July 26 of last year, we remain prepared to undertake a major reconstruction program throughout Indo-China, including North Vietnam, to help all these people recover from the ravages of a generation of war.

We will pursue any approach that will speed negotiations.

We are ready to negotiate the plan I have outlined tonight and conclude a comprehensive agreement on all military and political issues. Because some parts of this agreement could prove more difficult to negotiate than others, we would be willing to begin implementing certain military aspects while negotiations continue on the implementation of other issues, just as we suggested in our private proposal in October.

Or, as we proposed last May, we remain willing to settle only the military issues and leave the political issues to the Vietnamese alone. Under this approach, we would withdraw all U.S. and Allied forces within six months in exchange for an Indo-China cease-fire and the release of all prisoners.

The choice is up to the enemy.

This is a settlement offer which is fair to North Vietnam and fair to South Vietnam. It deserves the light of public scrutiny by these nations and by other nations throughout the world. And it deserves the united support of the American people.

We made the substance of this generous offer privately over three months ago. It has not been rejected, but it has been ignored. I reiterate that peace offer tonight. It can no longer be ignored. The only thing this plan does not do is to join our enemy to overthrow our ally, which the United States of America will never do. If the enemy wants peace, it will have to recognize the important difference between settlement and surrender.

This has been a long and agonizing struggle. But it is difficult to see how anyone, regardless of his past position on the war, could now say that we have not gone the extra mile in offering a settlement that is fair—fair to everybody concerned. By the steadiness of our withdrawal of troops, America has proved its resolution to end our involvement in the war. By our readiness to act in the spirit of conciliation, America has proved its desire to be involved in the building of a permanent peace throughout Indo-China.

We are ready to negotiate peace immediately. If the enemy rejects our offer to negotiate, we shall continue our program of ending American involvement in the war by withdrawing our remaining forces as the South Vietnamese develop the capability to defend themselves. If the enemy's answer to our peace offer is to step up their military attacks, I shall fully meet my responsibility as Commander in Chief of our armed forces to protect our remaining troops. We do not prefer this course of action.

We want to end the war not only for America but for all the people of Indo-China. The plan I have proposed tonight can accomplish that goal.

Some of our citizens have become accustomed to thinking that whatever our Government says must be false and whatever our enemies say must be true, as far as this war is concerned. Well, the record I have revealed tonight proves the contrary. We can now demonstrate publicly what we have long been demonstrating privately: that America has taken the initiative not only to end our participation in this war but to end the war itself for all concerned.

This has been the longest, the most difficult war in American history. Honest and patriotic Americans have disagreed as to whether we should have become involved at all nine years ago, and there has been disagreement on the conduct of the war. The proposal I have made tonight is one on which we all can agree.

Let us unite now—unite in our search for peace, a peace that is fair to both sides, a peace that can last.

❧12❧

The Soviet Union

T HE IMPORTANCE of understanding Soviet policy is self-evident. As one of the two superpowers possessing a nuclear capability of making the world essentially uninhabitable, its actions are of great meaning. What are the mainsprings of Soviet actions, and what accounts for their behavior? What is the future likely to be, given current Soviet actions and objectives?

These questions are not answered in exactly similar terms by scholars, although the degree of academic unanimity about parts of Soviet behavior is certainly increasing. Even so, there are different explanations possible of the Soviet decision to build a navy (and merchant marine) equal to or superior to that of the United States. There are different explanations given of the new Soviet interventions in Middle Eastern and Far Eastern affairs. Some analysts see these policy decisions as initiating out of a strategically defensive posture: to escape the increasing pressures on Soviet land frontiers by "outflanking NATO." To others, they are outward signs of an expansionist if not aggressive intention. Arguments continue, too, over the role of Communist ideology in motivating and directing Soviet behavior. These arguments are amply reflected in the readings in this chapter.

The first selection, "Moscow's Foreign Policy," by Vernon V. Aspaturian, Professor of Political Science at Pennsylvania State University and a Soviet expert, gives a broad and balanced overview of Soviet policy over a fifty-year period. Aspaturian shows how the ideological perspective of communism, through which the early Soviet leaders judged the outside world, could not overcome and supplant the traditional Russian national interest. He describes how the dilemma was kept at subcritical level so long as the Soviet Union was the only Communist state, and how the creation of a Communist bloc intensified the problem. As Soviet power grew, and with it the opportunity to pursue ideological goals, so too did the realization of the potential costs to Russia. One important offshoot was the Sino-Soviet dispute.

In the second selection, "Russia's Problems Increase," Frederick H. Hartmann agrees with Aspaturian's overall assessment of the "impressive range of [Soviet] accomplishments" in the first fifty years, but argues that a comparison between the Soviet position in 1945 with that of 1964 (when the second article was written) shows a substantial increase in Soviet problems. The Hartmann article indicates one important reason why four years later the Soviets felt forced to occupy Czechoslovakia but thereafter began to explore détente in Western Europe even as Sino-Soviet frictions deepened with the phase-out of the Vietnam War. Consider how much Soviet relations with Germany in the early 1970s have been influenced by pressures from other directions. What is the price for détente in Europe from the Soviet viewpoint? How did the Vietnam War spare Russia hard decisions?

In the third selection, "Changes and Chances in American-Soviet Relations," Hans J. Morgenthau, whose name should be familiar from its frequent mention in these pages, analyzes the "five factors [which] have transformed" the relations between the superpowers.

Morgenthau points out that the improvement in superpower relations has been partly due to U.S. preoccupation with Vietnam. He warns that many issues exist between them, and neither an easy optimism nor a simple pessimism is appropriate. As he notes, the outcome no longer depends exclusively on the superpowers "but to an increasing extent upon the actions of secondary power centers— China, Japan, West Germany . . . either alone or in concert with a politically and militarily united Europe—and the reactions of the two superpowers to them."

After assessing these three selections the reader should be in no doubt that being a superpower is by no means synonymous with being freed from anxiety and danger, even without taking the other superpower into account. While the superpowers and their decisions remain, as before, critical, they, too, are in large part unable to control the solution of their problems through their own unilateral efforts— or even in a cooperation limited to the two of them.

29

MOSCOW'S FOREIGN POLICY

Vernon V. Aspaturian[*]

The balance-sheet of Soviet foreign policy over the past fifty years shows an impressive range of accomplishments when measured against a comparable period for any other power of similar magnitude. An outlaw state in 1917, governed by a pariah regime, beset on all sides by powerful enemies, racked internally by social convulsions, civil war, fragmentation, and foreign occupation, whose chances for survival were extremely poor, the Soviet Union stands today as a modernised global power, second only to the United States in power, prestige, and influence. This evolution was no orderly unilinear development, preordained by history, but rather the outcome of periodic collisions between utopian hopes generated by ideology and the limitations imposed by the interests and ambitions of other states. For while it is true that "the record of Soviet diplomacy shows an inability to distinguish between the real and the imaginary, a series of miscalculations about the capabilities and intentions of foreign countries, and a record of clumsy co-ordination between diplomacy and propaganda," it is also true that the many spectacular failures of Soviet foreign policy have been more than matched by its spectacular successes.[1]

The incalculable factor of luck has undoubtedly played a crucial role in the successes of both Soviet external and internal policy, beginning with the revolution itself, although Soviet leaders have not been loath to capitalise on the follies and misjudgments of other states. If luck was the principle ingredient which explains Lenin's success in seizing power and preserving it against an impressive array of internal and external enemies, whose failure to co-ordinate their actions was decisive for the survival of the Soviet regime, luck was even more emphatically the crucial factor which rescued Stalin's Russia from defeat and annihilation during the second world war. Stalin's misjudgment of the internal social and political forces and trends in Germany in the years before Hitler's assumption of power, his near catastrophic miscalculation of the balance of power between the Axis and the western powers in 1939, and his imprudent rejection of all evidence of an

---

[*] Vernon V. Aspaturian, "Moscow's Foreign Policy," *Survey*, No. 65 (October 1967), pp. 35–46. Reprinted by permission.
[1] Max Beloff, *Foreign Policy and the Democratic Process* (Baltimore, 1955), p. 98.

impending German attack, by all logic should have resulted in the destruction of the Soviet state; but fate intervened in the form of Churchill's decision to accept Russia as an ally and Japan's attack upon Pearl Harbour which brought the United States into the war.

It would be absurd, of course, to attribute all Soviet successes in foreign policy to sheer luck, just as it would be unfounded to ascribe them all to an innate shrewdness of Soviet leaders, who perceived every opportunity, exploited every advantage, and capitalised on every blunder with uncanny astuteness. Since success and failure in foreign policy are highly relative and often symbiotically interdependent, it is both captious and self-deceiving to pretend that Soviet "successes" are in reality little more than the "failures" of other states. Yet it would be difficult to quarrel with George Kennan's judgment that "the standard components for a rousing Soviet diplomatic success" are "one part Soviet resourcefulness and singlemindedness of purpose, two parts amateurism, complacency, and disunity on the part of the West," and that it was this which enabled the Soviet Union to advance from "the initial weakness of 1921 to the pinnacle of power and success it occupies in the wake of World War II."[2]

Throughout most of its history, Soviet foreign policy has operated within a self-defined framework of a two-camp or bi-polar world with two basic players, communism (the Soviet Union) and capitalism (everybody else), so that all losses in the capitalist world were automatic gains for the Soviet Union. While such an image of the world was a crude distortion of reality, it is true that the Soviet addiction to this grim view could not but redefine the international situation and superimpose upon international politics the synthetic impression of a zero-sum game whereby a loss for one player was automatically a gain for the other. For nearly two decades the Cold War was pursued within this framework as the bi-polarisation of power around Moscow and Washington increasingly assumed the objective character of a zero-sum game as defined by Moscow and increasingly by western statesmen as well in response. The disintegration of the European colonial empires, the advent of weapons of instantaneous and universal destruction, the progressive dissolution of the Soviet bloc, the erosion of the NATO alliance, and the eruption of the fratricidal Sino-Soviet conflict, however, have all but destroyed the bi-polarised international community in which gains and losses could be registered with zero-sum gamelike simplicity.

While Soviet foreign policy achievements are impressive, this does not mean that the Soviet Union today has fulfilled the expectations of its founders and leaders, past and present. Actually, its present status and position in the world community represents a blend of objective success and subjective failure, i.e. it has been a resounding success when its achievements are measured against the traditional yardstick of power politics, but a

---

[2] George Kennan, *Russia and the West Under Lenin and Stalin* (Boston, 1961), p. 223.

conspicuous failure when measured against its initial ideological inspiration and purpose. Instead of transforming the world, it is the Soviet Union which has been transformed. From a self-anointed centre of world revolution dedicated to the destruction of the existing social and political status quo, it has been objectively transformed into a mature global power whose interest in stabilising the status quo now virtually matches its dedication to revolution. From an embryonic world communist state the Soviet Union has been objectively metamorphosed into an arrested Russianised multinational community, burdened by supplicants and blessed by clients and allies as well as harassed and tormented by enemies and rivals in both the sub-community which it inspired and created as well as in the world which it sought originally to subvert. From a self-perceived instrument of history ordained to save mankind from the evils and injustices of capitalism and mandated to construct a new world communist society of universal justice, liberated from class, national, and racial conflict, the Soviet Union is now content to offer itself as a model for rapid modernisation and industrialisation of under-developed societies, with its eschatological and apocalyptic rhetoric largely muted. And finally, its ideology has been transformed from a vehicle legitimising world revolution into one legitimising communist rule in Russia; instead of raising the standard of revolution abroad, Moscow emphasises raising the standard of living at home in the name of ideology; instead of justifying further social changes in the Soviet system, it rationalises the social status quo; instead of inspiring the masses to charge the barricades, Soviet ideology now erects barricades against the heresies of Peking.

If we employ the traditional criteria of success in foreign policy (power, influence, and prestige), it is indisputable that the Soviet Union has been more successful than any other state in the past fifty years, save the United States. The most significant factor in the simultaneous rise of Soviet power and decline in the power of other states was the second world war. Germany was dismembered and occupied; Japan was squeezed back into her main islands and disarmed; Italy was shorn of her colonial empire, while a weakened France, Great Britain, and Netherlands progressively relinquished theirs. During the same period, the Soviet Union annexed 250,000 square miles of territory in Europe and Asia, established vassal and subservient states in east Asia and eastern Europe, displacing Japan and Germany respectively as the dominant powers in those two regions. It supported a successful communist take-over in China, sponsored the growth and proliferation of communist parties abroad, which it manipulated as instruments of its foreign policy, and continued to maintain the largest military establishment in the world poised to move into new vacuums which might be created by the convulsions and agonies of colonial empires in dissolution and by the internal turmoil and political uncertainties which swept western Europe in the post-war period.

Although the Soviet Union has certainly failed in its original ideological mission of communising the world, its half-century attempt has left a lasting imprint upon the physiognomy of the globe and has fundamentally re-structured the social, political, economic, and ideological configurations of one-third of the world and reoriented the direction in which the rest is mov-ing. As a consequence of its endeavours, an international sub-system of four-teen communist states, comprising nearly one-third of the world's population and territory, has been established. These fourteen states not only share a common ideology, of which individual variants have emerged, but a com-mon socio-economic system with a distinctive set of property relationships, giving rise to a shared social structure, governed and regulated by highly similar political institutions and processes.

Furthermore, communist parties, large and small, powerful and insig-nificant, are to be found in some seventy additional countries on five con-tinents, ranging from miniscule and furtive illegal conspiratorial groups to large mass parties, such as those in France, Italy, and India. All these parties are inspired by variants of a common ideology, Marxism-Leninism, and are thus derivative emanations from the Bolshevik revolution of 1917.

The failure of the Soviet Union to achieve its ideological goal of universal communism is largely attributable to American power, which grew even more rapidly and spectacularly than Soviet power. Unlike the Soviet Union, however, the United States was a status quo power. Ironically, its strength was largely sustained and accelerated by the remarkable expansion of Soviet power and the threat it posed to the world at large. Unlike the growth of Soviet power, which was largely relative, due in large measure to the destruction of the great powers on her periphery, the growth in American power was largely incremental and absolute, although it experienced a relative enhancement of its power as well resulting from the corresponding shrinkage in the number of great powers after the war. While the Soviet Union avidly fell heir to the power spheres left vacant by the collapse of Japan and Germany because of its advantageous geographical position, the United States, reluctantly, erratically, and often inadvertently, progressively assumed the burdens carried by the declining and retreating western European powers. What the United States lacked in geographical advantage it more than made up for by its control of the seas, its inexhaustible eco-nomic resources, and its atomic monopoly. From the Soviet perspective, the only obstacle in the way of communist universalism was the American "rul-ing class" armed with nuclear weapons, and Soviet post-war foreign policy for over a decade was largely designed to nullify, immobilise, neutralise, skirt, surround, or even destroy this impediment, which ultimately proved impassable and insurmountable.

The failure of Soviet foreign policy to find its way around American power signalled the success of the containment policy which had been in-augurated in 1947. It is a silent but eloquent tribute to this policy that when the great colonial empires dissolved, not a single former colonial dependency was sucked into the communist orbit (save North Vietnam), although the Soviet Union had devoted considerable thought, energy, effort, and expense to capitalise upon an event which Soviet leaders had been predicting and expecting for decades.

Both Lenin and Stalin had formulated elaborate theories of colonialism, imperialism, and "bourgeois-nationalist" revolutions; they framed imaginative strategies of multi-staged revolutionary upheavals and multi-phased transition processes designed to adapt the exotic political ferments and forces in the colonies and semi-colonies to the general Marxist historical perspective. If ever a political leadership was psychologically poised and intellectually prepared to take advantage of one of history's most extensive and profound shifts in the global balance of power, it was the Soviet leadership, which had repeatedly predicted and eagerly awaited the revolutionary disintegration of the colonial empires, from which they expected a flood of recruits to the world of communism.

But the colonial empires dissolved in more or less orderly fashion into more than sixty new states, which then were shielded by the power of the United States from being sucked into the Soviet orbit. The American shield, however, not only protected the new states from being absorbed by the communist world but it also had the unfortunate effect in many cases of protecting unsavoury and oppressive native systems and regimes from their own disaffected populations, and this was bound to drive a wedge between the United States and many non-communist revolutionary movements and regimes in the new states. Thus, while the containment policy succeeded in arresting the expansion of Soviet and/or communist power, it also had the distressing tendency to contain and limit the range of non-communist options open to many of the new states in order to organise their social and political life.

Deprived first of its self-asserted character as an embryonic communist world state and then effectively denied its role as the centre of a world revolutionary movement articulating the interests of mankind, the Soviet Union was forced by objective circumstances to revert more and more to its irreducible role as a traditional great power, responding and reacting to its own national interests. And the more it reverted to its character as a great state, the more the other communist countries were likely to act as autonomous states rather than as parts of an organic movement.

The recrudescence of the nation-state as the state form of the communists has thus effectively demolished the pretensions of the Soviet Union as an embryonic universal state and has in effect forced its transformation into a modern version of the Russian Empire, purporting to represent the national interests not only of Russia but of all the major nations of the USSR.

These profound transmutations and revisions in the communist world have shattered the Marxist-Leninist expectation that a common ideology and a common social system would first surmount and then eradicate conflicts of national interests among communist states. After the reams of ideological nonsense written about the character of the new socialist international system, founded on the basis of mutual trust, harmony of interests, and the absence of conflict, it must come as a profound shock to Soviet ideologists to be now charged with the thankless task of justifying the dissolution of the communist bloc and explaining the Sino-Soviet dispute. Thus one Soviet writer, obviously dismayed by the gross inadequacy of Marxist-Leninist propositions, ruefully concedes that relations among socialist states, in spite of a common ideology and similar socio-economic systems, are still determined by factors traditionally associated with national distinctions:

The formation of the world socialist system—a commonwealth of sovereign socialist states with equal rights—gave rise to a number of great theoretical and political problems which communists had never encountered before. . . . When the international relations among national detachments of the working class turned into relations between states, a new situation arose that required creative application of the general principles of Marxism-Leninism, the development of a number of propositions of the theory and actualisation of political decisions. How are the national and state interests of each socialist country to be brought in line with the interests of the entire system? How are the diverse interests of separate socialist states to be harmonised? How is the turbulent flow of national consciousness and national pride, caused by the success of socialist construction and the acquisition of genuine national independence, to be directed along the course of socialist internationalism?

He then concedes the essential naïveté of the orthodox Marxist-Leninist proposition that a common social system would be sufficient to eradicate conflicts of national interests:

In our time such a formulation of the question seems natural and even trite. But to arrive at it required more than a year of intense searching that was frequently accompanied by practical errors and theoretical confusion. Let us recall the state of theory before the opening of the sixties. A formula of approximately this sort was set forth: All socialist states are of the same socio-economic nature, they have the same types of political power, and the same ideology prevails in them; consequently, there should not and cannot be any disagreements or contradictions in the relations among the countries of socialism. The very fact of the establishment of socialist production relations in a number of countries was considered to be an adequate guarantee of good relations among them, a guarantee that national and international interests would somehow automatically be harmonised.

Ideology, he points out, foundered on the traditional shoals of national interests, whose diversity and contradictory character have their source in the national peculiarities of history, culture, geography, and socio-economic development, whose significance had been seriously underrated. Optimistically, but without much conviction, the writer maintains that concerted policy should be able to overcome the baneful effects of national interests:

Life has proved to be more complicated and contradictory than this formula. The actual practice of contact among the countries of socialism has shown that this homogeneity of socio-economic, political, and ideological structures is a

necessary but insufficient prerequisite for the real establishment of the principles
of fraternity and cooperation, complete trust and mutual understanding in the
relations among socialist states. Historical experience bears witness to the fact
that a complex intertwining of objective and subjective factors connected with
the considerable disparity in the levels of socio-economic development of the individual countries of socialism, with differences of an historical-cultural and geographical nature, and with varying degrees of cognisance by the various parties
of the laws of development of socialism, can lead in practice to deviations from
the internationalist principles which are supposed to regulate relations in the
socialist commonwealth. And an abstract reliance on the fact of a single type of
ownership or state power is of no help here. Only the conscious, purposeful policy
of the ruling communist parties is able to neutralise the influence of factors that
lead to collisions and contradictions. Such a policy presupposes a determined
fight against attempts to present what is desired for what is real and to put actual
problems of the socialist system in a simplified, bureaucratically optimistic form.
Such a policy is based on the fact that each socialist state may have its own
national interests, connected with peculiarities of its history, geographical location,
economic development, etc. This is a fact that, when understood, is of direct
significance for correct—both theoretically and politically correct—application of
the basic principles of relations among socialist states.[3]

The failure of the Soviet Union as a universal state should not, however,
obscure its achievements as a traditional great power. In many respects, the
current position of the Soviet Union exceeds the fondest aspirations of its
Tsarist predecessor. Russia's historical irredenta have been largely rein-
corporated into the Soviet Union, and the new Soviet empire has been
consolidated into an integrated and stable modern society, with a broad
base of social and multinational support; the country is substantially self-
sufficient militarily and economically; it presides over a retinue of client
and allied states in eastern Europe; a dismembered Germany lies impotent
in the west, a disarmed Japan has been shoved back into its indigenous
islands in the east, and a belt of weak buffer states carved out of colonial
empires lies to the south. Only the revival of an expansionist China threatens
the Soviet Union as a state and as the abortive leader of a residual revolutionary movement.

When Lenin established Soviet power in the former Russian Empire, he
thought not only that he could sever irrevocably the umbilical cord with
Russia's past but that he could also rid the new state of traditional Russian
goals and purposes in foreign policy. Neither geography, nor history, nor
national interests would govern the behaviour of the Soviet state in its relations with the outside world; rather its outlook and conduct would be
uniquely and exclusively determined by its self-anointed ideological mission
of world revolution as inspired by the doctrines of Marx and Engels. There
is little doubt that at first Lenin was genuinely convinced that this was
possible and that the new Soviet state could unilaterally unburden itself not

---

[3] A. Bovin, "The International Principles of Socialism," *Izvestiya*, September 21, 1966.

only of Tsarist purposes and goals in foreign policy but also of Russia's heritage and culture, could overcome the deterministic influences of its geography, surmount the complex aggregate behaviour patterns of its population (national character), relieve itself of the manifold liabilities and dispel the enmities acquired by its Tsarist predecessor in the the pursuit of its aims, and of whatever designs, claims, grievances, and demands Russia's enemies might have against her. All this, however, was more easily asserted than accomplished, for while Lenin could plausibly abjure the goals and purposes of Russia's traditional foreign policy and could selectively retain the fruits of four centuries of Russian expansionism wherever possible, he could not entirely disown the objective consequences of Tsarist diplomacy nor dictate the attitude of other states towards the new regime. Even if the Soviet state refused to remain Russia, Japan remained Japan, Poland remained Poland, Germany remained Germany, the Straits remained the Straits, and Russians remained Russians.

Thus, partly by choice, partly of necessity, and partly against its will, the Soviet state could not but assume many of the contours of its predecessor in foreign policy. This fact served not only to complicate Soviet foreign policy for many decades but also to plunge into seemingly insoluble and futile controversy all discussion and analysis concerning its motivations and nature. Was the Soviet Union motivated by traditional Russian national interests and manipulating revolutionary ideology as an instrument of its national purposes, or was Russia merely the national vehicle for a messianic universalism?

While there is no intention here to rehash the innumerable variations on this theme, ranging from the pathetically simplistic to the inordinately sophisticated, with virtually all possibilities in between, some comment is indispensable. After fifty years, the role of ideology in Soviet foreign policy, as both a source of ends and an instrument of other purposes, emerges more clearly and can now perhaps finally be placed in definitive perspective. Historically, ideology appears as a protean force and influence on Soviet foreign policy behaviour, shaping its eschatological goals operatively rather than operationally, and also as a cognitive and epistemological philosophy, embracing a theory of socio-historical reality, a theory of human nature and behaviour, and a theory of international and interstate behaviour. Instrumentally, ideology has also functioned as a theory or strategy of action, i.e. as a framework for the analysis, mobilisation, and manipulation of social and political power in a variety of conditions and circumstances. It has enabled Soviet leaders to recognise that interstate and intrastate social conflicts, tensions, frustrations, and resentments are potential reservoirs of energy which can be tapped, mobilised, and transmuted into concrete political power subject to the manipulation of Soviet policy. In calculating what the Soviet leaders call the international correlation of forces, internal social forces and the direction of their movement have always assumed an important value in the balance-of-power equation. Furthermore, ideology serves to justify and rationalise Soviet behaviour and the social status quo in the Soviet Union; it serves as the foundation of legitimacy upon which Soviet rule reposes and provides ethical sanction for the extension or intensification of Soviet power.

The relative influence of ideology as a motivating factor in Soviet foreign policy has been indissolubly linked with the utility of the world communist movement as an instrument of Soviet foreign policy. Hypothetically, the Soviet state was merely the creator and advance guard of a wider entity, the international proletariat, but not its directing centre. This was the theory. It simply represented the Russian national section of the international proletariat which had seized power in its own country. Consequently its policies and behaviour were supposed to reflect the interests of the world revolution and the international proletariat, which would be determined by the Comintern and its Executive Committee. Instead of being the master of the Comintern, the Soviet state was supposed to be its instrument. But since the Soviet state was the only communist state in existence and the headquarters of the Comintern could be located only in Moscow, it was inevitable that, as prospects for additional revolutions faded away, the position of the Soviet party would be correspondingly enhanced and its role transformed.

The Soviet state soon assumed an identity and existence of its own, separate yet related to that of the Comintern. As a state, the conditions for survival were sharply different from those of a movement whose existence, independent of state organisation, was still possible. Consequently, the Soviet Union gradually assumed the contours of a traditional state operating within a system of states, yet in conflict with it. It assumed a configuration of interests not entirely congruent with those of the revolutionary movement, since the impulse and requirements for survival as a state frequently collided with its obligations as an instrument of the Comintern and the world revolutionary movement.

The entire history of the Soviet relationships, first with foreign communist parties, then with communist states, and then with rivals for leadership, has been determined by the two essentially contradictory purposes of either serving the interests of foreign constituencies (world revolution, foreign communist states, China), or responding to the interests of internal constituencies (survival as a state, national interests, Soviet elites). The first purpose necessarily implies self-abnegation since it demands that the interests of the Soviet Union's internal constituencies be subordinated to the interests of external constituencies, while the second is subversive of internationalism, since it gives higher priority to internal needs than to external obligations.

Tension between these two conflicting sets of demands was inevitable and not capable of easy resolution. One purpose was bound to subordinate the other. Either the Soviet state was to become an expendable instrument of the international proletariat, or the Comintern would be reduced to a creature supinely responsive to the demands of the Soviet state. This contradiction was resolved by adjusting the interests and behaviour of the Comintern and foreign communist parties to those of the Soviet state. Comintern interests were thus reshaped and subordinated to Soviet state interests in order to ensure full coordination of action and congruence of interests. This, of course, ran counter to the theory of their relationship, since the interests and behaviour of the Soviet state were supposed to be adjusted to meet the demands and requirements of the Comintern. The orthodox rendition of the Stalinist formula ran as follows:

The USSR has no interests at variance with the interests of world revolution, and the international proletariat naturally has no interests that are at variance with the Soviet Union.[4]

The basic philosophy justifying this submission to Moscow's control was defined by Stalin as "proletarian internationalism":

A revolutionary is he who, without evasions, unconditionally, openly, and honestly . . . is ready to uphold and defend the USSR. . . . An internationalist is he who unconditionally, without hesitation and without provisos, is ready to defend the USSR because the USSR is the base of the revolutionary movement, and to defend the advance of this movement is impossible without defending the USSR.[5]

With the installation of communist regimes in the countries of eastern Europe, the Soviet Union was automatically deprived of its unique position as the only communist state, whose ruling proletariat pre-empted the articulation of the class interests of the entire world proletariat languishing in oppression and exploitation in capitalist countries. As long as the Soviet Union was the only communist state, it could be argued that good communists everywhere should display first loyalty to the only fatherland of the proletariat. Loyalty, however, was not founded on the inherent moral superiority or priority of interests of the Soviet proletariat over all others; the international proletariat gave its loyalty to the Soviet Union on the premise that the Soviet Union was the only authentic representative of the class interests of proletarians in all countries. That it was the Russian proletariat which ruled the first communist state was historically fortuitous and legitimised neither its moral nor its political superiority.

Stalin, however, extrapolated his meaning of "proletarian internationalism" from the period of "capitalist encirclement" into the period of multiple communist party-states, each with its own ruling proletariat. Proletarian internationalism became, in effect, a device for converting

---

[4] W. K. Knorin, *Fascism, Social Democracy and the Communists* (Moscow, 1933).
[5] J. V. Stalin, *Sochineniya* (Moscow, 1949), X, p. 61.

party subservience into state vassalage. Entire countries were subjugated and their interests subordinated to that of the Soviet state. Some satellite leaders, however, demurred and interpreted the Stalinist theory of proletarian internationalism as applicable only to parties in capitalist countries; otherwise it was a philosophical justification for Soviet imperialism and colonialism. The divergence of interests between the Soviet Union and foreign communist parties, particularly those in power, was exemplified by the break with Yugoslavia in 1948, and the potential character of the conflict was discernible when Stalin directed the execution or removal of satellite leaders who betrayed even a faint tendency towards national autonomy—all in the name of proletarian internationalism.

While Stalin's death set the stage for the disintegration of the world communist movement into its constituent state and national parties, ironically enough the underlying cause of the divorce between Soviet interests and those of other communist parties was the rapid growth of Soviet power and capabilities. Hypothetically, this should have brought Soviet ideological goals into closer alignment with policy; but as Soviet power grew, so did the risks and costs of implementing an ideological foreign policy. And as these increased, the general tendency was for Soviet ideological goals to crumble into ritualistic rhetoric, while the growth in Soviet power created greater opportunities and more options for the achievement of traditional great-power goals in foreign policy. Thus as Soviet power has increased to the point where ideological purpose could have been converted into state policy, there has been a corresponding tendency for the costs and risks of converting ideology into policy to escalate as well. As Peking has been quick to point out, the expansion of Soviet capabilities has served to debase some cherished ideological goals into little more than propaganda rhetoric.

In the fourteen years since Stalin's death, the Soviet Union has been forced to adjust itself to changing configurations of interests and power at home, in the communist interstate community, in the world communist movement, and in the international community at large, which has resulted in a fundamental shift of priorities in Soviet foreign policy.

While Stalin subordinated the interests of foreign communist states and parties to the security and foreign policy interests of the Soviet state, he rarely viewed the material prosperity of the Soviet population as a significant factor in coordinating Soviet interests with those of the communist movement. Stalin catered to internal constituencies only to the degree necessary to maximise the effectiveness and power of the state at his command. Once the communist monolith started to disintegrate into its component parts, and external constituencies could articulate their demands upon the Soviet Union to discharge its international ideological obligations in accordance with the theory that the Soviet Union was a servant of the movement and not its master, Stalin's successors, under pressure from their own internal constituencies, altered both the priorities and the theory underlying them, so that in both theory and practice the interests of Soviet social constituencies now assume priority over those of external constituencies.

Not only does the Sino-Soviet dialogue on this point demonstrate how international ideological commitments can be subordinated to internal economic requirements by a developed and an underdeveloped communist state sharing a common ideological commitment; it also illustrates how each perceives its ideological obligations in such a way that their implementation automatically serves the internal interests of the state concerned. Thus, while Moscow asserts that rising Soviet standards of living help to promote world communism, Peking contests this view and argues that the world revolution can best be furthered if the developed communist states postpone their affluence in favour of bolstering up the economies of their deprived communist allies. In either case, it reduces itself to the crude formula "What's good for the Soviet Union (or China) is good for the world revolution." While in the past this formula was applied by Stalin almost entirely in terms of the foreign policy and security needs of the Soviet state as the bastion of the world communist movement, it is only since his death that this formula has been applied to purely domestic economic considerations. To be sure, Moscow insists that raising the standard of living in the Soviet Union strengthens the most powerful state and hence alters the global balance of power in favour of world revolution, psychologically if not militarily; but this proposition is both dubious and transparently self-serving. It also serves to support the Chinese charge that in the face of possible thermonuclear war, the Soviet leaders have lost their revolutionary militancy and may be willing to settle for a status quo which will allow them to divert resources and energies from a counter-productive and dysfunctional policy of revolutionary aggressiveness to improving the standard of living at home and expanding and consolidating the social legitimacy of their power and authority as a great power.

Soviet foreign policy over the past fifty years has thus passed through a succession of distinct phases, each with its characteristic patterns of behaviour . . . .

If it was Stalin who transformed the Soviet Union into a great power, it was under Khrushchev that Soviet Russia was transformed into a global power, directly challenging the United States for paramountcy and unilaterally claiming the right to intervene in any part of the world to assert an interest and influence developments. Stalin pursued essentially a cautious continental policy, oriented towards the communisation, first of the Soviet periphery and then of the new geographical periphery of the expanded communist bloc, relying on direct physical contiguity and the concentrically radiating expansion of communism from the Soviet base. The experience of the Hungarian Soviet Republic and other geographically isolated attempts to establish communist regimes after the 1914–18 war convinced Stalin that the capitalist world would never tolerate an isolated communist state in its midst; it would be crushed through internal subversion or direct assault.

Stalin was loath to overcommit the Soviet Union militarily, politically, or ideologically, and was reluctant to burden himself with obligations which he could not or preferred not to fulfil. This may explain his refusal to assume a legal obligation to defend Albania, which after 1948 was separated from the rest of the communist bloc by Yugoslavia's defection and hence was exposed to attack or subversion. Only with the creation of the Warsaw Pact in 1955 did Albania come under formal Soviet military and political protection. Similarly, Stalin abjured any legal commitments to North Korea and North Vietnam, both of which were parts of divided states and hence susceptible to involvement. It was apparently Stalin's design that as the communist periphery was gradually expanded outward from the centre, all communist states would be territorially adjacent to at least one other communist state. In the meantime, communist parties in non-contiguous countries would be supported and encouraged until the movement of the communist periphery to their borders created the possibility of their transformation into communist states.

Khrushchev, on the other hand, broke out of the shell in which Soviet diplomacy had been encapsulated and embarked upon a bold global strategy of reaching out over oceans and continents in search not only of possible recruits to the communist bloc but of diplomatic client states as well in any part of the world. Whereas Stalin divided the world into two hostile camps and worked largely through local communist parties, Khrushchev carved a generous 'zone of peace' out of the capitalist camp as the immediate object of Soviet diplomacy. Consisting largely of underdeveloped, newly emancipated countries, strongly influenced by the Leninist theory of imperialism and predisposed to socialism of various national hues, the countries in the "zone of peace" were perceived by Khrushchev as intrinsically anti-imperialist, anti-capitalist, and hence anti-western, rather than as bogus appendages of the capitalist camp.

Khrushchev's global strategy, pursued in the wake of Soviet space spectaculars which he tried to transform into military power, was designed to breach the non-communist world at its vulnerable points all along the "zone of peace"—in the Middle East, Southeast Asia, Africa, and even Latin America. In the process, Soviet foreign policy was largely, but not entirely, de-ideologised, since the maximisation of possible diplomatic gains in the non-communist world dictated a minimisation and dilution of the ideological content of Soviet foreign policy. Ultimately this was self-defeating, although advantageous momentarily, since it entailed the abandonment of certain foreign policy strategies associated with Moscow for decades. It meant, in some instances, sacrificing the future of local communist parties in return for diplomatic gains in the third world; it also meant the diversion of scarce resources from internal development and allied communist countries to seduce the newly independent countries of Asia and Africa with economic bribes; it meant the assumption of new risks, costs, and burdens in areas far removed from the centres of communist power and vulnerable to American sea and air power. For a time Khrushchev capitalised on the alleged "missile gap" to unfurl a protective nuclear-missile umbrella over the three continents of Asia, Africa, and Latin America, in the mistaken conviction that the United States could be deterred or dissuaded from resisting Soviet policy or local shifts of power promoted or encouraged by the Soviet Union.

While Khrushchev transformed the Soviet Union into a global power, he did it at the expense of weakening Soviet control in its own sphere, alienating Moscow's strongest ally, China, overcommitting the power and resources of the Soviet Union, and increasing the danger of thermonuclear war by his persistent prodding and probing of weak spots in the western world and forcing the United States into a series of confrontations, in the hope that this would result in the settlement of outstanding issues on Soviet terms and force the United States to withdraw from exposed positions. The Suez crisis of 1956, the Middle East crisis of 1958, the spasmodic Berlin crisis of 1958–61, and finally the Cuban missile crisis of 1962 were either manifestations or consequences of Soviet risk-taking in foreign policy in pursuit of substantial diplomatic gains.

It was also Khrushchev's fate to preside over the breakdown of the Sino-Soviet alliance, the disintegration of the Soviet bloc, and the dissolution of the world communist movement into captious states and fractious parties, unable to reconstruct a new consensus.

By denouncing Stalin, Khrushchev simultaneously, but unwittingly, shattered the foundations of Soviet ideological hegemony—the myths of Soviet moral superiority and doctrinal infallibility on which rested the Soviet claim to priority on the political loyalty of all communists and communist parties, and on the resources of communist states. By demolishing the "cult of Stalin", Khrushchev inadvertently unleashed tremendous convulsive reactions in eastern Europe and provoked the wrath of the Chinese leadership; the virtual dissolution of the Soviet bloc and the Sino-Soviet conflict followed within a few years.

While the condemnation of the Stalin cult resulted in profound changes in Soviet relations with the communist states and parties, it was Khrushchev's repudiation of certain specific doctrinal formulations associated with Stalin (and Lenin in some instances) which was to have profound consequences for Soviet foreign policy. By renouncing the Leninist-Stalinist thesis of the "fatal inevitability of wars", Khrushchev jettisoned the suicidal implications of a formula whose grotesque self-fulfilling properties inspired terror in friend and foe alike, since the inevitability of war between East and West in the thermonuclear age promised not the inevitable victory of world communism but the inevitability of co-extinction. By dismantling the Stalinist two-camp image and interposing a broad "zone of peace" between the capitalist and communist worlds, Khrushchev not only introduced a convenient buffer between two contending giants but also freed Soviet diplomacy from the dogmatic restraints of the Stalinist dictum that all non-communist states were by definition part of the capitalist camp and hence to be treated as enemies rather than potential friends or allies. By renouncing the doctrine of "capitalist encirclement", Khrushchev not only demolished the main ideological prop justifying the preservation of the apparatus of terror at home but also dispelled the psychological atmosphere of a Soviet state besieged on all sides by powerful enemies intent upon its annihilation. The renunciation of this doctrine enabled the Soviet Union to adopt a normal diplomatic posture although it served simultaneously to dilute its ideological content. Khrushchev thus sought to free the Soviet Union from its psychological self-encirclement so that it might, in turn, forge an encirclement of the remaining bastions of world capitalism, whose territorial and demographic dimensions had been substantially diminished by the loss of the "zone of peace".

Khrushchev's repudiation of another Stalinist concept, the doctrine of the progressive "intensification of the class struggle" as the final victory of communism drew nearer, also had important implications for Soviet foreign policy. Extrapolated onto the world scene, this doctrine dictated the progressive aggravation of relations between the two camps and the exacerbation of international tensions generally. Its renunciation enabled Khrushchev to de-dogmatise Soviet diplomacy, redefine "peaceful coexistence", and elevate it to doctrinal significance as something approximating a policy norm of Soviet foreign policy rather than an objective description of an unwanted equilibrium. The substantive meaning of peaceful coexistence, however, remains indeterminate and this absence of precision probably reflects disagreement among the Soviet leaders as to its precise contemporary ideological significance. What is clear is that the Stalinist concept of peaceful coexistence has been disavowed, and while it may not accord in all particulars to the Chinese charge that the new Soviet concept is indistinguishable from a rationalised acceptance of the international status quo, in some respects Soviet behaviour corresponds to the Chinese accusations.

Khrushchev's global strategies were marked by serious contradictions, ambivalent goals, blatant opportunism, inept execution, and frequent adventurist excursions bordering on the irrational. For over a decade he alternated threats and blandishments, militancy and diffidence, responsible behaviour and irresponsibility, decorum and outrageous personal conduct. This ambivalence, while apparent in Khrushchev's personal idio-syncrasies, actually reflected the increasing difficulty of choosing between the Soviet Union's role as a responsible global power, dictated by the objective conditions of its industrial and technological maturation, and its role as an agency of messianic revolution.

Increasingly, Soviet ideological responsibilities to its communist allies and the world communist movement come into conflict with its respon-sibilities and interests as the second most powerful state in the inter-national community. As a global power with proclaimed rights and responsibilities all over the world based upon its objective capabilities rather than upon the moral force of its ideology, to behave as the centre of a messianic movement would automatically limit the influence of the Soviet Union in areas where Soviet ideology is unwelcome. It should be noted, however, that at many points the role of the Soviet Union in the world communist system merges harmoniously with its self-assumed role in the general international system, particularly in its support of revolu-tionary movements and regimes in underdeveloped areas; occasionally they also collide, as the relations between the Soviet Union and radical nationalist regimes in Egypt, Indonesia, Guinea, Algeria, and elsewhere have demonstrated.

This dual role calls for both conflict and cooperation with the United States; conflict as the residuary leader of the communist movement ostensibly still seeking to universalise itself, and cooperation as a partner-rival in the general international scene, where it seeks to relax international tensions. This cooperation not only gives greater physical security but also enables greater attention to be given to domestic needs. On the other hand, it involves the possible sacrifice of the interests of some of its allies (China, Cuba, North Vietnam), and the postponement or abandonment of some of its diplomatic and ideological objectives in foreign policy.

To minimise these conflicts, Soviet leaders have devised surrogates for the obligations to the world communist movement which they have deferred or renounced. They are providing greater material assistance to communist countries, are allowing, tolerating, or acquiescing in the assertion of greater autonomy in external and internal affairs on the parts of their east European allies, and in the underdeveloped countries they are supporting a variety of revolutionary-nationalist regimes and movements, frequently to the detriment of local communist parties, who are left to their own devices. This has created a gap, that the Chinese are trying to exploit, between the Soviet-supported nationalist regimes and the more radical guerrilla communists in many underdeveloped coun-tries. As a global power the Soviet Union seeks client states of all political hues; as the residuary centre of a revolutionary movement, it welcomes ideological adherents. In an effort to merge these two objectives, Moscow hopes to attract the radical nationalist regimes into the Soviet diplomatic orbit and then guide their "ethnic" brands of socialism in a Soviet direction through the conversion from above of radical nationalist regimes into communist regimes.

The emergence of the Soviet Union as a thermonuclear-missile power with global interests and responsibilities transcending ideological allegiances and rivalries, the resurgence of national autonomy in the communist system, the appearance of China as a national threat to Russia and ideological rival to the Soviet Union, and the fear of thermonuclear annihilation have combined to give the Soviet Union a greater interest in maintaining the status quo than in attempting to alter it in its favour by pursuing high-risk policies, whether ideologically inspired or not. There is a certain pathos and more than a grain of truth in the Chinese charge that the fear of thermonuclear annihilation, given the ingrained Bolshevik instinct for survival first implanted by Lenin at Brest-Litovsk in 1918, has become the principal animating force of the Soviet leadership:

> The Soviet leaders seek only to preserve themselves and would let other people sink or swim. They have repeatedly said that so long as they themselves survive and develop, the people of the world will be saved. The fact is they are selling out the fundamental interests of the people of the world in order to seek their own momentary ease.[6]

The avoidance of thermonuclear war, which was established by Khrushchev as the highest priority item in Soviet foreign policy, thus continues to have top priority under his successors, and this almost automatically impels the Soviet Union to minimise its confrontations with the United States. The recent Middle East crisis was a striking illustration of this.

---

[6] Chinese statement of 15 August 1963, *Peking Review*, 16 August 1963.

30

RUSSIA'S PROBLEMS INCREASE

FREDRICK H. HARTMANN[*]

The foreign policy problems of the Soviet Union have lately been increasing rather steeply. Concurrently the means at hand for Russia to resolve those problems have largely ceased to increase—or have even declined. Some of the reasons for this adverse change are highly similar to, or

---

[*] Frederick H. Hartmann, "Russia's Problems Increase," *International Review of History and Political Science* (Meerut, India), Vol. 1, No. 1 (June 1964), pp. 53–62. Reprinted with the permission of the Managing Editor, International Review of History and Political Science.

identical to, factors which have made the conduct of United States foreign policy also more difficult. But the Soviet Union is faced with a problem of greater dimensions than the Western superpower because of special factors applying to it but not to the United States. Let us first look at the factors affecting both in a rather similar fashion, and then at the special factors compounding the Soviet Union's problems.

I

Both superpowers find it much more difficult today to have their views accepted. The day of the "bipolar world" is essentially gone and there is little argument any more that this is so. Indeed, the "two-power world" in the popular and over-simplified sense was in process of disappearing not too long after its existence was generally recognized.[1] As is so often the case, popular slogan lags behind actual situation. This is not to say that the United States and the Soviet Union are not the leading military powers in the world. They are. It is to say that the effect of their military power has been altered by other developments, and that military power is of limited use to them for the solution of many of their most difficult problems. Moreover, their "fixed" position in the balance of power as anchor points of rival coalitions, reduces their maneuvering ability and their total impact upon a world which in great part and important respects refuses to see their antagonism as of prime relevance.

It might be objected by a tough-minded "realist" that H-bombs in existence cast large shadows even on those who may ignore them. They do if there is real prospect for their use. But H-bombs can have no direct and useful effects other than to deter enemies—and only then if the threat is believed. One cannot very well use the H-bomb to force a friendly nation to stay friendly, or as a device to convince an unaligned nation of the value of being allies. A union or concert or alliance based on fear has no real value. Indeed, the superpowers are even at a disadvantage in using more conventional weapons for the furtherance of foreign policy objectives, since they may upset the delicate relationships now prevailing. Since the superpower confrontation is worldwide, so too is it true that each is limited in the exercise of its power almost everywhere. An obvious proof of this principle is the continued existence on the one hand of Castro's Cuba as a thorn in the American flesh, and on the other hand of West Berlin as an independent and free area within the Soviet orbit.

Another facet of the decline in bipolarity is the independence and power of third states. A corollary of the success of the Marshall Plan and United States encouragement of Western European cooperation and economic coordination is the ability of Great Britain to differ with one aspect of

---

[1] The author first called attention to this development in 1957 in the first edition of *The Relations of Nations.*

American policy while Gaullist France differs with still another. Powers whose economic well-being and political stability enable them to argue their own view of their own interests are not easily "managed"—and certainly do not even consider "obeying" the United States out of fear of the bomb!

The same kinds of problems affect the Soviet Union although not necessarily in the same degree. Even a completely evacuated Poland and Balkans could not afford the fully independent attitude toward Russia currently exhibited by England and France toward the United States. They are not that stable and viable. Nevertheless the Soviet Union can hardly afford to exercise control by stark and outright military power in the "satellite" states without immense drains on her prestige even if international complications are avoided. Russia cannot afford a series of Hungarian revolutions suppressed by force. Soviet concessions to Gomulka's Poland illustrate this consideration, as do the repeated olive-branches extended in the direction of Tito. Although there is no convincing evidence one way or the other, it is quite possible that the erection of the Berlin Wall in 1961 was not the preferred solution of the Soviets to the Berlin problem. The so-called "German Democratic Republic" had much to gain from it, for its life blood was draining out as people fled its jurisdiction through Berlin. The Soviets, on the other hand, increased drastically the likelihood of having anti-Communist pressures in East Germany boil up to confront them with a new dilemma.

To sum up, both superpowers find themselves presiding over coalitions which threaten to come apart. Their word is not law any more. What of the additional problems confronting the Soviets?

II

The first special difficulty for the Soviets is the success of the movement to dissolve the old colonial empires. The transformation since World War II is highly dramatic. Today only handfuls of people remain to be "freed." Why classify this as a "difficulty" for the Soviets? Have the Soviets not heartily backed this progress of the "national liberation" movement (as they term it)? And do not these new nations often vote against the United States in the UN? Have not some of these established quite close relations with Russia?

All of this is true, but the general trend is still working against the Soviet Union. It will take time for this to become fully apparent, especially since the ringing anti-imperialistic slogans of the Soviet Union still arouse the expected emotional responses. But the Soviet Union is professedly an anti-status quo power in the sense that she is against the existence of non-Communist governments anywhere in the world. The Soviets opposed imperialism not as inhumane or unjust in its own right but on principle since it represented capitalist exploitation. Colonial peoples, clamoring for freedom, were in no mood to listen to this fine nuance of meaning. The Soviets cannot be really sympathetic and friendly to the governments of newly freed peoples who retain a capitalist (i.e., non-Communist) system. Remember that according to Communist doctrine these people were twice enslaved: by foreign domination, by a locally maintained capitalist economic system. Doing away with one does not really "free" these peoples. The optimistic assumption in many of these new states that the Soviets accept semi-socialist institutions as the real thing is founded upon ignoring the great contempt traditionally lavished by the Communists upon socialists who retard the real "peoples' revolution."

The Soviet Union must either change its doctrine or eventually clash with most of these new states. Their interests are no longer automatically aligned. Interesting enough, Khrushchev has taken some steps in the direction of revision of the doctrine. As he said in February, 1956, at the 20th Party Congress of the Soviet Communist Party, communism might now come to power without a "revolutionary class struggle" in some countries. The workers "in a number of capitalist and former colonial" nations might win majorities in free elections. "Of course in countries where capitalism is still strong and where it controls an enormous military and police machine, the serious resistance of the reactionary forces is inevitable. There the transition to socialism (communism) will proceed amid conditions of an acute revolutionary class struggle."[2] But this effort at revisionism, although quite modest measured against the problem, is one of the reasons why the Sino-Soviet dispute could not be suppressed (of which more in a moment).

The point here is that the break-up of the colonial world carries with it the elimination of troubled waters in which the Soviets caught fish almost without effort.

A second special difficulty for the Soviets is the dispute with China. The argument is carried on, of course, in doctrinal terms, but it can readily be translated into the conventional terms of international relations.[3] In fact, it is necessary to do this if the dispute is to be seen in proper perspective.

The first thing one must grasp here is the newness of the problem for Russia in contemporary times in having a powerful China astride Soviet frontiers. The emergence of a strong (or at least potentially powerful independent China) was bound to affect the Soviets quite drastically. There was a time earlier, to be sure, when the same problem existed vis-à-vis the Tartars. Between 1480 and 1725 Russia was expanding from a small "Muscovy" to a domain extending into the Far East. The first Russian treaty with China, the Treaty of Nerchinsk in 1689, stipulated Russia's withdrawal from the Amur territory. But the Treaty of Aigun of 1858 was another story. The

---

[2] *New York Times*, February 15, 1956.

[3] This is not meant to imply that the doctrinal disagreements are not real per se but only that they in turn arise out of deeper problems of divergences of national backgrounds, attitudes, and interests.

Manchu dynasty of China increasingly presided over a China characterized by growing weakness. Prominent among the despoilers were the Russians who took much territory, only ceasing to expand when confronted with the locally superior power of Japan.

Now it is significant that the Russians never fought an all-out war to the death with Japan—the Russo-Japanese War was certainly not one. Indeed, even to the present day the Russians have fought no all-out war in the Far East anytime in the modern period. (The few days of World War II hardly count.) Thus Russia has never in the modern period been in a threatened position for her eastern areas at all comparable to what exists today if the tension there should produce outright conflict. While the period of Japanese occupation of the China mainland was a significant danger, Japan's limited power and other distractions kept it from realizing its full potential.

In short, Russia in modern times has not had to give serious thought to the danger of a powerful neighbor across the eastern-southern frontier in a position to wage war along much of that frontier. At the same time (as we shall see in more detail shortly) the Soviets have a dangerous neighbor in Germany which also has a territorial grievance against the Soviet Union. Consequently the Soviets are entering a period of increased military vulnerability in possessing potential important enemies *on both flanks* (quite apart from the United States and its Polaris submarine missiles). While this is a familiar circumstance to Germany, which resulted in defeat in two world wars, it is virtually a new situation for Russia in modern times, certainly so in its scope and dimensions.

The Sino-Soviet dispute is, as said, expressed in doctrinal terms. We must see what these are; but since the whole of Russia's change in circumstance and increased problems are really behind the revisionism of Khrushchev, this is best examined by returning to it after considering the third special problem—that of Germany.

Germany historically has been of special interest to the Russians, for she has reached deep into Russian territory in military offensives in two world wars. There is a tendency today in the West to discount Germany as a problem for Russia, since West Germany is within NATO and NATO is "defensive." The tendency of the Soviet Union is to treat Germany in two contrasting fashions. The minor theme is bluster: "If you Germans start anything you will be turned by us into one vast cemetery." But the major theme, expressed in countless diplomatic notes to the West over the years, is one of increasing anxiety and fear of German rearmament. And this fear is soundly based since it is not realistic to expect Germany to be content with the present abnormal situation. The West German government has for years explicitly declared that legally the frontiers of Germany are those of January 1, 1937. Thus, from the German point of view, Russia presently occupies German East Prussia simply by force rather than by right. The best the

Russians have been able to extract from this situation is a German declaration that they will not seek to alter the status quo by force.

The interesting thing about the German situation is that the retirement of Adenauer has permitted a more flexible and dynamic policy. The first fruits of this policy are the establishment of major trade missions in several of the satellites plus the opening of the Berlin Wall at Christmas, 1963. The policy under Adenauer of writing-off relations with this whole area, and making no attempt to extend German influence there, is now ended. And since the European satellites rest only very uncomfortably within the Soviet orbit, and have much to gain by a window on the West, this is a feasible policy for Germany to follow. While these areas (Poland and the Balkans) have suffered from the Germans, so too do they suffer today from the Russians. The increase of German influence in these areas has little to recommend it from a Soviet standpoint.

The nature of the implications of this point can be made clear over Poland. Poland can cling to the Soviet Union for protection, or she can seek an agreement with Germany which assures her some independence. So long as she does not come to terms with Germany she is automatically chained to Russia—and in the background there always lurks the shadow of a new Polish partition.

These problems are only beginning to make themselves manifest. For a long time the German contentedness to simply "build strength" in alliance with the West has served to obscure the nature of what is involved once Germany assumes the more active role. The simplest way of expressing the core of the relationships here is to say that a program of simply keeping things as they are over Germany must be based either on (a) East-West cooperation to that end, as in World War II, or, if East and West are not in agreement, (b) German passive inaction. The basis of the status quo of (a) has long been gone. Now (b) is going too. Consequently, the status quo will change. This coming event is a difficult special problem for the Soviet Union.

The Adenauer theory of how German reunification was to come about assumed that the Soviets would want to settle the issue once they got into trouble in their domestic economy or with China. Then Russia would be forced to give up East Germany without any real *quid pro quo*. The alternate view *within* the West German government coalition is that some return concessions would be necessary (i.e., withdrawal of West Germany from NATO). Both views agree that Russia's difficulties make for a fruitful climate for the realization of German goals. But since the Soviets may well react instead by increased stubbornness and refusal to cut commitments anywhere, a rather dangerous situation could result from this. Consequently it is clear that the increase in Russia's problems should not be construed too simply as outright advantage for the West.

III

It is now possible to understand some of the basic reasons for the Sino-Soviet dispute and why the argument takes the form it does.

Central to the controversy is the "inevitability of war" doctrine. Lenin held that the capitalist need to expand markets led to international conflict. Conversely, he held that without capitalism there could be no wars (since socialist states would not have any motivation). Consequently the Soviet Union might find itself at war as a result of direct attack by a capitalist state seeking its area for markets, or it might be drawn into a war fought by capitalist blocs. Orthodox Leninism in any event did not see the alignment of world forces as primarily capitalist vs. socialist blocs. Stalin in this respect remained an orthodox Leninist as he made clear shortly before his death. He wrote: "Some comrades affirm that . . . the contradictions between the camp of socialism and the camp of capitalism are greater than the contradictions among capitalist countries. . . . These comrades are mistaken."[4] While the factors working for peace were stronger they were "insufficient to eliminate altogether the inevitability of wars among capitalist countries . . . and consequently the inevitability of wars also remains." In the post-Stalin period Khrushchev has rejected this view and revised the doctrine. And this for a readily understandable reason: in an age of H-bombs, it cannot be appealing for most people to hear that the world "inevitably" is going to be destroyed because, capitalists being capitalists (and therefore bound to act as such), the world is fated to be plunged into disaster as the natural sequence of cause and effect works itself out. As *Kommunist* said in September, 1960, "the working class cannot conceive of the creation of a Communist civilization on the ruins of world centers of culture, on desolated land contaminated with thermonuclear fallout, which would be an inevitable consequence of such a war. For some peoples the question of socialism would in general cease to exist: they would physically vanish from the planet."[5] Nuclear war, it went on, could not bring the victory of socialism closer; rather it would set "the cause of the building of socialism and Communism back by many decades."

Khrushchev, at the same 20th Congress of the Soviet Communist Party mentioned earlier, said "there is no fatal inevitability of war" between Russia and the West. The socialist camp was no longer in real danger of attack by the capitalists because "the socialist camp is invincible." So now capitalists, confronting this new power relationship, are supposed to make a prudent estimate of what the consequences of aggression would be, and then behave peacefully!

---

[4] In Chapter 6, "The Question of the Inevitability of Wars Among Capitalist Countries," *Economic Problems of Socialism in the USSR* (published September, 1952).

[5] As cited in Zbigniew Brzezinski, "A Book the Russians Would Like to Forget," *The Reporter*, December 22, 1960. *Kommunist* is the Russian theoretical monthly.

Why does Mao for China denounce this revisionism and talk about nuclear war in quite another tone? Even in the "revised version," Mao says: "If worse comes to worst, half of humanity will perish but half will remain. But imperialism will be razed off the face of the earth and the whole world will go socialist."[6] In the original version of these remarks, according to the Russians, Mao was speaking "to those people who allege that in case a nuclear war is unleashed by imperialism mankind will perish. We," the Chinese leaders, "do not agree with those views, so pessimistic and full of depair. We say that if imperialism unleashes a nuclear war, it will at most bring death to half the population of the globe. . . . We are confident of the bright future of mankind."[7]

Why does Mao take this viewpoint? The answer is that China's situation is quite different from that of Russia. Russia does not seek a war. While she would be happy to make further gains, she does not want a major conflagration. The Soviet carefulness over the Cuban missile crisis, and the quiet shelving of the Berlin crisis when the United States stood firm, illustrate. The Soviets already may sense that they will do well to keep what they have, now that developments have created dangers on *both* flanks, plus the nuclear power of the United States to be reckoned with.

The situation of China, though, is quite different. China feels that her present *de facto* frontiers were imposed upon her in the days of her weakness. She sees herself hemmed in by the United States at every turn. She sees a pretender government for China in existence, which is galling to her. She is kept out of the UN. She loses "face" and she reacts with intervention in Korea, armies on the Indian frontier, aid to North Vietnam, and friction with Russia. In her self-image she is not a satiated power with things to lose, so much as a frustrated power not making progress fast enough. Consequently she faces the fact of nuclear weapons in line with her feelings. The alternative is for her to resign herself to what she sees as an unsatisfactory situation.

IV

What is happening in the contemporary period, then, represents some rather fundamental changes. Some of these apply to both great blocs. But the problems of the Soviet Union are greater because of the three special problems outlined above. It will not be easy for the Soviet Union to work out proper solutions to her problems. In the short run she may still gain some new "peoples republics" here and there, but the long range picture is not very favorable to her. She is finding, as the imperialists also found, that colonies by whatever name, like "ripe fruit," eventually fall off the mother tree. The pressures on both flanks of her frontiers are also increas-

---

[6] *Statement of the Soviet Government, September 21, 1963* (Crosscurrents Press, New York: 1963) reprints this quotation from Mao on p. 23.

[7] *Ibid.*, p. 22.

ing even though world opinion and awareness has not quite caught up with what is developing. The differences between China and the United States, although made much of in both countries, are much more minor than those between China and Russia. And the Soviets are only at the beginning of German pressures. Will the Soviets recognize the predicament and respond with some graceful retrenchments, or will they take a hard line? It is a rather important question.

31

CHANGES AND CHANCES IN AMERICAN-SOVIET RELATIONS

HANS J. MORGENTHAU*

Our reactions to Soviet foreign policy have a way of jumping from one extreme to another, both in the long and short run, with more regard for changing superficial appearances than permanent objective factors. During the last year of the Second World War, we tended to idealize the Russians, Stalin became "Uncle Joe" to be charmed by Roosevelt into cooperation, and the United Nations, having done away with "power politics," was supposed to be the vehicle of that cooperation. From 1947 onwards, the Kremlin was perceived as the headquarters of the devil on earth, causing all that was wrong with the world and, more particularly, scheming the destruction of the United Nations. These extreme swings of the pendulum can also be observed in much shorter time spans.

On August 27, 1970, *The New York Times* reported from San Clemente that "authoritative White House sources have declared that the United States is prepared to join the Soviet Union in a two-nation peace-keeping force to maintain a settlement of the Middle East conflict. . . ." The reader was left with the clear inference that both the President and Mr. Henry Kissinger, his adviser on national security, had something to do with this statement. If Mr. Nixon had made such a statement ten years ago, it would have been judged at best to be utterly eccentric and at worst might have jeopardized the then Vice President's political career, and if Professor Kissinger had made such a statement 20 years ago, the House Un-American Activities Committee might have investigated him as a likely subversive.

* Hans J. Morgenthau, "Changes and Chances in American-Soviet Relations," *Foreign Affairs*, Vol. 49, No. 3, (April 1971), pp. 429–441. Copyright © 1971 by the Council of Foreign Relations, New York. Reprinted by permission.

Yet less than a month passed, and the atmosphere was drastically transformed. For the Soviet Union had not only violated the ceasefire agreement in the Middle East on a massive scale but seemed to have intended doing so from the outset. Furthermore, the Soviet Union was suspected to be building a submarine base in Cuba. Thus, Secretary of State Rogers, at his news conference of December 23, 1970, discounted as "totally impractical" the idea of such a peacekeeping force as had been adumbrated in August and denied that the United States had ever given any thought to such a possibility.

Yet beneath these fluctuations of mood and tactics the perennial question about the future of American-Soviet relations persists in demanding an answer: Is it possible to move from sterile confrontation to meaningful negotiations? While 20 years ago such a question was purely rhetorical since the negative answer was a foregone conclusion, it can now be asked seriously, and it deserves a serious answer, derived not from the changing mood of the day but from the objective factors which in the long run determine the relations among nations. What has happened during the last 20 years to account for the possibility of posing that crucial question seriously?

II

Five factors have transformed the relations between the United States and the Soviet Union: the rejection of nuclear war as an instrument of national policy; the ideological decontamination of foreign policy at least with respect to each other; the failure of the competition for the allegiance of the third world; the implicit recognition by the United States of the status quo in Eastern Europe; and the Chinese threat to the Soviet Union.

The fear of mutual destruction through nuclear war has imposed effective restraints upon the foreign policies of the superpowers in two respects: the avoidance of direct military confrontation and, when it inadvertently occurs, its speedy liquidation. The United States has fought in Korea and Vietnam wars for limited objectives, falling short of military victory, because of the fear of such a confrontation. It has kept its hands off a series of East European revolts against Soviet domination. For the same reason, the Soviet Union has not followed up with action its repeated demands—twice in the form of ultimatums with a precise time limit—for a change in the status quo of West Berlin. In the Middle East, Russia has come close to a military confrontation with America, but the latter has not responded in kind, and both powers have joined in an initiative to restore peace. When there was military confrontation during the Cuban missile crisis of 1962, both sides went as far as they dared without compelling the other side to take steps that might lead to nuclear war, and retraced their steps in partial retreat.

Sharing the conviction of the suicidal irrationality of nuclear war, the

United States and the Soviet Union have thus in a sense helped each other to avoid it; they appear to have concluded that the sole legitimate purpose of nuclear arms is not to win a nuclear war but to deter it. Nevertheless, they have continued an unlimited nuclear arms race as though there did not exist an optimum of nuclear preparedness sufficient for deterrence, beyond which to go is utterly irrational. They have thus pursued the rational goal of nuclear deterrence with the irrational means of an unlimited nuclear arms race. Recognizing this irrationality, they have joined in the Strategic Arms Limitation Talks (SALT), searching for an agreement which could bring the nuclear arms race under control.

While the United States and the Soviet Union have begun to deal with each other as one great power with another, having certain interests in common and being at loggerheads with regard to others, there was a time, not much more than a decade ago, when we took the communist dogma much more seriously as a guide to policy than did, for instance, Stalin, who with utter cynicism and brutality used communism and communists as a means to further the traditional ends of the Russian state. Yet we saw in Stalin the heir of Trotsky who was out to accomplish the communization of the world, begun in Eastern Europe at the end of the Second World War, while in truth Stalin was the heir of the Tsars, seeking the traditional goals of Imperial Russia with the new instruments communism put at his disposal. The Russians, in turn, interpreted our insistence upon democratic governments in Eastern Europe and our verbal commitment to "rollback" and "liberation" as evidence of the undying hostility of capitalism which since 1917 had used every opportunity to try to destroy the Soviet Union.

The emancipation of American and Soviet foreign policies from these dogmatic ideological stereotypes—again I must emphasize, limited to their mutual relations—has been the result of the impact the facts of life have made upon the thoughts and actions of the governments concerned. Foremost among these facts has been their failure to win the ideological allegiance of the nations of the third world in Africa, Asia and Latin America. The third world was supposed to be the decisive battleground in the struggle for men's minds, a struggle which would decide the fate of the world. Khrushchev, for instance, used to assure us that the third world would follow the lead of the Soviet Union and thereby seal the doom of the West. Nothing of the kind happened. The new nations of the third world have apparently preferred to be miserable in their own way to being made happy by the United States or the U.S.S.R.

This failure of ideological competition has led both superpowers to the conclusion that it is not worth the expense and the risk of a direct military confrontation, and they have given it up. The absence of any ideological reference and the explicit disavowal of ideological commitment in President Nixon's message to Congress on the state of the world of March of last year at least provides verbal evidence of this fundamental change in our approach to certain aspects of foreign policy. On the other hand, the Soviet Union has banished, a few exceptions to the contrary notwithstanding, ideological considerations from its policies in the third world. It has very close relations with the United Arab Republic whose communists are in jail, and it supports Latin American dictators against their communist parties, which are in turn supported by Cuba, the ally of the Soviet Union. That is to say, it practices old-fashioned power politics, unencumbered by ideological considerations.

It is part and parcel of this victory of the facts of life over ideological blinders that the United States has for all practical purposes recognized the Soviet predominance in Eastern Europe. True enough, we have contained the Soviet Union at the line of military demarcation of 1945; but now we and the Soviet Union realize that the United States, too, has been contained at the very same line. This realization has removed from the cold war its main issue: the territorial status quo, especially with regard to the two Germanys. The recent treaty between the Soviet Union and West Germany makes explicit what had been implicit in the policies of the two superpowers: the recognition by all concerned of the territorial boundaries established at the end of the Second World War. This normalization of East-West relations in Europe has also deprived the status of West Berlin of much of the leverage which Stalin and Khrushchev used against the West. They threatened the status quo of West Berlin in order to compel the West to recognize the territorial status quo in Eastern Europe. Since that recognition has now been forthcoming, the status of West Berlin as a pawn in the hands of the Soviet Union has markedly decreased, although it still retains its usefulness as an instrument of annoyance.

Finally, even if these two developments had not greatly contributed to stability in Europe, the Soviet Union would have a vital interest in such stability. For the Soviet Union must cope at its Chinese frontier with endemic instability which might well escalate into war, and in such a contingency it must be reasonably certain that its western frontiers are secure. It needs that certainty in particular because its élite is obsessed with the fear the Americans will gang up with the Chinese. The Russian leaders suffer from the same "cauchemar des coalitions" which disturbed Bismarck's sleep (only he had better reasons than they). Thus they are not likely to provoke the United States in Europe as long as the insecurity at their eastern frontiers persists.

Considering the beneficial impact these factors have had on the relations between the United States and the Soviet Union, it is tempting to conclude that, undisturbed by contrary tendencies, these factors will continue to exert their pacifying and normalizing effect. This conclusion is particularly tempting for those who have conceived of our relations with the Soviet Union primarily, if not exclusively, in ideological, that is, anti-communist terms. Since we do not need to worry any more about the Soviet Union as the spearhead of communism bent upon destroying us, so the argument runs, there is really nothing at all to worry about. This position, simple if not simplistic and superficially attractive since it caters to our wishes, is, however, vulnerable to three arguments: the elimination of ideological considerations from our foreign policy is partial, and tenuous where it exists; the power politics of the Soviet Union contains residues of ideological commitment; the U.S.S.R. is a great power whose interests and the policies serving it, regardless of ideology, may run counter to the interests of the United States and the policies serving it.

Nor does the ideological decontamination of our relations with the Soviet Union signify that our foreign policy has been altogether freed of its ideological ingredients. We still think about foreign policy in demonological terms and allow our actions to be influenced by them. Why are we fighting in Indochina? In order to prevent the communist takeover of South Vietnam is the official answer. Why did we send our troops to the Dominican Republic? Because we cannot have another communist government in the Western Hemisphere, said President Johnson. Thus it appears that the struggle against communism still influences our actions. Only the devil's place of residence has changed. He could at a moment's notice move back to the Kremlin, and his reappearance in his old haunts would rekindle the ideological animosity between the United States and the Soviet Union. As William Graham Sumner put it: "The amount of superstition is not much changed, but it now attaches to politics, not religion," and, one can add, it attaches to one locale rather than another as circumstances seem to require.

This propensity for political demonology finds support in the nature of the Soviet state and the foreign policies it pursues. It is true that since Stalin the Soviet Union has used ideological factors as means to the end for the Soviet state and in consequence has been able to switch with great alacrity its ideological preferences and stigmatizations from one country to the other. Thus the German "fascist beasts" became comrades-in-arms against Western imperialism after the Molotov-Ribbentrop pact of August 1939, and the "neo-fascists" and "revanchists" of West Germany transformed themselves into respectable partners, once they were willing to recognize the territorial status quo. China was embraced as a junior partner in the world communist movement as long as it was satisfied with that junior position. It was read out of the Marxist-Leninist camp altogether when it struck out on its own in competition with the Soviet Union.

But it is also true that the Soviet Union regards itself not only as one nation among others but also as the "Fatherland of Socialism," the leader of all "progressive" forces throughout the world. It is this position, now to be maintained against China's competitive claims, that imposes upon Soviet foreign policy certain ideological burdens which the Soviet Union would not need to bear if it conceived of its national interests in strictly traditional terms. What happens in Cuba has no bearing upon the interests of the

Russian state traditionally conceived, but it bears heavily upon the position of the Soviet Union as leader of the "progressive" forces of the world. For that reason, the Soviet Union subsidizes Cuba to the tune of approximately $1,000,000 a day even though Castro supports subversion and civil war against the very Latin American governments with which the Soviet Union deals on a pragmatic basis. It is for the same reason that the Soviet Union supports North Vietnam with military aid, carefully limited so as not to provoke the United States to escalate the war, but sufficient to prevent an American military victory.

Thus the ideological conflict between the United States and the Soviet Union is not dead but only dormant. As long as the interests of the two superpowers do not openly clash, the ideological conflict may remain in its present state of suspended animation. But if and when one superpower shall again openly encroach upon the interests of the other, the ideological demons are also likely to be awakened from their slumber. Here is indeed the crux of the future relations between the United States and the Soviet Union. Can they pursue their respective interests without encroaching upon each other's?

III

Since the downfall of Khrushchev, the Soviet Union has unobtrusively and effectively expanded its political and military influence in the eastern Mediterranean, the Middle East, South Asia and the Indian Ocean in the best tradition of great-power politics and has enhanced its economic influence throughout the world in the best tradition of a capitalist trading nation. The pattern of that expansion has been constant: Russia has moved into the spaces left by the liquidation of the British and French Empires, thereby bringing close to consummation the Tsarist aspirations which during the better part of the nineteenth century had pitted Russia against Great Britain over the "Eastern Question."

Yet there are less spectacular and potentially as important achievements as well. The following story from the London *Financial Times* of February 14, 1968, points out that Moscow has seen considerable commercial advantage to gain from the blockage of the Suez Canal. Across the Soviet Union lie "straight-line" routes from Western Europe to most of Asia, and the Russians are beginning to exploit this fact.

Already [the Russians] have developed two alternative water routes of their own to the East—the waterway system linking the Baltic Sea with the Caspian, and the Northern Sea route from Europe through the Arctic Ocean to the Pacific. Distances by these routes are shorter than via Suez (unlike the corresponding Cape journeys) and in the event of a long closure could well capture some of the traffic permanently. Iran's use of the Baltic-Caspian waterway has reached an advanced stage already. This route . . . is cutting 2,700 miles off the Suez route between Germany and Iran.

The *Financial Times* goes on to report that Russia had also announced that she would be "opening her previously tightly guarded Arctic shipping lane across the top of Siberia to foreign ships." Such a new sea route would put Yokohama only 8,500 miles from London whereas the Suez passage totals 12,500 miles.

Instead of remembering how in the sixteenth century the center of power shifted from the Mediterranean to the nations bordering on the Atlantic in consequence of the opening of new trade routes, we have been hypnotized by the ideological aspects of the Indochina war. While we put our minds to beating the Russian communists to the moon and keeping the Vietnamese communists out of Saigon, the Soviet Union has occupied much of the middle ground between these cosmic and parochial goals. Thus the absence of open conflict between the United States and the Soviet Union or, to put it in positive terms, the improvement in U.S.-Soviet relations is in good measure the result not of the settlement of outstanding issues or of the absence of points of conflict, but of American failure to compete with and oppose a Soviet Union steadily expanding its power throughout the world. What looks to the naïve and the wishful thinkers as a new harmonious phase in American-Soviet relations is in truth a by-product of our military involvement in Indochina. We have been too busy with trying to save Indochina from communism to pay much attention to what the U.S.S.R. was doing in the rest of the world and to compete with it or oppose it as our interests require.

As long as our main national energies and human and natural resources remain absorbed by Indochina, we will continue to enjoy "good" relations with the Soviet Union. The "good" quality of these relations will be the result not of the identity or the parallelism of interests derived from the settlement of outstanding issues, but of letting the defense and promotion of our interests go by default. After all, it takes two to quarrel. If one side does not object to what the other is doing, there will be harmony, but it can be harmony at the former's expense. Thus, paradoxically enough, the lack of controversy in American-Soviet relations results in good measure from the pathological inversion of our national priorities caused by our involvement in the Indochina war. Once we terminate that involvement and conduct our foreign policies again on the basis of the rational assessment and ordering of our national interests, we are likely to find ourselves again in competition and conflict with the Soviet Union.

IV

Four issues, if they are not settled, are likely to revive the competition and opposition between America and Russia: the nuclear arms race, the status of Germany, the balance of power in the Middle East, and the ferment in the third world.

The restraints which the fear of mutual destruction has imposed upon the foreign policies of the United States and the Soviet Union are predicated upon the certainty of that destruction. That is to say, they depend upon what Churchill called a "balance of terror," in which B, after having suffered unacceptable damage from nuclear attack by A, would still be able with what remained of its retaliatory nuclear force to inflict unacceptable damage upon A, and vice versa. It is this psychological conviction that a nuclear war is a genocidal and suicidal absurdity which has preserved the peace and at least a modicum of order in the relations of the superpowers.

However, the indefinite persistence of this conviction cannot be taken for granted. It is threatend by two assumptions: that one or the other side has acquired a first-strike capability which would destroy the enemy's retaliatory capability or at worst reduce it to tolerable proportions, and that one or the other side or both sides have developed a defensive system which at worst would reduce nuclear damage to tolerable proportions. It is irrelevant for the purpose of this discussion whether or not these assumptions are correct; it is sufficient that they might be held. If they were held, they would be bound to exacerbate drastically the nuclear competition between the United States and the Soviet Union; for then the question before us would no longer be the relatively simple one of maintaining mutual deterrence, but how to assure for oneself, and deny to the enemy, the ability to wage a successful nuclear war. The restraints which, as we have seen, have characterized the foreign policies of the superpowers would then follow mutual deterrence into oblivion; for the avoidance of nuclear war appears no longer as a precondition for physical survival if a nation is convinced that it can win a nuclear war either through irresistible attack or impenetrable defense.

It is this dire possibility that makes the success of the SALT talks, seeking a way to control the nuclear arms race, so crucially important for the future of American-Soviet relations. If they fail, a drastic deterioration of these very relations is likely to result. If they succeed, they will not only have stabilized the nuclear arms race on a level sufficient for mutual deterrence, though not for a first strike or effective defense, but they will also have demonstrated the ability of the two superpowers to translate their common interest in survival into operative policies.

While this issue, overshadowing all others, is still in the balance, the normalization of the relations between West Germany and the Soviet Union through the former's recognition of the territorial status quo has brought to the fore a conventional issue which touches the vital interests of both the United States and the Soviet Union: the future orientation of West Germany. Almost 20 years ago, West Germany joined the Western alliance in order to contain the Soviet Union and to assure powerful backing for its claim to be the sole legitimate representative of the whole German people, East and West. It succeeded in the first, and failed in the second, objective. That failure was due to the East German government's staying power and the Soviet determination to contain the West at the 1945 demarcation line.

For West Germany, however, the relations with East Germany and West Berlin have remained crucial. Bonn has come to recognize that the only power which can improve and secure these relations is the Soviet Union. By the same token, the Soviet Union knows that the security of its European empire depends upon West Germany's position. A West Germany which is the dissatisfied spearhead of a hostile alliance is a constant threat; a neutralized and friendly West Germany is an invaluable asset. For a Russo-German combination would become the master of the Eurasian land mass, reducing what remains of Western Europe to an insignificant promontory. This has been the long-range aim of Soviet foreign policy at least since Khrushchev. Khrushchev expressed time and again in private conversation his conviction that there would be another Rapallo, that is, another understanding between Germany and the Soviet Union after the model of the Rapallo Treaty of 1922; that it would come not under him and not under his successor but under his successor's successor; that it was inevitable; and that the Soviet Union could wait. The Soviet Union, in the treaty with West Germany recently concluded, has taken the first step in the direction sketched by Khrushchev.

This treaty, on the face of it, performs the function of a peace treaty—a quarter of a century overdue—in which West Germany recognizes explicitly the territorial status quo of 1945. This recognition has been implicit in the policies which West Germany and the United States have pursued for two decades vis-à-vis the Soviet Union and the nations of Eastern Europe, but the revisionary rhetoric accompanying it, especially in the 1950s, could not help but create doubts as to whether that implicit recognition could be relied upon if opportunities for a change in the territorial status quo should arise. These doubts have now been laid to rest.

However, it is hardly necessary to point out that the development so confidently predicted by Khrushchev would run counter to the interests of the United States and would nullify the policies Washington has pursued in Europe since the end of the Second World War; for it was the major aim of these policies to prevent all of Germany from being drawn into the Russian orbit. In the course of such a development, the Soviet Union, by replacing the United States as the predominant power in Western Europe, would achieve another of its long-term aims: the expulsion of the United States from Europe.

Here is indeed a potential source of serious conflict between the United States and the Soviet Union. Whether or not that conflict will materialize depends upon two factors: what other steps may follow after the initial step taken by the Soviet Union and West Germany, and whether the United States, remaining aware of those interests in Europe over which it fought the cold war, is still willing to support those interests with appropriate policies. As concerns the last point, domestic support for the proposal to reduce drastically our military presence in West Germany must give us pause.

At present it is the Middle East which appears the most obvious point at which the interests and policies of the United States and the Soviet Union appear to collide. The Soviet Union seeks to maintain and expand its predominant presence in the region, while the United States tries to contain it. In order to realize its aim the Soviet Union must support the Arab aspirations up to the point where the survival of Israel is in jeopardy; for much of the Soviet leverage in the Arab world depends upon the continuation of the enmity between the Arabs and Israel. Paradoxically enough, the Soviet Union has an interest in the survival of Israel, however precariously placed in the midst of continuing Arab hostility. On the other hand, the United States, too, is interested in the survival of Israel, secured through the acceptance of the Arab states; for such acceptance would reduce the Soviet leverage to a minimum and improve the chances for American influence reasserting itself. Thus American and Soviet interests with regard to Israel are both contradictory and run for quite different reasons along parallel lines. They make for conflict as well as coöperation.

The third possible point of friction between the United States and the Soviet Union, the revolutionary ferment in the third world, differs from the others in that it is highly speculative. In theory, both superpowers are committed to incompatible positions on this issue. The Soviet Union has repeatedly come out in favor of "wars of national liberation," while the United States favors stability, which means in concrete terms the defense of the status quo against revolution from the Left. In consequence of these incompatible positions, the United States and the Soviet Union have found themselves on opposite sides of the fence in the Congo, the Middle East, Cuba, Vietnam. But, as pointed out before with regard to Latin America, the Soviet Union has not hesitated to abandon this position in favor of a pragmatic pursuit of its national interests as a great power. And the United States, after the Indochinese experience, is not likely to intervene openly in Africa or Latin America in order to defend the established order against revolutionary change. In view of the abatement of ideological commitment on both sides, this source of friction may appear remote at present, but it might become acute overnight if an unforeseen event, domestic or international, should suddenly awaken the slumbering ideological passions.

The amicable or at least peaceful settlement of the substantive issues outstanding between the United States and the Soviet Union is greatly complicated and under certain conditions may well be jeopardized by a peculiarity of the Soviet approach to negotiated settlements. The Soviet Union has been painstaking in keeping the agreements—both political and commercial—that were in its interests to keep, and this is about all one can expect from any nation; for all nations will disregard—either openly or surreptitiously—those agreements which no longer serve their interests. It is peculiar to the Soviet approach to negotiated settlements to enter some-times into such settlements with the intention not to honor them. It is one thing to disregard agreements when they no longer serve one's purposes; it is quite another to pledge one's word to an agreement with the intention not to honor it. The former is accepted diplomatic practice, however morally repugnant. The latter is treachery—Gromyko assuring Kennedy of the absence of Russian missiles in Cuba while the President had photo-graphic evidence to the contrary; the Soviet Union agreeing to a cease-fire for the Middle East and violating the agreement at the very moment of its coming into operation. The experience and the resulting expectation of such treachery may well make the difference between accord and conflict and, when the chips are down, between peace and war.

Thus the future of American-Soviet relations is shrouded in uncertainty. Neither amity nor enmity is foreordained. Those who proclaim the in-evitability of conflict on ideological grounds are as wrong as are those who assert the inevitability of peace, or even friendship, because the United States and the Soviet Union have become more restrained in words and deeds in dealing with each other. The future depends first of all upon how the two governments conceive of their respective interests and how they will go about defending and protecting them. If they conceive of them in compatible terms and pursue them with appropriate concern for each other's sensibilities, the future might well witness the realization of Roosevelt's dream, Stalin's grand design, and Mao's nightmare: the coöperation of the United States and the Soviet Union in establishing and maintaining a modicum of order in the world. Otherwise, the world will continue to hover on the brink of self-destruction.

The outcome, however, will no longer depend exclusively upon the actions of the superpowers vis-à-vis each other, but to an increasing extent upon the actions of secondary power centers—China, Japan, West Germany, either alone or in concert with a politically and militarily united Europe—and the reactions of the two superpowers to them. Thus the issues dividing the two superpowers will remain susceptible to peaceful settlements only in the measure that the superpowers are able to prevent their relations with the secondary power centers from exacerbating their relations with each other. When they deal with each other, they must also, as it were, look over their shoulders to see what other nations are doing and to anticipate what they are likely to do. While the freedom of manœuvre which the secondary power centers are likely to enjoy will introduce a new element of uncer-tainty and risk into the relations between the superpowers, concern with the interests and policies of the secondary powers may well strengthen the self-restraint with which America and Russia have been dealing with each other because of the fear of nuclear war.

❧Part Five❦

World in Crisis—
Contemporary Problems

≥13≤

Europe in Ferment:
East and West

DISCERNING IMPORTANT TRENDS in international relations takes a trained eye and an informed mind. Yet one thing we can be sure of: change is taking place.

Thus, a statesman or leader who aligns his nation against the trend of developments in the system detracts from the potential influence and effect of his nation's power and policy. On the other hand, what characterizes the greatest and most successful leaders is that they increased the impact and effect of their national policy by seeking ends ultimately compatible with the parameters of those trends. They have altered the course of events neither by reversing the trend nor merely accepting it, but by capitalizing upon it and giving it firmer and more precise direction. This is a more abstract way of making Carr's point as quoted in the Hartmann article in Chapter 1, that is, thorough-going realism is defective in concentrating on "what is," and yet, "what is" already constitutes part of what is becoming. The present is already part of its future, and looked at in retrospect, it is all seen as part of a continuous past.

These observations fit today's Europe in ferment, whether we mean East or West. Partly the powerful factors for change (and the growing unwillingness to accept Europe's continued division) reflect Europe's dissatisfaction with the preoccupation of the superpowers with events outside Europe, in Asia and the Middle East. Partly they reflect a very deep, pan-European feeling that Europe's Cold War division is both unnatural and unwise. In Western Europe in addition there is a feeling that a purely national approach to problems will keep Europe weak and unable to play its proper role. These impulses toward change find a somewhat different focus in an Eastern Europe concerned with reducing Soviet dominance. But in both Western and Eastern Europe there is ferment; and political sentiment, once aroused, is a very powerful force. There can be little question that out of this ferment will come significant change. But, as usual, the exact shape of what is to come remains unclear. And when it will come is quite unpredictable with the present clues. In the three selections which follow we shall see a sophisticated appraisal of this Europe as it begins its transition.

In the first selection, "A Hard Look at the Community," W. Horsfall Carter, who from 1951 to 1963 was head of the Publications Division in the Council of Europe, looks at developments in the (Western) European Community with a dispassionate eye. Rejecting the "dogma of the Europe Crusaders" which judges Community institutions essentially in terms of progress toward supranationalism, Carter succeeds in stripping "the prevalent Community image [of] the 'federalist' cant with which it has been overlaid." While he judges that the European Economic Community (the EEC or Common Market) "has succeeded in its primary aim of a customs union, and has considerable merits as an economic catalyst" to promote further change, Carter takes pains to show the failure of the "idea that the mobilization of economic interests and the organizing of economic processes would inevitably provide a springboard for political union" into one West European super state. Carter also points out that pan-European progress and West European union are at odds as goals.

In the second selection, "The Process of Détente in Europe," Laszlo Hadik of the Institute for Defense Analyses draws a very perceptive distinction between the meaning of détente to the superpowers and the meaning to Europeans on both sides of the Iron Curtain. His thesis is that Europeans, profiting from the "stalemate of the two alliances . . . are using it as a means of altering the political face of Europe . . ." Contrasting the superpowers' wish for "immobility" by achieving détente through the maintenance of a stability between the blocs, Hadik characterizes the European aim as one of changing the *status quo*. To Europeans, "the stability [of] the two blocs" is seen "as a necessary and welcome condition for regaining their own independence of action and addressing some of Europe's outstanding political problems." Hadik shows both subtlety and balance in his analysis of the delicately interlocking issues.

Robert F. Byrnes, Distinguished Professor of History at Indiana University, in the third selection, "Eastern Europe: The Unstable Element in the Soviet Empire," looks lastly at the East. His presentation was prepared for the U.S. Senate Subcommittee on National Security and International Operations, itself a healthy sign of the Senate's new determination to play a more active role in foreign policy (as we saw in Chapter 11). Byrnes' analysis of the weaknesses of the Soviet position in Eastern Europe, and the factors at work there, is very complete and quite acute. His analysis has also some sharp points of disagreement with Hadik. Who is right?

32

A HARD LOOK AT THE COMMUNITY

W. Horsfall Carter[*]

What is so fascinating, and disconcerting, about the making of "Europe," in our generation, is that it is, in the words of Altiero Spinelli, author of *The Eurocrats*,[1] "at the same time a cold bureaucratic operation and an extraordinary political adventure." Both these aspects of it, applied to the Community phenomenon, were reflected in the communiqué issued at the close of the "summit" meeting at The Hague in the first days of December 1969. Considering that, in the days and weeks preceding the conclave, most commentators in the press had been suggesting that the Community was in complete disarray, that the whole "ramshackle"[2] enterprise was breaking down, President Pompidou's initiative would seem to have amply justified itself; and, certainly, that communiqué must be adjudged a masterpiece of diplomatic carpentering.

The Brussels Community is a most ingenious economic and social compound; and, apart from the stimulus to the growth rate, it has fostered and assisted, both inside the close preserve of the Six and outside, a change of scale in economic thinking—what the Italians aptly call *ridimensionamento*. But to too many people it has become a sacred cow. It has been grossly "oversold" by its own public relations staff and the tame "Common Market Correspondents": above all, by its identification with the European idea, it has provided a happy hunting-ground for the utopians, the incorrigible ideologists, in which this country abounds. The purpose of this article is to suggest that enthusiasm for the "political adventure" has blinded many people to the limitations of the Community in practice. I shall not here seek to pronounce on Britain's third bid for full membership, under Article 237 of the Rome Treaty, which is, as it were, *sub judice*[3]: I would only say that, contrary to the generally accepted view, "European" allegiance is not

[*] W. Horsfall Carter, "A Hard Look at the Community," *International Affairs*, Vol. 46, No. 2 (April 1970), pp. 280–292. Reprinted by permission.
[1] *The Eurocrats: Conflict and Crisis in the European Community.* Trans. by C. Grove Haines (Baltimore: Johns Hopkins Press, 1966. London: Oxford University Press, 1967).
[2] Mr. Enoch Powell's epithet.
[3] The case for proceeding circumspectly, on the basis of Article 238, and, first, establishing Britain's European credibility (because the Six will never risk the break-up of the Community structure) was admirably presented by Mr. Stanley Henig, M.P. in an article in *The Times* on June 26, 1968.

necessarily to be identified with membership of the EEC: that, for some of us, the latter is not the open sesame for, not even a necessary condition of, participation in European political effort. And that the establishment of a political and security régime, for the whole of Europe, is the immediate and urgent task.

To mark the expiry of the "transitional period" prescribed in the Treaty, the panjandrums of the six Common Market States were concerned, they said: "to draw up a balance-sheet of the work already accomplished, to show their determination to continue it and to define the broad lines for the future." *Completion* of the Community endeavour, it was agreed, required, first and foremost, at this stage, the settling of the definitive financial arrangements for the common agricultural policy; and this was duly achieved, on paper, after some very hard bargaining, at a subsequent series of high-level Ministerial meetings ending up with the customary "marathon." The agreement, intended to start operating from January 1, 1971, visualises the Community having at its disposal its own funds, from various sources—and being fully self-financing by 1978. It includes a firm promise of an autonomous Community budget (in accordance with Article 201 of the Treaty) together with a pledge that the budgetary powers of the European Parliament would be strengthened—with the important proviso, however, that the latter scheme would not come into force until January 1, 1975. This was indeed grist to the mill of the Europe Crusaders. But a lot of things can happen in eight years (or five years): to begin with, the whole agreement requires ratification by the six Parliaments—and, in the light of recent evidence of the strength of the farmers' lobby in France and in Germany, there is no assurance that it is "in the bag."

There was, after this, a rather vague reference to "the subsequent action needed to strengthen the Community and promote its development into an economic union," combined with a more specific undertaking to work out during 1970 with the Commission—which had already presented proposals (the Barre Report) in February 1969—a stage-by-stage plan with a view to the creation of an economic and monetary union.[4] Here was due obeiance being made to the second objective which the Community champions had set themselves: *development in depth.* Well, we all know how far the authorities in charge of finance in the various States are from achieving a stable international régime of control: meanwhile, in the nice French phrase, *"on a la diplomatie de sa monnaie."* I am probably not alone in thinking that the agricultural policy is not really viable unless and until the monetary nettle has been grasped. Co-operation of the Six in the monetary sphere, it was explained, must depend on the harmonisation of economic policies: a

---

[4] Details of the Commission's 8–10 year plan for a European economic and monetary union were issued on March 5. It is being sent to the Council of Ministers for formal consideration. 1978 is the target date, this being the year that the new financial arrangements are due to come fully into effect.

tall order, to judge by the experience of these twelve years! One discerns here undoubtedly an act of faith, an element of wishful thinking, especially when the invocation of economic union is linked with the pious hope of expansion of the Community "to dimensions more in conformity with the present state of world economy and technology." This was the overture to the third of the objectives which the Ministers had set themselves: *enlargement*. Preparatory negotiations between the Community, on the one hand, and the applicant States, on the other hand, were to go ahead "as soon as practically and conveniently possible." No date was specified, in deference to French susceptibilities; but M. Maurice Schumann, France's Foreign Minister, made no bones about indicating, at a press conference the same day, that an agreed Community negotiating position should be possible to achieve by July 1970. Finally, among other professions of the Brussels creed, there was an *obbligato* on "the political objectives which give the Community its meaning and purpose"; and, specifically, the Ministers for Foreign Affairs were commissioned to study the best way of "achieving progress towards political union . . . within the context of enlargement."

Now, as was to be expected, the optimists in the press—the soothsayers I prefer to call them—have hailed this new phase of Community development, especially the commitment to a "federal-type" budget, as "a giant step forward that the Six are taking in the relations between nation-States."[5] This is surely a somewhat extravagant claim to make for a progress report which, when all is said and done, is no more than a magnificent job of camouflage work, masking the brutal fact that, for all the indefatigable labours of the Commission and the multiplicity of committees of experts, the Community has in fact made only modest progress in its mission of economic unification—and none at all in the matter of political union. The one solid achievement to date is the industrial customs union, with its external tariff—*plus* the framework of a collective agricultural system which everyone agrees is now due for a complete revision, whether the EEC remains a combine of six states or expands to ten. Actually, the existing economic "integration" process, with all the paraphernalia of Regulations, Decisions and Directives involved, goes no further, except in the sphere of agriculture, than an attempt to co-ordinate policies and harmonise national legislation. In this connection one can record the adoption in principle by the Six of the French value-added tax for export transactions (but no agreement yet on common rates), the concordance on patents, which is still far from being effective—and, of course, the establishment of common rules of trade competition. All the rest is still *à l'étude*—what the Germans call *Zukunftmusik*.

As promised in the Treaty, there is, nominally, within the boundaries of the Community, "free movement of goods, services and people." Workers

---

[5] David Spanier in *The Times,* January 9, 1970.

are entitled to migrate across frontiers—not, however, to seek employment but only to take up offers made. Architects, doctors, lawyers, on the other hand, are still penned in their national folds, hedged in by the barriers of national qualifications. On transport, which has a whole Section to itself in the Treaty, progress has been virtually nil. In 1968 a system of additional licenses for lorries was agreed, together with regulations about lorry drivers' conditions; but the 1962 proposals for common rates and conditions for rail, road and water traffic throughout the territory of the Community have remained in abeyance. In this sphere West Germany, with its own very independent transport policy, is now the nigger in the woodpile—but also there is still a certain recalcitrance from the Netherlands. Last year the target of a unified commercial policy towards "third countries" had to be abandoned. And the task of instituting a Community antitrust and cartel system has made little headway.

With regard to energy sources, common action, let alone integration, has been conspicuous by its absence. The Council of Ministers last November got as far as accepting the basic principles of a communal policy on power propounded by the Commission. But it was obvious that the differences of approach are crucial, with the French and the Dutch, as often happens, at the two opposite ends of the scale. Incidentally, the disappointed hopes in this important field date back more than ten years, to the sad story of the Coal and Steel Community. The founding fathers of the ECSC cherished the illusion that "European" responsibility for controlling (or, at any rate, policing) a limited sector would exert a decisive pull on the rest of the economy: whereas the converse proved to be the case. Because national governments are, and must be, responsible for economic policy, when the coal crisis developed in 1957—a structural and not just a cyclical crisis, due to the appearance on the market of ever greater supplies of petroleum and natural gas—each government had to take over and deal with the problem in its own way. As for EURATOM, we know, whatever benefits it has brought in the pooling of research, etc., that as a supra-national entity it never got off the ground, the French Government having refused from the outset to transfer to an extra-national authority the powers of its Commissariat for Atomic Energy.

Perhaps the most telling example of the Community's failure as yet to establish a European identity is the fact that, while there has been abundant concentration and remodelling of industrial structures within each member-State of the Six, it has not proved possible to build up any authentic European company: a working party is still trying to find the legal formula. The difficulties are indeed enormous. Each State has a different system of company law and different ways to protect shareholders. In each country, too, companies have a different, and delicate, relationship with their government; and, as national planning develops, the relationship gets more involved, and notions of patriotism and the national interest *cannot* be excluded [6] One remembers the partially successful action of President de Gaulle's Government to ward off the Fiat-Citroen merger. Nor should we forget the intervention of the West German Government to prevent the *Compagnie Française des Pétroles* from taking over Gelsenberg, the German oil company. But direct government interference is not by any means the main obstacle. The chief difficulties are psychological: the fact that the companies of the individual countries of the Six do not trust one another sufficiently. The case of the Gevaert-Agfa merger, which is usually cited in evidence, has in practice only underlined the incidence of national jealousies.[7] Trustification of business is, of course, a characteristic of our times, with British firms to the fore in the industries based on modern advanced technology. But in almost every case within the boundaries of the Community it is being promoted and controlled by American firms.

Facts and figures about this United States business penetration—which, of course, extends in equal, if not greater, measure to Britain—have been hurled at us in M. Jean-Jacques Servan-Schreiber's best-seller *Le Défi Américain,* one of the grim conclusions of which is that in ten years' time America-in-Europe is likely to be the third biggest industrial Power in the world. M. Michel Debré, then France's Minister of Finance, put this point rather more cynically—as might be expected—with the remark that Europewise the EEC had proved a considerable disappointment because it had been mainly characterised by competition among the Six to see which of them "could lean most heavily on American might in order to strengthen its own position within the Market." And he added that, in the absence of united political action—e.g., de Gaulle's "European" Europe—this process of American satellisation must develop further: the mere admission to the Community of new Members would only reinforce the existing trend. Actually, this dominance of United States business enterprise is not as shocking as it appears to be: allowing for the difference of scale, it is surely not so dissimilar from the impact of British business and City interests on the European continent, as in the rest of the world, during the heyday of the Victorian era.

This gloomy picture of the state of play is, as a matter of fact, borne out by the author of *The Eurocrats* whom I cited at the beginning of this article. Signor Spinelli—he was writing towards the end of 1967, but there has been little change since then—has to recognise that, whatever the dynamic effects of the Community venture on individual businesses, the power of decision in matters economic remains firmly in the hands of the individual

---

[6] *Cf. The New Europeans* by Anthony Sampson (London: Hodder & Stoughton, 1968).

[7] The difficulties arising in this particular merger were the subject of a talk by M. Albert Becker, a director of the Belgian company, at a seminar on *Business Strategies in Today's Europe* sponsored by the French National Association of Doctors of Economic Science in June [1969].

States, and that "the phantom of political union remains disembodied." Indeed, he came to the sad conclusion that "united Europe" was at that time (i.e., after ten years of the Community) very much as it had been defined by Jean Monnet in 1952: "the precarious ensemble of European action-centres committed to constructing its unity": that, in short, the "Europe of the offices," as he calls it, and not any political purpose, is the real "European connective tissue."

The positive merit of this "Europe of the offices" moving forward gradually in agreement with the parallel departments of the administration in the member States is not to be denied. And, in Signor Spinelli's view, the national administrations have responded in a substantially positive way: progress towards European "integration," slow though it may be, is ensured by the direct and continuous process of consultation, through the Permanent Representatives Council in Brussels, through industrial, commercial, labour and agricultural organisations geared to a "European" purpose—and, of course, through relations with political parties *via* the European Parliament. We can all agree, moreover, that, as a technical device, the continuing dialogue process between the Commission and the Council of Ministers of the Community is invaluable. But it is a technical device, not a prime factor in policy-making. De Gaulle was right. Supranationalism is *as yet* a fiction, an aspiration; and, as for federation, the EEC is nowhere near it. On this Sir Alec Douglas-Home and Harold Wilson are justifiably at one. Meanwhile, the "Europe of the States" holds the field.

Someone should undertake a sober analysis of the mythology of the Commission. In the meantime, for an understanding of the way in which the Community actually works I commend warmly a recent "Personal View" broadcast talk by Andrew Shonfield (published in *The Listener* of November 20, 1969). He was discussing the "Crisis in the Common Market," and specifically the Common Agricultural Policy, following the revaluation of the Deutsche Mark. Two months previously, France, on account of devaluation of the Franc, was up against the repercussions on her farm prices—and still further overproduction of surplus cereals—and the Commission had promptly authorised the introduction of countervailing taxes. The West German Government, now faced by lower-priced competition, had similarly imposed emergency dues on food imports from the other Common Market countries. The Commission pointed out that this was against the rules. But its protests went unheeded. And the limitations of the Community as an instrument for making collective decisions were thereby exposed. It just showed, as Mr. Shonfield says, that the Commission "can't boss Governments around on major questions of domestic policy. What it can do is to set the terms of new bargains among the member States: it can get them to accept a commitment to agree on some specific step at some specified date in the future which the national Governments, acting by themselves, would be unlikely to achieve . . . The task of the European Commission is to push out the frontier of collective decision-making. This is really what supra-nationalism is about in practice . . .": no more and no less. And, as Mr. Shonfield goes on to suggest, the Community is, admittedly, a very im-perfect instrument for doing what now needs to be done in this respect. It can, and no doubt will, be improved. "But, in trying to improve it, one must recognise it for what it really is, not a piece of ideology but another and more efficient way of doing business between nations."

"Not a piece of ideology." That is the key phrase. For it is the ideological zeal of champions of European unity of different categories—the federalists or proponents of a United States of Europe, such as Mr. John Pinder, Director of PEP and Dr. Roy Pryce, Director of European Studies at the University of Sussex,[8] some Eurocrats—and numerous politicians, like Mr. Michael Stewart, when taking a holiday from actual political decision-making, which has given people a distorted picture of the Community as it really is today. Typical of this confusion of vision was the celebrated asser-tion some years ago by Dr. Hallstein, then President of the European Com-mission, and now President of the European Movement: "What is emerging from all this is not just an economic union. Rather it is political union limited to the economic and social fields . . . The logic of economic integra-tion . . . leads on towards political unity by way of the fusion of economic interests."

Dr. Hallstein, who retains a touching faith in the metamorphosis of the Community into a European federal State, went even further into the in-tellectual stratosphere in his report on the institutional problems of the Common Market made to a gathering of the Action Committee for the United States of Europe in July 1969. He boldly affirmed that present trends must be reversed, that the powers of the Commission *vis-à-vis* the govern-ments must be strengthened and the majority principle reinforced. In other words, that the "Luxembourg compromise" of 1965 (whereby France and Germany agreed to differ about majority voting in the Council of Ministers in respect of matters of vital national interest) must be jettisoned. And he went on to argue that to bring in the four applicant States led by Britain would not strengthen the Community unless the occasion were taken to con-centrate more effective power at the centre.

With all respect to the hero of the Community's first decade, his "logic" begs all the fundamental questions. If, indeed, the EEC has succeeded in its primary aim of a customs union, and has considerable merits as an economic catalyst, the concomitant political theory has been utterly exploded: this idea that the mobilisation of economic interests and the organising of eco-nomic processes would inevitably provide a springboard for political union. There is, of course, interaction between politics and economics all the time. But the notion that economic considerations per se determine political

---

[8] *Europe After De Gaulle* (A Penguin Special. Harmondsworth: Penguin Books, 1969).

decisions contradicts all historical experience. Yet this automatic "spill-over" effect was the basic assumption on which the architects of the Community relied, as it is still the dogma of the Europe Crusaders.

Typical, too, of the ideological approach, and of the view that politics must take its cue from economics, is the author of *Le Défi Américain*. His prescription for remedying Europe's colossal technological gap *vis-à-vis* the United States is a homeopathic one—"a hair of the dog that bit them!" Because, like the "professional Europeans" he sees Europe in the American image, he considers our only salvation to be the construction of European federal-type political authorities, based on the Communities, to direct and control the mammoth undertakings operating beyond national boundaries. This is indeed the logical inference. But in matters of politics logic is at all times a poor guide. Europe is not America. And, so long as there is not the slightest sign that the super-Powers—the United States, the Soviet Union, China—are disposed to submit to any outside authority, the image of a tidy European "federal" segment, a Europe spinning along on its own orbit, is about as remote from reality as was the "Union Now" chimera of Clarence Streit and his disciples thirty years ago.

In the realm of theory, of course, the prophets and priests of a supra-national authority are quite right. For more than two generations now technology, communications, defence and large-scale industry have patently outrun the bounds of the national State; and, by the same token, if only we were all rational entities, and not human beings, the case for a world government superseding the continuing international anarchy—as made out, for example, by Emery Reves in *The Anatomy of Peace*—is unanswerable.[9] It happens that the inter-State relationship, one of interdependence but no more, is the pattern of the real world we live in. Statesmen must deal with the world as it is, not as they hope it will be.

The fact is that both the State and the Nation are still very much alive, and it is a peculiar chemical compound of the two which supplies the lubrication of national and international life. Whether we like it or not, now and in the foreseeable future, the nation-State is the only unit in international relations which provides a legitimate source of political authority, indeed which has any real political significance. And those who condemn and deplore "nationalism" are blinding themselves to a vital strand in the whole political process: they would appear deliberately to overlook the fact that the framework of the national State alone secures the political consensus which we call democracy—and to which we all pay lip-service. There is no such thing as a European nation. Charles de Gaulle, on whom so much abuse has been heaped for his nationalistic stance, was simply being

---

[9] The present writer may be forgiven for a certain malicious glee at the discomfiture of the reformers and blue-print apostles, since he was preaching, in vain, a similar gospel, in the world context, from the late Lord Davies' "New Commonwealth" pulpit thirty-seven years ago.

realistic, retailing the facts of political life (he sets no store, as we know, by ideology); and it was incumbent upon someone in a responsible position to state and re-state, as he did, the essential nature of a political community.

In his famous press conferences de Gaulle time and again expounded the "Europe of realities" in lapidary terms. Listen to him on September 5, 1960:

> To build Europe, that is to say, to unite Europe is manifestly an essential step. . . . Only, in a matter like this, the way forward must not be through dreams but in accordance with realities. Now, what are the realities of Europe? What are the pillars on which it can be erected? In sober truth, they are the States, which are certainly very different from one another but each one of which has its own history, its own language, its misfortunes, its glories, its own ambitions; and these States are the only entities that are entitled to give orders, the only bodies possessing authority to proceed to action. To imagine that there is the possibility of building something effective for action, and capable of securing the approval of the peoples, over and above the State is a chimera. . . . Certainly, pending the moment for coming to grips with the problem of Europe as a whole, it has proved possible to establish a number of more or less extra-national bodies. And such bodies have their technical value. But they have not, and they cannot have, authority and by the same token political efficacy. As long as nothing serious is happening, they function without much fuss, but from the moment when some dramatic development occurs, when there is some major problem to be resolved, it becomes plain that a so-called "High Authority" [the reference is, of course, to the Coal and Steel Community failure] has no authority over the various national categories and that the States alone possess such authority.

No one can quarrel with this insistence on the authority of "the State," which was the hall-mark of de Gaulle's policy at home during eleven eventful years. Heir to the Richelieu rather than the Napoleonic tradition, he was a master of statecraft, of what is called pejoratively *Realpolitik*. But he was, too, ever mindful of his democratic obligations; his monocracy was always carefully posited on the popular will, hence his frequent use of the referendum. The consequence in external policy was, of course, an obsession with political issues which made him a formidable opponent. In championing national interests, however, he was only doing what every other democratic statesman does. There was a determination to achieve maximum independence for France in world affairs, but there was no denial of interdependence, opposition to NATO as a vehicle of military integration but no repudiation of the Atlantic alliance. And, as his initiative in 1961–62 for the establishment of a European political union showed, and his unfurling of the banner of a "European" Europe for five years or so after that, he had his own target of a political and defence union of Western Europe, in the first place, then of a wider Europe, through détente with the East, which was at least as respectworthy as the Atlanticist view or the "federal" fantasy of the Community ideologists—and indeed was, in the sixties, far better adapted to the new political and strategic realities. French policy came to grief ostensibly on the question of British participation in European plans, but mainly on the counter-productive effects of de Gaulle's own crushing personality.

French leadership is a *sine qua non*. France must be, if only for reasons of history and geography, the core and centre of any European union; and Anglo-French partnership the indispensable nexus, the one guarantee of Europe playing an effective independent role on the world stage. As I wrote in my book—*Speaking European*,[10] "Present Franco-German connubiality is an important fortunate circumstance, but it is, after all, only a *pis aller* [as General de Gaulle himself was the first to admit], an interim phase of development, pending the full assumption by Britain of her European responsibilities and status." The tragedy of the last few years has been Anglo-French antagonism, which has blocked all progress—due, patently, to the cleaving by British policy-makers, in the nuclear power and monetary spheres, to a supposititious "special relationship" with the U.S.A. which is incompatibile with a "European" Europe. The essential passage from the General's famous press conference of January 14, 1963 deserves to be quoted and requoted:

> It is possible that one day Britain will transform herself sufficiently to participate in the European community without restriction or reservation and *preferring it to every other connection* (my italics), and in that case the Six would open the door and France would raise no objection. . . .

This is still the nub of the question.

It is, of course, common form in this country to fasten responsibility for the resurgence of nationalism, and the Community's slow march, on France, and specifically on de Gaulle's contumacy. But a closer scrutiny of the Brussels deliberations over the years will assuredly demonstrate that it is not only France that has been intent on driving hard bargains, that will not in present circumstances face further sacrifice of political authority. The situation has been disguised by the opposition of the "friendly Five" on the specific question of Britain's entry into the Community. Now that this issue has been resolved in principle—though it is not, of course, by any means out of the way—we shall come to realise the extent to which in recent years the Five have thankfully sheltered behind de Gaulle's broad shoulders. The stark truth is that neither France nor Britain, the only two European States possessing the semblance of decision-making capacity—Federal Germany, even under Willy Brandt's leadership remains "an economic colossus but a political dwarf"—are prepared, any more than the giants, to accept coercion on major policy issues by any outside authority. Hence Mr. Wilson's frank statement, made, in answer to a question in the House of Commons on February 6, 1969 that "we did not and do not support any federal or supranational structure for our relations with Europe"—repeated on January 12 this year in a notable Panorama television programme. Some of my readers will no doubt have taken note of the *mot* attributed to Georges Pompidou on the occasion of his first visit to the Brussels organisation: "Oh, yes, we have lost a President, but you have lost an alibi!"

Striking confirmation of this sober view of what is possible today—and

---

[10] London: Allen & Unwin. 1966.

politics *is* the art of the possible—was supplied by the Federal German Chancellor, Willy Brandt, in a number of public statements he made on the occasion of his eminently successful visit to London at the beginning of March. At the Foreign Press Association luncheon on March 3, for example, he said: "It is not possible at this stage to achieve a European political union on the basis of the supranational principle: that is a task for generations ahead of us."

One more quotation from de Gaulle, and I have done. On February 5, 1962, after the breakdown of his attempts to obtain agreement between France and her partners in the Six on a scheme of political union (the Fouchet, later Cattani, plan) he said: "We are applying our energies actively to rescuing 'European union' from the sphere of ideology and technocracy to bring it into the realm of reality, that is to say, *of politics*" (my italics).

Eight years later this is still, I venture to suggest, the task confronting those who have not allowed themselves to be mesmerised by the success story of the Community—those of us who remain unconvinced that European federalism (alas!) is anything but "a satisfying moral and intellectual idea."[11] The "crisis of the Community" has demonstrated once and for all the need for political direction of the economic unification process.

How a political consensus is to be achieved is anybody's guess. Some die-hards of the Community cause, like Lord Gladwyn, are still—while repudiating federalism as irrelevant to Europe's problem—convinced that the Brussels formula is our talisman—that the establishment of a political Commission, composed of nominated but "independent" Commissioners, on the lines of M. Jean Rey's team, with provision for the dialogue process and a weighted vote in the Council of Ministers, is the way forward. Others will suggest that this Community technique is really only a subterfuge, an expedient for Ministers to slough off to some extent their responsibilities. They pin their faith to the orthodoxy of "organised co-operation" (de Gaulle's phrase) the first instalment of which must obviously be the holding of regular meetings of the Foreign Ministers. Which means, of course, a great deal of hard bargaining, but it does not exclude the possibility of agreement, eventually, on the common objective. The outcome of the promised Brussels negotiations could conceivably be an extended free trade area linked to a political directorate of the senior European nations, including Britain—an elaboration of the French proposals made a year ago to H.M. Ambassador in Paris.

All responsible Ministers, anyway, have come to appreciate now, I think, that the military factor cannot be divorced from the political— that some kind of European defence mechanism, including nuclear capacity, is indispensable, as a complement to the American system. This, of course, raises the

---

[11] The phrase is taken from the unprejudiced conclusions of a journalist writing in the Northampton *Chronicle & Echo,* after a study tour of the Community's headquarters in Brussels.

whole question of the changed Europe-America relationship—acknowledged by President Nixon, thanks to his mentor, Henry Kissinger—which was the *raison d'être* of General de Gaulle's much-maligned and misunderstood policy. But discussion of this theme is outside the scope of the present article.

My object has been to correct the prevalent Community image, to strip off the "federalist" cant with which it has been overlaid. The detached observer can only marvel at the capacity of the "professional Europeans" for mixing hopes with reality—at the way in which the thurifers in attendance on the Brussels altar have consistently blurred the line between what is actually happening today and what they hope will happen tomorrow. The supreme fallacy of these ideologists, whose conception of European unity is in the American image, is, I suggest, the assumption—shared, it is true, by many enthusiastic businessmen—that economic interests and processes will by themselves infallibly bring about political union. This is a gross oversimplification of the politico-economic nexus. The primacy of politics over economics, and the fact that in these days of welfare the State inevitably plays a bigger part in economic decisions than ever before, is one lesson we should all have learnt from de Gaulle: for it explains, better than anything else, the persistent gap between harsh realities and the European dream.

33

THE PROCESS OF DÉTENTE IN EUROPE

LASZLO HADIK*

Any follower of European political developments will agree that events are happening faster than ever before, that the changes are greater than ever, and that many of these changes are both surprising and baffling. The meaning of any one event, let alone of the overall trend, is a matter of debate. Discussion soon surfaces the term détente, and on that concept a new discussion turns. Is there or is there not a détente? Does it signify a real improvement of relations? Can we rely on détente? . . .

Our uneasiness about détente is usually due to overlooking the substantially different ways in which the two superpowers on the one hand and the states of Europe on the other have experienced the past quarter-century. Despite fervent denials by U.S. officials, . . . the United States has become

* Laszlo Hadik, "The Process of Détente in Europe," *Orbis*, Vol. 13, No. 4 (Winter 1970), pp. 1008–1028. Published by the Foreign Policy Research Institute. Reprinted by permission.

predisposed to view security in Europe in a way that favors the status quo. The Soviet Union, of course, readily denounces any attempt to change the status quo as well as any state which implicitly fails to accept it. The preservation of the status quo is thus implicit in the superpower use of the concept of détente. It is used either in the sense of the absence of tensions and threats in the East-West relationship or to signify an atmosphere in which the opposing side is disposed to make concessions.

By contrast, Europeans have come to view détente as a flexible diplomacy, flux in European relationships, and the opportunity to change the political face of Europe. . . .

Europeans have come to differentiate between the territorial status quo, which cannot be changed without a war and which thus assures their defense, and the political status quo, which *can* be altered and in the changing of which they can see an opportunity to enhance their security. . . .

. . . .

Europeans have concluded that both superpowers are not only satisfied with the status quo which they cannot alter unilaterally, but also prefer its stability to the uncertainties that might be created by changing it. Neither in a friendly nor a belligerent mood has either superpower indicated serious preoccupation with problems that could not be solved within the framework of the present bipolar system. In the static view of the superpowers, the existence or nonexistence of détente is thus a measure of their success in making the status quo more stable and more acceptable.

The European Experience

The same twenty-five years of history are viewed differently from the standpoint of Europe. The sum total of European security interests at the outbreak of the Cold War consisted of defense and recovery, and these were to be found only in close alliance with the respective superpowers. As recipients of both military and economic aid from the United States, which guaranteed them security against aggression and subversion, West European members of NATO willingly submitted to a strict discipline. The regimes in the East were tied to the Soviet discipline on a bilateral basis both because of Stalin's methods and aims and because they were so unstable; the attraction of the strong and prosperous West to their suppressed and dissatisfied populations represented a constant threat.

It was characteristic of the Cold War era that each side viewed bloc solidarity as an attribute of strength. This gave rise to the concept of alignment, resulting in the search for unanimity where possible and in the absolute necessity of gaining respective superpower backing for individual European policies. Because room for maneuver outside the two groupings was nonexistent, in any case, European members of both alliances sought to advance their interests by eliciting support and frequently getting a commitment from the protecting superpower. The two alliances were conceived of by their members as the primary vehicle for a European political settlement. The strength provided by NATO was to be the basis for a restoration conforming to Western goals; the Warsaw Pact held out the promise of frustrating this restoration and creating a new order.

European members of the two alliances thus contributed to the division of Europe. Furthermore, they shared with their superpower protector a concern for strength and solidarity, not so much to stabilize the European confrontation as to enhance deterrence and defense. More conscious of unfinished business in Europe, they were less acutely concerned with stability than the superpowers were. Yet in the early stages of the stabilization process, Europeans too accepted the principle that the more stable the balance of terror the greater their own security.

Awareness in both Eastern and Western Europe of the political consequences of a more secure and stable balance between the superpowers was slow in coming. These consequences were of two types. First, maintenance of a stable deterrent relationship meant that the superpowers were unable to deliver on their commitment to advance the causes of their allies. Second, stability in Europe allowed Europeans to turn their attention to the problems left unsolved after World War II, made them feel the adverse consequences of Europe's division more keenly, and set in motion a process of change in national outlook and national values.

The division of Germany into two vastly differing social and political systems, several frontier changes, the self-isolation of the East European states, and many lingering hostilities in Europe became a source of worry to those who saw in them the seeds of future conflict. The division of Europe not only violated the common bond that European states have felt despite their frequent conflicts, but showed itself as a serious obstacle to economic growth, especially in the Eastern part of the continent. Finally, elimination of the fear of war in Europe led gradually and unevenly to a changed outlook in which ideology has a diminishing role and there is greater preoccupation with welfare, greater awareness of interdependence, and a willingness to transform Cold War relationships.

The process of détente is a product of these two factors: The confrontation of military blocs has largely eliminated the danger of war in Europe, but neither the blocs nor the superpowers that lead them have become attuned to Europe's emerging needs. In effect, Europeans have begun pursuing their own interests in a variety of ways, giving rise to the enormous growth of transbloc diplomatic activity we have witnessed in the past two or three years. For analytical purposes, one might describe the process of détente as the dialectical interaction of three elements: (1) a growing dissatisfaction with the status quo, (2) gradual espousal of a flexible approach to overcome the status quo, and (3) the exploration and definition of a new system of security in Europe.

The acceptance of Europe's postwar frontiers and of the communist regimes in Eastern Europe may have seemed like resignation to the unalterable, but they were a fact nevertheless. To change the situation in the East would be seen as a threat to the national existence of the states affected, and would constitute a return to the instability of the Cold War era. Acceptance of the status quo was thus a precondition for other changes in Europe. However, a distinction between various levels of status quo, which had been impossible to make in the atmosphere of the Cold War, became feasible under détente. As the European nations felt more secure, changes in relationship between states of different social systems, in the perceptions and outlooks of governments, in the aspirations and declared interests of populations and leaders, and in the methods of pursuing policy were no longer inherently threatening to national security. Regimes and leaderships began to react to such changes not by clinging more stubbornly to their positions, but by adapting themselves through modifications in their own outlooks and approaches.

Such a differentiated view of the status quo has permitted the hope that a sufficient number of mutually responsive and reinforcing changes would alter the political climate of the European system, creating a new environment without a threat to peace so that a new system could be constructed. Increasing flexibility in European politics came to represent a method of changing the political status quo peacefully, and thus provides an alternative to the Cold War dilemma of an indefinite stalemate or the triumph of one camp over the other.

In the European pursuit of détente there is an implicit recognition that only by increasing the options of all European actors can the system itself be brought into flux. Some East and West European states have, therefore, acted as though they were looking toward a chain reaction of exploration, experimentation and interaction. Many recent initiatives have been designed not for quick payoff but to set in motion processes whose end result will come much later, after many other changes have occurred.

In sum, while Europeans have perceived the superpowers to be biased in favor of immobility in Europe, their own aim has become to change the status quo. They have not seen the stability established by the two blocs as an end in itself, but as a necessary and welcome condition for regaining their own independence of action and addressing some of Europe's outstanding political problems. European détente relationships, therefore, are characterized by dynamism and flexibility.

The Changed Evaluation of the Threat

There is little question that Western Europe has come to feel safer than ever before from communist attack. East European regimes, with the possible exception of the GDR, have also found security against both Western aggression and subversion. In fact, this state of reduced tensions is often erroneously labeled as détente, rather than the process that emerged as a result of it. It is a tribute to the performance of NATO and the Warsaw Pact—or, more precisely, to the stalemated confrontation between them—that there appears to be no present danger to peace in Europe. There is no longer even an arms race at the regional level between the two military alliances, and there has been talk of a willingness to discuss balanced force reductions under certain conditions.[1]

The existence of apparently stable peace has not, however, reduced the preoccupation of Europeans with "security." What has changed is that the threat of war no longer obscures other threats and concerns. "Security" has become a broader concept than "defense" because the national interests that determine it have grown. As new national interests have emerged and as the horizon of European governments has widened, the forms and sources of threat have also expanded. These changing perceptions required a search for means and arrangements to deal with them. For this, political instruments of security have come to encroach upon primarily military ones. Thus, the bipolar alliance system has come under scrutiny from the vantage point of the new perceptions.

At the root of European worries about the present security system is that it is so dependent on the superpowers. While the growing relationship of the alliance leaders has stabilized Europe, Europeans are aware that this may not always be the case. The superpowers have global interests. Their relations may deteriorate dangerously over some extra-European issue such as Cuba, Viet Nam or the Middle East, or as a result of some drastic internal change of regime in one or both of them. In any case, Europeans feel they have almost no control over the European policies of the superpowers at this time, and this state of affairs could pose a threat in the future.

Now that Europe has gained stability and begun to acquire a taste for the fruits of cooperation, even a minor deterioration in superpower relations could be seriously threatening to European interests. A return to the "discipline" of the Cold War or to the overt threats and heightened tension of the immobile years could eradicate the progress achieved in gaining mutual confidence among European states.

A more abstract apprehension is that effective mutual deterrence might fail, bringing to an end the present standoff and stability in Europe, which is a precondition for détente. This fear is based not so much on the possibility that the superpowers will in the future court the chance of nuclear war against each other, as that they may risk limited war in Europe on the assumption that such a war between their two sides could remain limited. Europeans find it not inconceivable that the superpowers will stabilize the strategic arms balance between them in such a way as to diminish the value

[1] Despite some continuing territorial or interstate disputes within the blocs (Transylvania, Cyprus, South Tyrol, Macedonia), there is conspicuously little belligerent action being taken by the disputants, and only in the case of Greece and Turkey can one find evidence of a state arming against its Cold War ally.

of nuclear deterrence for their respective allies. This could destroy the bipolar defense system founded on mutual deterrence, which Europeans feel is needed as a contingency for some time to come.

As the superpower relationship has begun to take on structured form, Europeans have become apprehensive that in pursuing interests common to themselves the superpowers might violate some vital interest of a European state. This is not necessarily a fear of collusion, but simply a recognition that global powers of nuclear stature may have common interests which supersede the interests of their lesser allies. Already, the changing superpower relationship implicit in a rapid succession of agreements—the Nonproliferation Treaty, Strategic Arms Limitation Talks, a proposed discussion of balanced force reductions in Europe—has strained the European ability to appraise and adjust to its effects.

Perhaps even more real than the threats so far mentioned have been the foreseeable costs existing alliance commitments will impose on Europe in the future. For one thing, the level of armaments and the pace of arms competition tend to be set by the superpowers and tailored to their demands. Both East and West Europeans estimate that a modern army has to be re-equipped once every decade in order to stay abreast of military technology. Even at present levels this is a financial cost European governments cannot be confident of justifying unless the benefits are clearly worth it. There must also be a need for remaining constantly under arms, and this need is not something most Europeans want to perpetuate.

Nonfinancial costs as well, although largely immeasurable and perhaps even illusory, are looming ever larger in European calculations. The constraints placed by Ulbricht's sensitivities upon Hungarian and Czechoslovak attempts to improve relations with West Germany—in other words, to pursue détente—provide a lesson that will not be lost on other European states. U.S. petulance toward France for being the first European partner to act on assumptions much like those held by the United States is another case in point.[2] The Soviet Union has dominated its allies in the name of security. Even the requirements for consultation and coordination of policy that alliance membership imposes become burdensome in a period characterized by the increasing attractions and rewards of flexible diplomacy. A capricious veto by one or both superpowers is a threat that worries Europeans.

Taking a West European situation separately for illustration, one can see a further source of threat emerging. Recently, the United States has insisted on maintaining at least the present strength of both U.S. and European forces committed to NATO. Just prior to the Soviet invasion of Czechoslovakia, however, Washington was making no secret of its desire to reduce U.S. forces. A similar "state of détente" may again raise pressures for

---

[2] For an analysis of French security policy, see the author's "France's New Approach to Western European Security," *World Affairs,* December 1969, p. 209.

reducing U.S. forces in Europe. Washington might make its defense guarantee contingent upon the Europeans maintaining a sufficient conventional force under arms. West Europeans would then remain in a bipolar system in which they held the major responsibility for the conventional defense of one side without a large enough U.S. presence or a European say about the use of tactical nuclear weapons to make the deterrent effect of the whole credible. European security based upon two opposing systems would thus become an anachronism, especially as neither the United States nor the West Europeans would be willing to pay the cost of keeping up a Cold War in order to assure that the other side behaves. If Western Europe's security continues to depend solely on NATO, any doubts about the cohesion of NATO in a low-threat environment constitute a potential danger.

Finally, the European search for a status quo based on new relationships is also sparked by a fear that without a European initiative the superpowers might arrive at dispositions for European security which failed to account for European interests. The worst of these would be a superpower condominium in which the Europeans were intentionally denied a major role and voice. If the superpowers should move from détente to entente and collaboration before Europeans found some substitute for the present bipolar security system, they would lose most of their independence of action to a dual hegemony. . . .

The Goals: European Security and a Security System

Perhaps the most significant common denominator of the three attributes of European détente is that they are oriented toward change, action, and the future. This implies a purpose and some sort of goal. Both the more proximate and the more distant aims relate to security and are thus interdependent. The former is sometimes defined as a European peace settlement, while the more distant vision is referred to as a European or all-European security system.

The immediate purpose apparent in the actions of détente-oriented Europeans is to address outstanding issues and disputes piecemeal, in an effort to change the political climate of Europe. These might include the improvement of international understanding and communication, the establishment of new relationships and diplomatic practices, and the solution or elimination of contentious problems between states. As models, the postwar settlements of the Saar, Trieste and South Tyrol disputes come to mind, as does the Franco-German reconciliation.

Reference to only a few examples will indicate that this purpose is neither farfetched nor without some promise. Since many of the conflict-prone problems relate to Germany, the piecemeal solution of these has become a goal of both the Federal Republic and some of its interlocutors. The recent rapprochement with Poland was marked by attention to limited specific issues. One of these is the Oder-Neisse frontier, which forms the western border of Poland with East Germany. Bonn's formal acceptance of this frontier would moderate Polish fears that any future German government might reopen claims against Poland for territories lost after World War II. Reconciliation between Poland and Germany would lessen the opportunity for the Soviet Union or others to exploit a potential conflict situation to their own ends. Claims of German revanchism would lose their credibility in Eastern Europe, and thus reduce East European dependence on Soviet "protection."

In the course of the same Polish-West German exploration, Bonn's leaders have sought Polish guarantees for the continued freedom and independence of West Berlin—whose vulnerability to Soviet and East German threats is one of the more touchy issues in Europe. Once Poland and other East European states give such guarantees in the course of their bilateral "normalization" of relations with Bonn, it is hoped that these states will act to constrain any attempts within the Warsaw Pact to threaten West Berlin. At the same time, one of the subjects the two German governments are expected to discuss is the restoration of economic relations between West Berlin and East Germany. This would enhance the interdependence of the two units, further reducing West Berlin's insecurity.

There is a large component of economic motivation in the growing interaction between Europeans of the rival blocs. However, this does not explain the whole phenomenon. Expanding markets, cost-cutting joint ventures and technological improvements are not the only motives behind East-West economic contacts. East Europeans have their own complex urges, one of which is to achieve greater independence from the Soviet Union for their economies. Another post-Cold War preoccupation that has social and political consequences for change in Eastern Europe is the desire to better the standard of living. A broader aim is also evident in West European overtures toward the East. Deals are no longer based only on barter. The many forms they are taking reflect an effort to eliminate Eastern Europe's isolation, involve it in the growth of Western Europe, strengthen the independence of regimes from bloc constraints, enhance the position of pragmatic and flexible technocrats within the communist countries, and induce the regimes to change their aims, outlooks and opportunity expectations. In this way, it is hoped that a form of East-West interdependence will emerge to reinforce European security.

East Europeans, whose motives in calling for a European security conference are often suspected on the basis of our Cold War experiences, have their own individual purposes. One of these is to reduce the threat inherent in the German problem. Although the division of Germany may appear to them as the necessary basis for a final solution, it is not in itself a solution and the present arrangement does not offer sufficient guarantees for the future. To begin with, the GDR does not yet feel secure enough to end its self-isolation, and therefore acts to constrain the activities of its allies. Second,

FRG acceptance of the two Germanys cannot be considered final as long as a satisfactory modus vivendi between the two entities has not been achieved. Finally, a U.S.-West German axis, which for East Europeans is the core of the NATO residue, looks to them more like a potential threat than a stabilizing factor. For this reason, they are also interested in gaining West European guarantees that NATO members will not allow the FRG to exploit the alliance and its power against East European interests.

It is clear to East Europeans that they cannot throw off Soviet dominance by force. Predominance in the region is a key factor of Soviet security perceptions. Besides, East Europeans continue to perceive the need for Soviet protection. At the same time, they are increasingly opposed to the potential for interference in their domestic affairs that Soviet predominance offers. They cannot defend themselves against Soviet forces, and therefore their only security against the Brezhnev Doctrine consists in inducing gradual changes in Moscow's perceptions of security needs toward something less paranoiac and less hegemonic and in placing constraints on Soviet intervention. For this reason East Europeans have supported the signing of bilateral agreements renouncing the use of force between states, rather than an East-West agreement between the two blocs. Such agreements are not firm obstacles, but they do have a psychological effect and thus constitute a constraint on the use of force. Much more important is the excuse such agreements would give for members of the opposing alliances to oppose, and exclude themselves from, the use of force by a predominant member of the alliance. This would tend to weaken the offensive potential of the military blocs, without necessarily affecting their defensive potential.

These are only a few of the realistic and practical measures discernible in the current détente efforts of European governments. The goal behind the détente process is more than any one of these, however. It is to change the political climate of Europe through the cumulative effects of such concrete measures so that a new security system can be developed. The concept of all-European security is not merely a slogan for this goal, but a descriptive name for a system whose form and structures are still only dimly perceived. It is possible, nevertheless, to list some of the hopes pegged on such a system and some of the functions it is to perform.

The key to some future all-European security system appears to be interdependence among all of the states of Europe. The object is to emphasize common interests and to build from them a web of human, commercial, technological and political ties which will be stronger than the issues that continue to divide Europeans. It is hoped that eventually states will refrain from acting in a hostile fashion in the pursuit of their interests because they have more to lose than to gain from such a stance, rather than because they are effectively deterred through the threat of retaliation. All-European security thus would be based more on cooperation and conflict resolution than on deterrence and a high state of defense preparedness.

Another element of any all-European security system would be the creation of means for resolving conflict peacefully and thus eliminating open eruption and prolonged festering. This is to be approached at first by efforts to build confidence between former opponents, to create incentives for conciliation, and to facilitate compromise. One way of changing the security system in Europe is to induce nations to change their goals from conflicting to compatible ones, thereby eliminating the fear and insecurity that derive from incompatible goals. Much of this can be achieved through harmonization of interests in such indispensable common goals as prosperity, economic development and human fulfillment, as well as the common fear of potentially suicidal war, all of which transcend divisive national interests.

There is in the process of détente an appeal to a sense of common European destiny, mutual dependence and even pride. Implicit in characteristic détente thinking is the specter of an outside threat to Europe, which endangers the security of all Europeans and therefore should concern them all. Europeans view the superpowers ambivalently, as both necessary protectors and potential overlords: they share a common interest in avoiding situations where Europe would be at the mercy of the superpowers and in preventing them from gaining domination over Europe either singly or in concert. Europeans want to be able both to prevent conflicts among themselves and to defend themselves against outside threats.

In sum, Europeans want to create a Europe that is internally and externally safe, especially from the danger of nuclear war; a continent that can exploit its full development potential, that can play a role in the world. One analyst put it this way:

> What is involved is the establishment and stabilization of a state of peace valid for all Europeans and secure within a framework in which they are relatively free to develop. Nothing but a ruling opening the way for equal possibilities of development for all European peoples and delimiting equal boundaries to their egoism holds forth the prospect of a peaceful coexistence not jeopardized by internal upheavals.[3]

The distinction between security and defense has led some analysts to call for two overlapping systems.[4] One would be the present system of military alliances which would continue to guarantee the inviolability of national boundaries and keep the price of using force at prohibitive levels. The other would be a security system, whose function would be to harmonize interests, resolve disputes, prevent and control crises, and provide the environment for orderly and mutually beneficial change.

In the search for a new security system for Europe there is no need for

---

[3] Eberhard Schulz, "Reflections on a European Peace Settlement," *The German Tribune Quarterly Review*, December 1969, p. 1, reprinted from *Europa-Archiv*, Number 17/1969.

[4] Such a distinction has been made by André Beaufre in "Security and Defense in Western Europe," *Orbis*, Spring 1969, pp. 76–86.

imminent structural changes, a *renversement des alliances,* or the sudden abolition of NATO and the Warsaw Pact, although an upheaval of this magnitude may be the ulterior motivation of some. There is, however, an undercurrent to modify national goals and fears, national habits and practices, the environment and relationships, so as gradually to reduce the role of these alliances and minimize the need for them. In this sense, because the alliances represent the commitment and interest of the two superpowers —one of which is also a European state—the search for a new security system does not mean the ejection of the superpowers. All of Europe's small states are likely to insist, especially, on a role for the United States as a counterweight to the Soviet Union.

The European Security Conference

Although the importance of the proposed European security conference, or pan-European security conference as it is sometimes referred to, is obscured by the fact that the Soviet Union and its East European allies have taken and maintained the initiative on this issue, it is nevertheless a significant element of the détente process in Europe. It must be understood as part of this process and not dismissed as another disruptive Soviet gambit, because the Europeans are using the conference idea as a vehicle for their own interests.

Having received the endorsement of Warsaw Pact meetings as far back as the Bucharest meeting of July 1966, and the somewhat more reluctant endorsement of NATO at its Twentieth Anniversary meeting in April 1969 in Washington, the proposal for a security conference has been placed on the European agenda and a feverish preparatory dialogue between individual European members of the two pacts has begun. East-West contacts have, in fact, increased substantially since the Soviet occupation of Czechoslovakia. This web of bilateral contacts being conducted under the guise of "preparatory work" has speeded up the process of change in European relationships. One might almost say that the "conference" has already begun.

The tendency of U.S. observers has been to place the idea of this Eastern initiative in the context of the Cold War rather than of the détente process and to judge it as such. Some have denounced the conference as a communist plot to create euphoria in Western Europe and bring about the dissolution of NATO and the withdrawal of the United States. The official U.S. line appears to be to downgrade both the threat and the importance of the proposed talks on the ground that they are of interest only as a device to give East European countries greater freedom of contact with the West. In any case, Washington believes that the West Europeans are not greatly interested in such negotiations.

Because the United States has taken the idea of "conference" too literally, it has been U.S. policy in NATO to approach any talks with the utmost caution and only on the basis of a list of specific topics that are "negotiable."

This position is quite understandable. If a real sit-down conference were to convene without an agenda of issues that are negotiable and likely to result in agreement, there would be several possible dangers. First, euphoria might result from a great show of meaningless good will by the Soviet Union, something we suspect the Kremlin of being able to turn on and off at will. Another danger is that unreasonably high West European expectations would be dashed by Soviet belligerence, possibly resulting in a temptation to make unilateral concessions so as to restore Soviet friendliness. Third, an unstructured conference might turn into a free-for-all of recriminations and threats which would adversely affect superpower relationships and the SALT talks.

A further important reason why the United States prefers carefully structured talks is that the preparations would lead to a unified position by NATO. It is assumed that members of the Eastern bloc would put up a unified front and, therefore, a disorganized West could be in danger of being split. However, it is precisely because of this U.S. predilection to make the talks a bloc-to-bloc discussion that West Europeans are lukewarm about a sit-down conference. They prefer the flexible and selective approach that they have been pursuing with good results in the preparatory phase. Besides, many European leaders, including Chancellor Willy Brandt, believe NATO is not equipped to negotiate European détente, because talks between the pacts are merely alternate forms of negotiation between the superpowers. Brandt has an additional reason to oppose a sit-down conference at this time: the GDR would sit as an equal sovereign state alongside the FRG.

It is natural and reasonable to assume that the Soviet Union would try to control the actions of its allies at a conference. Whether it would be successful is open to debate. East Europeans have shown enough independence in action and motives for one to expect some divergence from the Moscow line. (One must always remember, however, that many East European security interests are identical to those of Moscow.) Given their incentive to retain some freedom of action in European security talks, they may refrain from insisting on a sit-down conference unless the preparatory activity fails to show progress. In any case, this explains why the East Europeans have always insisted on a conference of all European states rather than one between the two alliances.

It is both difficult and risky to postulate Soviet intentions. One can proceed from the worst assumption that the Soviet aim behind the security talks is to disrupt NATO and cause the United States to withdraw from Europe, leaving the field to the Kremlin. Such an assumption alone does not make the conference a threat to Western security, and it is by no means clear that all West Europeans would share the American interpretation. The conference is part of the détente process and not merely another grand design or package deal for gaining unilateral advantages in Europe. There is, of course, a remote danger that the Soviet Union could end up with a peaceful "conquest" of all of Europe, something it was unable to achieve under Stalin. Such a risk does not appear great enough so far, however, to have frightened either East or West Europeans, for whom such a "conquest" would be equally catastrophic.

It is intriguing and in a sense enticing to Europeans that the Soviet Union should be pursuing the European détente option, with all its implications, at a time when it has just gone through a traumatic crisis testing bloc cohesion. The thesis that the détente initiative is designed to cover up the memory of the Soviet invasion and continued occupation of Czechoslovakia is not convincing, because the Soviets must be as aware as other Europeans are of the uncertainties en route to détente. By engaging in the SALT talks and in bilateral talks with Bonn as well, the Soviets are showing an interest in détente and the process of European transformation. The question is whether they can control the process so as to gain unilateral advantage.

Implications

What do we gain by looking at the changing European scene as outlined in this article? For one thing, we can decide whether there is détente in Europe, not on the basis of the presence or absence of tension, but on the basis of whether a process of change is under way. For Europeans détente is not a comfortable state of inaction, but an often baffling and sometimes risky pursuit of various interests. Former French Premier Michel Debré epitomized this when he told the French Parliament, after the Soviet invasion of Czechoslovakia, that France would continue to press for détente. Just because there has been a major accident on the road, he said, did not mean that one should no longer use that road, especially if it remained the only road Europeans found worth traveling.

Perhaps the most important implication of the analysis here is that détente is aimed at a gradual transformation of the European political landscape. We should, therefore, expect further changes in outlook and relationships. To a great extent, it is again Europe's hour, made possible by our own efforts to make Western Europe safe from aggression and all of Europe safe from war. The process of détente is the European parallel to our own search for a stable modus vivendi with the Soviet Union.

Risks abound in any such process, especially one which has burst out from under the pressure built up by twenty years of East-West hostility and intrabloc conformity. The Europeans are not unaware of these risks, although they may look at them quite differently. For Americans, the greatest risk is to misinterpret these events and their meaning, and thus be out of tune with our allies as well as our own long-range interests. Conceivably, we could bring the process to a halt, but only at the risk of prohibitive damage to our relationships with our own allies, the bloc countries and the Soviet Union. A return to the Cold War in order to have a dormant Europe would be absurd.

The chief source of our apprehension seems to be the fact that the Soviet

Union is playing the détente game in Europe, even while hanging on to its hegemonic hold over Eastern Europe. There is in this asymmetry a danger of greater "dissolution" in the West than in the East. The American dilemma necessarily follows from the dual role of the Soviet Union as superpower and as European state. Are the Soviets opting for a looser Europe, or is this a predictable consequence of which they are not aware? Or, have the Soviets a different design for exploiting European détente of which neither we nor our West European allies are aware?

The one danger that does not appear to be acute is that we will be excluded against our wishes from participation in the process. Europeans, both East and West, continue to need the U.S. presence and defense guarantee, and it should not be impossible to find a U.S. role commensurate with our interests, Europe's needs, and the changing environment. This is the challenge of European détente for us in the next decade.

One way the United States can and must fulfill its role is to continue to maintain NATO as a "contingent defense system" for the protection of Western Europe and the maintenance of peace on the continent. We and NATO are committed to defending a large portion of Europe. What is this commitment worth if it does not cover our allies in the pursuit of interests they consider vital to their present and future security? Because of the changing environment, which includes a weakening bond of fear, NATO and the NATO concept might have to be modified. We must therefore work closely with our allies to adapt NATO for an equally effective but less costly and less constraining fulfillment of its defense function. We must ignore those pessimists who predict that the process of détente is merely a communist scheme to eject the United States from Europe and dissolve NATO. We cannot let all-European security mean Western insecurity. If Americans understand the process of détente in Europe and learn to participate in it, we might even find a way to reduce our own burden of European defense and thus ensure that we can carry this burden a great deal longer.

34

EASTERN EUROPE: THE UNSTABLE ELEMENT IN THE SOVIET EMPIRE

Robert F. Byrnes[*]

There is a finality, for better or worse, about what has happened in Eastern Europe.

If things go on as they are today, there will simply have to be some sort of an adjustment on the part of the peoples of Eastern Europe, even if it is one that takes the form of general despair, apathy, demoralization, and the deepest sort of disillusion with the West. The failure of recent popular uprisings to shake the Soviet military domination has now produced a bitter and dangerous despondency throughout large parts of Eastern Europe. If the taste or even the hope of independence dies out in the hearts of these peoples, then there will be no recovering it; then Moscow's victory will be complete.

These two statements were made by Ambassador George Kennan, one of our most perceptive analysts of Soviet politics and foreign policy. The first appeared in the spring of 1956, three months before the Poznan riots and six months before the revolt in Hungary. The other was made only two years later, ten years before the Soviet armed forces intervened in Czechoslovakia to crush the hopes there for "socialism with a human face." Thus even a perceptive analyst demonstrates a lack of understanding of and confidence in the peoples of Eastern Europe, their national response to foreign rule, and the immense challenge which their faith and Western intellectual and economic strengths combined pose for the Soviet Union.

Eastern Europe remains a part of Europe and therefore the very heart of the struggle between the Soviet Union and the United States. The thesis which Walter Lippmann emphasized in 1947 is still valid: the main problem is "whether, when, and under what conditions the Red Army can be prevailed upon to evacuate Europe," because the balance of power and peace can be achieved only with withdrawal. Soviet control of most of Eastern Europe has given it forward military bases and possession of the traditional invasion routes into Europe, especially across the northern plains. The

[*] Robert F. Byrnes, "Eastern Europe: The Unstable Element in the Soviet Empire," *Memorandum,* Prepared at the Request of Senate Subcommittee on National Security and International Operations of the Committee on Government Operations, September 8, 1970.

Soviet position constitutes a threat to the security of Western Europe, in fact a kind of pistol held at the head of the West. The peoples and resources of the area behind the Berlin Wall constitute an important increment to Soviet economic and military power. At the same time, the Soviet position gives the Soviet Union a veto not only over the unification of Germany but also over the unification or reconstruction of Europe as a whole. It also constitutes a permanent threat to the NATO system because Soviet control over Eastern Germany maintains the fear of another Russian-German alliance and therefore provides opportunities for Soviet diplomacy. By dividing Europe and perpetuating fear and tension, it therefore enables the Soviet Union to restrict the role which the European states can play in world politics.

The high position which Europe, including Eastern Europe, occupies in Soviet foreign policy is reflected in the constant efforts to undermine and destroy NATO and to acquire legitimacy for the Soviet position in Eastern Europe. Soviet expansion in the Middle East is in good part an effort to stage an end run (in Leninist terminology, one step backward in order to take two steps forward) around NATO, to strike at Europe by depriving it of access to 90 percent of its oil, and to undermine Greece, Turkey, Rumania, Yugoslavia, and Italy, and the Western position in the Mediterranean.

The Surface View of Soviet Authority

Soviet control over Bulgaria, Czechoslovakia, East Germany, Hungary, and Poland appears tighter and firmer than ever before, and the relative independence of Rumania is severely hedged by its geographical position. The force and skill with which Soviet-led ground forces crushed Czechoslovakia in August 1968 demonstrated to the Czechs, the Slovaks, and all those living under Soviet domination that the Soviet Union is powerful and resolute and that it would not tolerate significant modification of the Communist monopoly in these countries. Moreover, the crushing of Czechoslovak socialist humanism was accomplished at remarkably low cost. The Czechs and Slovaks received no support from friends and neighbors; in fact, their "allies" in the Warsaw Pact, except for Rumania, participated in the invasion. The diplomatic skill with which the Soviets handled the post-invasion situation was also exceptional. Neither the United States, its Western European allies, nor the United Nations provided effective criticism, and the cause of Czechoslovakia disappeared far more quickly from the international scene than did that of Hungary in 1956, or even that of Tibet. Even the losses within the international Communist movement were cleverly restricted. Moreover, the political skill with which the Soviet rulers have brought about change in the Czechoslovak political system since August 1968 has been most impressive. They have eliminated Dubcek, Smrkovski, Cernik, and their chief supporters and replaced them with

Soviet puppets with no outward manifestation of disaffection at any stage within Czechoslovakia or, indeed, anywhere in the world.

At the same time, the United States has taken no diplomatic or other action and seems to concentrate its diplomatic energies upon finding honorable and quick endings to crises caused in good part by Soviet aggressive actions, the war in Southeast Asia and the conflict in the Middle East, and on reaching an agreement in the SALT talks. As the Soviet outward thrust has created tensions in other parts of the world, and as weapons technology has proceeded through several revolutions, Eastern Europe has declined precipitously in the American public's system of priorities. Many Americans, like Ambassador Kennan, believe that Soviet authority and determination are so immense, the weaknesses of each of the peoples and states so manifest, and the disinterest and powerlessness of other governments so evident that those peoples now dominated by the Soviet Union are doomed to remain forever condemned to that situation. Others are still tempted by doctrines such as disengagement, or the belief that tensions in central Europe will decline if American and Soviet forces can only be withdrawn or reduced. Moreover, the United States, still the center of resistance to Soviet expansion, is swept by disillusion, weariness, a revival of isolationism, another wave of hedonism, and a kind of one-sided intellectual disarmament which clearly reduce our influence in world politics and which must affect the Soviet view of Soviet prospects. In fact, we often resemble Great Britain or France in the 1930's. In addition, most Americans, for understandable reasons, are increasingly preoccupied with domestic social problems, at the same time that many of our intellectuals and opinionmakers concentrate upon debunking American policy since the end of World War II.

Our allies in Europe, after the Soviet invasion of Czechoslovakia briefly interrupted some of their activities, also resumed their relationships with the Soviet Union and its East European allies. In fact, the West German government, with the full understanding and support of its allies, on August 12 signed a non-aggression agreement in Moscow which recognizes the inviolability of the present boundaries of Europe, which means apparent acceptance of the Soviet position in that critical area and may lead to some kind of status or recognition for East Germany. . . .

Western acceptance of Soviet hegemony and even perhaps of the German Democratic Republic helps explain the Soviet drive for a détente. The Soviets will also seek to soften and divide the West; to take advantage of the current American disarray and irresolution to ease the United States out of Europe; to destroy NATO; to paralyze West European efforts toward some kind of unity; to obtain trade and credits for itself and for the equally stagnant economies of Eastern Europe; and to attain some kind of security on their Western borders at a time of prolonged tension with Communist China. Indeed, some worried Western observers share the illusions expressed by Ambassador Kennan that Soviet resolution and skill will end once and for all hope of independence or even of gradual progress for self-determination throughout Eastern Europe.

In fact, as the Soviet rulers no doubt realize, the policy of détente also raises problems and challenges. Indeed, I believe that Soviet policy represents a great gamble and that it exposes its Western borderlands to developments it will be unable to control. Basically, West German acceptance of the present boundaries of Eastern Europe represents no real change: no Western states hoped or intended to change those boundaries, and no treaty can guarantee their permanence, any more than the Congress of Vienna ensured the permanence of the status quo of Europe then. Moreover, the August 12 agreement, other West German treaties with the several states under Soviet hegemony, and a European security agreement will not only reduce Czech and Polish fear of West Germany, which has helped turn them toward the Soviet Union, but will also help create a climate of trust, cooperation, and peaceful rivalry by reducing somewhat the danger of war. Soviet controls lose their justification and some of their potency when fear is reduced, while those elements of our strength become ever more effective as peaceful relations are more widely accepted. In short, moving the competition into fields where our weapons are most effective will enable the Western states to use their economic, intellectual, and diplomatic tools with the different countries in such a way as to undermine the Soviet position.

The Basic Instability of Communist Eastern Europe

Eastern Europe is a seriously unstable area and one which will test Soviet resourcefulness, and that of all of us, throughout the next few years. It constitutes, first of all, the Achilles heel of an overextended empire, an area which has already given Soviet leaders several serious cases of indigestion and one which will become more troublesome and burdensome in the years ahead. Eastern Europe is not Central Asia, or Tibet, and the Soviet Union will not be able to absorb its peoples as easily as Russia did those of Central Asia just one hundred years ago. Moreover, Eastern Europe is subject to the same economic, social, and intellectual forces which are causing rapid change everywhere in the world.

The basic problem for the Soviet Union is simple: its military and political rule is threatened by powerful economic, social, and intellectual forces which are not susceptible to the kinds of controls which have proved effective in the Soviet Union (and which will remain effective within that country). First of all, nationalism is a rising phenomenon throughout Eastern Europe, as it is in most other parts of the world. It enabled Tito to unite his country and to survive against both intensive Soviet pressure and enticements after 1948. It helped the Albanian Communist rulers successfully to switch their allegiance from Moscow to Peking when they suspected their country might be sacrificed as part of an attempted rapprochement between Yugoslavia and the Soviet Union. It has united most Rumanians behind the

Rumanian Communist leaders in their effort to carve out an independent role in economic development and in foreign policy. The peasants kept it alive during the dreadful years under Stalin and his puppets, "rolling with the punch" as they had under other foreign regimes. Now, the affection for the national history and culture, and for the national interest, has been adopted by the workers, the middle class, the students, and the intelligentsia as well. In fact, one of the ironies of the last twenty years is that Communist success in transforming the economies of the East European states has created new classes of skilled workers and trained men and women who have rediscovered their national past and who now direct more of their animosity against the Russians for recent restrictions than against the Germans, who were the hated enemies for the first two decades after the war. The recent trade and aid agreement completed between Bonn and Warsaw, the successful talks between Moscow and Bonn concerning the mutual renunciation of force and other issues, and the forthcoming discussions and, presumably, agreements between West Germany and the other countries now dominated by the Soviet Union will clearly increase the relationships and reduce the fear of West Germany. In any case, West Germany and the West in general will seem less a menace as the agreements eliminate the causes of fear and as their benefits become ever more evident. At the same time, of course, the Communists in countries now dominated by the Soviet Union will be increasingly attracted by national communism, as the Yugoslav, Chinese, Cuban, and other forms of communism continue to compete effectively as independent centers with the original Muscovite throne of the international movement.

The economic problems which the rulers and their Soviet overlords face make the countries of Eastern Europe especially vulnerable to Western strengths. Indeed, the combination of growing nationalism and of the pressures for modernization and then liberalization constitute the core of the Soviet problem. Basically, the East Europeans at enormous effort, including the sacrifice of most civil liberties, have modernized their economies quite significantly, and made substantial progress in industrial production. However, they find that the command economy methods have "taken them as far as they can go," and that the West Europeans in the same two decades have moved into a new economic era, one which leaves East Europeans even further behind than before. This discovery and the clear slowing down of the Czechoslovak economy in the mid-1960's were at the root of the Czechoslovak problem. The necessary economic changes introduced led almost ineluctably to social, cultural, and political changes as well, all in the name of Communism and directed by Communists.

Moreover, the economic and social problems of Czechoslovakia are even more fundamental and challenging than they were before the invasion, which in fact worsened them. The Czechoslovak government still needs to decentralize the economy, to increase investment in industry and agriculture, to increase the economic rate of growth, to raise the standard of living, to improve incentives, and to increase the quality of the industrial product. Internal resources for these needs do not exist. The Soviet Union does not have the materials or the understanding to provide assistance; indeed, it is hampered by the same scientific and technical lag. At the same time, its intervention in August 1968 and the restrictions since imposed have prevented the Czechoslovaks from obtaining economic and intellectual sustenance abroad. Consequently, the stagnant Czechoslovak economy will stagger on, with a working class ever less disposed to obey the commands of its rulers and with an industrial base ever less competent to meet the demands of the last third of the twentieth century.

Perhaps the best illustration of the Czech dilemma is reflected in their discovery several years ago that Czechoslovak textile equipment was, on the average, more than 60 years old, at a time when the Germans, the English, the Indians, and most other peoples were using automatic equipment manufactured within the previous five or ten years. The Soviet government was both unwilling and unable to provide new equipment for this Czechoslovak industry. At the same time, it would not allow the Czechs to borrow abroad or to increase their trade abroad so that they might obtain this equipment. In short, the Czechs and the Slovaks are condemned to economic stagnation, at a time when a new wave of the industrial revolution is sweeping the West. On the other hand, if the Soviet government should allow the Czechoslovak government to sign an agreement such as that which the Polish government signed in June with West Germany, and if German (or French or British) machinery is introduced and helps revive a flagging Czechoslovak industry, with Western engineers in Czechoslovakia to install the machinery; Czechoslovak workers and engineers sent abroad to study; new management principles (and managers), incentives, and quality standards introduced to enable Czechoslovak industries to produce goods for sale abroad to pay for the imported machinery and the instruction—in short, if necessary changes from abroad are introduced into the economy of Czechoslovakia (or Poland, or Bulgaria), those changes will inevitably reverberate throughout many sectors of the economy and into intellectual and political life, creating a threat similar to that raised by the "New Course" in the mid-'50's or by the Czechoslovak "spring." The Russians in turning to the West for technological and scientific aid for the flagging economies of Czechoslovakia or Poland are thus courting serious dangers. In contemporary terms, the Soviet Union in Eastern Europe is a closed system facing a modernization crisis of especial severity because it is compounded by imperial problems. The Russians are facing the hazard which de Tocqueville foresaw for any autocratic government which sought popularity or greater productivity. In an old Russian phrase, they seek a fire which will not burn.

Moreover, this new fire may not succeed in warming up the stagnant economies of these countries, but may only stimulate appetites and intensify problems. From 60 to 75 percent of their foreign trade is committed to the Soviet Union by long-term agreements, so they have little freedom of action. The arrangements which the Soviet Union has established constitute a form of imperialism which further cripples the Poles, the Hungarians, and others in trade with the West: generally, the East European states are obliged to ship their finest industrial products to Moscow, receiving in return various raw materials, such as oil, gas, and iron ore. In addition, the quality of the goods produced in Eastern Europe is generally far below the level sought by Western consumers, and East Europeans lack the marketing skills international trade requires. In short, prospects for greatly increased trade between Eastern and Western Europe are dim. Increased Western aid is also unlikely, for economic as well as political reasons.

An intellectual and philosophical vacuum also creates a dangerously unstable system in Eastern Europe for the Soviet Union. Briefly, Marxism-Leninism is considered less and less relevant even by Communist leaders in those countries. This is due in part to the changes in doctrine introduced since 1956; in part to the visible breakup of the solidarity of the international Communist movement and the development of various forms of Communism; in part to the rapid changes within these societies; in part to the revived interest in traditional beliefs, including religion; and in part to the irrelevance of Marxism-Leninism to help resolve the problems these states now face. As one high planner remarked, Marx was the world's greatest philosopher and Lenin the world's greatest man, but the issues which we face, such as those requiring increasing numbers of computers and automatic machinery, were not foreseen by these great men, one of whom died almost 90 years ago, and the other almost 50 years ago. In short, he said, we turn not to Marx and Lenin to resolve our economic problems, but to the Harvard Business School and to Western technology, which do provide some answers.

Above all, Eastern Europe is unstable because of the remarkable recovery and the growing vitality of the neighboring states in Western Europe, which reflect extraordinary vigor and which have an enormous impact in Eastern Europe, as they do elsewhere in the world. At a time when there is a silence in Russian culture, as Sir Isaiah Berlin pointed out, Western ideas and ideals and cultural influences of all kinds are overwhelming Eastern Europe and having significant impact in the Soviet Union as well. Movies, music, fashions, novels, economic theory, social relations between generations, and all of the qualitative achievements of Western science and technology are thoroughly known, respected, and envied throughout Eastern Europe. In fact, Western Europe is a magnet for the East, as it was before the First World War, and the sunflower turns to the West now rather than to Moscow. The vision Stalin had twenty years ago, one in which the economic transformation from Warsaw to Sofia would so impress the peoples of the West that the Soviet-East European magnet would draw Western Europe and then the rest of the world into the Communist system, has turned into a Soviet nightmare, because the electrifying progress has occurred in the West. Indeed, Moscow must on occasion see Eastern Europe as a carrier of Western infections, rather than a barrier or "cordon Stalinaire."

Unfortunately, from the Soviet point of view, Eastern Europe cannot be isolated from Western Europe and the rest of the world as it was during Stalin's time, and the prospects for increased external influence grow. In fact, Soviet efforts for a détente, as reflected in the agreement with West Germany, in Soviet proposals for a European security conference, and in agreements such as that for West German trade and aid with Poland will certainly increase Western influence throughout Eastern Europe. The impact of this flood is already obvious among those whom the Communist regimes have most favored, the workers, the students, and the intellectuals, who brought about the revolts in 1953 and 1956 and the move for "socialism with a human face" in Czechoslovakia. In fact, there is considerable evidence that the very highest levels of Communist parties in these countries have been deeply affected. Louis XIV's comment that nations meet only at the top does not apply in an age of mass culture, international travel and study, and revolution in communications, but nations still meet *first* at the top and foreign influences are absorbed first by today's political leaders as they were among earlier aristocrats.

In some ways, the Soviet dilemma in Eastern Europe is like that which the regimes of Alexander I and Nicholas I faced in the empire 150 years ago, except that the Soviet Union is even more deeply involved in European state politics and even more influenced by European ideas and economic vitality than was the other old regime. The Decembrists and the Polish revolt in 1830–1831 alarmed the early tsars just as the Budapest and Prague revolts have frightened their successors.

The question is, therefore: Can Soviet military and police power control these economic, social, and intellectual forces, or will these forces produce changes like those which undid the work of the Congress of Vienna 150 years ago? Will these forces lead to situations such as 1956 and 1968, but next time in several countries simultaneously and with more skilled leadership and even greater popular support? Will the intellectual and economic and social pressures produce a general softening, withering away, or nibbling at the power of those supported by the Soviet Union, a development which will not present a clear target for the Soviet leaders but one causing a slow and gradual erosion of will not unlike that which has afflicted other societies at other times? What will be the impact of such developments within the Soviet Union?

We should recognize this basic instability and be prepared to assist in the flowering of these developments in such a way as to aid these peoples towards self-determination and independence without causing another Soviet avalanche.

Our Strengths and Our Diplomacy

The economic and military strength of the United States alone is so vast that Americans do not understand its significance in world politics, while our power when added to that of our allies almost staggers the imagination. However, our greatest strength is almost invisible, because it is the social vitality, the effervescent intellectual vigor, and the freedom and openness in which we live and face our serious problems. This strength is contagious and compelling and represents the greatest force at our disposal.

Western Europe, most of which is allied with the United States and with which we share values, has the same kinds of resources. Its economic, political, and spiritual recovery would be considered miraculous by any Rip Van Winkle who returned for the first time since 1945. The vigor and vitality it demonstrates in every aspect of life proves that its brief period of decline is over, as is Japan's, and that it will soon assume a central role again in world affairs. The progress its states have made since 1950 towards some form of federal or other union has been remarkable. Moreover, the existence of several possibilities for union and the open-endedness of the various plans both constitute advantages in the 1970's, when some or all of the states of Eastern Europe, including the Soviet Union, may become associated. The role which the Federal Republic of Germany plays in Western Europe represents another great strength. The Soviet Union has legitimized the West German role by recognizing Western Germany in 1955 (when it was headed by a Christian Democrat, Adenauer) and in dealing with it for fifteen years, and then signing another significant agreement with a Soviet Democrat, Brandt.

A fourth strength of the United States and its European allies is their pragmatism and their leading role in introducing revolutionary scientific, technical, philosophical, and social concepts into political and international life. The Western states are equipped for change, lead in it, respect it, assume it. They are in fact helping to create a series of revolutionary changes as significant as those of the Renaissance and Reformation, but which are condensed into a shorter period of time, produce more elemental transformations within every society they touch, and are universal in their scope. In short, the West is riding, if not driving, a complex of revolutionary changes which recognize no frontiers. The Western states therefore possess a tremendous advantage over the Soviet Union, a most conservative society bothered by heresies which it cannot master and fearful of change throughout its empire.

We benefit also from our record in our dealings towards the Soviet Union and Eastern Europe. Our aid without strings to a threatened Yugoslavia;

our position on the national Communism of Rumania; the help we have given even to East Germany in times of food shortages; our determined avoidance of threats, as in the various crises over Berlin, and of needless killing, when planes stray over our territory; our proposals for building bridges and for peaceful engagement; and our performance in cultural exchanges and economic arrangements have won respect and friendship among the peoples of Eastern Europe, disarmed those who would make us responsible for tension, and now strengthen our cause with the governments and peoples of Europe east of Germany and Italy.

Finally, in the competition which lies ahead, economic, social, and political forces, which are among our greatest strengths, will play an increasingly important role in world politics in a situation in which those who work best in times of peace can act most effectively.

All of our strengths can be used effectively though only if we have confidence in ourselves and in the peoples of Eastern Europe, of whom we tend to know little and whom we often disparage. We must, first of all, maintain and increase when necessary our economic and military power. We should maintain our alliances, particularly NATO. We must continue to demonstrate resolution and perseverance in our relations with the Soviet Union, and we should under no circumstances allow anyone to doubt our strength and our resolution.

The central position in our foreign policy should remain the peaceful reconstruction of Europe, accomplished without alarming the Soviet Union but providing the states and peoples of Eastern Europe the independence and right to self-determination which they, like others, deserve and seek. No one should be misled by the waves of superficial conciliation released on occasion by Moscow, because Soviet military power continues to grow and the basic philosophical, political, and economic conflicts remain. Europe constitutes the center of the stage, and the principal problem for our diplomacy still consists of freeing the states and peoples of Eastern Europe from the Soviet armed forces.

In the immediate future, the principal goal for the United States and its allies should be ensuring the safety and security of West Berlin as an integral part of West Germany, which should have unhindered access. The euphoria produced by the August 12 agreement and the apparent progress on SALT should not divert our attention from that critical city, which was not a part of the Moscow agreement, for significant legal reasons. He who doubts the need for alert resolution with regard to West Berlin should ask himself: whatever became of East Berlin?

Our diplomacy should also continue to concentrate upon obtaining agreement on a monitored withdrawal of Russian and American troops from Europe. In particular, we should delay a European security conference until agreement has been reached on that issue because the kind of conference envisaged by the Soviets would only create a vague idea of détente and erode NATO.

I know of no dramatic step which we can take toward our long-term goals. In fact, while a new concept to replace those of containment, liberation, peaceful coexistence, and building bridges might be useful, we should seek to avoid dramatic steps or crises, which would increase the instability of Eastern Europe and alarm the Soviet peoples and their leaders, both extremely sensitive to their hard-won position on their Western borders. We should press for reconciliation and promote the new forces bringing change. We should also reiterate our continuing national interest in the application of self-determination to Eastern Europe and in the reconstruction of a peaceful Europe, accomplished with the support of the Soviet Union, which would benefit from the end of an unstable and dangerous situation.

The progress of Western Europe towards some kind of economic and political union has been painfully slow, until we remember the hatreds and disunities which helped bring on World War II and which were intensified by that war. So many concepts of the new Europe abound—the Atlantic Community, *Europe des patries,* Europe from the Atlantic to the Urals, Europe "within its historic boundaries," and Europe from San Francisco to Vladivostok—that no one can be certain which in the long run will be most compelling, but American diplomats should join in pressing for federal institutions which will bring Europe together in peace and at the same time satisfy the national interests of the United States and of the U.S.S.R.

. . . .

In the 19th century, the so-called Eastern question constituted one of the most critical diplomatic issues. The situation of the states of Eastern Europe today in many ways resembles that of the Balkan peoples under Ottoman rule. The Greeks, the Serbs, the Bulgars, and the other Balkan peoples obtained their independence after long and hard struggles, in which outside assistance played an important role. We should view the situation in Eastern Europe as a similarly long, tortuous, and involved struggle, one in which resolution, determination, and imagination are likely to prove as important as military power. These qualities have always been decisive. No one appreciates this more than the East Europeans. We should also.

⚕14⚕

Asian Affairs and the
Nixon Doctrine

FOR MORE than a quarter-century after World War II the United States, while maintaining close ties with an economically preoccupied Japan and pursuing a policy of bitter opposition to mainland China, intervened militarily in the rimlands of continental Asia. The consequent expenditure of both American blood and treasure, especially by the time of Vietnam, led to a serious erosion of public support and to the Nixon Doctrine.

Like any statement of a policy promising a transition to a less costly approach to maintaining U.S. security in Asia, the Nixon Doctrine was admittedly ambiguous. Coupled in 1971 with the announcement of President Nixon's visit to Peking (which took place in February, 1972), it aroused intense speculation.

In the first selection, "Conversation with the Chinese Premier in Peking," James Reston, the noted columnist of *The New York Times*, foreshadows the general approach of Premier Chou En-lai to the then forthcoming talks. Reston's transcript has the merit of indicating the substance of the Chinese approach to Nixon on many issues on which the official reports remain silent or vague.

The second selection, "The U.S.-Chinese Communiqué" at the end of the Nixon visit, is particularly interesting for the method used to record views. Where the two sides remained opposed in viewpoint, the policy of each was stated separately, thus avoiding bland clichés which paper over differences. China's concern over Japan's possible remilitarization is clearly apparent in both the first and second selections.

In the face of Nixon's visit to Peking, Moscow quite literally found it impossible to say nothing. In the third selection, "Radio Moscow Speaks to China," four Soviet broadcasts during March, 1972 (the month following Nixon's visit) are given. Each comments on the communiqué, each is addressed to the Chinese people in the Mandarin language. What makes the Soviet comments to China even more interesting is the silence of Radio Peking. In the same period Peking had nothing substantive or explanatory to say about the communiqué or the Soviet charges at all.

Not only is the Soviet Union highly interested in the changing Sino-Soviet relations, but so is Japan. In the fourth selection, "Japan: 'Same Bed, Different Dreams,'" T. C. Rhee, Professor of History at the University of Dayton, gives a provocative report on contemporary Japan. Just as Russia is reassessing her policies in the light of the changing American approach, so, too, is Japan. In Japan, now awakening from intensive self-preoccupation, issues long suspended are being reexamined. Which choices Japan will make cannot be judged, but Rhee indicates accurately the nature of the alternatives before her. Whether Rhee is overstating the new Japanese nationalist spirit or not, it is certain that Japan is confronting difficult choices. At the end of September, 1972, she made one: to reestablish diplomatic relations with Peking at the cost of her relations with Taiwan.

35

CONVERSATION WITH THE CHINESE PREMIER IN PEKING

James Reston*

Mr. Reston: I believe very frankly that we've come to an unusual moment in the history of the world that neither in your life nor in mine will we see again. In my own country there are great changes taking place, philosophical and political. In Europe we are seeing a transformation, with the British coming into the Common Market. In the Middle East we see more evidence, I think, that force does not prevail for anybody. The only place where force seems to have prevailed is for Russia in Czechoslovakia. And therefore what I've come here to do is to find out, during this long period when China had not been actively participating in these affairs of the U.N. and elsewhere, how you see the world of this great transformation? Do you really believe that the United States is ready for change, as I do, or do you feel that we are engaged again in maneuvers and manipulations for imperialist purposes, as you seem to be saying in your press?

Mr. Chou: We admit we also are seeing some changes. As you said to our friends, you are also seeing changes taking place in China. But there is one question and that is we will not barter away principles. And so once this question is raised, there is bound to be a dispute.

As for Taiwan, who occupied Taiwan? And so if you want to have a change, then you should act according to a Chinese saying, that is, it is for the doer to undo the knot.

The latest discussions between Japan and Taiwan were obviously designed to create an obstacle so that it would not be possible for us to get into the U.N. After [U.S. Secretary of State] Rogers's statement, the Japanese Acting Foreign Minister, Kimura, and the Secretary General of the ruling Japanese Liberal-Democratic party, Hori Shigeru, made similar statements.

Both Kimura and Hori Shigeru said that this basic policy of the United States was determined after many consultations between the United States and Japan. And Japan's demand was put forward after two secret talks held between the Chiang representative and Sato in the latter part of July and on Aug. 1.

And so the statement made by the so-called Foreign Ministry of Chiang

* James Reston, "Conversation With the Chinese Premier in Peking, *The New York Times,* August 10, 1971, pp. 14–15. © 1971 by The New York Times Company. Reprinted by permission.

Kai-shek did not touch on Rogers's statement at all but concentrated on attacking the Albanian resolution [to seat Communist China in Taiwan's UN seat].

Japan has ambitious designs with regard to Taiwan. Japan wants to control Taiwan in her hands. So it's not a simple matter that Japan is supporting Taiwan in the United Nations.

In fact, we can even go on further from there. That is, not only will there be a question of two Chinas or one China, one Taiwan—it's even conceivable that they are trying to separate Taiwan from China and, under the direction of Japan and also possibly with support from some quarters in the United States, to bring about a so-called independent Taiwan.

And because of this, we cannot but make our attitude very clear. We have stated very clearly that should a state of two Chinas or one China, one Taiwan appear in the U.N., or a similar absurd state of affairs take place in the U.N. designed to separate Taiwan from China to create a so-called independent Taiwan, we will firmly oppose it and under those circumstances we will absolutely not go into the U.N.

It is indeed true that the world is undergoing changes. But these changes must not cause further damage to the Chinese people. Over the past 20 years and more, it's not we who have caused harm to others, but the U.S. Government who have been causing harm to other countries and other peoples. We have waited already for more than 20 years and we can wait for another year. That doesn't matter. But there must be a just solution.

Mr. Reston: May I ask whether, in the event that your present position proves to be too pessimistic and the General Assembly and the Security Council without any veto by the United States decide to seat China, will you at this meeting of the Security Council go to New York yourself and represent China at this meeting of the General Assembly?

Mr. Chou: Will Chiang Kai-shek still be there or not?

Mr. Reston: No, on the assumption that he is not.

Mr. Chou: He has left?

Mr. Reston: Yes.

Mr. Chou: Only if he has really left can I express an attitude, and Taiwan must be a part of China. But if in the U.N. resolution there is anything to the effect that the status of Taiwan remains to be determined, then we will not go in.

Mr. Reston: I understand that. But I am assuming by my question that the Albanian resolution will have been put up and voted to your satisfaction in the General Assembly, and that you will go on and be voted into the Security Council, at which time Taiwan will be expelled, and my question is: Would you at that time personally go to New York?

Mr. Chou: But I was asking the question that would they still consider the status of Taiwan undetermined and the status of Taiwan an outstanding question? You cannot answer that question now, nor can I.

Mr. Reston: I don't see that that question would be a question for the

U.N. at all. At that time it's a question between you and the Taiwanese. As early as 1955 I believe that you said that this was an internal question and it should be settled between the Government of the People's Republic and the local authorities, I believe you called them at that time, on Taiwan. Is it still your view, that it should be settled in that way? And second, is there anything to Edgar Snow's remark that he believes there already has been contact between the People's Republic and officials on Taiwan?

Mr. Chou: I've said on many occasions that the liberation of Taiwan is China's internal affair which brooks no foreign interference. That is still our position now. At the same time, I've said that the United States has committed aggression against and occupied China's Taiwan Province and the Taiwan Strait, so we are willing to sit down and enter into negotiations with the U.S. Government for a settlement of this question.

This has been going on for 16 years, first in Geneva and then in Warsaw. And what is more, I've said that the Chinese people are friendly to the American people, the two peoples have been friendly with each other in the past, and in the future they should all the more live together in friendship, because the Chinese people have now stood up.

That was said far back in 1955 at the Bandung conference. Afterwards, we tried to accept the visit of some American correspondents to China, but John Foster Dulles's State Department did not approve of that. And so, since the way was blocked by the U.S. Government, then we on our side would no longer want any such contacts. We have thus been cut off for more than 20 years, but it doesn't matter.

But now since there are some changes in the world, then we should see to it no damage is done to anyone, that concern should be shown to the wronged party and the wronged party should not continue to be wronged. Therefore, the question of Taiwan is not merely an internal question. If it were merely an internal matter, then we will be able to settle it ourselves. The solution of this internal problem has been obstructed now for already 21 years, and so changes are taking place. And in this process some country has started to harbor ambitions. That is quite evident.

Mr. Reston: You mean by that Japan?

Mr. Chou: Yes.

Mr. Reston: May I ask you to state the principles again. You have been very clear about this in the past, you have told Snow, in '60 I believe. Principle one was nothing between us on Taiwan shall be settled by force or the threat of force. Principle two, there is only one China. Now are these the two and only two principles to be settled? What about withdrawal of forces, what about the question of the treaty between Washington and Taipei?

Mr. Chou: When you say us, you mean China and the United States?

Mr. Reston: Yes, the United States and China.

Mr. Chou: If Taiwan is to be returned to the motherland, the U.S. forces must withdraw, because otherwise how can it be returned to the mother-land? And since the United States is to withdraw all their troops and military installations from Taiwan and the Taiwan Strait area, then as a matter of course the so-called U.S.-Chiang mutual defense treaty, which we had all along considered to be illegal, would become invalid.

Mr. Reston: I understand. It is clear, I think, since the differences over Rogers's statement, that there is a lot of underbrush to be cleared away before you and the President are to meet. I wondered what ideas you have about whether preliminary technical talks at a lower level should take place and where, between now and the President's arrival?

Mr. Chou: It is possible. But if these questions are to be solved, they can only be solved when the President himself comes. He expressed a desire to come and we have invited him to come.

Mr. Reston: Could I ask one final question about the U.N. and China? In your mind, is there a conflict between the basic principle of the U.N., namely, that all disputes between nations shall be resolved without the use of force or the threat of force, and the principle of revolution and support for national liberation movements in the world as espoused by your Government in the past? Is there a conflict between these two things?

Mr. Chou: No. Who has committed aggression against other countries? China hasn't. Over the 22 years of the history of our People's Republic, we only went abroad to assist Korea, but that was under certain conditions. We made it very clear to the so-called U.N. Command composed of 16 countries led by the U.S. We said to them that if they press toward the Yalu River, then we will not sit idly by, although at that time our Taiwan and Taiwan Strait area had already been occupied by the U.S. Seventh Fleet and the U.S. Air Force. It was the U.S. which first committed aggression against China, and not vice versa. It was only after the U.S. forces had reached the Yalu River that we sent our C.P.V. [Chinese People's Volunteers] to resist American aggression and aid Korea.

As for our help to other countries of the world, that is in the case when they are subjected to aggression. And in the view of the U.N. itself, aggression is wrong and should be stopped. So we are merely helping them to resist aggression. And in the view of the U.N. itself, they should be given support. And a striking instance is Vietnam.

As for Vietnam, we will continue to give them assistance to the end, until the complete withdrawal of the U.S. forces. At present the most urgent question is still Vietnam. You wondered very much why I said to the Committee of Concerned Asian Scholars that it was our position that first of all the question of Vietnam and Indochina should be solved, and not the question of Taiwan or other questions.

Because the status quo of Taiwan has remained for 21 years. There is no war there. That is because of restraint on our part. But this is not the case with Vietnam. Not only did the U.S. send troops to commit aggression there, but the U.S. is expanding the war there. When President Nixon took office, he started withdrawing troops from Vietnam, that is anyhow changing the former situation. But in March last year, the peaceful rule of Samdech Norodom Sihanouk in Cambodia was subverted, and then the U.S. troops went in. Even your *New York Times* criticized that action.

Mr. Reston: Especially *The New York Times.*

Mr. Chou: And then this year there was the attack on Route 9. Isn't that an expansion of the war?

Mr. Reston: Yes, I think so.

Mr. Chou: And so that has brought even greater harm to the Vietnamese people and the Indochinese people as a whole. Such a small place as Indochina, with a small population. Yet such a huge sum has been spent. The American Government itself admitted that in 10 years' time it spent $120-billion and suffered such heavy casualties. And the American people are unhappy about the American casualties. We on our side feel they are needless casualties. But the Vietnamese people have suffered even greater casualties.

Mr. Reston: I agree.

Mr. Chou: Just take a look there and you can see that. Shouldn't we sympathize with them?

Mr. Reston: Absolutely. It's a tragedy.

Mr. Chou: So why shouldn't the United States. It's aggression?

Mr. Reston: Yes. Now what do you think we should do to stop it? I went straight there from Panmunjom in 1953, and I have been fighting against our involvement in that war ever since. As a matter of fact, when I went to Saigon in 1953 I saw the British brigadier who was the observer there at that time and I asked, was there any way in which the West can possibly deal with the Vietminh, as they were then called. And he said, yes, there may be one way: If you would give foreign aid, military program to the Vietminh, especially tanks, then you might be able to find them. That will be the only way, said he, the West will ever win a war in this part of the world.

Mr. Chou: You did some work, your *New York Times,* by making public some of the secret Pentagon papers.

Mr. Reston: Yes.

Mr. Chou: Indeed, back in the time of Truman, the U.S. Government started helping the French in their aggression and colonial war in Indochina. And after Dulles took over from Acheson, this further developed.

Mr. Reston: Are there some Peking papers on that period on the war that have not been published. If there are, then *The New York Times* would like to accommodate you and publish them.

Mr. Chou: We have no secret papers like that. But we did send some weapons to the Vietnamese people to help them in their resistance. The French Government is aware of that. Within less than half a year after the founding of our People's Republic, we recognized the DRVN [Democratic

Republic of Vietnam] headed by President Ho Chi Minh. Actually the French Government was prepared to recognize the P.R.C. [People's Republic of China], but because of that matter, France put off the recognition until the time of General de Gaulle. So if you are interested in secret documents, this is a document but not a secret one.

Mr. Reston: Yes. Your commentator the other day made it quite clear that your Government is opposed to the Geneva conference for a settlement of the Indochina war. Now, do you see the Laotian and the Cambodian questions being settled separately from the Vietnam question?

Mr. Chou: This is a matter within the sovereignty of the Government of the DRVN, of the provisional revolutionary government of the Republic of SVN [South Vietnam], of the royal government of national union of Cambodia and of the Laotian Patriotic Front. It is within their sovereignty to decide whether the Indochina question is to be settled together or separately.

Judging from the present situation, negotiations are going on now only on Vietnam. And so maybe the Vietnam question will be first solved. As for Cambodia, the U.S. refuses to recognize Prince Sihanouk's Government, and Prince Sihanouk has clearly stated his just position in his message No. 24 to his compatriots. I haven't heard anyone say anything more on that score. As for Laos, they are planning to discuss among themselves. And there is correspondence between Souvanna Phouma and Prince Souphanouvong, and the Laotian Patriotic Front has put forward a five-point proposal, one of which is cease-fire throughout Laos.

We support this five-point proposal of the Laotian Patriotic Front. As for the summit conference of the Indochinese peoples, the four sides of the three countries issued a joint statement in April last year and they put forward a common proposition. They demand all troops from countries outside of Indochina to completely withdraw and let the three peoples of Indochina solve their question by themselves. And we support this principle.

Mr. Reston: You are not interested in mediating this struggle between the U.S. and the North Vietnamese and Liberation Front?

Mr. Chou: We don't want to be a mediator in any way. And we were very badly taken in during the first Geneva conference. If you are interested, I can go into it now. If not, we can discuss it at the dinner table.

Mr. Reston: Yes, but I want to hear all about your confrontation with John Foster Dulles at dinner. You know, nothing has surprised me quite so much since coming here as the vehemence of your feeling about Japan.

Mr. Chou: You too were victims of Japanese militarism. But you said the Americans are more forgetful. But I know you still recall the Pearl Harbor incident.

Mr. Reston: Yes, but this is one of—in my view—the endearing qualities of the American people: They have no memory. They have every reason to be aggrieved, if not full of hatred, about Japan and about Germany. There is no hatred in our country toward Japan or Germany. And if there is one thing that has troubled me a bit since I have come here, it is a sense that, while you are, in your domestic policy, looking forward toward the 21st century, in your foreign policy I think you are looking backward to the old disputes. And that saddens me. Now am I being unfair to you? Because I don't want to be.

Mr. Chou: It is unfair. Because you didn't have any direct talk with us about our foreign policy, you just heard about some of our slogans.

Why is there such sentiment among the Americans? Because the U.S. benefited from both World Wars, and the U.S. losses were rather small. Why is it that the American people have a rather deep impression about the present U.S. war of aggression against Vietnam? Because they have really suffered. And so the American people demand the withdrawal of the American troops. It is not that the American people don't summarize their experience.

So I don't quite agree with your estimate that the American people are easily forgetful. Any nation is bound to summarize its own historical experience. Just yesterday I met a friend who had come from the U.S. some time ago, and he said that among the Americans there are now some changes toward the black people and that is a good thing. And it shows that many white people in the U.S. are becoming awakened to the fact that it is not right to continue the exploitation and oppression of the black people left over from history. So isn't that a summary of historical experience? And it is very good.

Mr. Reston: Yes.

Mr. Chou: We oppose the Japanese reactionaries. It is not that we have any hatred for the Japanese people. After the end of the Pacific war, we have not stopped our contacts with the Japanese people. New China has never imposed a blockade against them. The Japanese people have kept on visiting China, and we are also willing to go there.

The Japanese people are a diligent and brave people and a great nation. And it was the U.S. Government which after the war strengthened the Japanese reactionaries. And when they have developed to the present stage they are bound to develop militarism.

Just look at the economic development of Japan. According to your President, the steel output of Japan is about to catch up to that of the U.S., as he said in Kansas City on July 6. Why is it that Japan has developed so quickly? I've heard that you also admit that the reason was that not only was no indemnity exacted from Japan, but Japan was protected and provided with raw materials, markets, investments and technology.

And then there is another thing. That is, the U.S. has promoted the development of Japan toward militarism by the indefinite prolongation of the Japan-U.S. security treaty. The Japanese people are opposed to this treaty. And according to the report of the American congressmen who went to Japan to study the matter, Japan does not need such a huge defense budget for its fourth defense plan for the purpose of self-defense.

The budget for the fourth defense plan reached the amount of more than $16 billion. And Defense Secretary Laird himself admits that according to Japan's present economic strength and industrial and technical ability, she will not need five years (1972-1976) to complete that plan, and two to two and a half years will be sufficient.

In Japan, in South Korea and when he returned to Washington, Laird said that there were three pillars to the Nixon doctrine. The first is to arm your partners, and of these partners, the principal one will be Japan. The second is nuclear protection, and only thirdly is negotiation. And what is more, he made it clear that these negotiations have to proceed from a position of strength. And without the previous two pillars, there would not be the third.

Mr. Reston: Could I ask you, sir, what you want us to do about Japan? Because it seems to me there is a dilemma here. If we stay allied to Japan, with some control over her, particularly in the nuclear field, that is one thing. If we end the security pact with Japan, is it in your view that it is more likely then that Japan will become more militaristic or less militaristic?

It seems to me that, confronted by two nuclear powers in the Pacific, both China and the Soviet Union, and freed from us and our pact, she would almost certainly have to go nuclear, would she not? Therefore I find myself puzzled by your desire to see this pact with the U.S. broken.

Mr. Chou: That argument is quite a forced argument. Despite this treaty, Japan with her present industrial capabilities is fully able to produce all the means of delivery, she is able to manufacture ground-to-air, ground-to-ground missiles and sea-to-ground missiles. As for bombers, she is all the more capable of manufacturing them. The only thing lacking is the nuclear warhead.

Japan's output of nuclear power is increasing daily. The United States supply of enriched uranium to Japan is not enough for her requirement, and she is now importing enriched uranium from other countries. And so her nuclear weapons can be produced readily. She cannot be prevented from doing so merely by the treaty. You have helped her develop her economy to such a level. And she is bound to demand outward expansion.

Economic expansion is bound to bring about military expansion. And that cannot be restrained by a treaty. Look at all your nuclear bases in Japan. Even if you were able to withdraw your nuclear weapons, the nuclear bases are still there, and they can make use of them.

When you said that there is no militarism, well, I'll argue with you on that score. This is borne out by the film which we have shown you and by the activities of Mishima, who had committed suicide.

Just when you were ill in Peking, you probably heard of the incident of a Japanese fighter colliding with a Boeing civil airliner, causing heavy casualties. Why? Because the air corridor in Japan is very narrow.

You have been to Japan. You know that the Japanese air corridors are divided into several levels, the higher for the Boeings, the lower for the propeller-driven aircraft. And with the Japanese Air Force being equipped with more and more planes, they just fly everywhere with them at will for training. And the pilot of that fighter parachuted to safety but let his fighter collide with the Boeing. And when asked why they did that, the trainer just said there was no place for training. What could they do?

That of course gave rise to public indignation. And among those voicing indignation were the opposition with the ruling Liberal-Democratic party itself, who said this is one of the harms of militarism. It is not something said by the Chinese alone; they themselves are saying that.

Mr. Reston: You are really worried about Japan, aren't you?

Mr. Chou: Because you know we suffered a long time, for 50 years. Such calamities can be prevented by opposition from us and from the Japanese people together.

Of the four opposition parties in Japan, only the Japanese Communist party has differing views with China; that part supports Sato on this.

The Japanese Socialist party admits the revival of Japanese militarism. The Komeito party admits that Japanese militarism is being revived, the Democratic Socialist party does not deny this fact, and the opposition wing of the Liberal-Democratic party also admits this fact.

When you oppose a danger, you should oppose it when it is only budding. Only then can you arouse public attention. Otherwise, if you are to wait until it has already developed into a power, it will be too strenuous. If the Far East situation is really to move towards relaxation, and if Japan gives up its ambitions of aggression against Korea and China's Taiwan, then it will be possible for China and Japan to conclude a mutual nonaggression treaty on the basis of the five principles of peaceful coexistence.

Mr. Reston: Could I ask you at that point whether you can foresee an expansion of such a pact to include the United States and the Soviet Union?

Mr. Chou: That must go through a whole series of steps and I cannot at the present time give an immediate answer. Because at the present time the two superpowers, the U.S. and the Soviet Union, are involving themselves in affairs throughout the world. And it is not an easy thing to bring about a solution of world problems, so we would rather like to have a discussion with your President.

Mr. Reston: On this subject—

Mr. Chou: Various questions can be discussed. This question, too, may be discussed.

Mr. Reston: This is too serious a question to be dismissed lightly. Could you define as you have done so often in the past and so helpfully in the past, what are the principles that must precede such a far-sighted move as such a four power nonaggression pact.

Mr. Chou: This question can be thought about only after we come to it because international questions are too complicated. It is easy to say the five principles of peaceful coexistence which we advocate. But to go into an examination to see whether or not these principles are observed, then many problems will arise.

For instance, it was with India that we had first reached an agreement on the five principles of peaceful coexistence. Because both China and India are two big countries, and in history there was no aggression by either against the other, with the sole exception of Genghis Khan's descendants, who went to the subcontinent but then stayed here and intermarried with the local inhabitants.

As for the two peoples, we had lived together in friendship for generations. As for the boundary question, it was something left over by British imperialism. But precisely over this boundary question, they fell out with us.

On this question, it was India which occupied Chinese territory. They even crossed the so-called McMahon Line. As for us, we did not press forward and were ready to solve the question by negotiations. As for Aksai Chin, in the western sector, that had all along been Chinese territory, there was never a boundary dispute over that territory before, but suddenly they raised the question about the western sector.

I went to India to negotiate this boundary question with the Indians on three occasions, and no solution was reached. What is more, they want to further occupy our territory north of the so-called McMahon Line. You didn't know much about this. Now you should know about it. A very good proof of the facts about this situation was a book written by a British author, Mr. Maxwell.

Mr. Reston: Yes.

Mr. Chou: That book is similar to the Pentagon papers which you published. They did not make use of a single Chinese document. All are from Indian sources.

Mr. Reston: May I ask you, sir, how you view the control of nuclear arms? You are now one of the nuclear powers.

Mr. Chou: No, we are not a nuclear power. We are only in the experimental stage. And what is more, that has been the case throughout the period from 1964 to the present, seven years already. We will not test when there is no need. We know it is quite expensive and a waste. And it is not beneficial to the improvement of the livelihood of the people.

It is quite clear, we can see, that the two big powers, the United States and the Soviet Union, having embarked on the mass production of nuclear weapons—cannot get down from the horse, so to speak. But can they thereby monopolize nuclear weapons. No, they cannot.

We produced nuclear weapons by ourselves. We manufacture nuclear weapons because we are forced to do so in order to break the nuclear monopoly. And our aim is the complete prohibition and thorough destruction of nuclear weapons. And so every time we make a test, we declare that we will never be the first to use nuclear weapons. You will see what we Chinese say counts.

Mr. Reston: Do you want to see a world conference on this question? How can this ghastly problem be solved when the world is now spending about $220 billion a year on arms? It is a disgrace to the intelligence of the human family. What are we to do about this question, and what can China do to help?

Mr. Chou: We do not agree with the Soviet proposal for a conference of the five nuclear powers. They want to lasso us by that means. We have expressed our disapproval, Britain said that she would not take part in the conference, and France too now says that she would not take part either.

We are calling for the convening of a conference of all countries of the world, big or small—because all the countries of the world, regardless of their size, should be equal—for the purpose of reaching an agreement on the complete prohibition and thorough destruction of nuclear weapons, and as a first step, on the nonuse of nuclear weapons. Once everyone agrees on the nonuse of nuclear weapons then what will be the need for the production of nuclear weapons?

Mr. Reston: Why do you use the word "lasso"?

Mr. Chou: When I said "lasso," it means if they want to drag us into such an affair. They will, first of all, demand that we sign on the partial nuclear test ban treaty, on the nonproliferation treaty and so on. How can we sign them?

But we undertake not to be the first to use nuclear weapons. The people of the world have indeed noted the fact that these two big powers are using so much money on nuclear weapons. Your Defense Secretary, Laird, himself admits that with so many nuclear weapons it is not possible for the United States and the Soviet Union to fight a nuclear war. The two peoples will oppose such a war.

Mr. Reston: True.

Mr. Chou: Since you do not want to have a nuclear war, then the United States and the Soviet Union should first undertake forthrightly that neither of them will be the first to use nuclear weapons, and then to go on to the next business. Because by reaching such an agreement, people will feel at ease. Secretary Laird said, now the U.S. should be prepared for conventional warfare. So Laird is telling Japan to strengthen the modernization of conventional weapons in Japan.

Mr. Reston: Is there a conflict between the so-called Nixon doctrine or Guam doctrine and our efforts to reach an accommodation with China? The thought I have in mind is this: I am afraid there is a puzzling and troubling point here that as we try to reduce our commitments in the Pacific, we encourage Japan and other countries to assume a larger military role, and that, in turn, leads to a greater dismay and anxiety on the part of China. Is there a conflict here? Is this one of the things to talk about with President Nixon when he comes to Peking?

Mr. Chou: You put it well. It is indeed a contradiction. I also discovered this contradiction because this is to encourage the militarization of Japan. There should be an effort at relaxation by all parties concerned. Indeed, there are a lot of questions. And as you know, your President spoke to the correspondents on the fourth after Rogers made his statement. We have not yet seen the full text of his interview, we have read only a partial text. Have you seen it?

Mr. Reston: You mean the Rogers'?

Mr. Chou: No, Nixon's.

Mr. Reston: No, I have not seen it.

Mr. Chou: I have only received very fragmentary reports, and probably I might get the full text tonight. President Nixon said that there were no preconditions for the forthcoming talks with China. Neither side has made any commitments. That is, there was no tacit understanding previously reached between the two sides.

Mr. Reston: I think it is useful to clarify this point because I think your allies and ours have both been a bit suspicious on this point.

Mr. Chou: China is a country which was blockaded by the United States for more than 20 years. Now since there is a desire to come and look at China, it's all right. And since there is a desire to talk, we are also ready to talk. Of course, it goes without saying that the positions of our two sides are different. And there are a lot of differences between our points of view. To achieve relaxation, there must be a common desire for it, so various questions must be studied, and all these questions may be placed on the table for discussion. We do not expect a settlement of all questions at one stroke. That is not possible. That would not be practicable. But by contacting each other, we may be able to find out from where we should start in solving these questions.

Mr. Reston: We are a very impatient people, you know, Mr. Prime Minister. In the old grocery stores up in our countryside there used to be little signs which said the improbable we do today, the impossible tomorrow. How long do you anticipate that it will take for reasonable men to resolve these problems of Taiwan, Vietnam and get the principles solved and get down to diplomatic relations between these two countries?

Mr. Chou: We hope that the Indochina question will be solved first, because the war is still going on there. I have read some of your articles, and you said in one of your articles that you felt that your President lacked courage. But of course, in deciding to come to China this time, it is something which even the opposition party say others dare not do. So on this point he has some courage. Mr. Mansfield himself said that.

Mr. Reston: Courage or lack of courage, those are fighting words. What I was trying to say is that I do not think that he is a bold-minded man in the sense that de Gaulle was when de Gaulle said, "I was wrong about Algeria, therefore, I stop it, and I move to change it now."

I think the trend of the President's thought is bold and even right on both Vietnam and China. His timing and his politics are rather ambiguous. That was what I meant, not a lack of courage—it is not a lack of courage, it's a lack of clarity and definition and boldness to cut and end the killing and end the stupidity of isolation of China.

You asked me before about what did I mean by favoring China and the end of the Taiwan relationship. It's very simple. We cannot resolve the problems in the world without China. It's just that simple. We can resolve the problems of the world without Taiwan. It's not a question of sentiment, it's a question of reality and power.

That is why I want to see this resolved, and resolved at a moment when the country is ready for it. That is why I am worried about the China news agency and their story of the other night. If we leave it to journalists, the world will be in a mess. It has to get down to quiet diplomacy.

Mr. Chou: Well, some things can be dealt with quietly, but when some things have been openly declared by the other party for several times, then it must be openly answered in the press.

I agree to your estimate of the character of President Nixon, and of course there is also the question of the position he is now in. The then position of General de Gaulle in France was a bit different. But as there is going to be conversations between us, I hope he will clearly see the future, as you said, to look forward.

For instance, a complete withdrawal from Vietnam will be quite an honorable thing. What is there dishonorable about their withdrawal from Vietnam? I think that is most honorable. When General de Gaulle withdrew from Algeria, the whole world expressed their approval, and the Algerian people expressed approval, too. The relations between France and Algeria improved in de Gaulle's time.

Mr. Reston: I should say one thing to you privately about this. I think it is very important that you say you should look forward. I think the President does look forward. I think there are two things about him that are particularly interesting.

One, he is a Californian and he looks to the Pacific in the way that we who live on the other side of the continent do not. Second, he has an ambition. His ambition is to preside over the 200th anniversary of the Declaration of Independence in 1976. There is one small barrier in the way of that, which is he must get re-elected in 1972. And beyond that, I think he is a romantic, and I think he is dead serious about China.

I think he sees an historic opportunity here to repair the damage that has been done and even the injustice that has been done to China, and also perhaps in his own sense, a certain rebuke to his own past and a feeling that the role he has played in the cold war is something that might be altered by a great and generous move to unify the peoples of the Pacific before he ends his term.

Mr. Chou: Thank you for providing me with this information. And you are motivated by your concern about the over-all world situation.

Mr. Reston: Yes, one doesn't come abroad to criticize one's own President, and I don't do that. It is true and it is still part of the mythology of America —I believe it's true—that the White House—you know, Woodrow Wilson once said that in the White House a man either grows or he swells, but most men are ennobled by it, and I think President Nixon is focusing on China, where he sees a historic role. This I think is terribly important psychologically.

Mr. Chou: We've noted this.

Mr. Reston: May I, because I don't want to impose on or weary you. There is one thing I want to have you clarify for me if you will. You see we can talk philosophy, and that is interesting. But when we get down to it and I listen to all the specific conditions to which I've heard since I have come to Peking, I get rather depressed. The condition on Vietnam I understand, and I can see that it can be met. The conditions and the principles of Chou En-lai on Taiwan, I think, can be met. But when I hear General Huang say that we must withdraw from the Philippines, we must withdraw from Japan, we must withdraw from Thailand, I think this is asking us, in a way, to withdraw from the Pacific, and I get depressed at that point because this doesn't seem to me to be a realistic basis which any President could accept.

Mr. Chou: If one really wants to achieve a relaxation throughout the world and not the aggravation of tension, then the troops of all foreign countries, not only the U.S. troops, should be withdrawn from the territories of the countries they have occupied and let the peoples of various countries solve their own problems by themselves.

This is a question of principle. But as to when and where these withdrawals are to take place first, and how to discuss and reach agreement with the governments concerned, they are concrete matters.

When the principle has been put forward, and if one really goes in this direction, there are many specific details which have to be discussed for the implementation of this principle.

Mr. Reston: I have a feeling that perhaps we'd better end on this point. There are two great movements in the world today. There is a movement of withdrawal by the U.S. in Vietnam and a retrenchment of its commitment overseas, and, on the other hand, the most visible movement it seems to me is the enlargement and the expansion of Soviet power across the Middle East and along the southern shore of the Mediterranean, and once the Suez is opened, into the Indian Ocean and the Pacific. Is one justified in being troubled by this Soviet movement in your view? Are you bothered by it?

Mr. Chou: Of course, for us it is an even more urgent matter. The assistant managing editor of your paper, Mr. [Harrison] Salisbury had been to Mongolia. He testified to the fact that there are massive troops concentrated on our borders in the north. So, in general, we stand for the withdrawal of all foreign troops back to their own countries so that the people of various countries may settle their own questions by themselves.

This is a matter of principle. But to put that into concrete form, of course, requires a process. In a word, in the past 25 years, first the U.S. tried to manage affairs of the whole globe, and then after Khrushchev took office it was a matter of striving for hegemony between the two superpowers.

The so-called disarmament conference is in fact a conference for arms expansion. Although there has been no world war, yet small wars have never ceased. We are not for demanding only the U.S. withdrawal and not the Soviet withdrawal, because that would be unfair. We say so in general terms, and specific matters will be dealt with concretely.

So if you say one should relax the situation, it is indeed not an easy matter. The reason is they have a few more atom bombs. But we Chinese are not afraid of atom bombs. We are prepared against their attack, against their launching a pre-emptive attack on us. That is why we are digging underground tunnels. You probably heard about this.

Mr. Reston: Yes, I did. As a matter of fact, you have a great network of tunnels under Peking.

Mr. Chou: Not only Peking. The great majority of our big and medium cities now have a network of underground tunnels.

[*At this point the formal interview broke for dinner, but after dinner, though it was then past midnight, Mr. Chou asked that the formal discussion be resumed. The official transcript was renewed.*]

Mr. Chou: There is one thing I've forgotten to mention. We have just discussed the question of Japan without discussing the question of Korea. As you know, there is still only an armistice agreement in Korea, and there has been no peace treaty. In this connection, we have to revert to John Foster Dulles.

In the Geneva conference, the first stage was devoted to the Korean question. As for the armistice in Korea, on your side it was a result of the decision taken by President Eisenhower. One of your generals admitted that the Korean war was a wrong war fought at a wrong time at a wrong place.

Mr. Reston: Gen. Omar Bradley.

Mr. Chou: At the 1954 Geneva conference there should have been a result on the Korean question, at least a decision should have been made to continue the conference in the future. But even that was disrupted by Dulles. And so even now there is a demilitarized zone, a Military Armistice Commission which meets once every one or two weeks in Panmunjom.

On your side there is an American representative and a representative from what we call the puppet Government in South Korea. And on the northern side is a representative of the Democratic People's Republic of Korea and a representative of the Chinese People's Volunteers. So the state of war has not ended. And you may recall the two incidents caused by your side, one of the *Pueblo* spy ship and the other a spy plane which was downed.

Mr. Reston: Yes.

Mr. Chou: And so the situation remains tense. And this is a matter which should be discussed.

Mr. Reston: Yes. If you could give me your views about that, I would be very happy to report them.

Mr. Chou: Our people's volunteers were withdrawn back in 1958. And the troops of other countries under the so-called U.N.C. have also been withdrawn. Only American troops remain there. And of the 60,000 troops or more in Korea at that time, 20,000 troops have been withdrawn and 40,000 and more still remain. And the American troops should all be withdrawn.

To solve the Korean question, a way should be found to bring about a rapprochement between the two sides in Korea and to move toward a peaceful unification of Korea. That of course requires time. But this demand is reasonable.

Now in the U.N. there is still a so-called commission for the unification and rehabilitation of Korea which is completely unilateral, composed of those countries of the so-called U.N.C. participating in the Korean war, and not a commission of both sides.

That presents a problem too. And so the Korean question is also linked up with the problem of Japanese militarism. If things do not go well, Japan may use the treaty it has concluded with South Korea, i.e., the Japan-R.O.K. treaty, to get into South Korea immediately upon the withdrawal of the U.S. forces.

Mr. Reston: It is extremely useful to have this view . . . to define those questions . . . that really should be on the agenda when the President comes here.

Mr. Chou: The Korean question also involves a question of preventing the rise of Japanese militarism. If Japanese militarism is to expand outward, it will first aim at these two wings. Taiwan and this wing. I only dealt with Taiwan. This is just what I would like to add.

Mr. Reston: Prime Minister, thank you very much for your kindness. I would like to ask the Prime Minister while I am here, would it be presumptuous for me to ask whether it is at all possible to see the Chairman?

Mr. Chou: Not very possible this time, because the Chairman is preoccupied with other matters. But of course you can come with your President next time.

Mr. Reston: No, I don't think I'll do that. I'll worry about him from now till then, and let you worry about him after he gets here.

36

THE U.S.-CHINESE COMMUNIQUÉ—
NIXON'S PEKING VISIT*

... The leaders of the People's Republic of China and the United States of America found it beneficial to have this opportunity, after so many years without contact, to present candidly to one another their views on a variety of issues. They reviewed the international situation in which important changes and great upheavals are taking place and expounded their respective positions and attitudes.

The U.S. side stated:

Peace in Asia and peace in the world requires efforts both to reduce immediate tensions and to eliminate the basic causes of conflict. The United States will work for a just and secure peace: just, because it fulfills the aspirations of peoples and nations for freedom and progress; secure, because it removes the danger of foreign aggression. The United States supports individual freedom and social progress for all the peoples of the world, free of outside pressure or intervention.

The United States believes that the effort to reduce tensions is served by improving communications between countries that have different ideologies so as to lessen the risks of confrontation through accident, miscalculation or misunderstanding. Countries should treat each other with mutual respect and be willing to compete peacefully, letting performance be the ultimate judge. No country should claim infallibility and each country should be prepared to reexamine its own attitudes for the common good.

The United States stressed that the peoples of Indochina should be allowed to determine their destiny without outside intervention; its constant primary objective has been a negotiated solution; the eight-point proposal put forward by the Republic of Vietnam and the United States on Jan. 27, 1972, represents the basis for the attainment of that objective; in the absence of a negotiated settlement the United States envisages the ultimate withdrawal of all U.S. forces from the region consistent with the aim of self-determination for each country of Indochina.

The United States will maintain its close ties with and support for the Republic of Korea. The United States will support efforts of the Republic of

---

* Text from AP, *The New York Times*, February 28, 1972. The paragraphs omitted at beginning list the officials and refer to "earnest and frank discussions . . . on the normalization of relations . . ."

Korea to seek a relaxation of tension and increase communications in the Korean peninsula. The United States places the highest value on its friendly relations with Japan; it will continue to develop the existing close bonds. Consistent with the United Nations Security Council Resolution of Dec. 21, 1971, the United States favors the continuation of the cease-fire between India and Pakistan and the withdrawal of all military forces to within their own territories and to their own sides of the cease-fire line in Jammu and Kashmir; the United States supports the right of the peoples of South Asia to shape their own future in peace, free of military threat, and without having the area become the subject of big-power rivalry.

The Chinese side stated:

Wherever there is oppression, there is resistance. Countries want independence, nations want liberation and the people want revolution—this has become the irresistible trend of history. All nations, big or small, should be equal; big nations should not bully the small and strong nations should not bully the weak. China will never be a superpower and it opposes hegemony and power politics of any kind.

The Chinese side stated that it firmly supports the struggles of all oppressed people and nations for freedom and liberation and that the people of all countries have the right to choose their social systems according to their own wishes and the right to safeguard the independence, sovereignty and territorial integrity of their own countries and oppose foreign aggression, interference, control and subversion. All foreign troops should be withdrawn to their own countries.

The Chinese side expressed its firm support to the peoples of Vietnam, Laos and Cambodia in their efforts for the attainment of their goals and its firm support to the seven-point proposal of the Provisional Revolutionary Government of the Republic of South Vietnam and the elaboration of February this year on the two key problems in the proposal, and to the Joint Declaration of the Summit Conference of the Indochinese Peoples.

It firmly supports the eight-point program for the peaceful unification of Korea put forward by the Government of the Democratic People's Republic of Korea on April 12, 1971, and the stand for the abolition of the "U.N. Commission for the Unification and Rehabilitation of Korea." It firmly opposes the revival and outward expansion of Japanese militarism and firmly supports the Japanese people's desire to build an independent, democratic, peaceful and neutral Japan. It firmly maintains that India and Pakistan should, in accordance with the United Nations resolutions on the India-Pakistan question, immediately withdraw all their forces to their respective territories and to their own sides of the cease-fire line in Jammu and Kashmir and firmly supports the Pakistan Government and people in their struggle to preserve their independence and sovereignty and the people of Jammu and Kashmir in their struggle for the right of self-determination.

There are essential differences between China and the United States in their social systems and foreign policies. However, the two sides agreed that countries, regardless of their social systems, should conduct their relations on the principles of respect for the sovereignty and territorial integrity of all states, nonaggression against other states, noninterference in the internal affairs of other states, equality and mutual benefit, and peaceful coexistence. International disputes should be settled on this basis, without resorting to the use or threat of force. The United States and the People's Republic of China are prepared to apply these principles to their mutual relations.

With these principles of international relations in mind the two sides stated that:

1. Progress toward the normalization of relations between China and the United States is in the interests of all countries.

2. Both wish to reduce the danger of international military conflict.

3. Neither should seek hegemony in the Asia-Pacific region and each is opposed to the efforts by any other country or group of countries to establish such hegemony; and

4. Neither is prepared to negotiate on behalf of any third party or to enter into agreements or understandings with the other directed at other states.

Both sides are of the view that it would be against the interests of the peoples of the world for any major country to collude with another against other countries, or for major countries to divide up the world into spheres of interest.

The sides reviewed the long-standing serious disputes between China and the United States.

The Chinese side reaffirmed its position: The Taiwan question is the crucial question obstructing the normalization of relations between China and the United States; the Government of the People's Republic of China is the sole legal government of China; Taiwan is a province of China which has long been returned to the motherland; the liberation of Taiwan is China's internal affair in which no other country has the right to interfere; and all U.S. forces and military installations must be withdrawn from Taiwan. The Chinese government firmly opposes any activities which aim at the creation of "one China, or Taiwan," "one-China, two governments," "two Chinas" and "Independent Taiwan" or advocate that "the status of Taiwan remains to be determined."

The U.S. side declared: The United States acknowledges that all Chinese on either side of the Taiwan Strait maintain there is but one China and that Taiwan is a part of China. The United States Government does not challenge that position. It reaffirms its interest in a peaceful settlement of the Taiwan question by the Chinese themselves. With this prospect in mind, it affirms the ultimate objective of the withdrawal of all U.S. forces and military installations from Taiwan. In the meantime, it will progressively reduce its forces and military installations on Taiwan as the tension in the area diminishes.

The two sides agreed that it is desirable to broaden the understanding between the two peoples. To this end, they discussed specific areas in such fields as science, technology, culture, sports and journalism, in which people-to-people contacts and exchanges would be mutually beneficial. Each side undertakes to facilitate the further development of such contacts and exchanges.

Both sides view bilateral trade as another area from which mutual benefits can be derived, and agree that economic relations based on equality and mutual benefit are in the interest of the peoples of the two countries. They agree to facilitate the progressive development of trade between their two countries.

The two sides agree that they will stay in contact through various channels, including the sending of a senior U.S. representative to Peking from time to time for concrete consultations to further the normalization of relations between the two countries and continue to exchange views on issues of common interest.

The two sides expressed the hope that the gains achieved during this visit would open up new prospects for the relations between the two countries. They believe that the normalization of relations between the two countries is not only in the interest of the Chinese and American peoples but also contributes to the relaxation of tension in Asia and the world.

President Nixon, Mrs. Nixon and the American party express their appreciation for the gracious hospitality shown them by the government and people of the People's Republic of China.

37

RADIO MOSCOW SPEAKS TO CHINA

Peking's Anti-Soviet Policy Harms Chinese People*

Talk by Station Commentator Latyshev: "Taking an Antisocialist Stand"

[Text] Dear listeners, those of you who have had the chance to read the communique on the Sino-U.S. talks may have probably noticed this: Not a single word in the communique was devoted to the world socialist system nor to any problems existing in the mutual relationship between world socialism and world capitalism.

This is not because this communique is not a suitable form for carrying the viewpoints on such questions. On the contrary, both China and the United States have pointed out elsewhere in the communique their respective different opinions on many contemporary questions.

The Chinese leaders have completely and consciously failed to devote a single word to the socialist system. They have hinted to their opponent in the negotiations, U.S. President Nixon and those he represents, that they are not bound by the world socialist system.

The question of attitude toward the socialist system is vitally significant in terms of principle. The characteristics of the present era indicate that society is in a period of transition from capitalism to socialism. Therefore, the forefront of the major struggle of all political forces in the world today lies between world capitalism and world socialism.

The Chinese leaders have decided on their own stand in this struggle. They claim that they will advance together with other socialist countries. It seems that they will struggle against imperialism independently by using their own methods, including negotiations with the leader of the United States, the major imperialist country. . . .

It is quite clear at present that further cooperation with the socialist countries is not included in Mao Tse-tung's plan, because this cooperation is aimed at strengthening socialism in China as well as substantially strengthening the whole socialist system in its confrontation against imperialism.

The result of the Sino-U.S. talks has provided reason to believe that what is happening between the United States and China is, instead of a normal-

* Radio Moscow, broadcasting in Mandarin to China at 0730 GMT, March 7, 1972, as recorded by the U.S. Foreign Broadcast Information Service. See FBIS, *Daily Report, Soviet Union,* 8 March 1972.

ization of relations based on the principle of peaceful coexistence, a plan to develop a totally different kind of cooperation—the purpose of which is to oppose the world socialist system.

The question does not merely lie in China's omission in the communique of the struggle of world socialism against world capitalism. All the preparations for the Sino-U.S. talks, the talks themselves, and the propaganda on the results of the talks have all been carried out in a background of rampant anti-Sovietism. Chinese propaganda organs are doing their utmost to convince the masses that their major enemy is not U.S. imperialism, but the Soviet Union and other socialist countries.

There has never been a precedent in history in which a country was able to build socialism with the help of imperialism. There have been only many instances in history testifying that an anti-Soviet, antisocialist policy will surely put the maker of such a policy in the enemy's camp, in the laps of imperialism.

The Chinese leaders are now taking this dangerous road. It is dangerous because it will cause the Chinese people to suffer from misery and privation again. Imperialism is the enemy of the Chinese people.

Scrutiny of Peking Communique Bares PRC Concessions*

MASILEV COMMENTARY

[Text] Foreign newspapers have pointed out that the joint U.S.-Chinese communique obviously does not reflect the real content of the negotiations between the U.S. President and the Chinese leaders, and that some sections of this communique are ambiguous and superficial. These foreign newspapers also have emphatically pointed out Nixon's remarks about keeping the content of the negotiations secret.

As is universally known, the Chinese leaders are also concealing the real nature of the negotiations, not mentioning their content and results. Many observers believe that one of the reasons for the Chinese leaders' secrecy is that the political crisis in China is not yet over. It was reported that of the 25 members and candidate members of the CCP Central Committee Politburo, only five participated [in] the negotiations with Nixon and only Mao-Tse-tung and Chou En-lai participated in the negotiations on problems of a specially secret nature.

It was also reported that the interpreter during the negotiations was Mao Tse-tung's niece. All this shows that the Chinese party, state, and army activists are dissatisfied with Mao Tse-tung's policy of moving closer to the United States—the major imperialist country in the world. They cannot be blind to the fact that a rapprochement with the United States would be made

---

* Radio Moscow, broadcasting in Mandarin to China at 0830 GMT, March 13, 1972, as recorded by the U.S. Foreign Broadcast Information Service. See FBIS, *Daily Report, Soviet Union,* 14 March 1972.

at the cost of betraying or abandoning the fundamental principles of the CCP's previously formulated foreign policy.

Take the Taiwan issue, for example. Superficially, the Chinese side re-iterated its previous position on this issue, while the U.S. side made certain concessions to China. However, a careful analysis shows the contrary. As is universally known, in past discussions on the normalization of Sino-U.S. relations the Chinese leaders insisted that priority be given to solving the Taiwan issue on the ground that this was a question of principle in Chinese-U.S. relations. The Chinese leaders also repeatedly emphasized that other problems in Chinese-U.S. relations could be tackled only after the Taiwan issue was settled. Mao Tse-tung and his clique have now abandoned this principle and have made a great concession to the U.S. imperialists. They have agreed to develop relations in various fields with the United States before settling the Taiwan issue—the important problem in Chinese-U.S. relations.

What have the Chinese leaders achieved by such action? A careful read-ing of the section in the Sino-U.S. communique dealing with this issue will help one to realize that the Americans have made a concession on the sur-face only. The communique said: "The U.S. side declared that the United States acknowledges that all Chinese on either side of the Taiwan Strait maintain there is but one China and that Taiwan is a part of China." Please note the phrase "a part of China." The communique did not say that Tai-wan is "a part of the PRC." It is not an inadvertent wording because this is the same view held by Chiang Kai-shek, the U.S. imperialists' running dog, on the Taiwan question, and the United States supports him.

The U.S. side also pointed out in the communique that the United States "affirms the ultimate objective of the withdrawal of all U.S. forces and mili-tary installations from Taiwan" and that "in the meantime it will progres-sively reduce its forces and military installations on Taiwan as the tension in the area diminishes." What can we say about the so-called concession? First, it is worth noting that the communique set no definite date for ful-filling the so-called ultimate objective, that is, the withdrawal of the U.S. forces from Taiwan. Hence, the statement on the withdrawal has lost its mean-ing. Second, the progressive reduction, not the withdrawal, of the U.S. forces from Taiwan will be determined by the relaxation of the tension "in the area." What is behind this condition? What is "the area" referred to? This wording will enable Washington to make suitable interpretations of the word "Taiwan" and the situation in the other Asian areas adjacent to Taiwan, especially in Indochina. The CHRISTIAN SCIENCE MONITOR said that the clause that "as the tension in the area diminishes" in the com-munique means the military action in Indochina will be ended on U.S. terms and that Nixon has suggested that if the Chinese help persuade Hanoi to accept U.S. conditions—in fact, surrender to the United States—the United

States will leave Taiwan. Other well-informed U.S. newspapers have also expressed the same views.

Dear listeners, you can see that the so-called U.S. concession on the Taiwan issue is nothing but a disgraceful deal made by Washington and Peking behind the backs of the Vietnamese and the other Asian peoples. From the communique you can see that the United States has not abandoned its military treaty with the Taiwan regime and that the Chinese side dared not ask Nixon to sever U.S. relations with Chiang Kai-shek. On 6 March, after returning from his China trip, Nixon received the Chiang Kai-shek clique's ambassador to Washington. According to UPI, the allegation that Taiwan's position was undermined during the talks with the Chinese leaders was refuted. These and other facts show that before and after Nixon's visit to Peking the U.S. imperialists held to and are still holding to their policy of supporting Chiang Kai-shek.

Nixon's visit to Peking and the rapprochement between the United States and China are the results of the concession made by Mao Tse-tung and his clique. From the communique we can see that the Chinese leaders have divorced themselves from the class stand and that the Chinese side has completely ignored socialist practice. The communique did not say directly or indirectly that China protects the interests of socialism—as a socialist country has to do in its activities on [the] international stage. There was not a single word in the communique about the DRV. The communique also did not say that China supports the Arab people in their struggle against imperialism and Zionism. In short, the results of the U.S.-Chinese negotiations show that in order to make the rapprochement with the United States, Mao Tse-tung and his clique have abandoned the fundamental principles of a socialist country's foreign policy.

PRC-U.S. Communique Conceals Secret Agreements*

VALENTINOV COMMENTARY: "WHO WANTS SECRET DIPLOMACY?"

[Text] Lenin, the founder of the world's first socialist state, was firmly opposed to secret diplomacy. He pointed out that practicing politics stealthily behind the backs of the party and the people is incompatible with a worker-peasant regime. . . .

Thus, the secret diplomacy of the Chinese and U.S. leaders, carried out behind the backs of their own peoples, cannot help but arouse apprehension and distrust among all upright people. The peoples of the world are well aware of the treacherous schemes and tactics of the U.S. imperialist wolves and the hypocrisy of the Maoists. They realize that the secret, behind-the-scenes diplomacy between Peking and Washington is obviously directed

---

* Radio Moscow, broadcasting in Mandarin to China at 1230 GMT, March 15, 1972, as recorded by the U.S. Foreign Broadcast Information Service. See FBIS, *Daily Report, Soviet Union,* 16 March, 1972.

against their interests. If the American and Chinese leaders are indeed serious about easing tensions in Asia and in the world, as they have said in their joint communique, why then are they hiding the content of their talks from their own peoples and the peoples of other countries?

If the Chinese and American leaders are truly working to normalize their bilateral relations not at the expense of other peoples' interests, this is indeed in the interest of peace and international security. On this point, the communique said: Neither is prepared to negotiate on behalf of any third party or to enter into agreements or understandings with the other directed at other states.

But, may we ask, how are we to understand the military alliances between the United States and certain Asian countries which are directed at other countries and are left unmentioned in the joint communique? And what price did Nixon pay to reward this silence?

The authors of the American-Chinese joint communique may have used all sorts of clever words and expressions to camouflage the actual content of the talks. But it is not hard to realize that one of the secret premises for the rapprochement between the Maoists and the U.S. imperialists is their common antisocialist and anti-Soviet stand. Thus, one U.S. imperialist objective is to capitalize on the Chinese leaders' splittist scab policy. The U.S. capitalists are experienced manipulators of scabs in the revolutionary movement. For instance, the U.S. imperialists are now pinning their hopes on these scabs—the Maoist leadership—in their struggle against the national liberation movements in Asia.

The Sino-U.S. communique can only hoodwink a handful of people, certainly not the peoples in Indochina. The peoples in Indochina have long seen through the nature of the "Guam doctrine," the "Vietnamization of the war," the stinking "eight-point proposal" concerning Vietnam, and all other schemes of the U.S. strategists.

Washington's latest scheme is all the more vicious. It hopes to achieve its aims in Indochina through the scab Mao Tse-tung. As a payment for Mao Tse-tung's treachery, Washington has agreed to pull out the U.S. troops from Taiwan in the indefinite future.

Thus, the communique is but a propaganda wand for concealing the many secret agreements reached between the Peking and Washington leaders over a series of international issues, including the issues of Indochina and Taiwan. Many newspapers of the world have exposed this secret but not so deft diplomacy. For instance, the British GUARDIAN said: The United States hopes to link the solution of the Taiwan issue to the solutions of other pending issues in the Far East, including the Vietnam war. The mouthpiece of the U.S. ruling clique, the Washington POST, openly declared: A bargain of exchanging Taiwan for Vietnam was carried out at the talks.

Thus, the aim of the secret diplomacy between the American and Chinese leaders is not only to make deals behind the backs of their own peoples but also to collude behind the backs of the peoples of Vietnam and other Asian countries—to adjust their own positions at the expense of the interests of other peoples.

Undoubtedly, the secret diplomacy of the Chinese and American leaders is doomed to failure. They can never achieve their selfish ends by deceiving other peoples and behind-the-scenes collusions. This secret diplomacy is another eloquent proof of their inability to deliver themselves from the quagmire of contradictions.

The policy of subserviency to the imperialists is an indication of the Maoist leadership's betrayal of the socialist foundation of foreign policy. Such a policy is contrary to the national interests of the Chinese people. Only by putting China back on the road of proletarian internationalism and cooperation with the socialist countries can the Chinese people's national interests be safeguarded from the threat of imperialism.

Mao Switches Allegiance from Socialism to Imperialism*

UNATTRIBUTED COMMENTARY: "THERE IS NO OTHER ALTERNATIVE"

[Text] In the past Mao Tse-tung said: "The imperialists are opposed to the Soviet Union and the communists. If you go near them you will be asked to attack the north, and this would reduce your revolution to nothing. The present situation is obvious: If it is not a policy of uniting with Russia and the socialist countries, it must be one of uniting with the imperialists." These words are no longer heard in China, and they and the principle behind them are forgotten.

We quote these words to show that the speaker is a downright double-dealer. In the past, when he needed support and assistance from the Soviet Union and the CPSU, Mao Tse-tung spared no praise for the Soviet Union and Lenin's party. He is now practicing an altogether different policy. One of his past utterances is nothing but a slap in his own face. He said: "All imperialists in this world are our enemies. Without the support and assistance of the socialist countries and the international proletariat, China will not be able to gain independence." That was to say, it had to have Soviet support and assistance.

What else can this be but the guiding of China along this road? There are only two roads—marching along the broad avenue of socialist development together with the Soviet Union and the other fraternal socialist countries, or colluding with the imperialists and opposing socialism. There is no other alternative.

---

* Radio Moscow, broadcasting in Mandarin to China at 1230 GMT, March 22, 1972, as recorded by the U.S. Foreign Broadcast Information Service. See FBIS, *Daily Report, Soviet Union,* 23 March, 1972.

38

JAPAN: "SAME BED, DIFFERENT DREAMS"

T. C. RHEE*

Japan's booming economy cannot fail to have a determining influence on the future trend of her general policy. Largely due to a phenomenal growth rate, Japan has already become the third-ranking economic power in the world. It is now estimated that by 1980, Japan's gross national product will surpass that of all the Asian nations combined. Herman Kahn, of the Hudson Institute, and many others now predict that there is a strong possibility that Japan might even exceed the United States by the end of this century—both in terms of gross and net national product, and in terms of per capita income. According to James Abegglen, vice president of the Boston Consulting Group, Japan's economic growth "has no parallel in the world's economic history." He cites that the current Japanese growth rate (14 to 15 percent) is in real terms five times that of the United States. By 1970, Abegglen predicts, Japan's GNP will be about $200 billion, and will double that by 1975 (equaling the present economy of all the Common Market countries in Europe), and will double again by 1980—at which point it will genuinely threaten to surpass the American economic strength in "per capita" output.

Japan's economic advance has not been limited to any single area, but has been virtually "across the board—in production, domestic consumption, exports, industrial investment and just about every other key indicator."

Basking in this unprecedented prosperity, the people of Japan are not particularly happy with their image of mere "aggressive salesmen." Japan's world-renowned novelist, Yukio Mishima, sighs, "Our present culture has no roots. We don't know who we are or what we are." In the same vein, it was reported, Charles de Gaulle's portrayal of Japan's visiting Foreign Minister as a "transistor salesman" is nationally regarded as an unbearable insult. Among an increasing number of Japanese there is a deep sense of futility in their present mode of life, in their present degree of national prestige in global politics, and in their present severely introverted sense of self-imposed isolation.

Japan: Past and Future

Naturally, then, the pressing question of the 1970s is how Japan will translate her economic and industrial strength into a politico-military-diplo-

---

* T. C. Rhee, "Japan: 'Same Bed, Different Dreams,' " *Interplay*, Vol. 3, No. 11 (August 1970), pp. 4–10. Reprinted by permission.

matic role. Judging from the historical record of modern Japan—especially from the Meiji period—the present economic strength will eventually be harnessed to an extension of political and even military influence in Asia, if not immediately on a global scale.

More important in the recent past was the distinct tandem between Japanese economic and industrial growth and the rise of an aggressive foreign policy. The attempt to control Korea, which led to the Sino-Japanese war of 1894–95, the rivalry over Korea with the Russian Empire that led to the defeat of the Russian fleet at Tsushima Strait, all indicate certain parallels between the realities of economics and political aspiration. The controversies over the Taft-Knox Neutralization Plan and American Dollar Diplomacy should also be a valuable indicator of Japan's past record of translating her economic strength into a political claim of dominance. Indeed, there are more numerous, more clear-cut cases in the 20th century such as the Shantung Question, the Twenty-One Demands, the Tanaka Memorial, the Manchurian Crisis, the establishment of Manchukuo (leading to Japan's withdrawal from the League of Nations), and the turbulent diplomatic maneuverings of the 1930s which led to Pearl Harbor.

The present tendency in Japan points to a disturbing line of development. Not only is there a growing bitterness in "sharing" wealth or in involving other economies in joint ventures, but a disturbing number of Japanese now argue for a massive rearmament to enhance their international influence. Although at the moment Japan is peace-minded, indicated by the "anti-war" Constitution, if the economy maintains its present dynamism with the accompanying growth of national confidence and activism, then militaristic and aggressive expression of national strength may not be easily discounted. Under such circumstances, the rise of fierce nationalism is not a novelty. After a long period of "forced repentence," there is indeed a lively pace of "recasting" Japan's immediate past history. A mood of nostalgia for past glory and grandeur has virtually wiped out whatever pangs of conscience the people of Japan felt just after the war, which has been replaced with "re-glorification" of their achievements as an imperial power. More and more Japanese now not only justify their role in such events as the Manchurian crisis, the China "Incident," colonialism in Korea and Taiwan, but glorify them as their contribution to Asia. Kei Wakaizumi, professor at Kyoto Industrial University, wrote in *Foreign Affairs* that the present Japanese Constitution was "imposed" by the American occupation and, therefore, "sooner or later" the demand for an amendment would be "a metabolic demand of healthy national reassertion." Commenting on the basic change in Japan's thinking, he continued:

The present leaders of Japan (who will continue to hold power in the early 1970s) have personally experienced the Pacific war and its aftermath of defeat. This experience produced the "postwar hangover," a uniquely Japanese pattern of pathological consciousness compounded of resentment, humiliation and a sense of guilt about the violence and aggressiveness of Japan's militarists in subjugating other nations. *While Japanese feel shame at their behavior toward their neighbors, Hiroshima and Nagasaki erased the sense of guilt Japanese might have felt toward the United States because of Pearl Harbor* (italics added).

Renascent Nationalism

This renascent nationalism can be found in almost every important facet of Japanese life. Recently, art exhibits of wartime paintings drew enormous crowds of Japanese of all ages in Tokyo, who saw those wartime arts as nostalgic reflections of their former imperial glory. Wartime heroes such as Admiral Isoroku Yamamoto, supreme commander of Japan's high seas fleet which attacked Pearl Harbor, are being glorified in biographies, all on the bestsellers' list. There are growing numbers of "pilgrimages" to the grave of General Hideki Tojo who, for his responsibility in the Pacific war, was executed as the major war criminal by the Tokyo Tribunal. The Maritime Self-Defense Force maintains a naval museum depicting Japanese naval exploits and enshrining the hair of Admirals Togo and Yamamoto. All the postwar textbooks are being revised to accommodate sagas of military heroes, including kamikaze pilots, in Japan's history as an expression of national homage to past grandeur. Most of Japan's Shinto temples are firmly back in business, receiving numerous worshipers come to pay respect to fallen heroes of the Imperial war machine. Shintoism itself as an epitome of Japan's "manifest destiny" is regaining its symbolic strength as a national rallying point. Referring to Japan's rising national pride, Professor Wakaizumi said, "We surrendered in 1945. Twenty-three years is long enough for any nation, particularly a self-conscious, proud people like the Japanese, to lie low. We are tired of maintaining a low posture in the world. Now, we must once again be proud of our nation."

Candid discussion of military matters of all kinds is fast becoming a vogue in new Japan, so shy of all military matters since 1945. For the first time since the war, Emperor Hirohito was recently allowed to talk to the chiefs of staff and other top military commanders of the Self-Defense Forces. Furthermore, the world might soon see the Emperor's attendance in military reviews, perhaps even in a military uniform.

If all these are the natural accompaniments of a re-emerging nation, and therefore no particular cause for alarm or concern, there are other, more aggressive signs. First, there are widespread signs of Japanese ridicule of other nations, particularly the United States. Problems such as Negroes and the civil rights movement, national violence (i.e., the assassinations of the Kennedys, Martin Luther King, etc.), the Democratic Convention in Chicago, and the riots by the Negroes, students and police (i.e., police brutality) are being increasingly cited as showing the basic sickness of American society. These things are being discussed widely as an indirect comment on America's postwar attempt at Japan's "democratization," "liberalization" and "demilitarization." The argument is mainly directed at American "hypocrisy" and "self-righteousness." In this context the Vietnam conflict is being compared to Japan's own experiences in China in the 1930s, and the "moralistic" condemnation and the diplomatic inflexibility of Washington that "forced" Japan to an "inevitable attack" on Pearl Harbor are again being criticized. The My Lai massacre occupies an emotional niche in Japan as a parallel to the "crimes" judged by the Tokyo and Nuremberg tribunals, the "rape of Nanking," the Bataan "Death March," etc.

Japan's Military Strength

The possibility of Japan's massive rearmament merits special attention. For years, Japan's growing military establishment has been camouflaged under such unassuming designations as "Ground, Maritime and Air Self-Defense Forces." The present strength of the SDF stands at a puny 258,000 —a mere one-tenth of the old Imperial war machine. Nonetheless, Japan's existing conventional forces have already reached the point of sufficient self-defense capability. In terms of conventional firepower and mobility, Japan's military capability has clearly surpassed those of the Imperial military establishment. In terms of cadres, Japan's forces have all the features of the Weimar Republic's military establishment during the period of General Hans von Seeckt (after the Rapallo Agreement). Should the Japanese decide in favor of expanded military power in the future, they would not be hindered by the lack of a firm foundation.

Although spending a mere one percent of the GNP (less than Luxembourg's), Japan's defense spending is, in real terms, quite substantial. Should Japan reach at least the level of West Germany (4.5 percent), it will involve about $20 billion. Even if Japan continues the present rate of defense spending, it will soon surpass the Red Chinese budget (including Peking's nuclear spending) by about 1975. Japan's Finance Ministry reported in the draft national budget that the military allocation for fiscal year 1970 was $1.6 billion, an unprecedented increase of 17.7 percent over 1969 and the sharpest rise in defense spending since 1945. The increased spending will be utilized for production of tanks, surface-to-air missiles, naval vessels, aircraft and a rise in the number of military personnel.

A New Trend of Military Policy

By 1971, Japan will have completed its three-phase rearmament program involving some $6.5 billion, spent largely in increasing the firepower and mobility of the three services. Tanks and various other armored vehicles are being added in large numbers, along with a greater number of rapid-fire automatic weapons, to ground units than are normally available to standardized modern units of comparable size. The Maritime Self-Defense Forces have substantially increased their destroyer and submarine squadrons, widened their operational scope and increased the capacities of their naval anti-submarine aviation. Air units are being rapidly modernized to accommodate F-4E Phantom jets, which are produced in large numbers through licensing.

Besides this conventional military muscle, Japan is investing huge sums through official and private channels—mostly through large financial groups —in long-range research and development projects by major *Zaibatsu* combines, all involved in munitions production in Japan's past wars. Mitsubishi Heavy Industries, Nippon Steel, Kawasaki Aircraft, Sumimoto Company and Mitsubishi Electric, among others, are expanding their facilities for basic research in preparation for the mass production of various weapon systems.

In view of the well-known close relations between the financial and industrial leadership and the ruling Liberal-Democratic Party in Japan, one could well wonder why the pragmatic Japanese business circles would commit so much of their efforts to weapon systems development and research if there is no agreement on the future trend of Japan's military policy.

Along with this, Japan is undergoing a period of rapid psychological change in favor of predicted rearmament. Increasingly strong pressures are being brought to bear on the present Japanese government for rearmament, both conventional and nuclear. In 1968, Agriculture Minister Tadao Kuraishi was forced to resign "under public pressure," because of his statement favoring nuclear weapons and larger armed forces. Under the changed conditions of the 1970s, a man like him might not have to resign at all, but could be in a position of leadership. In 1969, former Prime Minister Nobusuke Kishi (brother of Eisaku Sato, and tried by the Tokyo Tribunal as a war criminal), and Takeshi Sakurada (head of the powerful Japan Federation of Employers Association) have lobbied for amending the Japanese Constitution for the sake of faster and greater rearmament. At the end of last year, Kenzo Okubo (President of the Japan Ordnance Association) was urging the government to "produce nuclear armaments and devote 4 percent of its gross national product [or about $6 billion] to defense." On Nagasaki Day, the powerful chairman of the LDP's security committee, Naka Funada, demanded the increase of Japan's military establishment by the creation of a million-strong "reserve defense corps" or "national militia." The new Director of Japan's Defense Agency, and a possible challenger to Sato's continued leadership of the LDP, Yasuhiro Nakasone, was "sharply critical of Japanese reliance on American defense" and pledged "an overall review" of the present force level to arrive at an expanded level compatible with Japan's economic status.

Public Opinion and Production of Nuclear Weapons

Japan's public opinion itself shows remarkable signs of conformity to the same posture. The recent opinion poll in Japan—conducted by the Prime Minister's office itself—showed that 81 percent of the Japanese people now favor national defense *without* outside help (i.e., the United States), while 45 percent favor acquisition of nuclear weapons. Concerning Japan's nuclear armament, there are some tough problems to deal with: (1) domestic opposition, especially from leftist political elements; (2) the strong possibility of adverse reactions from Asian nations which experienced Japanese aggression; (3) the uncertain reactions of major nuclear and non-nuclear powers, particularly Red China, the Soviet Union, the United States, India and Australia; and (4) the problem of ratification of the Nuclear Non-Proliferation Treaty.

Quite obviously, the LDP will have a hard time in warding off strong national pressures for massive rearmament. Should the present Sato leadership prove too timid in the eyes of more radical elements, it could be easily replaced in a sweeping realignment of factions in the LDP, a strong probability in the 1970s. Or Sato's faction itself may shift its position out of political expediency to a more radical expression of national goals. If one takes into account the radically chauvinistic positions of Komeito on many important issues (i.e., the reversion of the Kuriles), and its rapidly rising popularity, it is very hard to be optimistic.

Once her future domestic and foreign policies are settled, Japan could easily make gigantic headway toward producing nuclear weapons. According to the latest study, the amount of plutonium required for producing a nuclear weapon is about six kilograms. Under present conditions, Japan is expected to have nuclear electrical generating capacities of about 20,000 megawatts by 1980, which is equivalent to 5,000 kilograms of plutonium per year, enough for some 800 nuclear weapons. Japan's goal for 1985 is put at "at least" 30,000–40,000 megawatt capacity, an equivalent of 1,600 bombs per year. It is reported that Japanese scientists have successfully developed their own techniques for producing enriched uranium, sufficiently concentrated to manufacture nuclear weapons of substantial yield. The Radioisotope Laboratory of Tokai has spent two and one half years in completing experiments on equipment for "enriching natural uranium through the gaseous diffusion method."

Japan is presently dependent on the United States for the supply of enriched uranium, which is being used, through gaseous diffusion, to produce the fissionable material U-235. At present, however, some 30 Japanese companies are exploring African uranium resources in cooperation with the French Atomic Energy Commission. A joint company, "Overseas Uranium Resources Development Company," is soon to be established which will conclude an agreement to jointly develop uranium resources in the Akokan district of Niger. Annual production is estimated at 1,500 tons of yellow cake which will be shared with the French. In addition, Japan is seeking other uranium resources from "as many countries as possible," which indicates its intense desire to free itself from dependence on the United States.

The Non-Proliferation Treaty

Although, after a long delay, Japan has just signed the nuclear Non-Proliferation Treaty, final ratification is still highly uncertain. Japan's Foreign Office has a lengthy list of objections. The Japanese object to the unequal nature of the treaty. The nuclear powers have paid lip-service to nuclear disarmament in the preamble, but have failed to provide any significant provision to that effect. On the other hand, non-nuclear powers must not only pledge to give up nuclear weapons, but must also submit to unduly prohibitive inspections. Hence, Tokyo—like Bonn—feels that the treaty was designed solely to protect and perpetuate the present nuclear powers' monopoly, thus allowing them undue and unfair political and military leverage.

Inspection procedures are considered highly unfair to Japan. While the nuclear powers are not subject to inspection, the non-nuclear powers of Western Europe will be inspected only by EURATOM, "a family organization of six Western European states," with perhaps nominal participation by the International Atomic Energy Agency. Japan, on the other hand, will have to submit to inspection by an international agency, comprising 96 nations including the Soviet Union and other Communist nations.

Third, the Japanese argue that nuclear science is still in its infancy, and nobody can foretell the possibilities of future progress in the peaceful use of atomic energy. Should Japan accept the treaty, and the country be forced to submit to harsh inspections, peaceful uses of atomic energy in Japan could suffer serious setbacks.

Fourth, because Red China and France remain uncommitted, Japan feels the treaty has no universal applicability. Without such universality, the Japanese doubt the wisdom of tying their hands for an indefinite period.

Finally, the Japanese, like many European nations, maintain that the Americans have no justification for keeping the uranium-enrichment process to themselves since the treaty prohibits manufacture of atomic bombs. Japan's Foreign Minister Kiichi Aichi "has been compelled to pacify business and ultra-nationalist opponents by giving public and private assurances that Japan will not ratify the treaty unless a 'satisfactory' inspection compromise can be reached."

Rearmament . . .

Masami Takatsuji, Director of the Cabinet Legislation Bureau, stated in the House of Councillors that, although nuclear weapons were not authorized by the Constitution, under changed conditions the manufacture of "nuclear weapons which are in conformity with the purpose and within the limits of self-defense" would not be "necessarily unconstitutional." When later questioned, Prime Minister Sato pointedly noted that he found nothing in the statement that he felt compelled to correct. If the Constitution itself is to be amended, no such devious justification would have to be employed. Moreover, the cost of owning the nuclear weapons system is well within the economic capacity of growing Japan. Although the government presently eschews public statement to this effect, there has been no lack of allusion by many leaders of Japan, civilian as well as military, in or out of government circles. General Minoru Genda, former Chief of the Air Defense Force, said in an interview, "Japan can have 100 standard warheads [Hiroshima type] in less than ten years for less than $200 million."

Many leaders in Japan are convinced that the only way to achieve diplomatic parity with Washington, as well as with Peking and Moscow, and acquire added political influence in global affairs is through nuclear armament. The serious problem, then, is not the mere fact of the Japanese nuclear arsenal but the basic political intentions behind it. Washington's hopes that Japan may be persuaded to play a complementary role with the United States in maintaining the Asian balance of power could very well be illusory. Even supposing Japan's nominal cooperation, Tokyo's aims would *not* be to foster an Asian political climate likely to lead to harmony with American goals. Equally important is the beneath-the-surface intense anti-Americanism in Japan. The range of disagreements between Washington and Tokyo is already wide and deep. Besides the problems already discussed, there are the inflammatory problems of textile exports, of fishery disputes, of airline rights, and a multitude of trading problems between the two nations.

American Bases

This year the Japanese-American mutual defense arrangement will be exposed to lively national debate and controversy in Japan. Although no specific action is necessary for automatic extension of the treaty, the potentially volatile atmosphere of Japan's domestic opinion, including that of Sato's own cabinet members, would make it difficult for the Tokyo government to risk automatic continuation without attempting further renegotiation. American military bases in mainland Japan are sore points, reminders of Japan's defeat and national humiliation. As voices are raised for an independent posture, those bases will soon come under severe attack in Japan, not necessarily from the leftist parties alone.

Much more important, Japan feels that American involvement in Asia—even with the Nixon Doctrine—is still highly risky and provocative, and could easily entangle Japan in a political *cul de sac*. This fear is increased as the post-Vietnam prospect seems to point toward the general retrenchment of America's Asian commitment. Japan senses the growing incapacity and unwillingness of the United States to involve itself in future Asian crises, and is determined not to be involved by proxy (through the continued existence of American bases in Japan) in acts of "hostility" in Asia with which Japan herself will some day have to come to terms.

An increasing number of Japanese writers now attest the fact that these events are the natural and logical reflections of rising Japanese nationalism and confidence. Goto Motoo, deputy chief editorial writer of the *Asahi Shimbun* and the former head of the London Bureau, wrote that the widespread opposition to the American presence in Japan "could no longer be ignored as simply 'anti-American demonstrations by a left-wing minority'." He cited the growing attack of "middle-of-the-road" political parties, such as Komeito and the Democratic Socialist Party, against the Sato government's pro-American policy, which the Liberal-Democrats would no longer be able to ignore. Goto went on to point out that "it is extremely doubtful whether that facile and optimistic view of Japan-US relations really reflects the present situation." He quite clearly denied that the Liberal-Democrats' election victories in December 1969 meant the national desire for a continuing pro-American posture.

In the aftermath of the Socialist defeat, party leaders are reportedly pessimistic to the point of fearing their extinction as a viable and credible alternative political force in Japan. The surprising increase of Komeito's power may have further dashed their political hopes. Some are even reported to have argued for rejection of the Marxist line to make the party more appealing to the increasingly nationalistic electorate. The defeat indicates that the Japanese are against the Socialist parties' views of "unarmed neutrality" as Japan's future posture, and are in favor of large-scale rearmament as the only viable instrument of attaining a superpower's role.

The Ultra Chauvinistic Militants

The stunning election victory of Komeito (political arm of the Sokka Gakkai, a powerful organization of the militant Nichiren Buddhistic sect) will certainly be an important aspect of the rapidly radicalizing national mentality. This mass movement of 7,500,000 families remains as yet totally undefined, its programs so far unclarified. With a motto of "To redeem the world, largely through aggressive mass conversion tactics," the movement is said to have resorted to "a membership drive in a semi-gangster manner, using a military organization," and has been known to suppress the publication of true facts in Japan. Some Japanese and knowledgeable Japan watchers in the West are afraid that through Komeito Japan may soon "go the way of Hitler." Although the present Komeito leadership seems "reasonable," there is no way of knowing how they will use political power once they have attained leadership. Nearly doubling their Diet seats in the latest election, their mercurial rise in popularity—natural as well as coerced—could easily bring to the surface their true intentions, once they are well entrenched. Even now, there is no mistaking the fact that the Komeito stands for goals similar to those of neo-Shintoism which show an ultra-chauvinistic tendency reminiscent of General Araki and "New Japanism," and the unbalanced Kotoha (the Imperial Way faction) of the Japanese Army in the 1930s. Such a tendency will mean military-oriented expansionism abroad and totalitarian tendencies at home. Komeito's party membership may already have infiltrated other parties—particularly the ultra-conservative right-wing elements in the LDP. In view of the similar role played by most of the radical societies in the 1920s and the 1930s (i.e., Sakurakai, Kokuryokai, etc.), this aspect should not be lightly ruled out.

Communist Alliances

What, then, is Japan's future posture in Asia? Judging from the statements of Sato's government, Japan will soon concentrate her diplomatic efforts on Red China. Japan sees American efforts in Warsaw *vis-à-vis* the Chinese as potentially detrimental to her overtures to Peking, and will certainly try to outdo Washington's efforts in order to assure the fullest fruit of a diplomatic *rapprochement* with the Chinese. Through political recognition and other important agreements, Japan will want to precede America's entry into the China orbit. Any agreement with the Chinese will undoubtedly enhance Japan's bargaining position with the Soviet Union over reversion of Soviet-occupied islands north of Hokkaido. Tokyo has not given up hopes of regaining at least the southern half of the Kuriles—Habomai, Shikotan, Etorofu, Kunashir Islands.

Under present circumstances, Japan's relations with Moscow would not go beyond minor accords on an economic level—such as expansion of the Siberian agreement. For Japanese efforts to be successful, Tokyo might have to satisfy the Soviet Union with further clarification of future relations with the United States (i.e., a pledge of neutrality, for one), and some satisfactory assurances on China (i.e., either Japan's guarantee of neutrality or a pledge of non-support of Peking's position on the Sino-Soviet conflict), and a pledge of disengagement from the Nixon Doctrine in Asia.

Should Japan arm herself with nuclear weapons and pursue a policy of extreme nationalistic aspirations in Asia—bolstered by a continuing economic boom—one could hardly hope for repetition of the checks and balances applied against the aggressive powers in the 1930s. For one, the United States would have to rely on a completely new set of policies.

In this context, Japan's rise to a new superpower status in the future will have no historical precedent. It will neither encounter the same kind of challenges as those prior to 1941, nor will it have to expect a one-sided outcome as in 1945. There, indeed, lies the crucial importance of Japan's aspirations as a "refound" nation in the 1970s and beyond. Keiji Sakamoto, Japanese economist, put it in a nutshell: "If the US produced a chart of where it wants Japan to go in the coming years, Japan would accept it. But whether it would follow the chart is another matter. We have an expression: *Dosho imu*—Same bed, different dreams."

❧15❧

Revolution and Change in the Newer Nations

Nowhere in the world does politics proceed more out of the mouth of the gun than in the contemporary Middle East and Africa. In these areas, violence or the threat of violence is ubiquitous and military coups are frequent. In the Middle East there is the additional possibility of renewed Arab-Israeli fighting; in Black Africa instability in government and tension over the black-white issue continue to dominate politics.

In the first selection, "Conflict in the Middle East," Bernard Lewis, Professor of History of the Near and Middle East, University of London, makes the point that the Arab-Israeli dispute has become more than a "minor nuisance to the rest of the world" primarily because of great power intervention. Consequently, while Lewis explores the conflict in the Middle East, he does so primarily by examining Russian "aims and methods." His discussion is especially valuable for its carefully balanced evaluation of what the Soviets stand to gain or lose. In the process, Lewis contributes a somewhat unusual (and stimulating) perspective on the Middle East.

In the second selection, "The New Africa," Guy Hunter gives a thoughtful appraisal of an Africa beset by problems and in transition. His analysis sheds much light on the predominant role of the military and the precarious balance in contemporary African political institutions. Hunter's article is also very relevant to other poorer areas of the world.

488

Latin America today is an area of great and rapid change. With its population increasing very quickly, and industrialization gaining, it is an area beset by major problems. By comparison with the Middle East which has become a major area of superpower confrontation, Latin America has been largely protected by distance—but not entirely as the Cuban missile crisis showed. Unlike Africa, Latin America enjoys the comparative advantage of a lengthy experience with self-government. Now, as the 1970s unfold, Latin America is increasingly asserting itself in such areas as nationalization of foreign-held assets and protected (even exclusive) maritime belts far to sea. In these and in other areas the challenge has been posed to the United States to reexamine its policies and assumptions toward Latin America.

In the third selection, "Rockefeller Report on Latin America," Governor Nelson A. Rockefeller of New York discusses with the U.S. Senate Committee on Foreign Relations the results of a series of trips to twenty Latin American nations as the special emissary of President Nixon. In the give-and-take of the questioning over the substance of the report (not included here) the main issues are clearly outlined.

The fact that two of the selections in this chapter represent testimony before committees of the United States Senate is a hopeful sign of the reinvigoration of the Senate's role.

39

CONFLICT IN THE MIDDLE EAST

Bernard Lewis[*]

Contrary to the general impression which prevails, the Arab–Israel dispute is not the main world issue in the Middle East. It is basically a local issue, a conflict between local interests. Left alone, the participants would no doubt eventually reach some *modus vivendi* and, even if they did not, it would not constitute a major menace to world peace. Neither side is capable of inflicting a mortal wound on the other. Without a settlement, the quarrel might smoulder on, like Cyprus or Kashmir, troublesome but not critical for the participants, and a minor nuisance to the rest of the world.

In the Middle East as elsewhere, it is not small power quarrels which inflame great power conflict, but rather the reverse. The major issue and the major threat in the Middle East is the encounter between the United States and the Soviet Union, to which perhaps China may soon be added. It is this global confrontation which affects and transforms local conflicts, otherwise trivial, making them both more difficult and more dangerous.

. . . .

The immediate needs of the situation are therefore:

1. To assess the nature and purposes of the adversary, including the study of such questions as the relative importance of Russian interests and Communism, and the spectrum of policies and intentions in different sections of the Soviet leadership;

2. To devise appropriate methods of diplomacy and other techniques for the avoidance of conflict where possible and for success where not possible;

3. To evaluate local (i.e., Middle Eastern) factors and prospects and to devise and apply policies, in the light of the foregoing.

. . . .

In dealing, specifically, with the Soviet leaders, it is important to avoid the elementary but common error of assuming that they operate in the same way as we do, and within the same political and moral parameters. They do not. The present rulers of the Soviet Union are men who grew up in

---

[*] Bernard Lewis, "Conflict in the Middle East," Hearings Before the United States Senate, Subcommittee on National Security and International Operations of the Committee on Government Operations, 1971.

Stalin's Russia, and recognize no motive but interest or fear, no methods but guile and force. They have inherited the political traditions of the Tsarist state, but without the moral restraints of the orthodox church. For them, such concepts as legality, honesty, and fair play are without meaning. Educated on Marxist doctrine and Stalinist practice, they have no sense of sin or guilt, no compunction and compassion. In the short run, their contempt for law and public opinion gives them a freedom of action at home and abroad unattainable by Western statesmen; in the long run it is a source of weakness and danger.

The Soviet Union is like a house without a fuse-box, and no one knows when and where it will blow. Limited by training and outlook, the Soviet leaders are unable to understand any system that operates differently from theirs, and judge all on their own terms. Our Western leaders should not make the equivalent mistake.

Soviet Aims and Methods in the Middle East

I turn now to Russian aims and methods in the Middle East. A first question is the relative importance of Russian and Communist objectives. It is by now generally agreed that the Soviet Union acts as a great power pursuing national and indeed imperial objectives. Communism is dead as a revolutionary force in Russia and also in that part of the world Communist movement which is controlled by Russia. It is indeed now customary to call pro-Moscow elements in the Communist movement conservatives, a usage which can give rise to misunderstanding.

Communism survives as the legitimating ideology of the Soviet Union and bloc, with the double function of justifying the maintenance of hierarchy at home and of domination abroad—in contrast to our own so-called "ruling classes," which have lost the will to do either. It may be noted in passing that Communism is by far the most successful device which the 20th century has invented to keep the working classes down.

Communism is also important in that it inevitably and pervasively shapes both assessment and planning, both tactical and strategic, in a society where by now all have been brought up on Communist history, Communist logic and Communist morality. Even if the leaders of Soviet Russia no longer believe in anything but power, their thinking and behaviour are still shaped by Communist education, as the West is still shaped by the inherited values of the Judaeo-Christian tradition.

The question is sometimes asked whether Russian policy is offensive or defensive. This seems to me to be an artificial problem. Soviet policy could best be described as imperial; that is, imperial in the traditional rather than imperialist in the modern sense—the steady, cautious, but unrelenting expansion which earlier empire-builders ascribed to the will of God, and the Russians to the inexorable laws of history. These are seen as assigning a special role to both the Soviet system and the Great Russian people. . . .

Soviet leaders are haunted by many fears, but they still have the appetite, ferocity, smugness and sense of mission which are essential to the imperial mood, and which in the West have given way to satiety, guilt and doubt.

Senator Jackson [Chairman of the Subcommittee] has likened the Soviet Union, in its foreign relations, to a burglar walking down a hotel corridor, trying the door-handles and going in where he finds one unlocked. One might perhaps add a distinction between areas judged to be of vital Russian national interest, where the burglar carries tools and indeed weapons quite openly and continues his work even when detected, and those other areas, of less immediate concern, where he operates rather more like a sneak-thief. The burglar has, so to speak, been walking for many years round the vast periphery of the Russian Imperial frontier, testing and probing and moving on elsewhere when he encounters firm resistance. Stopped in their advance towards the Middle East by the Crimean War (1853–56), the Russians moved instead to the Amur River and the Far East and founded Vladivostok in 1860. Stopped again by the Treaty of Berlin (1878), which gave a further reprieve to the Turks, they advanced into Central Asia, and reached the borders of Afghanistan in 1884–85.

The post-war period shows a similar pattern. Talked out of Iran in 1946, the Russians took over Czechoslovakia and blockaded Berlin in 1948. Stopped short in Europe by the resistance of Tito and by the formation of NATO in 1949, they turned to the Far East. After the Korean peace in 1953 the time was ripe for another effort in the Middle East.

Soviet Aims in the Area

What are the aims of Soviet policy in the Middle East? The development of these may be seen in historical order in three phases:

The first and traditional objective was to exercise pressure on Turkey and Iran, and thus safeguard the southern approaches to the Russian Empire. In the course of their long journeys southwards and eastwards in search of a better frontier, the Russians came to dominate vast areas and many peoples. When this happened, the need for a stable frontier meant not only a good defensive frontier in military terms; it also meant protecting the subject peoples within the imperial frontier against influence or incitement from their unsubjugated kinsmen or co-religionists beyond the frontier. The defence of Moscow led to Warsaw and Prague, to Sofia, and, unsuccessfully, to Belgrade. The defence of Baku could lead to Baghdad and Basra. Where a territory could not conveniently be annexed or occupied, it was to be kept weak and isolated, and prevented from becoming the seat or the instrument of a powerful and potentially hostile state. Above all, it was to be kept out of the hands of a rival great power.

The Russian interest in the Middle East was for centuries therefore primarily concerned with Turkey and Iran, the countries immediately to the south of the frontier, and inhabited by peoples akin in language, culture and religion to those already incorporated by conquest within the imperial domain.

The first Soviet offensive in the Middle East immediately after the war was consequently directed against Turkey and Iran, with demands for bases in the Turkish Straits, for the annexation of parts of eastern Turkey and with the attempt to establish a puppet people's democracy in the Soviet-occupied zone of northern Iran. At that time, the Russian offensive against Turkey and Iran failed. Both countries held firm and, with Western help, were able to induce the Soviets to withdraw. By their own acts, the Soviets themselves created the situation which they had been trying to prevent, and demonstrated, to Turkey and Iran on the one hand and to the West on the other, both the danger and the remedy. Soviet action thus initiated the course of events which led to the Truman doctrine, the extension of NATO to Turkey and the creation of CENTO.

Turkey and Iran were the main objectives of the Soviet move against the Middle East in 1945–46; they remain a primary concern of Soviet policy in the Middle East to the present day.

Their second objective in the post-war period was to exclude Western influence from the Arab lands, which were then regarded as a potential base for attack on the Soviet Union or the territories which it dominates. It was for this reason that in 1947–48 the Soviet Union supported Israel rather than the Arabs. At that time, Britain was seen as the principal Western power in the Middle East, and support for Israel was the best way of getting the British out of Palestine. That result having been achieved, Soviet support was withdrawn and later diverted elsewhere.

The next and current stage came with the Soviet attempt first to penetrate and then to dominate the Arab lands. The initial purpose, perhaps even now the primary purpose of the Soviet adventure among the Arabs, was to bring new pressures to bear on Turkey and Iran, and thus induce them to realign, or at least to modify, their foreign policies. The frontal attacks on Turkey and Iran had failed, and a repetition was not feasible, now that both countries were buttressed by Western alliances. Instead, the Soviets adopted a tactic of leap-frogging and were thus able to take their southern neighbors from the rear. This policy has already achieved a certain measure of success. The Soviet advance, coupled with intermittent doubts about American judgment and reliability, has led both Turkey and Iran to reappraise their positions. Neither country has withdrawn from its alliances, but both have found it expedient to mend their fences in the North.

Significantly, the Soviets have so far refused to support Iraq in her quarrel with Iran over the Shatt al-Arab. They could of course do so at any time if they thought it expedient, just as they could support Syrian irredentist claims against Turkey. These are useful levers against both countries.

The apparent ease and speed of Soviet successes among the Arabs encouraged wider ambitions. The most obvious gain is the power to threaten the southern flank of NATO, both militarily and through its oil supplies. There are signs that the economies of the Soviet Union and its satellites may draw on Middle Eastern oil, but for the time being the direct economic interest in oil is less important than the strategic—i.e., the ability to threaten or cut the supply of Middle Eastern oil to the free world. A further temptation is the possibility of extending Russian influence from Egypt along the North African littoral and thus into the Western Mediterranean.

The confrontation with the United States remains a major Soviet concern in the area. In recent years, however, the confrontation with China, and the growing Chinese intervention in southern Arabia, East Africa, and elsewhere, has added a new dimension and a new perspective to Soviet strategy. The Middle East is the land bridge to Asia and Africa, the link between the Mediterranean and the Indian Ocean. The southern and eastern outlets— the Red Sea and the Persian Gulf—are acquiring a new significance.

The Soviet aim is, clearly, to preserve, consolidate, and extend their position in the Arab countries. To make full use of their position, they need to reopen the Canal, which would at once enormously strengthen their naval and therefore political position in the Red Sea and Indian Ocean. On the other hand the reopening of the Suez Canal would require a peaceful settlement, which would weaken and perhaps end their hold on Egypt. This is part of the Soviet dilemma in the Middle East. It is not the whole of it.

Soviet Assessment and Strategy

The strategy of the Soviet leaders, it would seem, is to maintain a state of tension short of war, thus ensuring the continuance of Arab dependence and need for their help. Soviet interests would thus appear to be opposed to a genuine peace in the area. But this situation is inherently unstable and therefore holds many dangers, especially to the Soviets themselves.

One is growing Arab disillusionment with Soviet friendship. The Soviet Union is a weighty protector—but the Arabs are more conscious of the weight than of the protection. The Soviets have a great need to gain some sort of victory over Israel in order to convince the Arabs of the value of their protection. For this, they must persuade the United States to provide them with one—a task that is not as difficult as it ought to be.

Another danger is that the situation could suddenly get out of control and escalate to the point of war, which would again confront the Soviets with an agonizing choice. In 1967 the Russians were confident that their protégés would win if left alone, and the Soviet representative at the Security Council at first fought hard to delay the cease-fire, so as to give the Arabs time to complete their victory. On that occasion the Russians were wrong. That error will not be repeated. Now both sides know that if war breaks out the choice before the Soviets will be between an Israeli victory, with the final discrediting of Russian patronage, and effective Russian military intervention which, in order to be effective, would have to be very considerable. Otherwise Russia could suffer her own *Pueblo* incident—on a larger scale, and with far more damaging effects.

The Soviet decision depends on American policy and more particularly on Soviet assessment of American policy. In the past the Russians have been guilty of grave errors of assessment which are perhaps excusable since others, even many Americans, have often erred in the same way. This was especially so last summer. In Russia the smallest challenge to authority is visited with immediate and condign punishment. Russian observers, seeing the highly publicized agony of the United States, appear to have assumed that the United States was falling apart and ceasing to be a real power capable of pursuing any kind of foreign policy in the Middle East or elsewhere. This assumption was reflected in the brazen and contemptuous violation of the standstill agreement from the very day of its signature, and received apparent confirmation in the agitated attempts by some Washington spokesmen to look the other way. The subsequent and unexpected vigour shown by the United States in the Middle East and other places brought second thoughts.

A further source of Russian anxiety was the hijack affair in September and its sequel. This reminded the Russians of what they had already had the opportunity to observe in 1967—the unpredictable, uncontrollable character of Arab politics. The Russians do not like the unpredictable and uncontrollable, and there have been signs of re-thinking and re-assessment in consequence. In 1967, the lesson they learned was the need to tighten their control over their Arab protégés. We do not know what lessons they are learning this time. If the Soviets decide that the present position is too unstable and hazardous for comfort and that the United States is really firm, then probably they will accept a stalemate as in Korea, or perhaps even allow—I say allow, rather than encourage—peace to be made. If, on the other hand, they decide that American firmness is a flash in the pan and will vanish within the next year or two, they will maintain a hard line and pursue it as far as they judge it to be safe. Given the necessary acquiescence, this could be very far indeed.

American Policy Needs

The future therefore depends very largely on American policy in the area. This might include the following aims:

1. To make clear to the Russians that direct intervention would involve unacceptable risks.

2. To clarify policy to both the Israelis and the Arabs so as neither to alarm by fear of betrayal, nor to encourage by tolerance of intransigence.

3. To distinguish between friends and enemies—the ability to do so is a necessary biological condition of survival for any animal. In the Middle East, perhaps more than elsewhere, one is expected to help one's friends and not one's enemies. It is of course better to win over enemies than to defeat

them. This is achieved not by courting them but by creating a situation in which they court you. If, as some desire, you appear as an unsafe friend and a harmless enemy, if you make it a practice to bully your friends and court your enemies—you must not be surprised if, at the end of the day, you have more enemies than friends.

4. To take adequate steps to protect vital Western interests, for example in the Gulf, in the Indian Ocean and in the Mediterranean, and to make clear that this will be done.

5. With all this, to continue to work for peace. At best, the Russians will permit a settlement. It is useless to count on them for help in procuring one. Negotiations, to have any chance of success, most ultimately, in some form, involve the parties themselves. This means the governments of Israel and the Arab states, and not such nebulous and intangible entities as the Jews, the Arabs, Zionism, Pan-Arabism, or Revolution. Peace will come about only when both sides realize that it is in their own hands, and that the powers will neither impose nor prevent it.

A final point. It may often be better to stand pat and do nothing rather than engage in activity. There is a common tendency, especially in the new world, to assume that action or even mere activism is always better than inaction in terms both of expediency and of morality. This is sometimes the reverse of the truth.

In a situation of deadlock, a burst of febrile activity can often lead to a weakening of one's own stand to the advantage of one's immobile and more stupid perhaps, but more patient, opponent.

The American and Soviet Positions

Contrary to the prevailing impression, the West has an easier and Russia a harder task in the Middle East, for a number of reasons. There are first the deficiencies in Russia's own position. Her economic and technological base is much weaker, so that her effort and investment cost her more, and accomplish proportionately less, than those of the West. Her political and cultural offerings, too, are less attractive, and have notably failed to arouse enthusiasm among those Arabs and others who have been able to observe them at close quarters. Such observation cannot be entirely prevented.

Russia's satellites are the poor states of the area, which are politically unstable and unpredictable, and economically very costly. This is a built-in and continuing disadvantage, since even rich states, on adopting revolutionary methods and turning towards Russia, became poor states. It will not take the revolution very long to reduce even the fabulously wealthy state of Libya to the same condition as successive revolutions have reduced a once prosperous Iraq.

Russia therefore operates under several disabilities. Her protégés are in constant need of both military aid and economic support, while America's protégés are, by comparison, strong and self-reliant. The Russians therefore have to carry an immense economic burden, which is relatively much heavier for them, and causes greater strain, than even the Vietnam war for the United States.[1] Militarily, the onus of intervention, with the consequent risks, lies on Russia. America's protégés are safer if both are left alone.

In the meantime, by her presence and action in the Arab lands Russia is building up very rapidly a reserve of exasperation and hatred of the kind previously encountered by the Western powers in the area and still encountered by the United States in other parts where she plays a parallel though not similar role. The Middle East is beginning, increasingly, to understand the facts of Russian imperialism and to cast wistful glances towards the West.

In view of all this, Russia's position is inherently unstable and precarious in the Middle East. She is therefore less well able to stand pat and await events than the West. It is natural that she should seek Western help in changing this situation to her advantage. It is not necessary that such help should be provided.

If the peace, even the present peace, is kept, there will probably be an evolution towards stabilization and eventual settlement of the Arab–Israel conflict. If Russia decides that the West is not serious, then grave dangers will follow. If Russia, in making such an assumption should prove correct, then the outlook will be very grim indeed, and not only for the Middle East.

---

[1] Estimates of Soviet aid in the Middle East and North Africa up to September 1970 are as follows: A total of $4 billion made up of; Iran $290 million; South Yemen $10 million; Yemen $65 million; The Sudan $60 million; Libya $25 million; Iraq $690 million; Syria $490 million; Algeria $275 million; and United Arab Republic $2,100 million. These figures do not include weapons etc., supplied since September 1970.

40

THE NEW AFRICA

Guy Hunter[*]

I

The problems which would beset post-colonial Africa were hardly recognized as the continent emerged into congeries of independent states ten years ago. Perhaps too great familiarity with detail made it hard for the colonial powers to see the problems clearly; too little familiarity with the realities made it hard for the United States; for both, and for the Africans

---

[*] Guy Hunter, "The New Africa," *Foreign Affairs*, Vol. 48, No. 4 (July 1970), pp. 712–725. Copyright © 1970 by the Council on Foreign Relations, Inc., New York. Reprinted by permission.

themselves, belief in the sovereign power of freedom blinded them to the risks and tests which freedom entails.

But the problems lying in wait (which had much in common, also, with those of the new Asian nations) were not long in coming. The most dangerous of them was the legitimacy of the political system—how to establish the authority and sovereignty of a constitution so that it should be unquestioned even if governments ruling by it should change. Unlike uncolonized Ethiopia—or, in Asia, Thailand—the modern countries of tropical Africa had no traditional rulers to whom power could be naturally entrusted. Universal suffrage, for largely illiterate populations, was used as the legitimizing tool.

The economic problems derived from the dual economy created by colonialism—the small, largely Westernized "modern sector" of sophisticated production and consumption, versus the huge hinterland of somewhat disturbed rural life, tribalism and ancient cultural tradition. There seemed to be only a choice of emphasizing this dualism by further development of the modern sector through close economic relations with the West, or of trying to escape neo-colonialism by sacrificing economic growth.

Certain ideological and moral dilemmas have also been deeply felt by African leaders who wanted to avoid the materialistic capitalism of the West, escape the horrors of the nineteenth-century industrial revolution, and invent an economy which put social services ahead of the production of material goods (which in the West had financed the Welfare State). The resulting variants of state socialism have often placed upon thinly manned governments and communities which are weak in commercial skills the major burden of generating wealth, a function which in the West was largely performed by private enterprise. In some cases the emphasis on social expenditure has preëmpted resources urgently needed to expand the productive base of the economy.

Apart from purely economic and ideological issues, the dual economy has posed a more profound problem for national integration—the synchronous development of economic, political, social and moral elements in the society. One obvious symptom of social disarray is seen in the growing imbalance between educational output and employment, the frustration of unemployed graduates which at Independence already showed among primary-school leavers and was later to overtake first the secondary schools and then even the liberal-arts graduates from universities. And at a deeper level, this lack of integration shows itself in the huge divergences in attitudes, values and cultural continuity between the modernized and the traditional sectors. Here the educational system is obviously critical, and here the high-level manpower planners inadvertently widened the gap still further. As I wrote in 1962:

To abstract from the whole Western system just those elements designed to produce engineers or geophysicists (rather than the whole, which is designed to produce citizens and men) could be to fall into a grave mistake. For what is in issue in Africa is the growth of new nations, new societies of men, not merely the construction of new economies. . . . It would be unwise to assume that merely by "planning" and massive expenditure on a technological education any African country can turn itself in two decades into the reality, rather than the façade, of a developed modern society. The real growth must have time to spread its roots deep and wide in the life of the community, aided by an education which fully replaces the old tribal training as a preparation for modern citizenship.[1]

There is a real dilemma here. To build into one and the same school system an education with a strong element of cultural continuity and a real relevance to the conditions of a slowly modernizing rural life, and a curriculum designed to produce the small but vital technical and administrative leadership with which to replace expatriates, has proved beyond the wit of politicians and planners and of their foreign advisers; it remains an unsolved and even more pressing problem today.

Finally, there was and is the problem of transfer of technology. Developing nations have been urged, and have been eager, to borrow both technology and institutions developed in and for a wholly different social and economic environment. But, as H. S. Frankel has pointed out: "Technical knowledge, the machine, and capital goods in general never exist in the abstract but always in the relatively fleeting form suited to the momentary situation and to that complex of unique problems to which they have been adapted. That is why they cannot readily be transferred from one situation to another." The dangers of transferring technology were fairly obvious; as to institutions—trade unions, universities, county councils—they were less quickly or clearly seen.

In a sophisticated age, so well stocked with analysts and critics, it is surprising that in face of this range of fundamental problems African independence was greeted first with such high expectations, and later with such disappointment and disillusion when the cracks began to show. There were critics, especially among the settlers and administrators who knew Africa best. But their voices were neglected, partly because they were seen as self-interested; partly (and very rightly) because they so often addressed themselves not to problems but to persons—to the alleged incapacity of Africans as such. If we turn now to the record, I think it can be demonstrated that it has been the problems rather than the persons which have made this decade a grueling experience—and yet still a hopeful one—for Africans and their well-wishers alike.

II

That the first independent governments should have been formed by "one man, one vote" elections was inevitable, because independence parties demanded it, because there was no other acceptable method, and because the colonial powers could not deny democratic ideals. That such a method

---

[1] I include this quotation, written in 1962, partly to avoid the obvious accusation of hindsight, and partly because it still expresses the situation today.

should be satisfactory as a continuing form of government was highly improbable. As Dr. Lucy Mair has said: "Conferred from above on a populace which is not aware of any desire to manage its own affairs, democracy can never be anything but a mechanical system, to be manipulated by a few individuals for their own ends, while the majority remain indifferent to its proceedings." The result has been faction; and worse still, too often tribal, communal or racial faction, since such loyalties are the easiest and strongest foundations on which factional leaders can build support.

Certainly in Africa the leaders who succeeded in the first elections recognized the dangers, and their early years have been spent in constant appeals for national unity and condemnation of tribal and communal faction. (Discrimination against expatriates and aliens was an allowable safety-valve, since they could not threaten any government's political position.) Perhaps half-consciously, some leaders also saw that elections would not give "authority" (in Hannah Arendt's sense of instinctive reverence for the *auctor* or founder of a national tradition), and that without authority, which democracy in new countries lacked, neither constitution nor government would be secure. It was thus that, in a great number of African and Asian states, the single charismatic leader, backed by a single national party, animated by some overtly expressed national philosophy (Nkrumah-ism, Nyerere-ism, Kaunda-ism, Senghor-ism in Africa; Gandhi-ism in India; Sukarno-ism in Indonesia; U Nu-ism in Burma) can be seen as an attempt to found a tradition around which authority would form and grow. Government would then be legitimized, not so much by votes as by its succession from the founding fathers and their philosophy.

If we look at a few African states, we see that Nyerere, Kaunda, Sékou-Touré, Houphouet-Boigny are perhaps on their way to achieving this result. Kenyatta, too identified by tribal background, may not succeed in passing on his national authority. Obote in Uganda, having reached power by political skill and sustained it by armed force, has only just adopted a national philosophy in his "Move to Left" proclamation of October 1969. Nkrumah overdid a cult of personalism and economic ambition, and crashed. The old Belgian Congo never had a start. Nigeria, lacking a dominating central figure, staggered through some years of compromise among three national loyalties and is now in political ruins. There are parallels in Asia: Sukarno, like Nkrumah, overplayed his personal hand and ignored the warnings of economic disaster; U Nu in Burma, perhaps too gentle and betrayed by bad economic advice, had not the strength to maintain his role; Prince Sihanouk in Cambodia for a long time achieved, with fascinating skill, a marriage of the "authority" of monarchy and the mythology of development, but now also seems to have fallen from the razor's edge.

The failure of some of the first leaders—and West Africa particularly is strewn with failures—has been due not only to their lesser skill or to tribalism: it is certainly in part due to failure to control the greed of their henchmen in the modern sector. Without a tradition to control them, ministers, businessmen and some officials gave way to an orgy of corruption, intrigue and repression (bitterly described by François Fanon as neo-colonialism), which was enough to discredit all authority and leadership, however charismatic.

When authority fails, force, the oldest authenticator of governments, returns. We are still in the phase of military takeovers (two took place while this article was being written). Sometimes the General attempts to create a "Founder's" tradition, as Mobutu may be doing, and as Ayub Khan attempted in Pakistan. Sometimes, as in Ghana or Sierra Leone, the military phase is a pause for reconstruction: Ghana's new democratic experiment, thoughtfully designed, will be of extreme interest. Pakistan faces this third phase with extreme anxiety and little hope.

This political analysis is made in terms of authority rather than of the pressures on governments, simply because these pressures, from tribal groups, from intellectuals, from rivals, from half-educated unemployed, were always certain to be strong. The critical issue is the strength of government to contain them while some unity and authority are building. Indeed, it is perhaps surprising that some of the successful leaders, such as Nyerere or Kaunda, have not insured themselves by a greater armed force: the East African military revolts, trivial as they were, showed what a perilously narrow margin of security they have.

If this analysis is correct, there are clear implications, at least for Africa. First, that classical democracy, as such, was an unsuitable form of government for most emerging nations; in most countries, it has not succeeded and there may be more failures to come. Second, that perhaps the best hope of stability for Africa may be in those countries where a national leader, protected by adequate armed force and supported by an ideology carried widely through the country by a single party, is in power long enough for authority to grow around him, around his memory as founder, and around a set of ideas which succession governments adopt. It is perhaps in this way that a national consensus, vital to the working of a democratic system, could grow.

III

A dual economy, reflecting the contrast between colonial administration and investment on the one hand, and the indigenous economy on the other, was bound to exist in Africa. The early independence policies of industrializing and building a top-quality modern infrastructure, which were reinforced by foreign aid, widened the gap still further, gradually substituting an African élite for a European one. The result has often been described in terms of modern capital cities (surrounded by shack towns), trunk roads, airports, tourist hotels, a few modern factories and at least one superb university structure in each country. The rapid growth of (usually) more modest primary and secondary schools and of the provision of teachers for them has been the biggest contribution of the aided modernizing process to a better balance in society.

The difficulty of escaping from this situation has been underemphasized; perhaps the briefest glance at history will make it more clear. When Europe entered the industrial revolution populations were small and grew at a moderate pace—the highest rate in a decade in Britain was 1.4 percent per annum (1820–30). There was therefore a good chance of absorbing the extra manpower into rapidly growing industries. Besides, between 1600 and 1900 northern and western Europe conquered or penetrated Canada, the United States, South America, Africa, much of the Near East, India and Burma, Indochina, Malaya, Indonesia, the Philippines, the Pacific islands, Australia and New Zealand—that does not leave much of the rest of the world save for Russia, China and Japan. The growing industrial nations had a decisive technological superiority. It was therefore not necessary for British industry to await the expansion of consumer demand within the nation's own agricultural community, for the markets of a conquered world were open. Public expenditure on education and social services was small (primary education did not become universal until the 1880s in Britain, long after the main technical expansion had taken place). Nationhood had been established for centuries.

Contrast with this story that of Africa. Population growth has preceded industrial development, and at two and one-half to three percent per annum. There is no new world to expand into; there is no technical superiority to wield in existing markets; industry must wait upon the growth of consumer demand from among the vast bulk of rural population—in the 1960s Tanzania was classified as 95 percent rural, five percent urban; education and social services have come before industrial development on a large scale; national unity is barely 10 years old.

This list of contrasts is, to my mind, staggering. It faces Africa, and to a lesser degree most other developing countries, with a situation which is unique in modern history. With no large external market for manufactures, and without the ability of a Britain or a Switzerland to import raw materials, apply special skills and reëxport them, the foundation of African economies had to be laid in primary production—lucky were those with oil or copper —using agricultural or mineral exports to purchase equipment for industry. But industry in turn was limited to the internal market, and low productivity and low incomes in the massive agricultural sector narrowly limited chances for industrial expansion or for the growth of small-scale processing, commerce, distributive and technical services from which a more solid economy could grow. The small modern sector typically was burdened with over-valued exchange rates (favoring imports of sophisticated machinery and élite consumption goods), excessively high differentials between urban and rural earnings, a stagnant agriculture and a growing menace of unemployment. The mineral-rich countries (Zambia, Nigeria and the oil countries of North Africa) find it even harder to unify the high-reward mining economy with the subsistence hinterland.

It is this situation, not confined to Africa, which has led to rich cash-crop exports alongside miserable subsistence agriculture and to the paradox of widespread malnutrition and even hunger alongside complaints of limited demand for agricultural output. In Latin America it has led to the dreary sequence of development expenditure in the industrial sector—inflation; crisis; retrenchment; stagnation; development expenditure—a sequence sadly familiar to the World Bank and the International Monetary Fund. In Asia, with a longer tradition of craft industry, metalworking and commerce, the duality has not been quite so marked, although even in India the neglect of food production gave a sharp lesson in 1966.

In short, the attempt to industrialize from the top downward by borrowing sophisticated techniques, while 60 to 70 percent of the population remained in a stagnant rural economy, represents an attempt to enter the twentieth-century world industrial economy before the domestic foundations have been properly laid. The worst symptom is unemployment, which will be the dominant problem of Africa in the 1970s; the way on is— "reculer pour mieux sauter"—to return to a really thorough development of the traditional agricultural sector, accompanied by a development of the processing, supply and consumer goods industries and services which a successful and modernized agriculture demands.

Unemployment is best illustrated by some simple figures on population growth, rural-urban distribution and salaried employment. When a two and one-half percent population growth is applied to a 75 percent rural population, the resulting increase in absolute rural numbers will far exceed the natural growth (two and one-half percent on 25 percent) in towns; it will exceed it even if growth plus immigration to towns adds up to six percent per annum. Thus, in the sharpest contrast to Western experience, the rural areas in Africa and Asia will have to give a livelihood to greatly increased absolute numbers for a generation or more. Even with a seven percent per annum growth in gross national product, in modern experience salaried employment seldom increases faster than two to three percent per annum. Thus, the towns will not be able to absorb their own growth; and the country will face ever-mounting pressure on land and jobs.

These grim calculations have been accepted only slowly. The first tendency in Africa, under the pressure of the foreign exchange drain in the modern sector, was to reëmphasize export crops, until markets began to be filled and the threat of unemployment sharpened. The second main response was to create very expensive settlement schemes; East and West Nigeria, Tanzania and Kenya have felt very sharply the cost and the small economic result (although in Kenya the political gain was worth the cost). Only in the last year or two has real attention moved to enriching, diversifying and commercializing internal food production, with its possible gains not only in nutrition but, above all, in employment. Hopefully, a highly intensive agriculture, with doubled farm incomes, could create a hum of construction as well as commercial, distributive, processing and servicing activity which could bring a substantial volume of wasted human and technical potential into productivity and start to build the economy from below.

The idea of the "green revolution" and the importance of agriculture are beginning to grow all over the developing world, and there have been remarkable successes in India, Pakistan, Taiwan, Mexico and at scattered points in Africa and Latin America. But there is still a long way to go before statements about the priority of the agricultural sector are borne out by priorities in resource-allocation: in physical investment, personnel, training, education, market incentives. How many countries still are content with one field extension officer to 1,500 or 2,000 farming families? Indeed, in Mexico and in India there are clear dangers that the green revolution will simply add a small group of the larger and more powerful farmers to the modern sector, leaving the other three-quarters of the rural economy relatively worse off.

IV

A dual economy has meant a dual educational system—full Westernized education for the lucky few who are destined for the modern sector, a bare taste of education (also Westernized) for the multitude destined to stay in the rural economy. Again, this seemed inevitable at the start. The demand for full equality for at least some few in the newly independent countries implied equality in educational "standards," which was often confused with content. Africa certainly was not to be fobbed off with rural polytechnics instead of universities. After the decline of the fashion for high-level manpower studies aimed exclusively at the modern sector, the pendulum has swung back to a revived concern for an education more related to environment, to national cultural tradition and to economic and educational needs at the lower and middle levels of society. It has proved hard to translate this new approach into practice, whether in syllabus or in structure. For one thing, the association of education with superior employment has had time to be deeply engraved in the minds of parents and pupils alike. But above all, an education really suited to the rural environment in which the great majority of Africans and Asians live can become both acceptable and genuinely functional only when that environment begins to offer real opportunity and to require skills and knowledge on a large scale, which an education revised both in content and structure could provide. It is useless to dream of a revolution in education without a revolution in the economy. While opportunity lies only in the Westernized top of the dual economy, education will remain in thrall to that small sector. It will produce first enough and then too many graduates, and the surplus will then emigrate to greener pastures in the developed countries.

Thus, education, employment and rural development are an almost metaphysical three-in-one. Perhaps the most forceful statement of this trinity in Africa was made at the Kericho Conference in Kenya in 1966; it was followed up by the Kenya government and the university with a series of a dozen pilot schemes of integrated rural development, scattered in contrasting environments all over Kenya, the first of which are now emerging from the planning stage into action. The Indian "block development" system, older and covering an immense area, moves in the same direction, though with less consciousness of the critical issue of employment for the mass of school-leavers.

Both the need for employment and the need for social integration require the growth, from below, of a bridging middle to the dual economy, and an educational system consonant with it—more demotic, more practical and based on those elements of tradition capable of survival in the twentieth century. It is mainly on the Left—in Tanzania, in Cuba—that such ideas are being given practical expression: the Right would be well advised to take heed. The growing body of unemployed young school-leavers exasperated by a flick of irrelevant education, and the continued existence of "two nations"—these are beyond question the two major dangers from now on.

V

Developing societies, especially in Africa, are necessarily borrowing societies; we have seen them borrowing political forms, technology, institutions. The peculiar nature of this borrowing process is worth a closer look, for the light which it can throw on the whole development process described here.

If we look at an African country of five or six million people—say Uganda —its economy has much in common with that of Britain in about the seventeenth century when its population was also five million. It may seem absurd for Uganda to borrow twentieth-century techniques and social forms, the outcome of 300 years of subsequent social and economic change. Yet, while there is much to be learned from the steps by which Britain was transformed from an agricultural and craft society to an industrial one, it is equally mistaken to suppose that these steps must be simply repeated. The environment of 1650 Britain was Europe in 1650; the environment of Uganda is the 1970 world. Developing countries have a single great advantage, as latecomers in this environment; the sciences, which Europe had to find, are there for the taking. If development which took Europe 300 years is to be achieved in 50, this great accelerator must be borrowed and fitted somehow into the local social structure.

In fact, some technologies *can* easily be borrowed; radio, electric power to drive an illiterate peasant's tubewell, bicycles, typewriters, sewing machines, the truck and the DC3 find a ready use in rural areas from China to Peru. Some, however, will not fit; high-speed mass production machinery requires conditions (mass market, skills, prices of labor) which disqualify it for use in totally different economies. The degree of suitability for the environment may well be one criterion for the transfer of technology. (The problem of adapting technology is largely a market problem. As the Japanese have shown, if there is a market for small tractors, small tractors will be produced.) But it should be emphasized that technology is not science: the latter is not vitally connected with the environment that houses it; it is true for the world, and from it technologies adapted to social circumstances can be borrowed.

Clearly, the borrowing of social institutions will be far more difficult. It has also been far less studied. Why were trade unions, with their social reference to nineteenth-century European history and traditions shouting to high heaven, introduced almost forcibly into Africa? Why has the Rochdale Coöperative model been exported to three-quarters of the world, as though it was a philosopher's stone for all sorts and conditions of men? Why has the cohort of consultants and aid agencies continued to stamp British, French or American institutions on developing countries? A reasoned theory of the growth and appropriateness of institutions, and the changes in them which should accompany the uniquely rapid process of change in developing countries, is still to be found.

To put this abstract argument into concrete terms, it is possible to find rational criteria for the types of institution likely to succeed (or fail) in the development of small-holding agriculture, which occupies such a vast mass of Africans and Asians. For example, even the most fervent devotee of private enterprise can hardly believe that commercial firms can pioneer the distribution of fertilizer to tens of thousands of scattered villages, mostly inaccessible by hard road, when demand is infinitesimal and credit nonexistent; yet at a later stage of growth they may be easily the best agency. Even—one would think—the most patriotic American could not believe that the American model of university extension (developed for literate farmers, on sizable farms, with good access roads, supported by a trade press and aggressive commercial selling) would work for illiterate villagers on three-acre holdings requiring the simplest advice; yet 20 years from now this method might become appropriate. Why should county councils, served by poorly paid officials, manned by small-time politicians and village magnates concerned with private power or gain or the smashing of political rivals, prove a suitable choice of institution for improving the lot of small peasantry? What are the conditions in which coöperatives normally succeed, and the conditions in which they almost invariably fail? There are plenty of examples of both in Africa, yet the tool is still used, without rational discrimination, alike in promising and in totally unpromising circumstances.

If we look at the record of African countries over the last 10 years, we thus see them seeking desperately to contain the demands of economic growth and alien technical change within a social and political structure partly borrowed, partly invented, seldom reinforced by indigenous tradition.

Alas, the tools chosen for this process, far from being closely adapted to local circumstances and stages of growth, have usually been "blanket" choices—of coöperatives, district commissioners, universities, development corporations or whatever—largely reflecting ideology, or fashion, or the home practice of the consultant who advises. In the 1970s the technical means of agricultural advance in the tropics will at last be widely available: now far more thought is needed on the administrative and institutional patterns through which the contribution of science—the one great accelerator—can be made effective in the unique combination of seventeenth-century society and twentieth-century technique.

VI

There is not much that the West can do to help the developing nations with the crisis of political authority at the center, or in the choice between the authoritative commissioner, elected council or party machine in local administration, except to avoid giving bad advice or chanting our own political hymns. But we can, through well-judged aid, help cure the evils of the dual economy, particularly in the agricultural sector; help with population control; and refrain from selling our own educational system to countries which need a radically different one.

We can also recognize, in relation to the transfer of technology and institutions, that the path of social and economic development in Africa (and elsewhere) will be unique, and will require its own social inventiveness. Indeed, development is becoming, and must increasingly become, a path chosen by developing countries for themselves. Patronage, aid with ideological or political strings, the "selling" of Western techniques and institutions will be increasingly resented, at least by those nations which have the political will to break the deadlock which a rich, Westernized modern sector and a stagnant rural economy are imposing on their society. Aid-givers will have to talk less, listen more and think more creatively if they are to find channels to help bring about widespread, indigenous, self-sustaining growth.

Finally, there is a growing coalescence of ideas, politically to the Left, which have been generated in very different circumstances in the developing world and in the rich, white world. From Asia and Latin America they come as protest against the old establishment of landlords, merchants, corrupt industrialists and politicians; from Africa, as rage against the new establishment of Westernized African privilege and self-seeking. In all three the figure who is seen to lurk behind the local enemy, blocking the door to social emancipation, racial equality, economic independence is the white capitalist or "racialist" or "imperialist," whether in Washington (and Vietnam), London (and Salisbury), or even Moscow (and Prague). From the developed world comes an answering cry of protest, not only from idealist and anarchic youth, not only from racial and social minorities, but from a growing group of normal adult men and women oppressed by the blemishes of our own system—by injustice, poverty amid riches, materialism, destruction of the environment, bureaucratic arrogance, lack of participation. The radical experiments of a Cuba or a Tanzania or a Zambia may seem far away from such concerns. But they strike a common chord of protest, and this is a protest upon which civilization itself depends for its renewal generation by generation.

Growing violence in our world is a sign that this protest is not being heeded fast enough. The West cannot afford, for its own health, to be ranged among the old against the young. John F. Kennedy, whatever he was in fact, was *seen* by the outer world as one who listened to the protest, and his death was widely mourned accordingly. General de Gaulle, in the heartland of rich Europe, was swept away because he heard it too late. We cannot afford to look at the developing world, of Africa or Asia or Latin America, without sympathy for those forces in it which, whatever their faults, nevertheless stand for renewal; for the same forces are also within our gates; we too need renewal. Perhaps the growing awareness of the blemishes of our own system will also help us to look less dogmatically at developing countries, especially in Africa; to realize that their problems are not those which we thought we had solved 100 years ago, and that our old solutions will not suit them; and to show more patience and generosity at least to those new nations which are sincerely seeking a new political and economic formula for their future.

41

ROCKEFELLER REPORT ON LATIN AMERICA

Nelson A. Rockefeller*

Senator Church: Thank you, Governor, for your statement this morning. . . .

. . . .

I thought we might start [with the fact that] this committee has been very much disturbed by the precipitous slide toward militarism in the hemisphere.

Free government, democratic government, has now become the exception

---

* Nelson A. Rockefeller, "Rockefeller Report on Latin America," presented to the United States Senate, Subcommittee on Western Hemisphere Affairs of the Committee on Foreign Relations, November 20, 1969.

to the rule. And in reading your report . . . I was disturbed to find language which all but approves the military juntas that have come to power.

For example, I read, "In short, a new type of military man is coming to the fore and often becoming a major force for constructive social change in the American Republics. Motivated by increasing impatience with corruption, inefficiency, and a stagnant political order, the new military man is prepared to adapt his authoritarian tradition to the goals of social and economic progress."

Well, language of that kind is reminiscent of the time when I was beginning to take my first interest in politics, when similar arguments were put forward in justification of the Fascist military dictatorships in Europe. I would like to start there, to give you an opportunity to clarify your own position with respect to the military governments that have come to dominate the politics of the hemisphere.

Governor Rockefeller: Well, Mr. Chairman, I appreciate your going to the heart of this question because I think this is probably the most important first step we have to face and understand in facing up to the broader problems of our relations.

Now I would say as far as the quote that you read is concerned, the real question is, is that an accurate description of the situation? . . .

I would like to say that in all frankness, I think that is an accurate description of the situation that exists today in this hemisphere.

Now, this is really the basic question. If it is true, then it is important we understand it.

If it is not true, then it is important we know that.

Now, let me just talk a little about this statement and the facts relating to it. Traditionally the military and the church have been the two forces in the hemisphere that have related to what was known as stability, the institution, and they supported the landowners and that was the ruling organization.

Both these institutions are going through—that is, the military and the church—are going through major, almost revolutionary changes and I think it is terribly important that we understand that and recognize it because neither of them are as I knew them, frankly, back in the early 1940's.

The military group we are talking about used to draw its leadership, its officers, from the landowning class and they were part of the structure.

The landowning class has moved importantly into industrial activity and into the cities and has lost interest in becoming involved in military life.

Today the bright leadership in the military is coming from working class people who are ambitious, who have a desire to get ahead, who have no chance for education.

They do not own any land. Their families are not professional. So they go into the military and they get an education and come on up through the ranks.

I would say that the predominant leadership today in the military in the Western Hemisphere come from the poor families of the country and have a deep and abiding concern for the people of the country. There are exceptions—and they have taken power because they have felt it necessary. Inflation has been one of the really great tragedies. We are worried about a 6-percent inflation and think it is killing us in this country.

There has been in another hemisphere country inflation as high as 130 percent in one year. There has been a tremendous period of inflation. And inflation, of course, is killing to those on fixed income, is destructive of the middle income groups which are the groups that are increasingly the strength and vitality of democracy in those countries, and they are the ones who have been most concerned and put the pressure on for change.

Now, we have to think of one other thing in discussing this. The democratic tradition of the Western Hemisphere and their belief in justice and human dignity is very real but it comes from Spain, or from Portugal, as against from England; and you have a different background there than we do. There is a much higher degree of "personalissimo" of the individual so that a man may believe very strongly in democracy and dignity and justice but his concept is importantly related to himself and his family; and that gentleman and his family who are strong advocates of this under a democratic government are much less willing to accept the procedures and the regulations and the rules of the democratic structure than we are here in this country.

So there is much instability and much less ability to achieve discipline which is essential in a free society.

Senator Church: Governor, I do not take issue with the statement that there are many able and dedicated young officers in the military in Latin America, or that democracy, as we know it, is not as deeply rooted there as it is in our own country. But I am concerned about the condition of freedom, or the lack of it, in the hemisphere.

Governor Rockefeller: So am I.

Senator Church: You would acknowledge, would you not, that the military governments that now control Argentina, Peru, Bolivia, Brazil, Panama, and other countries in the hemisphere, were not placed in power by the vote of the people?

Governor Rockefeller: That is correct.

Senator Church: They took power by force of arms. Isn't that correct?

Governor Rockefeller: Yes, in varying degrees.

Senator Church: Yes. This strikes me as ironical. . . .

I find it hard to understand why it is so important for us to secure free elections in South Vietnam, but so unimportant that there be free elections in South America.

Governor Rockefeller: . . . I think it is important to achieve free elections in South America and what I am trying to say in this report is the way I think that we can best achieve the restoration of democratic institutions in this hemisphere because this is the heart of the problem, Mr. Chairman, and you and I agree on the objective. It is a question of how we get there and what the method should be.

Senator Church: I think that is right.

The objective is certainly one that you and I would agree upon. I would like to turn to the methods.

. . . .

. . . I am somewhat perplexed by some, though surely not all, of your recommendations. We are faced in Latin America with military dictatorships that have usurped nearly full control. You have said that a very important part of the quality of life is free government. We are engaged in a war in Asia to obtain free elections for the people of South Vietnam. We agree that the ultimate objective of our policy should be to encourage the growth of democratic government, though there have been serious reversals on that score in our own hemisphere recently.

Then you recommend the expansion of the military assistance program for purposes of internal security.

Now, that means, to use the language of your report, that we will give very extensive military assistance to undemocratic governments for the purpose of internal security.

Governor Rockefeller: Not only these governments, all.

Senator Church: All governments. But most of these governments today—and the biggest ones—are military dictatorships.

I read your recommendations:

Internal security support: The United States should respond to requests for assistance of the police and security forces of the hemisphere nations by providing them with the essential tools to do their job.

Accordingly, the United States should meet reasonable requests from other hemisphere governments for trucks, jeeps, helicopters, and like equipment to provide mobility and logistical support for these forces; for radios, and other command control equipment for proper communication among the forces; and for small arms for security forces.

In furtherance of these objectives, the United States should provide, on request, military and technical training missions but should no longer maintain the permanent military missions in residence in other nations which too often have constituted too large and too visible a United States presence.

Governor, on the last part of the last sentence I am in full agreement.

Now, extending military assistance to foreign governments to help them obtain internal security is just a euphemism for maintaining internal order, and governments try to maintain internal order to keep themselves in control and prevent their own overthrow.

Do you think we should extend this kind of assistance, say, to the Government of Haiti?

Governor Rockefeller: Well, I would say that basically it is essential that it be extended and that we cooperate with the training and the equipment hemisphere-wide.

Senator Church: Then you would extend it to the Government of Haiti?

. . . .

Governor Rockefeller: Well, if you will excuse me, Senator, the present Government is not there through my policies and I am not here to justify that Government. I am here to talk to you about how do we prevent that in the Government and how do we encourage the evolution of those countries to democracy.

Senator Church: But you are advocating a military assistance program.

Governor Rockefeller: Which is essential.

Senator Church: And you have indicated you would make it hemisphere-wide.

Governor Rockefeller: Yes, sir.

Senator Church: And the effect of this is to help such governments as the Haitian Government and other dictatorial governments stay in power.

I do not see what that has to do either with the American tradition, which is based on the peoples' right to revolt against despotism, or with improving the quality of life for the people of the hemisphere.

Governor Rockefeller: Senator, I have to challenge a basic assumption, that if we do not send aid and if we cut off our relations we are going to achieve the goal that you want, restoration of democracy. This, in my opinion, is the fundamental error made in this country as to how we achieve the goals of human dignity and freedom and opportunity which are our objectives.

And I think we have no difference on the goals. It is how this is achieved. And I would like to give you a case in point of where there is still a democratic government and that it is fighting for its life, and to give you a little insight as to what we are up against and what really more importantly they are up against.

I would like to cite the case of Uruguay which has been held up as the Switzerland of the Americas and which has been going through utter chaos in recent years.

I had a visit with President Pacheco who is a man of infinite courage and who came into office because his President died in office. President Pacheco was a professor of law at the university, had never been in politics before, but was a man of tremendous integrity, a tremendous man. His country was almost bankrupt when I was there.

Prior to the arrival, the nationalists and the anarchistic group in the legislature tried to embarrass him by voting to stop the visit.

The General Motors building and showroom were burned with fire bombs, at a loss of about a million dollars, because the Tupamoros, which is a revolutionary group, said they had sold cars to the "pigs," the police, somewhat reminiscent of a situation in our own country, sir; and the Minister of Foreign Affairs' office was bombed with Molotov cocktails.

Two of his cars were overturned and burned.

The President went ahead with the visit. He could not guarantee security in the capital, Montevideo, so we had the meeting at Punta del Este. We had a lady who was meeting with women's groups on the trip. Three women showed. The others did not because they had been threatened before they arrived that their homes would be fire-bombed, that their cars would be run off the road, that their lives were in danger. Only three of them dared come; and they were so burned up, they came. There were general strikes in all government operations: 80 percent of the unions are led by Communist leadership.

The President flew over. I flew in from the Montevideo airport to Punta del Este, where we met and President Pacheco said, "I am determined to meet the problems of inflation, bankruptcy, and social disintegration of this country through the democratic process. But," he said, "I have got to have help from the United States to provide security forces and financing. We have not even got the money," he said, "to finance the crops for the next year's planting."

Now, I would like to read what is happening in just the last 2 months in Uruguay where he is fighting for his life.

Senator Church: Governor, I do not want to cut you short on your answer, because I think there are particular countries where strong arguments can be made for particular programs. Uruguay, being a democratic country, may be one of them.

I simply take issue with the position that we should undertake, on a hemisphere-wide basis, to supply more military assistance to help all governments stay in power. I do not see what interest the United States has in trying to help a government like Duvalier's regime in Haiti to stay in power. I think that does us more damage in the long run than adhering to our national tradition of recognizing that other people have the right to revolt and to overthrow tyranny, even if it does not happen to wear a red cloak, even if it is not Communist tyranny. That is not the only kind of tyranny in the world.

I cannot reconcile this kind of a sweeping recommendation, encompassing all the governments of Latin America, either with our traditional concepts as a nation or with our own national self-interest.

Governor Rockefeller: Obviously the executive has to have the right to determine where and how and in what form they would give aid of any kind, but what I am pleading for is that the Congress not try to dictate the powers and the authority and the approach of the executive so that their hands are tied.

Now, let's take your argument for the sake of discussion here, that we should not give any aid to Haiti, and let's see what has happened. We followed your policies——

Senator Church: I said military aid; that has been the subject of our exchange.

Governor Rockefeller: But we have followed the policy of giving no aid to Haiti——

Senator Church: That is another question.

Governor Rockefeller (continuing): —since 1963. And if everybody in Haiti goes down the drain because of the tragic conditions, the last person to go down is going to be Papa "Doc."

Now, our policy has been an utter and tragic failure in achieving our objectives in Haiti and I think it is time that we have the courage to face up to the realities of these things, that the methods we have been using are not working.

Since the Alliance for Progress, the goals of which I share, there have been 17 military coups—more than any other period. Therefore, I think it does bring us to a point where we have to say the cliches which we have been talking about are not as effective as we thought, and maybe we have to take a more realistic examination.

I would like to go to the question of why these coups have taken place, and I think that the perfect example is what is happening in Uruguay. They have held on but most of these countries did not have strong enough governments to be able to withstand these internal pressures.

Senator Church: I just want to reemphasize that my argument, Governor, has to do with military assistance. I think many of the recommendations you make with respect to economic aid can prove helpful in building a better standard of living and are, as I said before, highly praiseworthy. I simply cannot follow the logic of the argument you make on military assistance extended to the entire hemisphere as you have suggested.

Senator Case: I wonder if this colloquy and this very interesting discussion really aren't leading us to the proposition that each country must be treated on its own merits and that we should not try to prescribe broadly for the whole hemisphere on the same basis.

When you suggest that Congress ought not to tie the hands of the executive, I think I would agree, but I think I also would say the executive ought not follow a general proposition of either no military aid or military aid for everyone.

Governor Rockefeller: I agree.

· ·

. . . Would you let me use my illustration of Uruguay?

Senator Church: Yes.

Governor Rockefeller: Thank you.

I would like to say—you say by military action—the revolution in Brazil was started by the people in São Paulo in the State of Minas Gerais where 600,000 went into the streets to protest the Government. The military only came in at the end of the first week and there was not a shot fired and there was nobody killed.

Now, this is not what you would call a typical old-style military revolution. So that I think you have got to, Senator, understand the details of each country, the variations in the problems that they face, and to me what is the most important, which I find difficult to put across because I have not been able to make my point so you can feel what I am saying, that I feel very deeply, based on past experience and present experience, that our best chance of restoring the opportunity for free government is working with what I would consider in the majority of cases caretaker governments, transition governments, trying to stop inflation, restore some form of order, and restore the country.

Now, you saw a new president, a military president come in in Brazil. He reconfirmed the statement of his predecessor who made it when I was down there to me. They were going to reconvene the Congress. They would go to elections next year for the Congress and Governors, and they would go to a presidential election the following year.

Now, this is exactly the goal we are seeking and my basic thesis here is that we as a nation understand and separate the different types, characteristics, and so forth, through deep intimate understanding, that we can better help achieve these goals by working with the Government in power than we can by alienating ourselves from them and then giving them the kinds of support internally because they are then the defenders against the big colossus of the north.

Senator Church: Well, I think you have made your position plain, Governor.

Senator Case: I wonder if we might preserve the continuity of this discussion by allowing the Governor to talk about what has happened in the last 2 months.

Governor Rockefeller: I would just like to give you what Uruguay is up against and it is nip and tuck whether this lasts. Let me read you this:

On October 8, 1969, the Tupamoros, who have known links with Castro in Cuba, attempted to take over the town of Pando, approximately 20 kilometers from Montevideo. There was a plan to take Pando, take the money in the banks, control communications, and hold the town for a period. President Pacheco got wind of the plan, met the Tupamoros with a well-organized force of 200 police and army, defeated the Tupamoros and captured about 100 who are now in jail. Interrogation of the Tupamoros brought out the fact that occupation of Pando was to be a training exercise for a larger attempt in Uruguay.

About 2 weeks ago the Tupamoros kidnapped a Uruguayan banker and he has not yet been found. Last Saturday, November 15, a policeman was killed in Montevideo by six known Tupamoros.

These are just some of the incidents which are taking place.

Now, a government that is not strong, that hasn't the capacity to cope with these problems, can be nibbled away and finally destroyed so that any form of order, so that there can be economic development, education, sanitation programs, and so forth, is ended. These depend on a structure of government.

Now, if this government goes under, you will have another military dictatorship because the people——

Senator Church: Yes, I think that is true. And that would make the score nearly complete.

Governor Rockefeller: No. You have still got Chile and Venezuela.

Senator Church: Yes, you are right about Chile and Venezuela. But Chile is teetering on the brink of a military coup d'etat. In fact, just the other day, as you know, the Government came very close to being displaced.

Governor Rockefeller: That is right.

Senator Case: Isn't the point, Mr. Chairman, not that we have a choice in every case between the best and what we have, but between the best we can get and what we have? In other words, what is the alternative to our policies in regard to any particular government—not what the ideal solution would be?

Governor Rockefeller: Absolutely right, and they are sovereign nations. They are not dependencies of the United States.

Senator Church: I think the point, at least the point that the Chair has been trying to make, is not that we have a responsibility to set up democratic governments or attempt to establish democratic governments.

Governor Rockefeller: We couldn't.

Senator Church: We couldn't if we wanted to.

Governor Rockefeller: That is right. That is not the way democracy grows.

Senator Church: It is not our policy or objective to insist that Latin America develop in our image. I understand that. We will have to deal with governments as we find them. But the question is whether we should adopt a program of giving arms, equipment, and training to keep these governments in power in their own lands. That is the question.

Governor Rockefeller: But that is part of the question.

Senator Church: And on that question I differ fundamentally from your recommendation that we should adopt an overall hemispheric policy of giving military assistance to all governments, regardless of their character.

Governor Rockefeller: Senator, would it be fair for me to ask you what you think the cost is going to be if we follow the policy which you outlined?

Senator Church: Yes. I think it might reverse the very serious decline in attitudes in Latin America toward the United States which was so manifest during your own trip there. . . .

. . . .

. . . [I]f the United States were really to practice a policy of non-interventionism, and would not insist upon identifying itself so closely with dictatorial regimes, . . . the attitude of the people of Latin America toward us, particularly the young people who are going to have so much to say about the future, would markedly improve. It couldn't be much worse than it is today.

But to get into one other question, after which I will turn to the other committee members. I am sorry I have taken so much time.

Governor Rockefeller: This is a very key area, and some time during the course of this discussion I would like to give you my idea of what is going to happen if you follow the policies which you have outlined.

Senator Church: Very well. You have had something to say about economics and the importance of economic development. I think that is more important than giving Papa "Doc" machineguns. In that respect, in your report you refer to the population explosion. This seems to me to be central to the whole question. You say that:

> The fact that over 60 percent of the population is now under 24 years of age has greatly increased the demands on government for more schools, more health services, more housing and roads—services beyond their resources to provide. It produces an increasing labor supply which cannot find enough work, and thus adds to the frustrations and tensions. It results in slum growth and a multiplication of the problems of urban life, and it cancels out so much of the economic growth achieved as to make improvement of living standards difficult if not impossible.

I certainly concur with that. In fact, real economic growth has been kept to something less than 2 percent in Latin America, which is very unsatisfactory, owing to the population explosion. This is a fundamental problem to solve if we are really going to see economic growth on a significant scale in the hemisphere.

At another place in your report you say we must face this issue squarely, but I didn't see any recommendations on how we should face it or what we should do. I would like to have your ideas on that.

Governor Rockefeller: Well, if you are thinking about family planning, Senator, it seems to me that is something that is so obvious that it is hardly necessary for me to recommend to 23 or 24 sister sovereign nations that we impose family planning on a Catholic country. If they themselves in their own initiative, as is now happening in virtually all of the countries, recognize this problem and want to achieve the cooperation of this country in undertaking these programs, obviously that is something we would do, and that is the policy of this Government. But I felt that this is a very personal question, that it would be taken as an insult for me to express, as an individual, to the President of the United States what our friends in the Western Hemisphere should do about family planning. That is their problem. But we obviously would help them and that obviously has proven in other areas to be very useful.

. . . .

Senator Fulbright: Do you make a recommendation about the Hickenlooper amendment? Do you think it should be repealed?

Governor Rockefeller: Yes, sir; but if it is not repealed, then I think it should be left optional to the President. What it does in my opinion, Senator, is put the opportunity of involving the United States in the hands of any American corporation who, for one reason or another, knowingly or unknowingly, may get itself into trouble locally and be expropriated, which is certainly the right of another country. The question of compensation we all agree is essential but I think that if that is handled not with the threat of U.S. retaliation, that it can be handled much more effectively because these countries feel that this law impinges on their sovereignty. It is bitterly resented and I think it has a counter-productive effect.

. . . .

Senator Sparkman: The internal debt is quite a problem with many of the countries, isn't it?

Governor Rockefeller: It is disastrous. In Bolivia, where I had a chance to visit prior to this unfortunate coup, they have a national budget of $87 million; $12 million of that is for foreign debt. They have to pay that annually. So it takes up their foreign exchange. When you take a nation with a budget of $87 million and $12 million going for foreign debt, it is a pretty high percentage. It doesn't leave them anything to undertake any programs. I might say parenthetically, Senator, in my opinion that revolution could have been avoided. It was clearly understood what was happening and I think this was unnecessary.

This is the kind of thing I feel very strongly we should cope with on a more understanding basis and that the present structure of our Government doesn't permit that intimate understanding between the problems of the country and the decision-making process back here in our Government.

Senator Sparkman: I think you make quite a telling point when you point out that in order to meet their payments to us on what were loans at low-interest rates, they have to borrow money at a high-interest rate and that rescheduling these debts might well relieve them of that burden.

Governor Rockefeller: Exactly.

. . . .

Senator Church: Thank you very much, Senator Sparkman.

Before we pass to Senator Case, let me say that one of the most perplexing problems we face in this committee, Governor, relates to such provisions in the law as the Hickenlooper amendment. I do not know how we can overcome the tendency in Congress to politicize a bilateral aid program. Every kind of conduct by a foreign government that we view as mischievous ends up in some kind of a penalty provision that is attached to the aid program. This, in turn, leads to the feeling in recipient countries that we are highly paternalistic in our dealings with them.

Governor Rockefeller: Exactly.

Senator Church: And yet, despite the way this whole problem has been dramatized by the deterioration of our relations in Peru over the expropriation of the International Petroleum Co., and despite repeated urgings of this committee, we have not yet obtained any recommendation on the part of the administration concerning the repeal of either the Hickenlooper amendment or any other like provisions in the aid program. I am glad that you have made these recommendations, and I hope that the administration will now see fit to adopt them and urge them upon the Congress.

Governor Rockefeller: Senator, may I just comment on what you are saying because I agree with you and it seems to me that if the Congress could define its position on policy toward the Western Hemisphere, growing out of a position, let us say, taken by the President so that there is a dovetailing, I think that it might be possible to enunciate our policy and then to say in that resolution that all previous amendments or provisions of the law which are counter to this policy shall be superseded rather than go back and debate each one and then you get to the identification of the personalities. It would seem to me if Congress could at some point take a strong clear position on Western Hemisphere policy and have it supersede everything else that has been done it would be just fabulous.

Senator Church: That might be the way to cut the Gordian knot. Senator Case?

Senator Case: Thank you very much, Mr. Chairman.

Governor, it is nice to have you here.

Governor Rockefeller: Thank you, sir.

Senator Case: I wish it would be more often than once in a decade that you share your counsel with us.

Governor Rockefeller: Thank you.